The Java 3D™ API Specification, Second Edition

The Java™ Series

Lisa Friendly, Series Editor
Tim Lindholm, Technical Editor
Ken Arnold, Technical Editor of The Jini™ Technology Series
Jim Inscore, Technical Editor of The Java™ Series, Enterprise Edition

---

Ken Arnold, James Gosling, David Holmes
The Java™ Programming Language, Third Edition

Greg Bollella, James Gosling, Ben Brosgol, Peter Dibble,
Steve Furr, David Hardin, Mark Turnbull
The Real-Time Specification for Java™

Mary Campione, Kathy Walrath, Alison Huml
*The Java™ Tutorial, Third Edition:
A Short Course on the Basics*

Mary Campione, Kathy Walrath, Alison Huml,
Tutorial Team
The Java™ Tutorial Continued: The Rest of the JDK™

Patrick Chan
The Java™ Developers Almanac 2000

Patrick Chan, Rosanna Lee
*The Java™ Class Libraries, Second Edition, Volume 2:
java.applet, java.awt, java.beans*

Patrick Chan, Rosanna Lee
*The Java™ Class Libraries Poster, Fifth Edition: Covering
the Java™ 2 Platform, Standard Edition, v1.3*

Patrick Chan, Rosanna Lee, Douglas Kramer
*The Java™ Class Libraries, Second Edition, Volume 1:
java.io, java.lang, java.math, java.net, java.text, java.util*

Patrick Chan, Rosanna Lee, Douglas Kramer
*The Java™ Class Libraries, Second Edition, Volume 1:
Supplement for the Java™ 2 Platform,
Standard Edition, v1.2*

Zhiqun Chen
*Java Card™ Technology for Smart Cards:
Architecture and Programmer's Guide*

Li Gong
*Inside Java™ 2 Platform Security:
Architecture, API Design, and Implementation*

James Gosling, Bill Joy, Guy Steele, Gilad Bracha
The Java™ Language Specification, Second Edition

Jonni Kanerva
The Java™ FAQ

Doug Lea
*Concurrent Programming in Java™, Second Edition:
Design Principles and Patterns*

Rosanna Lee, Scott Seligman
*JNDI API Tutorial and Reference:
Building Directory-Enabled Java™ Applications*

Sheng Liang
*The Java™ Native Interface:
Programmer's Guide and Specification*

Tim Lindholm, Frank Yellin
The Java™ Virtual Machine Specification, Second Edition

Henry Sowizral, Kevin Rushforth, Michael Deering
The Java 3D™ API Specification, Second Edition

Kathy Walrath, Mary Campione
The JFC Swing Tutorial: A Guide to Constructing GUIs

Seth White, Maydene Fisher, Rick Cattell,
Graham Hamilton, Mark Hapner
*JDBC™ API Tutorial and Reference, Second Edition:
Universal Data Access for the Java™ 2 Platform*

Steve Wilson, Jeff Kesselman
Java™ Platform Performance: Strategies and Tactics

The Jini™ Technology Series

Ken Arnold, Bryan O'Sullivan, Robert W. Scheifler,
Jim Waldo, Ann Wollrath
The Jini™ Specification

Eric Freeman, Susanne Hupfer, Ken Arnold
JavaSpaces™ Principles, Patterns, and Practice

The Java™ Series, Enterprise Edition

Patrick Chan, Rosanna Lee
*The Java™ Class Libraries Poster, Enterprise Edition,
version 1.2*

Nicholas Kassem, Enterprise Team
*Designing Enterprise Applications with the Java™ 2
Platform, Enterprise Edition*

Bill Shannon, Mark Hapner, Vlada Matena, James
Davidson, Eduardo Pelegri-Llopart, Larry Cable,
Enterprise Team
*Java™ 2 Platform, Enterprise Edition:
Platform and Component Specifications*

http://www.javaseries.com

The Java 3D™ API Specification, Second Edition

Henry Sowizral
Kevin Rushforth
Michael Deering

ADDISON-WESLEY

Boston • San Francisco • New York • Toronto • Montreal
London • Munich • Paris • Madrid
Capetown • Sydney • Tokyo • Singapore • Mexico City

Library of Congress Cataloging-in-Publication Data is available.

The publisher offers discounts on this book when ordered in quantity for special sales. For more information, please contact:

    Pearson Education Corporate Sales Division
    One Lake Street
    Upper Saddle River, NJ 07458
    (800) 382-3419

Visit Addison-Wesley on the Web at www.awl.com/cseng/

ISBN 0-201-71041-2
Text printed on recycled and acid-free paper.
1 2 3 4 5 6 7 8 9—MA— 04 03 02 01 00
First Printing, June 2000

To Renee   —HAS

To Debbie, Trudy, and Jennifer   —KCR

Contents

Figures

Preface

THIS document describes the Java 3D™ API, version 1.2, and presents some details on the implementation of the API. This specification is not intended as a programmer's guide.

This specification is written for 3D graphics application programmers. We assume that the reader has at least a rudimentary understanding of computer graphics. This includes familiarity with the essentials of computer graphics algorithms as well as familiarity with basic graphics hardware and associated terminology.

Related Documentation

This specification is intended to be used in conjunction with the browser-accessible, javadoc-generated API reference.

Style Conventions

The following style conventions are used in this specification:

- Lucida type is used to represent computer code and the names of files and directories.
- **Bold Lucida type** is used for Java 3D API declarations.
- **Bold** type is used to represent variables.
- *Italic type* is used for emphasis and for equations.

Changes to the Java 3D API, version 1.2, are indicated by an icon in the margin. The icon ◀ New in 1.2 ▶ appears in the outside margin for all new methods and constructors.

Programming Conventions

Java 3D uses the following programming conventions:

- The default coordinate system is right-handed, with $+y$ being up, $+x$ horizontal to the right, and $+z$ directed toward the viewer.

- All angles or rotational representations are in radians.

- All distances are expressed in units or fractions of meters.

Acknowledgments

We gratefully acknowledge Warren Dale for writing the Sound API portion of this specification and Daniel Petersen for writing the scene graph sharing portion of the specification. We especially acknowledge Bruce Bartlett for his invaluable assistance with the editing, formatting, and indexing of the specification. Without Bruce's considerable help, this book would not have been possible.

We also thank the many individuals and companies that provided comments and suggestions. They have improved the Java 3D API.

Henry Sowizral
Kevin Rushforth
Michael Deering
Sun Microsystems, Inc.
April 2000

CHAPTER 1

Introduction to Java 3D

THE Java 3D API is an application programming interface used for writing three-dimensional graphics applications and applets. It gives developers high-level constructs for creating and manipulating 3D geometry and for constructing the structures used in rendering that geometry. Application developers can describe very large virtual worlds using these constructs, which provide Java 3D with enough information to render these worlds efficiently.

Java 3D delivers Java's "write once, run anywhere" benefit to developers of 3D graphics applications. Java 3D is part of the JavaMedia suite of APIs, making it available on a wide range of platforms. It also integrates well with the Internet because applications and applets written using the Java 3D API have access to the entire set of Java classes.

The Java 3D API draws its ideas from existing graphics APIs and from new technologies. Java 3D's low-level graphics constructs synthesize the best ideas found in low-level APIs such as Direct3D, OpenGL, QuickDraw3D, and XGL. Similarly, its higher-level constructs synthesize the best ideas found in several scene graph–based systems. Java 3D introduces some concepts not commonly considered part of the graphics environment, such as 3D spatial sound. Java 3D's sound capabilities help to provide a more immersive experience for the user.

1.1 Goals

Java 3D was designed with several goals in mind. Chief among them is high performance. Several design decisions were made so that Java 3D implementations can deliver the highest level of performance to application users. In particular, when trade-offs were made, the alternative that benefited runtime execution was chosen.

Other important Java 3D goals are to

- Provide a rich set of features for creating interesting 3D worlds, tempered by the need to avoid nonessential or obscure features. Features that could be layered on top of Java 3D were not included.

- Provide a high-level object-oriented programming paradigm that enables developers to deploy sophisticated applications and applets rapidly.

- Provide support for runtime loaders. This allows Java 3D to accommodate a wide variety of file formats, such as vendor-specific CAD formats, interchange formats, and VRML97.

1.2   Programming Paradigm

Java 3D is an object-oriented API. Applications construct individual graphics elements as separate objects and connect them together into a treelike structure called a *scene graph*. The application manipulates these objects using their predefined accessor, mutator, and node-linking methods.

1.2.1   The Scene Graph Programming Model

Java 3D's scene graph–based programming model provides a simple and flexible mechanism for representing and rendering scenes. The scene graph contains a complete description of the entire scene, or virtual universe. This includes the geometric data, the attribute information, and the viewing information needed to render the scene from a particular point of view. Chapter 3, "Scene Graph Basics," provides more information on the Java 3D scene graph programming model.

The Java 3D API improves on previous graphics APIs by eliminating many of the bookkeeping and programming chores that those APIs impose. Java 3D allows the programmer to think about geometric objects rather than about triangles—about the scene and its composition rather than about how to write the rendering code for efficiently displaying the scene.

1.2.2   Rendering Modes

Java 3D includes three different rendering modes: immediate mode, retained mode, and compiled-retained mode (see Chapter 13, "Execution and Rendering Model"). Each successive rendering mode allows Java 3D more freedom in optimizing an application's execution. Most Java 3D applications will want to take advantage of the convenience and performance benefits that the retained and compiled-retained modes provide.

1.2.2.1   Immediate Mode

Immediate mode leaves little room for global optimization at the scene graph level. Even so, Java 3D has raised the level of abstraction and accelerates immediate mode rendering on a per-object basis. An application must provide a Java 3D draw method with a complete set of points, lines, or triangles, which are then rendered by the high-speed Java 3D renderer. Of course, the application can build these lists of points, lines, or triangles in any manner it chooses.

1.2.2.2   Retained Mode

Retained mode requires an application to construct a scene graph and specify which elements of that scene graph may change during rendering. The scene graph describes the objects in the virtual universe, the arrangement of those objects, and how the application animates those objects.

1.2.2.3   Compiled-Retained Mode

Compiled-retained mode, like retained mode, requires the application to construct a scene graph and specify which elements of the scene graph may change during rendering. Additionally, the application can compile some or all of the subgraphs that make up a complete scene graph. Java 3D compiles these graphs into an internal format. The compiled representation of the scene graph may bear little resemblance to the original tree structure provided by the application, however, it is functionally equivalent. Compiled-retained mode provides the highest performance.

1.2.3   Extensibility

Most Java 3D classes expose only accessor and mutator methods. Those methods operate only on that object's internal state, making it meaningless for an application to override them. Therefore, Java 3D does not provide the capability to override the behavior of Java 3D attributes. To make Java 3D work correctly, applications must call "`super.setXxxxx`" for any attribute state set method that is overridden.

Applications can extend Java 3D's classes and add their own methods. However, they may not override Java 3D's scene graph traversal semantics because the nodes do not contain explicit traversal and draw methods. Java 3D's renderer retains those semantics internally.

Java 3D *does* provide hooks for mixing Java 3D–controlled scene graph rendering and user-controlled rendering using Java 3D's immediate mode constructs (see Section 14.1.2, "Mixed-Mode Rendering"). Alternatively, the application can stop Java 3D's renderer and do all its drawing in immediate mode (see Section 14.1.1, "Pure Immediate-Mode Rendering").

Behaviors require applications to extend the Behavior object and to override its methods with user-written Java code. These extended objects should contain references to those scene graph objects that they will manipulate at run time. Chapter 10, "Behaviors and Interpolators," describes Java 3D's behavior model.

1.3   High Performance

Java 3D's programming model allows the Java 3D API to do the mundane tasks, such as scene graph traversal, managing attribute state changes, and so forth, thereby simplifying the application's job. Java 3D does this without sacrificing performance. At first glance, it might appear that this approach would create more work for the API; however, it actually has the opposite effect. Java 3D's higher level of abstraction changes not only the amount but, more important, also the kind of work the API must perform. Java 3D does not need to impose the same type of constraints as do APIs with a lower level of abstraction, thus allowing Java 3D to introduce optimizations not possible with these lower-level APIs.

Additionally, leaving the details of rendering to Java 3D allows it to tune the rendering to the underlying hardware. For example, relaxing the strict rendering order imposed by other APIs allows parallel traversal as well as parallel rendering. Knowing which portions of the scene graph cannot be modified at run time allows Java 3D to flatten the tree, pretransform geometry, or represent the geometry in a native hardware format without the need to keep the original data.

1.3.1   Layered Implementation

Besides optimizations at the scene graph level, one of the more important factors that determines the performance of Java 3D is the time it takes to render the visible geometry. Java 3D implementations are layered to take advantage of the native, low-level API that is available on a given system. In particular, Java 3D implementations that use Direct3D and OpenGL are available. This means that Java 3D rendering will be accelerated across the same wide range of systems that are supported by these lower-level APIs.

1.3.2   Target Hardware Platforms

Java 3D is aimed at a wide range of 3D-capable hardware and software platforms, from low-cost PC game cards and software renderers at the low end, through midrange workstations, all the way up to very high-performance specialized 3D image generators.

Java 3D implementations are expected to provide useful rendering rates on most modern PCs, especially those with 3D graphics accelerator cards. On midrange workstations, Java 3D is expected to provide applications with nearly full-speed hardware performance.

Finally, Java 3D is designed to scale as the underlying hardware platforms increase in speed over time. Tomorrow's 3D PC game accelerators will support more complex virtual worlds than high-priced workstations of a few years ago. Java 3D is prepared to meet this increase in hardware performance.

1.4   Support for Building Applications and Applets

Java 3D neither anticipates nor directly supports every possible 3D need. Instead it provides support for adding those features through Java code.

Objects defined using a computer-aided design (CAD) system or an animation system may be included in a Java 3D-based application. Most such modeling packages have an external format (sometimes proprietary). Designers can export geometry designed using an external modeler to a file. Java 3D can use that geometric information, but only if an application provides a means for reading and translating the modeler's file format into Java 3D primitives.

Similarly, VRML loaders will parse and translate VRML files and generate the appropriate Java 3D objects and Java code necessary to support the file's contents.

1.4.1   Browsers

Today's Internet browsers support 3D content by passing such data to plug-in 3D viewers that render into their own window. It is anticipated that, over time, the display of 3D content will become integrated into the main browser display. In fact, some of today's 3D browsers display 2D content as 2D objects within a 3D world.

1.4.2   Games

Developers of 3D game software have typically attempted to wring out every last ounce of performance from the hardware. Historically they have been quite willing to use hardware-specific, nonportable optimizations to get the best performance possible. As such, in the past, game developers have tended to program below the level of easy-to-use software such as Java 3D. However, the trend in 3D games today is to leverage general-purpose 3D hardware accelerators and to use fewer "tricks" in rendering.

So, while Java 3D was not explicitly designed to match the game developer's every expectation, Java 3D's sophisticated implementation techniques should provide more than enough performance to support many game applications. One might argue that applications written using a general API like Java 3D may have a slight performance penalty over those employing special, nonportable techniques. However, other factors such as portability, time to market, and development cost must be weighed against absolute peak performance.

1.5   Overview of Java 3D Object Hierarchy

Java 3D defines several basic classes that are used to construct and manipulate a scene graph and to control viewing and rendering. Figure 1-1 shows the overall object hierarchy used by Java 3D. Subsequent chapters provide more detail for specific portions of the hierarchy.

1.6   Structuring the Java 3D Program

This section illustrates how a developer might structure a Java 3D application. The simple application in this example creates a scene graph that draws an object in the middle of a window and rotates the object about its center point.

1.6.1   Java 3D Application Scene Graph

The scene graph for the sample application is shown in Figure 1-2.

The scene graph consists of superstructure components—a VirtualUniverse object and a Locale object—and a set of branch graphs. Each branch graph is a subgraph that is rooted by a BranchGroup node that is attached to the superstructure. For more information, see Chapter 3, "Scene Graph Basics."

javax.media.j3d
VirtualUniverse
Locale
View
PhysicalBody
PhysicalEnvironment
Screen3D
Canvas3D (extends awt.Canvas)
SceneGraphObject
    Node
    Group
    Leaf
    NodeComponent
       Various component objects
Transform3D

javax.vecmath
Matrix classes
Tuple classes

Figure 1-1   Java 3D Object Hierarchy

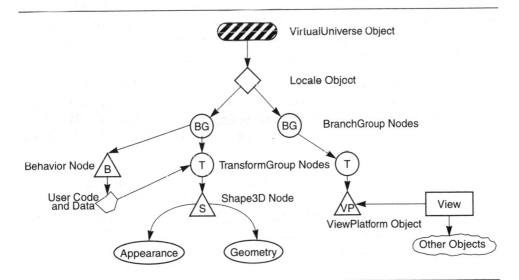

Figure 1-2   Application Scene Graph

A VirtualUniverse object defines a named universe. Java 3D permits the creation of more than one universe, though the vast majority of applications will use just one. The VirtualUniverse object provides a grounding for scene graphs. All

Java 3D scene graphs must connect to a VirtualUniverse object to be displayed. For more information, see Chapter 4, "Scene Graph Superstructure."

Below the VirtualUniverse object is a Locale object. The Locale object defines the origin, in high-resolution coordinates, of its attached branch graphs. A virtual universe may contain as many Locales as needed. In this example, a single Locale object is defined with its origin at (0.0, 0.0, 0.0).

The scene graph itself starts with the BranchGroup nodes (see Section 5.2, "BranchGroup Node"). A BranchGroup serves as the root of a subgraph, called a *branch graph*, of the scene graph. Only BranchGroup objects can attach to Locale objects.

In this example there are two branch graphs and, thus, two BranchGroup nodes. Attached to the left BranchGroup are two subgraphs. One subgraph consists of a user-extended Behavior leaf node. The Behavior node contains Java code for manipulating the transformation matrix associated with the object's geometry.

The other subgraph in this BranchGroup consists of a TransformGroup node that specifies the position (relative to the Locale), orientation, and scale of the geometric objects in the virtual universe. A single child, a Shape3D leaf node, refers to two component objects: a Geometry object and an Appearance object. The Geometry object describes the geometric shape of a 3D object (a cube in our simple example). The Appearance object describes the appearance of the geometry (color, texture, material reflection characteristics, and so forth).

The right BranchGroup has a single subgraph that consists of a TransformGroup node and a ViewPlatform leaf node. The TransformGroup specifies the position (relative to the Locale), orientation, and scale of the ViewPlatform. This transformed ViewPlatform object defines the end user's view within the virtual universe.

Finally, the ViewPlatform is referenced by a View object that specifies all of the parameters needed to render the scene from the point of view of the ViewPlatform. Also referenced by the View object are other objects that contain information, such as the drawing canvas into which Java 3D renders, the screen that contains the canvas, and information about the physical environment.

1.6.2   Recipe for a Java 3D Program

The following steps are taken by the example program to create the scene graph elements and link them together. Java 3D will then render the scene graph and display the graphics in a window on the screen:

1. Create a Canvas3D object and add it to the Applet panel.

2. Create a BranchGroup as the root of the scene branch graph.

3. Construct a Shape3D node with a TransformGroup node above it.

4. Attach a RotationInterpolator behavior to the TransformGroup.

5. Call the simple universe utility function to do the following:

   a. Establish a virtual universe with a single high-resolution Locale (see Chapter 3, "Scene Graph Basics").

   b. Create the PhysicalBody, PhysicalEnvironment, View, and ViewPlatform objects.

   c. Create a BranchGroup as the root of the view platform branch graph.

   d. Insert the view platform branch graph into the Locale.

6. Insert the scene branch graph into the simple universe's Locale.

The Java 3D renderer then starts running in an infinite loop. The renderer conceptually performs the following operations:

```
while(true) {
    Process input
    If (request to exit) break
    Perform Behaviors
    Traverse the scene graph and render visible objects
}
Cleanup and exit
```

1.6.3   HelloUniverse: A Sample Java 3D Program

Following are code fragments from a simple program, HelloUniverse.java, that creates a cube and a RotationInterpolator behavior object that rotates the cube at a constant rate of $\pi/2$ radians per second.

1.6.3.1   HelloUniverse Class

The HelloUniverse class, on the next page, creates the branch graph that includes the cube and the RotationInterpolator behavior. It then adds this branch graph to the Locale object generated by the SimpleUniverse utility.

```java
public class HelloUniverse extends Applet {
    public BranchGroup createSceneGraph() {
        // Create the root of the branch graph
        BranchGroup objRoot = new BranchGroup();

        // Create the TransformGroup node and initialize it to the
        // identity. Enable the TRANSFORM_WRITE capability so that
        // our behavior code can modify it at run time. Add it to
        // the root of the subgraph.
        TransformGroup objTrans = new TransformGroup();
        objTrans.setCapability(
                        TransformGroup.ALLOW_TRANSFORM_WRITE);
        objRoot.addChild(objTrans);

        // Create a simple Shape3D node; add it to the scene graph.
        objTrans.addChild(new ColorCube(0.4));

        // Create a new Behavior object that will perform the
        // desired operation on the specified transform and add
        // it into the scene graph.
        Transform3D yAxis = new Transform3D();
        Alpha rotationAlpha = new Alpha(-1, 4000);
        RotationInterpolator rotator = new RotationInterpolator(
                rotationAlpha, objTrans, yAxis,
                0.0f, (float) Math.PI*2.0f);
        BoundingSphere bounds =
            new BoundingSphere(new Point3d(0.0,0.0,0.0), 100.0);
        rotator.setSchedulingBounds(bounds);
        objRoot.addChild(rotator);

        // Have Java 3D perform optimizations on this scene graph.
        objRoot.compile();

        return objRoot;
    }

    public HelloUniverse() {
        <set layout of applet, construct canvas3d, add canvas3d>

        // Create the scene; attach it to the virtual universe
        BranchGroup scene = createSceneGraph();
        SimpleUniverse u = new SimpleUniverse(canvas3d);
        u.getViewingPlatform().setNominalViewingTransform();
        u.addBranchGraph(scene);
    }
}
```

CHAPTER 2

Java 3D Concepts

A specification serves to define objects, methods, and their actions precisely. It is not the best way to learn an API. Describing how to use an API belongs in a tutorial or programmer's reference manual—and that is well beyond the scope of this book. However, a short introduction to the main concepts in Java 3D can provide the context for understanding the detailed, but isolated, specification found in the remainder of this book.

This chapter introduces Java 3D concepts and illustrates them with some simple program fragments. Appendix H, "The Example Programs" describes the examples included with the CD-ROM and highlights particular code segments for some examples.

2.1 Basic Scene Graph Concepts

A scene graph is a "tree" structure that contains data arranged in a hierarchical manner. The scene graph consists of parent nodes, child nodes, and data objects. The parent nodes, called Group nodes, organize and, in some cases, control how Java 3D interprets their descendants. Group nodes serve as the glue that holds a scene graph together. Child nodes can be either Group nodes or Leaf nodes. Leaf nodes have no children. They encode the core semantic elements of a scene graph— for example, what to draw (geometry), what to play (audio), how to illuminate objects (lights), or what code to execute (behaviors). Leaf nodes refer to data objects, called NodeComponent objects. NodeComponent objects are not scene graph nodes, but they contain the data that Leaf nodes require, such as the geometry to draw or the sound sample to play.

A Java 3D application builds and manipulates a scene graph by constructing Java 3D objects and then later modifying those objects by using their methods. A

Java 3D program first constructs a scene graph, then, once built, hands that scene graph to Java 3D for processing.

The structure of a scene graph determines the relationships among the objects in the graph and determines which objects a programmer can manipulate as a single entity. Group nodes provide a single point for handling or manipulating all the nodes beneath it. A programmer can tune a scene graph appropriately by thinking about what manipulations an application will need to perform. He or she can make a particular manipulation easy or difficult by grouping or regrouping nodes in various ways.

2.1.1   Constructing a Simple Scene Graph

The code shown in Listing 2-1 constructs a simple scene graph consisting of a group node and two leaf nodes. It first constructs one leaf node, the first of two Shape3D nodes, using a constructor that takes both a Geometry and an Appearance NodeComponent object. It then constructs the second Shape3D node, with only a Geometry object. Next, since the second Shape3D node was created without an Appearance object, it supplies the missing Appearance object using the Shape3D node's setAppearance method. At this point both leaf nodes have been fully constructed.

Listing 2-1   Code for Constructing a Simple Scene Graph

```
Shape3D myShape1 = new Shape3D(myGeometry1, myAppearance1);
Shape3D myShape2 = new Shape3D(myGeometry2);
myShape2.setAppearance(myAppearance2);

Group myGroup = new Group();
myGroup.addChild(myShape1);
myGroup.addChild(myShape2);
```

The code next constructs a group node to hold the two leaf nodes. It uses the Group node's addChild method to add the two leaf nodes as children to the group node, finishing the construction of the scene graph. Figure 2-1 shows the constructed scene graph, all the nodes, the node component objects, and the variables used in constructing the scene graph.

2.1.2   A Place For Scene Graphs

Once a scene graph has been constructed, the question becomes what to do with it? Java 3D cannot start rendering a scene graph until a program "gives" it the scene graph. The program does this by inserting the scene graph into the virtual universe.

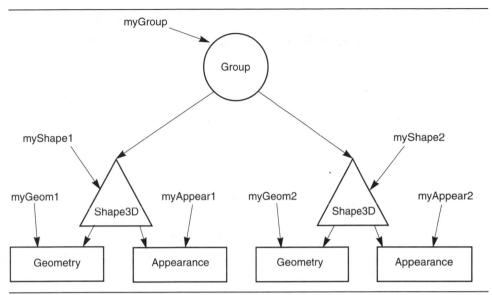

Figure 2-1   A Simple Scene Graph

Java 3D places restrictions on how a program can insert a scene graph into a universe.

A Java 3D environment consists of two superstructure objects, VirtualUniverse and Locale, and one or more graphs, rooted by a special BranchGroup node. Figure 2-2 shows these objects in context with other scene graph objects.

The VirtualUniverse object defines a universe. A universe allows a Java 3D program to create a separate and distinct arena for defining objects and their relationships to one another. Typically, Java 3D programs have only one VirtualUniverse object. Programs that have more than one VirtualUniverse may share NodeComponent objects but not scene graph node objects.

The Locale object specifies a fixed position within the universe. That fixed position defines an origin for all scene graph nodes beneath it. The Locale object allows a programmer to specify that origin very precisely and with very high dynamic range. A Locale can accurately specify a location anywhere in the known physical universe and at the precision of Plank's distance. Typically, Java 3D programs have only one Locale object with a default origin of (0, 0, 0). Programs that have more than one Locale object will set the location of the individual Locale objects so that they provide an appropriate local origin for the nodes beneath them. For example, to model the Mars landing, a programmer might create one Locale object with an origin at Cape Canaveral and another with an origin located at the landing site on Mars.

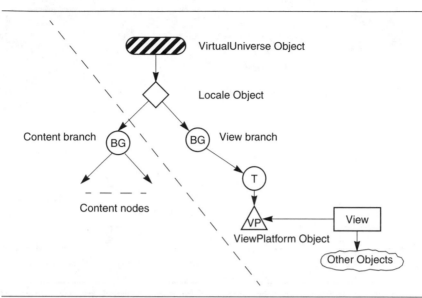

Figure 2-2   Content Branch, View Branch, and Superstructure

The BranchGroup node serves as the root of a *branch graph*. Collectively, the BranchGroup node and all of its children form the branch graph. The two kinds of branch graphs are called content branches and view branches. A *content branch* contains only content-related leaf nodes, while a *view branch* contains a ViewPlatform leaf node and may contain other content-related leaf nodes. Typically, a universe contains more than one branch graph—one view branch, and any number of content branches.

Besides serving as the root of a branch graph, the BranchGroup node has two special properties: It alone may be inserted into a Locale object, and it may be compiled. Java 3D treats uncompiled and compiled branch graphs identically, though compiled branch graphs will typically render more efficiently.

We could not insert the scene graph created by our simple example (Listing 2-1) into a Locale because it does not have a BranchGoup node for its root. Listing 2-2 shows a modified version of our first code example that creates a simple content branch graph and the minimum of superstructure objects. Of special note, Locales do not have children, and they are not part of the scene graph. The method for inserting a branch graph is addBranchGraph, whereas addChild is the method for adding children to all group nodes.

Listing 2-2 Code for Constructing a Scene Graph and Some Superstructure Objects

```
Shape3D myShape1 = new Shape3D(myGeometry1, myAppearance1);
Shape3D myShape2 = new Shape3D(myGeometry2, myAppearance2);

BranchGroup myBranch = new BranchGroup();
myBranch.addChild(myShape1);
myBranch.addChild(myShape2);
myBranch.compile();

VirtualUniverse myUniverse = new VirtualUniverse();
Locale myLocale = new Locale(myUniverse);
myLocale.addBranchGraph(myBranch);
```

2.1.3 SimpleUniverse Utility

Most Java 3D programs build an identical set of superstructure and view branch objects, so the Java 3D utility packages provide a universe package for constructing and manipulating the objects in a view branch. The classes in the universe package provide a quick means for building a single view (single window) application. Listing 2-3 shows a code fragment for using the SimpleUniverse class. Note that the SimpleUniverse constructor takes a Canvas3D as an argument, in this case referred to by the variable myCanvas.

Listing 2-3 Code for Constructing a Scene Graph Using the Universe Package

```
import com.sun.j3d.utils.universe.*;

Shape3D myShape1 = new Shape3D(myGeometry1, myAppearance1);
Shape3D myShape2 = new Shape3D(myGeometry2, myAppearance2);

BranchGroup myBranch = new BranchGroup();
myBranch.addChild(myShape1);
myBranch.addChild(myShape2);
myBranch.compile();

SimpleUniverse myUniv = new SimpleUniverse(myCanvas);
myUniv.addBranchGraph(myBranch);
```

2.1.4 Processing a Scene Graph

When given a scene graph, Java 3D processes that scene graph as efficiently as possible. How a Java 3D implementation processes a scene graph can vary, as long as the implementation conforms to the semantics of the API. In general, a Java 3D implementation will render all visible objects, play all enabled sounds, execute all triggered behaviors, process any identified input devices, and check for and generate appropriate collision events.

The order that a particular Java 3D implementation renders objects onto the display is carefully not defined. One implementation might render the first Shape3D object and then the second. Another might first render the second Shape3D node before it renders the first one. Yet another implementation may render both Shape3D nodes in parallel.

2.2   Features of Java 3D

Java 3D allows a programmer to specify a broad range of information. It allows control over the shape of objects, their color, and transparency. It allows control over background effects, lighting, and environmental effects such as fog. It allows control over the placement of all objects (even nonvisible objects such as lights and behaviors) in the scene graph and over their orientation and scale. It allows control over how those objects move, rotate, stretch, shrink, or morph over time. It allows control over what code should execute, what sounds should play, and how they should sound and change over time.

Java 3D provides different techniques for controlling the effect of various features. Some techniques act fairly locally, such as getting the color of a vertex. Other techniques have broader influence, such as changing the color or appearance of an entire object. Still other techniques apply to a broad number of objects. In the first two cases, the programmer can modify a particular object or an object associated with the affected object. In the latter case, Java 3D provides a means for specifying more than one object spatially.

2.2.1   Bounds

Bounds objects allow a programmer to define a volume in space. There are three ways to specify this volume: as a box, a sphere, or a set of planes enclosing a space.

Bounds objects specify a volume in which particular operations apply. Environmental effects such as lighting, fog, alternate appearance, and model clipping planes use bounds objects to specify their region of influence. Any object that falls within the space defined by the bounds object has the particular environmental effect applied. The proper use of bounds objects can ensure that these environmental effects are applied only to those objects in a particular volume, such as a light applying only to the objects within a single room.

Bounds objects are also used to specify a region of action. Behaviors and sounds execute or play only if they are close enough to the viewer. The use of behavior and sound bounds objects allows Java 3D to cull away those behaviors and sounds that are too far away to affect the viewer (listener). By using bounds properly, a programmer can ensure that only the relevant behaviors and sounds execute or play.

Finally, bounds objects are used to specify a region of application for per-view operations such as background, clip, and soundscape selection. For example, the background node whose region of application is closest to the viewer is selected for a given view.

2.2.2 Nodes

All scene graph nodes have an implicit location in space of (0, 0, 0). For objects that exist in space, this implicit location provides a local coordinate system for that object, a fixed reference point. Even abstract objects that may not seem to have a well-defined location, such as behaviors and ambient lights, have this implicit location. An object's location provides an origin for its local coordinate system and, just as importantly, an origin for any bounding volume information associated with that object.

2.2.3 Live and/or Compiled

All scene graph objects, including nodes and node component objects, are either part of an active universe or not. An object is said to be *live* if it is part of an active universe. Additionally, branch graphs are either *compiled* or not. When a node is either live or compiled, Java 3D enforces access restrictions to nodes and node component objects. Java 3D allows only those operations that are enabled by the program before a node or node component becomes live or is compiled. It is best to set capabilities when you build your content. Listing 2-4 shows an example where we create a TransformGroup node and enable it for writing.

Listing 2-4   Capabilities Example

```
TransformGroup myTrans = new TransformGroup();
myTrans.setCapability(Transform.ALLOW_TRANSFORM_WRITE);
```

By setting the capability to write the transform, Java 3D will allow the following code to execute:

```
myTrans.setTransform3D(myT3D);
```

However, the following code will cause an exception:

```
myTrans.getTransform3D(myT3D);
```

The reason for the exception is that the TransformGroup is not enabled for reading (ALLOW_TRANSFORM_READ).

It is important to ensure that all needed capabilities are set and that unnecessary capabilities are not set. The process of compiling a branch graph examines the capability bits and uses that information to reduce the amount of computation needed to run a program.

CHAPTER 3

Scene Graph Basics

A scene graph consists of Java 3D objects, called *nodes*, arranged in a tree structure. The user creates one or more scene subgraphs and attaches them to a virtual universe. The individual connections between Java 3D nodes always represent a directed relationship: parent to child. Java 3D restricts scene graphs in one major way: Scene graphs may not contain cycles. Thus, a Java 3D scene graph is a directed acyclic graph (DAG). See Figure 3-1.

Java 3D refines the Node object class into two subclasses: Group and Leaf node objects. Group node objects group together one or more child nodes. A group node can point to zero or more children but can have only one parent. The SharedGroup node cannot have any parents (although it allows sharing portions of a scene graph, as described in Chapter 7, "Reusing Scene Graphs"). Leaf node objects contain the actual definitions of shapes (geometry), lights, fog, sounds, and so forth. A leaf node has no children and only one parent. The semantics of the various group and leaf nodes are described in subsequent chapters.

3.1 Scene Graph Structure

A scene graph organizes and controls the rendering of its constituent objects. The Java 3D renderer draws a scene graph in a consistent way that allows for concurrence. The Java 3D renderer can draw one object independently of other objects. Java 3D can allow such independence because its scene graphs have a particular form and cannot share state among branches of a tree.

3.1.1 Spatial Separation

The hierarchy of the scene graph encourages a natural spatial grouping on the geometric objects found at the leaves of the graph. Internal nodes act to group their children together. A group node also defines a spatial bound that contains all the geometry defined by its descendants. Spatial grouping allows for efficient implementation of operations such as proximity detection, collision detection, view frustum culling, and occlusion culling.

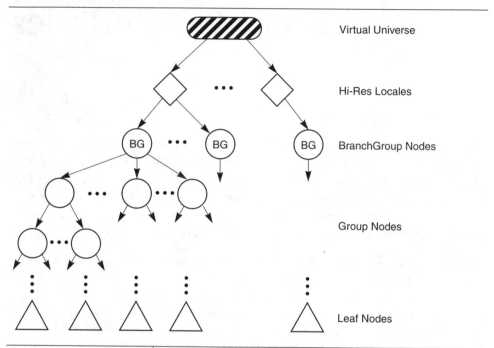

Figure 3-1   A Java 3D Scene Graph Is a DAG (Directed Acyclic Graph)

3.1.2   State Inheritance

A leaf node's state is defined by the nodes in a direct path between the scene graph's root and the leaf. Because a leaf's graphics context relies only on a linear path between the root and that node, the Java 3D renderer can decide to traverse the scene graph in whatever order it wishes. It can traverse the scene graph from left to right and top to bottom, in level order from right to left, or even in parallel. The only exceptions to this rule are spatially bounded attributes such as lights and fog.

This characteristic is in marked contrast to many older scene graph–based APIs (including PHIGS and SGI's Inventor) where, if a node above or to the left of a node changes the graphics state, the change affects the graphics state of all nodes below it or to its right.

The most common node object, along the path from the root to the leaf, that changes the graphics state is the TransformGroup object. The TransformGroup object can change the position, orientation, and scale of the objects below it.

Most graphics state attributes are set by a Shape3D leaf node through its constituent Appearance object, thus allowing parallel rendering. The Shape3D node also has a constituent Geometry object that specifies its geometry—this permits different shape objects to share common geometry without sharing material attributes (or vice versa).

3.1.3   Rendering

The Java 3D renderer incorporates all graphics state changes made in a direct path from a scene graph root to a leaf object in the drawing of that leaf object. Java 3D provides this semantic for both retained and compiled-retained modes.

3.2   Scene Graph Objects

A Java 3D scene graph consists of a collection of Java 3D node objects connected in a tree structure. These node objects reference other scene graph objects called *node component objects*. All scene graph node and component objects are subclasses of a common SceneGraphObject class. The SceneGraphObject class is an abstract class that defines methods that are common among nodes and component objects.

Scene graph objects are constructed by creating a new instance of the desired class and are accessed and manipulated using the object's set and get methods. Once a scene graph object is created and connected to other scene graph objects to form a subgraph, the entire subgraph can be attached to a virtual universe—via a high-resolution Locale object—making the object *live* (see Section 4.6.2, "Locale Object"). Prior to attaching a subgraph to a virtual universe, the entire subgraph can be *compiled* into an optimized, internal format (see Section 5.2, "BranchGroup Node").

An important characteristic of all scene graph objects is that they can be accessed or modified only during the creation of a scene graph, except where explicitly allowed. Access to most set and get methods of objects that are part of a live or compiled scene graph is restricted. Such restrictions provide the scene graph compiler with usage information it can use in optimally compiling or rendering a scene graph. Each object has a set of capability bits that enable certain functionality when the object is live or compiled. By default, all capability bits are disabled (cleared). Only those set and get methods corresponding to capability bits that are explicitly enabled (set) prior to the object being compiled or made live are legal. The methods for setting and getting capability bits are described next.

Constructors

The SceneGraphObject specifies one constructor.

public SceneGraphObject()

Constructs a new SceneGraphObject with default parameters:

Parameters	Default Values
capability bits	clear (all bits)
isLive	false
isCompiled	false
userData	null

Methods

The following methods are available on all scene graph objects:

public final boolean isCompiled()
public final boolean isLive()

The first method returns a flag that indicates whether the node is part of a scene graph that has been compiled. If so, only those capabilities explicitly allowed by the object's capability bits are allowed. The second method returns a flag that indicates whether the node is part of a scene graph that has been attached to a virtual universe via a high-resolution Locale object.

public final boolean getCapability(int bit)
public final void setCapability(int bit)
public final void clearCapability(int bit)

These three methods provide applications with the means for accessing and modifying the capability bits of a scene graph object. The bit positions of the capability bits are defined as public static final constants on a per-object basis. Every instance of every scene graph object has its own set of capability bits. An example of a capability bit is the ALLOW_BOUNDS_WRITE bit in node objects. Only those methods corresponding to capabilities that are enabled *before* the object is first compiled or made live are subsequently allowed for that object. A Restricted-AccessException is thrown if an application calls setCapability or clearCapability on live or compiled objects. Note that only a single bit may be set or cleared per method invocation—bits may *not* be ORed together.

```
public void setUserData(Object userData)
public Object getUserData()
```

These methods access or modify the userData field associated with this scene graph object. The userData field is a reference to an arbitrary object and may be used to store any user-specific data associated with this scene graph object—it is not used by the Java 3D API. If this object is cloned, the userData field is copied to the newly cloned object.

3.2.1 Node Objects

Node objects divide into group node objects and leaf node objects. Group nodes serve to group their child node objects together according to the group node's semantics. Leaf nodes specify the actual elements that Java 3D uses in rendering: specifically, geometric objects, lights, and sounds. These node objects are described in Chapter 5, "Group Node Objects" and Chapter 6, "Leaf Node Objects."

Constants

Node object constants allow an application to enable runtime capabilities individually. These capability bits are enforced only when the node is part of a live or compiled scene graph.

```
public static final int ALLOW_BOUNDS_READ
public static final int ALLOW_BOUNDS_WRITE
```

These bits, when set using the setCapability method, specify that the node will permit an application to invoke the getBounds and setBounds methods, respectively. An application can choose to enable a particular set method but not the associated get method, or vice versa. The application can choose to enable both methods or, by default, leave the method(s) disabled.

```
public static final int ALLOW_AUTO_COMPUTE_BOUNDS_READ
public static final int ALLOW_AUTO_COMPUTE_BOUNDS_WRITE
```

These bits, when set using the setCapability method, specify that the node will permit an application to invoke the getBoundsAutoCompute and setBoundsAutoCompute methods, respectively. An application can choose to enable a particular set method but not the associated get method, or vice versa. The application can choose to enable both methods or, by default, leave the method(s) disabled.

`public static final int ENABLE_PICK_REPORTING`

This flag specifies that this node will be reported in a SceneGraphPath. By default, this is disabled.

`public static final int ALLOW_PICKABLE_READ`
`public static final int ALLOW_PICKABLE_WRITE`

These flags specify that this Node can have its pickability read or changed.

`public static final int ENABLE_COLLISION_REPORTING`

This flag specifies that this Node will be reported in the collision SceneGraph-Path if a collision occurs. This capability is specifiable only for Group nodes; it is ignored for Leaf nodes. The default for Group nodes is false. Only interior nodes that have this flag set to true will be reported in the SceneGraphPath (unless they are needed for uniqueness).

`public static final int ALLOW_COLLIDABLE_READ`
`public static final int ALLOW_COLLIDABLE_WRITE`

These flags specify that this Node allows read or write access to its collidability state.

`public static final int ALLOW_LOCAL_TO_VWORLD_READ`

This flag specifies that this node allows read access to its local-coordinates-to-virtual-world-(Vworld)-coordinates transform.

Constructors

The Node object specifies the following constructor:

`public Node()`

This constructor constructs and initializes a Node object with default values. The Node class provides an abstract class for all group and leaf nodes. It provides a common framework for constructing a Java 3D scene graph, specifically, bounding volumes. The default values are:

Parameters	Default Value
pickable	true
collidable	true
boundsAutoCompute	true
bounds	N/A (automatically computed)

Methods

The following methods are available on Node objects, subject to the capabilities that are enabled for live or compiled nodes:

public Node getParent()

Retrieves the parent of this node, or `null` if this node has no parent. This method is valid only during the construction of the scene graph. If this object is part of a live or compiled scene graph, a `RestrictedAccessException` will be thrown.

public Bounds getBounds()
public void setBounds(Bounds bounds)

These methods access or modify this node's geometric bounds.

public void getLocalToVworld(Transform3D t)
public void getLocalToVworld(SceneGraphPath path, Transform3D t)

These methods access the local-coordinates-to-virtual-world-coordinates transform for this node and place the result into the specified Transform3D argument. The first form is used for nodes that are *not* part of a shared subgraph; the second form is used for nodes that *are* part of a shared subgraph. The local-coordinates-to-Vworld-coordinates transform is the composite of all transforms in the scene graph from the root down to this node (via the specified Link nodes, in the second case). It is valid only for nodes that are part of a live scene graph. An exception will be thrown if the node is not part of a live scene graph or if the appropriate capability is not set. Additionally, the first form will throw an exception if the node is part of a shared subgraph.

public void setBoundsAutoCompute(boolean autoCompute)
public boolean getBoundsAutoCompute()

These methods set and get the value that determines whether the node's geometric bounds are computed automatically, in which case the bounds will be read-only, or are set manually, in which case the value specified by `setBounds` will be used. The default is automatic.

public void setPickable(boolean pickable)
public boolean getPickable()

These methods set and retrieve the flag indicating whether this node can be picked. A setting of `false` means that this node and its children are all unpickable.

```
public void setCollidable(boolean collidable)
public boolean getCollidable()
```

The set method sets the collidable value. The get method returns the collidable value. This value determines whether this node and its children, if a group node, can be considered for collision purposes. If the value is false, neither this node nor any children nodes will be traversed for collision purposes. The default value is true. The collidable setting is the way that an application can perform collision culling.

3.2.2   NodeComponent Objects

Node component objects include the actual geometry and appearance attributes used to render the geometry. These component objects are described in Chapter 8, "Node Component Objects."

Constructors

The NodeComponent object specifies the following constructor:

```
public NodeComponent()
```

This constructor constructs and initializes a NodeComponent object with default parameters. The NodeComponent class provides an abstract class for all component objects. The default values are as follows:

Parameters	Default Value
duplicateOnCloneTree	false

Methods

The following methods are available on NodeComponent objects:

```
public void setDuplicateOnCloneTree(boolean duplicate)
public boolean getDuplicateOnCloneTree()
```

These methods access or modify the duplicateOnCloneTree value of the Node-Component object. The duplicateOnCloneTree value is used by the cloneTree method to determine if NodeComponent objects should be duplicated or just referenced in the cloned leaf object.

3.3   Scene Graph Superstructure Objects

Java 3D defines two scene graph superstructure objects, VirtualUniverse and Locale, which are used to contain collections of subgraphs that comprise the scene graph. These objects are described in more detail in Chapter 4, "Scene Graph Superstructure."

3.3.1   VirtualUniverse Object

A VirtualUniverse object consists of a list of Locale objects that contain a collection of scene graph nodes that exist in the universe. Typically, an application will need only one VirtualUniverse, even for very large virtual databases. Operations on a VirtualUniverse include enumerating the Locale objects contained within the universe. See Section 4.6.1, "VirtualUniverse Object," for more information.

3.3.2   Locale Object

The Locale object acts as a container for a collection of subgraphs of the scene graph that are rooted by a BranchGroup node. A Locale also defines a location within the virtual universe using high-resolution coordinates (HiResCoord) to specify its position. The HiResCoord serves as the origin for all scene graph objects contained within the Locale.

A Locale has no parent in the scene graph but is implicitly attached to a virtual universe when it is constructed. A Locale may reference an arbitrary number of BranchGroup nodes but has no explicit children.

The coordinates of all scene graph objects are relative to the HiResCoord of the Locale in which they are contained. Operations on a Locale include setting or getting the HiResCoord of the Locale, adding a subgraph, and removing a subgraph (see Section 4.6.2, "Locale Object," for more information).

3.4   Scene Graph Viewing Objects

Java 3D defines five scene graph viewing objects that are not part of the scene graph per se but serve to define the viewing parameters and to provide hooks into the physical world. These objects are Canvas3D, Screen3D, View, PhysicalBody, and PhysicalEnvironment. They are described in more detail in Chapter 9, "View Model," and Appendix C, "View Model Details."

3.4.1   Canvas3D Object

The Canvas3D object encapsulates all of the parameters associated with the window being rendered into (see Section 9.9, "The Canvas3D Object"). When a Canvas3D object is attached to a View object, the Java 3D traverser renders the specified view onto the canvas. Multiple Canvas3D objects can point to the same View object.

3.4.2   Screen3D Object

The Screen3D object encapsulates all of the parameters associated with the physical screen containing the canvas, such as the width and height of the screen in pixels, the physical dimensions of the screen, and various physical calibration values (see Section 9.8, "The Screen3D Object").

3.4.3   View Object

The View object specifies information needed to render the scene graph. Figure 3-2 shows a View object attached to a simple scene graph for viewing the scene.

The View object is the central Java 3D object for coordinating all aspects of viewing (see Section 9.7, "The View Object"). All viewing parameters in Java 3D are directly contained either within the View object or within objects pointed to by a View object. Java 3D supports multiple simultaneously active View objects, each of which can render to one or more canvases.

3.4.4   PhysicalBody Object

The PhysicalBody object encapsulates all of the parameters associated with the physical body, such as head position, right and left eye position, and so forth. (see Section 9.10, "The PhysicalBody Object").

3.4.5   PhysicalEnvironment Object

The PhysicalEnvironment object encapsulates all of the parameters associated with the physical environment, such as calibration information for the tracker base for the head or hand tracker (see Section 9.11, "The PhysicalEnvironment Object").

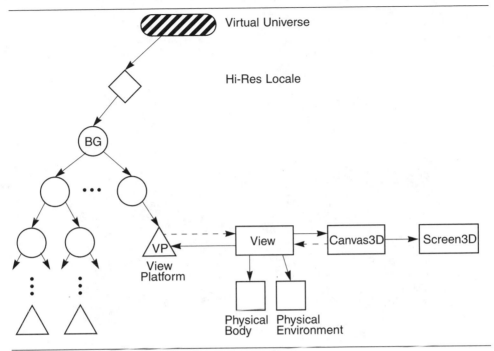

Figure 3-2   Viewing a Scene Graph

CHAPTER 4

Scene Graph Superstructure

JAVA 3D's superstructure consists of one or more VirtualUniverse objects, each of which contains a set of one or more high-resolution Locale objects. The Locale objects, in turn, contain collections of subgraphs that comprise the scene graph (see Figure 4-1).

4.1 The Virtual Universe

Java 3D defines the concept of a *virtual universe* as a three-dimensional space with an associated set of objects. Virtual universes serve as the largest unit of aggregate representation, and can also be thought of as databases. Virtual universes can be very large, both in physical space units and in content. Indeed, in most cases a single virtual universe will serve an application's entire needs.

Virtual universes are separate entities in that no node object may exist in more than one virtual universe at any one time. Likewise, the objects in one virtual universe are not visible in, nor do they interact with objects in, any other virtual universe.

To support large virtual universes, Java 3D introduces the concept of Locales that have *high-resolution coordinates* as an origin. Think of high-resolution coordinates as "tie-downs" that precisely anchor the locations of objects specified using less precise floating-point coordinates that are within the range of influence of the high-resolution coordinates.

A Locale, with its associated high-resolution coordinates, serves as the next level of representation down from a virtual universe. All virtual universes contain one or more high-resolution-coordinate Locales, and all other objects are attached to a Locale. High-resolution coordinates act as an upper-level translation-only transform node. For example, the coordinates of all objects that are attached to a particular Locale are all relative to the location of that Locale's high-resolution coordinates.

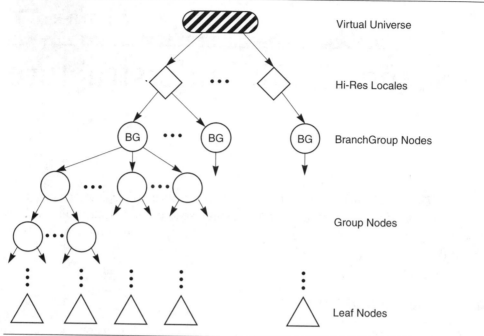

Figure 4-1   The Virtual Universe

While a virtual universe is similar to the traditional computer graphics concept of a scene graph, a given virtual universe can become so large that it is often better to think of a scene graph as the descendant of a high-resolution-coordinate Locale.

4.2   Establishing a Scene

To construct a three-dimensional scene, the programmer must execute a Java 3D program. The Java 3D application must first create a VirtualUniverse object and attach at least one Locale to it. Then the desired scene graph is constructed, starting with a BranchGroup node and including at least one ViewPlatform object, and the scene graph is attached to the Locale. Finally, a View object that references the ViewPlatform object (see Section 1.6, "Structuring the Java 3D Program") is constructed. As soon as a scene graph containing a ViewPlatform is attached to the VirtualUniverse, Java 3D's rendering loop is engaged, and the scene will appear on the drawing canvas(es) associated with the View object.

4.3   Loading a Virtual Universe

Java 3D is a runtime application programming interface (API), not a file format. As an API, Java 3D provides no direct mechanism for loading or storing a virtual universe. Constructing a scene graph involves the execution of a Java 3D program. However, loaders to convert a number of standard 3D file formats to or from Java 3D virtual universes are expected to be generally available.

4.4   Coordinate Systems

By default, Java 3D coordinate systems are right-handed, with the orientation semantics being that $+y$ is the local gravitational up, $+x$ is horizontal to the right, and $+z$ is directly toward the viewer. The default units are meters.

4.5   High-Resolution Coordinates

Double-precision floating-point, single-precision floating-point, or even fixed-point representations of three-dimensional coordinates are sufficient to represent and display rich 3D scenes. Unfortunately, scenes are not worlds, let alone universes. If one ventures even a hundred miles away from the (0.0, 0.0, 0.0) origin using only single-precision floating-point coordinates, representable points become quite quantized, to at very best a third of an inch (and much more coarsely than that in practice).

To "shrink" down to a small size (say the size of an IC transistor), even very near (0.0, 0.0, 0.0), the same problem arises.

If a large contiguous virtual universe is to be supported, some form of higher-resolution addressing is required. Thus the choice of 256-bit positional components for "high-resolution" positions.

4.5.1   Java 3D High-Resolution Coordinates

Java 3D high-resolution coordinates consist of three 256-bit fixed-point numbers, one each for x, y, and z. The fixed point is at bit 128, and the value 1.0 is defined to be exactly 1 meter. This coordinate system is sufficient to describe a universe in excess of several hundred billion light years across, yet still define objects smaller than a proton (down to below the planck length). Table 4-1 shows how many bits are needed above or below the fixed point to represent the range of interesting physical dimensions.

33

2^n Meters	Units
Table 4-1	**Java 3D High-Resolution Coordinates**
87.29	Universe (20 billion light years)
69.68	Galaxy (100,000 light years)
53.07	Light year
43.43	Solar system diameter
23.60	Earth diameter
10.65	Mile
9.97	Kilometer
0.00	Meter
−19.93	Micron
−33.22	Angstrom
−115.57	Planck length

A 256-bit fixed-point number also has the advantage of being able to directly represent nearly any reasonable single-precision floating-point value *exactly*.

High-resolution coordinates in Java 3D are used only to embed more traditional floating point coordinate systems within a much higher-resolution substrate. In this way a visually seamless virtual universe of any conceivable size or scale can be created, without worry about numerical accuracy.

4.5.2   Java 3D Virtual World Coordinates

Within a given virtual world coordinate system, positions are expressed by three floating point numbers. The virtual world coordinate scale is in meters, but this can be affected by scale changes in the object hierarchy.

4.5.3   Details of High-Resolution Coordinates

High-resolution coordinates are represented as signed, two's-complement, fixed-point numbers consisting of 256 bits. Although Java 3D keeps the internal representation of high-resolution coordinates opaque, users specify such coordinates using 8-element integer arrays. Java 3D treats the integer found at index 0 as containing the most significant bits and the integer found at index 7 as containing the least significant bits of the high-resolution coordinate. The binary point is located at bit position 128, or between the integers at index 3 and 4. A high-resolution coordinate of 1.0 is 1 meter.

The semantics of how file loaders deal with high-resolution coordinates is up to the individual file loader, as Java 3D does not directly define any file-loading semantics. However, some general advice can be given (note that this advice is *not* officially part of the Java 3D specification).

For "small" virtual universes (on the order of hundreds of meters across in relative scale), a single Locale with high-resolution coordinates at location (0.0, 0.0, 0.0) as the root node (below the VirtualUniverse object) is sufficient; a loader can automatically construct this node during the loading process, and the point in high-resolution coordinates does not need any direct representation in the external file.

Larger virtual universes are expected to be constructed usually like computer directory hierarchies, that is, as a "root" virtual universe containing mostly external file references to embedded virtual universes. In this case, the file reference object (user-specific data hung off a Java 3D group or hi-res node) defines the location for the data to be read into the current virtual universe.

The data file's contents should be parented to the file object node while being read, thus inheriting the high-resolution coordinates of the file object as the new relative virtual universe origin of the embedded scene graph. If this scene graph itself contains high-resolution coordinates, it will need to be offset (translated) by the amount in the file object's high-resolution coordinates and then added to the larger virtual universe as new high-resolution coordinates, with their contents hung off below them. Once again, this procedure is not part of the official Java 3D specification, but some more details on the care and use of high-resolution coordinates in external file formats will probably be available as a Java 3D application note.

Authoring tools that directly support high-resolution coordinates should create additional high-resolution coordinates as a user creates new geometry "sufficiently" far away (or of different scale) from existing high-resolution coordinates.

Semantics of widely moving objects. Most fixed and nearly-fixed objects stay attached to the same high-resolution Locale. Objects that make wide changes in position or scale may periodically need to be reparented to a more appropriate high-resolution Locale. If no appropriate high-resolution Locale exists, the application may need to create a new one.

Semantics of viewing. The ViewPlatform object and the associated nodes in its hierarchy are very often widely moving objects. Applications will typically attach the view platform to the most appropriate high-resolution Locale. For display, all objects will first have their positions translated by the difference between the location of their high-resolution Locale and the view platform's high-resolution Locale. (In the common case of the Locales being the same, no translation is necessary.)

4.6   API for Superstructure Objects

This section describes the API for the VirtualUniverse, Locale, and HiResCoord objects.

4.6.1   VirtualUniverse Object

The VirtualUniverse object consists of a set of Locale objects.

Constructors

The VirtualUniverse object has the following constructors:

```
public VirtualUniverse()
```

This constructs a new VirtualUniverse object. This VirtualUniverse can then be used to create Locale objects.

Methods

The VirtualUniverse object has the following methods:

```
public Enumeration getAllLocales()
public int numLocales()
```

The first method returns the Enumeration object of all Locales in this virtual universe. The numLocales method returns the number of Locales.

◀ New in 1.2 ▶ `public void removeLocale(Locale locale)`

This method removes a Locale and its associates branch graphs from this universe. All branch graphs within the specified Locale are detached, regardless of whether their ALLOW_DETACH capability bits are set. The Locale is then marked as being dead: No branch graphs may subsequently be attached.

◀ New in 1.2 ▶ `public void removeAllLocales()`

This method removes all Locales and their associates branch graphs from this universe. All branch graphs within each Locale are detached, regardless of whether their ALLOW_DETACH capability bits are set. Each Locale is then marked as being dead: No branch graphs may subsequently be attached. This method should be called by applications and applets to allow Java 3D to clean up its resources.

```
public static void setJ3DThreadPriority(int priority)
public static int getJ3DThreadPriority()
```

◀ New in 1.2 ▶
◀ New in 1.2 ▶

These methods set and retrieve the priority of all Java 3D threads. The default value is the priority of the thread that started Java 3D.

4.6.2   Locale Object

The Locale object consists of a point, specified using high-resolution coordinates, and a set of subgraphs, rooted by BranchGroup node objects.

Constructors

The Locale object has the following constructors:

```
public Locale(VirtualUniverse universe)
public Locale(VirtualUniverse universe, int x[], int y[], int z[])
public Locale(VirtualUniverse universe, HiResCoord hiRes)
```

These three constructors create a new high-resolution Locale object in the specified VirtualUniverse. The first form constructs a Locale object located at (0.0, 0.0, 0.0). The other two forms construct a Locale object using the specified high-resolution coordinates. In the second form, the parameters x, y, and z are arrays of eight 32-bit integers that specify the respective high-resolution coordinate.

Methods

The Locale object has the following methods. For the Locale picking methods, see Section 11.3.2, "BranchGroup Node and Locale Node Pick Methods."

```
public VirtualUniverse getVirtualUniverse()
```

This method retrieves the virtual universe within which this Locale object is contained.

```
public void setHiRes(int x[], int y[], int z[])
public void setHiRes(HiResCoord hiRes)
public void getHiRes(HiResCoord hiRes)
```

These methods set or get the high-resolution coordinates of this Locale.

```
public void addBranchGraph(BranchGroup branchGroup)
public void removeBranchGraph(BranchGroup branchGroup)
public void replaceBranchGraph(BranchGroup oldGroup,
        BranchGroup newGroup)
public int numBranchGraphs()
public Enumeration getAllBranchGraphs()
```

The first three methods add, remove, and replace a branch graph in this Locale. Adding a branch graph has the effect of making the branch graph "live." The fourth method retrieves the number of branch graphs in this Locale. The last method retrieves an Enumeration object of all branch graphs.

4.6.3   HiResCoord Object

A HiResCoord object defines a point using a set of three high-resolution coordinates, each of which consists of three two's-complement fixed-point numbers. Each high-resolution number consists of 256 total bits with a binary point at bit 128. Java 3D uses integer arrays of length eight to define or extract a single 256-bit coordinate value. Java 3D interprets the integer at index 0 as the 32 most significant bits and the integer at index 7 as the 32 least significant bits.

Constructors

The HiResCoord object has the following constructors:

```
public HiResCoord(int x[], int y[], int z[])
public HiResCoord(HiResCoord hc)
public HiResCoord()
```

The first constructor generates the high-resolution coordinate point from three integer arrays of length eight. The integer arrays specify the coordinate values corresponding with their name. The second constructor creates a new high-resolution coordinate point by cloning the high-resolution coordinates hc. The third constructor creates new high-resolution coordinates with value (0.0, 0.0, 0.0).

Methods

```
public void setHiResCoord(int x[], int y[], int z[])
public void setHiResCoord(HiResCoord hiRes)
public void setHiResCoordX(int x[])
public void setHiResCoordY(int y[])
public void setHiResCoordZ(int z[])
```

These five methods modify the value of high-resolution coordinates this. The first method resets all three coordinate values with the values specified by the three integer arrays. The second method sets the value of this to that of high-resolution coordinates hiRes. The third, fourth, and fifth methods reset the corresponding coordinate of this.

```
public void getHiResCoord(int x[], int y[], int z[])
public void getHiResCoord(HiResCoord hc)
public void getHiResCoordX(int x[])
public void getHiResCoordY(int y[])
public void getHiResCoordZ(int z[])
```

These five methods retrieve the value of the high-resolution coordinates this. The first method retrieves the high-resolution coordinates' values and places those values into the three integer arrays specified. All three arrays must have length greater than or equal to eight. The second method updates the value of the high-resolution coordinates hc to match the value of this. The third, fourth, and fifth methods retrieve the coordinate value that corresponds to their name and update the integer array specified, which must be of length eight or greater.

```
public void add(HiResCoord h1, HiResCoord h2)
public void sub(HiResCoord h1, HiResCoord h2)
```

These two methods perform arithmetic operations on high-resolution coordinates. The first method adds h1 to h2 and stores the result in this. The second method subtracts h2 from h1 and stores the result in this.

```
public void scale(int scale, HiResCoord h1)
public void scale(int scale)
```

These methods scale a high-resolution coordinate point. The first method scales h1 by the scalar value scale and places the scaled coordinates into this. The second method scales this by the scalar value scale and places the scaled coordinates back into this.

```
public void negate(HiResCoord h1)
public void negate()
```

These two methods negate a high-resolution coordinate point. The first method negates h1 and stores the result in this. The second method negates this and stores its negated value back into this.

`public void difference(HiResCoord h1, Vector3d v)`

This method subtracts h1 from `this` and stores the resulting difference vector in the double-precision floating-point vector v. Note that although the individual high-resolution coordinate points cannot be represented accurately by double-precision numbers, this difference vector between them *can* be accurately represented by doubles for many practical purposes, such as viewing.

`public boolean equals(HiResCoord h1)`
`public boolean equals(Object o1)`

The first method performs an arithmetic comparison between `this` and h1. It returns `true` if the two high-resolution coordinate points are equal; otherwise, it returns `false`. The second method returns true if the Object o1 is of type HiRes-Coord and all of the data members of o1 are equal to the corresponding data members in this HiResCoord.

`public double distance(HiResCoord h1)`

This method computes the linear distance between high-resolution coordinate points `this` and h1 and returns this value expressed as a double. Note that although the individual high-resolution coordinate points cannot be represented accurately by double precision numbers, this distance between them *can* be accurately represented by a double for many practical purposes.

CHAPTER 5

Group Node Objects

Gᴿᴼᵁᴾ nodes are the glue elements used in constructing a scene graph. The following subsections list the seven group nodes (see Figure 5-1) and their definitions. All group nodes can have a variable number of child node objects—including other group nodes as well as leaf nodes. These children have an associated index that allows operations to specify a particular child. However, unless one of the special ordered group nodes is used, the Java 3D renderer can choose to render a group node's children in whatever order it wishes (including rendering the children in parallel).

```
SceneGraphObject
    Node
        Group
            BranchGroup
            OrderedGroup
                DecalGroup
            SharedGroup
            Switch
            TransformGroup
```

Figure 5-1   Group Node Hierarchy

5.1   Group Node

The Group node object is a general-purpose grouping node. Group nodes have exactly one parent and an arbitrary number of children that are rendered in an unspecified order (or in parallel). Null children are allowed; no operation is performed on a null child node. Operations on Group node objects include adding, removing, and enumerating the children of the Group node. The subclasses of Group node add additional semantics.

Constants

```
public static final int ALLOW_CHILDREN_READ
public static final int ALLOW_CHILDREN_WRITE
public static final int ALLOW_CHILDREN_EXTEND
```

These flags, when enabled using the setCapability method, specify that this Group node will allow the following methods, respectively:

- numChildren, getChild, getAllChildren
- setChild, insertChild, removeChild
- addChild, moveTo

These capability bits are enforced only when the node is part of a live or compiled scene graph.

```
public static final int ALLOW_COLLISION_BOUNDS_READ
public static final int ALLOW_COLLISION_BOUNDS_WRITE
```

These flags, when enabled using the setCapability method, specify that this Group node will allow reading and writing of its collision bounds.

Constructors

```
public Group()
```

Constructs and initializes a Group node object with default parameters:

collision bounds = null
alternate collision target = false

Methods

The Group node class defines the following methods:

```
public int numChildren()
public Node getChild(int index)
```

The first method returns a count of the number of children. The second method returns the child at the specified index.

```
public void setChild(Node child, int index)
public void insertChild(Node child, int index)
public void removeChild(int index)
```

The first method replaces the child at the specified index with a new child. The second method inserts a new child before the child at the specified index. The third method removes the child at the specified index. Note that if this Group node is part of a live or compiled scene graph, only BranchGroup nodes may be added to or removed from it—and only if the appropriate capability bits are set.

public Enumeration getAllChildren()

This method returns an Enumeration object of all children.

public void addChild(Node child)

This method adds a new child as the last child in the group. Note that if this Group node is part of a live or compiled scene graph, only BranchGroup nodes may be added to it—and only if the appropriate capability bits are set.

public void moveTo(BranchGroup branchGroup)

This method moves the specified BranchGroup node from its old location in the scene graph to the end of this group, in an atomic manner. Functionally, this method is equivalent to the following lines:

```
branchGroup.detach();
this.addChild(branchGroup);
```

If either this Group or the specified BranchGroup is part of a live or compiled scene graph, the appropriate capability bits must be set in the affected nodes.

public Bounds setCollisionBounds(Bounds bounds)
public Bounds getCollisionBounds()

These methods set and retrieve the collision bounding object for a node.

public void setAlternateCollisionTarget(boolean target)
public boolean getAlternateCollisionTarget()

The set method causes this Group node to be reported as the collision target when collision is being used and this node or any of its children are in a collision. The default is false. This method tries to set the capability bit Node.ENABLE_COLLISION_REPORTING. The get method returns the collision target state.

For collision with USE_GEOMETRY set, the collision traverser will check the geometry of all the Group node's leaf descendants. For collision with USE_BOUNDS set, the collision traverser will check the bounds at this Group

43

node. In both cases, if there is a collision, this Group node will be reported as the colliding object in the SceneGraphPath.

5.2   BranchGroup Node

A BranchGroup is the root of a subgraph of a scene that may be compiled as a unit, attached to a virtual universe, or included as a child of a group node in another subgraph. A subgraph, rooted by a BranchGroup node, can be thought of as a compile unit. The following may be done with BranchGroup:

- A BranchGroup may be compiled by calling its `compile` method. This causes the entire subgraph to be compiled. If any BranchGroup nodes are contained within the subgraph, they are compiled as well (along with their descendants).

- A BranchGroup may be inserted into a virtual universe by attaching it to a Locale. The entire subgraph is then said to be *live*.

- A BranchGroup that is contained within another subgraph may be reparented or detached at run time if the appropriate capabilities are set. See Figure 5-2.

Note that if a BranchGroup is included in another subgraph, as a child of some other group node, it may not be attached to a Locale.

Constants

The BranchGroup class adds the following new constant:

`public static final int ALLOW_DETACH`

This flag, when enabled using the `setCapability` method, allows this Branch-Group node to be detached from its parent group node. This capability flag is enforced only when the node is part of a live or compiled scene graph.

Constructors

`public BranchGroup()`

Constructs and initializes a new BranchGroup node object.

Methods

The BranchGroup class defines the following methods:

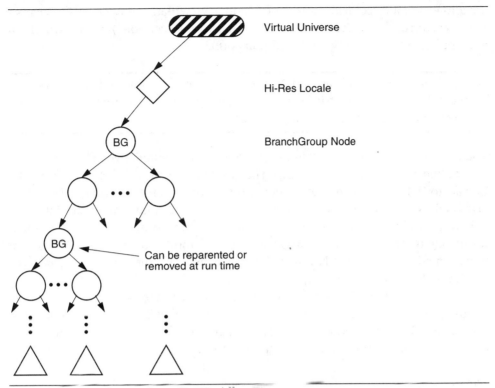

Figure 5-2   Altering the Scene Graph at Run Time

public void compile()

This method compiles the scene graph rooted at this BranchGroup and creates and caches a newly compiled scene graph.

public void detach()

This method detaches the BranchGroup node from its parent.

5.3   TransformGroup Node

The TransformGroup node specifies a single spatial transformation—via a Transform3D object (see Section 8.1.29, "Transform3D Object")—that can position, orient, and scale all of its children.

The specified transformation must be affine. Further, if the TransformGroup node is used as an ancestor of a ViewPlatform node in the scene graph, then the transformation must be congruent—only rotations, translations, and uniform scales are allowed in a direct path from a Locale to a ViewPlatform node. A `BadTransformException` (see Section D.1, "BadTransformException") is thrown if an attempt is made to specify an illegal transform.

Note: Even though arbitrary affine transformations are allowed, better performance will result if all matrices within a branch graph are congruent—containing only rotations, translation, and *uniform* scale.

The effects of transformations in the scene graph are cumulative. The concatenation of the transformations of each TransformGroup in a direct path from the Locale to a Leaf node defines a composite model transformation (CMT) that takes points in that Leaf node's local coordinates and transforms them into Virtual World (Vworld) coordinates. This composite transformation is used to transform points, normals, and distances into Vworld coordinates. Points are transformed by the CMT. Normals are transformed by the inverse-transpose of the CMT. Distances are transformed by the scale of the CMT. In the case of a transformation containing a nonuniform scale or shear, the maximum scale value in any direction is used. This ensures, for example, that a transformed bounding sphere, which is specified as a point and a radius, continues to enclose all objects that are also transformed using a nonuniform scale.

Constants

The TransformGroup class adds the following new flags:

```
public static final int ALLOW_TRANSFORM_READ
public static final int ALLOW_TRANSFORM_WRITE
```

These flags, when enabled using the `setCapability` method, allow this node's Transform3D to be read or written. They are used only when the node is part of a live or compiled scene graph.

Constructors

```
public TransformGroup()
public TransformGroup(Transform3D t1)
```

These construct and initialize a new TransformGroup. The first form initializes the node's Transform3D to the identity transformation; the second form initializes the node's Transform3D to a copy of the specified transform.

Methods

The TransformGroup class defines the following methods:

```
public void setTransform(Transform3D t1)
public void getTransform(Transform3D t1)
```

These methods retrieve or set this node's attached Transform3D object by copying the transform to or from the specified object.

```
public Node cloneNode(boolean forceDuplicate)
public void duplicateNode(Node originalNode,
        boolean forceDuplicate)
```

The first method creates a new instance of the node. This method is called by cloneTree to duplicate the current node. The second method copies all the node information from the originalNode into the current node. This method is called from the cloneNode method, which in turn is called by the cloneTree method.

For each NodeComponent object contained by the object being duplicated, the NodeComponent's duplicateOnCloneTree flag is used to determine whether the NodeComponent should be duplicated in the new node or a reference to the current node should be placed in the new node. This flag can be overridden by setting the forceDuplicate parameter in the cloneTree method to true.

5.4 OrderedGroup Node

The OrderedGroup node guarantees that Java 3D will render its children in their index order. Only the OrderedGroup node and its subclasses make any use of the order of their children during rendering.

Constructors

```
public OrderedGroup()
```

Constructs and initializes a new OrderedGroup node object.

5.5 DecalGroup Node

The DecalGroup node is a subclass of the OrderedGroup node. The DecalGroup node is an ordered group node used for defining decal geometry on top of other geometry. The DecalGroup node specifies that its children should be rendered in index order and that they generate coplanar objects. Examples include painted decals or text on surfaces and a checkerboard layered on top of a table.

The first child, at index 0, defines the surface on top of which all other children are rendered. The geometry of this child must encompass all other children; otherwise, incorrect rendering may result. The polygons contained within each of the children must be facing the same way. If the polygons defined by the first child are front facing, then all other surfaces should be front facing. In this case, the polygons are rendered in order. The renderer can use knowledge of the coplanar nature of the surfaces to avoid Z-buffer collisions. (If, for example, the underlying implementation supports stenciling or polygon offset, then these techniques may be employed.) If the main surface is back facing, then all other surfaces should be back facing and need not be rendered (even if back-face culling is disabled).

Note that using the DecalGroup node does not guarantee that Z-buffer collisions are avoided. An implementation of Java 3D may fall back to treating DecalGroup node as an ordinary OrderedGroup node.

Constructors

`public DecalGroup()`

Constructs and initializes a new DecalGroup node object.

5.6   Switch Node

The Switch group node allows a Java 3D application to choose dynamically among a number of subgraphs. The Switch node contains an ordered list of children and a switch value. The switch value determines which child or children Java 3D will render. Note that the index order of children is used only for selecting the appropriate child or children—it does not specify rendering order.

Constants

```
public static final int ALLOW_SWITCH_READ
public static final int ALLOW_SWITCH_WRITE
```

These flags, when enabled using the `setCapability` method, allow reading and writing of the values that specify the child-selection criteria. They are used only when the node is part of a live or compiled scene graph.

```
public static final int CHILD_NONE
public static final int CHILD_ALL
public static final int CHILD_MASK
```

These values, when used in place of a nonnegative integer index value, indicate which children of the Switch node are selected for rendering. A value of CHILD_NONE indicates that no children are rendered. A value of CHILD_ALL indicates that all children are rendered, effectively making this Switch node operate as an ordinary Group node. A value of CHILD_MASK indicates that the childMask BitSet is used to select the children that are rendered.

Constructors

public Switch()

Constructs a Switch node with default parameters:

Parameters	Default Values
child selection index	CHILD_NONE
child selection mask	false (for all children)

public Switch(int whichChild)
public Switch(int whichChild, BitSet childMask)

These constructors initialize a new Switch node using the specified parameters.

Methods

The Switch node class defines the following methods:

public void setWhichChild(int whichChild)
public int getWhichChild()

These methods access or modify the index of the child that the Switch object will draw. The value may be a nonnegative integer, indicating a specific child, or it may be one of the following constants: CHILD_NONE, CHILD_ALL, or CHILD_MASK. If the specified value is out of range, then no children are drawn.

public void setChildMask(BitSet childMask)
public BitSet getChildMask()

These methods access or modify the mask used to select the children that the Switch object will draw when the whichChild parameter is CHILD_MASK. This parameter is ignored during rendering if the whichChild parameter is a value other than CHILD_MASK.

`public Node currentChild()`

This method returns the currently selected child. If `whichChild` is out of range, or is set to CHILD_MASK, CHILD_ALL, or CHILD_NONE, then `null` is returned.

5.7   SharedGroup Node

A SharedGroup node provides a mechanism for sharing the same subgraph in different parts of the tree via a Link node. See Section 7.1.1, "SharedGroup Node," for a description of this node.

CHAPTER 6

Leaf Node Objects

LEAF nodes define atomic entities such as geometry, lights, and sounds. The leaf nodes and their associated meanings follow.

6.1 Leaf Node

The Leaf node is an abstract class for all scene graph nodes that have no children. Leaf nodes specify lights, geometry, and sounds; provide special linking and instancing capabilities for sharing scene graphs; and provide a view platform for positioning and orienting a view in the virtual world. Figure 6-1 shows the Leaf node object hierarchy.

Constructors

```
public Leaf()
```

Constructs and initializes a new Leaf object.

6.2 Shape3D Node

The Shape3D leaf node object specifies all geometric objects. It contains a list of one or more Geometry component objects and a single Appearance component object. The Geometry objects define the shape node's geometric data. The Appearance object specifies that object's appearance attributes, including color, material, texture, and so on. See Chapter 8, "Node Component Objects" for details of the Geometry and Appearance objects.

```
SceneGraphObject
    Node
        Leaf
            AlternateAppearance
            Background
            Behavior
                Predefined behaviors
            BoundingLeaf
            Clip
            Fog
                ExponentialFog
                LinearFog
            Light
                AmbientLight
                DirectionalLight
                PointLight
                    SpotLight
            Link
            Morph
            Shape3D
                OrientedShape3D
            Sound
                BackgroundSound
                PointSound
                    ConeSound
            Soundscape
            ViewPlatform
```

Figure 6-1   Leaf Node Hierarchy

The list of geometry objects must all be of the same equivalence class; that is, the same basic type of primitive. For subclasses of GeometryArray, all point objects are equivalent, all line objects are equivalent, and all polygon objects are equivalent. For other subclasses of Geometry, only objects of the same subclass are equivalent. The equivalence classes are as follows:

- GeometryArray (point): [Indexed]PointArray

- GeometryArray (line): [Indexed]{LineArray, LineStripArray}

- GeometryArray (polygon): [Indexed]{TriangleArray, TriangleStripArray, TriangleFanArray, QuadArray}

- CompressedGeometry

- Raster

- Text3D

Constants

The Shape3D node object defines the following flags:

```
public static final int ALLOW_GEOMETRY_READ
public static final int ALLOW_GEOMETRY_WRITE
public static final int ALLOW_APPEARANCE_READ
public static final int ALLOW_APPEARANCE_WRITE
public static final int ALLOW_COLLISION_BOUNDS_WRITE
public static final int ALLOW_COLLISION_BOUNDS_READ
public static final int ALLOW_APPEARANCE_OVERRIDE_WRITE
public static final int ALLOW_APPEARANCE_OVERRIDE_READ
```

◀ New in 1.2 ▶
◀ New in 1.2 ▶

These flags, when enabled using the `setCapability` method, allow reading and writing of the Geometry and Appearance component objects, the collision bounds, and the appearance override enable, respectively. These capability flags are enforced only when the node is part of a live or compiled scene graph.

Constructors

The Shape3D node object defines the following constructors:

public Shape3D()

Constructs a Shape3D node with default parameters:

Parameter	Default Value
appearance	null (default values are used for all appearance attributes)
geometry	{ null }
collisionBounds	null
appearanceOverrideEnable	false

The list of geometry components is initialized with a null geometry component as the single element with an index of 0. A null geometry component specifies that no geometry is drawn. A null appearance component specifies that default values are used for all appearance attributes.

public Shape3D(Geometry geometry, Appearance appearance)
public Shape3D(Geometry geometry)

The first form constructs and initializes a new Shape3D object with the specified geometry and appearance components. The second form uses the specified geometry and a null appearance component. The list of geometry components is initialized with the specified geometry component as the single element with an index of 0. If the geometry component is null, no geometry is drawn. A null appearance component specifies that default values are used for all appearance attributes.

Methods

The Shape3D node object defines the following methods:

```
                 public void setGeometry(Geometry geometry)
New in 1.2    public void setGeometry(Geometry geometry, int index)
                 public Geometry getGeometry()
New in 1.2    public Geometry getGeometry(int index)
```

These methods access or modify the Geometry component object associated with this Shape3D node. The first `setGeometry` method replaces the geometry component at index 0 in this Shape3D node's list of geometry components with the specified geometry component. The second `setGeometry` method replaces the geometry component at the specified index in this Shape3D node's list of geometry components with the specified geometry component. If there are existing geometry components in the list (besides the one being replaced), the new geometry component must be of the same equivalence class (point, line, polygon, CompressedGeometry, Raster, Text3D) as the others. The first `getGeometry` method retrieves the geometry component at index 0 from this Shape3D node's list of geometry components. The second `getGeometry` method retrieves the geometry component at the specified index from this Shape3D node's list of geometry components.

```
New in 1.2    public void insertGeometry(Geometry geometry, int index)
New in 1.2    public void removeGeometry(int index)
```

These methods insert and remove the specified geometry component into or from this Shape3D node's list of geometry components. The `insertGeometry` method inserts the specified geometry component into this Shape3D node's list of geometry components at the specified index. If there are existing geometry components in the list, the new geometry component must be of the same equivalence class (point, line, polygon, CompressedGeometry, Raster, Text3D) as the others. The `removeGeometry` method removes the geometry component at the specified index from this Shape3D node's list of geometry components.

```
New in 1.2    public void addGeometry(Geometry geometry)
```

This method appends the specified geometry component to this Shape3D node's list of geometry components. If there are existing geometry components in the list, the new geometry component must be of the same equivalence class (point, line, polygon, CompressedGeometry, Raster, Text3D) as the others.

`public Enumeration getAllGeometries()`   ◀ New in 1.2 ▶

This method returns an enumeration of this Shape3D node's list of geometry components.

`public int numGeometries()`   ◀ New in 1.2 ▶

This method appends the specified geometry component to this Shape3D node's list of geometry components. If there are existing geometry components in the list, the new geometry component must be of the same equivalence class (point, line, polygon, CompressedGeometry, Raster, Text3D) as the others.

`public void setAppearance(Appearance appearance)`
`public Appearance getAppearance()`

These methods access or modify the Appearance component object associated with this Shape3D node. Setting it to `null` results in default attribute use.

`public void setCollisionBounds(Bounds bounds)`
`public Bounds getCollisionBounds()`

These methods set and retrieve the collision bounds for this node.

`public boolean intersect(SceneGraphPath path, PickShape pickShape)`
`public boolean intersect(SceneGraphPath path, PickRay pickRay,`
`        double[] dist)`

These two methods check if the geometry component of this shape node under path intersects with the pickShape.

`public void setAppearanceOverrideEnable(boolean flag)`   ◀ New in 1.2 ▶
`public boolean getAppearanceOverrideEnable()`   ◀ New in 1.2 ▶

These methods set and retrieve the flag that indicates whether this node's appearance can be overridden. If the flag is true, this node's appearance may be overridden by an AlternateAppearance leaf node, regardless of the value of the `ALLOW_APPEARANCE_WRITE` capability bit. The default value is false. See Section 6.15, "AlternateAppearance Node."

6.2.1 OrientedShape3D Node   ◀ New in 1.2 ▶

The OrientedShape3D leaf node is a Shape3D node that is oriented along a specified axis or about a specified point. It defines an alignment mode and a rotation point or axis. This will cause the local +z axis of the object to point at the viewer's eye position. This is done regardless of the transforms above this OrientedShape3D node in the scene graph.

The OrientedShape3D node is similar in functionality to the Billboard behavior (see Section 10.8, "Billboard Behavior"), but OrientedShape3D nodes will orient themselves correctly for each view, and they can be used within a SharedGroup.

If the alignment mode is ROTATE_AXIS, the rotation will be around the specified axis. If the alignment mode is ROTATE_ABOUT_POINT, the rotation will be about the specified point, with an additional rotation to align the +*y* axis of the TransformGroup with the +*y* axis in the View.

OrientedShape3D nodes are ideal for drawing screen-aligned text or for drawing roughly symmetrical objects. A typical use might consist of a quadrilateral that contains a texture of a tree.

Constants

The OrientedShape3D node object defines the following flags:

◀ New in 1.2 ▶ `public static final int ALLOW_MODE_READ`
◀ New in 1.2 ▶ `public static final int ALLOW_MODE_WRITE`
◀ New in 1.2 ▶ `public static final int ALLOW_AXIS_READ`
◀ New in 1.2 ▶ `public static final int ALLOW_AXIS_WRITE`
◀ New in 1.2 ▶ `public static final int ALLOW_POINT_READ`
◀ New in 1.2 ▶ `public static final int ALLOW_POINT_WRITE`

These flags, when enabled using the `setCapability` method, allow reading and writing of the alignment mode, alignment axis, and rotation point information, respectively. These capability flags are enforced only when the node is part of a live or compiled scene graph.

◀ New in 1.2 ▶ `public static final int ROTATE_ABOUT_AXIS`

Specifies that rotation should be about the specified axis.

◀ New in 1.2 ▶ `public static final int ROTATE_ABOUT_POINT`

Specifies that rotation should be about the specified point and that the children's *y*-axis should match the view object's *y*-axis.

Constructors

The OrientedShape3D node specifies the following constructors:

`public OrientedShape3D()`   ◀ New in 1.2 ▶

Constructs an OrientedShape3D node with default parameters. The default values are as follows:

Parameter	Default Value
alignmentMode	ROTATE_ABOUT_AXIS
alignmentAxis	y-axis (0,1,0)
rotationPoint	(0,0,1)

`public OrientedShape3D(Geometry geometry, Appearance appearance,`   ◀ New in 1.2 ▶
     `int mode, Vector3f axis)`
`public OrientedShape3D(Geometry geometry, Appearance appearance,`   ◀ New in 1.2 ▶
     `int mode, Point3f point)`

The first constructor constructs an OrientedShape3D node with the specified geometry component, appearance component, mode, and axis. The second constructor constructs an OrientedShape3D node with the specified geometry component, appearance component, mode, and rotation point.

Methods

`public void setAlignmentMode(int mode)`   ◀ New in 1.2 ▶
`public int getAlignmentMode()`   ◀ New in 1.2 ▶

These methods set and retrieve the alignment mode. The alignment mode is one of ROTATE_ABOUT_AXIS or ROTATE_ABOUT_POINT.

`public void setAlignmentAxis(Vector3f axis)`   ◀ New in 1.2 ▶
`public void setAlignmentAxis(float x, float y, float z)`   ◀ New in 1.2 ▶
`public void getAlignmentAxis(Vector3f axis)`   ◀ New in 1.2 ▶

These methods set and retrieve the alignment axis. This is the ray about which this OrientedShape3D rotates when the mode is ROTATE_ABOUT_AXIS.

`public void setRotationPoint(Point3f point)`   ◀ New in 1.2 ▶
`public void setRotationPoint(float x, float y, float z)`   ◀ New in 1.2 ▶
`public void getRotationPoint(Point3f point)`   ◀ New in 1.2 ▶

These methods set and retrieve the rotation point. This is the point about which the OrientedShape3D rotates when the mode is ROTATE_ABOUT_POINT.

6.3 BoundingLeaf Node

The BoundingLeaf node defines a bounding region object that can be referenced by other leaf nodes to define a region of influence (Fog and Light nodes), an activation region (Background, Clip, and Soundscape nodes), or a scheduling region (Sound and Behavior nodes). The bounding region is defined in the local coordinate system of the BoundingLeaf node. A reference to a BoundingLeaf node can be used in place of a locally defined bounds object for any of the aforementioned regions.

This allows an application to specify a bounding region in one coordinate system (the local coordinate system of the BoundingLeaf node) other than the local coordinate system of the node that references the bounds. For an example of how this might be used, consider a closed room with a number of track lights. Each light can move independently of the other lights and, as such, needs its own local coordinate system. However, the bounding volume is used by all the lights in the boundary of the room, which doesn't move when the lights move. In this example, the BoundingLeaf node allows the bounding region to be defined in the local coordinate system of the room, rather than in the local coordinate system of a particular light. All lights can then share this single bounding volume.

Constants

The BoundingLeaf node object defines the following flags:

```
public static final int ALLOW_REGION_READ
public static final int ALLOW_REGION_WRITE
```

These flags, when enabled using the setCapability method, allow an application to invoke methods that respectively read and write the bounding region object.

Constructors

The BoundingLeaf node object defines the following constructors:

```
public BoundingLeaf()
```

Constructs a BoundingLeaf node with a null (empty) bounding region.

```
public BoundingLeaf(Bounds region)
```

Constructs a BoundingLeaf node with the specified bounding region.

Methods

```
public void setRegion(Bounds region)
public Bounds getRegion()
```

These methods set and retrieve the BoundingLeaf node's bounding region.

6.4 Background Node

The Background leaf node defines either a solid background color or a background image that is used to fill the window at the beginning of each new frame. It also specifies an application region in which this Background node is active. A Background node is active when its application region intersects the ViewPlatform's activation volume. If multiple Background nodes are active, the Background node that is "closest" to the eye will be used. If no Background nodes are active, then the window is cleared to black.

Constants

The Background node object defines the following flags:

```
public static final int ALLOW_APPLICATION_BOUNDS_READ
public static final int ALLOW_APPLICATION_BOUNDS_WRITE
public static final int ALLOW_IMAGE_READ
public static final int ALLOW_IMAGE_WRITE
public static final int ALLOW_COLOR_READ
public static final int ALLOW_COLOR_WRITE
public static final int ALLOW_GEOMETRY_READ
public static final int ALLOW_GEOMETRY_WRITE
```

These flags, when enabled using the setCapability method, allow an application to invoke methods that respectively read and write the application region, the image, the color, and the background geometry. These capability flags are enforced only when the node is part of a live or compiled scene graph.

Constructors

The Background node object defines the following constructors:

```
public Background()
```

Constructs a Background leaf node with default parameters:

Parameter	Default Value
color	black (0,0,0)
image	null
geometry	null
applicationBounds	null
applicationBoundingLeaf	null

```
public Background(Color3f color)
public Background(float r, float g, float b)
public Background(ImageComponent2D image)
public Background(Branchgroup branch)
```

The first two forms construct a Background leaf node with the specified color.
The second form constructs a Background leaf node with the specified 2D image.
The final form constructs a Background leaf node with the specified geometry.

Methods

The Background node object defines the following methods:

```
public void getColor(Color3f color)
public void setColor(Color3f color)
public void setColor(float r, float g, float b)
```

These three methods access or modify the background color.

```
public ImageComponent2D getImage()
public void setImage(ImageComponent2D image)
```

These two methods access or modify the background image. If the image is not
null then it is used in place of the color.

```
public void setGeometry(BranchGroup branch)
public BranchGroup getGeometry()
```

These two methods access or modify the Background geometry. The setGeome-
try method sets the background geometry to the specified BranchGroup node. If
non-null, this background geometry is drawn on top of the background color or
image using a projection matrix that essentially puts the geometry at infinity. The
geometry should be pretessellated onto a unit sphere.

```
public void setApplicationBounds(Bounds region)
public Bounds getApplicationBounds()
```

These two methods access or modify the Background node's application bounds. This bounds is used as the application region when the application bounding leaf is set to null. The getApplicationBounds method returns a copy of the associated bounds.

```
public void setApplicationBoundingLeaf(BoundingLeaf region)
public BoundingLeaf getApplicationBoundingLeaf()
```

These two methods access or modify the Background node's application bounding leaf. When set to a value other than null, this bounding leaf overrides the application bounds object and is used as the application region.

6.5   Clip Node

The Clip leaf node defines the far clipping plane used to clip objects in the virtual universe. It also specifies an application region in which this Clip node is active. A Clip node is active when its application region intersects the ViewPlatform's activation volume. If multiple Clip nodes are active, the Clip node that is "closest" to the eye will be used. The back distance value specified by this Clip node overrides the value specified in the View object. If no Clip nodes are active, then the back clip distance is used from the View object.

Constants

```
public static final int ALLOW_APPLICATION_BOUNDS_READ
public static final int ALLOW_APPLICATION_BOUNDS_WRITE
public static final int ALLOW_BACK_DISTANCE_READ
public static final int ALLOW_BACK_DISTANCE_WRITE
```

These flags, when enabled using the setCapability method, allow an application to invoke methods that respectively read and write the application region and the back distance. These capability flags are enforced only when the node is part of a live or compiled scene graph.

Constructors

The Clip node object defines the following constructors:

public Clip()

Constructs a Clip node with default parameters:

Parameter	Default Value
backDistance	100
applicationBounds	null
applicationBoundingLeaf	null

public Clip(double backDistance)

Constructs a Clip leaf node with the rear clip plane at the specified distance, in the local coordinate system, from the eye.

Methods

The Clip node object defines the following methods:

public void setBackDistance(double backDistance)
public double getBackDistance()

These methods access or modify the back-clipping distances in the Clip node. This distance specifies the back-clipping plane in the local coordinate system of the node. There are several considerations that need to be taken into account when choosing values for the front and back clip distances. See Section 9.7.3, "Projection and Clip Parameters," for details.

public void setApplicationBounds(Bounds region)
public Bounds getApplicationBounds()

These two methods access or modify the Clip node's application bounds. This bounds is used as the application region when the application bounding leaf is set to null. The getApplicationBounds method returns a copy of the associated bounds.

public void setApplicationBoundingLeaf(BoundingLeaf region)
public BoundingLeaf getApplicationBoundingLeaf()

These two methods access or modify the Clip node's application bounding leaf. When set to a value other than null, this bounding leaf overrides the application bounds object and is used as the application region.

6.6   ModelClip Node

The ModelClip leaf node defines a set of six arbitrary clipping planes in the virtual universe. The planes are specified in the local coordinate system of this node, and may be individually enabled or disabled. This node also specifies a region of influence in which this set of planes is active.

A ModelClip node also contains a list of Group nodes that specifies the hierarchical scope of this ModelClip. If the scope list is empty, the ModelClip node has *universe scope*; all nodes within the region of influence are affected by this ModelClip node. If the scope list is nonempty, then only those Leaf nodes under the Group nodes in the scope list are affected by this ModelClip node (subject to the influencing bounds).

If the regions of influence of multiple ModelClip nodes overlap, the Java 3D system will choose a single set of model clip planes for those objects that lie in the intersection. This is done in an implementation-dependent manner, but in general, the ModelClip node that is "closest" to the object is chosen.

The individual planes specify a half space defined by the following equation:

$$Ax + By + Cz + D \leq 0$$

where A, B, C, and D are the parameters that specify the plane.

The parameters are passed in the *x, y, z,* and *w* fields, respectively, of a Vector4d object. The intersection of the set of half spaces corresponding to the enabled planes in this ModelClip node defines a region in which points are accepted. Points in this acceptance region will be rendered (subject to view clipping and other attributes). Points that are not in the acceptance region will not be rendered.

Constants

The ModelClip node object defines the following flags:

```
public static final int ALLOW_INFLUENCING_BOUNDS_READ        ◀ New in 1.2 ▶
public static final int ALLOW_INFLUENCING_BOUNDS_WRITE       ◀ New in 1.2 ▶
public static final int ALLOW_PLANE_READ                     ◀ New in 1.2 ▶
public static final int ALLOW_PLANE_WRITE                    ◀ New in 1.2 ▶
public static final int ALLOW_ENABLE_READ                    ◀ New in 1.2 ▶
public static final int ALLOW_ENABLE_WRITE                   ◀ New in 1.2 ▶
public static final int ALLOW_SCOPE_READ                     ◀ New in 1.2 ▶
public static final int ALLOW_SCOPE_WRITE                    ◀ New in 1.2 ▶
```

These flags, when enabled using the `setCapability` method, allow an application to invoke methods that respectively read and write the influencing bounds and bounding leaf, planes, enable, and scope flags. These capability flags are enforced only when the node is part of a live or compiled scene graph.

Constructors

The ModelClip node object defines the following constructors:

◀ New in 1.2 ▶ **public ModelClip()**

Constructs a ModelClip node with default parameters:

Parameter	Default Value
planes[0]	$x \leq 1$ (1,0,0,–1)
planes[1]	$-x \leq 1$ (–1,0,0,–1)
planes[2]	$y \leq 1$ (0,1,0,–1)
planes[3]	$-y \leq 1$ (0–1,0–1)
planes[4]	$z \leq 1$ (0,0,1,–1)
planes[5]	$-z \leq 1$ (0,0,–1,–1)
enables	all planes enabled
scope	empty (universe scope)
influencingBounds	null
influencingBoundingLeaf	null

◀ New in 1.2 ▶ **public ModelClip(Vector4d[] planes, boolean[] enables)**
◀ New in 1.2 ▶ **public ModelClip(Vector4d[] planes)**

These constructors construct a new ModelClip node. The first constructor uses the specified planes and enable flags. The second constructor uses the specified parameters and uses defaults for those parameters not specified. Default values are described above.

Methods

The ModelClip node object defines the following methods:

◀ New in 1.2 ▶ **public void setInfluencingBounds(Bounds region)**
◀ New in 1.2 ▶ **public Bounds getInfluencingBounds()**

These methods access or modify the ModelClip node's influencing region. This is used when the influencing bounding leaf is set to null.

```
public void setInfluencingBoundingLeaf(BoundingLeaf region)          ◀ New in 1.2 ▶
public BoundingLeaf getInfluencingBoundingLeaf()                      ◀ New in 1.2 ▶
```

These methods access or modify the ModelClip node's influencing region. When set to a value other than null, this overrides the influencing bounds object.

```
public void setPlanes(Vector4d[] planes)                             ◀ New in 1.2 ▶
public void setPlane(int planeNum, Vector4d plane)                   ◀ New in 1.2 ▶
public void getPlanes(Vector4d[] planes)                            ◀ New in 1.2 ▶
public void getPlane(int planeNum, Vector4d plane)                  ◀ New in 1.2 ▶
```

These methods access or modify the specified ModelClip node's clipping planes. The planes are an array of six model clipping planes. The set methods copy the individual planes into this node. The get methods copy the individual planes into the specified planes, which must be allocated by the caller.

```
public void setEnables(boolean[] enables)                           ◀ New in 1.2 ▶
public void setEnable(int planeNum, boolean enable)                ◀ New in 1.2 ▶
public void getEnables(boolean[] enables)                          ◀ New in 1.2 ▶
public boolean getEnable(int planeNum)                             ◀ New in 1.2 ▶
```

These methods access or modify the specified ModelClip node's enable flag. The enables are an array of six booleans.

```
public void setScope(Group scope, int index)                       ◀ New in 1.2 ▶
```

This method replaces the node at the specified index in this ModelClip node's list of scopes with the specified Group node. By default, ModelClip nodes are scoped only by their influencing bounds. This allows them to be scoped further by a list of nodes in the hierarchy.

```
public Group getScope(int index)                                   ◀ New in 1.2 ▶
```

This method retrieves the Group node at the specified index from this ModelClip node's list of scopes.

```
public void insertScope(Group scope, int index)                    ◀ New in 1.2 ▶
```

This method inserts the specified Group node into this ModelClip node's list of scopes at the specified index. By default, ModelClip nodes are scoped only by their influencing bounds. This allows them to be scoped further by a list of nodes in the hierarchy.

```
public void removeScope(int index)                                 ◀ New in 1.2 ▶
```

This method removes the node at the specified index from this ModelClip node's list of scopes. If this operation causes the list of scopes to become empty, this

ModelClip will have universe scope; all nodes within the region of influence will be affected by this ModelClip node.

◀ New in 1.2 ▶ `public Enumeration getAllScopes()`

This method returns an enumeration of this ModelClip node's list of scopes.

◀ New in 1.2 ▶ `public void addScope(Group scope)`

This method appends the specified Group node to this ModelClip node's list of scopes. By default, ModelClip nodes are scoped only by their influencing bounds. This allows them to be scoped further by a list of nodes in the hierarchy.

◀ New in 1.2 ▶ `public int numScopes()`

This method returns the number of nodes in this ModelClip node's list of scopes. If this number is 0, the list of scopes is empty and this ModelClip node has universe scope: All nodes within the region of influence are affected by this Model-Clip node.

6.7   Fog Node

The Fog leaf node is an abstract class that defines a common set of attributes that control fog, or depth cueing, in the scene. The Fog node includes a parameter that specifies the fog color and a Bounds object that specifies the region of influence for the Fog node.

Objects whose bounding volumes intersect the Fog node's region of influence have fog applied to their color after lighting and texturing have been applied. The Fog node also contains a list of Group nodes that indicates the hierarchical scope of this fog. If the list of scoping nodes is empty, the fog has universe scope and will apply to all nodes in the virtual universe that are within the Fog node's region of influence.

If the regions of influence of multiple Fog nodes overlap, the Java 3D system will choose a single set of fog parameters for those objects that lie in the intersection. This is done in an implementation-dependent manner, but in general, the Fog node that is "closest" to the object is chosen.

Constants

The Fog node object defines the following flags:

```
public static final int ALLOW_INFLUENCING_BOUNDS_READ
public static final int ALLOW_INFLUENCING_BOUNDS_WRITE
public static final int ALLOW_COLOR_READ
public static final int ALLOW_COLOR_WRITE
public static final int ALLOW_SCOPE_READ
public static final int ALLOW_SCOPE_WRITE
```

These flags, when enabled using the setCapability method, allow an application to invoke methods that respectively read and write the region of influence, read and write color, and read and write scope information. These capability flags are enforced only when the node is part of a live or compiled scene graph.

Constructors

The Fog node object defines the following constructors:

public Fog()

Constructs a Fog node with default parameters:

Parameter	Default Value
color	black (0,0,0)
scope	empty (universe scope)
influencingBounds	null
influencingBoundingLeaf	null

public Fog(float r, float g, float b)
public Fog(Color3f color)

These constructors construct a new Fog node. The first constructor uses default values for all parameters. The second constructor uses the specified parameters and uses defaults for those parameters not specified. Default values are described above.

Methods

The Fog node object defines the following methods:

public void setColor(float r, float g, float b)
public void setColor(Color3f color)
public void getColor(Color3f color)

These three methods access or modify the Fog node's color. An application will typically set this to the same value as the background color.

```
public void setInfluencingBounds(Bounds region)
public Bounds getInfluencingBounds()
```

These methods access or modify the Fog node's influencing bounds. This bounds is used as the region of influence when the influencing bounding leaf is set to null. The Fog node operates on all objects that intersect its region of influence. The getInfluencingBounds method returns a copy of the associated bounds.

```
public void setInfluencingBoundingLeaf(BoundingLeaf region)
public BoundingLeaf getInfluencingBoundingLeaf()
```

These methods access or modify the Fog node's influencing bounding leaf. When set to a value other than null, this overrides the influencing bounds object, and it is used as the region of influence.

```
public void setScope(Group scope, int index)
public Group getScope(int index)
public void addScope(Group scope)
public void insertScope(Group scope, int index)
public void removeScope(int index)
public int numScopes()
public Enumeration getAllScopes()
```

These methods access or modify the Fog node's hierarchical scope. By default, Fog nodes are scoped only by their regions of influence. These methods allow them to be scoped further by a Group node in the hierarchy. The hierarchical scoping of a Fog node cannot be accessed or modified if the node is part of a live or compiled scene graph.

6.7.1   ExponentialFog Node

The ExponentialFog leaf node extends the Fog leaf node by adding a fog density that is used as the exponent of the fog equation. For more information on the fog equation, see Appendix E, "Equations."

The density is defined in the local coordinate system of the node, but the actual fog equation will ideally take place in eye coordinates.

Constants

The ExponentialFog node object defines the following flags:

```
public static final int ALLOW_DENSITY_READ
public static final int ALLOW_DENSITY_WRITE
```

These flags, when enabled using the `setCapability` method, allow an application to invoke methods that respectively read and write the density values. These capability flags are enforced only when the node is part of a live or compiled scene graph.

Constructors

The ExponentialFog node object defines the following constructors:

`public ExponentialFog()`

Constructs an ExponentialFog node with default parameters:

Parameter	Default Value
density	1.0

```
public ExponentialFog(float r, float g, float b)
public ExponentialFog(Color3f color)
public ExponentialFog(float r, float g, float b, float density)
public ExponentialFog(Color3f color, float density)
```

Each of these constructors creates a new ExponentialFog node using the specified parameters and use defaults for those parameters not specified.

Methods

The ExponentialFog node object defines the following methods:

```
public void setDensity(float density)
public float getDensity()
```

These two methods access or modify the density in the ExponentialFog object.

6.7.2   LinearFog Node

The LinearFog leaf node extends the Fog leaf node by adding a pair of distance values, in *z*, at which fog should start obscuring the scene and should maximally obscure the scene.

The front and back fog distances are defined in the local coordinate system of the node, but the actual fog equation will ideally take place in eye coordinates. For more information on the fog equation, see Appendix E, "Equations."

Constants

The LinearFog node object defines the following flags:

```
public static final int ALLOW_DISTANCE_READ
public static final int ALLOW_DISTANCE_WRITE
```

These flags, when enabled using the `setCapability` method, allow an application to invoke methods that respectively read and write the distance values. These capability flags are enforced only when the node is part of a live or compiled scene graph.

Constructors

The LinearFog node object defines the following constructors:

```
public LinearFog()
```

Constructs a LinearFog node with default parameters:

Parameter	Default Value
frontDistance	0.1
backDistance	1.0

```
public LinearFog(float r, float g, float b)
public LinearFog(Color3f color)
public LinearFog(float r, float g, float b, double frontDistance,
      double backDistance)
public LinearFog(Color3f color, double frontDistance,
      double backDistance)
```

These constructors construct a new LinearFog node with the specified parameters and use defaults for those parameters not specified.

Methods

The LinearFog node object defines the following methods:

```
public void setFrontDistance(float frontDistance)
public float getFrontDistance()
public void setBackDistance(float backDistance)
public float getBackDistance()
```

These four methods access or modify the front and back distances in the LinearFog object. The front distance is the distance at which the fog starts obscuring objects; the back distance is the distance at which the fog fully obscures objects.

Objects drawn closer than the front fog distance are not affected by fog. Objects drawn farther than the back fog distance are drawn entirely in the fog color.

6.8   Light Node

The Light leaf node is an abstract class that defines the properties common to all Light nodes. A light has associated with it a color, a state (whether it is on or off), and a Bounds object that specifies the region of influence for the light. Objects whose bounding volumes intersect the Light node's region of influence are lit by this light. The Light node also contains a Group node that indicates the hierarchical scope of this light. If no scoping node is specified, then the light has *universe scope* and applies to all nodes in the virtual universe that are within the light's region of influence.

The Java 3D lighting model is based on a subset of the OpenGL lighting model.

Constants

The Light node object defines the following flags:

```
public static final int ALLOW_INFLUENCING_BOUNDS_READ
public static final int ALLOW_INFLUENCING_BOUNDS_WRITE
public static final int ALLOW_STATE_READ
public static final int ALLOW_STATE_WRITE
public static final int ALLOW_COLOR_READ
public static final int ALLOW_COLOR_WRITE
public static final int ALLOW_SCOPE_READ
public static final int ALLOW_SCOPE_WRITE
```

These flags, when enabled using the setCapability method, allow reading and writing of the region of influence, the state, the color, and the scope information, respectively. These capability flags are enforced only when the node is part of a live or compiled scene graph.

Constructors

The Light node object defines the following constructors:

```
public Light()
```

Constructs and initializes a light with the following default values:

Parameter	Default Value
enable	true
color	white (1,1,1)
scope	empty (universe scope)
influencingBounds	null
influencingBoundingLeaf	null

```
public Light(Color3f color)
public Light(boolean lightOn, Color3f color)
```

These two constructors construct and initialize a light with the specified values.

Methods

The Light node object defines the following methods:

```
public void setEnable(boolean state)
public boolean getEnable()
```

These methods access or modify the state of this light (that is, whether the light is enabled).

```
public void setColor(Color3f color)
public void getColor(Color3f color)
```

These methods access or modify the current color of this light.

```
public setInfluencingBounds(Bounds region)
public Bounds getInfluencingBounds()
```

These methods access or modify the Light node's influencing bounds. This bounds is used as the region of influence when the influencing bounding leaf is set to null. The Light node operates on all objects that intersect its region of influence. The getInfluencingBounds method returns a copy of the associated bounds.

```
public setInfluencingBoundingLeaf(BoundingLeaf region)
public BoundingLeaf getInfluencingBoundingLeaf()
```

These methods access or modify the Light node's influencing bounding leaf. A value other than null overrides the influencing bounds object and it is used as the region of influence.

```
public void setScope(Group scope, int index)
public Group getScope(int index)
public void addScope(Group scope)
public void insertScope(Group scope, int index)
public void removeScope(int index)
public int numScopes()
public Enumeration getAllScopes()
```

These methods access or modify the Light node's hierarchical scope. By default, Light nodes are scoped only by their regions of influence bounds. These methods allow them to be scoped further by a node in the hierarchy.

6.8.1   AmbientLight Node

An AmbientLight node defines an ambient light source. It has the same attributes as the abstract Light node.

Constructors

The AmbientLight node defines the following constructors:

```
public AmbientLight()
public AmbientLight(Color3f color)
public AmbientLight(boolean lightOn, Color3f color)
```

The first constructor constructs and initializes a new AmbientLight node using default parameters. The next two constructors construct and initialize a new AmbientLight node using the specified parameters. The color parameter is the color of the light source. The lightOn flag indicates whether this light is on or off.

6.8.2   DirectionalLight Node

A DirectionalLight node defines an oriented light with an origin at infinity. It has the same attributes as a Light node, with the addition of a direction vector to specify the direction in which it shines.

Constants

The DirectionalLight node object defines the following flags:

73

```
public static final int ALLOW_DIRECTION_READ
public static final int ALLOW_DIRECTION_WRITE
```

These flags, when enabled using the setCapability method, allow an application to invoke methods that respectively read or write the associated direction. These capability flags are enforced only when the node is part of a live or compiled scene graph.

The DirectionalLight's direction vector is defined in the local coordinate system of the node.

Constructors

The DirectionalLight node object defines the following constructors:

```
public DirectionalLight()
```

Constructs and initializes a directional light with default parameters:

Parameter	Default Value
direction	(0,0,–1)

```
public DirectionalLight(Color3f color, Vector3f direction)
public DirectionalLight(boolean LightOn, Color3f color,
        Vector3f direction)
```

These constructors construct and initialize a directional light with the parameters provided.

Methods

The DirectionalLight node object defines the following methods:

```
public void setDirection(Vector3f direction)
public void setDirection(float x, float y, float z)
public void getDirection(Vector3f direction)
```

These methods access or modify the light's current direction.

6.8.3   PointLight Node

A PointLight node defines a point light source located at some point in space and radiating light in all directions (also known as a *positional light*). It has the same attributes as a Light node, with the addition of location and attenuation parameters.

The PointLight's position is defined in the local coordinate system of the node.

Constants

The PointLight node object defines the following flags:

```
public static final int ALLOW_POSITION_READ
public static final int ALLOW_POSITION_WRITE
public static final int ALLOW_ATTENUATION_READ
public static final int ALLOW_ATTENUATION_WRITE
```

These flags, when enabled using the setCapability method, allow an application to invoke methods that respectively read position, write position, read attenuation parameters, and write attenuation parameters. These capability flags are enforced only when the node is part of a live or compiled scene graph.

Constructors

The PointLight Node defines the following constructors:

```
public PointLight()
```

Constructs and initializes a point light source with the following default parameters:

Parameter	Default Value
position	(0,0,0)
attenuation	(1,0,0)

```
public PointLight(Color3f color, Point3f position,
        Point3f attenuation)
public PointLight(boolean lightOn, Color3f color,
        Point3f position, Point3f attenuation)
```

These constructors construct and initialize a point light with the specified parameters.

Methods

The PointLight node object defines the following methods:

```
public void setPosition(Point3f position)
public void setPosition(float x, float y, float z)
public void getPosition(Point3f position)
```

These methods access or modify the point light's current position.

```
public void setAttenuation(Point3f attenuation)
public void setAttenuation(float constant, float linear,
      float quadratic)
public void getAttenuation(Point3f attenuation)
```

These methods access or modify the point light's current attenuation. The values presented to the methods specify the coefficients of the attenuation polynomial, with `constant` providing the constant term, `linear` providing the linear coefficient, and `quadratic` providing the quadratic coefficient.

6.8.4   SpotLight Node

A SpotLight node defines a point light source located at some point in space and radiating in a specific direction. It has the same attributes as a PointLight node, with the addition of a direction of radiation, a spread angle to specify its limits, and a concentration factor that specifies how quickly the light intensity attenuates as a function of the angle of radiation as measured from the direction of radiation.

Constants

The SpotLight node object defines the following flags:

```
public static final int ALLOW_SPREAD_ANGLE_READ
public static final int ALLOW_SPREAD_ANGLE_WRITE
public static final int ALLOW_CONCENTRATION_READ
public static final int ALLOW_CONCENTRATION_WRITE
public static final int ALLOW_DIRECTION_READ
public static final int ALLOW_DIRECTION_WRITE
```

These flags, when enabled using the `setCapability` method, allow an application to invoke methods that respectively read and write spread angle, concentration, and direction. These capability flags are enforced only when the node is part of a live or compiled scene graph.

The SpotLight's direction vector and spread angle are defined in the local coordinate system of the node.

Constructors

The SpotLight node object defines the following constructors:

```
public SpotLight()
```

Constructs and initializes a new spotlight with the default values:

Parameter	Default Value
direction	(0,0 –1)
spreadAngle	π radians
concentration	0.0

```
public SpotLight(Color3f color, Point3f position,
       Point3f attenuation, Vector3f direction, float spreadAngle,
       float concentration)
public SpotLight(boolean lightOn, Color3f color, Point3f position,
       Point3f attenuation, Vector3f direction, float spreadAngle,
       float concentration)
```

These construct and initialize a new spotlight with the parameters specified.

Methods

The SpotLight node object defines the following methods:

```
public void setSpreadAngle(float spreadAngle)
public float getSpreadAngle()
```

These methods access or modify the spread angle, in radians, of this spotlight.

```
public void setConcentration(float concentration)
public float getConcentration()
```

These methods access or modify the concentration of this spotlight.

```
public void setDirection(float x, float y, float z)
public void setDirection(Vector3f direction)
public void getDirection(Vector3f direction)
```

These methods access or modify the direction of this spotlight.

6.9   Sound Node

The Sound leaf node is an abstract class that defines the properties common to all Sound nodes. A scene graph can contain multiple sounds. Each Sound node contains a reference to the sound data, an amplitude scale factor, a release flag denoting that the sound associated with this node is to play to the end when the sound is disabled, the number of times the sound is to be repeated, a state (whether the sound is on or off), a scheduling region, a priority, and a flag denoting if the sound is to continue playing "silently" even while it is inactive. Whenever the listener is within the Sound node's scheduling bounds, the sound is potentially audible.

Constants

The Sound object contains the following flags:

```
public static final int ALLOW_SOUND_DATA_READ
public static final int ALLOW_SOUND_DATA_WRITE
public static final int ALLOW_INITIAL_GAIN_READ
public static final int ALLOW_INITIAL_GAIN_WRITE
public static final int ALLOW_LOOP_READ
public static final int ALLOW_LOOP_WRITE
public static final int ALLOW_RELEASE_READ
public static final int ALLOW_RELEASE_WRITE
public static final int ALLOW_CONT_PLAY_READ
public static final int ALLOW_CONT_PLAY_WRITE
public static final int ALLOW_ENABLE_READ
public static final int ALLOW_ENABLE_WRITE
public static final int ALLOW_SCHEDULING_BOUNDS_READ
public static final int ALLOW_SCHEDULING_BOUNDS_WRITE
public static final int ALLOW_PRIORITY_READ
public static final int ALLOW_PRIORITY_WRITE
public static final int ALLOW_DURATION_READ
public static final int ALLOW_CHANNELS_USED_READ
public static final int ALLOW_IS_PLAYING_READ
public static final int ALLOW_IS_READY_READ
```

These flags, when enabled using the `setCapability` method, allow an application to invoke methods that respectively read and write the sound data, the initial gain information, the loop information, the release flag, the continuous play flag, the sound on/off switch, the scheduling region, the prioritization value, the duration information, and the sound playing information. These capability flags are enforced only when the node is part of a live or compiled scene graph.

`public static final float NO_FILTER`

This constant defines a floating point value that denotes that no filter value is set. Filters are described in Section 6.9.3, "ConeSound Node."

`public static final int DURATION_UNKNOWN`

This constant denotes that the sound's duration could not be calculated; a fallback for `getDuration` of a noncached sound.

Constructors

The Sound node object defines the following constructors:

public Sound()

Constructs and initializes a new Sound node object that includes the following defaults for its fields:

Parameter	Default Value
soundData	null
initialGain	1.0
loop	0
releaseEnable flag	false
continuousEnable flag	false
enable	false
schedulingBounds	null (cannot be scheduled)
schedulingBoundingLeaf	null
priority	1.0

public Sound(MediaContainer soundData, float initialGain)

Constructs and initializes a new Sound node object using the provided data and gain parameter values and defaults for all other fields. This constructor implicitly loads the sound data associated with this node if the implementation uses sound caching.

**public Sound(MediaContainer soundData, float initialGain,
        int loopCount, boolean release, boolean continuous,
        boolean enable, Bounds region, float priority)**

Constructs and initializes a new Sound node object using the provided parameter values.

Methods

The Sound node object defines the following methods:

public void setSoundData(MediaContainer soundData)
public MediaContainer getSoundData()

These methods provide a way to associate different types of audio data with a Sound node. This data can be cached (buffered) or noncached (unbuffered or streaming). If the AudioDevice has been attached to the PhysicalEnvironment, the sound data is made ready to begin playing. Certain functionality cannot be applied to true streaming sound data: sound duration is unknown, looping is disabled, and the sound cannot be restarted. Furthermore, depending on the implementation of the AudioDevice used, streaming, noncached data may not be fully spatialized.

```
public void setInitialGain(float amplitude)
public float getInitialGain()
```

This gain is a scale factor that is applied to the sound data associated with this sound source to increase or decrease its overall amplitude.

```
public void setLoop(int loopCount)
public int getLoop()
```

Data for nonstreaming sound (such as a sound sample) can contain two loop points marking a section of the data that is to be looped a specific number of times. Thus, sound data can be divided into three segments: the *attack* (before the begin loop point), the *sustain* (between the begin and end loop points), and the *release* (after the end loop point). If there are no loop begin and end points defined as part of the sound data (say for Java Media Player types that do not contain sound samples), then the begin loop point is set at the beginning of the sound data, and the end loop point at the end of the sound data. If this is the case, looping the sound means repeating the whole sound. However, these begin and end loop points can be placed anywhere within the sound data, allowing a portion in the middle of the sound to be looped.

A sound can be looped a specified number of times after it is activated and before it is completed. The loop count value explicitly sets the number of times the sound is looped. Any nonnegative number is a valid value. A value of 0 denotes that the looped section is not repeated but is played only once. A value of −1 denotes that the loop is repeated indefinitely.

Changing the loop count of a sound after the sound has been started will not dynamically affect the loop count currently used by the sound playing. The new loop count will be used the next time the sound is enabled.

```
public void setReleaseEnable(boolean state)
public boolean getReleaseEnable()
```

When a sound is disabled, its playback would normally stop immediately no matter what part of the sound data was currently being played. By setting the Release flag to true for nodes with nonstreaming sound data, the sound is allowed to play from its current position in the sound data to the end of the data (without repeats), thus playing the release portion of the sound before stopping.

```
public void setContinuousEnable(boolean state)
public boolean getContinuousEnable()
```

For some applications, it's useful to turn a sound source "off" but to continue playing the sound "silently" so that when it is turned back "on," the sound picks up playing in the same location (over time) it would have played if the sound had never been disabled (turned off). Setting the continuous flag to true causes the sound renderer to keep track of where (over time) the sound would be playing even when the sound is disabled.

```
public setSchedulingBounds(Bounds region)
public Bounds getSchedulingBounds()
```

These two methods access or modify the Sound node's scheduling bounds. This bounds is used as the scheduling region when the scheduling bounding leaf is set to null. A sound is scheduled for activation when its scheduling region intersects the ViewPlatform's activation volume. The getSchedulingBounds method returns a copy of the associated bounds.

```
public void setSchedulingBoundingLeaf(BoundingLeaf region)
public BoundingLeaf getSchedulingBoundingLeaf()
```

These two methods access or modify the Sound node's scheduling bounding leaf. When set to a value other than null, this bounding leaf overrides the scheduling bounds object and is used as the scheduling region.

```
public void setPriority(float ranking)
public float getPriority()
```

These methods access or modify the Sound node's priority, which is used to rank concurrently playing sounds in order of importance during playback. When more sounds are started than the AudioDevice can handle, the Sound node with the lowest priority ranking is deactivated. If a sound is deactivated (due to a sound with a higher priority being started), it is automatically reactivated when resources become available (for example, when a sound with a higher priority finishes playing) or when the ordering of sound nodes is changed due to a change in a Sound node's priority.

If a sound cannot be played due to a lack of channels, a lower priority sound requiring fewer channels will be played. For example, assume we have eight channels available for playing sounds. After ordering four sounds, we begin playing them in order, checking if the required channels to play a given sound are actually available before the sound is played. Furthermore, say the first sound needs three channels to play, the second sound needs four channels, the third sound needs three channels, and the fourth sound needs only one channel. The first and second sounds can be started because they require seven of the eight available channels. The third sound cannot be audibly started because it requires three channels and only one is still available. Consequently, the third sound starts playing "silently." The fourth sound can and will be started since it requires only one channel. The third sound will be made audible when three channels become available (that is, when the first or second sound is finished playing).

Sounds given the same priority are ordered randomly. If the application wants a specific ordering it must assign unique priorities to each sound.

Methods to determine what audio output resources are required for playback of a Sound node on a particular AudioDevice and to determine the currently available audio output resources are described in Chapter 12, "Audio Devices."

```
public void setEnable(boolean state)
public boolean getEnable()
```

These two methods access or modify the playing state of this sound (that is, whether the sound is enabled). When enabled, the sound source is started and thus can potentially be heard, depending on its activation state, gain control parameters, continuation state, and spatialization parameters. If the continuous state is `true` and the sound is not active, enabling the sound starts the sound silently "playing" so that when the sound is activated, the sound is (potentially) heard from somewhere in the middle of the sound data. The activation state can change from active to inactive any number of times without stopping or starting the sound. To restart a sound at the beginning of its data, re-enable the sound by calling `setEnable` with a value of `true`.

Setting the enable flag to `true` during construction will act as a request to start the sound playing "as soon as it can" be started. This could be close to immediately in limited cases, but several conditions, following, must be met for a sound to be ready to be played.

```
public boolean isReady()
```

This method retrieves the sound's "ready" status. If this sound is fully prepared for playing (either audibly or silently) on all initialized audio devices, this method returns `true`. Sound data associated with a Sound node, either during construction (when the MediaContainer is passed into the constructor as a parameter) or by calling `setSoundData()`, it can be prepared to begin playing only after the following conditions are satisfied:

- The Sound node has non-null sound data associated with it.
- The Sound node is live.
- There is an active View in the Universe.
- There is an initialized AudioDevice associated with the PhysicalEnvironment.

Depending on the type of MediaContainer the sound data is and on the implementation of the AudioDevice used, sound data preparation could consist of opening, attaching, loading, or copying into memory the associated sound data. The query method, `isReady()`, returns `true` when the sound is fully preprocessed so that it is playable (audibly if active, silently if not active).

public boolean isPlaying()

A sound source will not be heard unless it is both enabled (turned on) and activated. If this sound is audibly playing on any initialized audio device, this method will return a status of `true`.

When the sound finishes playing its sound data (including all loops), it is implicitly disabled.

public boolean isPlayingSilently()

This method returns the sound's silent status. If this sound is silently playing on any initialized audio device, this method returns `true`.

public long getDuration()

This method returns the length of time (in milliseconds) that the sound media associated with the sound source could run (including the number of times its loop section is repeated) if it plays to completion. If the sound media type is streaming or if the sound is looped indefinitely, a value of −1 (implying infinite length) is returned.

public int getNumberOfChannelsUsed()

When a sound is started it could use more than one channel on the selected AudioDevice it is to be played on. This method retrieves the number of channels that are being used to render this sound on the audio device associated with the VirtualUniverse's primary view. The method returns 0 if sound is not playing.

6.9.1 BackgroundSound Node

A BackgroundSound node defines an unattenuated, nonspatialized sound source that has no position or direction. It has the same attributes as a Sound node. This type of sound is simply added to the sound mix without modification and is useful for playing a mono or stereo music track or an ambient sound effect. Unlike a Background (visual) node, more than one BackgroundSound node can be simultaneously enabled and active.

Constructors

The BackgroundSound node specifies the following constructor:

```
public BackgroundSound()
```

Constructs a BackgroundSound node object using the default parameters for Sound nodes.

```
public BackgroundSound(MediaContainer soundData,
        float initialGain)
public BackgroundSound(MediaContainer soundData,
        float initialGain, int loopCount, boolean release,
        boolean continuous, boolean enable, Bounds region,
        float priority)
```

The first constructor constructs a new BackgroundSound node using only the provided parameter values for the sound data and initial gain. The second constructor uses the provided parameter values for the sound data, initial gain, the number of times the loop is looped, a flag denoting whether the sound data is played to the end, a flag denoting whether the sound plays silently when disabled, a flag denoting whether sound is switched on or off, the sound activation region, and a priority value denoting the playback priority ranking.

6.9.2 PointSound Node

The PointSound node defines a spatially located sound whose waves radiate uniformly in all directions from some point in space. It has the same attributes as a Sound object, with the addition of a location and the specification of distance-based gain attenuation for listener positions between an array of distances.

The sound's amplitude is attenuated based on the distance between the listener and the sound source position. A piecewise linear curve (defined in terms of pairs consisting of a distance and a gain scale factor) specifies the gain scale factor slope.

The PointSound's location and attenuation distances are defined in the local coordinate system of the node.

Constants

The PointSound object contains the following flags:

```
public static final int ALLOW_POSITION_READ
public static final int ALLOW_POSITION_WRITE
public static final int ALLOW_DISTANCE_GAIN_READ
public static final int ALLOW_DISTANCE_GAIN_WRITE
```

These flags, when enabled using the setCapability method, allow an application to invoke methods that respectively read and write the position and the distance gain array. These capability flags are enforced only when the node is part of a live or compiled scene graph.

Constructors

The PointSound node object defines the following constructors:

public PointSound()

Constructs a PointSound node object that includes the defaults for a Sound object plus the following defaults for its own fields:

Parameter	Default Value
position	(0.0, 0.0, 0.0)
distanceGain	null (no attenuation performed)

public PointSound(MediaContainer soundData, float initialGain, Point3f position)
public PointSound(MediaContainer soundData, float initialGain, float posX, float posY, float posZ)

Both of these constructors construct a PointSound node object using only the provided parameter values for sound data, sample gain, and position. The remaining fields are set to the default values specified earlier. The first form uses vectors as input for its position; the second form uses individual float parameters for the elements of the position vector.

```
public PointSound(MediaContainer soundData, float initialGain,
       int loopCount, boolean release, boolean continuous,
       boolean enable, Bounds region, float priority,
       Point3f position, Point2f distanceGain[])
public PointSound(MediaContainer soundData, float initialGain,
       int loopCount, boolean release, boolean continuous,
       boolean enable, Bounds region, float priority, float posX,
       float posY, float posZ, Point2f distanceGain[])
public PointSound(MediaContainer soundData, float initialGain,
       int loopCount, boolean release, boolean continuous,
       boolean enable, Bounds region, float priority,
       Point3f position, float attenuationDistance[],
       float attenuationGain[])
public PointSound(MediaContainer soundData, float initialGain,
       int loopCount, boolean release, boolean continuous,
       boolean enable, Bounds region, float priority, float posX,
       float posY, float posZ, float attenuationDistance[],
       float attenuationGain[])
```

These four constructors construct a PointSound node object using the provided parameter values. The first and third forms use points as input for the position. The second and fourth forms use individual float parameters for the elements of the position. The first and second forms accept an array of Point2f for the distance attenuation values where each pair in the array contains a distance and a gain scale factor. The third and fourth forms accept separate arrays for the components of distance attenuation, namely, the distance and gain scale factors. See the description for the setDistanceGain method, below, for details on how the separate arrays are interpreted.

Methods

The PointSound node object defines the following methods:

```
public void setPosition(Point3f position)
public void setPosition(float x, float y, float z)
public void getPosition(Point3f position)
```

These methods set and retrieve the position in 3D space from which the sound radiates.

```
public void setDistanceGain(Point2f attenuation[])
public void setDistanceGain(float distance[], float gain[])
public int getDistanceGainLength()
public void getDistanceGain(Point2f attenuation[])
public void getDistanceGain(float distance[], float gain[])
```

These methods set and retrieve the sound's distance attenuation. If this is not set, no distance gain attenuation is performed (equivalent to using a gain scale factor of 1.0 for all distances). See Figure 6-2. Gain scale factors are associated with distances from the listener to the sound source via an array of distance and gain scale factor pairs. The gain scale factor applied to the sound source is determined by finding the range of values distance[i] and distance[i+1] that includes the current distance from the listener to the sound source then linearly interpolating the corresponding values gain[i] and gain[i+1] by the same amount.

If the distance from the listener to the sound source is less than the first distance in the array, the first gain scale factor is applied to the sound source. This creates a spherical region around the listener within which all sound gain is uniformly scaled by the first gain in the array.

If the distance from the listener to the sound source is greater than the last distance in the array, the last gain scale factor is applied to the sound source.

The first form of setDistanceGain takes these pairs of values as an array of Point2f. The second form accepts two separate arrays for these values. The distance and gainScale arrays should be of the same length. If the gainScale array length is greater than the distance array length, the gainScale array elements beyond the length of the distance array are ignored. If the gainScale array is shorter than the distance array, the last gainScale array value is repeated to fill an array of length equal to distance array.

There are two methods for getDistanceGain. one returning an array of points, the other returning separate arrays for each attenuation component.

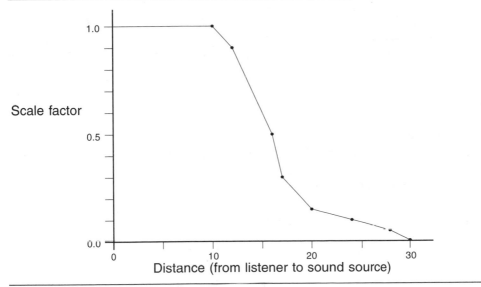

Figure 6-2   PointSound Distance Gain Attenuation

Distance elements in this array of Point2f are a monotonically increasing set of floating-point numbers measured from the location of the sound source. Gain scale factor elements in this list of pairs can be any positive floating-point numbers. While for most applications this list of gain scale factors will usually be monotonically decreasing, they do not have to be.

Figure 6-2 shows a graphical representation of a distance gain attenuation list. The values given for distance/gain pairs would be

((10.0, 1.0), (12.0, 0.9), (16.0, 0.5), (17.0, 0.3),
    (20.0, 0.16), (24.0, 0.12), (28.0, 0.05), (30.0, 0.0))

Thus if the current distance from the listener to the sound source is 22 units, a scale factor of 0.14 would be applied to the sound amplitude. If the current distance from the listener to the sound source is less than 10 units, the scale factor of 1.0 would be applied to the sound amplitude. If the current distance from the listener to the sound source is greater than 30 units, the scale factor of 0.0 would be applied to the sound amplitude.

The `getDistanceGainLength` method returns the length of the distance gain attenuation arrays. Arrays passed into `getDistanceGain` methods should all be at least this size.

6.9.3   ConeSound Node

The ConeSound node object defines a PointSound node whose sound source is directed along a specific vector in space. A ConeSound source is attenuated by gain scale factors and filters based on the angle between the vector from the source to the listener, and the ConeSound's direction vector. This attenuation is either a single spherical distance gain attenuation (as for a general PointSound source) or dual front and back distance gain attenuations defining elliptical attenuation volumes. The angular filter and the active AuralAttribute component filter define what filtering is applied to the sound source.

This node has the same attributes as a PointSound node, with the addition of a direction vector and an array of points that each contain an angular distance (in radians), a gain scale factor, and a filter (which for now consists of a lowpass filter cutoff frequency). Similar to the definition of the distance gain array for PointSounds, a piecewise linear curve (defined in terms of radians from the axis) specifies the slope of these additional attenuation values.

Figure 6-3 shows an approximation of angular attenuation (disregarding distance attenuation).

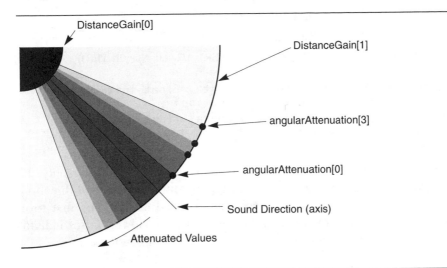

Figure 6-3   ConeSound

Constants

The ConeSound object contains the following flags:

```
public static final int ALLOW_DIRECTION_READ
public static final int ALLOW_DIRECTION_WRITE
public static final int ALLOW_ANGULAR_ATTENUATION_READ
public static final int ALLOW_ANGULAR_ATTENUATION_WRITE
```

These flags, when enabled using the `setCapability` method, allow an application to invoke methods that respectively read and write the direction and the angular attenuation array. These capability flags are enforced only when the node is part of a live or compiled scene graph.

Constructors

The ConeSound node object defines the following constructors:

public ConeSound()

Constructs a ConeSound node object that includes the defaults for a PointSound object plus the following defaults for its own fields:

Parameter	Default Value
direction	(0.0, 0.0, 1.0)
angularAttenuation	((0.0, 1.0, NO_FILTER),(π/2, 0.0, NO_FILTER))

```
public ConeSound(MediaContainer soundData, float initialGain,
      Point3f position, Vector3f direction)
public ConeSound(MediaContainer soundData, float initialGain,
      float posX, float posY, float posZ, float dirX, float dirY,
      float dirZ)
```

Both of these constructors construct a ConeSound node object using only the provided parameter values for sound, overall initial gain, position, and direction. The remaining fields are set to the default values listed earlier. The first form uses points as input for its position and direction. The second form uses individual float parameters for the elements of the position and direction vectors.

```
public ConeSound(MediaContainer soundData, float initialGain,
      int loopCount, boolean release, boolean continuous,
      boolean enable, Bounds region, float priority,
      Point3f position, Point2f frontDistanceAttenuation[],
      Point2f backDistanceAttenuation[], Vector3f direction)
public ConeSound(MediaContainer soundData, float initialGain,
      int loopCount, boolean release, boolean continuous,
      boolean enable, Bounds region, float priority, float posX,
      float posY, float posZ, float frontDistance[],
      float frontDistanceGain[], float backDistance[],
      float backDistanceGain[], float dirX, float dirY, float dirZ)
```

These constructors construct a ConeSound node object using the provided parameter values. The first form uses points or vectors as input for its position, direction, and front/back distance attenuation arrays. The second form uses individual float parameters for the elements of the position, direction, and two distance attenuation arrays.

Unlike the single distance gain attenuation array for PointSounds, which define spherical areas about the sound source between which gains are linearly interpolated, this directed ConeSound can have two distance gain attenuation arrays that define ellipsoidal attenuation areas. See the setDistanceGain PointSound method for details on how the separate distance and distanceGain arrays are interpreted.

The ConeSound's direction vector and angular measurements are defined in the local coordinate system of the node.

90

```
public ConeSound(MediaContainer soundData, float initialGain,
        int loopCount, boolean release, boolean continuous,
        boolean enable, Bounds region, float priority,
        Point3f position, Point2f distanceAttenuation[],
        Vector3f direction, Point3f angularAttenuation[])
public ConeSound(MediaContainer soundData, float initialGain,
        int loopCount, boolean release, boolean continuous,
        boolean enable, Bounds region, float priority, float posX,
        float posY, float posZ, float distance[],
        float distanceGain[], float dirX, float dirY, float dirZ,
        float angle[], float angularGain[], float frequencyCutoff[])
```

These constructors construct a ConeSound node object using the provided parameter values, which include a single spherical distance attenuation array. The first form uses points and vectors as input for its position, direction, single spherical `distanceAttenuation` array, and `angularAttenuation` array. The second form uses individual float parameters for the elements of the position, direction, `distanceAttenuation` array, and `angularAttenuation` array.

The first form accepts arrays of points for the distance attenuation and angular values. Each Point2f in the `distanceAttenuation` array contains a distance and a gain scale factor. Each Point3f in the `angularAttenuation` array contains an angular distance, a gain scale factor, and a filtering value (which is currently defined as a simple cutoff frequency).

The second form accepts separate arrays for the distance and gain scale factor components of distance attenuation, and separate arrays for the angular distance, angular gain, and filtering components of angular attenuation. See the setDistanceGain PointSound method for details on how the separate `distance` and `distanceGain` arrays are interpreted. See the setAngularAttenuation ConeSound method for details on how the separate `angularDistance`, `angularGain`, and `filter` arrays are interpreted.

```
public ConeSound(MediaContainer soundData, float initialGain,
        int loopCount, boolean release, boolean continuous,
        boolean enable, Bounds region, float priority,
        Point3f position, Point2f frontDistanceAttenuation[],
        Point2f backDistanceAttenuation[], Vector3f direction,
        Point3f angularAttenuation[])
public ConeSound(MediaContainer soundData, float initialGain,
        int loopCount, boolean release, float priority,
        boolean continuous, boolean enable, Bounds region,
        float posX, float posY, float posZ, float frontDistance[],
        float frontDistanceGain[], float backDistance[],
        float backDistanceGain[], float dirX, float dirY, float dirZ,
        float angle[], float angularGain[], float frequencyCutoff[])
```

These constructors construct a ConeSound node object using the provided parameter values, which include two distance attenuation arrays defining elliptical distance attenuation regions. The first form uses points and vectors as input for its position, direction, and attenuation arrays. The second form uses individual float parameters for these same elements.

These two constructors differ from the previous two constructors only in the definition of the two distinct front and back distance attenuation arrays. See the setDistanceGain ConeSound method for details on how the separate distance and distanceGain arrays are interpreted. See the setAngularAttenuation ConeSound method for details on how the separate angularDistance, angular-Gain, and filter arrays are interpreted.

Methods

The ConeSound node object defines the following methods:

```
public void setDistanceGain(Point2f frontAttenuation[], Point2f
        backAttenuation[])
public void setDistanceGain(float frontDistance[],
        float frontGain[], float backDistance[], float backGain[])
public void setBackDistanceGain(Point2f attenuation[])
public void setBackDistanceGain(float distance[], float gain[])
public void getDistanceGain(Point2f frontAttenuation[], Point2f
        backAttenuation[])
public void getDistanceGain(float frontDistance[],
        float frontGain[], float backDistance[], float backGain[])
```

These methods set and retrieve the ConeSound's two distance attenuation arrays. If these are not set, no distance gain attenuation is performed (equivalent to using a distance gain of 1.0 for all distances). If only one distance attenuation array is set, spherical attenuation is assumed (see Figure 6-4). If both a front and back distance attenuation are set, elliptical attenuation regions are defined (see Figure 6-5). Use the PointSound setDistanceGain method to set the front distance attenuation array separately from the back distance attenuation array.

A front distance attenuation array defines monotonically increasing distances from the sound source origin along the position direction vector. A back distance attenuation array (if given) defines monotonically increasing distances from the sound source origin along the negative direction vector. The two arrays must be of the same length. The backDistance[i] gain values must be less than or equal to frontDistance[i] gain values.

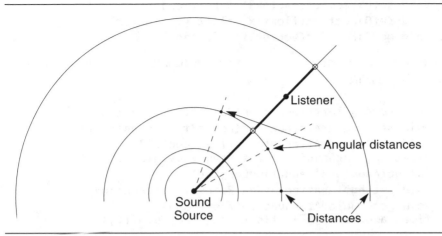

Figure 6-4   ConeSound with a Single Distance Gain Attenuation Array

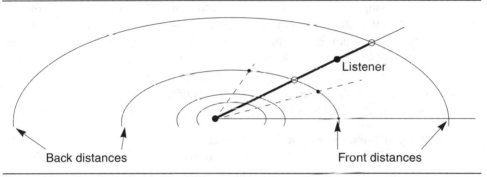

Figure 6-5   ConeSound with Two Distance Gain Attenuation Arrays

Gain scale factors are associated with distances from the listener to the sound source via an array of distance and gain scale factor pairs (see Figure 6-2 on page 87). The gain scale factor applied to the sound source is the linear interpolated gain value within the distance value range that includes the current distance from the listener to the sound source.

The getDistanceGainLength method (defined in PointSound) returns the length of all distance gain attenuation arrays, including the back distance gain arrays. Arrays passed into getBackDistanceGain methods should all be at least this size.

```
public void setDirection(Vector3f direction)
public void setDirection(float x, float y, float z)
public void getDirection(Vector3f direction)
```

This value is the sound source's direction vector. It is the axis from which angular distance is measured.

```
public void setAngularAttenuation(Point2f attenuation[])
public void setAngularAttenuation(Point3f attenuation[])
public void setAngularAttenuation(float angle[],
     float angularGain[], float frequencyCutoff[])
public int getAngularAttenuationLength()
public void getAngularAttenuation(Point3f attenuation[])
public void getAngularAttenuation(float angle[],
     float angularGain[], float frequencyCutoff[])
```

These methods set and retrieve the sound's angular gain and filter attenuation arrays. If these are not set, no angular gain attenuation or filtering is performed (equivalent to using an angular gain scale factor of 1.0 and an angular filter of NO_FILTER for all distances). This attenuation is defined as a triple of angular distance, gain scale factor, and filter values. The distance is measured as the angle in radians between the ConeSound's direction vector and the vector from the sound source position to the listener. Both the gain scale factor and filter applied to the sound source are the linear interpolation of values within the distance value range that includes the angular distance from the sound source axis.

If the angular distance from the listener-sound-position vector and the sound's direction vector is less than the first distance in the array, the first gain scale factor and first filter are applied to the sound source. This creates a conical region around the listener within which the sound is uniformly attenuated by the first gain and the first filter in the array.

If the distance from the listener-sound-position vector and the sound's direction vector is greater than the last distance in the array, the last gain scale factor and last filter are applied to the sound source.

Distance elements in this array of points are a monotonically increasing set of floating point numbers measured from 0 to π radians. Gain scale factor elements in this list of points can be any positive floating-point numbers. While for most applications this list of gain scale factors will usually be monotonically decreasing, they do not have to be. The filter (for now) is a single simple frequency cutoff value.

In the first form of setAngularAttenuation, only the angular distance and angular gain scale factor pairs are given. The filter values for these tuples are implicitly set to NO_FILTER. In the second form of setAngularAttenuation, an array of all three values is supplied.

The third form of setAngularAttenuation accepts three separate arrays for these angular attenuation values. These arrays should be of the same length. If the angularGain or filtering array length is greater than the angularDistance array length, the array elements beyond the length of the angularDistance array are ignored. If the angularGain or filtering array is shorter than the angularDistance array, the last value of the short array is repeated to fill an array of length equal to the angularDistance array.

The getAngularAttenuationArrayLength method returns the length of the angular attenuation arrays. Arrays passed into getAngularAttenuation methods should all be at least this size.

There are two methods for getAngularAttenuation, one returning an array of points, the other returning separate arrays for each attenuation component.

Figure 6-3 on page 89 shows an example of an angular attenuation defining four points of the form (radiant distance, gain scale factor, cutoff filter frequency):

((0.12, 0.8, NO_FILTER), (0.26, 0.6, 18000.0), (0.32, 0.4, 15000.0), (0.40, 0.2, 11000.0))

6.10 Soundscape Node

The Soundscape leaf node defines the attributes that characterize the listener's aural environment. This node defines an application region and an associated aural attribute component object that controls reverberation and atmospheric properties that affect sound source rendering. (Aural attributes are described in Section 8.1.17, "AuralAttributes Object.") Multiple Soundscape nodes can be included in a single scene graph.

The Soundscape application region, different from a Sound node's scheduling region, is used to select which Soundscape (and thus which aural attribute object) is to be applied to the sounds being rendered. This selection is based on the position of the ViewPlatform (the "listener"), not on the position of the sound.

It will be common for multiple Soundscape regions to be contained within a scene graph. Figure 6-6 shows application regions for two Soundscape nodes: a region with a large open area on the right, and a smaller, more constricted, less reverberant area on the left.

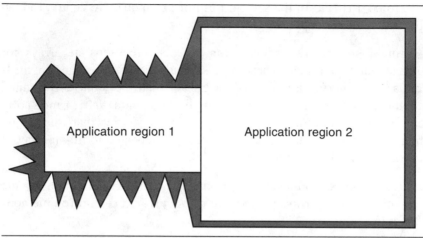

Figure 6-6   Multiple Soundscape Application Regions

The reverberation attributes for these two regions could be set to represent their physical differences so that active sounds are rendered differently depending on which region the listener is in.

Constants

The Soundscape node object defines the following flags:

```
public static final int ALLOW_APPLICATION_BOUNDS_READ
public static final int ALLOW_APPLICATION_BOUNDS_WRITE
public static final int ALLOW_ATTRIBUTES_READ
public static final int ALLOW_ATTRIBUTES_WRITE
```

These flags, when enabled using the `setCapability` method, allow an application to invoke methods that respectively read and write the application region and the aural attributes. These capability flags are enforced only when the node is part of a live or compiled scene graph.

Constructors

The Soundscape node object defines the following constructors:

```
public Soundscape()
```

Constructs a Soundscape node object that includes the following defaults for its elements:

Parameter	Default Value
applicationBounds	null (no active region)
auralAttributes	null (uses default aural attributes)

public Soundscape(Bounds region, AuralAttributes attributes)

This method constructs a Soundscape node object using the specified application region and aural attributes.

Methods

The Soundscape node object defines the following methods:

public void setApplicationBounds(Bounds region)
public Bounds getApplicationBounds()

These two methods access or modify the Soundscape node's application bounds. This bounds is used as the application region when the application bounding leaf is set to null. The aural attributes associated with this Soundscape are used to render the active sounds when this application region intersects the ViewPlatform's activation volume. The getApplicationBounds method returns a copy of the associated bounds.

public void setApplicationBoundingLeaf(BoundingLeaf region)
public BoundingLeaf getApplicationBoundingLeaf()

These two methods access or modify the Soundscape node's application bounding leaf. When set to a value other than null, this bounding leaf overrides the application bounds object and is used as the application region.

public void setAuralAttributes(AuralAttributes attributes)
public AuralAttributes getAuralAttributes()

These two methods access or modify the aural attributes of this Soundscape. Setting it to null results in default attribute use.

6.11 ViewPlatform Node

The ViewPlatform node object defines a viewing platform that is referenced by a View object. The location, orientation, and scale of the composite transforms in the scene graph from the root to the ViewPlatform specify where the viewpoint is located and in which direction it is pointing. A viewer navigates through the virtual universe by changing the transform in the scene graph hierarchy above the ViewPlatform.

Constants

The ViewPlatform node object defines the following flags:

```
public static final int ALLOW_POLICY_READ
public static final int ALLOW_POLICY_WRITE
```

These flags, when enabled using the `setCapability` method, allow an application to invoke methods that respectively read and write the view attach policy. These capability flags are enforced only when the node is part of a live or compiled scene graph.

Constructors

```
public ViewPlatform()
```

Constructs and initializes a new ViewPlatform leaf node object with default parameters:

Parameter	Default Value
viewAttachPolicy	View.NOMINAL_HEAD
activationRadius	62

Methods

The ViewPlatform node object defines the following methods:

```
public void setActivationRadius(float activationRadius)
public float getActivationRadius()
```

The activation radius defines an activation volume surrounding the center of the ViewPlatform. This activation volume intersects with the scheduling regions and application regions of other leaf node objects to determine which of those objects may affect rendering.

Different leaf objects interact with the ViewPlatform's activation volume differently. The Background, Clip, and Soundscape leaf objects each define a set of attributes and an application region in which those attributes are applied. If more than one node of a given type (Background, Clip, or Soundscape) intersects the ViewPlatform's activation volume, the "most appropriate" node is selected.

Sound leaf objects begin playing their associated sounds when their scheduling region intersects a ViewPlatform's activation volume. Multiple sounds may be active at the same time.

Behavior objects act somewhat differently. Those Behavior objects with scheduling regions that intersect a ViewPlatform's activation volume become candidates for scheduling. Effectively, a ViewPlatform's activation volume becomes an additional qualifier on the scheduling of all Behavior objects. See Chapter 10, "Behaviors and Interpolators," for more details.

```
public void setViewAttachPolicy(int policy)
public int getViewAttachPolicy()
```

The view attach policy determines how Java 3D places the user's virtual eye point as a function of head position. See Section 9.4.3, "View Attach Policy," for details.

6.12 Behavior Node

The Behavior leaf node allows an application to manipulate a scene graph at run time. Behavior is an abstract class that defines properties common to all Behavior objects in Java 3D. There are several predefined behaviors that are subclasses of Behavior. Additionally, a Behavior leaf node may be subclassed by the user. Behaviors are described in Chapter 10, "Behaviors and Interpolators."

6.13 Morph Node

The Morph leaf node permits an application to morph between multiple GeometryArrays. The Morph node contains a single Appearance node, an array of GeometryArray objects, and an array of corresponding weights. The Morph node combines these GeometryArrays into an aggregate shape based on each GeometryArray's corresponding weight. Typically, Behavior nodes will modify the weights to achieve various morphing effects.

Constants

The Morph node specifies the following flags:

```
public static final int ALLOW_GEOMETRY_ARRAY_READ
public static final int ALLOW_GEOMETRY_ARRAY_WRITE
public static final int ALLOW_APPEARANCE_READ
public static final int ALLOW_APPEARANCE_WRITE
public static final int ALLOW_WEIGHTS_READ
public static final int ALLOW_WEIGHTS_WRITE
public static final int ALLOW_COLLISION_BOUNDS_READ
public static final int ALLOW_COLLISION_BOUNDS_WRITE
```

`public static final int ALLOW_APPEARANCE_OVERRIDE_READ`
`public static final int ALLOW_APPEARANCE_OVERRIDE_WRITE`

These flags, when enabled using the `setCapability` method, allow an application to invoke methods that respectively read and write the node's array of GeometryArray objects, appearance, weights, collision Bounds, and appearance override enable components.

Constructors

The Morph node specifies the following constructors:

public Morph(GeometryArray geometryArrays[])

Constructs and initializes a new Morph leaf node with the specified array of GeometryArray objects. Default values are used for all other parameters:

Parameter	Default Value
appearance	null
weights	[1, 0, 0, 0, ...]
collisionBounds	null
appearanceOverrideEnable	false

A null appearance object specifies that default values are used for all appearance attributes.

public Morph(GeometryArray geometryArrays[], Appearance appearance)

Constructs and initializes a new Morph leaf node with the specified array of GeometryArray objects and the specified Appearance object. The length of the `geometryArrays` parameter determines the number of weighted geometry arrays in this Morph node. If `geometryArrays` is `null`, then a `NullPointerException` is thrown. If the Appearance component is `null`, then default values are used for all appearance attributes.

Methods

The Morph node specifies the following methods:

public void setGeometryArrays(GeometryArray geometryArrays[])

This method sets the array of GeometryArray objects in the Morph node. Each GeometryArray component specifies colors, normals, and texture coordinates. The length of the `geometryArrays` parameter must be equal to the length of the array with which this Morph node was created; otherwise, an `Illegal-ArgumentException` is thrown.

public GeometryArray getGeometryArray(int index)

This method retrieves a single geometry array from the Morph node. The `index` parameter specifies which array is returned.

public void setAppearance(Appearance appearance)
public Appearance getAppearance()

These methods set and retrieve the Appearance component of this Morph node. The Appearance component specifies material, texture, texture environment, transparency, or other rendering parameters. Setting it to `null` results in default attribute use.

public void setWeights(double weights[])
public double[] getWeights()

These methods set and retrieve the morph weight vector component of this Morph node. The Morph node "weights" the corresponding GeometryArray by the amount specified. The length of the `weights` parameter must be equal to the length of the array with which this Morph node was created; otherwise, an `IllegalArgumentException` is thrown.

public void setCollisionBounds(Bounds bounds)
public Bounds getCollisionBounds()

These methods set and retrieve the collision bounding object of this node.

public boolean intersect(SceneGraphPath path, PickShape pickShape)
public boolean intersect(SceneGraphPath path, PickRay pickRay,
        double[] dist)

These methods check if the geometry component of this morph node under path intersects with the pickShape.

public void setAppearanceOverrideEnable(boolean flag)   ◀ New in 1.2 ▶
public boolean getAppearanceOverrideEnable()   ◀ New in 1.2 ▶

These methods set and retrieve the flag that indicates whether this node's appearance can be overridden. If the flag is true, this node's appearance may be overridden by an AlternateAppearance leaf node, regardless of the value of the `ALLOW_APPEARANCE_WRITE` capability bit. The default value is false. See Section 6.15, "AlternateAppearance Node."

6.14 Link Node

The Link leaf node allows an application to reference a shared subgroup, rooted by a SharedGroup node, from within a branch of the scene graph. Any number of Link nodes can refer to the same SharedGroup node. See Section 7.1.2, "Link Leaf Node," for a description of this node.

6.15 AlternateAppearance Node

The AlternateAppearance leaf node is used for overriding the Appearance component of selected nodes. It defines an Appearance component object and a region of influence in which this AlternateAppearance node is active. An AlternateAppearance node also contains a list of Group nodes that specifies the hierarchical scope of this AlternateAppearance. If the scope list is empty, the AlternateAppearance node has universe scope; all nodes within the region of influence are affected by this AlternateAppearance node. If the scope list is non-empty, only those Leaf nodes under the Group nodes in the scope list are affected by this AlternateAppearance node (subject to the influencing bounds).

An AlternateAppearance node affects Shape3D and Morph nodes by overriding their appearance component with the appearance component in this AlternateAppearance node. Only those Shape3D and Morph nodes that explicitly allow their appearance to be overridden are affected. The AlternateAppearance node has no effect on Shape3D and Morph nodes that do not allow their appearance to be overridden.

If the regions of influence of multiple AlternateAppearance nodes overlap, the Java 3D system will choose a single alternate appearance for those objects that lie in the intersection. This is done in an implementation-dependent manner, but in general, the AlternateAppearance node that is "closest" to the object is chosen.

Constants

The AlternateAppearance node specifies the following flags:

◀ New in 1.2 ▶ `public static final int ALLOW_INFLUENCING_BOUNDS_READ`
◀ New in 1.2 ▶ `public static final int ALLOW_INFLUENCING_BOUNDS_WRITE`
◀ New in 1.2 ▶ `public static final int ALLOW_APPEARANCE_READ`
◀ New in 1.2 ▶ `public static final int ALLOW_APPEARANCE_WRITE`
◀ New in 1.2 ▶ `public static final int ALLOW_SCOPE_READ`
◀ New in 1.2 ▶ `public static final int ALLOW_SCOPE_WRITE`

These flags, when enabled using the `setCapability` method, allow an application to invoke methods that respectively read and write the node's influencing bounds and bounds leaf information, appearance information, and scope information components.

Constructors

The AlternateAppearance node specifies the following constructors:

public AlternateAppearance()   ◀ New in 1.2 ▶

Constructs an AlternateAppearance node with default parameters. The default values are as follows:

Parameter	Default Value
appearance	null
scope	empty (universe scope)
influencingBounds	null
influencingBoundingLeaf	null

public AlternateAppearance(Appearance appearance)   ◀ New in 1.2 ▶

Constructs an AlternateAppearance node with the specified appearance.

Methods

The AlternateAppearance node specifies the following methods:

public void setAppearance(Appearance appearance)   ◀ New in 1.2 ▶
public Appearance getAppearance()   ◀ New in 1.2 ▶

These methods set and retrieve the appearance of this AlternateAppearance node. This appearance overrides the appearance in those Shape3D and Morph nodes affected by this AlternateAppearance node.

public void setInfluencingBounds(Bounds region)   ◀ New in 1.2 ▶
public Bounds getInfluencingBounds()   ◀ New in 1.2 ▶

These methods set and retrieve the AlternateAppearance's influencing region to the specified bounds. This is used when the influencing bounding leaf is set to null.

public void setInfluencingBoundingLeaf(BoundingLeaf region)   ◀ New in 1.2 ▶
public BoundingLeaf getInfluencingBoundingLeaf()   ◀ New in 1.2 ▶

These methods set and retrieve the AlternateAppearance's influencing region to the specified bounding leaf. When set to a value other than null, this overrides the influencing bounds object.

◀ New in 1.2 ▶ **public void setScope(Group scope, int index)**
◀ New in 1.2 ▶ **public Group getScope(int index)**

The first method replaces the node at the specified index in this AlternateAppearance node's list of scopes with the specified Group node. The second method retrieves the Group node at the specified index from this AlternateAppearance node's list of scopes. By default, AlternateAppearance nodes are scoped only by their influencing bounds. This allows them to be scoped further by a list of nodes in the hierarchy.

◀ New in 1.2 ▶ **public void insertScope(Group scope, int index)**
◀ New in 1.2 ▶ **public void removeScope(int index)**

The first method inserts the specified Group node into this AlternateAppearance node's list of scopes at the specified index. The second method removes the node at the specified index from this AlternateAppearance node's list of scopes. If this operation causes the list of scopes to become empty, this AlternateAppearance will have universe scope; all nodes within the region of influence will be affected by this AlternateAppearance node. By default, AlternateAppearance nodes are scoped only by their influencing bounds. This allows them to be scoped further by a list of nodes in the hierarchy.

◀ New in 1.2 ▶ **public Enumeration getAllScopes()**

This method returns an enumeration of this AlternateAppearance node's list of scopes.

◀ New in 1.2 ▶ **public void addScope(Group scope)**

This method appends the specified Group node to this AlternateAppearance node's list of scopes. By default, AlternateAppearance nodes are scoped only by their influencing bounds. This allows them to be scoped further by a list of nodes in the hierarchy.

◀ New in 1.2 ▶ **public int numScopes()**

This method returns the number of nodes in this AlternateAppearance node's list of scopes. If this number is 0, the list of scopes is empty and this AlternateAppearance node has universe scope; all nodes within the region of influence are affected by this AlternateAppearance node.

CHAPTER 7

Reusing Scene Graphs

JAVA 3D provides application programmers with two different means for reusing scene graphs. First, multiple scene graphs can share a common subgraph. Second, the node hierarchy of a common subgraph can be cloned, while still sharing large component objects such as geometry and texture objects. In the first case, changes in the shared subgraph affect all scene graphs that refer to the shared subgraph. In the second case, each instance is unique—a change in one instance does not affect any other instance.

7.1 Sharing Subgraphs

An application that wishes to share a subgraph from multiple places in a scene graph must do so through the use of the Link leaf node and an associated SharedGroup node. The SharedGroup node serves as the root of the shared subgraph. The Link leaf node refers to the SharedGroup node. It does not incorporate the shared scene graph directly into its scene graph.

7.1.1 SharedGroup Node

A SharedGroup node allows multiple Link leaf nodes to share its subgraph (see Figure 7-1) according to the following semantics:

- A SharedGroup may be referenced by one or more Link leaf nodes. Any runtime changes to a node or component object in this shared subgraph affect all graphs that refer to this subgraph.

- A SharedGroup may be compiled by calling its `compile` method prior to being referenced by any Link leaf nodes.

- Only Link leaf nodes may refer to SharedGroup nodes. A SharedGroup node cannot have parents or be attached to a Locale.

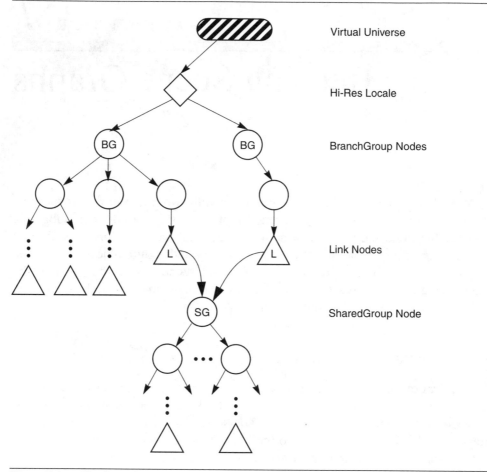

Figure 7-1   Sharing a Subgraph

A shared subgraph may contain any group node, except an embedded
SharedGroup node (SharedGroup nodes cannot have parents). However, only the
following leaf nodes may appear in a shared subgraph:

- Light
- Link
- Morph
- Shape
- Sound

An IllegalSharingException is thrown if any of the following leaf nodes
appear in a shared subgraph:

- AlternateAppearance
- Background
- BoundingLeaf
- Behavior
- Clip
- Fog
- ModelClip
- Soundscape
- ViewPlatform

Constructors

```
public SharedGroup()
```

Constructs and initializes a new SharedGroup node object.

Methods

The SharedGroup node defines the following methods:

```
public void compile()
```

This method compiles the source SharedGroup associated with this object and creates and caches a newly compiled scene graph.

7.1.2 Link Leaf Node

The Link leaf node allows an application to reference a shared graph, rooted by a SharedGroup node, from within a branch graph or another shared graph. See Figure 7-1 on page 106. Any number of Link nodes can refer to the same SharedGroup node.

Constants

The Link node object defines two flags.

```
public static final int ALLOW_SHARED_GROUP_READ
public static final int ALLOW_SHARED_GROUP_WRITE
```

These flags, when enabled using the setCapability method, allow an application to invoke methods that respectively read and write the SharedGroup node pointed to by this Link node. These capability flags are enforced only when the node is part of a live or compiled scene graph.

Constructors

The Link node object defines two constructors.

```
public Link()
public Link(SharedGroup sharedGroup)
```

The first form constructs a Link node object that does not yet point to a SharedGroup node. The second form constructs a Link node object that points to the specified SharedGroup node.

Methods

The Link node object defines two methods.

```
public void setSharedGroup(SharedGroup sharedGroup)
public SharedGroup getSharedGroup()
```

These methods access and modify the SharedGroup node associated with this Link leaf node.

7.2   Cloning Subgraphs

An application developer may wish to reuse a common subgraph without completely sharing that subgraph. For example, the developer may wish to create a parking lot scene consisting of multiple cars, each with a different color. The developer might define three basic types of cars, such as convertible, truck, and sedan. To create the parking lot scene, the application will instantiate each type of car several times. Then the application can change the color of the various instances to create more variety in the scene. Unlike shared subgraphs, each instance is a separate copy of the scene graph definition: Changes to one instance do not affect any other instance.

Java 3D provides the cloneTree method for this purpose. The cloneTree method allows the programmer to change some attributes (NodeComponent objects) in a scene graph, while at the same time sharing the majority of the scene graph data—the geometry.

Methods

```
public Node cloneTree()
public Node cloneTree(boolean forceDuplicate)
public Node cloneTree(boolean forceDuplicate,
      boolean allowDanglingReferences)
public Node cloneTree(NodeReferenceTable referenceTable)
public Node cloneTree(NodeReferenceTable referenceTable,
      boolean forceDuplicate)
public Node cloneTree(NodeReferenceTable referenceTable,
      boolean forceDuplicate, boolean allowDanglingReferences)
```

◀ New in 1.2 ▶

◀ New in 1.2 ▶

◀ New in 1.2 ▶

These methods start the cloning of the subgraph. The optional `forceDuplicate` parameter, when set to `true`, causes leaf NodeComponent objects to ignore their `duplicateOnCloneTree` value and always be duplicated (see Section 7.2.1, "References to Node Component Objects"). The `allowDanglingReferences` parameter, when set to `true`, will permit the cloning of a subgraph even when a dangling reference is generated (see Section 7.2.3, "Dangling References"). Setting `forceDuplicate` and `allowDanglingReferences` to `false` is the equivalent of calling `cloneTree` without any parameters. This will result in NodeComponent objects being either duplicated or referenced in the cloned node, based on their `duplicateOnCloneTree` value. A `DanglingReferenceException` will be thrown if a dangling reference is encountered.

When the `cloneTree` method is called on a node, that node is duplicated along with its entire internal state. If the node is a Group node, `cloneTree` is then called on each of the node's children.

The `cloneTree` method cannot be called on a live or compiled scene graph.

7.2.1   References to Node Component Objects

When `cloneTree` reaches a leaf node, there are two possible actions for handling the leaf node's NodeComponent objects (such as Material, Texture, and so forth). First, the cloned leaf node can reference the original leaf node's NodeComponent object—the NodeComponent object itself is not duplicated. Since the cloned leaf node shares the NodeComponent object with the original leaf node, changing the data in the NodeComponent object will effect a change in both nodes. This mode would also be used for objects that are read-only at run time.

Alternatively, the NodeComponent object can be duplicated, in which case the new leaf node would reference the duplicated object. This mode allows data referenced by the newly created leaf node to be modified without that modification affecting the original leaf node.

109

Figure 7-2 shows two instances of NodeComponent objects that are shared and one NodeComponent element that is duplicated for the cloned subgraph.

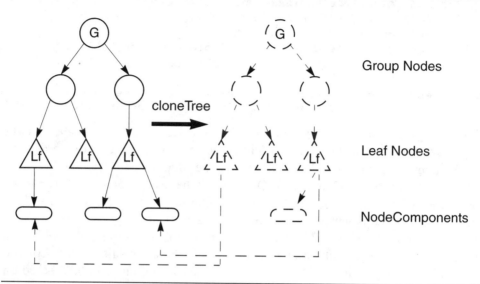

Figure 7-2   Referenced and Duplicated NodeComponent Objects

Methods

```
public void setDuplicateOnCloneTree(boolean)
public void getDuplicateOnCloneTree()
```

These methods set a flag that controls whether a NodeComponent object is duplicated or referenced on a call to `cloneTree`. By default this flag is `false`, meaning that the NodeComponent object will not be duplicated on a call to `cloneTree`—newly created leaf nodes will refer to the original NodeComponent object instead.

If the `cloneTree` method is called with the `forceDuplicate` parameter set to `true`, the `duplicateOnCloneTree` flag is ignored and the entire scene graph is duplicated.

7.2.2   References to Other Scene Graph Nodes

Leaf nodes that contain references to other nodes (for example, Light nodes reference a Group node) can create a problem for the `cloneTree` method. After the `cloneTree` operation is performed, the reference in the cloned leaf node will still refer to the node in the original subgraph—a situation that is most likely incorrect (see Figure 7-3).

To handle these ambiguities, a callback mechanism is provided.

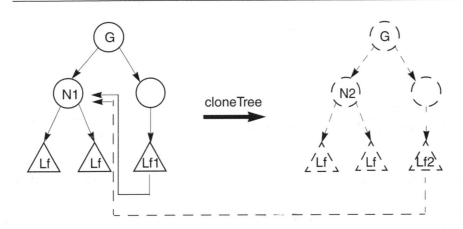

Figure 7-3   References to Other Scene Graph Nodes

A leaf node that needs to update referenced nodes upon being duplicated by a call to `cloneTree` must implement the `updateNodeReferences` method. By using this method, the cloned leaf node can determine if any nodes referenced by it have been duplicated and, if so, update the appropriate references to their cloned counterparts.

Suppose, for instance, that the leaf node Lf1 in Figure 7-3 implemented the `updateNodeReferences` method. Once all nodes had been duplicated, the `cloneTree` method would then call each cloned leaf's node `updateNodeReferences` method. When cloned leaf node Lf2's method was called, Lf2 could ask if the node N1 had been duplicated during the `cloneTree` operation. If the node had been duplicated, leaf Lf2 could then update its internal state with the cloned node, N2 (see Figure 7-4).

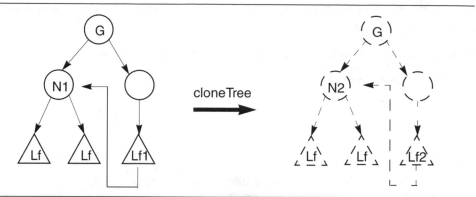

Figure 7-4   Updated Subgraph after `updateNodeReferences` Call

All predefined Java 3D nodes will automatically have their `updateNodeRefer-ences` method defined. Only subclassed nodes that reference other nodes need to have this method overridden by the user.

Methods

`public void updateNodeReferences(NodeReferenceTable referenceTable)`

This SceneGraphObject node method is called by the `cloneTree` method after all nodes in the subgraph have been cloned. The user can query the NodeReference-Table object (see Section 7.2.5, "NodeReferenceTable Object") to determine if any nodes that the SceneGraphObject node references have been duplicated by the `cloneTree` call and, if so, what the corresponding node is in the new sub-graph. If a user extends a predefined Java 3D object and adds a reference to another node, this method must be defined in order to ensure proper operation of the `cloneTree` method. The first statement in the user's `updateNodeReferences` method must be `super.updateNodeReferences(referenceTable)`. For pre-defined Java 3D nodes, this method will be implemented automatically.

The NodeReferenceTable object is passed to the `updateNodeReferences` method and allows references from the old subgraph to be translated into references in the cloned subgraph. The translation is performed by the `getNew-NodeReference` method.

`public final SceneGraphObject getNewObjectReference(SceneGraphObject oldReference)`

This method takes a reference to the node in the original subgraph as an input parameter and returns a reference to the equivalent node in the just-cloned subgraph. If the equivalent node in the cloned subgraph does not exist, either an exception is thrown or a reference to the original node is returned (see Section 7.2.3, "Dangling References").

7.2.3   Dangling References

Because `cloneTree` is able to start the cloning operation from any node, there is a potential for creating *dangling references*. A dangling reference can occur only when a leaf node that contains a reference to another scene graph node is cloned. If the referenced node is not cloned, a dangling reference situation exists: There are now two leaf nodes that access the same node (Figure 7-5). A dangling reference is discovered when a leaf node's `updateNodeReferences` method calls the `getNewNodeReference` method and the cloned subgraph does not contain a counterpart to the node being looked up.

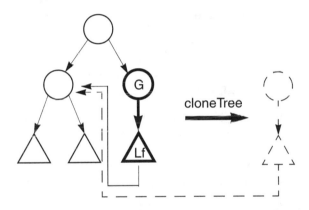

Figure 7-5   Dangling Reference: Bold Nodes Are Being Cloned

When a dangling reference is discovered, `cloneTree` can handle it in one of two ways. If `cloneTree` is called without the `allowDanglingReferences` parameter set to `true`, a dangling reference will result in a `DanglingReferenceException` being thrown. The user can catch this exception if desired. If `cloneTree` is called with the `allowDanglingReferences` parameter set to `true`, the `update-NodeReferences` method will return a reference to the same object passed into the `getNewNodeReference` method. This will result in the `cloneTree` operation completing with dangling references, as in Figure 7-5.

7.2.4   Subclassing Nodes

All Java 3D predefined nodes (for example, Interpolators and LOD nodes) auto-matically handle all node reference and duplication operations. When a user sub-classes a Leaf object or a NodeComponent object, certain methods must be provided in order to ensure the proper operation of `cloneTree`.

Leaf node subclasses (for example, Behaviors) that contain any user node-spe-cific data that needs to be duplicated during a `cloneTree` operation must define the following two methods:

```
Node cloneNode(boolean forceDuplicate);
void duplicateNode(Node n, boolean forceDuplicate)
```

The `cloneNode` method consists of three lines:

```
    UserSubClass usc = new UserSubClass();
    usc.duplicateNode(this, forceDuplicate);
    return usc;
```

The `duplicateNode` method must first call `super.duplicateNode` before dupli-cating any necessary user-specific data or setting any user-specific state.

NodeComponent subclasses that contain any user node-specific data must define the following two methods:

```
NodeComponent cloneNodeComponent();
```
◀ New in 1.2 ▶ `void duplicateNodeComponent(NodeComponent nc,`
`        boolean forceDuplicate);`

The `cloneNodeComponent` method consists of three lines:

```
    UserNodeComponent unc = new UserNodeComponent();
    unc.duplicateNodeComponent(this, forceDuplicate);
    return un;
```

The `duplicateNodeComponent` must first call `super.duplicateNodeComponent` and then can duplicate any user-specific data or set any user-specific state as nec-essary.

7.2.5   NodeReferenceTable Object

The NodeReferenceTable object is used by a leaf node's `updateNodeReferences` method called by the `cloneTree` operation. The NodeReferenceTable maps nodes from the original subgraph to the new nodes in the cloned subgraph. This information can than be used to update any cloned leaf node references to reference nodes in the cloned subgraph. This object can be created only by Java 3D.

Constructors

`public NodeReferenceTable()`   ◀ New in 1.2 ▶

Constructs an empty NodeReferenceTable.

Methods

`public SceneGraphObject getNewObjectReference(SceneGraphObject`
      `oldReference)`

This method takes a reference to the node in the original subgraph as an input parameter and returns a reference to the equivalent node in the just-cloned subgraph. If the equivalent node in the cloned subgraph does not exist, either an exception is thrown or a reference to the original node is returned (see Section 7.2.3, "Dangling References").

7.2.6   Example User Behavior Node

The following is an example of a user-defined Behavior object to show properly how to define a node to be compatible with the `cloneTree` operation.

```
class RotationBehavior extends Behavior {
    TransformGroup objectTransform;
    WakeupOnElapsedFrames w;

    Matrix4d rotMat = new Matrix4d();
    Matrix4d objectMat = new Matrix4d();
    Transform3D t = new Transform3D();

    // Override Behavior's initialize method to set up wakeup
    // criteria
    public void initialize() {
        // Establish initial wakeup criteria
        wakeupOn(w);
    }
```

```
        // Override Behavior's stimulus method to handle the event
        public void processStimulus(Enumeration criteria) {
            // Rotate by another PI/120.0 radians
            objectMat.mul(objectMat, rotMat);
            t.set(objectMat);
            objectTransform.setTransform(t);

            // Set wakeup criteria for next time
            wakeupOn(w);
        }

        // Constructor for rotation behavior.
        public RotationBehavior(TransformGroup tg, int numFrames) {
            w = new WakeupOnElapsedFrames(numFrames);
            objectTransform = tg;
            objectMat.setIdentity();

            // Create a rotation matrix that rotates PI/120.0
            // radians per frame
            rotMat.rotX(Math.PI/120.0);

            // Note: When this object is duplicated via cloneTree,
            // the cloned RotationBehavior node needs to point to
            // the TransformGroup in the just-cloned tree.
        }

        // Sets a new TransformGroup.
        public void setTransformGroup(TransformGroup tg) {
            objectTransform = tg;
        }

        // The next two methods are needed for cloneTree to operate
        // correctly.
        // cloneNode is needed to provide a new instance of the user
        // derived subclass.
        public Node cloneNode(boolean forceDuplicate) {
            // Get all data from current node needed for
            // the constructor
            int numFrames = w.getElapsedFrameCount();
```

```
        RotationBehavior r =
            new RotationBehavior(objectTransform, numFrames);
        r.duplicateNode(this, forceDuplicate);
        return r;
    }
    // duplicateNode is needed to duplicate all super class
    // data as well as all user data.
    public void duplicateNode(Node originalNode, boolean
     forceDuplicate) {
        super.duplicateNode(originalNode, forceDuplicate);
        // Nothing to do here - all unique data was handled
        // in the constructor in the cloneNode routine.
    }

    // duplicateNode is needed to duplicate all super class
    // data as well as all user data.
    public void duplicateNode(Node originalNode, boolean
     forceDuplicate) {
        super.duplicateNode(originalNode, forceDuplicate);
        // Nothing to do here - all unique data was handled
        // in the constructor in the cloneNode routine.
    }

    // Callback for when this leaf is cloned. For this object
    // we want to find the cloned TransformGroup node that this
    // clone Leaf node should reference.
    public void updateNodeReferences(NodeReferenceTable t) {
        super.updateNodeReferences(t);

        // Update node's TransformGroup to proper reference
        TransformGroup newTg =
         (TransformGroup)t.getNewObjectReference(
            objectTransform);
        setTransformGroup(newTg);
    }
}
```

CHAPTER **8**

Node Component Objects

NODE component objects include the actual geometry and appearance attributes used to render the geometry.

8.1 Node Component Objects: Attributes

Node objects by themselves do not fully specify their exact semantics. They contain information that further refines their exact meaning. Some of that information is specified as an attribute and an associated floating-point or integer value. In many cases, however, the information consists of references to more complex entities called *node component objects*. Node component objects encapsulate related state information in a single entity. See Figure 8-1.

8.1.1 Alpha Object

The Alpha node component object provides common methods for converting a time value into an alpha value (a value in the range 0.0 to 1.0). See Section 10.6, "Interpolator Behaviors," for a description of the Alpha object.

8.1.2 Appearance Object

The Appearance object is a component object of a Shape3D node that defines all rendering state attributes for that shape node. If the Appearance object in a Shape3D node is null, default values will be used for all rendering state attributes.

Constants

The Appearance component object defines the following flags:

```
SceneGraphObject
    NodeComponent
        Alpha
        Appearance
        AuralAttributes
        ColoringAttributes
        LineAttributes
        PointAttributes
        PolygonAttributes
        RenderingAttributes
        TextureAttributes
        TransparencyAttributes
        Material
        MediaContainer
        TextureUnitState
        TexCoordGeneration
        Texture
            Texture2D
            Texture3D
        ImageComponent
            ImageComponent2D
            ImageComponent3D
        DepthComponent
            DepthComponentFloat
            DepthComponentInt
            DepthComponentNative
Bounds
    BoundingBox
    BoundingPolytope
    BoundingSphere
Transform3D
```

Figure 8-1   Attribute Component Object Hierarchy

```
public static final int ALLOW_MATERIAL_READ
public static final int ALLOW_MATERIAL_WRITE
public static final int ALLOW_TEXTURE_READ
public static final int ALLOW_TEXTURE_WRITE
public static final int ALLOW_TEXGEN_READ
public static final int ALLOW_TEXGEN_WRITE
public static final int ALLOW_TEXTURE_ATTRIBUTES_READ
public static final int ALLOW_TEXTURE_ATTRIBUTES_WRITE
public static final int ALLOW_COLORING_ATTRIBUTES_READ
public static final int ALLOW_COLORING_ATTRIBUTES_WRITE
public static final int ALLOW_TRANSPARENCY_ATTRIBUTES_READ
public static final int ALLOW_TRANSPARENCY_ATTRIBUTES_WRITE
```

```
public static final int ALLOW_RENDERING_ATTRIBUTES_READ
public static final int ALLOW_RENDERING_ATTRIBUTES_WRITE
public static final int ALLOW_POLYGON_ATTRIBUTES_READ
public static final int ALLOW_POLYGON_ATTRIBUTES_WRITE
public static final int ALLOW_LINE_ATTRIBUTES_READ
public static final int ALLOW_LINE_ATTRIBUTES_WRITE
public static final int ALLOW_POINT_ATTRIBUTES_READ
public static final int ALLOW_POINT_ATTRIBUTES_WRITE
public static final int ALLOW_TEXTURE_UNIT_STATE_READ         ◀ New in 1.2 ▶
public static final int ALLOW_TEXTURE_UNIT_STATE_WRITE        ◀ New in 1.2 ▶
```

These flags, when enabled using the `setCapability` method, allow an application to invoke methods that read and write the specified component object reference (material, texture, texture coordinate generation, and so forth). These capability flags are enforced only when the object is part of a live or compiled scene graph.

Constructors

The Appearance object has the following constructor:

public Appearance()

Constructs and initializes an Appearance object using defaults for all state variables. All component object references are initialized to null.

Methods

The Appearance object has the following methods:

public void setMaterial(Material material)
public Material getMaterial()

The Material object specifies the desired material properties used for lighting. Setting it to null disables lighting.

public void setTexture(Texture texture)
public Texture getTexture()

The Texture object specifies the desired texture map and texture parameters. Setting it to null disables texture mapping. Applications must not set individual texture component objects (texture, textureAttributes, or texCoordGeneration) and the texture unit state array in the same Appearance object. Doing so will result in an exception being thrown.

```
public void setTextureAttributes(TextureAttributes
     textureAttributes)
public TextureAttributes getTextureAttributes()
```

These methods set and retrieve the TextureAttributes object. Setting it to `null` results in default attribute use. Applications must not set individual texture component objects (texture, textureAttributes, or texCoordGeneration) and the texture unit state array in the same Appearance object. Doing so will result in an exception being thrown.

```
public void setColoringAttributes(ColoringAttributes
     coloringAttributes)
public ColoringAttributes getColoringAttributes()
```

These methods set and retrieve the ColoringAttributes object. Setting it to `null` results in default attribute use.

```
public void setTransparencyAttributes(
     TransparencyAttributes transparencyAttributes)
public TransparencyAttributes getTransparencyAttributes()
```

These methods set and retrieve the TransparencyAttributes object. Setting it to `null` results in default attribute use.

```
public void setRenderingAttributes(RenderingAttributes
     renderingAttributes)
public RenderingAttributes getRenderingAttributes()
```

These methods set and retrieve the RenderingAttributes object. Setting it to `null` results in default attribute use.

```
public void setPolygonAttributes(PolygonAttributes
     polygonAttributes)
public PolygonAttributes getPolygonAttributes()
```

These methods set and retrieve the PolygonAttributes object. Setting it to `null` results in default attribute use.

```
public void setLineAttributes(LineAttributes lineAttributes)
public LineAttributes getLineAttributes()
```

These methods set and retrieve the LineAttributes object. Setting it to `null` results in default attribute use.

```
public void setPointAttributes(PointAttributes pointAttributes)
public PointAttributes getPointAttributes()
```

These methods set and retrieve the PointAttributes object. Setting it to `null` results in default attribute use.

```
public void setTexCoordGeneration(TexCoordGeneration
      texCoordGeneration)
public TexCoordGeneration getTexCoordGeneration()
```

These methods set and retrieve the TexCoordGeneration object. Setting it to `null` disables texture coordinate generation.

```
public void setTextureUnitState(TextureUnitState[] stateArray)    ◀ New in 1.2 ▶
public void setTextureUnitState(int index, TextureUnitState state)◀ New in 1.2 ▶
public TextureUnitState[] getTextureUnitState()                   ◀ New in 1.2 ▶
public TextureUnitState getTextureUnitState(int index)           ◀ New in 1.2 ▶
```

These methods set and retrieve the texture-unit state for this Appearance object (see Section 8.1.15, "TextureUnitState Object"). The first method sets the texture unit state array to the specified array. A shallow copy of the array of references to the TextureUnitState objects is made. If the specified array is null or if the length of the array is 0, multitexture is disabled. Within the array, a null Texture-UnitState element disables the corresponding texture unit. The second method sets the texture unit state array object at the specified index within the texture unit state array to the specified object. If the specified object is null, the corresponding texture unit is disabled. The index must be within the range [0, stateArray.length–1]. Applications must not set individual texture component objects (texture, textureAttributes, or texCoordGeneration) and the texture unit state array in the same Appearance object. Doing so will result in an exception being thrown.

```
public int getTextureUnitCount()                                 ◀ New in 1.2 ▶
```

This method retrieves the length of the texture unit state array from this Appearance object. The length of this array specifies the maximum number of texture units that will be used by this appearance object. If the array is null, a count of 0 is returned.

8.1.3 ColoringAttributes Object

The ColoringAttributes object defines attributes that apply to color mapping.

Constants

```
public static final int ALLOW_COLOR_READ
public static final int ALLOW_COLOR_WRITE
public static final int ALLOW_SHADE_MODEL_READ
public static final int ALLOW_SHADE_MODEL_WRITE
```

These flags, when enabled using the `setCapability` method, allow an application to invoke methods that respectively read and write its color component and shade model component information.

Constructors

```
public ColoringAttributes()
```

Constructs a ColoringAttributes node with default parameters:

Parameter	Default Value
color	white (1,1,1)
shadeModel	SHADE_GOURAUD

```
public ColoringAttributes(Color3f color, int shadeModel)
public ColoringAttributes(float red, float green, float blue,
        int shadeModel)
```

These constructors create a ColoringAttributes object with the specified values.

Methods

```
public void setColor(Color3f color)
public void setColor(float r, float g, float b)
public void getColor(Color3f color)
```

These methods set and retrieve the intrinsic color of this ColoringAttributes component object. This color is used only for unlit geometry. If lighting is enabled, the material colors are used in the lighting equation to produce the final color. When vertex colors are present in unlit geometry, those vertex colors are used in place of this ColoringAttributes color unless the vertex colors are ignored.

```
public void setShadeModel(int shadeModel)
public int getShadeModel()
```

These methods set and retrieve the shade model for this ColoringAttributes component object. The shade model is one of the following:

- FASTEST: Uses the fastest available method for shading.

- NICEST: Uses the nicest (highest quality) available method for shading.
- SHADE_FLAT: Does not interpolate color across the primitive.
- SHADE_GOURAUD: Smoothly interpolates the color at each vertex across the primitive.

8.1.4 LineAttributes Object

The LineAttributes object defines attributes that apply to line primitives.

Constants

The LineAttributes object specifies the following variables:

```
public static final int ALLOW_WIDTH_READ
public static final int ALLOW_WIDTH_WRITE
public static final int ALLOW_PATTERN_READ
public static final int ALLOW_PATTERN_WRITE
public static final int ALLOW_ANTIALIASING_READ
public static final int ALLOW_ANTIALIASING_WRITE
```

These flags, when enabled using the setCapability method, allow an application to invoke methods that read and write its individual component field information.

```
public static final int PATTERN_SOLID
```

Draws a solid line with no pattern.

```
public static final int PATTERN_DASH
```

Draws a dashed line. Ideally, this will be drawn with a repeating pattern of eight pixels on and eight pixels off.

```
public static final int PATTERN_DOT
```

Draws a dotted line. Ideally, this will be drawn with a repeating pattern of one pixel on and seven pixels off.

```
public static final int PATTERN_DASH_DOT
```

Draws a dashed-dotted line. Ideally, this will be drawn with a repeating pattern of seven pixels on, four pixels off, one pixel on, and four pixels off.

◀ New in 1.2 ▶ **public static final int PATTERN_USER_DEFINED**

Draws lines with a user-defined line pattern. The line pattern is specified with a pattern mask and a scale factor.

Constructors

public LineAttributes()

Constructs a LineAttributes object with default parameters:

Parameter	Default Value
lineWidth	1
linePattern	PATTERN_SOLID
lineAntialiasing	false

**public LineAttributes(float lineWidth, int linePattern,
        boolean lineAntialiasing)**

Constructs a LineAttributes object with specified values of line width, pattern, and whether antialiasing is enabled or disabled.

Methods

public void setLineWidth(float lineWidth)
public float getLineWidth()

These methods respectively set and retrieve the line width, in pixels, for this Line-Attributes component object.

public void setLinePattern(int linePattern)
public int getLinePattern()

These methods respectively set and retrieve the line pattern for this LineAttributes component object. The linePattern value describes the line pattern to be used, which is one of the following: PATTERN_SOLID, PATTERN_DASH, PATTERN_DOT, or PATTERN_DASH_DOT.

public void setLineAntialiasingEnable(boolean state)
public boolean getLineAntialiasingEnable()

The set method enables or disables line antialiasing for this LineAttributes component object. The get method retrieves the state of the line antialiasing flag. The flag is true if line antialiasing is enabled, false if line antialiasing is disabled.

```
public void setPatternMask(int mask)
public int getPatternMask()
```
◀ New in 1.2 ▶
◀ New in 1.2 ▶

These methods respectively set and retrieve the line pattern mask. The line pattern mask is used when the linePattern attribute is set to PATTERN_USER_DEFINED.

In this mode, the pattern is specified using a 16-bit mask that specifies on and off segments. Bit 0 in the pattern mask corresponds to the first pixel of the line or line strip primitive. A value of 1 for a bit in the pattern mask indicates that the corresponding pixel is drawn, while a value of 0 indicates that the corresponding pixel is not drawn. After all 16 bits in the pattern are used, the pattern is repeated. For example, a mask of 0x00ff defines a dashed line with a repeating pattern of eight pixels on followed by eight pixels off. A value of 0x0101 defines a dotted line with a repeating pattern of one pixel on and seven pixels off.

The pattern continues around individual line segments of a line strip primitive. It is restarted at the beginning of each new line strip. For line array primitives, the pattern is restarted at the beginning of each line.

```
public void setPatternScaleFactor(int scaleFactor)
public int getPatternScaleFactor()
```
◀ New in 1.2 ▶
◀ New in 1.2 ▶

These methods respectively set and retrieve the line pattern scale factor. The line pattern scale factor is used in conjunction with the patternMask when the linePattern attribute is set to PATTERN_USER_DEFINED. The pattern is multiplied by the scale factor such that each bit in the pattern mask corresponds to that many consecutive pixels. For example, a scale factor of 3 applied to a pattern mask of 0x001f would produce a repeating pattern of 15 pixels on followed by 33 pixels off. The valid range for this attribute is [1,15]. Values outside this range are clamped.

8.1.5 PointAttributes Object

The PointAttributes object defines attributes that apply to point primitives.

Constants

The PointAttributes object specifies the following variables:

```
public static final int ALLOW_SIZE_READ
public static final int ALLOW_SIZE_WRITE
```

```
public static final int ALLOW_ANTIALIASING_READ
public static final int ALLOW_ANTIALIASING_WRITE
```

These flags, when enabled using the setCapability method, allow an application to invoke methods that read and write its individual component field information.

Constructors

```
public PointAttributes()
```

Constructs a PointAttributes object with default parameters:

Parameter	Default Value
pointSize	1
pointAntialiasingEnable	false

```
public PointAttributes(float pointSize,
       boolean pointAntialiasing)
```

Constructs a PointAttributes object with specified values.

Methods

```
public void setPointSize(float pointSize)
public float getPointSize()
```

These methods set and retrieve the point size, in pixels, for this Appearance component object.

```
public void setPointAntialiasingEnable(boolean state)
public boolean getPointAntialiasingEnable()
```

The set method enables or disables point antialiasing for this PointAttributes component object. The get method retrieves the state of the point antialiasing flag. The flag is true if point antialiasing is enabled; false if point antialiasing is disabled.

8.1.6   PolygonAttributes Object

The PolygonAttributes object defines attributes for rendering polygon primitives.

Constants

The PolygonAttributes object specifies the following variables:

```
public static final int ALLOW_CULL_FACE_READ
public static final int ALLOW_CULL_FACE_WRITE
public static final int ALLOW_MODE_READ
public static final int ALLOW_MODE_WRITE
public static final int ALLOW_OFFSET_READ
public static final int ALLOW_OFFSET_WRITE
public static final int ALLOW_NORMAL_FLIP_READ
public static final int ALLOW_NORMAL_FLIP_WRITE
```

These flags, when enabled using the `setCapability` method, allow an application to invoke methods that read and write its individual component field information.

Constructors

public PolygonAttributes()

Constructs a PolygonAttributes object with default parameters:

Parameter	Default Value
cullFace	CULL_BACK
backFaceNormalFlip	false
polygonMode	POLYGON_FILL
polygonOffset	0.0
polygonOffsetFactor	0.0

```
public PolygonAttributes(int polygonMode, int cullFace,
      float polygonOffset)
public PolygonAttributes(int polygonMode, int cullFace,
      float polygonOffset, boolean backFaceNormalFlip)
public PolygonAttributes(int polygonMode, int cullFace,
      float polygonOffsct, boolean backFaceNormalFlip,
      float polygonOffsetFactor)
```

◀ New in 1.2 ▶

These constructors create a new PolygonAttributes object with the specified values.

Methods

public void setCullFace(int cullFace)
public int getCullFace()

These methods set and retrieve the face culling flag for this PolygonAttributes component object. The face culling flag is one of the following:

- CULL_NONE: Performs no face culling.
- CULL_FRONT: Culls all front-facing polygons.
- CULL_BACK: Culls all back-facing polygons.

public void setBackFaceNormalFlip(boolean backFaceNormalFlip)
public boolean getBackFaceNormalFlip()

These methods set and retrieve the back-face normal flip flag. This flag indicates whether vertex normals of back-facing polygons should be flipped (negated) prior to lighting. When this flag is set to true and back-face culling is disabled, polygons are rendered as if the polygon had two sides with opposing normals. This feature is disabled by default.

public void setPolygonMode(int polygonMode)
public int getPolygonMode()

These methods set and retrieve the polygon rasterization mode for this Appearance component object. The polygon rasterization mode is one of the following:

- POLYGON_POINT: Renders polygonal primitives as points drawn at the vertices of the polygon.
- POLYGON_LINE: Renders polygonal primitives as lines drawn between consecutive vertices of the polygon.
- POLYGON_FILL: Renders polygonal primitives by filling the interior of the polygon.

public void setPolygonOffset(float polygonOffset)
public float getPolygonOffset()

These methods set and retrieve the constant polygon offset. This screen-space offset is added to the final, device coordinate z value of polygon primitives.

◀ New in 1.2 ▶ **public void setPolygonOffsetFactor(float polygonOffsetFactor)**
◀ New in 1.2 ▶ **public float getPolygonOffsetFactor()**

These methods set and retrieve the polygon offset factor. This factor is multiplied by the slope of the polygon and then added to the final device coordinate z value of polygon primitives.

8.1.7 RenderingAttributes Object

The RenderingAttributes object defines common rendering attributes for all primitive types.

Constants

```
public static final int ALLOW_ALPHA_TEST_VALUE_READ
public static final int ALLOW_ALPHA_TEST_VALUE_WRITE
public static final int ALLOW_ALPHA_TEST_FUNCTION_READ
public static final int ALLOW_ALPHA_TEST_FUNCTION_WRITE
public static final int ALLOW_DEPTH_ENABLE_READ
public static final int ALLOW_VISIBLE_READ                         ◀ New in 1.2 ▶
public static final int ALLOW_VISIBLE_WRITE                        ◀ New in 1.2 ▶
public static final int ALLOW_IGNORE_VERTEX_COLORS_READ            ◀ New in 1.2 ▶
public static final int ALLOW_IGNORE_VERTEX_COLORS_WRITE           ◀ New in 1.2 ▶
public static final int ALLOW_RASTER_OP_READ                       ◀ New in 1.2 ▶
public static final int ALLOW_RASTER_OP_WRITE                      ◀ New in 1.2 ▶
```

These flags, when enabled using the setCapability method, allow an application to invoke methods that respectively read and write its individual test value and function information.

Constructors

public RenderingAttributes()

Constructs a RenderingAttributes object with default parameters:

Parameter	Default Value
depthBufferEnable	true
depthBufferWriteEnable	true
alphaTestFunction	ALWAYS
alphaTestValue	0.0
visible	true
ignoreVertexColors	false
rasterOpEnable	false
rasterOp	ROP_COPY

```
public RenderingAttributes(boolean depthBufferEnable,
        boolean depthBufferWriteEnable, float alphaTestValue,
        int alphaTestFunction)
public RenderingAttributes(boolean depthBufferEnable,          ◀ New in 1.2 ▶
        boolean depthBufferWriteEnable, float alphaTestValue,
        int alphaTestFunction, boolean visible,
        boolean ignoreVertexColors, boolean rasterOpEnable,
        int rasterOp)
```

Constructs a RenderingAttributes object with specified values.

Methods

```
public void setDepthBufferEnable(boolean state)
public boolean getDepthBufferEnable()
```

These methods set and retrieve the depth buffer enable flag for this RenderingAt-tributes component object. The flag is `true` if the depth buffer mode is enabled, `false` if disabled.

```
public void setDepthBufferWriteEnable(boolean state)
public boolean getDepthBufferWriteEnable()
```

These methods set and retrieve the depth buffer write enable flag for this Render-ingAttributes component object. The flag is `true` if the depth buffer mode is writable, `false` if the depth buffer is read-only.

```
public void setAlphaTestValue(float value)
public float getAlphaTestValue()
```

These methods set and retrieve the alpha test value used by the alpha test func-tion. This value is compared to the alpha value of each rendered pixel.

```
public void setAlphaTestFunction(int function)
public int getAlphaTestFunction()
```

These methods set and retrieve the alpha test function. The alpha test function is one of the following:

- ALWAYS: Indicates pixels are always drawn irrespective of the alpha val-ue. This effectively disables alpha testing.

- NEVER: Indicates pixels are never drawn irrespective of the alpha value.

- EQUAL: Indicates pixels are drawn if the pixel alpha value is equal to the alpha test value.

- NOT_EQUAL: Indicates pixels are drawn if the pixel alpha value is not equal to the alpha test value.

- LESS: Indicates pixels are drawn if the pixel alpha value is less than the alpha test value.

- LESS_OR_EQUAL: Indicates pixels are drawn if the pixel alpha value is less than or equal to the alpha test value.

- GREATER: Indicates pixels are drawn if the pixel alpha value is greater than the alpha test value.

- GREATER_OR_EQUAL: Indicates pixels are drawn if the pixel alpha val-ue is greater than or equal to the alpha test value.

```
public void setVisible(boolean visible)
public boolean getVisible()
```
◀ New in 1.2 ▶
◀ New in 1.2 ▶

These methods set and retrieve the visibility flag for this RenderingAttributes component object. Invisible objects are not rendered (subject to the visibility policy for the current view), but they can be picked or collided with.

```
public void setIgnoreVertexColors(boolean ignoreVertexColors)
public boolean getIgnoreVertexColors()
```
◀ New in 1.2 ▶
◀ New in 1.2 ▶

These methods set and retrieve the flag that indicates whether vertex colors are ignored for this RenderingAttributes object. If `ignoreVertexColors` is false, per-vertex colors are used, when present in the associated Geometry objects, taking precedence over the ColoringAttributes color and Material diffuse color. If `ignoreVertexColors` is true, per-vertex colors are ignored. In this case, if lighting is enabled, the Material diffuse color will be used as the object color. If lighting is disabled, the ColoringAttributes color will be used. The default value is false.

```
public void setRasterOpEnable(boolean rasterOpEnable)
public boolean getRasterOpEnable()
```
◀ New in 1.2 ▶
◀ New in 1.2 ▶

These methods set and retrieve the rasterOp enable flag for this RenderingAttributes component object. When set to true, this enables logical raster operations as specified by the `setRasterOp` method. Enabling raster operations effectively disables alpha blending, which is used for transparency and antialiasing. Raster operations, especially XOR mode, are primarily useful when rendering to the front buffer in immediate mode. Most applications will not wish to enable this mode.

```
public void setRasterOp(int rasterOp)
public int getRasterOp()
```
◀ New in 1.2 ▶
◀ New in 1.2 ▶

These methods set and retrieve the raster operation function for this Rendering-Attributes component object. The rasterOp is one of the following:

- ROP_COPY: DST = SRC
- ROP_XOR: DST = SRC ∧ DST

8.1.8 TextureAttributes Object

The TextureAttributes object defines attributes that apply to texture mapping.

Constants

```
public static final int ALLOW_MODE_READ
public static final int ALLOW_MODE_WRITE
public static final int ALLOW_BLEND_COLOR_READ
public static final int ALLOW_BLEND_COLOR_WRITE
public static final int ALLOW_TRANSFORM_READ
public static final int ALLOW_TRANSFORM_WRITE
public static final int ALLOW_COLOR_TABLE_READ
public static final int ALLOW_COLOR_TABLE_WRITE
```

◀ New in 1.2 ▶ (for `ALLOW_COLOR_TABLE_READ`)
◀ New in 1.2 ▶ (for `ALLOW_COLOR_TABLE_WRITE`)

These flags, when enabled using the `setCapability` method, allow an application to invoke methods that respectively read and write its individual component field information.

Constructors

public TextureAttributes()

Constructs a TextureAttributes object with default parameters:

Parameter	Default Value
textureMode	REPLACE
textureBlendColor	black (0,0,0,0)
transform	identity
perspectiveCorrectionMode	NICEST
textureColorTable	null

public TextureAttributes(int textureMode, Transform3D transform, Color4f textureBlendColor, int perspCorrectionMode)

These constructors create a new TextureAttributes object with the specified parameters.

Methods

public void setTextureMode(int textureMode)
public int getTextureMode()

These methods set and retrieve the texture mode parameter for this Texture-Attributes component object. The texture mode is one of the following:

- MODULATE: Modulates the object color with the texture color.
- DECAL: Applies the texture color to the object as a decal.

- BLEND: Blends the texture blend color with the object color.
- REPLACE: Replaces the object color with the texture color.

```
public void setTextureBlendColor(Color4f textureBlendColor)
public void setTextureBlendColor(float r, float g, float b,
    float a)
public void getTextureBlendColor(Color4f textureBlendColor)
```

These methods set and retrieve the texture blend color for this TextureAttributes component object. The texture blend color is used when the texture mode parameter is BLEND.

```
public void setTextureColorTable(int[][] table)
```
◀ New in 1.2 ▶

This method sets the texture color table from the specified table. The individual integer array elements are copied. The array is indexed first by color component (*r*, *g*, *b*, and *a*, respectively) and then by color value; `table.length` defines the number of color components, and `table[0].length` defines the texture color table size. If the table is non-null, the number of color components must be either three, for *rgb* data, or four, for *rgba* data. The size of each array for each color component must be the same and must be a power of 2. If `table` is null or if the texture color table size is 0, the texture color table is disabled. If the texture color table size is greater than the device-dependent maximum texture color table size for a particular Canvas3D, the texture color table is ignored for that canvas.

When enabled, the texture color table is applied after the texture filtering operation and before texture application. Each of the *r*, *g*, *b*, and *a* components is clamped to the range [0,1], multiplied by `textureColorTableSize–1`, and rounded to the nearest integer. The resulting value for each component is then used as an index into the respective table for that component. If the texture color table contains three components, alpha is passed through unmodified.

```
public void getTextureColorTable(int[][] table)
```
◀ New in 1.2 ▶

This method retrieves the texture color table and copies it into the specified array. If the current texture color table is null, no values are copied. The array must be allocated by the caller and must be large enough to hold the entire table (that is, `int[numTextureColorTableComponents][textureColorTableSize]`).

```
public int getNumTextureColorTableComponents()
```
◀ New in 1.2 ▶

This method retrieves the number of color components in the current texture color table. A value of 0 is returned if the texture color table is null.

135

◀ New in 1.2 ▶ `public int getTextureColorTableSize()`

This method retrieves the size of the current texture color table. A value of 0 is returned if the texture color table is null.

```
public void setTextureTransform(Transform3D transform)
public void getTextureTransform(Transform3D transform)
```

These methods set and retrieve the texture transform object used to transform texture coordinates. A copy of the specified Transform3D object is stored in this TextureAttributes object.

```
public void setPerspectiveCorrectionMode(int mode)
public int getPerspectiveCorrectionMode()
```

These methods set and retrieve the perspective correction mode to be used for color and texture coordinate interpolation. The perspective correction mode is one of the following:

- NICEST: Uses the nicest (highest quality) available method for texture mapping perspective correction.

- FASTEST: Uses the fastest available method for texture mapping perspective correction.

8.1.9   TransparencyAttributes Object

The TransparencyAttributes object defines all attributes affecting the transparency of the object.

Constants

```
                public static final int ALLOW_MODE_READ
                public static final int ALLOW_MODE_WRITE
                public static final int ALLOW_VALUE_READ
                public static final int ALLOW_VALUE_WRITE
◀ New in 1.2 ▶ public static final int ALLOW_BLEND_FUNCTION_READ
◀ New in 1.2 ▶ public static final int ALLOW_BLEND_FUNCTION_WRITE
```

These flags, when enabled using the `setCapability` method, allow an application to invoke methods that respectively read and write its individual component field information.

Constructors

public TransparencyAttributes()

Constructs a new TransparencyAttributes object with default values:

Parameter	Default Value
transparencyMode	NONE
transparencyValue	0.0
srcBlendFunction	BLEND_SRC_ALPHA
dstBlendFunction	BLEND_ONE_MINUS_SRC_ALPHA

public TransparencyAttributes(int tMode, float tVal)
public TransparencyAttributes(int tMode, float tVal, int srcBlendFunction, int dstBlendFunction)

◀ New in 1.2 ▶

Constructs a new TransparencyAttributes object with specified values.

Methods

public void setTransparencyMode(int transparencyMode)
public int getTransparencyMode()

These methods set and retrieve the transparency mode for this Appearance component object. The transparency mode is one of the following:

- FASTEST: Uses the fastest available method for transparency.
- NICEST: Uses the nicest available method for transparency.
- SCREEN_DOOR: Uses screen-door transparency. This is done using an on/off stipple pattern in which the percentage of transparent pixels is approximately equal to the value specified by the transparency parameter.
- BLENDED: Uses alpha blended transparency. The blend equation is specified by the srcBlendFunction and dstBlendFunction attributes. The default equation is: alpha*src + (1-alpha)*dst, where alpha is 1 − transparency.
- NONE: No transparency; opaque object.

public void setTransparency(float transparency)
public float getTransparency()

These methods set and retrieve this Appearance object's transparency value. The transparency value is in the range [0.0, 1.0], with 0.0 being fully opaque and 1.0 being fully transparent.

137

◀ New in 1.2 ▶ `public void setSrcBlendFunction(int blendFunction)`
◀ New in 1.2 ▶ `public int getSrcBlendFunction()`

These methods set and retrieve the source blend function used in blended transparency and antialiasing operations. The source function specifies the factor that is multiplied by the source color. This value is added to the product of the destination factor and the destination color. The default source blend function is `BLEND_SRC_ALPHA`. The source blend function is one of the following:

- BLEND_ZERO: The blend function is $f = 0$.
- BLEND_ONE: The blend function is $f = 1$.
- BLEND_SRC_ALPHA: The blend function is $f = alpha_{src}$.
- BLEND_ONE_MINUS_SRC_ALPHA: The blend function is $f = 1 - alpha_{src}$.

◀ New in 1.2 ▶ `public void setDstBlendFunction(int blendFunction)`
◀ New in 1.2 ▶ `public int getDstBlendFunction()`

These methods set and retrieve the destination blend function used in blended transparency and antialiasing operations. The destination function specifies the factor that is multiplied by the destination color. This value is added to the product of the source factor and the source color. The default destination blend function is `BLEND_ONE_MINUS_SRC_ALPHA`.

8.1.10 Material Object

The Material object is a component object of an Appearance object that defines the material properties used when lighting is enabled. If the Material object in an Appearance object is `null`, lighting is disabled for all nodes that use that Appearance object.

Constants

The Material object defines two flags.

```
public static final int ALLOW_COMPONENT_READ
public static final int ALLOW_COMPONENT_WRITE
```

These flags, when enabled using the `setCapability` method, allow an application to invoke methods that respectively read and write its individual component field information.

Constructors

The Material object has the following constructors:

public Material()

Constructs and initializes a Material object using default values for all attributes. The default values are as follows:

Parameter	Default Value
lightingEnable	true
ambientColor	(0.2, 0.2, 0.2)
emissiveColor	(0.0, 0.0, 0.0)
diffuseColor	(1.0, 1.0, 1.0)
specularColor	(1.0, 1.0, 1.0)
shininess	64

public Material(Color3f ambientColor, Color3f emissiveColor,
**   Color3f diffuseColor, Color3f specularColor, float shininess)**

Constructs and initializes a new Material object using the specified parameters. The ambient color, emissive color, diffuse color, specular color, and shininess parameters are specified.

Methods

The Material object has the following methods:

public void setAmbientColor(Color3f color)
public void setAmbientColor(float r, float g, float b)
public void getAmbientColor(Color3f color)

This parameter specifies this material's ambient color, that is, how much ambient light is reflected by the material's surface.

public void setEmissiveColor(Color3f color)
public void setEmissiveColor(float r, float g, float b)
public void getEmissiveColor(Color3f color)

This parameter specifies the color of light, if any, that the material emits. This color is added to the color produced by applying the lighting equation.

```
public void setDiffuseColor(Color3f color)
public void setDiffuseColor(float r, float g, float b)
public void setDiffuseColor(float r, float g, float b, float a)
public void getDiffuseColor(Color3f color)
```

This parameter specifies the color of the material when illuminated by a light source. In addition to the diffuse color (red, green, and blue), the alpha value is used to specify transparency such that transparency = (1 − alpha). When vertex colors are present in geometry that is being lit, those vertex colors are used in place of this diffuse color in the lighting equation unless the vertex colors are ignored.

```
public void setSpecularColor(Color3f color)
public void setSpecularColor(float r, float g, float b)
public void getSpecularColor(Color3f color)
```

This parameter specifies the specular highlight color of the material.

```
public void setShininess(float shininess)
public float getShininess()
```

This parameter specifies a material specular scattering exponent, or shininess. It takes a floating-point number in the range [1.0, 128.0], with 1.0 being not shiny and 128.0 being very shiny.

```
public void setLightingEnable(boolean state)
public boolean getLightingEnable()
```

These methods set and retrieve the current state of the lighting enable flag (true or false) for this Appearance component object.

```
public String toString()
```

This method returns a string representation of this Material's values. If the scene graph is live, only those values with their capability bit set will be displayed.

8.1.11 Texture Object

The Texture object is a component object of an Appearance object that defines the texture properties used when texture mapping is enabled. If the Texture object in an Appearance object is null, then texture mapping is disabled for all nodes that use that Appearance object. The Texture object is an abstract class. As such, all texture objects must be created as either a Texture2D object or a Texture3D object.

Constants

The Texture object defines the following flags:

```
public static final int ALLOW_ENABLE_READ
public static final int ALLOW_ENABLE_WRITE
public static final int ALLOW_BOUNDARY_MODE_READ
public static final int ALLOW_FILTER_READ
public static final int ALLOW_IMAGE_READ
public static final int ALLOW_IMAGE_WRITE
public static final int ALLOW_MIPMAP_MODE_READ
public static final int ALLOW_BOUNDARY_COLOR_READ
public static final int ALLOW_FORMAT_READ
public static final int ALLOW_SIZE_READ
```

◀ New in 1.2 ▶

◀ New in 1.2 ▶
◀ New in 1.2 ▶

These flags, when enabled using the setCapability method, allow an application to invoke methods that read, and in some cases write, its individual component field information. The size information includes width, height, and number of mipmap levels.

Constructors

The Texture object has the following constructor:

```
public Texture()
```

This constructor is not very useful as the default width and height are 0. The other default values are as follows:

Parameter	Default Value
enable Flag	true
width	0
height	0
mipMapMode	BASE_LEVEL
format	RGB
boundaryModeS	WRAP
boundaryModeT	WRAP
minificationFilter	BASE_LEVEL_POINT
magnificationFilter	BASE_LEVEL_POINT
boundaryColor	black (0,0,0,0)
array of images	null

public Texture(int mipMapMode, int format, int width, int height)

Constructs an empty Texture object with specified mipmapMode format, width, and height. Defaults are used for all other parameters. If mipMapMode is set to BASE_LEVEL, the image at level 0 must be set by the application using the set-Image method or the setImages method. If mipMapMode is set to MULTI_LEVEL_MIPMAP, then images for all levels must be set. The mipmapMode can be one of the following:

- BASE_LEVEL: Indicates that this Texture object has only a base-level image. If multiple levels are needed, they will be implicitly computed.

- MULTI_LEVEL_MIPMAP: Indicates that this Texture object has multiple images—one for each mipmap level (that is, $\log_2(\max(\text{width,height})) + 1$ separate images). If mipmapMode is set to MULTI_LEVEL_MIPMAP, images for *all* levels must be set.

The format is the data of textures saved in this object. The format can be one of the following:

- INTENSITY: Specifies Texture contains only intensity values.

- LUMINANCE: Specifies Texture contains only luminance values.

- ALPHA: Specifies Texture contains only alpha values.

- LUMINANCE_ALPHA: Specifies Texture contains luminance and alpha values.

- RGB: Specifies Texture contains red, green, and blue color values.

- RGBA: Specifies Texture contains red, green, and blue color values and an alpha value.

Methods

The Texture object has the following methods:

```
public void setBoundaryModeS(int boundaryModeS)
public int getBoundaryModeS()
public void setBoundaryModeT(int boundaryModeT)
public int getBoundaryModeT()
```

These parameters specify the boundary mode for the S and T coordinates in this Texture object. The boundary mode is as follows:

- CLAMP: Clamps texture coordinates to be in the range [0, 1]. A constant boundary color is used for U,V values that fall outside this range.

- WRAP: Repeats the texture by wrapping texture coordinates that are outside the range [0, 1]. Only the fractional portion of the texture coordinates is used; the integer portion is discarded.

```
public void setMinFilter(int minFilter)
public int getMinFilter()
```

This parameter specifies the minification filter function. This function is used when the pixel being rendered maps to an area greater than one texel. The minification filter is one of the following:

- FASTEST: Uses the fastest available method for processing geometry.

- NICEST: Uses the nicest available method for processing geometry.

- BASE_LEVEL_POINT: Selects the nearest texel in the level 0 texture map.

- BASE_LEVEL_LINEAR: Performs a bilinear interpolation on the four nearest texels in the level 0 texture map.

- MULTI_LEVEL_POINT: Selects the nearest texel in the nearest mipmap.

- MULTI_LEVEL_LINEAR: Performs trilinear interpolation of texels between four texels each from the two nearest mipmap levels.

```
public void setMagFilter(int magFilter)
public int getMagFilter()
```

This parameter specifies the magnification filter function. This function is used when the pixel being rendered maps to an area less than or equal to one texel. The value is one of the following:

- FASTEST: Uses the fastest available method for processing geometry.

- NICEST: Uses the nicest available method for processing geometry.

- BASE_LEVEL_POINT: Selects the nearest texel in the level 0 texture map.

- BASE_LEVEL_LINEAR: Performs a bilinear interpolation on the four nearest texels in the level 0 texture map.

```
public void setImage(int level, ImageComponent image)
public ImageComponent getImage(int level)
```

These methods set and retrieve the image for a specified mipmap level. Level 0 is the base level.

◀ New in 1.2 ▶ `public void setImages(ImageComponent[] images)`
◀ New in 1.2 ▶ `public ImageComponent[] getImages()`

These methods set and retrieve the array of images for all mipmap levels.

`public void setBoundaryColor(Color4f boundaryColor)`
`public void setBoundaryColor(float r, float g, float b, float a)`
`public void getBoundaryColor(Color4f boundaryColor)`

This parameter specifies the texture boundary color for this Texture object. The texture boundary color is used when boundaryModeS or boundaryModeT is set to CLAMP. The magnification filter affects the boundary color as follows: For BASE_ LEVEL_POINT, the boundary color is ignored since the filter size is 1 and the border is unused. For BASE_LEVEL_LINEAR, the boundary color is used.

`public void setEnable(boolean state)`
`public boolean getEnable()`

These methods set and retrieve the state of texture mapping for this Texture object. A value of `true` means that texture mapping is enabled; `false` means that texture mapping is disabled.

`public void setMipMapMode(int mipMapMode)`
`public int getMipMapMode()`

These methods set and retrieve the mipmap mode for texture mapping for this Texture object. The mipmap mode is either BASE_LEVEL or MULTI_LEVEL_MIP_ MAP.

◀ New in 1.2 ▶ `public int numMipMapLevels()`

This method retrieves the number of mipmap levels needed for this Texture object.

◀ New in 1.2 ▶ `public int getFormat()`

This method retrieves the format of this Texture object.

◀ New in 1.2 ▶ `public int getWidth()`

This method retrieves the width of this Texture object.

◀ New in 1.2 ▶ `public int getHeight()`

This method retrieves the height of this Texture object.

8.1.12 Texture2D Object

The Texture2D object is a subclass of the Texture class. It extends the Texture class by adding a constructor for setting a 2D texture image.

Constructors

The Texture2D object has the following constructors:

`public Texture2D()`

This constructor is not very useful as the default width and height are 0.

`public Texture2D(int mipmapMode, int format, int width, int height)`

Constructs and initializes a Texture2D object with the specified attributes. The `mipmapMode` parameter is either `BASE_LEVEL` or `MULTI_LEVEL_MIPMAP`. The format parameter is one of the following: `INTENSITY`, `LUMINANCE`, `ALPHA`, `LUMINANCE_ALPHA`, `RGB`, or `RGBA`.

8.1.13 Texture3D Object

The Texture3D object is a subclass of the Texture class. It extends the Texture class by adding a third texture coordinate and by adding a constructor for setting a 3D texture image. If 3D texture mapping is not supported on a particular Canvas3D, 3D texture mapping is ignored for that canvas.

Constructors

The Texture3D object has the following constructors:

`public Texture3D()`

Constructs a Texture3D object with default parameters.

Parameter	Default Value
depth	0
boundaryModeR	WRAP

`public Texture3D(int mipmapMode, int format, int width, int height, int depth)`

Constructs and initializes a Texture3D object using the specified attributes. The `mipmapMode` parameter is either `BASE_LEVEL` or `MULTI_LEVEL_MIPMAP`. The format parameter is one of `INTENSITY`, `LUMINANCE`, `ALPHA`, `LUMINANCE_ALPHA`, `RGB`, or `RGBA`. The default value for a Texture3D object is as follows:

Parameter	Default Value
boundaryModeR	WRAP

Methods

The Texture3D object has the following methods:

```
public void setBoundaryModeR(int boundaryModeR)
public int getBoundaryModeR()
```

This parameter specifies the boundary mode for the R coordinate in this Texture object. The boundary mode is as follows:

- CLAMP: Clamps texture coordinates to be in the range [0, 1]. A constant boundary color is used for R values that fall outside this range.

- WRAP: Repeats the texture by wrapping texture coordinates that are outside the range [0, 1]. Only the fractional portion of the texture coordinates is used; the integer portion is discarded.

◀ New in 1.2 ▶ `public int getDepth()`

This method retrieves the depth of this Texture3D object.

8.1.14 TexCoordGeneration Object

The TexCoordGeneration object is a component object of an Appearance object that defines the parameters used when texture coordinate generation is enabled. If the TexCoordGeneration object in an Appearance object is `null`, texture coordinate generation is disabled for all nodes that use that Appearance object.

Constants

The TexCoordGeneration object specifies the following variables:

```
public static final int ALLOW_ENABLE_READ
public static final int ALLOW_ENABLE_WRITE
public static final int ALLOW_FORMAT_READ
public static final int ALLOW_MODE_READ
public static final int ALLOW_PLANE_READ
```

These flags, when enabled using the `setCapability` method, allow an application to invoke methods that read, and in some cases write, its individual component field information.

`public static final int OBJECT_LINEAR`

Generates texture coordinates as a linear function in object coordinates.

`public static final int EYE_LINEAR`

Generates texture coordinates as a linear function in eye coordinates.

`public static final int SPHERE_MAP`

Generates texture coordinates using a spherical reflection mapping in eye coordinates.

`public static final int TEXTURE_COORDINATE_2`

Generates 2D texture coordinates (S and T).

`public static final int TEXTURE_COORDINATE_3`

Generates 3D texture coordinates (S, T, and R).

Constructors

The TexCoordGeneration object has the following constructors:

`public TexCoordGeneration()`

Constructs a TexCoordGeneration object with the following default parameters:

Parameter	Default Value
enable	true
genMode	OBJECT_LINEAR
format	TEXTURE_COORDINATE_2
planeS	(1,0,0,0)
planeT	(0,1,0,0)
planeR	(0,0,0,0)

```
public TexCoordGeneration(int genMode, int format)
public TexCoordGeneration(int genMode, int format,
      Vector4f planeS)
public TexCoordGeneration(int genMode, int format,
      Vector4f planeS, Vector4f planeT)
public TexCoordGeneration(int genMode, int format,
      Vector4f planeS, Vector4f planeT, Vector4f planeR)
```

These constructors construct a TexCoordGeneration object by initializing the specified fields. Default values are used for those state variables not specified in the constructor. The parameters are as follows:

- genMode: Texture generation mode. One of `OBJECT_LINEAR`, `EYE_LINEAR`, or `SPHERE_MAP`.
- format: Texture format (2D or 3D). Either `TEXTURE_COORDINATE_2` or `TEXTURE_COORDINATE_3`.
- planeS: Plane equation for the S coordinate.
- planeT: Plane equation for the T coordinate.
- planeR: Plane equation for the R coordinate.

Methods

The TexCoordGeneration object has the following methods:

```
public void setEnable(boolean state)
public boolean getEnable()
```

This parameter enables or disables texture coordinate generation for this Appearance component object. The value is `true` if texture coordinate generation is enabled, `false` if texture coordinate generation is disabled.

```
public void setFormat(int format)
public int getFormat()
```

This parameter specifies the format, or dimension, of the generated texture coordinates. The format value is either `TEXTURE_COORDINATE_2` or `TEXTURE_COORD-INATE_3`.

```
public void setGenMode(int genMode)
public int getGenMode()
```

This parameter specifies the texture coordinate generation mode. The value is one of `OBJECT_LINEAR`, `EYE_LINEAR`, or `SPHERE_MAP`.

```
public void setPlaneS(Vector4f planeS)
public void getPlaneS(Vector4f planeS)
```

This parameter specifies the S coordinate plane equation. This plane equation is used to generate the S coordinate in `OBJECT_LINEAR` and `EYE_LINEAR` texture generation modes.

```
public void setPlaneT(Vector4f planeT)
public void getPlaneT(Vector4f planeT)
```

This parameter specifies the T coordinate plane equation. This plane equation is used to generate the T coordinate in OBJECT_LINEAR and EYE_LINEAR texture generation modes.

```
public void setPlaneR(Vector4f planeR)
public void getPlaneR(Vector4f planeR)
```

This parameter specifies the R coordinate plane equation. This plane equation is used to generate the R coordinate in OBJECT_LINEAR and EYE_LINEAR texture generation modes.

8.1.15 TextureUnitState Object   ◀ New in 1.2 ▶

The TextureUnitState object defines all texture mapping state for a single texture unit. An Appearance object contains an array of texture unit state objects to define the state for multiple texture mapping units. The texture unit state consists of the following:

- Texture: Defines the texture image and filtering parameters used when texture mapping is enabled. These attributes are defined in a Texture object.

- Texture attributes: Defines the attributes that apply to texture mapping, such as the texture mode, texture transform, blend color, and perspective correction mode. These attributes are defined in a TextureAttributes object.

- Texture coordinate generation: Defines the attributes that apply to texture coordinate generation, such as whether texture coordinate generation is enabled; coordinate format (2D or 3D coordinates); coordinate generation mode (object linear, eye linear, or spherical reflection mapping); and the R, S, and T coordinate plane equations. These attributes are defined in a Tex-CoordGeneration object.

Constants

The TextureUnitState object has the following flags:

```
public static final int ALLOW_STATE_READ                ◀ New in 1.2 ▶
public static final int ALLOW_STATE_WRITE               ◀ New in 1.2 ▶
```

These flags, when enabled using the setCapability method, allow an application to invoke methods that read or write this object's texture, texture attribute, or texture coordinate generation component information.

Constructors

The TextureUnitState object has the following constructors:

◀ New in 1.2 ▶ `public TextureUnitState()`
◀ New in 1.2 ▶ `public TextureUnitState(Texture texture,`
`                TextureAttributes textureAttributes,`
`                TexCoordGeneration texCoordGeneration)`

Construct and initialize a TextureUnitState component object. The first constructor uses defaults for all state variables. All component object references are initialized to null. The second constructor uses the specified component objects.

Methods

The TextureUnitState object has the following methods:

◀ New in 1.2 ▶ `public void set(Texture texture,`
`                TextureAttributes textureAttributes,`
`                TexCoordGeneration texCoordGeneration)`

This method sets the texture, texture attributes, and texture coordinate generation components in this TextureUnitState object to the specified component objects.

◀ New in 1.2 ▶ `public void setTexture(Texture texture)`
◀ New in 1.2 ▶ `public Texture getTexture()`

These methods set and retrieve the texture object. Setting it to null disables texture mapping for the texture unit corresponding to this TextureUnitState object.

◀ New in 1.2 ▶ `public void setTextureAttributes(TextureAttributes`
`                textureAttributes)`
◀ New in 1.2 ▶ `public TextureAttributes getTextureAttributes()`

These methods set and retrieve the textureAttributes object. Setting it to null will result in default attribute usage for the texture unit corresponding to this TextureUnitState object.

◀ New in 1.2 ▶ `public void setTexCoordGeneration(TexCoordGeneration`
`                texCoordGeneration)`
◀ New in 1.2 ▶ `public TexCoordGeneration getTexCoordGeneration()`

These methods set and retrieve the texCoordGeneration object. Setting it to null disables texture coordinate generation for the texture unit corresponding to this TextureUnitState object.

8.1.16 MediaContainer Object

The MediaContainer object defines all sound data: cached state flag and associated sound media. Currently, this references the sound media in one of three forms: URL string, URL object, or InputStream object. In a future release of Java 3D, media data will include references to Java Media Player objects.

Only one type of sound media data specified using setURLString, setURLObject, or setInputStream may be non-null (or they may all be null). An attempt to set more than one of these attributes to a non-null reference will result in an exception being thrown. If all sound media data references are null, there is no sound associated with this MediaContainer, and Sound nodes referencing this object cannot be played.

Constants

The MediaContainer object has the following flags:

```
public static final int ALLOW_CACHE_READ
public static final int ALLOW_CACHE_WRITE
public static final int ALLOW_URL_READ
public static final int ALLOW_URL_WRITE
```

These flags, when enabled using the setCapability method, allow an application to invoke methods that read or write its cached flag and its URL string.

Constructors

The MediaContainer object has the following constructors:

```
public MediaContainer()
```

Constructs and initializes a new MediaContainer object using the following default values:

Parameter	Default Value
URLString data	null
URLObject data	null
inputStream data	null
cacheEnable	true

```
public MediaContainer(String path)
public MediaContainer(URL url)
public MediaContainer(InputStream stream)
```

◀ New in 1.2 ▶

Construct and initialize a new MediaContainer object using the specified parameters.

Methods

The Sound object has the following methods:

```
public void setCacheEnable(boolean flag)
public boolean getCacheEnable()
```

This parameter specifies whether this component contains a noncached reference to the sound data or explicit cached sound data.

```
public void setURL(String path)
public void setURL(URL url)
public String getURL()
```

These methods are deprecated in Java 3D version 1.2. Use the setURLString, setURLObject, and getURLString methods instead.

◀ New in 1.2 ▶ `public void setURLString(String path)`
◀ New in 1.2 ▶ `public String getURLString()`

These methods set and retrieve the string of URL containing the sound data.

◀ New in 1.2 ▶ `public void setURLObject(URL url)`
◀ New in 1.2 ▶ `public URL getURLObject()`

These methods set and retrieve the URL containing the sound data.

◀ New in 1.2 ▶ `public void setInputStream(InputStream stream)`
◀ New in 1.2 ▶ `public InputStream getInputStream()`

These methods set and retrieve the input stream object containing the sound data.

8.1.17 AuralAttributes Object

The AuralAttributes object is a component object of a Soundscape node that defines environmental audio parameters that affect sound rendering. These attributes include gain scale factor; atmospheric rolloff; and parameters controlling reverberation, distance frequency filtering, and velocity-activated Doppler effect.

8.1.17.1 Attribute Gain Rolloff

The rolloff scale factor is used to model atmospheric changes from the normal speed of sound. The base value, 0.344 meters per millisecond used to approximate the speed of sound through air at room temperature, is multiplied by this scale factor whenever the speed of sound is applied during spatialization calculations. Valid values are ≥ 0.0. Values > 1.0 increase the speed of sound, while values < 1.0 decrease its speed. A value of zero makes the sound silent (although the sound continues to play).

8.1.17.2   Reverberation

Within Java 3D's simple model for auralization, there are three components to sound reverberation for a particular listening space:

- Delay time: Approximates the time from the start of a sound until it reaches the listener, after reflecting once off the surfaces in the region.

- Reflection coefficient: Attenuates the reverberated sound uniformly (for all frequencies) as it bounces off surfaces.

- Feedback loop: Controls the maximum number of times a sound is reflected off the surfaces.

None of these parameters is affected by sound position. Figure 8-2 shows the interaction of these parameters.

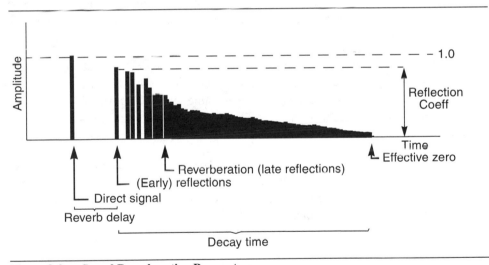

Figure 8-2   Sound Reverberation Parameters

The reflection coefficient for reverberation is a single scale factor used to approximate the overall reflective or absorptive characteristics of the surfaces in a reverberation region in which the listener is located. This scale factor is applied to the sound's amplitude regardless of the sound's position. A value of 1.0 represents complete (unattenuated) sound reflection, while a value of 0.0 represents full absorption (reverberation is disabled).

The reverberation delay time is set either explicitly (in milliseconds) or implicitly by supplying an additional bounds volume (so the delay time can be calculated). The bounds of the reverberation space do not have to be the same as the application region of the Soundscape node using this object.

The reverberation order defines the number of reverberation (feedback) loop iterations to be executed while a sound is played. As long as the reflection coefficient is small enough, the reverberated sound decreases (as it would naturally) each successive iteration. A value of 0 disables reverberation, a value of 1 creates a single echo (given that the reverb delay is long enough), and a value of –1 signifies that reverberation is to loop until it reaches an amplitude of *effective zero* (>60 dB or 1/1000 of sound amplitude). All other positive values are used as the number of loop iterations.

8.1.17.3 Doppler Effect

Doppler effect can be used to create a greater sense of movement of sound sources and can help unambiguate front-to-back localization errors. The frequency of sound waves emanating from the source are raised or lowered based on the speed of the source in relation to the listener and on several `AuralAttributes` parameters.

The frequency scale factor can be used to increase or reduce the change of frequency associated with the normal Doppler calculation or to shift the pitch of the sound directly if Doppler-effect is disabled. Values must be > 0.0 for sounds to be heard. If the value is 0.0, sounds affected by this `AuralAttributes` object are paused.

To simulate Doppler effect, the relative velocity (change in distance in the local coordinate system between the sound source and the listener over time, in meters per second) is calculated. This calculated velocity is multiplied by the given velocity scale factor. Values must be ≥ 0.0. If the scale factor value is 0.0, Doppler effect is not calculated or applied to the sound.

Constants

The AuralAttributes object has the following flags:

```
public static final int ALLOW_ATTRIBUTE_GAIN_READ
public static final int ALLOW_ATTRIBUTE_GAIN_WRITE
public static final int ALLOW_ROLLOFF_READ
```

```
public static final int ALLOW_ROLLOFF_WRITE
public static final int ALLOW_REFLECTION_COEFFICIENT_READ
public static final int ALLOW_REFLECTION_COEFFICIENT_WRITE
public static final int ALLOW_REVERB_DELAY_READ
public static final int ALLOW_REVERB_DELAY_WRITE
public static final int ALLOW_REVERB_ORDER_READ
public static final int ALLOW_REVERB_ORDER_WRITE
public static final int ALLOW_DISTANCE_FILTER_READ
public static final int ALLOW_DISTANCE_FILTER_WRITE
public static final int ALLOW_FREQUENCY_SCALE_FACTOR_READ
public static final int ALLOW_FREQUENCY_SCALE_FACTOR_WRITE
public static final int ALLOW_VELOCITY_SCALE_FACTOR_READ
public static final int ALLOW_VELOCITY_SCALE_FACTOR_WRITE
```

These flags, when enabled using the `setCapability` method, allow an application to invoke methods that read or write the associated parameters.

Constructors

The AuralAttributes object has the following constructors:

public AuralAttributes()

Constructs and initializes a new AuralAttributes object using the following default values:

Parameter	Default Value
attributeGain	1.0
rolloff	1.0
reflectionCoeff	0.0
reverbDelay	0.0
reverbBounds	null
reverbOrder	0
distanceFilter	null (no filtering performed)
frequencyScaleFactor	1.0
velocityScaleFactor	1.0

```
public AuralAttributes(float gain, float rolloff,
       float reflectionCoefficient, float reverbDelay,
       int reverbOrder, Point2f distanceFilter[],
       float frequencyScaleFactor, float velocityScaleFactor)
```

```
public AuralAttributes(float gain, float rolloff,
        float reflectionCoefficient, float reverbDelay,
        int reverbOrder, float distance[], float frequencyCutoff,
        float frequencyScaleFactor, float velocityScaleFactor)
```

Construct and initialize a new AuralAttributes object using the specified parameters.

Methods

The AuralAttributes object has the following methods:

```
public void setAttributeGain(float gain)
public float getAttributeGain()
```

This parameter specifies an amplitude scale factor applied to all sounds amplitude active within this region. This factor attenuates both direct and reflected/reverberated amplitudes. Valid values are ≥ 0.0.

```
public void setRolloff(float rolloff)
public float getRolloff()
```

The rolloff scale factor is used to model atmospheric changes from the normal speed of sound. The base value of 0.344 meters per millisecond is used to approximate the speed factor whenever the speed of sound is applied during spatialization calculations. Valid values are ≥ 0.0. Values > 1.0 increase the speed of sound; a value of 0.0 makes the sound silent (although the sound continues to play).

```
public void setReflectionCoefficient(float coefficient)
public float getReflectionCoefficient()
```

This parameter specifies an average amplitude scale factor used to approximate the average reflective or absorptive characteristics of the composite surfaces in the region the listener is in. This scale factor is applied to the sound's amplitude regardless of the sound's position. There is currently no method to assign different reflective audio properties to individual surfaces. The range of values is 0.0 to 1.0. A value of 1.0 denotes that reflections are unattenuated—the amplitude of reflected sound waves is not decreased. A value of 0.0 represents full absorption of reflections by the surfaces in the listening space.

```
public void setReverbDelay(float reverbDelay)
public float getReverbDelay()
```

This parameter specifies the delay time between each order of reflection while reverberation is being rendered. In the first form of setReverbDelay, an explicit delay time is given in milliseconds. In the second form, a reverberation bounds volume is specified, and then the delay time is calculated, becoming the new reverb time delay. A value of 0.0 for delay time disables reverberation.

```
public void setReverbDelay(Bounds reverbVolume)
```

This method is deprecated in Java 3D 1.2. Use setReverbBounds(Bounds) method instead.

```
public void setReverbBounds(Bounds reverbVolume)              ◀ New in 1.2 ▶
public Bounds getReverbBounds()                               ◀ New in 1.2 ▶
```

These methods set and retrieve the reverberation bounds volume. In this form the reverberation bounds volume parameter is used to calculate the reverb delay time and the reverb decay. Specification of a non-null bounding volume causes the explicit values given for reverb delay and decay to be overridden by the implicit values calculated from these bounds.

```
public void setReverbOrder(int reverbOrder)
public int getReverbOrder()
```

This parameter limits the number of times reflections are added to the reverberation being rendered. When the amplitude of the nth reflection reaches effective zero, no further reverberations need be added to the sound image. A value of 0 disables reverberation. A nonpositive value specifies an unbounded number of reflections.

```
public void setDistanceFilter(Point2f attenuation[])
public void setDistanceFilter(float distance[],
      float frequencyCutoff[])
public int getDistanceFilterLength()
public void getDistanceFilter(Point2f attenuation[])
public void getDistanceFilter(float distance[],
      float frequencyCutoff[])
```

This parameter specifies a (distance, filter) attenuation pairs array. If this is not set, no distance filtering is performed (equivalent to using a distance filter of Sound.NO_FILTER for all distances). Currently, this filter is a low-pass cutoff frequency. This array of pairs defines a piecewise linear slope for a range of values. This attenuation array is similar to the PointSound node's distanceAttenuation pair array, except that frequency values are paired with distances in this list. Using these pairs, distance-based, low-pass frequency filtering can be applied during sound rendering. Distances, specified in the local coordinate system in meters, must be > 0. Frequencies (in Hz) must be > 0.

If the distance from the listener to the sound source is less than the first distance in the array, the first filter is applied to the sound source. This creates a spherical region around the listener within which a sound is uniformly attenuated by the first filter in the array. If the distance from the listener to the sound source is greater than the last distance in the array, the last filter is applied to the sound source.

The first form of `setDistanceFilter` takes these pairs of values as an array of Point2f. The second form accepts two separate arrays for these values. The `distance` and `frequencyCutoff` arrays should be of the same length. If the `frequencyCutoff` array length is greater than the `distance` array length, the `frequencyCutoff` array elements beyond the length of the `distance` array are ignored. If the `frequencyCutoff` array is shorter than the `distance` array, the last `frequencyCutoff` array value is repeated to fill an array of length equal to the `distance` array.

The `getDistanceFilterLength` method returns the length of the distance filter arrays. Arrays passed into `getDistanceFilter` methods should all be at least this size.

There are two methods for `getDistanceFilter`: one returning an array of points, the other returning separate arrays for each attenuation component.

Distance elements in this array of pairs are a monotonically increasing set of floating-point numbers measured from the location of the sound source. Frequency cutoff elements in this list of pairs can be any positive float. While for most applications this list of values will usually be monotonically decreasing, they do not have to be.

public void setFrequencyScaleFactor(float frequencyScaleFactor)
public float getFrequencyScaleFactor()

This parameter specifies a scale factor applied to the frequency of sound during rendering playback. If the Doppler effect is disabled, this scale factor can be used to increase or decrease the original pitch of the sound. During rendering, this scale factor expands or contracts the usual frequency shift applied to the sound source due to Doppler-effect calculations. Valid values are ≥ 0.0; a value of 0.0 pauses the sound.

public void setVelocityScaleFactor(float velocityScaleFactor)
public float getVelocityScaleFactor()

This parameter specifies a scale factor applied to the *relative velocity* of the sound relative to the listener's position and movement in relation to the sound's position and movement over time. This scale factor is multiplied by the calculated velocity portion of the Doppler-effect equation used during sound rendering. This allows the application to exaggerate or reduce the relative velocity calculated by the standard Doppler equation. Valid values are ≥ 0.0. A value of 0.0 disables any Doppler calculation.

8.1.18 ImageComponent Object

The ImageComponent classes are used for texture and background images. The ImageComponent object is an abstract class that is used to define 2D or 3D ImageComponent classes used in a Java 3D scene graph.

Image data may be passed to this ImageComponent object in one of two ways: by copying the image data into this object or by accessing the image data by reference.

- By copying: By default, the set and get image methods copy the image data into or out of this ImageComponent object. This is appropriate for many applications since the application may reuse the RenderedImage object after copying it to the ImageComponent.

- By reference: A new feature in Java 3D version 1.2 allows image data to be accessed by reference, directly from the RenderedImage object. To use this feature, you need to construct an ImageComponent object with the by-Reference flag set to true. In this mode, a reference to the input data is saved but the data itself is not necessarily copied (although it may be, depending on the value of the yUp flag, the format of the ImageComponent, and the format of the RenderedImage). Image data referenced by an ImageComponent object must not be modified. Applications must exercise care not to violate this rule. If any referenced RenderedImage is modified after it has been passed to an ImageComponent object, the results are undefined. Another restriction in by-reference mode is that if the specified RenderedImage is not an instance of BufferedImage, this ImageComponent cannot be used for readRaster or off-screen rendering operations, since these operations modify the ImageComponent data.

An image component object also specifies whether the orientation of its image data is "y-up" or "y-down" (the default). y-up mode causes images to be interpreted as having their origin at the lower left (rather than the default upper left) of a texture or raster image with successive scan lines moving up. This is more consistent with texture mapping data onto a surface, and maps directly into the way textures are used in OpenGL and other 3D APIs. Setting the yUp flag to true in conjunction with setting the byReference flag to true makes it possible for Java 3D to avoid copying the texture map in some cases.

Note that all color fields are treated as unsigned values, even though Java does not directly support unsigned variables. This means, for example, that an Image-Component using a format of FORMAT_RGB5 can represent red, green, and blue values between 0 and 31, while an ImageComponent using a format of FORMAT_RGB8 can represent color values between 0 and 255. Even when byte values are used to create a RenderedImage with 8-bit color components, the resulting colors (bytes) are interpreted as if they were unsigned. Values greater than 127 can be assigned to a byte variable using a type cast. For example,

```
byteVariable = (byte) intValue;// intValue can be > 127
```

If intValue is greater than 127, byteVariable will be negative. The correct value will be extracted when it is used (by masking off the upper bits).

Constants

The ImageComponent object has the following flags:

```
public static final int ALLOW_SIZE_READ
public static final int ALLOW_FORMAT_READ
public static final int ALLOW_IMAGE_READ
```

These flags, when enabled using the setCapability method, allow an application to invoke methods that read the associated parameters.

The ImageComponent object specifies the following variables, used to define 2D or 3D ImageComponent classes. These variables specify the format of the pixel data.

public static final int FORMAT_RGB

Specifies that each pixel contains three eight-bit channels, one each for red, green, and blue. This is the same as FORMAT_RGB8.

public static final int FORMAT_RGBA

Specifies that each pixel contains four eight-bit channels, one each for red, green, blue, and alpha. This is the same as FORMAT_RGBA8.

public static final int FORMAT_RGB8

Specifies that each pixel contains three eight-bit channels, one each for red, green, and blue. This is the same as FORMAT_RGB.

public static final int FORMAT_RGBA8

Specifies that each pixel contains four eight-bit channels, one each for red, green, blue, and alpha. This is the same as FORMAT_RGBA.

public static final int FORMAT_RGB5

Specifies that each pixel contains three five-bit channels, one each for red, green, and blue.

public static final int FORMAT_RGB5_A1

Specifies that each pixel contains three five-bit channels, one each for red, green, and blue, and a one-bit channel for alpha.

public static final int FORMAT_RGB4

Specifies that each pixel contains three four-bit channels, one each for red, green, and blue.

public static final int FORMAT_RGBA4

Specifies that each pixel contains four four-bit channels, one each for red, green, blue, and alpha.

public static final int FORMAT_LUM4_ALPHA4

Specifies that each pixel contains two four-bit channels, one each for luminance and alpha.

public static final int FORMAT_LUM8_ALPHA8

Specifies that each pixel contains two eight-bit channels, one each for luminance and alpha.

public static final int FORMAT_R3_G3_B2

Specifies that each pixel contains two three-bit channels, one each for red and green, and a two-bit channel for blue.

public static final int FORMAT_CHANNEL8

Specifies that each pixel contains one eight-bit channel. The channel can be used only for luminance, alpha, or intensity.

Constructors

The ImageComponent object defines the following constructor:

public ImageComponent(int format, int width, int height)

This constructor constructs and initializes a new ImageComponent object using the specified format, width, and height. Default values are used for all other parameters. The default values are as follows:

Parameter	Default Value
byReference	false
yUp	false

◀ New in 1.2 ▶ **public ImageComponent(int format, int width, int height, boolean byReference, boolean yUp)**

Constructs an image component object using the specified format, width, height, byReference flag, and yUp flag.

Methods

The ImageComponent object defines the following methods:

public int getWidth()
public int getHeight()
public int getFormat()

These methods retrieve the width, height, and format of this image component object.

◀ New in 1.2 ▶ **public boolean isByReference()**

This method retrieves the data access mode for this ImageComponent object.

◀ New in 1.2 ▶ **public void setYUp(boolean yUp)**

This method sets the *y*-orientation of this ImageComponent object to *y*-up or *y*-down.

◀ New in 1.2 ▶ **public boolean isYUp()**

This method retrieves the *y*-orientation for this ImageComponent object.

8.1.19 ImageComponent2D Object

The ImageComponent2D class defines a 2D image component. This is used for texture images, background images, and raster components of Shape3D nodes. Prior to Java 3D 1.2, only BufferedImage objects could be used as the input to an ImageComponent2D object. As of Java 3D 1.2, an ImageComponent2D accepts any RenderedImage object (BufferedImage is an implementation of the RenderedImage interface). The methods that set/get a BufferedImage object are left in for compatibility. The new methods that set/get a RenderedImage are a superset of the old methods. In particular, the two set methods in the following example are equivalent:

```
BufferedImage bi;
RenderedImage ri = bi;
ImageComponent2D ic;

// Set the image to the specified BufferedImage
ic.set(bi);

// Set the image to the specified RenderedImage
ic.set(ri);
```

Constructors

The ImageComponent2D object defines the following constructors:

```
public ImageComponent2D(int format, int width, int height)
public ImageComponent2D(int format, BufferedImage image)
public ImageComponent2D(int format, RenderedImage image)
```
◀ New in 1.2 ▶

The first constructor constructs and initializes a 2D image component object using the specified format, width, height, and a null image. The second and third constructors construct and initialize a 2D image component object using the specified format and image. A copy of the image is made.

```
public ImageComponent2D(int format, int width, int height,
        boolean byReference, boolean yUp)
```
◀ New in 1.2 ▶
```
public ImageComponent2D(int format, BufferedImage image,
        boolean byReference, boolean yUp)
```
◀ New in 1.2 ▶
```
public ImageComponent2D(int format, int width, int height,
        boolean byReference, boolean yUp)
```
◀ New in 1.2 ▶

The first constructor constructs a 2D image component object using the specified format, width, height, byReference flag, yUp flag, and a null image. The second and third constructors construct a 2D image component object using the specified format, image, byReference flag, and yUp flag.

Methods

The ImageComponent2D object defines the following methods:

```
public void set(BufferedImage image)
```
◀ New in 1.2 ▶ `public void set(RenderedImage image)`

These methods set the image in this ImageComponent2D object to the specified BufferedImage or RenderedImage object. If the data access mode is not by-reference, the image data is copied into this object. If the data access mode is by-reference, a reference to the image is saved, but the data is not necessarily copied.

```
public BufferedImage getImage()
```
◀ New in 1.2 ▶ `public RenderedImage getRenderedImage()`

These methods retrieve the image from this ImageComponent2D object. If the data access mode is not by-reference, a copy of the image is made. If the data access mode is by-reference, the reference is returned.

8.1.20 ImageComponent3D Object

The ImageComponent3D class defines a 3D image component. This is used for texture images. Prior to Java 3D 1.2, only BufferedImage objects could be used as the input to an ImageComponent3D object. As of Java 3D 1.2, an Image-Component3D accepts an array of arbitrary RenderedImage object (BufferedImage is an implementation of the RenderedImage interface). The methods that set/get a BufferedImage object are left in for compatibility. The new methods that set/get a RenderedImage are a superset of the old methods. In particular, the two set methods in the following example are equivalent:

```
BufferedImage bi;
RenderedImage ri = bi;
ImageComponent3D ic;

// Set image 0 to the specified BufferedImage
ic.set(0, bi);

// Set image 0 to the specified RenderedImage
ic.set(0, ri);
```

Constructors

The ImageComponent3D object defines the following constructors:

```
public ImageComponent3D(int format, int width, int height,
        int depth)
```

Constructs and initializes a 3D image component object using the specified format, width, height, and depth. Default values are used for all other parameters. The default values are as follows:

Parameter	Default Value
array of images	null

```
public ImageComponent3D(int format, BufferedImage[] images)
public ImageComponent3D(int format, RenderedImage[] images)    ◀ New in 1.2 ▶
```

These two constructors construct and initialize a 3D image component object using the specified format and array of images. Default values are used for all other parameters.

```
public ImageComponent3D(int format, int width, int height,     ◀ New in 1.2 ▶
        int depth, boolean byReference, boolean yUp)
```

This constructor constructs a 3D image component object using the specified format, width, height, depth, byReference flag, and yUp flag. Default values are used for all other parameters.

```
public ImageComponent3D(int format, BufferedImage[] images,    ◀ New in 1.2 ▶
        boolean byReference, boolean yUp)
public ImageComponent3D(int format, RenderedImage[] images,    ◀ New in 1.2 ▶
        boolean byReference, boolean yUp)
```

These two constructors construct a 3D image component object using the specified format, BufferedImage or RenderedImage array, byReference flag, and yUp flag. Default values are used for all other parameters.

Methods

The ImageComponent3D object defines the following methods:

```
public int getDepth()
```

This method retrieves the depth of this 3D image component object.

```
public void set(RenderedImage[] images)     ◀ New in 1.2 ▶
public void set(BufferedImage[] images)
```

These methods set the array of images in this image component to the specified array of RenderedImage or BufferedImage objects. If the data access mode is not by-reference, the data is copied into this object. If the data access mode is by-reference, a shallow copy of the array of references to the objects is made, but the data is not necessarily copied.

◀ New in 1.2 ▶ `public RenderedImage[] getRenderedImage()`
◀ New in 1.2 ▶ `public RenderedImage getRenderedImage(int index)`

These methods retrieve the images or image from this ImageComponent3D object. If the data access mode is not by-reference, a copy of the images is made. If the data access mode is by-reference, the references are returned.

```
public BufferedImage[] getImage()
public BufferedImage getImage(int index)
```

These methods retrieve a copy of the images in this ImageComponent3D object. If the data access mode is not by-reference, a copy of the images is made. If the data access mode is by-reference, the references are returned.

◀ New in 1.2 ▶ `public void set(int index, RenderedImage image)`
`public void set(int index, BufferedImage image)`

These methods set this image component at the specified index to the specified RenderedImage or BufferedImage object. If the data access mode is not by-reference, the data is copied into this object. If the data access mode is by-reference, a reference to the image is saved, but the data is not necessarily copied.

8.1.21 DepthComponent Object

The DepthComponent object is an abstract base class that defines a 2D array of depth (z) values.

Constants

The DepthComponent object has the following flags:

```
public static final int ALLOW_SIZE_READ
public static final int ALLOW_DATA_READ
```

These flags, when enabled using the `setCapability` method, allow an application to invoke methods that read the associated parameters.

Methods

```
public int getWidth()
public int getHeight()
```

These methods get the width and height of this object.

8.1.22 DepthComponentFloat Object

The DepthComponentFloat object extends the DepthComponent object and defines a 2D array of depth (z) values in floating-point format in the range $[0, 1]$. A value of 0.0 indicates the closest z value to the user, while a value of 1.0 indicates the farthest z value.

Constructors

The DepthComponentFloat object defines the following constructors:

```
public DepthComponentFloat(int width, int height)
```

Constructs a new floating-point depth (z-buffer) component object with the specified width and height.

Methods

```
public void setDepthData(float depthData[])
public void getDepthData(float depthData[])
```

These methods set and retrieve the specified depth data for this object.

8.1.23 DepthComponentInt Object

The DepthComponentInt object extends the DepthComponent object and defines a 2D array of depth (z) values in integer format. Values are in the range $[0, (2^n) - 1]$, where n is the z-buffer pixel depth.

Constructors

The DepthComponentInt object defines the following constructor:

```
public DepthComponentInt(int width, int height)
```

Constructs a new integer depth (z-buffer) component object with the specified width and height.

Methods

```
public void setDepthData(int depthData[])
public void getDepthData(int depthData[])
```

These methods set and retrieve the specified depth data for this object.

8.1.24 DepthComponentNative Object

The DepthComponentNative object extends the DepthComponent object and defines a 2D array of depth (z) values stored in the most efficient format for a particular device. Values are not accessible by the user and may be used only to read the z values and subsequently to write them back.

Constructors

The DepthComponentNative object defines the following constructor:

public DepthComponentNative(int width, int height)

Constructs a new native depth (z-buffer) component object with the specified width and height.

8.1.25 Bounds Object

Bounds objects define three varieties of containing volumes. Java 3D uses these containing volumes to support various culling operations. The types of bounds include an axis-aligned-box volume, a spherical volume, and a bounding polytope.

Constructors

The Bounds object defines the following constructor:

public Bounds()

Constructs a new Bounds object.

Methods

The Bounds object defines the following methods:

public abstract Object clone()

Clones this object.

public abstract void set(Bounds boundsObject)

This method sets the value of this Bounds object to enclose the specified bounding object.

```
public abstract boolean intersect(Point3d origin,
        Point3d direction)
public abstract boolean intersect(Point3d point)
public abstract boolean intersect(Bounds boundsObject)
public abstract boolean intersect(Bounds boundsObjects[])
```

These methods test for the intersection of this Bounds object with a ray, a point, another Bounds object, or an array of Bounds objects, respectively.

```
public abstract Bounds closestIntersection(Bounds boundsObjects[])
```

This method finds the closest bounding object that intersects this bounding object.

```
public abstract void combine(Bounds boundsObject)
public abstract void combine(Bounds boundsObjects[])
public abstract void combine(Point3d point)
public abstract void combine(Point3d points[])
```

These methods combine this Bounds object with a bounding object, an array of bounding objects, a point, or an array of points, respectively.

```
public abstract void transform(Bounds bounds, Transform3D trans)
public abstract void transform(Transform3D trans)
```

The first method tranforms a Bounds object so that it bounds a volume that is the result of transtorming the given bounding object by the given transform. The second method transforms the Bounds object by the given transform.

```
public abstract boolean equals(Object bounds)                    ◀ New in 1.2 ▶
```

This method indicates whether the specified bounds object is equal to this Bounds object. They are equal if both the specified bounds object and this Bounds are instances of the same Bounds subclass and all of the data members of bounds are equal to the corresponding data members in this Bounds.

```
public abstract int hashCode()                                   ◀ New in 1.2 ▶
```

This method returns a hash code for this Bounds object based on the data values in this object. Two different Bounds objects of the same type with identical data values (that is, Bounds.equals returns true) will return the same hash code. Two Bounds objects with different data members may return the same hash code value, although this is not likely.

```
public abstract boolean isEmpty()
```

This method tests whether the bounds is empty. A bounds is empty if it is null (either by construction or as the result of a null intersection) or if its volume is negative. A bounds with a volume of zero is *not* empty.

8.1.26 BoundingBox Object

BoundingBox objects are axis-aligned bounding box volumes.

Constructors

The BoundingBox object defines the following constructors:

```
public BoundingBox()
public BoundingBox(Point3d lower, Point3d upper)
public BoundingBox(Bounds boundsObject)
public BoundingBox(Bounds bounds[])
```

The first constructor constructs and initializes a 2X unity BoundingBox about the origin. The second constructor constructs and initializes a BoundingBox from the given minimum and maximum in *x*, *y*, and *z*. The third constructor constructs and initializes a BoundingBox from a bounding object. The fourth constructor constructs and initializes a BoundingBox from an array of bounding objects.

Methods

The BoundingBox object defines the following methods:

```
public void getLower(Point3d p1)
public void setLower(Point3d p1)
public void setLower(double xmin, double ymin, double zmin)
```

This parameter specifies the lower corner of this bounding box.

```
public void getUpper(Point3d p1)
public void setUpper(Point3d p1)
public void setUpper(double xmax, double ymax, double zmax)
```

This parameter specifies the upper corner of this bounding box.

```
public void set(Bounds boundsObject)
```

Sets the value of this bounding region to enclose the specified bounding object.

public Object clone()

Creates a copy of this bounding box.

public void combine(Bounds boundsObject)
public void combine(Bounds boundsObjects[])
public void combine(Point3d point)
public void combine(Point3d points[])

These methods combine this bounding box with a bounding object, an array of bounding objects, a point, or an array of points, respectively.

public void transform(Bounds boundsObject, Transform3D matrix)
public void transform(Transform3D matrix)

The first method transforms a bounding box so that it bounds a volume that is the result of transforming the given bounding object by the given transform. The second method transforms the bounding box by the given transform.

public boolean intersect(Point3d origin, Vector3d direction)
public boolean intersect(Point3d point)
public boolean intersect(Bounds boundsObject)
public boolean intersect(Bounds boundsObjects[])

These methods test for the intersection of this bounding box with a ray, a point, another Bounds object, and an array of Bounds objects, respectively.

public boolean intersect(Bounds boundsObject,
        BoundingBox newBoundBox)
public boolean intersect(Bounds boundsObjects[],
        BoundingBox newBoundBox)

These methods compute a new BoundingBox that bounds the volume created by the intersection of this BoundingBox with another Bounds object or array of Bounds objects.

public Bounds closestIntersection(Bounds boundsObjects[])

This method finds the closest bounding object that intersects this bounding box.

public boolean equals(Object bounds)   ◀ New in 1.2 ▶

This method indicates whether the specified bounds object is equal to this BoundingBox object. They are equal if the specified bounds object is an instance of BoundingBox and all of the data members of bounds are equal to the corresponding data members in this BoundingBox.

`public int hashCode()`

This method returns a hash code value for this BoundingBox object based on the data values in this object. Two different BoundingBox objects with identical data values (that is, `BoundingBox.equals` returns true) will return the same hash code value. Two BoundingBox objects with different data members may return the same hash code value, although this is not likely.

`public boolean isEmpty()`

This method tests whether the bounding box is empty. A bounding box is empty if it is `null` (either by construction or as the result of a null intersection) or if its volume is negative. A bounding box with a volume of zero is *not* empty.

8.1.27 BoundingSphere Object

The BoundingSphere object defines a spherical bounding volume. It has two associated values: the center point and the radius of the sphere.

Constructors

The BoundingSphere object defines the following constructors:

```
public BoundingSphere()
public BoundingSphere(Point3D center, double radius)
public BoundingSphere(Bounds boundsObject)
public BoundingSphere(Bounds boundsObjects[])
```

The first constructor constructs and initializes a BoundingSphere to unity (radius = 1.0 and center at 0.0, 0.0, 0.0). The second constructor constructs and initializes a BoundingSphere from a center and radius. The third constructor constructs and initializes a BoundingSphere from a bounding object. The fourth constructor constructs and initializes a BoundingSphere from an array of bounding objects.

Methods

The BoundingSphere object defines the following methods:

```
public double getRadius()
public void setRadius(double r)
```

This parameter specifies the bounding sphere radius.

```
public void getCenter(Point3d center)
public void setCenter(Point3d center)
```

This parameter defines the position of the bounding sphere.

```
public void set(Bounds boundsObject)
```

Sets the value of this bounding sphere to enclose the volume specified by the Bounds object.

```
public Object clone()
```

Creates a copy of the bounding sphere.

```
public void combine(Bounds boundsObject)
public void combine(Bounds boundsObjects[])
public void combine(Point3d point)
public void combine(Point3d points[])
```

These methods combine this bounding sphere with a bounding object, an array of bounding objects, a point, or an array of points, respectively.

```
public boolean intersect(Point3d origin, Point3d direction)
public boolean intersect(Point3d point)
public boolean intersect(Bounds boundsObject)
public boolean intersect(Bounds boundsObjects[])
```

These methods test for the intersection of this bounding sphere with the given ray, point, another Bounds object, or an array of Bounds objects.

```
public boolean intersect(Bounds boundsObject,
       BoundingSphere newBoundSphere)
public boolean intersect(Bounds boundsObjects[],
       BoundingSphere newBoundSphere)
```

These methods compute a new BoundingSphere that bounds the volume created by the intersection of this BoundingSphere with another Bounds object or array of Bounds objects.

```
public Bounds closestIntersection(Bounds boundsObjects[])
```

This method finds the closest bounding object that intersects this bounding sphere.

```
public void transform(Bounds boundsObject, Transform3D matrix)
public void transform(Transform3D matrix)
```

The first method transforms a bounding sphere so that it bounds a volume that is the result of transforming the given bounding object by the given transform. The second method transforms the bounding sphere by the given transform. Note that when transforming a bounding sphere by a transformation matrix containing a nonuniform scale or a shear, the result is a bounding sphere with a radius equal to the maximal scale in any direction—the bounding sphere does not transform into an ellipsoid.

◀ New in 1.2 ▶ `public boolean equals(Object bounds)`

This method indicates whether the specified bounds object is equal to this BoundingSphere object. They are equal if the specified bounds object is an instance of BoundingSphere and all of the data members of bounds are equal to the corresponding data members in this BoundingSphere.

◀ New in 1.2 ▶ `public int hashCode()`

This method returns a hash code value for this BoundingSphere object based on the data values in this object. Two different BoundingSphere objects with identical data values (that is, `BoundingSphere.equals` returns true) will return the same hash code value. Two BoundingSphere objects with different data members may return the same hash code value, although this is not likely.

`public String toString()`

This method returns a string representation of this class.

`public boolean isEmpty()`

This method tests whether the bounding sphere is empty. A bounding sphere is empty if it is `null` (either by construction or as the result of a null intersection) or if its volume is negative. A bounding sphere with a volume of zero is *not* empty.

8.1.28 BoundingPolytope Object

A BoundingPolytope object defines a polyhedral bounding region using the intersection of three or more half spaces. The region defined by a BoundingPolytope is always convex and must be closed.

Each plane in the BoundingPolytope specifies a half space defined by the equation:

$$Ax + By + Cz + D \leq 0$$

where A, B, C, D are the parameters that specify the plane.

The parameters are passed in the x, y, z, and w fields, respectively, of a Vector4d object. The intersection of the set of half spaces corresponding to the planes in this BoundingPolytope defines the bounding region.

Constructors

The BoundingPolytope object defines the following constructors:

public BoundingPolytope()

This constructor constructs and initializes a BoundingPolytope to a set of six planes that define a cube, such that $-1 \leq x,y,z \leq 1$. The values of the planes are as follows:

planes[0]	$x \leq 1$ (1,0,0,–1)
planes[1]	$-x \leq 1$ (–1,0,0,–1)
planes[2]	$y \leq 1$ (0,1,0,–1)
planes[3]	$-y \leq 1$ (0,–1,0,–1)
planes[4]	$z \leq 1$ (0,0,1,–1)
planes[5]	$-z \leq 1$ (0,0,–1,–1)

public BoundingPolytope(Vector4d planes[])
public BoundingPolytope(Bounds boundsObject)
public BoundingPolytope(Bounds boundsObjects[])

The first constructor constructs and initializes a BoundingPolytope from an array of bounding planes. The second constructor constructs and initializes a BoundingPolytope from a Bounds object. The new polytope will circumscribe the region specified by the input bounds. The final constructor constructs and initializes a BoundingPolytope from an array of Bounds objects. The new polytope will circumscribe the union of the regions specified by the input bounds objects.

Methods

The BoundingPolytope object defines the following methods:

public void setPlanes(Vector4d planes[])
public void getPlanes(Vector4d planes[])

These methods set and retrieve the bounding planes for this BoundingPolytope object.

```
public int getNumPlanes()
```

This method returns the number of bounding planes for this bounding polytope.

```
public void set(Bounds boundsObject)
```

This method sets the planes for this BoundingPolytope by keeping its current number and direction of the planes and by computing new plane positions to enclose the given Bounds object.

```
public Object clone()
```

This method creates a copy of the BoundingPolytope object.

```
public void combine(Bounds boundsObject)
public void combine(Bounds boundsObjects[])
public void combine(Point3d point)
public void combine(Point3d points[])
```

These methods combine this BoundingPolytope with a bounding object, an array of bounding objects, a point, or an array of points, respectively.

```
public void transform(Bounds bounds, Transform3D matrix)
public void transform(Transform3D matrix)
```

The first method tranforms a bounding polytope so that it bounds a volume that is the result of transforming the given bounding object by the given transform. The second method transforms the bounding polytope by the given transform.

```
public boolean intersect(Point3d origin, Vector3d direction)
public boolean intersect(Point3d point)
public boolean intersect(Bounds boundsObject)
public boolean intersect(Bounds boundsObjects[])
```

These methods test for the intersection of this BoundingPolytope with the given ray, point, another Bounds object, or array of Bounds objects, respectively.

```
public boolean intersect(Bounds boundsObject,
      BoundingPolytope newBoundPolytope)
public boolean intersect(Bounds boundsObjects[],
      BoundingPolytope newBoundPolytope)
```

These methods compute a new BoundingPolytope that bounds the volume created by the intersection of this BoundingPolytope with another Bounds object or array of Bounds objects.

```
public Bounds closestIntersection(Bounds boundsObjects[])
```

This method finds the closest bounding object that intersects this bounding polytope.

```
public boolean equals(Object bounds)
```
◀ New in 1.2 ▶

This method indicates whether the specified bounds object is equal to this BoundingPolytope object. They are equal if the specified bounds object is an instance of BoundingPolytope and all of the data members of bounds are equal to the corresponding data members in this BoundingPolytope.

```
public int hashCode()
```
◀ New in 1.2 ▶

This method returns a hash code value for this BoundingPolytope object based on the data values in this object. Two different BoundingPolytope objects with identical data values (that is, `BoundingPolytope.equals` returns true) will return the same hash code value. Two BoundingPolytope objects with different data members may return the same hash code value, although this is not likely.

```
public boolean isEmpty()
```

This method tests whether the bounding polytope is empty. A bounding polytope is empty if it is null (either by construction or as the result of a null intersection) or if its volume is negative. A bounding polytope with a volume of zero is *not* empty.

8.1.29 Transform3D Object

Transformations are represented by matrix multiplication and include such operations as rotation, scaling, and translation. The Transform3D object is represented internally as a 4×4 double-precision floating-point matrix. The mathematical representation is row major, as in traditional matrix mathematics.

Constants

```
public static final int ZERO
public static final int IDENTITY
public static final int SCALE
public static final int TRANSLATION
public static final int ORTHOGONAL
public static final int RIGID
public static final int CONGRUENT
```

```
public static final int AFFINE
public static final int NEGATIVE_DETERMINANT
```

A Transform3D has an associated type that is internally computed when the transform object is constructed and updated any time it is modified. A matrix will typically have multiple types. For example, the type associated with an identity matrix is the result of ORing all of the types, except for ZERO and NEGATIVE_ DETERMINANT, together. There are public methods available to get the ORed type of the transformation, the sign of the determinant, and the least general matrix type. The matrix type flags are defined as follows:

- ZERO: Zero matrix.

- IDENTITY: Identity matrix.

- SCALE: This matrix is a uniform scale matrix—there are no rotational or translation components.

- TRANSLATION: This matrix has translation components only. The scale is unity, and there are no rotational components.

- ORTHOGONAL: The four row vectors that make up an orthogonal matrix form a basis, meaning that they are mutually orthogonal. The scale is unity, and there are no translation components.

- RIGID: The upper 3×3 of the matrix is orthogonal, and there is a translation component—the scale is unity.

- CONGRUENT: This is an angle- and length-preserving matrix, meaning that it can translate, rotate, and reflect about an axis and scale by an amount that is uniform in all directions. These operations preserve the distance between any two points and the angle between any two intersecting lines.

- AFFINE: An affine matrix can translate, rotate, reflect, scale anisotropically, and shear. Lines remain straight, and parallel lines remain parallel, but the angle between intersecting lines can change.

A matrix is also classified by the sign of its determinant:

- NEGATIVE_DETERMINANT: This matrix has a negative determinant. An orthogonal matrix with a positive determinant is a rotation matrix. An orthogonal matrix with a negative determinant is a reflection and rotation matrix.

The Java 3D model for 4×4 transformations is

$$\begin{bmatrix} m00 & m01 & m02 & m03 \\ m10 & m11 & m12 & m13 \\ m20 & m21 & m22 & m23 \\ m30 & m31 & m32 & m33 \end{bmatrix} \cdot \begin{bmatrix} x \\ y \\ z \\ w \end{bmatrix} = \begin{bmatrix} x' \\ y' \\ z' \\ w' \end{bmatrix}$$

$$x' = m00 \cdot x + m01 \cdot y + m02 \cdot z + m03 \cdot w$$
$$y' = m10 \cdot x + m11 \cdot y + m12 \cdot z + m13 \cdot w$$
$$z' = m20 \cdot x + m21 \cdot y + m22 \cdot z + m23 \cdot w$$
$$w' = m30 \cdot x + m31 \cdot y + m32 \cdot z + m33 \cdot w$$

Note: When transforming a Point3f or a Point3d, the input w is set to 1. When transforming a Vector3f or Vector3d, the input w is set to 0.

Constructors

The Transform3D object defines the following constructors:

```
public Transform3D()
```

This constructs and initializes a new Transform3D object to the identity transformation.

```
public Transform3D(Transform3D t1)
```

This constructs and initializes a new Transform3D object from the specified transform.

```
public Transform3D(Matrix3f m1, Vector3d t1, double s)
public Transform3D(Matrix3d m1, Vector3d t1, double s)
public Transform3D(Matrix3f m1, Vector3f t1, float s)
```

These construct and initialize a new Transform3D object from the rotation matrix, translation, and scale values. The scale is applied only to the rotational component of the matrix (upper 3×3) and not to the translational components of the matrix.

```
public Transform3D(Matrix4f m1)
public Transform3D(Matrix4d m1)
```

These construct and initialize a new Transform3D object from the 4×4 matrix. The type of the constructed transform is classified automatically.

179

```
public Transform3D(float matrix[])
public Transform3D(double matrix[])
```

These construct and initialize a new Transform3D object from the array of length 16. The top row of the matrix is initialized to the first four elements of the array, and so on. The type of the constructed transform is classified automatically.

```
public Transform3D(Quat4d q1, Vector3d t1, double s)
public Transform3D(Quat4f q1, Vector3d t1, double s)
public Transform3D(Quat4f q1, Vector3f t1, float s)
```

These construct and initialize a new Transform3D object from the quaternion q1, the translation t1, and the scale s. The scale is applied only to the rotational components of the matrix (the upper 3×3) and not to the translational components of the matrix.

```
public Transform3D(GMatrix m1)
```

This constructs and initializes a new Transform3D object and initializes it to the upper 4×4 of the specified GMatrix. If the specified matrix is smaller than 4×4, the remaining elements in the transformation matrix are assigned to zero.

Methods

The Transform3D object defines the following methods:

```
public final int getType()
```

This method retrieves the type of this matrix. The type is an ORed bitmask of all of the type classifications to which it belongs.

```
public final int getBestType()
```

This method retrieves the least general type of this matrix. The order of generality from least to most is as follows: ZERO, IDENTITY, SCALE, TRANSLATION, ORTHOGONAL, RIGID, CONGRUENT, and AFFINE. If the matrix is ORTHOGONAL, calling the method getDeterminantSign will yield more information.

```
public final void setAutoNormalize(boolean autoNormalize)
public final boolean getAutoNormalize()
```

These methods set and retrieve the state of autonormalization. Autonormalization performs an automatic singular value decomposition (SVD) normalization of the rotational components (upper 3×3) of this matrix after every subsequent matrix operation on this object, unless the boolean is subsequently set to false. The default value for this parameter is false.

public final boolean getDeterminantSign()

This method returns the sign of the determinant of this matrix. A return value of `true` indicates a positive determinant; a return value of `false` indicates a negative determinant. In general, an orthogonal matrix with a positive determinant is a pure rotation matrix; an orthogonal matrix with a negative determinant is both a rotation and a reflection matrix.

public final void setIdentity()

This method sets this transform to the identity matrix.

public final void setZero()

This method sets this transform to all zeros.

public final void setEuler(Vector3d euler)

This method sets the rotational component (upper 3×3) of this transform to the rotation matrix converted from the Euler angles provided. The `euler` parameter is a Vector3d consisting of three rotation angles applied first about the x, then the y, then the z axis. These rotations are applied using a static frame of reference. In other words, the orientation of the y rotation axis is not affected by the x rotation and the orientation of the z rotation axis is not affected by the x or y rotation.

public final void setRotation(Matrix3d m1)
public final void setRotation(Matrix3f m1)

These methods set the rotational component (upper 3×3) of this transform to the values in the specified matrix; the other elements of this transform are unchanged. A singular value decomposition is performed on this object's upper 3×3 matrix to factor out the scale, then this object's upper 3×3 matrix components are replaced by the input rotational components, and finally the scale is reapplied to the rotational components.

public final void setRotation(Quat4f q1)
public final void setRotation(Quat4d q1)

These methods set the rotational component (upper 3×3) of this transform to the appropriate values derived from the specified quaternion; the other elements of this transform are unchanged. A singular value decomposition is performed on this object's upper 3×3 matrix to factor out the scale, then this object's upper 3×3 matrix components are replaced by the matrix equivalent of the quaternion, and finally the scale is reapplied to the rotational components.

```
public final void setRotation(AxisAngle4d a1)
public final void setRotation(AxisAngle4f a1)
```

These methods set the rotational component (upper 3×3) of this transform to the appropriate values derived from the specified axis angle; the other elements of this transform are unchanged. A singular value decomposition is performed on this object's upper 3×3 matrix to factor out the scale, then this object's upper 3×3 matrix components are replaced by the matrix equivalent of the axis angle, and finally the scale is reapplied to the rotational components.

```
public final void setScale(double scale)
public final double getScale()
```

The set method sets the scale component of this transform by factoring out the current scale from the rotational component and multiplying by the new scale. The get method performs an SVD normalization of this transform to calculate and return the scale factor; this transform is not modified. If the matrix has non-uniform scale factors, the largest of the x, y, and z scale factors will be returned.

```
public final void setScale(Vector3d scale)
public final void getScale(Vector3d scale)
```

The set method sets the possibly nonuniform scale component to the current transform. Any existing scale is first factored out of the existing transform before the new scale is applied. The get method returns the possibly nonuniform scale components of the current transform and places them into the scale vector.

```
public final void setNonUniformScale(double xScale, double yScale,
        double zScale)
```

This is a deprecated method; use setScale(Vector3d) instead. Note that the setScale method modifies only the scale component.

```
public final void scaleAdd(double s, Transform3D t1,
        Transform3D t2)
public final void scaleAdd(double s, Transform3D t1)
```

The first method scales transform t1 by a uniform scale matrix with scale factor s, then adds transform t2 (this = S * t1 + t2). The second method scales this transform by a uniform scale matrix with scale factor s, then adds transform t1 (this = S * this + t1).

```
public final void setRotationScale(Matrix3f m1)
public final void setRotationScale(Matrix3d m1)
public final void getRotationScale(Matrix3f m1)
```

```
public final void getRotationScale(Matrix3d m1)
```

The set methods replace the upper 3×3 matrix values of this transform with the values in the matrix m1. The get methods retrieve the upper 3×3 matrix values of this transform and place them in the matrix m1.

```
public String toString()
```

This method returns the matrix elements of this transform as a string.

```
public final void add(Transform3D t1)
public final void add(Transform3D t1, Transform3D t2)
public final void sub(Transform3D t1)
public final void sub(Transform3D t1, Transform3D t2)
```

The first add method adds this transform to the transform t1 and places the result back into this. The second add method adds the transforms t1 and t2 and places the result into this. The first sub method subtracts transform t1 from this transform and places the result back into this. The second sub method subtracts transform t2 from t1 and places the result into this.

```
public final void add(double scalar)
public final void add(double scalar, Transform3D t1)
```

The first method adds a scalar to each component of this transform. The second method adds a scalar to each component of the transform t1 and places the result into this. Transform t1 is not modified.

```
public final void transpose()
public final void transpose(Transform3D t1)
```

The first method transposes this matrix in place. The second method transposes transform t1 and places the value into this transform. The transform t1 is not modified.

```
public void rotX(double angle)
public void rotY(double angle)
public void rotZ(double angle)
```

These three methods set the value of this matrix to a rotation matrix about the specified axis. The matrices rotate in a counter-clockwise (right-handed) direction. The angle to rotate is specified in radians.

```
public final void setTranslation(Vector3f trans)
public final void setTranslation(Vector3d trans)
```

This method modifies the translational components of this transform to the values of the argument. The other values of this transform are not modified.

```
public final void set(Quat4f q1)
public final void set(Quat4d q1)
```

These methods set the value of this transform to the matrix conversion of the quaternion argument.

```
public final void set(Quat4d q1, Vector3d t1, double s)
public final void set(Quat4f q1, Vector3d t1, double s)
public final void set(Quat4f q1, Vector3f t1, float s)
```

These methods set the value of this matrix from the rotation expressed by the quaternion q1, the translation t1, and the scale s.

```
public final void set(Vector3d trans)
public final void set(Vector3f trans)
```

These methods set the translational value of this matrix to the specified vector parameter values and set the other components of the matrix as if this transform were an identity matrix.

```
public final void set(Vector3d v1, double scale)
public final void set(Vector3f v1, float scale)
```

These methods set the value of this transform to a scale and translation matrix; the translation is scaled by the scale factor, and all of the matrix values are modified.

```
public final void set(Transform3D t1)
```

This method sets the matrix, type, and state of this transform to the matrix, type, and state of the transform t1.

```
public final void set(double matrix[])
public final void set(float matrix[])
```

These methods set the matrix values of this transform to the specified matrix values.

```
public final void set(double scale)
public final void set(double scale, Vector3d v1)
public final void set(float scale, Vector3f v1)
```

The first method sets the value of this transform to a uniform scale; all of the matrix values are modified. The next two methods set the value of this transform to a scale and translation matrix; the scale is not applied to the translation, and all of the matrix values are modified.

```
public final void set(Matrix4d m1)
public final void set(Matrix4f m1)
```

These methods set the matrix values of this transform to the matrix values in the specified matrix.

```
public final void set(Matrix3f m1)
public final void set(Matrix3d m1)
```

These methods set the rotational and scale components (upper 3×3) of this transform to the matrix values in the specified matrix. The remaining matrix values are set to the identity matrix. All values of the matrix are modified.

```
public final void set(Matrix3f m1, Vector3f t1, float s)
public final void set(Matrix3f m1, Vector3d t1, double s)
public final void set(Matrix3d m1, Vector3d t1, double s)
```

These methods set the value of this matrix from the rotation expressed by the rotation matrix m1, the translation t1, and the scale s. The scale is applied only to the rotational component of the matrix (upper 3×3) and not to the translational component of the matrix.

```
public final void set(GMatrix matrix)
```

These methods set the matrix values of this transform to the matrix values in the specified matrix. The GMatrix object must specify a 4×4, 3×4, or 3×3 matrix.

```
public final void set(AxisAngle4f a1)
public final void set(AxisAngle4d a1)
```

These methods set the rotational component (upper 3×3) of this transform to the matrix conversion of the specified axis-angle argument. The remaining matrix values are set to the identity matrix. All values of the matrix are modified.

```
public final void get(double matrix[])
public final void get(float matrix[])
```

These methods place the values of this transform into the specified matrix of length 16. The first four elements of the array will contain the top row of the transform matrix, and so on.

```
public final void get(Matrix4d matrix)
public final void get(Matrix4f matrix)
```

These methods place the values of this transform into the `matrix` argument.

```
public final void get(Matrix3d m1)
public final void get(Matrix3f m1)
```

These methods place the normalized rotational component of this transform into the 3×3 matrix argument.

```
public final double get(Matrix3d m1, Vector3d t1)
public final float get(Matrix3f m1, Vector3f t1)
public final double get(Matrix3f m1, Vector3d t1)
```

These methods place the normalized rotational component of this transform into the m1 parameter and the translational component into the t1 parameter.

```
public final void get(Quat4d q1)
public final void get(Quat4f q1)
```

These methods perform an SVD normalization of this matrix to acquire the normalized rotational component. The values are placed into the quaternion q1 parameter.

```
public final double get(Quat4d q1, Vector3d t1)
public final float get(Quat4f q1, Vector3f t1)
public final double get(Quat4f q1, Vector3d t1)
```

These methods perform an SVD normalization of this transform to calculate the rotation as a quaternion, the translation, and the scale. None of the matrix values is modified.

```
public final void get(Vector3d trans)
public final void get(Vector3f trans)
```

These methods retrieve the translational components of this transform.

```
public final void invert()
public final void invert(Transform3D t1)
```

The first method inverts this transform in place. The second method sets the value of this transform to the inverse of the transform t1. Both of these methods use the transform type to determine the optimal algorithm for inverting the transform.

```
public final double determinant()
```

This method calculates and returns the determinant of this transform.

```
public final void mul(Transform3D t1)
public final void mul(Transform3D t1, Transform3D t2)
```

The first method sets the value of this transform to the result of multiplying itself with transform t1 (this = this * t1). The second method sets the value of this transform to the result of multiplying transform t1 by transform t2 (this = t1 * t2).

```
public final void mul(double scalar)
public final void mul(double scalar, Transform3D t1)
```

The first method multiplies this transform by the scalar constant. The second method multiplies transform t1 by the scalar constant and places the value into this transform.

```
public final void mulInverse(Transform3D t1)
public final void mulInverse(Transform3D t1, Transform3D t2)
```

The first method multiplies this transform by the inverse of transform t1 and places the result into this transform (this = this * $t1^{-1}$). The second method multiplies transform t1 by the inverse of transform t2 and places the result into this transform (this = t1 * $t2^{-1}$).

```
public final void mulTransposeRight(Transform3D t1,Transform3D t2)
public final void mulTransposeLeft(Transform3D t1, Transform3D t2)
public final void mulTransposeBoth(Transform3D t1, Transform3D t2)
```

The first method multiplies the transform t1 by the transpose of transform t2 and places the result into this transform (this = t1 * transpose(t2)). The second method multiplies the transpose of transform t1 by transform t2 and places the result into this transform (this = transpose(t1) * t2). The third method multiplies the transpose of transform t1 by the transpose of t2 and places the result into this transform (this = transpose(t1) * transpose(t2)).

187

```
public final void normalize()
public final void normalize(Transform3D t1)
```

Both of these methods use an SVD normalization. The first `normalize` method normalizes the rotational components (upper 3×3) of matrix `this` and places the results back into `this`. The second `normalize` method normalizes the rotational components (upper 3×3) of transform `t1` and places the result in `this`.

```
public final void normalizeCP()
public final void normalizeCP(Transform3D t1)
```

Both of these methods use a cross-product (CP) normalization. The first `normalizeCP` method normalizes the rotational components (upper 3×3) of this transform and places the result into this transform. The second `normalizeCP` method normalizes the rotational components (upper 3×3) of transform `t1` and places the result into `this` transform.

```
public boolean equals(Transform3D t1)
public boolean equals(Object o1)
```

The first method returns `true` if all of the data members of transform `t1` are equal to the corresponding data members in `this` transform. The second method returns true if the Object `o1` is of type Transform3D and all of the data members of `o1` are equal to the corresponding data members in this Transform3D.

```
public boolean epsilonEquals(Transform3D t1, double epsilon)
```

This method returns `true` if the L∞ distance between this transform and transform `m1` is less than or equal to the epsilon parameter; otherwise, it returns `false`. The L∞ distance is equal to

$$\text{MAX}[i=0,1,2,3 \; ; j=0,1,2,3 \; ; abs[(this.m(i,j) - m1.m(i,j)]$$

```
public int hashCode()
```

This method returns a hash number based on the data values in this object. Two different Transform3D objects with identical data values (that is, `true` is returned for `trans.equals(Transform3D)`) will return the same hash number. Two Transform3D objects with different data members may return the same hash value, although this is not likely.

```
public final void transform(Vector4d vec, vector4d vecOut)
public final void transform(Vector4f vec, Vector4f vecOut)
public final void transform(Vector4d vec)
public final void transform(Vector4f vec)
```

The first two methods transform the vector vec by this transform and place the result into vecOut. The last two methods transform the vector vec by this transform and place the result back into vec.

```
public final void transform(Point3d point, Point3d pointOut)
public final void transform(Point3f point, point3f pointOut)
public final void transform(Point3d point)
public final void transform(Point3f point)
```

The first two methods transform the point parameter by this transform and place the result into pointOut. The last two methods transform the point parameter by this transform and place the result back into point. In both cases, the fourth element of the point input parameter is assumed to be 1.

```
public final void transform(Vector3d normal, Vector3d normalOut)
public final void transform(Vector3f normal, Vector3f normalOut)
public final void transform(Vector3d normal)
public final void transform(Vector3f normal)
```

The first two methods transform the normal parameter by this transform and place the value into normalOut. The third and fourth methods transform the normal parameter by this transform and place the value back into normal.

8.1.29.1 View Model Compatibility Mode Methods: Viewing Matrix

```
public void lookAt(Point3d eye, Point3d center, Vector3d up)
```

This is a utility method that specifies the position and orientation of a viewing transformation. It works very much like the similar function in OpenGL. The inverse of this transform can be used to control the ViewPlatform object within the scene graph. Alternatively, this transform can be passed directly to the View's VpcToEc transform via the compatibility mode viewing functions defined in Section C.11.2, "Using the Camera-Based View Model."

8.1.29.2 View Model Compatibility Mode Methods: Projection Matrix

```
public void frustum(double left, double right, double bottom,
        double top, double near, double far)
public void perspective(double fovx, double aspect, double zNear,
        double zFar)
public void ortho(double left, double right, double bottom,
        double top, double near, double far)
```

These three utility methods allow an application to create a perspective or parallel (orthographic) projection matrix. These three methods work very much like the similar functions in OpenGL. The resulting Transform3D can be used to set directly the View's left and right projection transforms when in compatibility mode. See Section C.11.2, "Using the Camera-Based View Model," for details. The fovx parameter specifies the field of view in the *x* direction in radians.

8.2   Node Component Objects: Geometry

A Geometry object is an abstract class that specifies the geometry component information required by a Shape3D node. Geometry objects describe both the geometry and topology of the Shape3D nodes that reference them. Geometry objects consist of four generic geometric types: CompressedGeometry, GeometryArray, Raster, and Text3D (see Figure 8-3). Each of these geometric types defines a visible object or set of objects. A Geometry object is used as a component object of a Shape3D leaf node.

```
SceneGraphObject
    NodeComponent
        Geometry
            CompressedGeometry
            Raster
            Text3D
            GeometryArray
                GeometryStripArray
                    LineStripArray
                    TriangleStripArray
                    TriangleFanArray
                LineArray
                PointArray
                QuadArray
                TriangleArray
                IndexedGeometryArray
                    IndexedGeometryStripArray
                        IndexedLineStripArray
                        IndexedTriangleStripArray
                        IndexedTriangleFanArray
                    IndexedLineArray
                    IndexedPointArray
                    IndexedQuadArray
                    IndexedTriangleArray
```

Figure 8-3   Geometry Component Object Hierarchy

Constants

The Geometry object defines the following constant:

public static final int ALLOW_INTERSECT

This flag specifies that this Geometry object allows the intersect operation.

Constructors

public Geometry()

Constructs a new Geometry object.

8.2.1 GeometryArray Object

A GeometryArray object is an abstract class from which several classes are derived to specify a set of geometric primitives. A GeometryArray contains separate arrays of the following vertex components: coordinates, colors, normals, and texture coordinates and a bitmask indicating which of these components are present.

Vertex data may be passed to this geometry array in one of two ways: by copying the data into the array using the existing methods or by passing a reference to the data.

- By copying: The existing methods for setting positional coordinates, colors, normals, and texture coordinates (such as setCoordinate and set-Colors) copy the data into this GeometryArray. This is appropriate for many applications and offers an application much flexibility in organizing its data. This is the default mode.

- By reference: A new set of methods in Java 3D version 1.2 allows data to be accessed by reference, directly from the user's arrays. To use this feature, set the BY_REFERENCE bit in the vertexFormat field of the constructor for this GeometryArray. In this mode, the various set methods for coordinates, normals, colors, and texture coordinates are not used. Instead, new methods are used to set a reference to user-supplied coordinate, color, normal, and texture coordinate arrays (such as setCoordRefFloat and set-ColorRefFloat). Data in any array that is referenced by a live or compiled GeometryArray object may be modified only via the updateData method (subject to the ALLOW_REF_DATA_WRITE capability bit). Applications must exercise care not to violate this rule. If any referenced geometry data is modified outside of the updateData method, the results are undefined.

A single GeometryArray contains a predefined collection of per-vertex information; all of the vertices in a GeometryArray object have the same format and primitive type. Different GeometryArrays can contain different per-vertex information. One GeometryArray might contain only three-space coordinates; another might contain per-vertex coordinates, normals, colors, and texture coordinates; yet another might contain any subset of the previous example.

All colors used in the GeometryArray object must be in the range [0.0, 1.0]. Values outside this range will cause undefined results. All normals used in the GeometryArray object must be unit length vectors; that is, their geometric length must be 1.0. Normals that are not unit length vectors will cause undefined results.

Note that the term *coordinate*, as used in the method names and method descriptions, actually refers to a set of *x*, *y*, and *z* coordinates representing the position of a single vertex. The term *coordinates* (plural) is used to indicate sets of *x*, *y*, and *z* coordinates for multiple vertices. This is somewhat at odds with the mathematical definition of a coordinate but is used as a convenient shorthand. Similarly, the term *texture coordinate* is used to indicate a set of texture coordinates for a single vertex, while the term *texture coordinates* (plural) is used to indicate sets of texture coordinates for multiple vertices.

Constants

The GeometryArray object defines the following flags:

```
public static final int ALLOW_COORDINATE_READ
public static final int ALLOW_COORDINATE_WRITE
```

These flags specify that the GeometryArray object allows reading or writing of the array of coordinates.

```
public static final int ALLOW_COLOR_READ
public static final int ALLOW_COLOR_WRITE
```

These flags specify that the GeometryArray object allows reading or writing of the array of colors.

```
public static final int ALLOW_NORMAL_READ
public static final int ALLOW_NORMAL_WRITE
```

These flags specify that the GeometryArray object allows reading or writing of the array of normals.

```
public static final int ALLOW_TEXCOORD_READ
public static final int ALLOW_TEXCOORD_WRITE
```

These flags specify that the GeometryArray object allows reading or writing of the array of texture coordinates.

```
public static final int ALLOW_COUNT_READ
public static final int ALLOW_COUNT_WRITE
```
◀ New in 1.2 ▶

These flags specify that the GeometryArray object allows reading or writing of any count or initial index data (such as the vertex count) associated with the GeometryArray.

```
public static final int ALLOW_FORMAT_READ
```

This flag specifies that the GeometryArray object allows reading the vertex format associated with the GeometryArray.

```
public static final int ALLOW_REF_DATA_READ
public static final int ALLOW_REF_DATA_WRITE
```
◀ New in 1.2 ▶
◀ New in 1.2 ▶

These flags specify that this GeometryArray allows reading or writing the geometry data reference information for this object. The second flag also enables writing the referenced data itself, via the GeometryUpdater interface. These are used only in by-reference geometry mode.

```
public static final int BY_REFERENCE
```
◀ New in 1.2 ▶

This flag specifies that the position, color, normal, and texture coordinate data for this GeometryArray are accessed by reference.

```
public static final int INTERLEAVED
```
◀ New in 1.2 ▶

This flag specifies that the position, color, normal, and texture coordinate data for this GeometryArray are accessed via a single interleaved, floating-point array reference. All of the data values for each vertex are stored in consecutive memory locations. This is valid only in conjunction with the BY_REFERENCE flag.

Constructors

The GeometryArray object has the following constructors:

```
public GeometryArray(int vertexCount, int vertexFormat)
```

Constructs an empty GeometryArray object with the specified vertex format and number of vertices. The vertexCount parameter specifies the number of vertex elements in this array. The vertexFormat parameter is a mask indicating which vertex components are present in each vertex. The vertex format is specified as a set of flags that are bitwise ORed together to describe the per-vertex data. The following vertex formats are supported:

- COORDINATES: Specifies that this vertex array contains coordinates. This bit must be set.

- NORMALS: Specifies that this vertex array contains normals.

- COLOR_3: Specifies that this vertex array contains colors without alpha. Colors are specified as floating-point values in the range [0.0, 1.0].

- COLOR_4: Specifies that this vertex array contains colors with alpha. Colors are specified as floating-point values in the range [0.0, 1.0]. This takes precedence over COLOR_3.

- TEXTURE_COORDINATE_2: Specifies that this vertex array contains 2D texture coordinates (S and T).

- TEXTURE_COORDINATE_3: Specifies that this vertex array contains 3D texture coordinates (S, T, and R). This takes precedence over TEXTURE_COORDINATE_2.

- BY_REFERENCE: Indicates that the data is passed by reference rather than by copying.

- INTERLEAVED: Indicates that the referenced data is interleaved in a single array.

The GeometryArray object is constructed with the following default values:

Parameter	Default Value
texCoordSetCount	1
texCoordSetMap	{ 0 }
validVertexCount	vertexCount
initialVertexIndex	0
initialCoordIndex	0
initialColorIndex	0
initialNormalIndex	0
initialTexCoordIndex	0
all data array values	0.0
all data array references	null

◀ New in 1.2 ▶ `public GeometryArray(int vertexCount, int vertexFormat, int texCoordSetCount, int[] texCoordSetMap)`

Constructs an empty GeometryArray object with the specified number of vertices, vertex format, number of texture coordinate sets, and texture coordinate mapping array. Defaults are used for all other parameters.

The texCoordSetCount parameter specifies the number of texture coordinate sets in this GeometryArray object. If the vertexFormat parameter does not include one of TEXTURE_COORDINATE_2 or TEXTURE_COORDINATE_3, the texCoordSetCount parameter is not used.

The texCoordSetMap parameter specifies an array that maps texture coordinate sets to texture units. The array is indexed by texture unit number for each texture unit in the associated Appearance object. The values in the array specify the texture coordinate set within this GeometryArray object that maps to the corresponding texture unit. All elements within the array must be less than texCoordSetCount. A negative value specifies that no texture coordinate set maps to the texture unit corresponding to the index.

If there are more texture units in any associated Appearance object than elements in the mapping array, the extra elements are assumed to be –1. The same texture coordinate set may be used for more than one texture unit. Each texture unit in every associated Appearance must have a valid source of texture coordinates: Either a nonnegative texture coordinate set must be specified in the mapping array, or texture coordinate generation must be enabled. Texture coordinate generation will take precedence for those texture units for which a texture coordinate set is specified and texture coordinate generation is enabled. If vertexFormat does not include one of TEXTURE_COORDINATE_2 or TEXTURE_COORDINATE_3, the texCoordSetMap array is not used. The following example illustrates the use of the texCoordSetMap array.

Index	Element	Description
0	1	Use texture coordinate set 1 for texture unit 0
1	–1	Use no texture coordinate set for texture unit 1
2	0	Use texture coordinate set 0 for texture unit 2
3	1	Reuse texture coordinate set 1 for texture unit 3

Methods

GeometryArray methods provide access (get and set methods) to individual vertex component arrays in two different modes: as individual elements or as arrays of multiple elements.

public int getVertexCount()

Retrieves the number of vertices in the GeometryArray.

```
public int getVertexFormat()
```

Retrieves the vertex format of the GeometryArray.

◀ New in 1.2 ▶ `public void updateData(GeometryUpdater updater)`

This method updates geometry array data that is accessed by reference. This method calls the updateData method of the specified GeometryUpdater object to synchronize updates to vertex data that is referenced by this GeometryArray object. Applications that wish to modify such data must perform all updates via this method.

This method may also be used to set multiple references atomically (for example, to coordinate and color arrays) or to change multiple data values atomically through the geometry data copying methods.

◀ New in 1.2 ▶ `public void setValidVertexCount(int validVertexCount)`
◀ New in 1.2 ▶ `public int getValidVertexCount()`

Sets or retrieves the valid vertex count for this GeometryArray object. This count specifies the number of vertices actually used in rendering or other operations such as picking and collision. This attribute is initialized to vertexCount.

◀ New in 1.2 ▶ `public void setInitialVertexIndex(int initialVertexIndex)`
◀ New in 1.2 ▶ `public int getInitialVertexIndex()`

Sets or retrieves the initial vertex index for this GeometryArray object. This index specifies the first vertex within this geometry array that is actually used in rendering or other operations such as picking and collision. This attribute is initialized to 0. This attribute is used only when the data mode for this geometry array object is not BY_REFERENCE.

```
public void setCoordinate(int index, float coordinate[])
public void getCoordinate(int index, float coordinate[])
public void setCoordinate(int index, double coordinate[])
public void getCoordinate(int index, double coordinate[])
```

Sets or retrieves the coordinate associated with the vertex at the specified index of this object. The index parameter is the vertex index in this geometry array. The coordinate parameter is an array of three values containing the new coordinate.

```
public void setCoordinate(int index, Point3f coordinate)
public void getCoordinate(int index, Point3f coordinate)
public void setCoordinate(int index, Point3d coordinate)
public void getCoordinate(int index, Point3d coordinate)
```

Sets or retrieves the coordinate associated with the vertex at the specified index. The index parameter is the vertex index in this geometry array. The coordinate parameter is a vector containing the new coordinate.

```
public void setCoordinates(int index, float coordinates[])
public void getCoordinates(int index, float coordinates[])
public void setCoordinates(int index, double coordinates[])
public void getCoordinates(int index, double coordinates[])
```

Sets or retrieves the coordinates associated with the vertices starting at the specified index. The index parameter is the starting vertex index in this geometry array. The coordinates parameter is an array of $3n$ values containing n new coordinates. The length of the coordinates array determines the number of vertices copied.

```
public void setCoordinates(int index, Point3f coordinates[])
public void getCoordinates(int index, Point3f coordinates[])
public void setCoordinates(int index, Point3d coordinates[])
public void getCoordinates(int index, Point3d coordinates[])
```

Sets or retrieves the coordinates associated with the vertices starting at the specified index. The index parameter is the starting vertex index in this geometry array. The coordinates parameter is an array of points containing new coordinates. The length of the coordinates array determines the number of vertices copied.

```
public void setCoordinates(int index, Point3d coordinates[],
      int start, int length)
public void setCoordinates(int index, Point3f coordinates[],
      int start, int length)
public void setCoordinates(int index, float coordinates[],
      int start, int length)
public void setCoordinates(int index, double coordinates[],
      int start, int length)
```

These methods set the coordinates associated with the vertices starting at the specified index for this object, using coordinate data starting from vertex index start for length vertices. The index parameter is the starting destination vertex index in this geometry array.

```
public void setColor(int index, float color[])
public void getColor(int index, float color[])
public void setColor(int index, byte color[])
public void getColor(int index, byte color[])
```

Sets or retrieves the color associated with the vertex at the specified index. The index parameter is the vertex index in this geometry array. The color parameter is an array of three or four values containing the new color.

```
public void setColor(int index, Color3f color)
public void getColor(int index, Color3f color)
public void setColor(int index, Color4f color)
public void getColor(int index, Color4f color)
public void setColor(int index, Color3b color)
public void getColor(int index, Color3b color)
public void setColor(int index, Color4b color)
public void getColor(int index, Color4b color)
```

Sets or retrieves the color associated with the vertex at the specified index. The index parameter is the vertex index in this geometry array. The color parameter is a vector containing the new color.

```
public void setColors(int index, float colors[])
public void getColors(int index, float colors[])
public void setColors(int index, byte colors[])
public void getColors(int index, byte colors[])
```

Sets or retrieves the colors associated with the vertices starting at the specified index. The index parameter is the starting vertex index in this geometry array. The colors parameter is an array of $3n$ or $4n$ values containing n new colors. The length of the colors array determines the number of vertices copied.

```
public void setColors(int index, Color3f colors[])
public void getColors(int index, Color3f colors[])
public void setColors(int index, Color4f colors[])
public void getColors(int index, Color4f colors[])
public void setColors(int index, Color3b colors[])
public void getColors(int index, Color3b colors[])
public void setColors(int index, Color4b colors[])
public void getColors(int index, Color4b colors[])
```

Sets or retrieves the colors associated with the vertices starting at the specified index. The index parameter is the starting vertex index in this geometry array. The colors parameter is an array of vectors containing the new colors. The length of the colors array determines the number of vertices copied.

198

```
public void setColors(int index, float colors[], int start,
      int length)
public void setColors(int index, byte colors[], int start,
      int length)
```

These methods set the colors associated with the vertices starting at the specified index for this object, using data in colors starting at index start for length colors. The index parameter is the starting destination vertex index in this geometry array. The colors parameter is an array of $3n$ or $4n$ values containing n new colors.

```
public void setColors(int index, Color3f colors[], int start,
      int length)
public void setColors(int index, Color4f colors[], int start,
      int length)
public void setColors(int index, Color3b colors[], int start,
      int length)
public void setColors(int index, Color4b colors[], int start,
      int length)
```

These methods set the colors associated with the vertices starting at the specified index for this object, using data in colors starting at index start for length colors. The index parameter is the starting destination vertex index in this geometry array. The colors parameter is an array of vectors containing new colors.

```
public void setNormal(int index, float normal[])
public void getNormal(int index, float normal[])
```

Sets or retrieves the normal associated with the vertex at the specified index. The index parameter is the vertex index in this geometry array. The normal parameter is the new normal.

```
public void setNormal(int index, Vector3f normal)
public void getNormal(int index, Vector3f normal)
```

Sets or retrieves the normal associated with the vertex at the specified index. The index parameter is the vertex index in this geometry array. The normal parameter is a vector containing the new normal.

```
public void setNormals(int index, float normals[])
public void getNormals(int index, float normals[])
```

Sets or retrieves the normals associated with the vertices starting at the specified index. The index parameter is the starting vertex index in this geometry array. The normals parameter is an array of $3n$ values containing n new normals. The length of the normals array determines the number of vertices copied.

```
public void setNormals(int index, Vector3f normals[])
public void getNormals(int index, Vector3f normals[])
```

Sets or retrieves the normals associated with the vertices starting at the specified index. The `index` parameter is the starting vertex index in this geometry array. The `normals` parameter is an array of vectors containing new normals. The length of the `normals` array determines the number of vertices copied.

```
public void setNormals(int index, float normals[], int start,
        int length)
public void setNormals(int index, Vector3f normals[], int start,
        int length)
```

These methods set the normals associated with the vertices starting at the specified index for this object, using data in `normals` starting at index `start` and ending at index `start+length`. The `index` parameter is the starting destination vertex index in this geometry array.

◀ New in 1.2 ▶ `public int getTexCoordSetCount()`

This method retrieves the number of texture coordinate sets in this Geometry-Array object.

◀ New in 1.2 ▶ `public int getTexCoordSetMapLength()`

This method retrieves the length of the texture coordinate set mapping array of this GeometryArray object.

◀ New in 1.2 ▶ `public void getTexCoordSetMap(int[] texCoordSetMap)`

This method retrieves the texture coordinate set mapping array from this GeometryArray object.

◀ New in 1.2 ▶ `public void setTextureCoordinate(int texCoordSet, int index,`
`        float[] texCoord)`
◀ New in 1.2 ▶ `public void setTextureCoordinate(int texCoordSet, int index,`
`        TexCoord2f texCoord)`
◀ New in 1.2 ▶ `public void setTextureCoordinate(int texCoordSet, int index,`
`        TexCoord3f texCoord)`
◀ New in 1.2 ▶ `public void getTextureCoordinate(int texCoordSet, int index,`
`        float[] texCoord)`
◀ New in 1.2 ▶ `public void getTextureCoordinate(int texCoordSet, int index,`
`        TexCoord2f texCoord)`
◀ New in 1.2 ▶ `public void getTextureCoordinate(int texCoordSet, int index,`
`        TexCoord3f texCoord)`

These methods set and retrieve the texture coordinate associated with the vertex at the specified index in the specified texture coordinate set for this object.

200

```
public void setTextureCoordinates(int texCoordSet, int index,      ◀ New in 1.2 ▶
     float[] texCoords)
public void setTextureCoordinates(int texCoordSet, int index,      ◀ New in 1.2 ▶
     TexCoord2f[] texCoords)
public void setTextureCoordinates(int texCoordSet, int index,      ◀ New in 1.2 ▶
     TexCoord3f[] texCoords)
public void getTextureCoordinates(int texCoordSet, int index,      ◀ New in 1.2 ▶
     float[] texCoords)
public void getTextureCoordinates(int texCoordSet, int index,      ◀ New in 1.2 ▶
     TexCoord2f[] texCoords)
public void getTextureCoordinates(int texCoordSet, int index,      ◀ New in 1.2 ▶
     TexCoord3f[] texCoords)
```

These methods set and retrieve the texture coordinates associated with the vertices starting at the specified index in the specified texture coordinate set for this object. The set methods copy the entire source array to this geometry array. For the get methods, the length of the destination array determines the number of texture coordinates copied.

```
public void setTextureCoordinates(int texCoordSet, int index,      ◀ New in 1.2 ▶
     float[] texCoords, int start, int length)
public void setTextureCoordinates(int texCoordSet, int index,      ◀ New in 1.2 ▶
     TexCoord2f[] texCoords, int start, int length)
public void setTextureCoordinates(int texCoordSet, int index,      ◀ New in 1.2 ▶
     TexCoord3f[] texCoords, int start, int length)
```

These methods set and retrieve the texture coordinates associated with the vertices starting at the specified index in the specified texture coordinate set for this object using data in texCoords starting at index start and ending at index start+length.

```
public void setTextureCoordinate(int index, float texCoord[])
public void getTextureCoordinate(int index, float texCoord[])
public void setTextureCoordinate(int index, Point2f texCoord)
public void getTextureCoordinate(int index, Point2f texCoord)
public void setTextureCoordinate(int index, Point3f texCoord)
public void getTextureCoordinate(int index, Point3f texCoord)
public void setTextureCoordinates(int index, float texCoords[])
public void getTextureCoordinates(int index, float texCoords[])
public void setTextureCoordinates(int index, Point2f texCoords[])
public void getTextureCoordinates(int index, Point2f texCoords[])
public void setTextureCoordinates(int index, Point3f texCoords[])
public void getTextureCoordinates(int index, Point3f texCoords[])
public void setTextureCoordinates(int index, float texCoords[],
     int start, int length)
public void setTextureCoordinates(int index, Point2f texCoords[],
     int start, int length)
```

201

```
public void setTextureCoordinates(int index, Point3f texCoords[],
        int start, int length)
```

These methods are deprecated in Java 3D version 1.2.

◀ New in 1.2 ▶ `public void setInitialCoordIndex(int initialCoordIndex)`
◀ New in 1.2 ▶ `public int getInitialCoordIndex()`

Sets or retrieves the initial coordinate index for this GeometryArray object. This index specifies the first coordinate within the array of coordinates referenced by this geometry array that is actually used in rendering or in other operations such as picking and collision. This attribute is initialized to 0. This attribute is used only when the data mode for this geometry array object is BY_REFERENCE.

◀ New in 1.2 ▶ `public void setInitialColorIndex(int initialColorIndex)`
◀ New in 1.2 ▶ `public int getInitialColorIndex()`

Sets or retrieves the initial color index for this GeometryArray object. This index specifies the first color within the array of colors referenced by this geometry array that is actually used in rendering or other operations such as picking and collision. This attribute is initialized to 0. This attribute is used only when the data mode for this geometry array object is BY_REFERENCE.

◀ New in 1.2 ▶ `public void setInitialNormalIndex(int initialNormalIndex)`
◀ New in 1.2 ▶ `public int getInitialNormalIndex()`

Sets or retrieves the initial normal index for this GeometryArray object. This index specifies the first normal within the array of normals referenced by this geometry array that is actually used in rendering or other operations such as picking and collision. This attribute is initialized to 0. This attribute is used only when the data mode for this geometry array object is BY_REFERENCE.

◀ New in 1.2 ▶
```
public void setInitialTexCoordIndex(int texCoordSet,
        int initialTexCoordIndex)
```
◀ New in 1.2 ▶ `public int getInitialTexCoordIndex(int texCoordSet)`

Sets or retrieves the initial texture coordinate index for the specified texture coordinate set for this GeometryArray object. This index specifies the first texture coordinate within the array of texture coordinates referenced by this geometry array that is actually used in rendering or other operations such as picking and collision. This attribute is initialized to 0. This attribute is used only when the data mode for this geometry array object is BY_REFERENCE.

◀ New in 1.2 ▶ `public void setCoordRefFloat(float[] coords)`
◀ New in 1.2 ▶ `public float[] getCoordRefFloat()`
◀ New in 1.2 ▶ `public void setCoordRefDouble(double[] coords)`

public double[] getCoordRefDouble() ◀ New in 1.2 ▶

Sets or retrieves the coordinate array reference to the specified array. The array contains *x*, *y*, and *z* values for each vertex (for a total of 3*n values, where *n* is the number of vertices). Only one of coordRefFloat, coordRefDouble, coordRef3f, or coordRef3d may be non-null (or they may all be null). An attempt to set more than one of these attributes to a non-null reference will result in an exception being thrown. If all coordinate array references are null, the entire geometry array object is treated as if it were null—any Shape3D or Morph node that uses this geometry array will not be drawn.

public void setCoordRef3f(Point3f[] coords) ◀ New in 1.2 ▶
public Point3f[] getCoordRef3f() ◀ New in 1.2 ▶
public void setCoordRef3d(Point3d[] coords) ◀ New in 1.2 ▶
public Point3d[] getCoordRef3d() ◀ New in 1.2 ▶

Sets or retrieves the coordinate array reference to the specified array. The array contains a Point3f or Point3d object for each vertex. Only one of coordRefFloat, coordRefDouble, coordRef3f, or coordRef3d may be non-null (or they may all be null). An attempt to set more than one of these attributes to a non-null reference will result in an exception being thrown. If all coordinate array references are null, the entire geometry array object is treated as if it were null—any Shape3D or Morph node that uses this geometry array will not be drawn.

public void setColorRefFloat(float[] colors) ◀ New in 1.2 ▶
public float[] getColorRefFloat() ◀ New in 1.2 ▶
public void setColorRefByte(byte[] colors) ◀ New in 1.2 ▶
public byte[] getColorRefByte() ◀ New in 1.2 ▶

Sets or retrieves the color array reference to the specified array. The array contains *red*, *green*, *blue*, and, optionally, *alpha* values for each vertex (for a total of 3*n or 4*n values, where *n* is the number of vertices). Only one of colorRefFloat, colorRefByte, colorRef3f, colorRef4f, colorRef3b, or colorRef4b may be non-null (or they may all be null). An attempt to set more than one of these attributes to a non-null reference will result in an exception being thrown. If all color array references are null and colors are enabled (that is, the vertexFormat includes either COLOR_3 or COLOR_4), the entire geometry array object is treated as if it were null—any Shape3D or Morph node that uses this geometry array will not be drawn.

public void setColorRef3f(Color3f[] colors) ◀ New in 1.2 ▶
public Color3f[] getColorRef3f() ◀ New in 1.2 ▶
public void setColorRef4f(Color4f[] colors) ◀ New in 1.2 ▶
public Color4f[] getColorRef4f() ◀ New in 1.2 ▶

203

◀ New in 1.2 ▶ `public void setColorRef3b(Color3b[] colors)`
◀ New in 1.2 ▶ `public Color3b[] getColorRef3b()`
◀ New in 1.2 ▶ `public void setColorRef4b(Color4b[] colors)`
◀ New in 1.2 ▶ `public Color4b[] getColorRef4b()`

Sets or retrieves the color array reference to the specified array. The array contains a Color 3f, Color4f, Color3b, or Color4b object for each vertex. Only one of `colorRefFloat`, `colorRefByte`, `colorRef3f`, `colorRef4f`, `colorRef3b`, or `colorRef4b` may be non-null (or they may all be null). An attempt to set more than one of these attributes to a non-null reference will result in an exception being thrown. If all color array references are null and colors are enabled (that is, the vertexFormat includes either COLOR_3 or COLOR_4), the entire geometry array object is treated as if it were null—any Shape3D or Morph node that uses this geometry array will not be drawn.

◀ New in 1.2 ▶ `public void setNormalRefFloat(float[] normals)`
◀ New in 1.2 ▶ `public float[] getNormalRefFloat()`

Sets or retrieves the float normal array reference to the specified array. The array contains floating-point *nx*, *ny*, and *nz* values for each vertex (for a total of $3*n$ values, where n is the number of vertices). Only one of `normalRefFloat` or `normalRef3f` may be non-null (or they may all be null). An attempt to set more than one of these attributes to a non-null reference will result in an exception being thrown. If all normal array references are null and normals are enabled (that is, the vertexFormat includes NORMAL), the entire geometry array object is treated as if it were null—any Shape3D or Morph node that uses this geometry array will not be drawn.

◀ New in 1.2 ▶ `public void setNormalRef3f(Vector3f[] normals)`
◀ New in 1.2 ▶ `public Vector3f[] getNormalRef3f()`

Sets or retrieves the normal array reference to the specified array. The array contains a Vector3f object for each vertex. Only one of `normalRefFloat` or `normalRef3f` may be non-null (or they may all be null). An attempt to set more than one of these attributes to a non-null reference will result in an exception being thrown. If all normal array references are null and normals are enabled (that is, the vertexFormat includes NORMAL), the entire geometry array object is treated as if it were null—any Shape3D or Morph node that uses this geometry array will not be drawn.

◀ New in 1.2 ▶ `public void setTexCoordRefFloat(int texCoordSet,`
`        float[] texCoords)`
◀ New in 1.2 ▶ `public float[] getTexCoordRefFloat(int texCoordSet)`

Sets or retrieves the float texture coordinate array reference for the specified texture coordinate set to the specified array. The array contains floating-point s, t, and, optionally, r values for each vertex (for a total of $2*n$ or $3*n$ values, where n is the number of vertices). Only one of `texCoordRefFloat`, `texCoordRef2f`, or texCoordRef3f may be non-null (or they may all be null). An attempt to set more than one of these attributes to a non-null reference will result in an exception being thrown. If all texCoord array references are null and texture coordinates are enabled (that is, the vertexFormat includes either TEXTURE_ COORDINATE_2 or TEXTURE_COORDINATE_3), the entire geometry array object is treated as if it were null—any Shape3D or Morph node that uses this geometry array will not be drawn.

```
public void setTexCoordRef2f(int texCoordSet,          ◀ New in 1.2 ▶
    TexCoord2f[] texCoords)
public TexCoord2f[] getTexCoordRef2f(int texCoordSet)  ◀ New in 1.2 ▶
public void setTexCoordRef3f(int texCoordSet,          ◀ New in 1.2 ▶
    TexCoord3f[] texCoords)
public TexCoord3f[] getTexCoordRef3f(int texCoordSet)  ◀ New in 1.2 ▶
```

Sets the texture coordinate array reference for the specified texture coordinate set to the specified array. The array contains a TexCoord2f or TexCoord3f object for each vertex. Only one of `texCoordRefFloat`, texCoordRef2f, or texCoordRef3f may be non-null (or they may all be null). An attempt to set more than one of these attributes to a non-null reference will result in an exception being thrown. If all texCoord array references are null and texture coordinates are enabled (that is, the vertexFormat includes either TEXTURE_COORDINATE_2 or TEXTURE_ COORDINATE_3), the entire geometry array object is treated as if it were null— any Shape3D or Morph node that uses this geometry array will not be drawn.

```
public void setInterleavedVertices(float[] vertexData)  ◀ New in 1.2 ▶
public float[] getInterleavedVertices()                 ◀ New in 1.2 ▶
```

Sets or retrieves the interleaved vertices array reference to the specified array. The vertex components must be stored in a predetermined order in the array. The order is texture coordinates, colors, normals, and positional coordinates. Only those components that are enabled appear in the vertex. The number of words per vertex depends on which vertex components are enabled. Texture coordinates, if enabled, use two words per vertex for TEXTURE_COORDINATE_2 or three words per vertex for TEXTURE_COORDINATE_3. Colors, if enabled, use three words per vertex for COLOR_ 3 or four words per vertex for COLOR_4. Normals, if enabled, use three words per vertex. Positional coordinates, which are always enabled, use three words per vertex. For example, the format of interleaved data for a GeometryArray object whose vertexFormat includes COORDINATES, COLOR_3, and NORMALS would be _red, green,_ *blue, Nx, Ny, Nz, x, y, z.* All components of a vertex are stored in adjacent memory locations. The first component of vertex 0 is stored beginning at index 0 in the array. The first component of vertex 1 is stored beginning at index *words_per_vertex* in the array. The total number of words needed to store *n* vertices is *words_per_vertex*n.*

8.2.2   GeometryUpdater Interface

The GeometryUpdater interface is used in updating geometry data that is accessed by reference from a live or compiled GeometryArray object (see Section 8.2.1, "GeometryArray Object"). Applications that wish to modify such data must define a class that implements this interface. An instance of that class is then passed to the `updateData` method of the GeometryArray object to be modified.

Methods

◀ New in 1.2 ▶ `public void updateData(Geometry geometry)`

This method updates geometry data that is accessed by reference. This method is called by the `updateData` method of a GeometryArray object to effect safe updates to vertex data that is referenced by that object. Applications that wish to modify such data must implement this method and perform all updates within it.

Note: Applications should not call this method directly.

8.2.3   PointArray Object

The PointArray object extends GeometryArray and provides no additional methods. Objects of this class draw the array of vertices as individual points.

Constructors

`public PointArray(int vertexCount, int vertexFormat)`

Constructs an empty PointArray object with the specified vertex format and number of vertices.

◀ New in 1.2 ▶ `public PointArray(int vertexCount, int vertexFormat,`
`                int texCoordSetCount, int[] texCoordSetMap)`

Constructs an empty PointArray object with the specified number of vertices, vertex format, number of texture coordinate sets, and texture coordinate mapping array.

8.2.4   LineArray Object

The LineArray object extends GeometryArray and provides no additional methods. Objects of this class draw the array of vertices as individual line segments. Each pair of vertices defines a line segment to be drawn.

Constructors

```
public LineArray(int vertexCount, int vertexFormat)
```

Constructs an empty LineArray object with the specified vertex format and number of vertices.

```
public LineArray(int vertexCount, int vertexFormat,
        int texCoordSetCount, int[] texCoordSetMap)
```
◀ New in 1.2 ▶

Constructs an empty LineArray object with the specified number of vertices, vertex format, number of texture coordinate sets, and texture coordinate mapping array.

8.2.5   TriangleArray Object

The TriangleArray object extends GeometryArray and provides no additional methods. Objects of this class draw the array of vertices as individual triangles. Each group of three vertices defines a triangle to be drawn.

Constructors

```
public TriangleArray(int vertexCount, int vertexFormat)
```

Constructs an empty TriangleArray object with the specified vertex format and number of vertices.

```
public TriangleArray(int vertexCount, int vertexFormat,
        int texCoordSetCount, int[] texCoordSetMap)
```
◀ New in 1.2 ▶

Constructs an empty TriangleArray object with the specified number of vertices, vertex format, number of texture coordinate sets, and texture coordinate mapping array.

8.2.6   QuadArray Object

The QuadArray object extends GeometryArray and provides no additional methods. Objects of this class draw the array of vertices as individual quadrilaterals. Each group of four vertices defines a quadrilateral to be drawn. A quadrilateral must be planar and convex or results are undefined. A quadrilateral may be rendered as a pair of triangles with either diagonal line arbitrarily chosen to split the quad.

Constructors

```
public QuadArray(int vertexCount, int vertexFormat)
```

Constructs an empty QuadArray object with the specified vertex format and number of vertices.

◀ New in 1.2 ▶
```
public QuadArray(int vertexCount, int vertexFormat,
        int texCoordSetCount, int[] texCoordSetMap)
```

Constructs an empty QuadArray object with the specified number of vertices, vertex format, number of texture coordinate sets, and texture coordinate mapping array.

8.2.7   GeometryStripArray Object

GeometryStripArray is an abstract class from which all strip primitives (line strip, triangle strip, and triangle fan) are derived. In addition to specifying the array of vertex elements, which is inherited from GeometryArray, the GeometryStripArray class specifies an array of per-strip vertex counts that specifies where the separate strips appear in the vertex array.

Constructors

The GeometryStripArray object has the following constructors:

```
public GeometryStripArray(int vertexCount, int vertexFormat,
        int stripVertexCounts[])
```

Constructs an empty GeometryStripArray object with the specified number of vertices, vertex format, and an array of vertex counts per strip. The `vertexCount` parameter specifies the number of vertex elements in this array.

The `stripVertexCounts` parameter is an array that specifies the count of the number of vertices for each separate strip. The length of this array specifies the number of separate strips. The sum of the vertex counts for all strips, as specified by the `stripVertexCounts` array, must equal the total count of all vertices as specified by the `vertexCount` parameter.

```
public GeometryStripArray(int vertexCount, int vertexFormat,          ◀ New in 1.2 ▶
        int texCoordSetCount, int[] texCoordSetMap,
        int[] stripVertexCounts)
```

Constructs an empty GeometryStripArray object with the specified number of vertices, vertex format, number of texture coordinate sets, texture coordinate mapping array, and array of per-strip vertex counts.

Methods

The GeometryStripArray object has the following methods:

```
public int getNumStrips()
```

This method returns the number of strips in the GeometryStripArray.

```
public void getStripVertexCounts(int stripVertexCounts[])
```

This method gets an array containing a list of vertex counts for each strip.

8.2.8   LineStripArray Object

The LineStripArray extends GeometryStripArray and provides no additional methods. Objects of this class draw an array of vertices as a set of connected line strips. An array of per-strip vertex counts specifies where the separate strips appear in the vertex array. For every strip in the set, each vertex, beginning with the second vertex in the array, defines a line segment to be drawn from the previous vertex to the current vertex.

Constructors

```
public LineStripArray(int vertexCount, int vertexFormat,
        int stripVertexCounts[])
```

Constructs an empty LineStripArray object with the specified number of vertices, vertex format, and array of vertex counts per strip.

```
public LineStripArray(int vertexCount, int vertexFormat,              ◀ New in 1.2 ▶
        int texCoordSetCount, int[] texCoordSetMap,
        int[] stripVertexCounts)
```

Constructs an empty LineStripArray object with the specified number of vertices, vertex format, number of texture coordinate sets, texture coordinate mapping array, and array of per-strip vertex counts.

209

8.2.9   TriangleStripArray Object

The TriangleStripArray extends GeometryStripArray and provides no additional methods. Objects of this class draw an array of vertices as a set of connected triangle strips. An array of per-strip vertex counts specifies where the separate strips appear in the vertex array. For every strip in the set, each vertex, beginning with the third vertex in the array, defines a triangle to be drawn using the current vertex and the two previous vertices.

Constructors

```
public TriangleStripArray(int vertexCount, int vertexFormat,
      int stripVertexCounts[])
```

Constructs an empty TriangleStripArray object with the specified number of vertices, vertex format, and array of vertex counts per strip.

◀ New in 1.2 ▶
```
public TriangleStripArray(int vertexCount, int vertexFormat,
      int texCoordSetCount, int[] texCoordSetMap,
      int[] stripVertexCounts)
```

Constructs an empty TriangleStripArray object with the specified number of vertices, vertex format, number of texture coordinate sets, texture coordinate mapping array, and array of per-strip vertex counts.

8.2.10   TriangleFanArray Object

The TriangleFanArray extends GeometryStripArray and provides no additional methods. Objects of this class draw an array of vertices as a set of connected triangle fans. An array of per-strip vertex counts specifies where the separate strips (fans) appear in the vertex array. For every strip in the set, each vertex, beginning with the third vertex in the array, defines a triangle to be drawn using the current vertex, the previous vertex, and the first vertex. This can be thought of as a collection of convex polygons.

Constructors

```
public TriangleFanArray(int vertexCount, int vertexFormat,
      int stripVertexCounts[])
```

Constructs an empty TriangleFanArray object with the specified number of vertices, vertex format, and array of vertex counts per strip.

```
public TriangleFanArray(int vertexCount, int vertexFormat,
      int texCoordSetCount, int[] texCoordSetMap,
      int[] stripVertexCounts)
```
◀ New in 1.2 ▶

Constructs an empty TriangleFanArray object with the specified number of vertices, vertex format, number of texture coordinate sets, texture coordinate mapping array, and array of per-strip vertex counts.

8.2.11 IndexedGeometryArray Object

An IndexedGeometryArray object is an abstract class that extends Geometry-Array to allow vertex data to be accessed via a level of indirection. In addition to the separate arrays of coordinates, colors, normals, and texture coordinates—inherited from GeometryArray—an IndexedGeometryArray object adds corresponding arrays of coordinate indices, color indices, normal indices, and texture coordinate indices.

Constants

The IndexedGeometryArray object defines the following flags:

```
public static final int ALLOW_COORDINATE_INDEX_READ
public static final int ALLOW_COORDINATE_INDEX_WRITE
```

These flags specify that the IndexedGeometryArray object allows reading or writing of the array of coordinate indices.

```
public static final int ALLOW_COLOR_INDEX_READ
public static final int ALLOW_COLOR_INDEX_WRITE
```

These flags specify that the IndexedGeometryArray object allows reading or writing of the array of color indices.

```
public static final int ALLOW_NORMAL_INDEX_READ
public static final int ALLOW_NORMAL_INDEX_WRITE
```

These flags specify that the IndexedGeometryArray object allows reading or writing of the array of normal indices.

```
public static final int ALLOW_TEXCOORD_INDEX_READ
public static final int ALLOW_TEXCOORD_INDEX_WRITE
```

These flags specify that the IndexedGeometryArray object allows reading or writing of the array of texture coordinate indices.

Constructors

The IndexedGeometryArray object has two constructors that accept the same parameters as GeometryArray.

```
public IndexedGeometryArray(int vertexCount, int vertexFormat,
        int indexCount)
```

Constructs an empty IndexedGeometryArray object with the specified number of vertices, vertex format, and number of indices. The index values in each of the four index arrays (coordinates, colors, normals, and texture coordinates) are all initialized to 0.

◀ New in 1.2 ▶
```
public IndexedGeometryArray(int vertexCount, int vertexFormat,
        int texCoordSetCount, int[] texCoordSetMap, int indexCount)
```

Constructs an empty IndexedGeometryArray object with the specified number of vertices, vertex format, number of texture coordinate sets, texture coordinate mapping array, and number of indices. The index values in each of the four index arrays (coordinates, colors, normals, and texture coordinates) are all initialized to zero.

Methods

IndexedGeometryArray methods provide access (get and set methods) to the individual vertex component index arrays that are used when rendering the geometry. This access is allowed in two different modes: as individual index elements or as arrays of multiple index elements.

```
public void setCoordinateIndex(int index, int coordinateIndex)
public int getCoordinateIndex(int index)
```

Sets or retrieves the coordinate index associated with the vertex at the specified index.

```
public void setCoordinateIndices(int index,
        int coordinateIndices[])
public void getCoordinateIndices(int index,
        int coordinateIndices[])
```

Sets or retrieves the coordinate indices associated with the vertices starting at the specified index.

```
public void setColorIndex(int index, int colorIndex)
public int getColorIndex(int index)
```

Sets or retrieves the color index associated with the vertex at the specified index.

```
public void setColorIndices(int index, int colorIndices[])
public void getColorIndices(int index, int colorIndices[])
```

Sets or retrieves the color indices associated with the vertices starting at the specified index.

```
public void setNormalIndex(int index, int normalIndex)
public int getNormalIndex(int index)
```

Sets or retrieves the normal index associated with the vertex at the specified index.

```
public void setnormalIndices(int index, int normalIndices[])
public void getNormalIndices(int index, int normalIndices[])
```

Sets or retrieves the normal indices associated with the vertices starting at the specified index.

```
public void setTextureCoordinateIndex(int texCoordSet, int index,      ◀ New in 1.2 ▶
    int texCoordIndex)
public int getTextureCoordinateIndex(int texCoordSet, int index)       ◀ New in 1.2 ▶
```

These methods set and retrieve the texture coordinate index associated with the vertex at the specified index in the specified texture coordinate set for this object.

```
public void setTextureCoordinateIndices(int texCoordSet,               ◀ New in 1.2 ▶
    int index, int[] texCoordIndices)
public void getTextureCoordinateIndices(int texCoordSet,               ◀ New in 1.2 ▶
    int index, int[] texCoordIndices)
```

These methods set and retrieve the texture coordinate indices associated with the vertices starting at the specified index in the specified texture coordinate set for this object.

```
public void setTextureCoordinateIndex(int index,
    int texCoordIndex)
public int getTextureCoordinateIndex(int index)
public void setTextureCoordinateIndices(int index,
    int texCoordIndices[])
public void getTextureCoordinateIndices(int index,
    int texCoordIndices[])
```

These methods are deprecated in Java 3D version 1.2.

```
public int getIndexCount()
```

Retrieves the number of indices for this IndexedGeometryArray.

8.2.12 IndexedPointArray Object

The IndexedPointArray object extends IndexedGeometryArray and provides no additional methods. Objects of this class draw the array of vertices as individual points.

Constructors

The IndexedPointArray object has the following constructors:

```
public IndexedPointArray(int vertexCount, int vertexFormat,
    int indexCount)
```

Constructs an empty IndexedPointArray object with the specified number of vertices, vertex format (see Section 8.2.1, "GeometryArray Object," for a description of the supported vertex formats), and the number of indices in this array.

◀ New in 1.2 ▶
```
public IndexedPointArray(int vertexCount, int vertexFormat,
    int texCoordSetCount, int[] texCoordSetMap, int indexCount)
```

Constructs an empty IndexedPointArray object with the specified number of vertices, vertex format, number of texture coordinate sets, texture coordinate mapping array, and number of indices.

8.2.13 IndexedLineArray Object

The IndexedLineArray object extends IndexedGeometryArray and provides no additional methods. Objects of this class draw the array of vertices as individual line segments. Each pair of vertices defines a line segment to be drawn.

Constructors

The IndexedLineArray object has the following constructors:

```
public IndexedLineArray(int vertexCount, int vertexFormat,
    int indexCount)
```

Constructs an empty IndexedLineArray object with the specified number of vertices, vertex format, and the number of indices in this array. The `vertexFormat` is a mask indicating which components are present in each vertex (see Section 8.2.1, "GeometryArray Object," for a description of the supported vertex formats).

◀ New in 1.2 ▶
```
public IndexedLineArray(int vertexCount, int vertexFormat,
    int texCoordSetCount, int[] texCoordSetMap, int indexCount)
```

Constructs an empty IndexedLineArray object with the specified number of vertices, vertex format, number of texture coordinate sets, texture coordinate mapping array, and number of indices.

8.2.14 IndexedTriangleArray Object

The IndexedTriangleArray object extends IndexedGeometryArray and provides no additional methods. Objects of this class draw the array of vertices as individual triangles. Each group of three vertices defines a triangle to be drawn.

Constructors

The IndexedTriangleArray object has the following constructors:

```
public IndexedTriangleArray(int vertexCount, int vertexFormat,
        int indexCount)
```

Constructs an empty IndexedTriangleArray object with the specified number of vertices, vertex format, and the number of indices in this array. The vertexFormat is a mask indicating which components are present in each vertex (see Section 8.2.1, "GeometryArray Object," for a description of the supported vertex formats).

```
public IndexedTriangleArray(int vertexCount, int vertexFormat,
        int texCoordSetCount, int[] texCoordSetMap, int indexCount)
```
◀ New in 1.2 ▶

Constructs an empty IndexedTriangleArray object with the specified number of vertices, vertex format, number of texture coordinate sets, texture coordinate mapping array, and number of indices.

8.2.15 IndexedQuadArray Object

The IndexedQuadArray object extends IndexedGeometryArray and provides no additional methods. Objects of this class draw the array of vertices as individual quadrilaterals. Each group of four vertices defines a quadrilateral to be drawn. A quadrilateral must be planar and convex or results are undefined. A quadrilateral may be rendered as a pair of triangles with either diagonal line arbitrarily chosen to split the quad.

Constructors

The IndexedQuadArray object has the following constructors:

```
public IndexedQuadArray(int vertexCount, int vertexFormat,
        int indexCount)
```

Constructs an empty IndexedQuadArray object with the specified number of vertices, vertex format (see Section 8.2.1, "GeometryArray Object," for a description of the supported vertex formats), and the number of indices in this array.

◀ New in 1.2 ▶
```
public IndexedQuadArray(int vertexCount, int vertexFormat,
        int texCoordSetCount, int[] texCoordSetMap, int indexCount)
```

Constructs an empty IndexedQuadArray object with the specified number of vertices, vertex format, number of texture coordinate sets, texture coordinate mapping array, and number of indices.

8.2.16   IndexedGeometryStripArray Object

IndexedGeometryStripArray is an abstract class from which all strip primitives (line strip, triangle strip, and triangle fan) are derived. In addition to specifying the array of vertex elements, which is inherited from IndexedGeometryArray, the IndexedGeometryArrayStrip class specifies an array of per-strip index counts that specifies where the separate strips appear in the indexed vertex array.

Constructors

The IndexedGeometryStripArray object has the following constructors:

```
public IndexedGeometryStripArray(int vertexCount,
        int vertexFormat, int indexCount, int stripIndexCounts[])
```

Constructs an empty IndexedGeometryStripArray object with the specified number of vertices, vertex format, number of indices in the array, and an array of index counts per strip. The vertexCount parameter specifies the number of vertex elements in this array. The vertexFormat parameter is a mask indicating which vertex components are present in each vertex. The indexCount parameter specifies the number of indices in this array. The stripIndexCounts parameter is an array that specifies the count of the number of indices for each separate strip. The length of this array specifies the number of separate strips. The sum of the index counts for all strips, as specified by the stripIndexCounts array, must equal the total count of all indices as specified by the indexCount parameter.

◀ New in 1.2 ▶
```
public IndexedGeometryStripArray(int vertexCount,
        int vertexFormat, int texCoordSetCount,
        int[] texCoordSetMap, int indexCount,
        int[] stripIndexCounts)
```

216

Constructs an empty IndexedGeometryStripArray object with the specified number of vertices, vertex format, number of texture coordinate sets, texture coordinate mapping array, number of indices, and array of per-strip index counts.

Methods

The IndexedGeometryArrayStrip object has the following methods:

public int getNumStrips()

Gets the number of strips in the IndexedGeometryStripArray.

public void getStripIndexCounts(int stripIndexCounts[])

Gets a list of the indexCounts for each strip.

8.2.17 IndexedLineStripArray Object

The IndexedLineStripArray extends IndexedGeometryStripArray and provides no additional methods. Objects of this class draw an array of vertices as a set of connected line strips. An array of per-strip index counts specifies where the separate strips appear in the indexed vertex array. For every strip in the set, each vertex, beginning with the second vertex in the array, defines a line segment to be drawn from the previous vertex to the current vertex.

Constructors

The IndexedLineStripArray object has the following constructors:

public IndexedLineStripArray(int vertexCount, int vertexFormat, int indexCount, int stripIndexCounts[])

Constructs an empty IndexedLineStrip object with the specified number of vertices, vertex format, number of indices in this array, and an array that specifies the number of indices for each strip. The vertexFormat parameter is a mask indicating which components are present in each vertex. This is specified as one or more individual flags that are bitwise ORed together to describe the per-vertex data (see Section 8.2.1, "GeometryArray Object," for a description of the supported vertex formats).

◀ New in 1.2 ▶
```
public IndexedLineStripArray(int vertexCount, int vertexFormat,
        int texCoordSetCount, int[] texCoordSetMap, int indexCount,
        int[] stripIndexCounts)
```

Constructs an empty IndexedLineStripArray object with the specified number of vertices, vertex format, number of texture coordinate sets, texture coordinate mapping array, number of indices, and array of per-strip index counts.

8.2.18 IndexedTriangleStripArray Object

The IndexedTriangleStripArray extends IndexedGeometryStripArray and provides no additional methods. Objects of this class draw an array of vertices as a set of connected triangle strips. An array of per-strip index counts specifies where the separate strips appear in the indexed vertex array. For every strip in the set, each vertex, beginning with the third vertex in the array, defines a triangle to be drawn using the current vertex and the two previous vertices.

Constructors

The IndexedTriangleStripArray object has the following constructors:

```
public IndexedTriangleStripArray(int vertexCount,
        int vertexFormat, int indexCount, int stripIndexCounts[])
```

Constructs an empty IndexedTriangleStripArray object with the specified number of vertices, vertex format, number of indices in this array, and an array of index counts per strip. The `vertexFormat` parameter is a mask indicating which components are present in each vertex. This is specified as one or more individual flags that are bitwise ORed together to describe the per-vertex data (see Section 8.2.1, "GeometryArray Object," for a description of the supported vertex formats).

◀ New in 1.2 ▶
```
public IndexedTriangleStripArray(int vertexCount,
        int vertexFormat, int texCoordSetCount,
        int[] texCoordSetMap, int indexCount,
        int[] stripIndexCounts)
```

Constructs an empty IndexedTriangleStripArray object with the specified number of vertices, vertex format, number of texture coordinate sets, texture coordinate mapping array, number of indices, and array of per-strip index counts.

8.2.19 IndexedTriangleFanArray Object

The IndexedTriangleFanArray extends IndexedGeometryStripArray and provides no additional methods. Objects of this class draw an array of vertices as a set of connected triangle fans. An array of per-strip index counts specifies where the separate strips (fans) appear in the indexed vertex array. For every strip in the set, each vertex, beginning with the third vertex in the array, defines a triangle to be drawn using the current vertex, the previous vertex, and the first vertex. This can be thought of as a collection of convex polygons.

Constructors

The IndexedTriangleFanArray object has the following constructors:

```
public IndexedTriangleFanArray(int vertexCount, int vertexFormat,
        int indexCount, int stripIndexCounts[])
```

Constructs an empty IndexedTriangleFanArray object with the specified number of vertices, vertex format, number of indices in this array, and an array of index counts per strip. The vertexFormat parameter is a mask indicating which components are present in each vertex. This is specified as one or more individual flags that are bitwise ORed together to describe the per-vertex data (see Section 8.2.1, "GeometryArray Object," for a description of the supported vertex formats).

```
public IndexedTriangleFanArray(int vertexCount, int vertexFormat, ◀ New in 1.2 ▶
        int texCoordSetCount, int[] texCoordSetMap, int indexCount,
        int[] stripIndexCounts)
```

Constructs an empty IndexedTriangleFanArray object with the specified number of vertices, vertex format, number of texture coordinate sets, texture coordinate mapping array, number of indices, and array of per-strip index counts.

8.2.20 CompressedGeometry Object

The CompressedGeometry object is used to store geometry in a compressed format. CompressedGeometry objects use a special format for representing geometric information in one order of magnitude less space. The representation, though lossy, preserves significant object quality during compression. There will be parameters to allow the user to specify the degree of lossy-ness (for example, a space versus quality knob).

For more information, see Appendix B, "3D Geometry Compression."

Compressed geometry may be passed to this CompressedGeometry object in one of two ways: by copying the data into this object using the existing constructor or by passing a reference to the data.

- By copying: The existing CompressedGeometry constructor copies the buffer of compressed geometry data into this CompressedGeometry object. This is appropriate for many applications and allows Java 3D to verify the data once and then not to worry about it again.

- By reference: A new constructor and set of methods in Java 3D version 1.2 allows compressed geometry data to be accessed by reference, directly from the user's array. To use this feature, you need to construct a CompressedGeometry object with the byReference flag set to true. In this mode, a reference to the input data is saved, but the data itself is not necessarily copied. Note that the compressed geometry header is still copied into this compressed geometry object. Data referenced by a CompressedGeometry object must not be modified after the CompressedGeometry object has been constructed. Applications must exercise care not to violate this rule. If any referenced compressed geometry data is modified after construction, the results are undefined.

Constants

The CompressedGeometry object specifies the following variables:

```
public static final int ALLOW_COUNT_READ
public static final int ALLOW_HEADER_READ
public static final int ALLOW_GEOMETRY_READ
```

These flags, when enabled using the setCapability method, allow an application to invoke methods that read its individual component field information.

◀ New in 1.2 ▶ `public static final int ALLOW_REF_DATA_READ`

This flag specifies that this CompressedGeometry allows reading the geometry data reference information for this object. This is used only in by-reference geometry mode.

Constructors

```
public CompressedGeometry(CompressedGeometryHeader hdr,
        byte geometry[])
```

Constructs a CompressedGeometry NodeComponent by copying the specified compressed geometry data into this object. The hdr field is copied into the CompressedGeometry object. The geometry parameter must conform to the compressed geometry format as described in Appendix B, "3D Geometry Compression." If the version number of compressed geometry, as specified by the CompressedGeometryHeader, is incompatible with the supported version of compressed geometry in the current version of Java 3D, the compressed geometry object will not be rendered.

public CompressedGeometry(CompressedGeometryHeader hdr,   ◀ New in 1.2 ▶
    byte[] compressedGeometry, boolean byReference)

Creates a new CompressedGeometry NodeComponent. The specified compressed geometry data is either copied into this object or accessed by reference. If the version number of compressed geometry, as specified by the CompressedGeometryHeader, is incompatible with the supported version of compressed geometry in the current version of Java 3D, the compressed geometry object will not be rendered.

Methods

public int getByteCount()

This method retrieves the size, in bytes, of the compressed geometry buffer.

public void getCompressedGeometryHeader
    (CompressedGeometryHeader hdr)

This method retrieves the header for this CompressedGeometry object (see Section 8.2.21, "CompressedGeometryHeader Object"). The header is copied into the CompressedGeometryHeader object provided.

public void getCompressedGeometry(byte compGeom[])

This method retrieves the compressed geometry associated with the CompressedGeometry object. It copies the compressed geometry from the CompressedGeometry object into the given array.

public byte[] getCompressedGeometryRef()   ◀ New in 1.2 ▶

This method retrieves the compressed geometry data reference with which this CompressedGeometry object was constructed. It is valid only in by-reference mode.

public Shape3D[] decompress()

This method decompresses the compressed geometry. It returns an array of Shape nodes containing the decompressed geometry objects.

public boolean isByReference()   ◀ Now in 1.2 ▶

This method retrieves the data access mode for this CompressedGeometry object.

221

8.2.21 CompressedGeometryHeader Object

The CompressedGeometryHeader object is used in conjunction with the CompressedGeometry object. The CompressedGeometryHeader object contains information specific to the compressed geometry data stored in the CompressedGeometry NodeComponent object. This header is used to aid in the processing of the compressed geometry by decompression routines. All members in the CompressedGeometryHeader node are public, so no `get` or `set` routines are provided. The CompressedGeometryHeader object should be created, and all values should be set, by the geometry compression utility.

Constants

```
public static final int POINT_BUFFER
public static final int LINE_BUFFER
public static final int TRIANGLE_BUFFER
```

These flags indicate whether the compressed geometry is made up of individual points, line segments, or triangles.

```
public static final int COLOR_IN_BUFFER
public static final int ALPHA_IN_BUFFER
public static final int NORMAL_IN_BUFFER
```

These flags indicate whether RGB, alpha color, or normal information is initialized in the compressed geometry buffer.

```
public int majorVersionNumber
public int minorVersionNumber
public int minorMinorVersionNumber
```

These flags indicate the major, minor, and minor-minor version numbers for the compressed geometry format that was used to compress the geometry. If the version number of compressed geometry is incompatible with the supported version of compressed geometry in the current version of Java 3D, the compressed geometry object will not be rendered.

```
public int bufferType
```

This flag describes the type of data in the compressed geometry buffer. Only one type may be present in any given compressed geometry buffer.

```
public int bufferDataPresent
```

This flag indicates whether a particular data component (for example, color) is present in the compressed geometry buffer, preceding any geometric data. If a particular data type is not present then this information will be inherited from the Appearance object.

public int size

This flag indicates the size of the compressed geometry, in bytes, that needs to be applied to every point in the compressed geometry buffer to restore the geometry to its original (uncompressed) position.

public int start

This flag contains the offset in bytes of the start of the compressed geometry from the beginning of the compressed geometry buffer.

public Point3d lowerBound   ◀ New in 1.2 ▶
public Point3d upperBound   ◀ New in 1.2 ▶

These two flags specify two points that specify the upper and lower bounds of the x, y, and z components for all positions in the compressed geometry buffer. If null, a lower bound of $(-1,-1,-1)$ and an upper bound of $(1,1,1)$ is assumed. Java 3D will use this information to construct a bounding box around compressed geometry objects that are used in nodes for which the auto compute bounds flag is true. The default value for both points is null.

Constructor

public CompressedGeometryHeader()

Creates a new CompressedGeometryHeader object used for the creation of a CompressedGeometry NodeComponent object. All instance data is declared public, and no get or set methods are provided. All values are set to 0 by default and must be filled in by the application.

8.2.22 Raster Object

The Raster object extends Geometry to allow drawing a raster image that is attached to a 3D location in the virtual world. The Raster object contains a point that is defined in the local object coordinate system of the Shape3D node that references the Raster. The Raster object also contains a type specifier, a reference to an ImageComponent2D object or a DepthComponent object, an integer x,y offset, and a size (width, height) to allow reading or writing of a portion of the referenced image. In addition to being used as a type of geometry for drawing, a Raster object may be used to read back pixel data (color and z-buffer) from the frame buffer in immediate mode.

The geometric extent of a Raster object is a single 3D point, specified by the raster position. This means that geometry-based picking or collision with a Raster object will intersect the object only at this single point; the 2D raster image is neither pickable nor collidable.

Constants

The Raster object defines the following flags:

```
public static final int ALLOW_POSITION_READ
public static final int ALLOW_POSITION_WRITE
public static final int ALLOW_OFFSET_READ
public static final int ALLOW_OFFSET_WRITE
public static final int ALLOW_IMAGE_READ
public static final int ALLOW_IMAGE_WRITE
public static final int ALLOW_DEPTH_COMPONENT_READ
public static final int ALLOW_DEPTH_COMPONENT_WRITE
public static final int ALLOW_SIZE_READ
public static final int ALLOW_SIZE_WRITE
public static final int ALLOW_TYPE_READ
```

These flags specify that the Raster object allows reading or writing of the position, offset, image, depth component, or size, or reading of the type.

```
public static final int RASTER_COLOR
```

Specifies a Raster object with color data. In this mode, the ImageComponent reference must point to a valid ImageComponent object.

```
public static final int RASTER_DEPTH
```

Specifies a Raster object with depth (*z*-buffer) data. In this mode, the depth component reference must point to a valid DepthComponent object.

```
public static final int RASTER_COLOR_DEPTH
```

Specifies a Raster object with both color and depth (*z*-buffer) data. In this mode, the image component reference must point to a valid ImageComponent object, and the depth component reference must point to a valid DepthComponent object.

Constructors

```
public Raster()
```

Constructs and initializes a new Raster object with default values:

Parameter	Default Value
type	RASTER_COLOR
position	(0,0,0)
offset	(0,0)
size	(0,0)
image	null
depthComponent	null

```
public Raster(Point3f pos, int type, int xOffset, int yOffset,
        int width, int height, ImageComponent2D image,
        DepthComponent depthComponent)
public Raster(Point3f pos, int type, Point offset, Dimension size,
        ImageComponent2D image, DepthComponent depthComponent)
```

Constructs and initializes a new Raster object with the specified values.

Methods

```
public void setPosition(Point3f pos)
public void getPosition(Point3f pos)
```

These methods set and retrieve the position, in object coordinates, of this raster. This position is transformed into device coordinates and is used as the upper-left corner of the raster.

```
public void setType(int type)
public int getType()
```

These methods set and retrieve the type of this Raster object. The type is one of the following: RASTER_COLOR, RASTER_DEPTH, or RASTER_COLOR_DEPTH.

```
public void setOffset(int xOffset, int yOffset)
public void setOffset(Point offset)
public void getOffset(Point offset)
```

These methods set and retrieve the offset within the array of pixels at which to start copying.

```
public void setSize(int width, int height)
public void setSize(Dimension size)
public void getSize(Dimension size)
```

These methods set and retrieve the number of pixels to be copied from the pixel array.

225

```
public void setImage(ImageComponent2D image)
public ImageComponent2D getImage()
```

These methods set and retrieve the pixel array used to copy pixels to or from a Canvas3D. This is used when the type is RASTER_COLOR or RASTER_COLOR_DEPTH.

```
public void setDepthComponent(DepthComponent depthComponent)
public DepthComponent getDepthComponent()
```

These methods set and retrieve the DepthComponent used to copy pixels to or from a Canvas3D. This is used when the `type` is RASTER_DEPTH or RASTER_COLOR_DEPTH.

8.2.23 Font3D Object

The Font3D object is used to contain 3D glyphs used in rendering 3D text. These 3D glyphs are constructed from a Java 2D font object and a FontExtrusion object (see Section 8.2.24, "FontExtrusion Object"). To ensure correct rendering, the 2D font object should be created with the default transform.

A 3D Font consists of a Java 2D font, a tessellation tolerance, and an extrusion path. The extrusion path describes how the edge of a glyph varies in the *z* axis.

Constructors

```
public Font3D(java.awt.Font font, FontExtrusion extrudePath)
```

Creates a Font3D object from the specified Font and FontExtrusion objects, using the default value for the tesselation tolerance. The default value is as follows:

Parameter	Default Value
tesselationTolerance	0.01

The FontExtrusion object (see Section 8.2.24, "FontExtrusion Object") contains the extrusion path to use on the 2D font glyphs. To ensure correct rendering, the font must be created with the default AffineTransform. Passing in a `null` FontExtrusion object results in no extrusion being done.

◀ New in 1.2 ▶
```
public Font3D(Font font, double tessellationTolerance,
              FontExtrusion extrudePath)
```

Creates a Font3D object from the specified Font and FontExtrusion objects, using the specified tessellation tolerance. The FontExtrusion object (see

Section 8.2.24, "FontExtrusion Object") contains the extrusion path to use on the 2D Font glyphs. To ensure correct rendering, the font must be created with the default AffineTransform. Passing in a `null` FontExtrusion object results in no extrusion being done. The `tessellationTolerance` parameter corresponds to the `flatness` parameter in the `java.awt.Shape.getPathIterator` method.

Methods

`public void getBoundingBox(int glyphCode, BoundingBox bounds)`

This method returns the 3D bounding box of the specified glyph code.

`public Font getFont()`

This method returns the Java 2D font used to create this Font3D object.

`public void getFontExtrusion(FontExtrusion extrudePath)`

This method retrieves the FontExtrusion object used to create this Font3D object and copies it into the specified parameter. For information about the FontExtrusion object, see Section 8.2.24, "FontExtrusion Object."

`public double getTessellationTolerance()`   ◀ New in 1.2 ▶

This method returns the tessellation tolerance with which this Font3D was created.

8.2.24 FontExtrusion Object

The FontExtrusion object is used to describe the extrusion path for a Font3D object (see Section 8.2.23, "Font3D Object"). The extrusion path is used in conjunction with a Font2D object. The extrusion path defines the edge contour of 3D text. This contour is perpendicular to the face of the text. The contour has its origin at the edge of the glyph, with 1.0 being the height of the tallest glyph. Contour must be monotonic in x. The user is responsible for data sanity and must make sure that extrusionShape does not cause intersection of adjacent glyphs or within a single glyph, otherwise undefined output may be generated.

Constructors

`public FontExtrusion()`

Creates a FontExtrusion object with default parameters. The default parameters are as follows:

Parameter	Default Value
extrusionShape	null
tesselationTolerance	0.01

A null extrusion shape specifies that a straight line from 0.0 to 0.2 (straight bevel) is used.

public FontExtrusion(java.awt.Shape extrusionShape)

Creates a FontExtrusion object with the specified extrusion shape, using the default tesselation tolerance. The extrusionShape parameter is used to construct the edge contour of a Font3D object. Each shape begins with an implicit point at 0.0. Contour must be monotonic in *x*. An IllegalArgumentException is thrown if multiple contours in extrusionShape, contour is not monotonic, or least *x*-value of a contour point is not 0.0f.

◀ New in 1.2 ▶ **public FontExtrusion(Shape extrusionShape,
                    double tessellationTolerance)**

Creates a FontExtrusion object with the specified shape, using the specified tessellation tolerance. The specified shape is used to construct the edge contour of a Font3D object. Each shape begins with an implicit point at 0.0. Contour must be monotonic in x. The tessellationTolerance parameter corresponds to the flatness parameter in the java.awt.Shape.getPathIterator method.

Methods

**public void setExtrusionShape(java.awt.Shape extrusionShape)
public java.awt.Shape getExtrusionShape()**

These methods set and retrieve the 2D shape object associated with this FontExtrusion object. The Shape object describes the extrusion path used to create a 3D glyph from a 2D glyph. The set method sets the FontExtrusion's shape parameter. The get method gets the FontExtrusion's shape parameter.

◀ New in 1.2 ▶ **public double getTessellationTolerance()**

This method returns the tessellation tolerance with which this FontExtrusion was created.

8.2.25 Text3D Geometry Object

A Text3D object is a text string that has been converted to 3D geometry. The Font3D object (see Section 8.2.23, "Font3D Object") determines the appearance of the Text3D NodeComponent object. Each Text3D object has a text position—a point in 3D space where the text should be placed. The 3D text can be placed around this position using different alignments and paths. An OrientedShape3D node may also be used for drawing screen-aligned text (see Section 6.2.1, "OrientedShape3D Node").

If 3D texture mapping is not supported on a particular Canvas3D, 3D texture mapping is ignored for that canvas.

Constants

The Text3D object defines the following flags:

```
public static final int ALLOW_FONT3D_READ
public static final int ALLOW_FONT3D_WRITE
public static final int ALLOW_STRING_READ
public static final int ALLOW_STRING_WRITE
public static final int ALLOW_POSITION_READ
public static final int ALLOW_POSITION_WRITE
public static final int ALLOW_ALIGNMENT_READ
public static final int ALLOW_ALIGNMENT_WRITE
public static final int ALLOW_PATH_READ
public static final int ALLOW_PATH_WRITE
public static final int ALLOW_CHARACTER_SPACING_READ
public static final int ALLOW_CHARACTER_SPACING_WRITE
public static final int ALLOW_BOUNDING_BOX_READ
```

These flags control reading and writing of the Font3D component information for Font3D, the String object, the text position value, the text alignment value, the text path value, the character spacing, and the bounding box.

Constructors

public Text3D()

Creates a new Text3D object with the following default parameters:

Parameter	Default Value
font3D	null
string	null
position	(0,0,0)
alignment	ALIGN_FIRST
path	PATH_RIGHT
characterSpacing	0.0

```
public Text3D(Font3D font3D)
public Text3D(Font3D font3D, String string)
public Text3D(Font3D font3D, String string, Point3f position)
public Text3D(Font3D font3D, String string, Point3f position,
        int alignment, int path)
```

Create a new Text3D object with the defined parameters.

Methods

```
public Font3D getFont3D()
public void setFont3D(Font3D font3d)
```

These methods get and set the Font3D object associated with this Text3D object.

```
public String getString()
public void setString(String string)
```

These methods get and set the character string associated with this Text3D object.

```
public void getPosition(Point3f position)
public void setPosition(Point3f position)
```

These methods get and set the text position. The `position` parameter is used to determine the initial placement of the string. The text position is used in conjunction with the alignment and path to determine how the glyphs are to be placed in the scene. The default value is (0.0, 0.0, 0.0).

```
public void setAlignment(int alignment)
public int getAlignment()
```

These methods set and get the text alignment policy for this Text3D NodeComponent object (see Figure 8-4). The `alignment` parameter is used to specify how glyphs in the string are placed in relation to the `position` field. Valid values for the alignment field are

- ALIGN_CENTER: places the center of the string on the position point.
- ALIGN_FIRST: places the first character of the string on the position point.
- ALIGN_LAST: places the last character of the string on the position point.

The default value of this field is ALIGN_FIRST.

```
public void setPath(int path)
public int getPath()
```

These methods set and get the node's path field. This field is used to specify how succeeding glyphs in the string are placed in relation to the previous glyph (see Figure 8-4). The path is relative to the local coordinate system of the Text3D node. The default coordinate system (see Section 4.4, "Coordinate Systems") is right-handed with $+y$ being up, $+x$ horizontal to the right, and $+z$ directed toward the viewer. Valid values for this field are as follows:

- PATH_LEFT: places succeeding glyphs to the left (the $-x$ direction) of the current glyph.

- PATH_RIGHT: places succeeding glyphs to the right (the $+x$ direction) of the current glyph.

- PATH_UP: places succeeding glyphs above (the $+y$ direction) the current glyph.

- PATH_DOWN: places succeeding glyphs below (the $-y$ direction) the current glyph.

The default value of this field is PATH_RIGHT.

```
public void getBoundingBox(BoundingBox bounds)
```

This method retrieves the 3D bounding box that encloses this Text3D object.

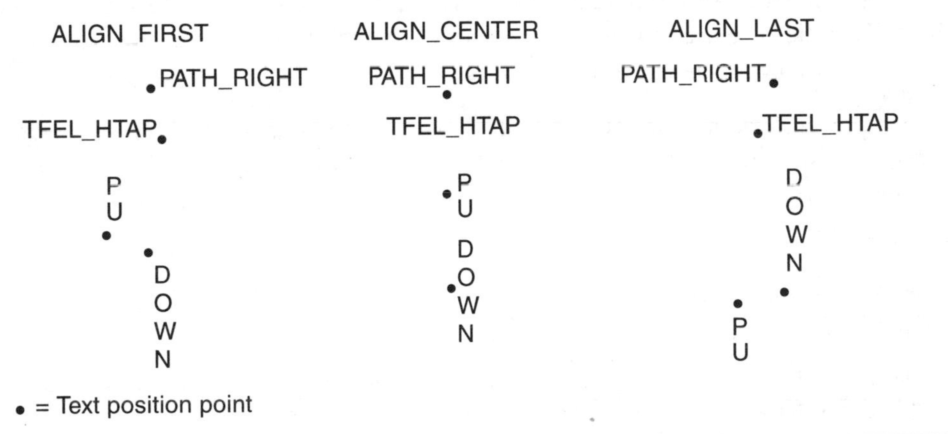

ALIGN FIRST	ALIGN_CENTER	ALIGN_LAST
•PATH_RIGHT	PATH_RIGHT	PATH_RIGHT•
TFEL_HTAP•	TFEL_HTAP	•TFEL_HTAP
P	•P	D
U	U	O
•	D	W
•	•O	N
D	W	•
O	N	•
W		P
N		U

• = Text position point

Figure 8-4   Various Text Alignments and Paths

```
public void setCharacterSpacing(float characterSpacing)
public float getCharacterSpacing()
```

These methods set and get the character spacing used to construct the Text3D
string. This spacing is in addition to the regular spacing between glyphs as
defined in the Font object. A value of 1.0 in this space is measured as the width
of the largest glyph in the 2D font. The default value is 0.0.

8.3   Math Component Objects

Java 3D defines a number of additional objects that are used in the construction
and manipulation of other Java 3D objects. These objects provide low-level storage and manipulation control for users. They provide methods for representing
vertex components (for example, color and position), volumes, vectors, and
matrices.

The tuple and matrix math classes are not part of Java 3D per se, but they are
needed by Java 3D and are defined here for convenience. Java 3D uses these
classes internally and also makes them available for use by applications. These
classes will be delivered in a separate `javax.vecmath` package. The tuple and
matrix math classes are described in detail in Appendix A, "Math Objects."

8.3.1   Tuple Objects

The tuple objects, listed in Table 8-1, store tuples of length two, three, and four.
Java 3D tuples are used to store various kinds of information such as colors, normals, texture coordinates, vertices, and so forth.

The tuple classes are further subdivided by storage type, such as point, vector,
color, and so forth, and by class—whether the vector consists of single- or double-precision floating-point numbers or bytes. Only the floating-point tuple
classes support math operations.

Table 8-1   **Tuple Objects**

Class	Description

Tuple2d	Used to represent two-component coordinates in double-precision floating-point format. This class is further divided into the following:
	  Point2d: Represents *x,y* point coordinates.
	  Vector2d: Represents *x,y* vector coordinates.

Table 8-1   Tuple Objects (Continued)

Class	Description
Tuple2f	Used to represent two-component coordinates in single-precision floating-point format. This class is further divided into the following: 　Point2f: Represents x,y point coordinates. 　TexCoord2f: Represents x,y texture coordinates. 　Vector2f: Represents x,y vector coordinates.
Tuple3b	Used to represent three-component color information stored as three bytes. This class is further divided into the following: 　Color3b: Represents RGB color values.
Tuple3d	Used to represent point and vector coordinates in double-precision floating-point format. This class is further divided into the following: 　Point3d: Represents x,y,z point coordinates. 　Vector3d: Represents x,y,z vector coordinates.
Tuple3f	Used to represent three-component colors, point coordinates, texture coordinates, and vectors in single-precision floating-point format. This class is further divided into the following: 　Color3f: Represents RGB color values. 　Point3f: Represents x,y,z point coordinates. 　TexCoord3f: Represents x,y,z texture coordinates. 　Vector3f: Represents x,y,z vector coordinates.
Tuple3i	Used to represent three-component point coordinates in signed integer format. This class is further divided into the following: 　Point3i: Represents x,y,z point coordinates.
Tuple4b	Used to represent four-component color information stored as four bytes. This class is further divided into the following: 　Color4b: Represents RGBα color values.
Tuple4d	Used to represent four-component color information, quaternions, and vectors stored in double-precision floating-point format. This class is further divided into the following: 　Point4d: Represents x,y,z,w point coordinates. 　Quat4d: Represents x,y,z,w quaternion coordinates. 　Vector4d: Represents x,y,z,w vector coordinates.
Tuple4f	Used to represent four-component color information, point coordinates, quaternions, and vectors in single-precision floating-point format. This class is further divided into the following: 　Color4f: Represents RGBα color values. 　Point4f: Represents x,y,z,w point coordinates. 　Quat4f: Represents x,y,z,w quaternion coordinates. 　Vector4f: Represents x,y,z,w vector coordinates.
Tuple4i	Used to represent four-component point coordinates in signed integer format. This class is further divided into the following: 　Point4i: Represents x,y,z,w point coordinates.

233

Table 8-1   Tuple Objects (Continued)

Class	Description
AxisAngle4d	Used to represent four-component axis-angle rotations consisting of double-precision floating-point x, y, and z coordinates and a rotation angle in radians.
AxisAngle4f	Used to represent four-component axis-angle rotations consisting of single-precision floating point x, y, and z coordinates and a rotation angle in radians.
GVector	Used to represent a general, dynamically resizeable, one-dimensional vector class.

These are described in more detail in Appendix A, "Math Objects."

8.3.2   Matrix Objects

The matrix objects, listed in Table 8-2, define a complete 3×3 or 4×4 floating-point transformation matrix. All the vector subclasses operate using this one matrix type.

Table 8-2   Matrix Objects

Class	Description
Matrix3d	Used to represent a double-precision floating-point 3×3 matrix.
Matrix3f	Used to represent a single-precision floating-point 3×3 matrix.
Matrix4d	Used to represent a double-precision floating-point 4×4 matrix.
Matrix4f	Used to represent a single-precision floating-point 4×4 matrix.
GMatrix	A double-precision, general, dynamically resizeable $N \times M$ matrix class.

These are described in more detail in Appendix A, "Math Objects."

CHAPTER 9

View Model

$\mathbf{J}$AVA 3D introduces a new view model that takes Java's vision of "write once, run anywhere" and generalizes it to include display devices and six-degrees-of-freedom input peripherals such as head trackers. This "write once, view everywhere" nature of the new view model means that an application or applet written using the Java 3D view model can render images to a broad range of display devices, including standard computer displays, multiple-projection display rooms, and head-mounted displays, without modification of the scene graph. It also means that the same application, once again without modification, can render stereoscopic views and can take advantage of the input from a head tracker to control the rendered view.

Java 3D's view model achieves this versatility by cleanly separating the virtual and the physical world. This model distinguishes between how an application positions, orients, and scales a ViewPlatform object (a viewpoint) within the virtual world and how the Java 3D renderer constructs the final view from that viewpoint's position and orientation. The application controls the ViewPlatform's position and orientation; the renderer computes what view to render using this position and orientation, a description of the end-user's physical environment, and the user's position and orientation within the physical environment.

This chapter first explains why Java 3D chose a different view model and some of the philosophy behind that choice. It next describes how that model operates in the simple case of a standard computer screen without head tracking—the most common case. Finally, it presents the relevant parts of the API from a developer's perspective. Appendix C, "View Model Details," describes the Java 3D view model from an advanced developer and Java 3D implementor's perspective.

9.1   Why a New Model?

Camera-based view models, as found in low-level APIs, give developers control over all rendering parameters. This makes sense when dealing with custom applications, less sense when dealing with systems that wish to have broader applicability: systems such as viewers or browsers that load and display whole worlds as a single unit or systems where the end users view, navigate, display, and even interact with the virtual world.

Camera-based view models emulate a camera in the virtual world, not a human in a virtual world. Developers must continuously reposition a camera to emulate "a human in the virtual world."

The Java 3D view model incorporates head tracking directly, if present, with no additional effort from the developer, thus providing end users with the illusion that they actually exist inside a virtual world.

The Java 3D view model, when operating in a non-head-tracked environment and rendering to a single, standard display, acts very much like a traditional camera-based view model, with the added functionality of being able to generate stereo views transparently.

9.1.1   The Physical Environment Influences the View

Letting the application control all viewing parameters is not reasonable in systems in which the physical environment dictates some of the view parameters.

One example of this is a head-mounted display (HMD), where the optics of the head-mounted display directly determine the field of view that the application should use. Different HMDs have different optics, making it unreasonable for application developers to hard-wire such parameters or to allow end users to vary that parameter at will.

Another example is a system that automatically computes view parameters as a function of the user's current head position. The specification of a world and a predefined flight path through that world may not exactly specify an end-user's view. HMD users would expect to look and thus see to their left or right even when following a fixed path through the environment—imagine an amusement park ride with vehicles that follow fixed paths to present content to their visitors, but visitors can continue to move their heads while on those rides.

Depending on the physical details of the end-user's environment, the values of the viewing parameters, particularly the viewing and projection matrices, will vary widely. The factors that influence the viewing and projection matrices include the size of the physical display, how the display is mounted (on the user's head or on a table), whether the computer knows the user's head location in three space, the head mount's actual field of view, the display's pixels per inch, and other such parameters. For more information, see Appendix C, "View Model Details."

9.2   Separation of Physical and Virtual

The Java 3D view model separates the virtual environment, where the application programmer has placed objects in relation to one another, from the physical environment, where the user exists, sees computer displays, and manipulates input devices.

Java 3D also defines a fundamental correspondence between the user's physical world and the virtual world of the graphic application. This physical-to-virtual-world correspondence defines a single common space, a space where an action taken by an end user affects objects within the virtual world and where any activity by objects in the virtual world affects the end user's view.

9.2.1   The Virtual World

The virtual world is a common space in which virtual objects exist. The virtual world coordinate system exists relative to a high-resolution Locale—each Locale object defines the origin of virtual world coordinates for all of the objects attached to that Locale. The Locale that contains the currently active ViewPlatform object defines the virtual world coordinates that are used for rendering. Java3D eventually transforms all coordinates associated with scene graph elements into this common virtual world space.

9.2.2   The Physical World

The physical world is just that—the real, physical world. This is the space in which the physical user exists and within which he or she moves his or her head and hands. This is the space in which any physical trackers define their local coordinates and in which several calibration coordinate systems are described.

The physical world is a space, not a common coordinate system between different execution instances of Java 3D. So while two different computers at two different physical locations on the globe may be running at the same time, there is no mechanism directly within Java 3D to relate their local physical world coordinate systems with each other. Because of calibration issues, the local tracker (if any) defines the local physical world coordinate system known to a particular instance of Java 3D.

9.3   The Objects That Define the View

Java 3D distributes its view model parameters across several objects, specifically, the View object and its associated component objects, the PhysicalBody object, the PhysicalEnvironment object, the Canvas3D object, and the Screen3D object. Figure 9-1 shows graphically the central role of the View object and the subsidiary role of its component objects.

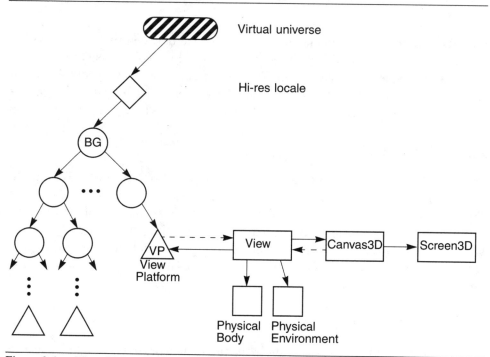

Figure 9-1   **View Object, Its Component Objects, and Their Interconnection**

The view-related objects shown in Figure 9-1 and their roles are as follows. For each of these objects, the portion of the API that relates to modifying the virtual world and the portion of the API that is relevant to non-head-tracked standard display configurations are derived in this chapter. The remainder of the details are described in Appendix C, "View Model Details."

- *ViewPlatform*: A leaf node that locates a view within a scene graph. The ViewPlatform's parents specify its location, orientation, and scale within the virtual universe. See Section 6.11, "ViewPlatform Node," and Section 9.4, "ViewPlatform: A Place in the Virtual World," for more information.

- *View*: The main view object. It contains many pieces of view state. See Section 9.7, "The View Object," for more information.

- *Canvas3D*: The 3D version of the Abstract Windowing Toolkit (AWT) Canvas object. It represents a window in which Java 3D will draw images. It contains a reference to a Screen3D object and information describing the Canvas3D's size, shape, and location within the Screen3D object. See Section 9.9, "The Canvas3D Object," for more information.

- *Screen3D*: An object that contains information describing the display screen's physical properties. Java 3D places display-screen information in a separate object to prevent the duplication of screen information within every Canvas3D object that shares a common screen. See Section 9.8, "The Screen3D Object," for more information.

- *PhysicalBody*: An object that contains calibration information describing the user's physical body. See Section 9.10, "The PhysicalBody Object," for more information.

- *PhysicalEnvironment*: An object that contains calibration information describing the physical world, mainly information that describes the environment's six-degrees-of freedom tracking hardware, if present. See Section 9.11, "The PhysicalEnvironment Object," for more information.

Together, these objects describe the geometry of viewing rather than explicitly providing a viewing or projection matrix. The Java 3D renderer uses this information to construct the appropriate viewing and projection matrices. The geometric focus of these view objects provides more flexibility in generating views—a flexibility needed to support alternative display configurations.

9.4 ViewPlatform: A Place in the Virtual World

A ViewPlatform leaf node defines a coordinate system, and thus a reference frame with its associated origin or reference point, within the virtual world. The ViewPlatform serves as a point of attachment for View objects and as a base for determining a renderer's view.

Figure 9-2 shows a portion of a scene graph containing a ViewPlatform node. The nodes directly above a ViewPlatform determine where that ViewPlatform is located and how it is oriented within the virtual world. By modifying the Transform3D object associated with a TransformGroup node anywhere directly above a ViewPlatform, an application or behavior can move that ViewPlatform anywhere within the virtual world. A simple application might define one TransformGroup node directly above a ViewPlatform, as shown in Figure 9-2.

A VirtualUniverse may have many different ViewPlatforms, but a particular View object can attach itself only to a single ViewPlatform. Thus, each rendering onto a Canvas3D is done from the point of view of a single ViewPlatform.

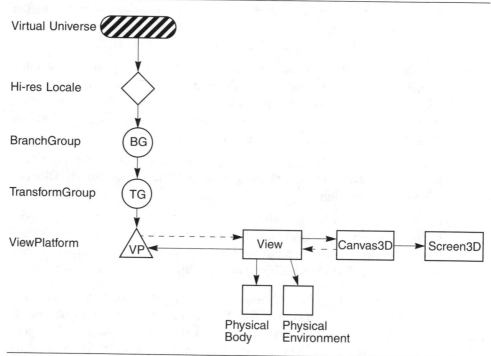

Figure 9-2   A Portion of a Scene Graph Containing a ViewPlatform Object

9.4.1   Moving through the Virtual World

An application navigates within the virtual world by modifying a ViewPlatform's parent TransformGroup. Examples of applications that modify a ViewPlatform's location and orientation include browsers, object viewers that provide navigational controls, applications that do architectural walkthroughs, and even search-and-destroy games.

Controlling the ViewPlatform object can produce very interesting and useful results. Our first simple scene graph (see Figure 1-2 on page 7) defines a scene graph for a simple application that draws an object in the center of a window and rotates that object about its center point. In that figure, the Behavior object modifies the TransformGroup directly above the Shape3D node.

An alternative application scene graph, shown in Figure 9-3, leaves the central object alone and moves the ViewPlatform around the world. If the shape node contains a model of the earth, this application could generate a view similar to that seen by astronauts as they orbit the earth.

Had we populated this world with more objects, this scene graph would allow navigation through the world via the Behavior node.

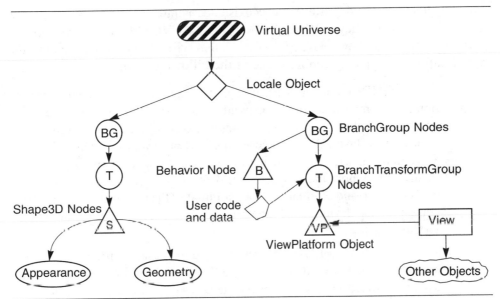

Figure 9-3   A Simple Scene Graph with View Control

Applications and behaviors manipulate a TransformGroup through its access methods. These methods (defined in Section 5.3, "TransformGroup Node") allow an application to retrieve and set the Group node's Transform3D object. Transform3D Node methods include `getTransform` and `setTransform`.

9.4.2   Dropping in on a Favorite Place

A scene graph may contain multiple ViewPlatform objects. If a user detaches a View object from a ViewPlatform and then reattaches that View to a different ViewPlatform, the image on the display will now be rendered from the point of view of the new ViewPlatform. For more information, see Section 9.7, "The View Object."

9.4.3   View Attach Policy

The actual view that Java 3D's renderer draws depends on the view attach policy specified within the currently attached ViewPlatform. The ViewPlatform defines the following methods for setting and retrieving the view attach policy:

Methods

```
public void setViewAttachPolicy(int policy)
public int getViewAttachPolicy()
```

These methods set and retrieve the coexistence center in virtual world policy. The default attach policy is View.NOMINAL_HEAD. A ViewPlatform's *view attach policy* determines how Java 3D places the virtual eyepoint within the ViewPlatform. The policy can have one of the following values:

- View.NOMINAL_HEAD: Ensures that the end user's nominal eye position in the physical world corresponds to the virtual eye's nominal eye position in the virtual world (the ViewPlatform's origin). In essence, this policy tells Java 3D to position the virtual eyepoint relative to the ViewPlatform origin in the same way as the physical eyepoint is positioned relative to its nominal physical-world origin. Deviations in the physical eye's position and orientation from nominal in the physical world generate corresponding deviations of the virtual eye's position and orientation in the virtual world.

- View.NOMINAL_FEET: Ensures that the end user's virtual feet always touch the virtual ground. This policy tells Java 3D to compute the physical-to-virtual-world correspondence in a way that enforces this constraint. Java 3D does so by appropriately offsetting the physical eye's position by the end user's physical height. Java 3D uses the nominalEyeHeightFrom-Ground parameter found in the PhysicalBody object (see Section 9.10, "The PhysicalBody Object") to perform this computation.

- View.NOMINAL_SCREEN: Allows an application always to have the virtual eyepoint appear at some "viewable" distance from a point of interest. This policy tells Java 3D to compute the physical-to-virtual-world correspondence in a way that ensures that the renderer moves the nominal virtual eyepoint away from the point of interest by the amount specified by the nominalEyeOffsetFromNominalScreen parameter found in the PhysicalBody object (see Section 9.10, "The PhysicalBody Object").

9.4.4 Associating Geometry with a ViewPlatform

Java 3D does not have any built-in semantics for displaying a visible manifestation of a ViewPlatform within the virtual world (an *avatar*). However, a developer can construct and manipulate an avatar using standard Java 3D constructs.

A developer can construct a small scene graph consisting of a TransformGroup node, a behavior leaf node, and a shape node and insert it directly under the BranchGroup node associated with the ViewPlatform object. The shape node would contain a geometric model of the avatar's head. The behavior node would change the TransformGroup's transform periodically to the value stored in a View object's `UserHeadToVworld` parameter (see Appendix C, "View Model Details"). The avatar's virtual head, represented by the shape node, will now move around in lock-step with the ViewPlatform's TransformGroup *and* any relative position and orientation changes of the user's actual physical head (if a system has a head tracker).

9.5 Generating a View

Java 3D generates viewing matrices in one of a few different ways, depending on whether the end user has a head-mounted or a room-mounted display environment and whether head tracking is enabled. This section describes the computation for a non-head-tracked, room-mounted display—a standard computer display. Other environments are described in Appendix C, "View Model Details."

In the absence of head tracking, the ViewPlatform's origin specifies the virtual eye's location and orientation within the virtual world. However, the eye location provides only part of the information needed to render an image. The renderer also needs a projection matrix. In the default mode, Java 3D uses the projection policy, the specified field-of-view information, and the front and back clipping distances to construct a viewing frustum.

9.5.1 Composing Model and Viewing Transformations

Figure 9-4 shows a simple scene graph. To draw the object labeled "S," Java 3D internally constructs the appropriate model, view platform, eye, and projection matrices. Conceptually, the model transformation for a particular object is computed by concatenating all the matrices in a direct path between the object and the VirtualUniverse. The view matrix is then computed—again, conceptually—by concatenating all the matrices between the VirtualUniverse object and the

ViewPlatform attached to the current View object. The eye and projection matrices are constructed from the View object and its associated component objects.

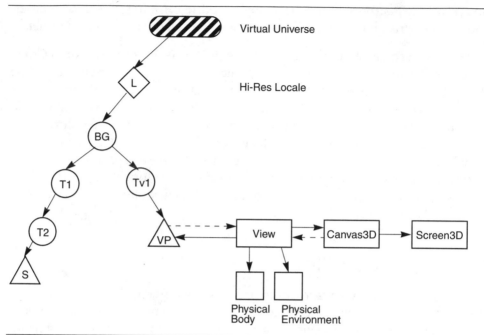

Figure 9-4   Object and ViewPlatform Transformations

In our scene graph, what we would normally consider the model transformation would consist of the following three transformations: $\mathbf{LT_1T_2}$. By multiplying $\mathbf{LT_1T_2}$ by a vertex in the shape object, we would transform that vertex into the virtual universe's coordinate system. What we would normally consider the view platform transformation would be $(\mathbf{LT_{v1}})^{-1}$ or $\mathbf{T_{v1}}^{-1}\mathbf{L}^{-1}$. This presents a problem since coordinates in the virtual universe are 256-bit fixed-point values, which cannot be used to represent transformed points efficiently.

Fortunately, however, there is a solution to this problem. Composing the model and view platform transformations gives us

$$\mathbf{T_{v1}}^{-1}\mathbf{L}^{-1}\mathbf{LT_1T_2} = \mathbf{T_{v1}}^{-1}\mathbf{IT_1T_2} = \mathbf{T_{v1}}^{-1}\mathbf{T_1T_2},$$

the matrix that takes vertices in an object's local coordinate system and places them in the ViewPlatform's coordinate system. Note that the high-resolution Locale transformations cancel each other out, which removes the need to actually transform points into high-resolution VirtualUniverse coordinates. The general formula of the matrix that transforms object coordinates to ViewPlatform coordinates is $\mathbf{T_{vn}}^{-1}\dots\mathbf{T_{v2}}^{-1}\mathbf{T_{v1}}^{-1}\mathbf{T_1T_2}\dots\mathbf{T_m}$.

As mentioned earlier, the View object contains the remainder of the view information, specifically, the eye matrix, $\mathbf{E}$, that takes points in the ViewPlatform's local coordinate system and translates them into the user's eye coordinate system, and the projection matrix, $\mathbf{P}$, that projects objects in the eye's coordinate system into clipping coordinates. The final concatenation of matrices for rendering our shape object "S" on the specified Canvas3D is $\mathbf{PET}_{v1}^{-1}\mathbf{T}_1\mathbf{T}_2$. In general this is $\mathbf{PET}_{vn}^{-1}...\mathbf{T}_{v2}^{-1}\mathbf{T}_{v1}^{-1}\mathbf{T}_1\mathbf{T}_2...\mathbf{T}_m$.

The details of how Java 3D constructs the matrices $\mathbf{E}$ and $\mathbf{P}$ in different end-user configurations are described in Appendix C, "View Model Details."

9.5.2 Multiple Locales

Java 3D supports multiple high-resolution Locales. In some cases, these Locales are close enough to each other that they can "see" each other, meaning that objects can be rendered even though they are not in the same Locale as the ViewPlatform object that is attached to the View. Java 3D automatically handles this case without the application having to do anything. As in the previous example, where the ViewPlatform and the object being rendered are attached to the same Locale, Java 3D internally constructs the appropriate matrices for cases in which the ViewPlatform and the object being rendered are *not* attached to the same Locale.

Let's take two Locales, L_1 and L_2, with the View attached to a ViewPlatform in L_1. According to our general formula, the modeling transformation—the transformation that takes points in object coordinates and transforms them into VirtualUniverse coordinates—is $\mathbf{LT}_1\mathbf{T}_2...\mathbf{T}_m$. In our specific example, a point in Locale L_2 would be transformed into VirtualUniverse coordinates by $\mathbf{L}_2\mathbf{T}_1\mathbf{T}_2...\mathbf{T}_m$. The view platform transformation would be $(\mathbf{L}_1\mathbf{T}_{v1}\mathbf{T}_{v1}...\mathbf{T}_{vn})^{-1}$ or $\mathbf{T}_{vn}^{-1}...\mathbf{T}_{v2}^{-1}\mathbf{T}_{v1}^{-1}\mathbf{L}_1^{-1}$. Composing these two matrices gives us

$$\mathbf{T}_{vn}^{-1}...\mathbf{T}_{v2}^{-1}\mathbf{T}_{v1}^{-1}\mathbf{L}_1^{-1}\mathbf{L}_2\mathbf{T}_1\mathbf{T}_2...\mathbf{T}_m.$$

Thus, to render objects in another Locale, it is sufficient to compute $\mathbf{L}_1^{-1}\mathbf{L}_2$ and use that as the starting matrix when composing the model transformations. Given that a Locale is represented by a single high-resolution coordinate position, the transformation $\mathbf{L}_1^{-1}\mathbf{L}_2$ is a simple translation by $\mathbf{L}_2 - \mathbf{L}_1$. Again, it is not actually necessary to transform points into high-resolution VirtualUniverse coordinates.

In general, Locales that are close enough that the difference in their high-resolution coordinates can be represented in double precision by a noninfinite value are close enough to be rendered. In practice, more sophisticated culling techniques can be used to render only those Locales that really are "close enough."

9.6   A Minimal Environment

An application must create a minimal set of Java 3D objects before Java 3D can render to a display device. In addition to a Canvas3D object, the application must create a View object, with its associated PhysicalBody and PhysicalEnvironment objects, and the following scene graph elements:

- A VirtualUniverse object
- A high-resolution Locale object
- A BranchGroup node object
- A TransformGroup node object with associated transform
- A ViewPlatform leaf node object that defines the position and orientation within the virtual universe for generating views

9.7   The View Object

The View object coordinates all aspects of the rendering process. It contains all the parameters or references to objects containing the parameters that determine how to render images to the windows represented by its Canvas3D objects. It also contains the set of canvases that represent various "windows" onto a view.

Java 3D allows applications to specify multiple simultaneously active View objects, each controlling its own set of canvases. For more details on a View object's internals, see Section C.5, "The View Object."

Constructors

The View object specifies the following constructor:

```
public View()
```

Constructs and initializes a new View object with the following default parameters:

Parameter	Default Value
view policy	SCREEN_VIEW
projection policy	PERSPECTIVE_PROJECTION
screen scale policy	SCALE_SCREEN_SIZE
window resize policy	PHYSICAL_WORLD
window movement policy	PHYSICAL_WORLD
window eyepoint policy	RELATIVE_TO_FIELD_OF_VIEW

Parameter	Default Value
monoscopic view policy (deprecated in this class)	CYCLOPEAN_EYE_VIEW
front clip policy	PHYSICAL_EYE
back clip policy	PHYSICAL_EYE
visibility policy	VISIBILITY_DRAW_VISIBLE
coexistence centering flag	true
compatibility mode	false
left projection	identity
right projection	identity
vpc to ec transform	identity
physical body	null
physical environment	null
screen scale	1.0
field of view	$\pi/4$
left manual eye in coexistence	(-0.033, 0.0, 0.4572)
right manual eye in coexistence	(0.033, 0.0, 0.4572)
front clip distance	0.1
back clip distance	10.0
tracking enable	false
user head to vworld enable	false
list of Canvas3D objects	empty
depth buffer freeze transparent	true
scene antialiasing	false
local eye lighting	false
view platform	null
behavior scheduler running	true
view running	true
minimum frame duration	0

Methods

The View object specifies the following methods:

```
public void setPhysicalBody(PhysicalBody physicalBody)
public PhysicalBody getPhysicalBody()
```

These methods set and retrieve the View's PhysicalBody object. See Section 9.10, "The PhysicalBody Object," for more information on the Physical-Body object.

```
public void setPhysicalEnvironment(PhysicalEnvironment
        physicalEnvironment)
public PhysicalEnvironment getPhysicalEnvironment()
```

These methods set and retrieve the View's PhysicalEnvironment object. See Section 9.11, "The PhysicalEnvironment Object," for more information on the PhysicalEnvironment object.

```
public void attachViewPlatform(ViewPlatform vp)
```

This method attaches a ViewPlatform leaf node to this View, replacing the existing ViewPlatform. If the ViewPlatform is part of a live scene graph, or is subsequently made live, the scene graph is rendered into all canvases in this View object's list of Canvas3D objects. To remove a ViewPlatform without attaching a new one—causing the View to no longer be rendered—a null reference may be passed to this method. In this case, the behavior is as if rendering were simultaneously stopped on all canvases attached to the View—the last frame that was rendered in each remains visible until the View is again attached to a live ViewPlatform object. See Section 6.11, "ViewPlatform Node," for more information on ViewPlatform objects.

```
public ViewPlatform getViewPlatform()
```

This method retrieves the currently attached ViewPlatform object.

```
public Canvas3D getCanvas3D(int index)
public void setCanvas3D(Canvas3D canvas3D, int index)
public void addCanvas3D(Canvas3D canvas3D)
public void insertCanvas3D(Canvas3D canvas3D, int index)
public void removeCanvas3D(int index)
public void removeCanvas3D(Canvas3D canvas3D)
```

These methods set, retrieve, add to, insert after, and remove a Canvas3D object from this View. The index specifies the reference to the Canvas3D object within the View object. See Section 9.9, "The Canvas3D Object" for more information on Canvas3D objects.

```
public int numCanvas3Ds()
```
                                                                                    ◀ New in 1.2 ▶

This method returns the the number of Canvas3Ds in this View.

```
public Enumeration getAllCanvas3Ds()
```

This method gets the Enumeration object of all the Canvas3Ds.

9.7.1   Projection Policy

The projection policy informs Java 3D whether it should generate a parallel projection or a perspective projection. This policy is attached to the Java 3D View object.

Methods

```
public void setProjectionPolicy(int policy)
public int getProjectionPolicy()
```

These two methods set and retrieve the current projection policy for this view. The projection policies are as follows:

- PARALLEL_PROJECTION: Specifies that Java 3D should compute a parallel projection.

- PERSPECTIVE PROJECTION: Specifies that Java 3D should compute a perspective projection. This is the default setting.

```
public void setLocalEyeLightingEnable(boolean flag)
public boolean getLocalEyeLightingEnable()
```

These methods set and retrieve the local eye lighting flag, which indicates whether the local eyepoint is used in lighting calculations for perspective projections. If this flag is set to true, the view vector is calculated per vertex based on the direction from the actual eyepoint to the vertex. If this flag is set to false, a single view vector is computed from the eyepoint to the center of the view frustum. This is called *infinite eye lighting*. Local eye lighting is disabled by default and is ignored for parallel projections.

9.7.1.1   Window Sizing and Movement

When users resize or move windows, Java 3D can choose to think of the window as attached either to the physical world or to the virtual world. The *window resize policy* allows an application to specify how the view model will handle resizing requests. The window resize policies are specified by two constants.

Constants

public static final int PHYSICAL_WORLD

This variable specifies the policy for resizing and moving windows and is used in specifying `windowResizePolicy` and `windowMovementPolicy`. This variable specifies that the specified action takes place only in the physical world.

public static final int VIRTUAL_WORLD

This variable specifies that Java 3D applies the associated policy in the virtual world.

Methods

public void setWindowResizePolicy(int policy)
public int getWindowResizePolicy()

This variable specifies how Java 3D modifies the view when a user resizes a window. A value of PHYSICAL_WORLD states that Java 3D will treat window resizing operations as happening *only* in the physical world. This implies that rendered objects continue to fill the same percentage of the newly sized window, using more or fewer pixels to draw those objects, depending on whether the window grew or shrank in size. A value of VIRTUAL_WORLD states that Java 3D will treat window resizing operations as also happening in the virtual world whenever a resizing occurs in the physical world. This implies that rendered objects remain the same size (use the same number of pixels), but since the window becomes larger or smaller, the user sees more or less of the virtual world. The default value is PHYSICAL_WORLD.

public void setWindowMovementPolicy(int policy)
public int getWindowMovementPolicy()

This variable specifies what part of the virtual world Java 3D will draw as a function of the window location on the display screen. A value of PHYSICAL_WORLD states that the window acts as if it moves *only* on the physical screen. As the user moves the window on the screen, the window's position on the screen changes, but Java 3D continues to draw exactly the same image within that window. A value of VIRTUAL_WORLD states that the window acts as if it also moves within the virtual world. As the user moves the window on the physical screen, the window's position on the screen changes, and the image that Java 3D draws changes as well to match what would be visible in the virtual world from a window in that new position. The default value is PHYSICAL_WORLD.

9.7.2   Clip Policies

The clip policies determine how Java 3D interprets clipping distances to both the near and far clip planes. The policies can contain one of four values specifying whether a distance measurement should be interpreted in the physical or the virtual world and whether that distance measurement should be interpreted relative to the physical eyepoint or the physical screen.

Methods

```
public void setFrontClipPolicy(int policy)
public int getFrontClipPolicy()
public void setBackClipPolicy(int policy)
public int getBackClipPolicy()
```

The *front clip policy* determines where Java 3D places the front clipping plane. The value is one of the following: PHYSICAL_EYE, PHYSICAL_SCREEN, VIRTUAL_EYE, or VIRTUAL_SCREEN. The default value is PHYSICAL_EYE.

The *back clip policy* determines where Java 3D places the back clipping plane. The value is one of the following: PHYSICAL_EYE, PHYSICAL_SCREEN, VIRTUAL_EYE, or VIRTUAL_SCREEN. The default value is PHYSICAL_EYE.

These policies are defined as follows.

- PHYSICAL_EYE: Specifies that the plane is located relative to the eye's position as measured in the physical space (in meters).

- PHYSICAL_SCREEN: Specifies that the plane is located relative to the screen (that is, the image plate) as measured in physical space (in meters).

- VIRTUAL_EYE: Specifies that the plane is located relative to the virtual eyepoint as measured in virtual world coordinates.

- VIRTUAL_SCREEN: Specifies that the plane is located relative to the screen (that is, the image plate) as measured in virtual world coordinates.

9.7.3   Projection and Clip Parameters

The projection and clip parameters determine the view model's field of view and the front and back clipping distances.

```
public void setFieldOfView(double fieldOfView)
public double getFieldOfView()
```

In the default non-head-tracked mode, this value specifies the view model's horizontal field of view in radians. This value is ignored when the view model is operating in head-tracked mode or when the Canvas3D's window eyepoint policy is set to a value other than the default setting of RELATIVE_TO_FIELD_OF_VIEW (see Section C.5.3, "Window Eyepoint Policy").

```
public void setFrontClipDistance(double distance)
public double getFrontClipDistance()
```

This value specifies the distance away from the clip origin, specified by the front clip policy variable, in the direction of gaze where objects stop disappearing. Objects closer than the clip origin (eye or screen) plus the front clip distance are not drawn. Measurements are done in the space (physical or virtual) that is specified by the associated front clip policy parameter.

```
public void setBackClipDistance(double distance)
public double getBackClipDistance()
```

This value specifies the distance away from the clip origin (specified by the back clip policy variable) in the direction of gaze where objects begin disappearing. Objects farther away from the clip origin (eye or screen) plus the back clip distance are not drawn. Measurements are done in the space (physical or virtual) that is specified by the associated back clip policy parameter. The View object's back clip distance is ignored if the scene graph contains an active Clip leaf node (see Section 6.5, "Clip Node").

There are several considerations that need to be taken into account when choosing values for the front and back clip distances.

- The front clip distance must be greater than 0.0 in physical eye coordinates.

- The front clipping plane must be in front of the back clipping plane; that is, the front clip distance must be less than the back clip distance in physical eye coordinates.

- The front and back clip distances, in physical eye coordinates, must be less than the largest positive single-precision floating-point value, Float.MAX_VALUE. In practice, since these physical eye coordinate distances are in meters, the values should be *much* less than that.

- The ratio of the back distance divided by the front distance, in physical eye coordinates, affects *z*-buffer precision. This ratio should be less than about

3000 to accommodate 16-bit z-buffers. Values of 100 to less than 1000 will produce better results.

Violating any of the above rules will result in undefined behavior. In many cases, no picture will be drawn.

9.7.4   Frame Start Time, Duration, and Number

The following methods are used to get information about system execution and performance:

`public long getCurrentFrameStartTime()`

This method returns the time at which the most recent rendering frame started. It is defined as the number of milliseconds since January 1, 1970, 00:00:00 GMT. Since multiple canvases might be attached to this View, the start of a frame is defined as the point just prior to clearing any canvas attached to this View.

`public long getLastFrameDuration()`

This method returns the duration, in milliseconds, of the most recently completed rendering frame. The time taken to render all canvases attached to this View is measured. This duration is computed as the difference between the start of the most recently completed frame and the end of that frame. Since multiple canvases might be attached to this View, the start of a frame is defined as the point just prior to clearing any canvas attached to this View, while the end of a frame is defined as the point just after swapping the buffer for all canvases.

`public long getFrameNumber()`

This method returns the frame number for this view. The frame number starts at 0 and is incremented prior to clearing all the canvases attached to this view.

`public static int getMaxFrameStartTimes()`

This method retrieves the implementation-dependent maximum number of frames whose start times will be recorded by the system. This value is guaranteed to be at least 10 for all implementations of the Java 3D API.

`public long getFrameStartTimes(long times[])`

This method copies the last k frame start-time values into the user-specified array. The most recent frame start time is copied to location 0 of the array, the next most recent frame start time is copied into location 1 of the array, and so on. If `times.length` is smaller than `maxFrameStartTimes`, only the last `times.length` values are copied. If `times.length` is greater than `maxFrame-StartTimes`, all array elements after index `maxFrameStartTimes − 1` are set to 0.

◀ New in 1.2 ▶ `public void setMinimumFrameCycleTime(long duration)`
◀ New in 1.2 ▶ `public long getMinimumFrameCycleTime()`

These methods set and retrieve the minimum frame cycle time, in milliseconds, for this view. The Java 3D renderer will ensure that the duration between each frame is at least the specified number of milliseconds. The default value is 0.

9.7.5   View Traversal and Behavior Scheduling

The following methods control the traversal, the rendering, and the execution of the behavior scheduler for this view:

```
public final long[] stopBehaviorScheduler()
public final void startBehaviorScheduler()
public final boolean isBehaviorSchedulerRunning()
```

The first method stops the behavior scheduler after all currently scheduled behaviors are executed. Any frame-based behaviors scheduled to wake up on the next frame will be executed at least once before the behavior scheduler is stopped. The method returns a pair of integers that specify the beginning and ending time (in milliseconds since January 1, 1970, 00:00:00 GMT) of the behavior scheduler's last pass. The second method starts the behavior scheduler running after it has been stopped. The third method retrieves a flag that indicates whether the behavior scheduler is currently running.

```
public final void stopView()
public final void startView()
public final boolean isViewRunning()
```

The first method stops traversing this view after the current state of the scene graph is reflected on all canvases attached to this view. The renderers associated with these canvases are also stopped. The second method starts traversing this view and starts the renderers associated with all canvases attached to this view. The third method returns a flag indicating whether the traverser is currently running on this view.

Note: The above six methods are heavy-weight methods intended for verification and image capture (recording). They are not intended to be used for flow control.

---

public void renderOnce()   ◀ New in 1.2 ▶

This method renders one frame for a stopped View. Functionally, this method is equivalent to startView() followed by stopview(), except that it is atomic, which guarantees that only one frame is rendered.

public void repaint()   ◀ New in 1.2 ▶

This method requests that this View be scheduled for rendering as soon as possible. The repaint method may return before the frame has been rendered. If the view is stopped or if the view is continuously running (for example, due to a free-running interpolator), this method will have no effect. Most applications will not need to call this method, since any update to the scene graph or to viewing parameters will automatically cause all affected views to be rendered.

9.7.6   Scene Antialiasing

```
public void setSceneAntialiasingEnable(boolean flag)
public boolean getSceneAntialiasingEnable()
```

These methods set and retrieve the scene antialiasing flag. Scene antialiasing is either enabled or disabled for this view. If enabled, the entire scene will be antialiased on each canvas in which scene antialiasing is available. Scene antialiasing is disabled by default.

Note: Line and point antialiasing are independent of scene antialiasing. If antialiasing is enabled for lines and points, the lines and points will be antialiased prior to scene antialiasing.

9.7.7   Depth Buffer

```
public void setDepthBufferFreezeTransparent(boolean flag)
public boolean getDepthBufferFreezeTransparent()
```

The set method enables or disables automatic freezing of the depth buffer for objects rendered during the transparent rendering pass (that is, objects rendered using alpha blending) for this view. If enabled, depth buffer writes are disabled during the transparent rendering pass regardless of the value of the depth-buffer-write-enable flag in the RenderingAttributes object for a particular node. This flag is enabled by default. The get method retrieves this flag.

9.8   The Screen3D Object

The Screen3D object provides a 3D version of the AWT screen object. It contains the screen's physical properties. Java 3D will support multiple active Screen3D objects as soon as AWT support is available. Of course, multiple screens are available only if the machine configuration has multiple output screens. Java 3D primarily needs to know the physical size (in meters) of the Screen3D's visible, addressable raster (the *image plate*) and, in head-tracking mode, the position and orientation of this raster relative to a well-defined physical world coordinate system, specifically, the tracker base coordinate system. Java 3D also needs to know how many pixels the raster can display in both the x and y dimensions. This information allows Java 3D to calculate a pixel's physical dimension.

Calibration utilities can change a Screen3D's physical characteristics or calibration transforms. See Section C.6, "The Screen3D Object."

The Screen3D object has no public constructors. Instead, the Screen3D object associated with a particular Canvas3D object can be obtained from the canvas by calling the `getScreen3D` method. See Section 9.9.3, "Other Canvas3D Parameters."

Default values for Screen3D parameters are as follows:

Parameter	Default Value
physical screen width	0.0254/90.0 * screen width (in pixels)
physical screen height	0.0254/90.0 * screen height (in pixels)
tracker base to image plate transform	identity
head tracker to left image plate transform	identity
head tracker to right image plate transform	identity
off-screen size	(0,0)

Methods

These methods provide applications with information concerning the underlying display hardware, such as the screen's width and height in pixels or in meters.

```
public Dimension getSize()
public Dimension getSize(Dimension rv)
```
◀ New in 1.2 ▶

These methods retrieve the width and height (in pixels) of this Screen3D. The second method copies the width and height into the specified Dimension object.

```
public double getPhysicalScreenWidth()
public double getPhysicalScreenHeight()
```

These methods retrieve the screen's (image plate's) physical width and height in meters.

9.8.1   Off-Screen Rendering

New for Java 3D 1.2 is an off-screen mode that allows rendering to a memory image, which is possibly larger than the screen.

```
public void setSize(int width, int height)                    ◀ New in 1.2 ▶
public void setSize(Dimension d)                              ◀ New in 1.2 ▶
```

These methods set the width and height (in pixels) of this off-screen Screen3D. The default size for off-screen Screen3D objects is (0,0).

Note: The off-screen size, physical width, and physical height must be set prior to rendering to the associated off-screen canvas. Failure to do so will result in an exception.

9.9   The Canvas3D Object

The Canvas3D object extends the `java.awt.Canvas` object to include 3D-related information such as the size of the canvas in pixels, the Canvas3D's location (also in pixels) within a Screen3D object, and whether or not the canvas has stereo enabled. The Canvas3D class is used either for on-screen rendering or for off-screen rendering. Because all Canvas3D objects contain a reference to a Screen3D object and because Screen3D objects define the size of a pixel in physical units, Java 3D can convert a Canvas3D size in pixels to a physical world size in meters. It can also determine the Canvas3D's position and orientation in the physical world.

The Canvas3D class is used either for on-screen rendering or for off-screen rendering. On-screen Canvas3Ds are added to AWT or Swing Container objects like any other canvas. Java 3D automatically and continuously renders to all on-screen canvases that are attached to an active View object. On-screen Canvas3Ds can be either single or double buffered and they can be either stereo or monoscopic.

Off-screen Canvas3Ds must not be added to any Container. Java 3D renders to off-screen canvases in response to the `renderOffScreenBuffer` method (see Section 9.9.2, "Off-Screen Rendering"). Off-screen Canvas3Ds are single buffered. However, on many systems, the actual rendering is done to an off-screen hardware buffer or to a 3D library-specific buffer and copied only to the off-screen buffer of the Canvas when the rendering is complete, at "buffer swap" time. Off-screen Canvas3Ds are monoscopic.

Constructors

The Canvas3D object specifies the following constructors:

public Canvas3D(GraphicsConfiguration graphicsConfiguration)

This constructs and initializes a new Canvas3D object that Java 3D can render into. The following Canvas3D parameters are initialized to default values as shown:

Parameter	Default Value
left manual eye in image plate	(0.142, 0.135, 0.4572)
right manual eye in image plate	(0.208, 0.135, 0.4572)
stereo enable	true
double buffer enable	true
monoscopic view policy	View.CYCLOPEAN_EYE_VIEW
off-screen mode	false
off-screen buffer	null
off-screen location	(0,0)

◀ New in 1.2 ▶ **public Canvas3D(GraphicsConfiguration graphicsConfiguration,
                boolean offScreen)**

This constructs and initializes a new Canvas3D object that Java 3D can render into.

Java 3D can render into this Canvas3D object. If the `graphicsConfiguration` argument is `null`, a GraphicsConfiguration object will be constructed using the default GraphicsConfigTemplate3D (see Section 9.9.4, "GraphicsConfigTemplate3D Object").

For more information on the GraphicsConfiguration object, see the Java 2D specification, which is part of the AWT in JDK 1.2.

9.9.1   Window System–Provided Parameters

Java 3D specifies the size of a Canvas3D in pixels. It extracts this information directly from the AWT's window system. Java 3D allows applications only to access these values, not to change them.

```
public Dimension getLocationOnScreen()
public Dimension getSize()
```

These methods, inherited from the parent Canvas class, retrieve the Canvas3D's screen position and size in pixels.

9.9.2   Off-Screen Rendering

New for Java 3D 1.2 is an off-screen mode that allows rendering to a memory image, which is possibly larger than the screen.

```
public boolean isOffScreen()
```
◀ New in 1.2 ▶

This method retrieves the state of the renderer for this Canvas3D object.

```
public void setOffScreenBuffer(ImageComponent2D buffer)
public ImageComponent2D getOffScreenBuffer()
```
◀ New in 1.2 ▶
◀ New in 1.2 ▶

The first method sets the off-screen buffer for this Canvas3D. The specified image is written into by the Java 3D renderer. The size of the specified Image-Component determines the size, in pixels, of this Canvas3D—the size inherited from Component is ignored. The second method retrieves the off-screen buffer for this Canvas3D.

Note: The size, physical width, and physical height of the associated Screen3D must be set explicitly prior to rendering. Failure to do so will result in an exception.

```
public void renderOffScreenBuffer()
```
◀ New in 1.2 ▶

This method schedules the rendering of a frame into this Canvas3D's off-screen buffer. The rendering is done from the point of view of the View object to which this Canvas3D has been added. No rendering is performed if this Canvas3D object has not been added to an active View. This method does not wait for the rendering to actually happen. An application that wishes to know when the rendering is complete must either subclass Canvas3D and override the postSwap method or call waitForOffScreenRendering. An IllegalStateException is thrown if this Canvas3D is not in off-screen mode, if either the width or the height of the associated Screen3D's size is ≤ 0, or if the associated Screen3D's physical width or height is ≤ 0.

◀ New in 1.2 ▶ `public void waitForOffScreenRendering()`

This method waits for this Canvas3D's off-screen rendering to be done. This method will wait until the `postSwap` method of this off-screen Canvas3D has completed. If this Canvas3D has not been added to an active view or if the renderer is stopped for this Canvas3D, this method will return immediately. This method must not be called from a render callback method of an off-screen Canvas3D.

◀ New in 1.2 ▶ `public void setOffScreenLocation(int x, int y)`
◀ New in 1.2 ▶ `public void setOffScreenLocation(Point p)`

These methods set the location of this off-screen Canvas3D. The location is the upper-left corner of the Canvas3D relative to the upper-left corner of the corresponding off-screen Screen3D. The function of these methods is similar to that of `Component.setLocation` for on-screen Canvas3D objects. The default location is (0,0).

◀ New in 1.2 ▶ `public Point getOffScreenLocation()`
◀ New in 1.2 ▶ `public Point getOffScreenLocation(Point rv)`

These methods retrieve the location of this off-screen Canvas3D. The location is the upper-left corner of the Canvas3D relative to the upper-left corner of the corresponding off-screen Screen3D. The function of these methods is similar to that of `Component.getLocation` for on-screen Canvas3D objects. The second method stores the location in the specified Point object. This method is useful if the caller wants to avoid allocating a new Point object on the heap.

9.9.3 Other Canvas3D Parameters

`public boolean getStereoAvailable()`

This method specifies whether the underlying hardware supports field-sequential stereo on this canvas. This is equivalent to

```
((Boolean)queryProperties().get("stereoAvailable")).
    booleanValue()
```

```
public boolean getStereoEnable()
public void setStereoEnable(boolean flag)
```

These methods set or retrieve the flag indicating whether this Canvas3D has stereo enabled. If enabled, Java 3D generates left and right eye images. If the Canvas3D's StereoAvailable flag is false, Java 3D displays only the *left* eye's view even if an application sets StereoEnable to true. This parameter allows applications to enable or disable stereo on a canvas-by-canvas basis.

```
public void getDoubleBufferAvailable()
```

This method specifies whether the underlying hardware supports double buffering on this canvas. This is equivalent to

```
((Boolean)queryProperties().get("doubleBufferAvailable")).
    booleanValue()
```

```
public boolean getDoubleBufferEnable()
public void setDoubleBufferEnable(boolean flag)
```

These methods set or retrieve the flag indicating whether this Canvas3D has double buffering enabled. If disabled, all drawing is to the front buffer, and no buffer swap will be done between frames. It should be stressed that running Java 3D with double buffering disabled is not recommended.

```
public boolean getSceneAntialiasingAvailable()
```

This method specifies whether the underlying hardware supports scene-level antialiasing on this canvas. This is equivalent to

```
((Boolean)queryProperties().get("sceneAntialiasingAvailable")).
    booleanValue()
```

```
public View getView()
```

Retrieves the View object that points to this Canvas3D.

```
public Screen3D getScreen3D()
```

Retrieves the Screen3D object to which this Canvas3D is attached.

```
public final Map queryProperties()
```
◀ New in 1.2 ▶

This method returns a read-only Map object containing key-value pairs that define various properties for this Canvas3D. All of the keys are String objects. The values are key-specific, but most will be Boolean, Integer, Double, or String objects. The currently-defined keys are

Key (String)	Value Type	Description
doubleBufferAvailable	Boolean	A Boolean indicating whether double buffering is available for this Canvas3D. This is equivalent to the `getDoubleBufferAvailable` method. If this flag is false, the Canvas3D will be rendered in single buffer mode; requests to enable double buffering will be ignored.
stereoAvailable	Boolean	A Boolean indicating whether stereo is available for this Canvas3D. This is equivalent to the `getStereoAvailable` method. If this flag is false, the Canvas3D will be rendered in monoscopic mode; requests to enable stereo will be ignored.
sceneAntialiasingAvailable	Boolean	A Boolean indicating whether scene antialiasing is available for this Canvas3D. This is equivalent to the `getSceneAntialiasingAvailable` method. If this flag is false, requests to enable scene antialiasing will be ignored.
texture3DAvailable	Boolean	A Boolean indicating whether 3D Texture mapping is available for this Canvas3D. If this flag is false, 3D texture mapping is either not supported by the underlying rendering layer or is otherwise unavailable for this particular Canvas3D. All use of 3D texture mapping will be ignored in this case.
textureColorTableSize	Integer	An Integer indicating the maximum size of the texture color table for this Canvas3D. If the size is 0, the texture color table either is not supported by the underlying rendering layer or is otherwise unavailable for this particular Canvas3D. An attempt to use a texture color table larger than `textureColorTableSize` will be ignored; no color lookup will be performed.
compressedGeometry.majorVersionNumber	Integer	An Integer indicating the major version number of the version of compressed geometry supported by this version of Java 3D.
compressedGeometry.minorVersionNumber	Integer	An Integer indicating the minor version number of the version of compressed geometry supported by this version of Java 3D.
compressedGeometry.minorMinorVersionNumber	Integer	An Integer indicating the minor-minor version number of the version of compressed geometry supported by this version of Java 3D.

9.9.4   GraphicsConfigTemplate3D Object

This GraphicsConfigTemplate3D class is used to obtain a valid GraphicsConfiguration that can be used by Java 3D. A user instantiates one of these objects and then sets all nondefault attributes as desired. The `getGraphicsConfiguration` method found in the `java.awt.GraphicsDevice` class is then called with this GraphicsConfigTemplate. A valid GraphicsConfiguration that meets or exceeds what was requested in the `java.awt.GraphicsConfigTemplate` is returned.

Constructors

public GraphicsConfigTemplate3D()

This constructor constructs a new GraphicsConfigTemplate3D and sets all values to their default:

Parameter	Default Value
doubleBuffer	REQUIRED
stereo	UNNECESSARY
sceneAntialiasing	UNNECESSARY
depthSize	16
redSize	2
greenSize	2
blueSize	2

Methods

public void setDoubleBuffer(int value)
public int getDoubleBuffer()

These methods set and retrieve the double-buffering attribute. The valid values are REQUIRED, PREFERRED, and UNNECESSARY.

public void setStereo(int value)
public int getStereo()

These methods set and retrieve the stereo attribute. The valid values are REQUIRED, PREFERRED, and UNNECESSARY.

public void setSceneAntialiasing(int value)
public int getSceneAntialiasing()

These methods set and retrieve the scene antialiasing attribute. The valid values are REQUIRED, PREFERRED, and UNNECESSARY.

```
public void setDepthSize(int value)
public int getDepthSize()
```

These methods set and retrieve the depth buffer size requirement.

```
public void setRedSize(int value)
public int getRedSize()
public void setGreenSize(int value)
public int getGreenSize()
public void setBlueSize(int value)
public int getBlueSize()
```

These methods set and retrieve the number of red, green, and blue bits requested by this template.

```
public java.awt.GraphicsConfiguration
       getBestConfiguration(java.awt.GraphicsConfiguration[] gc)
```

This method returns the "best" possible configuration that passes the criteria defined in the GraphicsConfigTemplate3D.

```
public boolean
       isGraphicsConfigSupported(java.awt.GraphicsConfiguration
       gc)
```

This method returns a boolean indicating whether the given GraphicsConfiguration can be used to create a drawing surface that can be rendered to. This method returns true if this GraphicsConfiguration object can be used to create surfaces that can be rendered to, false if the GraphicsConfiguration cannot be used to create a drawing surface usable by this API.

9.10 The PhysicalBody Object

Java 3D defines a PhysicalBody object that contains information concerning the end user's physical characteristics. The head parameters allow end users to specify their own head's characteristics, such as the location of the eyes and the interpupilary distance. See Section C.8, "The PhysicalBody Object," for details. The default values are sufficient for applications that are running in a non-head-tracked environment and do not manually set the eyepoint.

Constructors

```
public PhysicalBody()
```

This constructor constructs and initializes a default PhysicalBody object.

9.11 The PhysicalEnvironment Object

The PhysicalEnvironment object defines several methods that are described in Section C.9, "The PhysicalEnvironment Object." The default values are sufficient for applications that do not use continuous input devices that are run in a non-head-tracked display environment.

Constructors

`public PhysicalEnvironment()`

Constructs and initializes a default PhysicalEnvironment object.

CHAPTER 10

Behaviors and Interpolators

BEHAVIOR nodes provide the means for animating objects, processing keyboard and mouse inputs, reacting to movement, and enabling and processing pick events. Behavior nodes contain Java code and state variables. A Behavior node's Java code can interact with Java objects, change node values within a Java 3D scene graph, change the behavior's internal state—in general, perform any computation it wishes.

Simple behaviors can add surprisingly interesting effects to a scene graph. For example, one can animate a rigid object by using a Behavior node to repetitively modify the TransformGroup node that points to the object one wishes to animate. Alternatively, a Behavior node can track the current position of a mouse and modify portions of the scene graph in response.

10.1 Behavior Object

A Behavior leaf node object contains a scheduling region and two methods: an `initialize` method called once when the behavior becomes "live" and a `processStimulus` method called whenever appropriate by the Java 3D behavior scheduler. The Behavior object also contains the state information needed by its `initialize` and `processStimulus` methods.

The **scheduling region** defines a spatial volume that serves to enable the scheduling of Behavior nodes. A Behavior node is *active* (can receive stimuli) whenever a ViewPlatform's activation volume intersects a Behavior object's scheduling region. Only active behaviors can receive stimuli.

The `initialize` method allows a Behavior object to initialize its internal state and specify its initial wakeup condition(s). Java 3D invokes a behavior's initialize code when the behavior's containing BranchGroup node is added to the virtual universe. Java 3D does not invoke the `initialize` method in a new thread.

Thus, for Java 3D to regain control, the `initialize` method must not execute an infinite loop: It must return. Furthermore, a wakeup condition must be set or else the behavior's `processStimulus` method is never executed.

The `processStimulus` method receives and processes a behavior's ongoing messages. The Java 3D behavior scheduler invokes a Behavior node's `processStimulus` method when a ViewPlatform's activation volume intersects a Behavior object's scheduling region and all of that behavior's wakeup criteria are satisfied. The `processStimulus` method performs its computations and actions (possibly including the registration of state change information that could cause Java 3D to wake other Behavior objects), establishes its next wakeup condition, and finally exits.

10.1.1   Code Structure

When the Java 3D behavior scheduler invokes a Behavior object's `processStimulus` method, that method may perform any computation it wishes. Usually, it will change its internal state and specify its new wakeup conditions. Most probably, it will manipulate scene graph elements. However, the behavior code can change only those aspects of a scene graph element permitted by the capabilities associated with that scene graph element. A scene graph's capabilities restrict behavioral manipulation to those manipulations explicitly allowed.

The application must provide the Behavior object with references to those scene graph elements that the Behavior object will manipulate. The application provides those references as arguments to the behavior's constructor when it creates the Behavior object. Alternatively, the Behavior object itself can obtain access to the relevant scene graph elements either when Java 3D invokes its `initialize` method or each time Java 3D invokes its `processStimulus` method.

Behavior methods have a very rigid structure. Java 3D assumes that they always run to completion (if needed, they can spawn threads). Each method's basic structure consists of the following:

- Code to decode and extract references from the WakeupCondition enumeration that caused the object's awakening.
- Code to perform the manipulations associated with the WakeupCondition.
- Code to establish this behavior's new WakeupCondition.
- A path to Exit (so that execution returns to the Java 3D behavior scheduler).

10.1.2   WakeupCondition Object

A WakeupCondition object is an abstract class specialized to fourteen different WakeupCriterion objects and to four combining objects containing multiple WakeupCriterion objects.

A Behavior node provides the Java 3D behavior scheduler with a WakeupCondition object. When that object's WakeupCondition has been satisfied, the behavior scheduler hands that same WakeupCondition back to the Behavior via an enumeration.

10.1.3   WakeupCriterion Object

Java 3D provides a rich set of wakeup criteria that Behavior objects can use in specifying a complex WakeupCondition. These wakeup criteria can cause Java 3D's behavior scheduler to invoke a behavior's `processStimulus` method whenever

- The center of a ViewPlatform enters a specified region.
- The center of a ViewPlatform exits a specified region.
- A behavior is activated.
- A behavior is deactivated.
- A specified TransformGroup node's transform changes.
- Collision is detected between a specified Shape3D node's Geometry object and any other object.
- Movement occurs between a specified Shape3D node's Geometry object and any other object with which it collides.
- A specified Shape3D node's Geometry object no longer collides with any other object.
- A specified Behavior object posts a specific event.
- A specified AWT event occurs.
- A specified time interval elapses.
- A specified number of frames have been drawn.
- The center of a specified Sensor enters a specified region.
- The center of a specified Sensor exits a specified region.

A Behavior object constructs a WakeupCriterion by constructing the appropriate criterion object. The Behavior object must provide the appropriate arguments (usually a reference to some scene graph object and possibly a region of interest). Thus,

269

to specify a WakeupOnViewPlatformEntry, a behavior would specify the region that will cause the behavior to execute if a ViewPlatform enters it.

10.1.4 Composing WakeupCriterion Objects

A Behavior object can combine multiple WakeupCriterion objects into a more powerful, composite WakeupCondition. Java 3D behaviors construct a composite WakeupCondition in one of the following ways:

- WakeupAnd: An array of WakeupCriterion objects ANDed together.

    ```
    WakeupCriterion && WakeupCriterion && ...
    ```

- WakeupOr: An array of WakeupCriterion objects ORed together.

    ```
    WakeupCriterion || WakeupCriterion || ...
    ```

- WakeupAndOfOrs: An array of WakeupOr WakeupCondition objects that are then ANDed together.

    ```
    WakeupOr && WakeupOr && ...
    ```

- WakeupOrOfAnds: An array of WakeupAnd WakeupCondition objects that are then ORed together.

    ```
    WakeupAnd || WakeupAnd || ...
    ```

10.2 Composing Behaviors

Behavior objects can condition themselves to awaken only when signaled by another Behavior node. The WakeupOnBehaviorPost WakeupCriterion takes as arguments a reference to a Behavior node and an integer. These two arguments allow a behavior to limit its wakeup criterion to a specific post by a specific behavior.

The WakeupOnBehaviorPost WakeupCriterion permits behaviors to chain their computations, allowing parenthetical computations—one behavior opens a door and the second closes the same door, or one behavior highlights an object and the second unhighlights the same object.

10.3 Scheduling

As a virtual universe grows large, Java 3D must carefully husband its resources to ensure adequate performance. In a 10,000-object virtual universe with 400 or so Behavior nodes, a naive implementation of Java 3D could easily end up consuming the majority of its compute cycles in executing the behaviors associated with the 400 Behavior objects before it draws a frame. In such a situation, the frame rate could easily drop to unacceptable levels.

Behavior objects are usually associated with geometric objects in the virtual universe. In our example of 400 Behavior objects scattered throughout a 10,000-object virtual universe, only a few of these associated geometric objects would be visible at a given time. A sizable fraction of the Behavior nodes—those associated with nonvisible objects—need not be executed. Only those relatively few Behavior objects that are associated with visible objects must be executed.

Java 3D mitigates the problem of a large number of Behavior nodes in a high-population virtual universe through execution culling—choosing to invoke only those behaviors that have high relevance.

Java 3D requires each behavior to have a *scheduling region* and to post a wakeup condition. Together a behavior's scheduling region and wakeup condition provide Java 3D's behavior scheduler with sufficient domain knowledge to selectively prune behavior invocations and invoke only those behaviors that absolutely need to be executed.

10.4 How Java 3D Performs Execution Culling

Java 3D finds all scheduling regions associated with Behavior nodes and constructs a scheduling/volume tree. It also creates an AND/OR tree containing all the Behavior node wakeup criteria. These two data structures provide the domain knowledge Java 3D needs to prune unneeded behavior execution (to perform "execution triage").

Java 3D must track a behavior's wakeup conditions only if a ViewPlatform object's activation volume intersects with that Behavior object's scheduling region. If the ViewPlatform object's activation volume does not intersect with a behavior's scheduling region, Java 3D can safely ignore that behavior's wakeup criteria.

In essence, the Java 3D scheduler performs the following checks:

- Find all Behavior objects with scheduling regions that intersect the ViewPlatform object's activation volume.

- For each Behavior object within the ViewPlatform's activation volume, if that behavior's WakeupCondition is `true`, schedule that Behavior object for execution.

Java 3D's behavior scheduler executes those Behavior objects that have been scheduled by calling the behavior's `processStimulus` method.

10.5 The Behavior API

The Java 3D behavior API spreads its functionality across three objects: the Behavior leaf node, the WakeupCondition object and its subclasses, and the WakeupCriterion objects.

10.5.1 The Behavior Node

The Behavior object is an abstract class that contains the framework for all behavioral components in Java 3D.

Constructor

The Behavior leaf node class defines the following constructor:

public Behavior()

Constructs a Behavior node with default parameters:

Parameter	Default Value
enable flag	true
schedulingBounds	null
schedulingBoundingLeafnull	

Methods

The Behavior leaf node class defines the following methods:

public abstract void initialize()

This method, invoked by Java 3D's behavior scheduler, is used to initialize the behavior's state variables and to establish its WakeupConditions. Classes that extend Behavior must provide their own `initialize` method. Applications should *not* call this method.

public abstract void processStimulus(Enumeration criteria)

This method processes stimuli destined for this behavior. The behavior scheduler invokes this method if its WakeupCondition is satisfied. Classes that extend

Behavior must provide their own `processStimulus` method. Applications should *not* call this method.

`public void setSchedulingBounds(Bounds region)`
`public Bounds getSchedulingBounds()`

These two methods access or modify the Behavior node's scheduling bounds. This bounds is used as the scheduling region when the scheduling bounding leaf is set to `null`. A behavior is scheduled for activation when its scheduling region intersects the ViewPlatform's activation volume (if its wakeup criteria have been satisfied). The `getSchedulingBounds` method returns a copy of the associated bounds.

`public void setSchedulingBoundingLeaf(BoundingLeaf region)`
`public BoundingLeaf getSchedulingBoundingLeaf()`

These two methods access or modify the Behavior node's scheduling bounding leaf. When set to a value other than `null`, this bounding leaf overrides the scheduling bounds object and is used as the scheduling region.

`protected void wakeupOn(WakeupCondition criteria)`

This method defines this behavior's wakeup criteria. This method may be called only from a Behavior object's `initialize` or `processStimulus` methods to (re)arm the next wakeup. It should be the last thing done by those methods.

`public void postId(int postId)`

This method, when invoked by a behavior, informs the Java 3D scheduler of the identified event. The scheduler will schedule other Behavior objects that have registered interest in this posting.

`protected View getView()`

This method returns the primary view associated with this behavior. This method is useful with certain types of behaviors, such as Billboard and LOD, that rely on per-View information and with behaviors in general in regards to scheduling (the distance from the view platform determines the active behaviors). The "primary" view is defined to be the first View attached to a live ViewPlatform, if there is more than one active View. So, for instance, Billboard behaviors would be oriented toward this primary view, in the case of multiple active views into the same scene graph.

10.5.2 WakeupCondition Object

WakeupCondition is an abstract class that is extended by the WakeupCriterion, WakeupOr, WakeupAnd, WakeupOrOfAnds, and WakeupAndOfOr classes. A Behavior node hands a WakeupCondition object to the behavior scheduler, and the behavior scheduler hands back an enumeration of that WakeupCondition.

Methods

The Java 3D API provides two methods for constructing WakeupCondition enumerations:

```
public Enumeration allElements()
public Enumeration triggeredElements()
```

These two methods create enumerators that sequentially access this WakeupCondition's wakeup criteria. The first method creates an enumerator that sequentially presents all wakeup criteria that were used to construct this WakeupCondition. The second method creates an enumerator that sequentially presents only those wakeup criteria that have been satisfied.

10.5.3 The WakeupCriterion Objects

WakeupCriterion is an abstract class that consists of several subclasses. Each subclass specifies one particular wakeup criterion, that criterion's associated arguments (if any), and either a flag that indicates whether this criterion caused a Behavior object to awaken or a return field containing the information that caused the Behavior object to awaken.

Methods

```
public boolean hasTriggered()
```

This predicate method returns `true` if this WakeupCriterion contributed to waking a Behavior object.

10.5.3.1 WakeupOnAWTEvent

This WakeupCriterion object specifies that Java 3D should awaken a behavior when the specified AWT event occurs.

Constructors

```
public WakeupOnAWTEvent(int AWTId)
public WakeupOnAWTEvent(long eventMask)
```

The first constructor creates a WakeupOnAWTEvent object that informs the Java 3D scheduler to wake up the specified Behavior object whenever the AWT event specified by AWTId occurs. The second constructor creates a WakeupOnAWTEvent object that informs the Java 3D scheduler to wake up the specified Behavior object whenever any of the specified AWT EVENT_MASK events occur. The eventMask consists of an ORed collection of EVENT_MASK values.

Methods

```
public AWTEvent[] getAWTEvent()
```

This method returns the array of consecutive AWT events that triggered this WakeupCriterion to awaken the Behavior object. The Behavior object can retrieve the AWTEvent array and process it in any way it wishes.

10.5.3.2 WakeupOnActivation

The WakeupOnActivation object specifies a wakeup the first time the ViewPlatform's activation region intersects with this object's scheduling region. This gives the behavior an explicit means of executing code when it is activated.

Constructors

```
public WakeupOnActivation()
```

This constructor creates a WakeupOnActivation criterion.

10.5.3.3 WakeupOnBehaviorPost

This WakeupCriterion object specifies that Java 3D should awaken this behavior when the specified behavior posts the specified ID.

Constructors

```
public WakeupOnBehaviorPost(Behavior behavior, int postId)
```

This constructor creates a WakeupOnBehaviorPost object that informs the Java 3D scheduler to wake up this Behavior object whenever the specified behavior posts the specified postId. A postId of 0 specifies that this behavior should awaken on any post from the specified behavior. Specifying a `null` behavior implies that this behavior should awaken whenever any behavior posts the specified `postId`.

Methods

`public int getPostId()`

This method returns the `postId` used in creating this WakeupCriterion.

`public Behavior getBehavior()`

This method returns the behavior specified in this object's constructor.

`public int getTriggeringPostId()`

This method returns the postid that caused the behavior to wake up. If the postid used to construct this wakeup criterion was not zero, the triggering postid will always be equal to the postid used in the constructor.

`public Behavior getTriggeringBehavior()`

This method returns the behavior that triggered this wakeup. If the arming behavior used to construct this object was not null, the triggering behavior will be the same as the arming behavior.

10.5.3.4   WakeupOnDeactivation

The WakeupOnDeactivation object specifies a wakeup on the first detection of a ViewPlatform's activation region no longer intersecting with this object's scheduling region. This gives the behavior an explicit means of executing code when it is deactivated.

Constructors

`public WakeupOnDeactivation()`

This constructor creates a new WakeupOnDeactivation criterion.

10.5.3.5   WakeupOnElapsedFrames

This WakeupCriterion object specifies that Java 3D should awaken this behavior after it has rendered the specified number of frames. A value of 0 implies that Java 3D will awaken this behavior at the next frame. The wakeup criterion can be either passive or nonpassive. If a behavior uses a nonpassive WakeupOnElapsed-Frames, the rendering system will run continuously.

Constructors

`public WakeupOnElapsedFrames(int frameCount)`

This constructor creates a nonpassive WakeupOnElapsedFrames object that informs the Java 3D scheduler to wake up the specified Behavior object after it has drawn `frameCount` frames. A `frameCount` value of *N* means wake up at the end of frame *N*, where the current frame is 0. A `frameCount` value of 0 means wake up at the end of the current frame.

`public WakeupOnElapsedFrames(int frameCount, boolean passive)`   ◀ New in 1.2 ▶

This constructor creates a WakeupOnElapsedFrames criterion. The `passive` flag indicates whether this behavior is passive. A nonpassive behavior will cause the rendering system to run continuously. A passive behavior will run only when some other event causes a frame to be run.

Methods

`public int getElapsedFrameCount()`

This method returns the frame count that was specified when constructing this object.

`public boolean isPassive()`   ◀ New in 1.2 ▶

This method retrieves the state of the passive flag that was used when constructing this object.

10.5.3.6   WakeupOnElapsedTime

This WakeupCriterion object specifies that Java 3D should awaken this behavior after an elapsed number of milliseconds.

Constructors

`public WakeupOnElapsedTime(long milliseconds)`

This constructor creates a WakeupOnElapsedTime object that informs the Java 3D scheduler to wake up the specified Behavior object after the specified number of milliseconds.

Note: The Java 3D scheduler will schedule the object after the specified number of milliseconds have elapsed, not before. However, the elapsed time may actually be slightly greater than the time specified.

Methods

```
public long getElapsedFrameTime()
```

This method returns the WakeupCriterion's elapsed time value in milliseconds.

10.5.3.7 WakeupOnSensorEntry

This WakeupCriterion object specifies that Java 3D should awaken this behavior when any sensor enters the specified region.

Note: There can be situations in which a sensor may enter and then exit an armed region so rapidly that neither the Entry nor Exit condition is engaged.

Constructors

```
public WakeupOnSensorEntry(Bounds region)
```

This constructor creates a WakeupOnSensorEntry object that informs the Java 3D scheduler to wake up the specified Behavior object whenever it detects a sensor within the specified `region` for the first time.

Methods

```
public Bounds getBounds()
```

This method returns the Bounds object used in creating this WakeupCriterion.

◀ New in 1.2 ▶ `public Sensor getTriggeringSensor()`

This method retrieves he Sensor object that caused the wakeup.

10.5.3.8 WakeupOnSensorExit

This WakeupCriterion object specifies that Java 3D should awaken this behavior when any sensor, already marked as within the region, is no longer in that region.

Note: This semantic guarantees that an Exit condition is engaged if its corresponding Entry condition was engaged.

Constructors

public WakeupOnSensorExit(Bounds region)

This constructor creates a WakeupOnSensorExit object that informs the Java 3D scheduler to wake up the specified Behavior object the first time it detects that a sensor has left the specified `region`.

Methods

public Bounds getBounds()

This method returns the Bounds object used in creating this WakeupCriterion.

public Sensor getTriggeringSensor()   ◀ New in 1.2 ▶

This method retrieves the Sensor object that caused the wakeup.

10.5.3.9   WakeupOnCollisionEntry

This WakeupCriterion object specifies that Java 3D should awaken the WakeupOnCollisionEntry behavior when the specified object collides with any other object in the scene graph.

Constants

```
public static final int USE_GEOMETRY
public static final int USE_BOUNDS
```

These constants specify whether collision against a Group, Shape, or Morph node is done using the actual geometry or whether the geometric bounds are used as an approximation.

Constructors

```
public WakeupOnCollisionEntry(SceneGraphPath armingPath)
public WakeupOnCollisionEntry(SceneGraphPath armingPath,
      int speedHint)
public WakeupOnCollisionEntry(Node armingNode)
public WakeupOnCollisionEntry(Node armingNode, int speedHint)
public WakeupOnCollisionEntry(Bounds armingBounds)
```

These constructors create a WakeupOnCollisionEntry object that informs the Java 3D scheduler to wake up the specified Behavior object if the specified "armed" node's geometry or the specified "armed" bounds collides with any other object in the scene graph. The `speedHint` flag is either `USE_GEOMETRY` or `USE_BOUNDS`.

Methods

```
public SceneGraphPath getArmingPath()
public Bounds getArmingBounds()
```

These methods return the "collidable" path or bounds object used in specifying the collision detection.

```
public SceneGraphPath getTriggeringPath()
public Bounds getTriggeringBounds()
```

These methods return the path or bounds object that caused the collision.

10.5.3.10 WakeupOnCollisionExit

This WakeupCriterion object specifies that Java 3D should awaken the WakeupOnCollisionExit behavior when the specified object no longer collides with any other object in the scene graph.

Constants

```
public static final int USE_GEOMETRY
public static final int USE_BOUNDS
```

These constants specify whether collision against a Group, Shape, or Morph node is done using the actual geometry or whether the geometric bounds are used as an approximation.

Constructors

```
public WakeupOnCollisionExit(SceneGraphPath armingPath)
public WakeupOnCollisionExit(SceneGraphPath armingPath,
       int speedHint)
public WakeupOnCollisionExit(Node armingNode)
public WakeupOnCollisionExit(Node armingNode, int speedHint)
public WakeupOnCollisionExit(Bounds armingBounds)
```

These constructors create a WakeupOnCollisionExit object that informs the Java 3D scheduler to wake up the specified Behavior object if the specified "armed" node's geometry or the specified "armed" bounds no longer collides with any other object in the scene graph. The `speedHint` flag is either `USE_GEOMETRY` or `USE_BOUNDS`.

Methods

```
public SceneGraphPath getArmingPath()
public Bounds getArmingBounds()
```

These methods return the "collidable" path or bounds object used in specifying the collision detection.

```
public SceneGraphPath getTriggeringPath()
public Bounds getTriggeringBounds()
```

These methods return the path or bounds object that caused the collision.

10.5.3.11 WakeupOnCollisionMovement

This WakeupCriterion object specifies that Java 3D should awaken the WakeupOnCollisionMovement behavior when the specified object moves while in a state of collision with any other object in the scene graph.

Constants

```
public static final int USE_GEOMETRY
public static final int USE_BOUNDS
```

These constants specify whether collision against a Group, Shape, or Morph node is done using the actual geometry or whether the geometric bounds are used as an approximation.

Constructors

```
public WakeupOnCollisionMovement(SceneGraphPath armingPath)
public WakeupOnCollisionMovement(SceneGraphPath armingPath,
        int speedHint)
public WakeupOnCollisionMovement(Node armingNode)
public WakeupOnCollisionMovement(Node armingNode, int speedHint)
public WakeupOnCollisionMovement(Bounds armingBounds)
```

These constructors create a WakeupOnCollisionMovement object that informs the Java 3D scheduler to wake up the specified Behavior object if the specified node's geometry or the specified bounds collides with any other object in the scene graph. The speedHint flag is either USE_GEOMETRY or USE_BOUNDS.

Methods

```
public SceneGraphPath getArmingPath()
public Bounds getArmingBounds()
```

These methods return the "collidable" path or bounds object used in specifying the collision detection.

```
public SceneGraphPath getTriggeringPath()
public Bounds getTriggeringBounds()
```

These methods return the path or bounds object that caused the collision.

10.5.3.12 WakeupOnViewPlatformEntry

This WakeupCriterion object specifies that Java 3D should awaken the WakeupOnViewPlatformEntry behavior when any ViewPlatform enters the specified region.

Note: There can be situations in which a ViewPlatform may enter and then exit an armed region so rapidly that neither the Entry nor Exit condition is engaged.

Constructors

```
public WakeupOnViewPlatformEntry(Bounds region)
```

This constructor creates a WakeupOnViewPlatformEntry object that informs the Java 3D scheduler to wake up the specified Behavior object whenever it detects a ViewPlatform center within the specified `region` for the first time.

Methods

```
public Bounds getBounds()
```

This method returns the Bounds object used in creating this WakeupCriterion.

10.5.3.13 WakeupOnViewPlatformExit

This WakeupCriterion object specifies that Java 3D should awaken the WakeupOnViewPlatformExit behavior when any ViewPlatform, already marked as within the region, is no longer in that region.

Note: This semantic guarantees that an Exit condition gets engaged if its corresponding Entry condition was engaged.

Constructors

`public WakeupOnViewPlatformExit(Bounds region)`

This constructor creates a WakeupOnViewPlatformExit object that informs the Java 3D scheduler to wake up the specified Behavior object the first time it detects that a ViewPlatform has left the specified `region`.

Methods

`public Bounds getBounds()`

This method returns the Bounds object used in creating this WakeupCriterion.

10.5.3.14 WakeupOnTransformChange

The WakeupOnTransformChange object specifies a wakeup when the transform within a specified TransformGroup changes.

Constructors

`public WakeupOnTransformChange(TransformGroup node)`

This constructor creates a new WakeupOnTransformChange criterion.

Methods

`public TransformGroup getTransformGroup()`

This method returns the TransformGroup node used in creating this WakeupCriterion.

10.5.3.15 WakeupAnd

The WakeupAnd class specifies any number of wakeup conditions ANDed together. This WakeupCondition object specifies that Java 3D should awaken this Behavior when all of the WakeupCondition's constituent wakeup criteria become valid.

Constructors

`public WakeupAnd(WakeupCriterion conditions[])`

This constructor creates a WakeupAnd object that informs the Java 3D scheduler to wake up this Behavior object when all the conditions specified in the array of WakeupCriterion objects have become valid.

10.5.3.16 WakeupOr

The WakeupOr class specifies any number of wakeup conditions ORed together. This WakeupCondition object specifies that Java 3D should awaken this Behavior when any of the WakeupCondition's constituent wakeup criteria becomes valid.

Constructors

```
public WakeupOr(WakeupCriterion conditions[])
```

This constructor creates a WakeupOr object that informs the Java 3D scheduler to wake up this Behavior object when any condition specified in the array of WakeupCriterion objects becomes valid.

10.5.3.17 WakeupAndOfOrs

The WakeupAndOfOrs class specifies any number of OR wakeup conditions ANDed together. This WakeupCondition object specifies that Java 3D should awaken this Behavior when all of the WakeupCondition's constituent WakeupOr conditions become valid.

Constructors

```
public WakeupAndOfOrs(WakeupOr conditions[])
```

This constructor creates a WakeupAndOfOrs object that informs the Java 3D scheduler to wake up this Behavior object when all of the WakeupOr conditions specified in the array of WakeupOr objects become valid.

10.5.3.18 WakeupOrOfAnds

The WakeupOrOfAnds class specifies any number of AND wakeup conditions ORed together. This WakeupCondition object specifies that Java 3D should awaken this Behavior when any of the WakeupCondition's constituent Wakeup And conditions becomes valid.

Constructors

```
public WakeupOrOfAnds(WakeupAnd conditions[])
```

This constructor creates a WakeupOrOfAnds object that informs the Java 3D scheduler to wake up this Behavior object when any of the WakeupAnd conditions specified in the array of WakeupAnd objects becomes valid.

10.6 Interpolator Behaviors

This section describes Java 3D's predefined Interpolator behaviors. They are called *interpolators* because they smoothly interpolate between the two extreme values that an interpolator can produce. Interpolators perform simple behavioral acts, yet they provide broad functionality.

The Java 3D API provides interpolators for a number of functions: manipulating transforms within a TransformGroup, modifying the values of a Switch node, and modifying Material attributes such as color and transparency.

These predefined Interpolator behaviors share the same mechanism for specifying and later for converting a temporal value into an alpha value. Interpolators consist of two portions: a generic portion that all interpolators share and a domain-specific portion.

The generic portion maps time in milliseconds onto a value in the range [0.0, 1.0] inclusive. The domain-specific portion maps an alpha value in the range [0.0, 1.0] onto a value appropriate to the predefined behavior's range of outputs. An alpha value of 0.0 generates an interpolator's minimum value, an alpha value of 1.0 generates an interpolator's maximum value, and an alpha value somewhere in between generates a value proportionally in between the minimum and maximum values.

10.6.1 Mapping Time to Alpha

Several parameters control the mapping of time onto an alpha value. That mapping is deterministic as long as its parameters do not change. Thus, two different interpolators with the same parameters will generate the same alpha value given the same time value. This means that two interpolators that do not communicate can still precisely coordinate their activities, even if they reside in different threads or even different processors—as long as those processors have consistent clocks.

Figure 10-1 shows the components of an interpolator's time-to-alpha mapping. Time is represented on the horizontal axis. Alpha is represented on the vertical axis. As we move from left to right, we see the alpha value start at 0.0, rise to 1.0, and then decline back to 0.0 on the right-hand side.

On the left-hand side, the trigger time defines when this interpolator's waveform begins in milliseconds. The region directly to the right of the trigger time, labeled Phase Delay, defines a time period where the waveform does not change.

During phase delays alpha is either 0 or 1, depending on which region it precedes.

Phase delays provide an important means for offsetting multiple interpolators from one another, especially where the interpolators have all the same parameters. The next four regions, labeled α increasing, α at 1, α decreasing, and α at 0, all specify durations for the corresponding values of alpha.

Interpolators have a loop count that determines how many times to repeat the sequence of alpha increasing, alpha at 1, alpha decreasing, and alpha at 0; they also have associated mode flags that enable either the increasing or decreasing portions, or both, of the waveform.

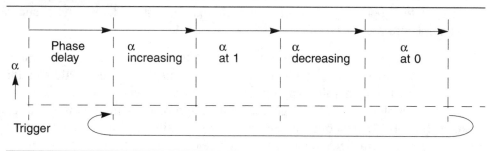

Figure 10-1   An Interpolator's Generic Time-to-Alpha Mapping Sequence

Developers can use the loop count in conjunction with the mode flags to generate various kinds of actions. Specifying a loop count of 1 and enabling the mode flag for only the alpha-increasing and alpha-at-1 portion of the waveform, we would get the waveform shown in Figure 10-2.

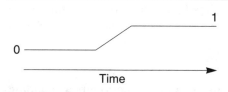

Figure 10-2   An Interpolator Set to a Loop Count of 1 with Mode Flags Set to Enable Only the Alpha-Increasing and Alpha-at-1 Portion of the Waveform

In Figure 10-2, the alpha value is 0 before the combination of trigger time plus the phase delay duration. The alpha value changes from 0 to 1 over a specified interval of time, and thereafter the alpha value remains 1 (subject to the reprogramming of the interpolator's parameters). A possible use of a single alpha-increasing value might be to combine it with a rotation interpolator to program a door opening.

Similarly, by specifying a loop count of 1 and a mode flag that enables only the alpha-decreasing and alpha-at-0 portion of the waveform, we would get the waveform shown in Figure 10-3.

In Figure 10-3, the alpha value is 1 before the combination of trigger time plus the phase delay duration. The alpha value changes from 1 to 0 over a specified interval; thereafter the alpha value remains 0 (subject to the reprogramming of the interpolator's parameters). A possible use of a single α-decreasing value might be to combine it with a rotation interpolator to program a door closing.

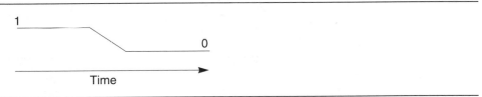

Figure 10-3   An Interpolator Set to a Loop Count of 1 with Mode Flags Set to Enable Only the Alpha-Decreasing and Alpha-at-0 Portion of the Waveform

We can combine both of the above waveforms by specifying a loop count of 1 and setting the mode flag to enable both the alpha-increasing and alpha-at-1 portion of the waveform as well as the alpha decreasing and alpha-at-0 portion of the waveform. This combination would result in the waveform shown in Figure 10-4.

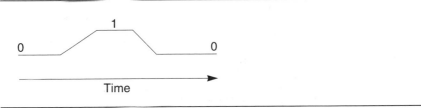

Figure 10-4   An Interpolator Set to a Loop Count of 1 with Mode Flags Set to Enable All Portions of the Waveform

In Figure 10-4, the alpha value is 0 before the combination of trigger time plus the phase delay duration. The alpha value changes from 0 to 1 over a specified period of time, remains at 1 for another specified period of time, then changes from 1 to 0 over a third specified period of time; thereafter the alpha value remains 0 (subject to the reprogramming of the interpolator's parameters). A possible use of an alpha-increasing value followed by an alpha-decreasing value might be to combine it with a rotation interpolator to program a door swinging open and then closing.

By increasing the loop count, we can get repetitive behavior, such as a door swinging open and closed some number of times. At the extreme, we can specify a loop count of –1 (representing infinity).

We can construct looped versions of the waveforms shown in Figure 10-2, Figure 10-3, and Figure 10-4. Figure 10-5 shows a looping interpolator with mode flags set to enable only the alpha-increasing and alpha-at-1 portion of the waveform.

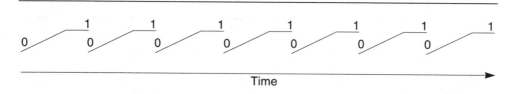

Figure 10-5   An Interpolator Set to Loop Infinitely and Mode Flags Set to Enable Only the Alpha-Increasing and Alpha-at-1 Portion of the Waveform

In Figure 10-5, alpha goes from 0 to 1 over a fixed duration of time, stays at 1 for another fixed duration of time, and then repeats.

Similarly, Figure 10-6 shows a looping interpolator with mode flags set to cnable only the alpha-decreasing and alpha-at-0 portion of the waveform.

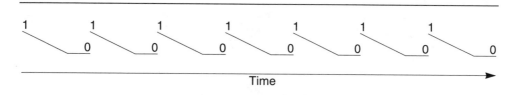

Figure 10-6   An Interpolator Set to Loop Infinitely and Mode Flags Set to Enable Only the Alpha-Decreasing and Alpha-at-0 Portion of the Waveform

Finally, Figure 10-7 shows a looping interpolator with both the increasing and decreasing portions of the waveform enabled.

In all three cases shown by Figure 10-5, Figure 10-6, and Figure 10-7, we can compute the exact value of alpha at any point in time.

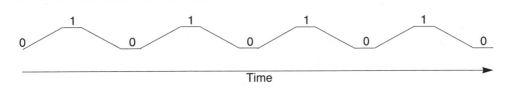

Figure 10-7   An Interpolator Set to Loop Infinitely and Mode Flags Set to Enable All Portions of the Waveform

Java 3D's preprogrammed behaviors permit other behaviors to change their parameters. When such a change occurs, the alpha value changes to match the state of the newly parameterized interpolator.

10.6.2   Acceleration of Alpha

Commonly, developers want alpha to change slowly at first and then to speed up until the change in alpha reaches some appropriate rate. This is analogous to accelerating your car up to the speed limit—it does not start off immediately at the speed limit. Developers specify this "ease-in, ease-out" behavior through two additional parameters, the increasingAlphaRampDuration and the decreasing AlphaRampDuration.

Each of these parameters specifies a period within the increasing or decreasing alpha duration region during which the "change in alpha" is accelerated (until it reaches its maximum per-unit-of-time step size) and then symmetrically decelerated. Figure 10-8 shows three general examples of how the increasingAlphaRampDuration method can be used to modify the alpha waveform. A value of 0 for the increasing ramp duration implies that α is not accelerated; it changes at a constant rate. A value of 0.5 or greater (clamped to 0.5) for this increasing ramp duration implies that the change in α is accelerated during the first half of the period and then decelerated during the second half of the period. For a value of n that is less than 0.5, alpha is accelerated for duration n, held constant for duration $(1.0 - 2n)$, then decelerated for duration n of the period.

10.6.3   The Alpha Class

The Alpha node component object provides common methods for converting a time value into an alpha value (a value in the range 0.0 to 1.0). The Alpha object is effectively a function of time that generates alpha values in the range [0,1] when sampled: $f_t = [0,1]$. The function f_t and the characteristics of the Alpha object are determined by the following user-definable parameters:

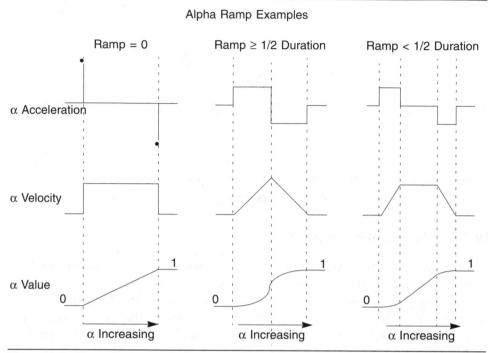

Figure 10-8   How an Alpha-Increasing Waveform Changes with Various Values of `increasingAlphaRampDuration`

- loopCount: Specifies the number of times to run this Alpha. A value of -1 specifies that the Alpha loops indefinitely.

- triggerTime: Specifies the time in milliseconds since the start time that this object first triggers. If `startTime + triggerTime` is less than `currentTime`, the Alpha object is started as soon as possible by the system.

- phaseDelayDuration: Specifies the number of milliseconds to wait after `triggerTime` before actually starting this Alpha.

- mode: The mode can be set to INCREASING_ENABLE or DECREASING_ENABLE or the ORed value of the two. INCREASING_ENABLE activates the increasing Alpha parameters described later. DECREASING_ENABLE activates the decreasing Alpha parameters listed later.

The increasing Alpha parameters are

- increasingAlphaDuration: Specifies the time period during which Alpha goes from zero to one.

- increasingAlphaRampDuration: Specifies the time period during which the Alpha step size increases at the beginning of the `increasingAlphaDuration` and, correspondingly, decreases at the end of the `increasingAlphaDuration`. This parameter is clamped to half of `increasingAlphaDuration`. When this parameter is nonzero, one gets constant acceleration while it is in effect; constant positive acceleration at the beginning of the ramp and constant negative acceleration at the end of the ramp. If this parameter is zero, the effective velocity of the Alpha value is constant and the acceleration is zero (that is, linearly increasing alpha ramp).

- alphaAtOneDuration: Specifies the time period that Alpha stays at one.

The decreasing Alpha parameters are

- decreasingAlphaDuration: Specifies the time period during which Alpha goes from one to zero.

- decreasingAlphaRampDuration: Specifies the time period during which the Alpha step size increases at the beginning of the `decreasingAlphaDuration` and, correspondingly, decreases at the end of the `decreasingAlphaDuration`. This parameter is clamped to half of `decreasingAlphaDuration`. When this parameter is nonzero, one gets constant acceleration while it is in effect—constant positive acceleration at the beginning of the ramp and constant negative acceleration at the end of the ramp. If this parameter is zero, the effective velocity of the Alpha value is constant and the acceleration is zero (that is, a linearly-decreasing alpha ramp).

- alphaAtZeroDuration: Specifies the time period that Alpha stays at zero.

Constants

```
public static final int INCREASING_ENABLE
public static final int DECREASING_ENABLE
```

These flags specify that this alpha's mode is to use the increasing or decreasing component of the alpha, respectively.

Constructors

```
public Alpha()
```

Constructs an Alpha object with the following default parameters:

Parameter	Default Value
loopCount	−1
mode	INCREASING_ENABLE

Parameter	Default Value
triggerTime	0
phaseDelayDuration	0
increasingAlphaDuration	1000
increasingAlphaRampDuration	0
alphaAtOneDuration	0
decreasingAlphaDuration	0
decreasingAlphaRampDuration	0
alphaAtZeroDuration	0

```
public Alpha(int loopCount, long increasingAlphaDuration)
    public Alpha(int loopCount, long triggerTime,
    long phaseDelayDuration, long increasingAlphaDuration,
    long increasingAlphaRampDuration, long alphaAtOneDuration)
public Alpha(int loopCount, int mode, long triggerTime,
    long phaseDelayDuration, long increasingAlphaDuration,
    long increasingAlphaRampDuration, long alphaAtOneDuration,
    long decreasingAlphaDuration,
    long decreasingAlphaRampDuration, long alphaAtZeroDuration)
```

Constructs a new Alpha object using the specified parameters to define the alpha phases for the object.

Methods

```
public float value()
public float value(long atTime)
```

These methods return the alpha value (between 0.0 and 1.0 inclusive) based on the time-to-alpha parameters established for this interpolator. The first method returns the alpha for the current time. The second method returns the alpha for an arbitrary given time. If the alpha mapping has not started, the starting alpha value is returned. If the alpha mapping has completed, the ending alpha value is returned.

```
public void setStartTime(long startTime)
public long getStartTime()
```

These methods set and retrieve this alpha's start time, the base for all relative time specifications. The default value of startTime is the system start time, defined to be a global time base representing the start of Java 3D execution.

```
public void setLoopCount(int loopCount)
public int getLoopCount()
```

These methods set and retrieve this alpha's loop count.

```
public void setMode(int mode)
public int getMode()
```

These methods set and retrieve this alpha's mode, which defines which of the alpha regions are active. The mode is one of the following values: INCREASING_ENABLE, DECREASING_ENABLE, or both (when both of these modes are ORed together).

If the mode is INCREASING_ENABLE, the increasingAlphaDuration, increasingAlphaRampDuration, and alphaAtOneDuration are active. If the mode is DECREASING_ENABLE, the decreasingAlphaDuration, decreasingAlphaRampDuration, and alphaAtZeroDuration are active. If the mode is both constants ORed, all regions are active. Active regions are all preceded by the phase delay region.

```
public void setTriggerTime(long triggerTime)
public long getTriggerTime()
```

These methods set and retrieve this alpha's trigger time.

```
public void setPhaseDelayDuration(long phaseDelayDuration)
public long getPhaseDelayDuration()
```

These methods set and retrieve this alpha's phase delay duration.

```
public void setIncreasingAlphaDuration(long
        increasingAlphaDuration)
public long getIncreasingAlphaDuration()
```

These methods set and retrieve this alpha's increasingAlphaDuration.

```
public void setIncreasingAlphaRampDuration(long
        increasingAlphaRampDuration)
public long getIncreasingAlphaRampDuration()
```

These methods set and retrieve this alpha's increasingAlphaRampDuration.

```
public long getAlphaAtOneDuration()
```

This method sets and retrieves this alpha's alphaAtOneDuration.

```
public void setDecreasingAlphaDuration(long
        decreasingAlphaDuration)
public long getDecreasingAlphaDuration()
```

These methods set and retrieve this alpha's decreasingAlphaDuration.

```
public void setDecreasingAlphaRampDuration(long
        decreasingAlphaRampDuration)
public long getDecreasingAlphaRampDuration()
```

These methods set and retrieve this alpha's decreasingAlphaRampDuration.

```
public long getAlphaAtZeroDuration()
```

This method sets and retrieves this alpha's alphaAtZeroDuration.

```
public boolean finished()
```

This method returns true if this Alpha object is past its activity window—that is, if it has finished all its looping activity. This method returns false if this Alpha object is still active.

10.6.4   The Interpolator Base Class

Interpolator is an abstract behavior class from which several subclasses are derived. The base Interpolator class contains an Alpha object that provides the means for converting a time value (in milliseconds) into an alpha value in the range [0.0, 1.0] inclusive. Its subclasses map this alpha value into domain-specific values in their range.

Constants

```
protected WakeupCriterion defaultWakeupCriterion
```

This is the default WakeupCondition for all interpolators. The wakeupOn method of Behavior, which takes a WakeupCondition as the method parameter, will need to be called at the end of the processStimulus method of any class that subclasses Interpolator. This is done with the following method call:

```
wakeupOn(defaultWakeupCriterion);
```

Constructors

The Interpolator behavior class has the following constructors:

```
public Interpolator()
```

Constructs and initializes a new Interpolator with a null alpha value.

```
public Interpolator(Alpha alpha)
```

Constructs and initializes a new Interpolator with the specified alpha value. This constructor provides the common initialization code for all specializations of Interpolator.

Methods

```
public void setAlpha(Alpha alpha)
public Alpha getAlpha()
```

These methods set and retrieve this interpolator's Alpha object. Setting it to null causes the Interpolator to stop running.

```
public void setEnable(boolean state)
public boolean getEnable()
```

These methods set and retrieve this Interpolator's enabled state—the default is enabled.

```
public void initialize()
```

This is the generic predefined interpolator `initialize` method. It schedules the behavior to awaken at the next frame.

10.6.5   PositionInterpolator Object

The PositionInterpolator class extends Interpolator. It modifies the translational component of its target TransformGroup by linearly interpolating between a pair of specified positions (using the value generated by the specified Alpha object). The interpolated position is used to generate a translation transform along the local *X*-axis of this interpolator.

Constructors

The PositionInterpolator object specifies the following constructors:

```
public PositionInterpolator(Alpha alpha, TransformGroup target)
```

Constructs a trivial position interpolator with a specified target, an `axisOf-Translation` set to the identity transformation, a `startPosition` of 0.0, and an `endPosition` of 1.0 along the *X*-axis.

295

```
public PositionInterpolator(Alpha alpha, TransformGroup target,
    Transform3D axisOfTranslation, float startPosition,
    float endPosition)
```

Constructs and initializes a new PositionInterpolator that varies the target TransformGroup node's translational component (`startPosition` and `endPosition`).
The `axisOfTranslation` parameter specifies the transform that defines the local
coordinate system in which this interpolator operates. The translation is done
along the *X*-axis of this local coordinate system.

Methods

The PositionInterpolator object specifies the following methods:

```
public void setStartPosition(float position)
public float getStartPosition()
```

These two methods set and get the Interpolator's start position.

```
public void setEndPosition(float position)
public float getEndPosition()
```

These two methods set and get the Interpolator's end position.

```
public void setTarget(TransformGroup target)
public TransformGroup getTarget()
```

These two methods set and get the Interpolator's target TransformGroup node.

```
public void setAxisOfTranslation(Transform3D axis)
public Transform3D getAxisOfTranslation()
```

These two methods set and get the Interpolator's axis of translation.

```
public void processStimulus(Enumeration criteria)
```

This method is invoked by the behavior scheduler every frame. It maps the alpha
value that corresponds to the current time into a translation value, computes a
transform based on this value, and updates the specified TransformGroup node
with this new transform.

10.6.6   RotationInterpolator Object

The RotationInterpolator class extends Interpolator. It modifies the rotational
component of its target TransformGroup by linearly interpolating between a pair
of specified angles (using the value generated by the specified Alpha object). The

interpolated angle is used to generate a rotation transform about the local *Y*-axis of this interpolator.

Constructors

`public RotationInterpolator(Alpha alpha, TransformGroup target)`

Constructs a trivial rotation interpolator with a specified `target`, an `axisOf-Rotation` set to identity, a minimum angle of 0 radians, and a maximum angle of 2π radians.

```
public RotationInterpolator(Alpha alpha, TransformGroup target,
      Transform3D axisOfRotation, float minimumAngle,
      float maximumAngle)
```

Constructs a new rotation interpolator that varies the target TransformGroup node's rotational component. The `minimumAngle` parameter is the starting angle, in radians; `maximumAngle` is the ending angle, in radians. The `axisOfRotation` parameter specifies the transform that defines the local coordinate system in which this interpolator operates. The rotation is done about the *Y*-axis of this local coordinate system.

Methods

```
public void setMinimumAngle(float angle)
public float getMinimumAngle()
```

These two methods set and get the interpolator's minimum rotation angle, in radians.

```
public void setMaximumAngle(float angle)
public float getMaximumAngle()
```

These two methods set and get the interpolator's maximum rotation angle, in radians.

```
public void setAxisOfRotation(Transform3D axis)
public Transform3D getAxisOfRotation()
```

These two methods set and get the interpolator's axis of rotation.

```
public void setTarget(TransformGroup target)
public TransformGroup getTarget()
```

These two methods set and get the interpolator's target TransformGroup node.

297

```
public void processStimulus(Enumeration criteria)
```

This method is invoked by the behavior scheduler every frame. It maps the alpha value that corresponds to the current time into a rotation angle, computes a transform based on this angle, and updates the specified TransformGroup node with this new transform.

10.6.7 ColorInterpolator Object

The ColorInterpolator class extends Interpolator. It modifies the diffuse color of its target material object by linearly interpolating between a pair of specified colors (using the value generated by the specified Alpha object).

Constructors

```
public ColorInterpolator(Alpha alpha, Material target)
```

Constructs a trivial color interpolator with a specified target, a start color of black, and an end color of white.

```
public ColorInterpolator(Alpha alpha, Material target,
    Color3f startColor, color3f endColor)
```

Constructs a new ColorInterpolator object that varies the diffuse color of the target material between two color values (startColor and endColor).

Methods

```
public void setStartColor(Color3f color)
public void getStartColor(Color3f color)
```

These two methods set and get the interpolator's start color.

```
public void setEndColor(Color3f color)
public void getEndColor(Color3f color)
```

These two methods set and get the interpolator's end color.

```
public void setTarget(Material target)
public Material getTarget()
```

These two methods set and get the interpolator's target Material component object.

```
public void processStimulus(Enumeration criteria)
```

This method is invoked by the behavior scheduler every frame. It maps the alpha value that corresponds to the current time into a color value and updates the diffuse color of the target Material object with this new color value.

10.6.8   ScaleInterpolator Object

The ScaleInterpolator class extends Interpolator. It modifies the uniform scale component of its target TransformGroup by linearly interpolating between a pair of specified scale values (using the value generated by the specified Alpha object). The interpolated scale value is used to generate a scale transform in the local coordinate system of this interpolator.

Constructors

```
public ScaleInterpolator(Alpha alpha, TransformGroup target)
```

Constructs a trivial scale interpolator that varies its target TransformGroup node between the two scale values, using the specified alpha, an identity matrix, a minimum scale of 0.1, and a maximum scale of 1.0.

```
public ScaleInterpolator(Alpha alpha, TransformGroup target,
        Transform3D axisOfScale, float minimumScale,
        float maximumScale)
```

Constructs a new ScaleInterpolator object that varies the target TransformGroup node's scale component between two scale values (minimumScale and maximumScale). The axisOfScale parameter specifies the transform that defines the local coordinate system in which this interpolator operates. The scale is done about the origin of this local coordinate system.

Methods

```
public void setMinimumScale(float scale)
public float getMinimumScale()
```

These two methods set and get the interpolator's minimum scale.

```
public void setMaximumScale(float scale)
public float getMaximumScale()
```

These two methods set and get the interpolator's maximum scale.

```
public void setAxisOfScale(Transform3D axis)
public Transform3D getAxisOfScale()
```

These two methods set and get the interpolator's axis of scale.

```
public void setTarget(TransformGroup target)
public TransformGroup getTarget()
```

These two methods set and get the interpolator's target TransformGroup node.

```
public void processStimulus(Enumeration criteria)
```

This method is invoked by the behavior scheduler every frame. It maps the alpha value that corresponds to the current time into a scale value, computes a transform based on this value, and updates the specified TransformGroup node with this new transform.

10.6.9 SwitchValueInterpolator Object

The SwitchValueInterpolator class extends Interpolator. It modifies the selected child of the target Switch node by linearly interpolating between a pair of specified child index values (using the value generated by the specified Alpha object).

Constructors

```
public SwitchValueInterpolator(Alpha alpha, Switch target)
public SwitchValueInterpolator(Alpha alpha, Switch target,
        int firstChildIndex, int lastChildIndex)
```

Constructs a new SwitchValueInterpolator object that varies the target Switch node's child index between the two values provided (firstChildIndex, the index of the first children in the Switch node to select; and lastChildIndex, the index of the last children in the Switch node to select).

Methods

```
public void setFirstChildIndex(int firstIndex)
public int getFirstChildIndex()
```

These two methods set and get the interpolator's first child index.

```
public void setLastChildIndex(int lastIndex)
public int getLastChildIndex()
```

These two methods set and get the interpolator's last child index.

```
public void setTarget(Switch target)
public Switch getTarget()
```

These two methods set and get the interpolator's target Switch node.

```
public void processStimulus(Enumeration criteria)
```

This method is invoked by the behavior scheduler every frame. It maps the alpha value that corresponds to the current time into a child index value and updates the specified Switch node with this new child index value.

10.6.10　TransparencyInterpolator Object

The TransparencyInterpolator class extends Interpolator. It modifies the transparency of its target TransparencyAttributes object by linearly interpolating between a pair of specified transparency values (using the value generated by the specified Alpha object).

Constructors

```
public TransparencyInterpolator(Alpha alpha,
        TransparencyAttributes target)
```

Constructs a trivial transparency interpolator with a specified target, a minimum transparency of 0.0 and a maximum transparency of 1.0.

```
public TransparencyInterpolator(Alpha alpha,
        TransparencyAttributes target, float minimumTransparency,
        float maximumTransparency)
```

Constructs a new TransparencyInterpolator object that varies the target material's transparency between the two transparency values (minimumTransparency, the starting transparency; and maximumTransparency, the ending transparency).

Methods

```
public void setMinimumTransparency(float transparency)
public float getMinimumTransparency()
```

These two methods set and get the interpolator's minimum transparency.

```
public void setMaximumTransparency(float transparency)
public float getMaximumTransparency()
```

These two methods set and get the interpolator's maximum transparency.

301

```
public void setTarget(TransparencyAttributes target)
public TransparencyAttributes getTarget()
```

These two methods set and get the interpolator's target TransparencyAttributes component object.

```
public void processStimulus(Enumeration criteria)
```

This method is invoked by the behavior scheduler every frame. It maps the alpha value that corresponds to the current time into a transparency value and updates the specified TransparencyAttributes object with this new transparency value.

10.6.11 PathInterpolator Object

The PathInterpolator class extends Interpolator. This class defines the base class for all path interpolators. Subclasses have access to the computePathInterpolation method, which computes the currentInterpolationValue given the current time and alpha. The method also computes the currentKnotIndex, which is based on the currentInterpolationValue.

The currentInterpolationValue is calculated by linearly interpolating among a series of predefined knot and orientation, pairs (using the value generated by the specified Alpha object). The last knot must have a value of 1.0; an intermediate knot with index k must have a value strictly greater than any knot with index less than k.

Constants

```
protected float currentInterpolationValue
```

This value is the ratio between knot values indicated by the currentKnotIndex variable. So if a subclass wanted to interpolate between knot values, it would use the currentKnotIndex to get the bounding knots for the "real" value and then use the currentInterpolationValue to interpolate between the knots. To calculate this variable, a subclass needs to call the computePathInterpolation method from the subclass's processStimulus method. Then this variable will hold a valid value that can be used in further calculations by the subclass.

```
protected int currentKnotIndex
```

This value is the index of the current base knot value, as determined by the alpha function. A subclass wishing to interpolate between bounding knots would use this index and the one following it and would use the currentInterpolation-Value variable as the ratio between these indices. To calculate this variable, a subclass needs to call the computePathInterpolation method from the subclass's `processStimulus` method. Then this variable will hold a valid value that can be used in further calculations by the subclass.

Constructors

public PathInterpolator(Alpha alpha, float knots[])

Constructs a new `PathInterpolator` object that varies the target Transform-Group node's transform.

Methods

public int getArrayLengths()

This method retrieves the length of the knot and position arrays (which are the same length).

public void setKnot(int index, float knot)
public float getKnot(int index)

These methods set and retrieve the knot at the specified index for this interpolator.

protected void setKnots(float[] knots)   ◀ New in 1.2 ▶
public void getKnots(float[] knots)   ◀ New in 1.2 ▶

These methods set and retrieve an array of knot values. The set method replaces the existing array with the specified array. The get method copies the array of knots from this interpolator into the specified array. The array must be large enough to hold all of the knots.

protected void computePathInterpolation()

This method computes the base knot index and interpolation value, given the current value of alpha and the knots[] array. If the index is 0 and there should be no interpolation, both the index variable and the interpolation variable are set to 0. Otherwise, `currentKnotIndex` is set to the lower index of the two bounding knot points, and the `currentInterpolationValue` variable is set to the ratio of the alpha value between these two bounding knot points.

10.6.12 PositionPathInterpolator Object

The PositionPathInterpolator class extends PathInterpolator. It modifies the translational component of its target TransformGroup by linearly interpolating among a series of predefined knot/position pairs (using the value generated by the specified

Alpha object). The interpolated position is used to generate a translation transform in the local coordinate system of this interpolator.

The first knot must have a value of 0.0. The last knot must have a value of 1.0. An intermediate knot with index k must have a value strictly greater than any knot with index less than k.

Constructors

```
public PositionPathInterpolator(Alpha alpha,
        TransformGroup target, Transform3D axisOfTranslation,
        float knots[], Point3f positions[])
```

Constructs a new PositionPathInterpolator that varies the translation of the target TransformGroup's transform. The `axisOfTranslation` parameter specifies the transform that defines the local coordinate system in which this interpolator operates. The `knots` parameter specifies an array of knot values that specifies a spline. The `positions` parameter specifies an array of position values at the knots.

Methods

```
public void setPosition(int index, Point3f position)
public void getPosition(int index, Point3f position)
```

These two methods set and get the interpolator's indexed position.

◀ New in 1.2 ▶ `public void getPositions(Point3f[] positions)`

This method copies the array of position values from this interpolator into the specified array. The array must be large enough to hold all of the positions. The individual array elements must be allocated by the caller.

```
public void setAxisOfTranslation(Transform3D axis)
public Transform3D getAxisOfTranslation()
```

These two methods set and get the interpolator's axis of translation.

```
public void setTarget(TransformGroup target)
public TransformGroup getTarget()
```

These two methods set and get the interpolator's target TransformGroup object.

public void setPathArrays(float[] knots, Point3f[] positions)   ◀ New in 1.2 ▶

This method replaces the existing arrays of knot values and position values with the specified arrays. The arrays of knots and positions are copied into this interpolator object.

public void processStimulus(Enumeration criteria)

This method is invoked by the behavior scheduler every frame. It maps the alpha value that corresponds to the current time into a translation value, computes a transform based on this value, and updates the specified TransformGroup node with this new transform.

10.6.13   RotPosPathInterpolator Object

The RotPosPathInterpolator class extends PathInterpolator. It modifies the rotational and translational components of its target TransformGroup by linearly interpolating among a series of predefined knot/position and knot/orientation pairs (using the value generated by the specified Alpha object). The interpolated position and orientation are used to generate a transform in the local coordinate system of this interpolator.

The first knot must have a value of 0.0. The last knot must have a value of 1.0. An intermediate knot with index k must have a value strictly greater than any knot with index less than k.

Constructors

public RotPosPathInterpolator(Alpha alpha, TransformGroup target, Transform3D axisOfRotPos, float knots[], Quat4f quats[], Point3f positions[])

This constructor constructs a new RotPosPathInterpolator that varies the rotation and translation of the target TransformGroup's transform. The `axisOfRotPos` parameter specifies the transform that defines the local coordinate system in which this interpolator operates. The `knots` parameter specifies an array of knot values that specifies a spline. The `quats` parameter specifies an array of quaternion values at the knots. The `positions` parameter specifies an array of position values at the knots.

Methods

```
public void setQuat(int index, Quat4f quat)
public void getQuat(int index, Quat4f quat)
```

These two methods set and get the interpolator's indexed quaternion value.

◀ New in 1.2 ▶ `public void getQuats(Quat4f[] quats)`

This method copies the array of quaternion values from this interpolator into the specified array. The array must be large enough to hold all of the quats. The individual array elements must be allocated by the caller.

```
public void setPosition(int index, Point3f position)
public void getPosition(int index, Point3f position)
```

These two methods set and get the interpolator's indexed position.

◀ New in 1.2 ▶ `public void getPositions(Point3f[] positions)`

This method copies the array of position values from this interpolator into the specified array. The array must be large enough to hold all of the positions. The individual array elements must be allocated by the caller.

```
public void setAxisOfRotPos(Transform3D axisOfRotPos)
public Transform3D getAxisOfRotPos()
```

These two methods set and get the interpolator's axis of rotation and translation.

```
public void setTarget(TransformGroup target)
public TransformGroup getTarget()
```

These two methods set and get the interpolator's target TransformGroup object.

◀ New in 1.2 ▶ `public void setPathArrays(float[] knots, Quat4f[] quats, Point3f[] positions)`

This method replaces the existing arrays of knot values, quaternion values, and position values with the specified arrays. The arrays of knots, quats, and positions are copied into this interpolator object.

`public void processStimulus(Enumeration criteria)`

This method is invoked by the behavior scheduler every frame. It maps the alpha value that corresponds to the current time into translation and rotation values, computes a transform based on these values, and updates the specified TransformGroup node with this new transform.

10.6.14 RotPosScalePathInterpolator Object

The RotPosScalePathInterpolator class extends PathInterpolator. It varies the rotational, translational, and scale components of its target TransformGroup by linearly interpolating among a series of predefined knot/position, knot/orientation, and knot/scale pairs (using the value generated by the specified Alpha object). The interpolated position, orientation, and scale are used to generate a transform in the local coordinate system of this interpolator.

The first knot must have a value of 0.0. The last knot must have a value of 1.0. An intermediate knot with index k must have a value strictly greater than any knot with index less than k.

Constructors

```
public RotPosScalePathInterpolator(Alpha alpha,
    TransformGroup target, Transform3D axisOfRotPosScale,
    float knots[], Quat4f quats[], Point3f positions[],
    float scales[])
```

This constructor constructs a new RotPosScalePathInterpolator that varies the rotation, translation, and scale of the target TransformGroup's transform. The axisOfRotPosScale parameter specifies the transform that defines the local coordinate system in which this interpolator operates. The knots parameter specifies an array of knot values that specifies a spline. The quats parameter specifies an array of quaternion values at the knots. The positions parameter specifies an array of position values at the knots. The scale parameter specifies the scale component value.

Methods

```
public void setScale(int index, float scale)
public float getScale(int index)
```

These two methods set and get the interpolator's indexed scale value.

```
public void getScales(float[] scales)
```
     ◀ New in 1.2 ▶

This method copies the array of scale values from this interpolator into the specified array. The array must be large enough to hold all of the scales.

```
public void setQuat(int index, Quat4f quat)
public void getQuat(int index, Quat4f quat)
```

These two methods set and get the interpolator's indexed quaternion value.

◀ New in 1.2 ▶ `public void getQuats(Quat4f[] quats)`

This method copies the array of quaternion values from this interpolator into the specified array. The array must be large enough to hold all of the quats. The individual array elements must be allocated by the caller.

`public void setPosition(int index, Point3f position)`
`public void getPosition(int index, Point3f position)`

These two methods set and get the interpolator's indexed position.

◀ New in 1.2 ▶ `public void getPositions(Point3f[] positions)`

This method copies the array of position values from this interpolator into the specified array. The array must be large enough to hold all of the positions. The individual array elements must be allocated by the caller.

`public void setAxisOfRotPosScale(Transform3D axisOfRotPosScale)`
`public Transform3D getAxisOfRotPosScale()`

These two methods set and get the interpolator's axis of rotation, translation, and scale.

`public void setTarget(TransformGroup target)`
`public TransformGroup getTarget()`

These two methods set and get the interpolator's target TransformGroup object.

◀ New in 1.2 ▶ `public void setPathArrays(float[] knots, Quat4f[] quats,`
`        Point3f[] positions, float[] scales)`

This method replaces the existing arrays of knot values, quaternion values, position values, and scale values with the specified arrays. The arrays of knots, quats, positions, and scales are copied into this interpolator object.

`public void processStimulus(Enumeration criteria)`

This method is invoked by the behavior scheduler every frame. It maps the alpha value that corresponds to the current time into translation, rotation, and scale values; computes a transform based on these values; and updates the specified TransformGroup node with this new transform.

10.6.15 RotationPathInterpolator Object

The RotationPathInterpolator class extends the PathInterpolator class. It varies the rotational component of its target TransformGroup by linearly interpolating among a series of predefined knot/orientation pairs (using the value generated by the specified Alpha object). The interpolated orientation is used to generate a rotation transform in the local coordinate system of this interpolator.

The first knot must have a value of 0.0. The last knot must have a value of 1.0. An intermediate knot with index k must have a value strictly greater than any knot with index less than k.

Constructors

```
public RotationPathInterpolator(Alpha alpha,
      TransformGroup target, Transform3D axisOfRotation,
      float knots[], Quat4f quats[])
```

This constructor constructs a new RotationPathInterpolator object that varies the target TransformGroup node's transform. The `axisOfRotation` parameter speci- fies the transform that defines the local coordinate system in which this interpo- lator operates. The `knots` parameter specifies an array of knot values that specifies a spline. The `quats` parameter specifies an array of quaternion values at the knots.

Methods

```
public void setQuat(int index, Quat4f quat)
public void getQuat(int index, Quat4f quat)
```

These two methods set and get the interpolator's indexed quaternion value.

```
public void setAxisOfRotation(Transform3D axisOfRotation)
public Transform3D getAxisOfRotation()
```

These two methods set and get the interpolator's axis of rotation.

```
public void setTarget(TransformGroup target)
public TransformGroup getTarget()
```

These two methods set and get the interpolator's target TransformGroup object.

```
public void setPathArrays(float[] knots, Quat4f[] quats)
```
◀ New in 1.2 ▶

This method replaces the existing arrays of knot values and quaternion values with the specified arrays. The arrays of knots and quats are copied into this inter- polator object.

309

◄ New in 1.2 ► `public void getQuats(Quat4f[] quats)`

This method copies the array of quaternion values from this interpolator into the specified array. The array must be large enough to hold all of the quats. The individual array elements must be allocated by the caller.

`public void processStimulus(Enumeration criteria)`

This method is invoked by the behavior scheduler every frame. It maps the alpha value that corresponds to the current time into a rotation angle, computes a transform based on this angle, and updates the specified TransformGroup node with this new transform.

10.7 Level-of-Detail Behaviors

The LOD (Level of Detail) leaf node is an abstract behavior class that operates on a list of Switch group nodes to select one of the children of the Switch nodes. Specializations of the LOD abstract behavior node implement various level-of-detail policies.

10.7.1 LOD Object

The LOD behavior node is an abstract class that is subclassed to implement selection among two or more levels of detail using an LOD selection criteria defined by the subclass.

Constructors

`public LOD()`

Constructs and initializes a new LOD node.

Methods

The LOD node class defines the following methods:

```
public void addSwitch(Switch switchNode)
public void setSwitch(Switch switchNode, int index)
public void insertSwitch(Switch switchNode, int index)
public void removeSwitch(int index)
public Switch getSwitch(int index)
public int numSwitches()
```

The addSwitch method appends the specified Switch node to this LOD's list of switches. The setSwitch method replaces the specified Switch node with the Switch node provided. The insertSwitch method inserts the specified Switch node at the specified index. The removeSwitch method removes the Switch node at the specified index. The getSwitch method returns the Switch node specified by the index. The numSwitches method returns a count of this LOD's switches.

public Enumeration getAllSwitches()

This method returns the Enumeration object of all switches.

10.7.2   DistanceLOD Object

The DistanceLOD behavior node implements a distance-based LOD policy. It operates on a Switch group node to select one of the children of that Switch node based on the distance of this LOD node from the viewer. An array of n monotonically increasing distance values is specified, such that distances[0] is associated with the highest level of detail, and distances[$n-1$] is associated with the lowest level of detail. Based on the actual distance from the viewer to this DistanceLOD node, these n distance values [0, $n-1$] select from among $n+1$ levels of detail [0, n]. If d is the distance from the viewer to the LOD node, then the equation for determining which level of detail (child of the Switch node) is selected is

$$0, \text{ if } d \leq \text{distances}[0]$$
$$i, \text{ if distances}[i-1] < d \leq \text{distances}[i]$$
$$n, \text{ if } d > \text{distances}[n-1]$$

Both the position of this node and the array of LOD distances are defined in the local coordinate system of this node.

Constructors

public DistanceLOD()

This constructor creates a DistanceLOD object with a single distance value set to 0.0 and is, therefore, not very useful.

public DistanceLOD(float distances[])
public DistanceLOD(float distances[], Point3f position)

Construct and initialize a new DistanceLOD node. The distances parameter specifies a vector of doubles representing LOD cutoff distances. The position parameter specifies the position of this node in local coordinates. The default position is (0,0,0).

Methods

```
public void setPosition(Point3f position)
public void getPosition(Point3f position)
```

These methods set and retrieve the position parameter for this DistanceLOD node. This position is specified in the local coordinates of this node, and is the position from which the distance to the viewer is computed.

```
public int numDistances()
public double getDistance(int whichDistance)
public void setDistance(int whichDistance, double distance)
```

The numDistances method returns a count of the number of LOD distance cutoff parameters. The getDistance method returns a particular LOD cutoff distance. The setDistance method sets a particular LOD cutoff distance.

```
public void initialize()
```

This method sets up the initial wakeup criteria.

```
public void processStimulus(Enumeration criteria)
```

This method computes the appropriate level of detail.

10.8   Billboard Behavior

The Billboard behavior node operates on the TransformGroup node to cause the local +z axis of the TransformGroup to point at the viewer's eye position. This is done regardless of the transforms above the specified TransformGroup node in the scene graph.

Billboard nodes provide the most benefit for complex, roughly symmetric objects. A typical use might consist of a quadrilateral that contains a texture map of a tree.

The Billboard node is similar in functionality to the OrientedShape3D node. See also Section 6.2.1, "OrientedShape3D Node."

Constants

The Billboard class adds the following new constants:

```
public static final int ROTATE_ABOUT_AXIS
```

Specifies that rotation should be about the specified axis.

public static final int ROTATE_ABOUT_POINT

Specifies that rotation should be about the specified point and that the children's *y*-axis should match the ViewPlatform's *Y*-axis.

Constructors

The Billboard class specifies the following constructors:

public Billboard()

Constructs a Billboard node with the following default parameters:

Parameter	Default Value
alignmentMode	ROTATE_ABOUT_AXIS
alignmentAxis	*y*-axis (0,1,0)
rotationPoint	(0,0,1)
target transform group	null

public Billboard(TransformGroup tg)

Constructs a Billboard node with default parameters that operates on the specified TransformGroup node. The default alignment mode is ROTATE_ABOUT_AXIS rotation with the axis pointing along the *y*-axis.

public Billboard(TransformGroup tg, int mode, Vector3f axis)
public Billboard(TransformGroup tg, int mode, Point3f point)

The first constructor constructs a Billboard behavior node with default parameters that operates on the specified target TransformGroup node. The default alignment mode is ROTATE_ABOUT_AXIS, with the axis along the *Y*-axis. The next two constructors construct a Billboard behavior node with the specified axis and mode that operate on the specified TransformGroup node. The axis parameter specifies the ray about which the billboard rotates. The point parameter specifies the position about which the billboard rotates. The mode parameter is the alignment mode and is either ROTATE_ABOUT_AXIS or ROTATE_ABOUT_POINT.

Methods

The Billboard class defines the following methods:

```
public void setAlignmentMode(int mode)
public int getAlignmentMode()
```

These methods, if enabled by the appropriate flag, permit an application to either retrieve or set the Billboard node's alignment mode, one of ROTATE_ABOUT_AXIS or ROTATE_ABOUT_POINT.

```
public void setAlignmentAxis(Vector3f axis)
public void setAlignmentAxis(float x, float y, float z)
public void getAlignmentAxis(Vector3f axis)
```

These methods, if enabled by the appropriate flag, permit an application to set or retrieve the Billboard node's alignment axis.

```
public void setTarget(TransformGroup tg)
public TransformGroup getTarget()
```

These methods set or retrieve the target TransformGroup node for this Billboard object.

```
public void setRotationPoint(float x, float y, float z)
public void setRotationPoint(Point3f point)
public void getRotationPoint(Point3f point)
```

The first two methods set the rotation point. The third method gets the rotation point and sets the parameter to this value.

```
public void initialize()
```

This method sets up the initial wakeup criteria.

```
public void processStimulus(Enumeration criteria)
```

This method computes the appropriate transform.

CHAPTER 11

Input Devices and Picking

JAVA 3D provides access to keyboards and mice using the standard Java API for keyboard and mouse support. Additionally, Java 3D provides access to a variety of continuous-input devices such as six-degrees-of-freedom (6DOF) trackers and joysticks.

Continuous-input devices like 6DOF trackers and joysticks have well-defined continuous inputs. Trackers produce a position and orientation that Java 3D stores internally as a transformation matrix. Joysticks produce two continuous values in the range $[-1.0, 1.0]$ that Java 3D stores internally as a transformation matrix with an identity rotation (no rotation) and one of the joystick values as the x translation and the other value as the y translation component.

Unfortunately, continuous-input devices do not have the same level of consistency when it comes to their associated switches or buttons. Still, the number of buttons or switches attached to a particular sensing element remains constant across all sensing elements associated with a single device.

11.1 InputDevice Interface

The InputDevice interface specifies an abstract input device that a developer can use in implementing a device driver for a particular device. All implementations of an InputDevice interface must implement all of its methods. Java 3D's input device scheduler uses these methods to interact with specific devices and incorporate their input. In addition to the generic methods that all InputDevices must provide, implementations of an InputDevice will contain whatever device-specific information and methods are necessary to maintain that device's proper functioning.

All input devices consist of a number of Sensor objects that have a direct one-to-one relationship with that device's physical detectors. Sensor objects serve double duty. Not only do they represent actual physical detectors, but they also serve as abstract six-degrees-of-freedom transformations that a Java 3D application can access. The Sensor class is described in more detail in Section 11.2.3, "The Sensor Object."

11.1.1 The Abstract Interface

All input devices implement a consistent interface that allows the initialization, processing of input, and finalization of a particular input device. A device-driver programmer would implement the following methods in whatever device-specific manner is necessary to perform the specified operations:

Constants

```
public static final int BLOCKING
public static final int NON_BLOCKING
public static final int DEMAND_DRIVEN
```

These three flags control how Java 3D schedules reads. The BLOCKING flag signifies that the driver for a device is a *blocking driver* and that it should be scheduled for regular reads by Java 3D. A blocking driver is a driver that can cause the thread accessing the driver (the Java 3D implementation thread calling the poll-AndProcessInput method) to block while the data is being accessed from the driver. The NON_BLOCKING flag signifies that the driver for a device is a nonblocking driver and that it should be scheduled for regular reads by Java 3D. The DEMAND_DRIVEN flag signifies that the Java 3D implementation should not schedule regular reads on the sensors of this device; the Java 3D implementation will call only pollAndProcessInput when the getRead method for one of the device's sensors is called. A DEMAND_DRIVEN driver must always provide the current value of the sensor on demand whenever pollAndProcessInput is called. This means that DEMAND_DRIVEN drivers are nonblocking by definition.

Methods

```
public abstract boolean initialize()
```

This method initializes the device. It returns true if initialization succeeded, false otherwise.

```
public abstract void setProcessingMode(int mode)
public abstract int getProcessingMode()
```

These methods set and retrieve this device's processing mode, one of BLOCKING, NON_BLOCKING, or DEMAND_DRIVEN.

public int getSensorCount()

This method returns the number of Sensor objects associated with this device.

public Sensor getSensor(int sensorIndex)

This method returns the specified Sensor associated with this device.

public abstract void setNominalPositionAndOrientation()

This method sets the device's current position and orientation as the device's nominal position and orientation (that is, it establishes its reference frame relative to the "tracker base" reference frame). This method is most useful in defining a nominal pose in immersive head-tracked situations.

public abstract void pollAndProcessInput()

This method first polls the device for data values and then processes the values received from the device. For BLOCKING and NON_BLOCKING drivers, this method is called regularly and the Java 3D implementation can cache the sensor values. For DEMAND_DRIVEN drivers, this method is called each time one of the Sensor.getRead methods is called; it is not otherwise called.

public abstract void processStreamInput()

This method will not be called by the Java 3D implementation and should be implemented as an empty method.

public abstract void close()

This method cleans up the device and relinquishes the associated resources. This method should be called after the device has been unregistered from Java 3D via the PhysicalEnvironment.removeInputDevice(InputDevice) method.

11.1.2   Instantiating and Registering a New Device

A browser or applications developer must instantiate whatever system-specific input devices that he or she needs and whatever exists on the system. This available-device information typically exists in a site configuration file. The browser or application will instantiate the viewing environment as requested by the end user.

The API for instantiating devices is site-specific, but it consists of a device object with a constructor and at least all of the methods specified in the Input-Device interface.

Once instantiated, the browser or application must register the device with the Java 3D input device scheduler. The API for registering devices is specified in Section 9.7, "The View Object." The addInputDevice method introduces new devices to the Java 3D environment, and the allInputDevices method produces an enumeration that allows examination of all available devices within a Java 3D environment.

11.2 Sensors

The Java 3D API provides only an abstract concept of a device. Rather than focusing on issues of devices and device models, it instead defines the concept of a sensor. A sensor consists of a timestamped sequence of input values and the state of the buttons or switches at the time that Java 3D sampled the value. A sensor also contains a hotspot offset specified in that sensor's local coordinate system. If not specified, the hotspot is (0.0, 0.0, 0.0).

Since a typical hardware environment contains multiple sensing elements, Java 3D maintains an array of sensors. Users can access a sensor directly from their Java code or they can assign a sensor to one of Java 3D's predefined 6DOF entities such as UserHead.

11.2.1   Using and Assigning Sensors

Using a sensor is as easy as accessing an object. The application developer writes Java code to extract the associated sensor value from the array of sensors. The developer can then directly apply that value to an element in a scene graph or process the sensor values in whatever way necessary.

Java 3D includes three special six-degrees-of-freedom (6DOF) entities. These include UserHead, DominantHand, and NondominantHand. An application developer can assign or change which sensor drives one of these predefined entities. Java 3D uses the specified sensor to drive the 6DOF entity—most visibly the View. Application developers should use this facility carefully, as it is quite easy to get the effect of a WristCam—and very disconcerting as well.

11.2.2   Behind the (Sensor) Scenes

Java 3D does not provide raw tracker or joystick-generated data in a sensor. At a minimum, Java 3D normalizes the raw data using the registration and calibration parameters either provided by or provided for the end user. Additionally, it may filter and process the data to remove noise and improve latency. The application programmer can suppress this latter effect on a sensor-by-sensor basis.

Unfortunately, tracker or sensor hardware may not always be available or be operational. Thus, Java 3D provides both an available and an enable flag on a per-sensor basis.

11.2.3   The Sensor Object

Java 3D stores its sensor array in the PhysicalEnvironment object. Each Sensor in the array consists of a fixed number of SensorRead objects. Also associated with each SensorRead is its timestamp and the state of that sensor's buttons.

Constants

The Sensor object specifies the following constants:

```
public static final int PREDICT_NONE
public static final int PREDICT_NEXT_FRAME_TIME
```

These flags define the Sensor's predictor type. The first flag defines no prediction. The second flag specifies to generate the value to correspond with the next frame time.

```
public static final int NO_PREDICTOR
public static final int HEAD_PREDICTOR
public static final int HAND_PREDICTOR
```

These flags define the Sensor's predictor policy. The first flag specifies to use no prediction policy. The second flag specifies to assume that the sensor is predicting head position or orientation. The third flag specifies to assume that the sensor is predicting hand position or orientation.

```
public static final int DEFAULT_SENSOR_READ_COUNT
```

This constant specifies the default number of SensorRead objects constructed when no SensorRead count is specified.

Constructors

The Sensor object specifies the following constructors:

```
public Sensor(InputDevice device)
```

Constructs a Sensor object for the specified input device using default parameters:

Parameter	Default Value
sensorReadCount	0
sensorButtonCount	0
hotspot	(0,0,0)
predictor	PREDICT_NONE
predictionPolicy	NO_PREDICTOR

public Sensor(InputDevice device, int sensorReadCount)
public Sensor(InputDevice device, int sensorReadCount,
        int sensorButtonCount)

These methods construct a new Sensor object associated with the specified device. They consist of either a default number of SensorReads or sensorRead-Count number of SensorReads and a hot spot at (0.0, 0.0, 0.0) specified in the sensor's local coordinate system. The default for sensorButtonCount is zero.

public Sensor(InputDevice device, Point3d hotspot)
public Sensor(InputDevice device, int sensorReadCount,
        Point3d hotspot)
public Sensor(InputDevice device, int sensorReadCount,
        int sensorButtonCount, Point3d hotspot)

These methods construct a new Sensor object associated with the specified device and consist of either sensorReadCount number of SensorReads or a default number of SensorReads and an offset defining the sensor's hot spot in the sensor's local coordinate system. The default for sensorButtonCount is zero.

Methods

public void setSensorReadCount(int count)
public int getSensorReadCount()
public int getSensorButtonCount()

These methods set and retrieve the number of SensorRead objects associated with this sensor and the number of buttons associated with this sensor. Both the number of SensorRead objects and the number of buttons are determined at Sensor construction time.

public void getHotspot(Point3d hotspot)
public void setHotspot(Point3d hotspot)

These methods set and retrieve the sensor's hotspot offset. The hotspot is specified in the sensor's local coordinate system.

```
public void lastRead(Transform3D read)
public void lastRead(Transform3D read, int kth)
```

These methods extract the most recent sensor reading and the *k*th most recent sensor reading from the Sensor object. In both cases, the methods copy the sensor value into the specified argument.

```
public void getRead(Transform3D read)
public void getRead(Transform3D read, long deltaT)
```

The first method computes the sensor reading consistent with the prediction policy and copies that value into the read matrix. The second method computes the sensor reading consistent as of time deltaT in the future and copies that value into the read matrix. All times are in milliseconds.

```
public long lastTime()
public long lastTime(int k)
```

These methods return the time associated with the most recent sensor reading and with the *k*th most recent sensor reading, respectively.

```
public int lastButtons(int values[])
public void lastButtons(int k, int values[])
```

The first method places the most recent sensor reading value for each button into the array parameter. The second method places the *k*th most recent sensor reading value for each button into the array parameter, where 0 is the most recent sensor reading, 1 is the next most recent sensor reading, and so on. These methods will throw an ArrayIndexOutOfBoundsException if values.length is less than the number of buttons.

```
public void setPredictor(int predictor)
public int getPredictor()
```

These methods set and retrieve the sensor's predictor policy. The predictor policy is either PREDICT_NONE or PREDICT_NEXT_FRAME_TIME.

```
public void setPredictionPolicy(int policy)
public int getPredictionPolicy()
```

These methods set and retrieve the sensor's predictor type. The predictor type is one of the following: NO_PREDICTOR, HEAD_PREDICTOR, or HAND_PREDICTOR.

```
public void setDevice(InputDevice device)
public InputDevice getDevice()
```

These methods set and retrieve the sensor's input device.

321

```
public SensorRead getCurrentSensorRead()
```

This method returns the current number of SensorRead objects per sensor.

```
public void setNextSensorRead(long time, Transform3D transform,
    int[] values)
public void setNextSensorRead(SensorRead read)
```

The first method sets the next sensor read to the specified values; once these values are set via this method, they become the current values returned by methods such as lastRead(), lastTime() and lastButtons(): Note that if there are no buttons associated with this sensor, then values can just be an empty array. The second method sets the next SensorRead object to the specified values, including the next SensorRead's associated time, transformation, and button state array.

11.2.4   The SensorRead Object

A SensorRead object encapsulates all the information associated with a single reading of a sensor, including a timestamp, a transform, and, optionally, button values.

Constants

```
public static final int MAXIMUM_SENSOR_BUTTON_COUNT
```

This flag determines the maximum number of sensor-attached buttons tracked on a per-sensor basis.

Constructors

The SensorRead object specifies the following constructor:

```
public SensorRead()
```

Constructs a SensorRead object with the following default parameters:

Parameter	Default Value
numButtons	0
button values	0 (for all array elements)
transform	identity
time	current time

```
public SensorRead(int numButtons)
```

Constructs a SensorRead object with the specified number of buttons.

Methods

```
public void set(Transform3D t1)
public void get(Transform3D result)
```

These methods set and retrieve the SensorRead object's transform. They allow a device to store a new rotation and orientation value into the SensorRead object and a consumer of that value to access it.

```
public void setTime(long time)
public long getTime()
```

These methods set and retrieve the SensorRead object's timestamp. They allow a device to store a new timestamp value into the SensorRead object and a consumer of that value to access it.

```
public void setButtons(int values[])
public void getButtons(int values[])
```

These methods set and retrieve the SensorRead object's button values. They allow a device to store an integer that encodes the button values into the Sensor-Read object and a consumer of those values to access the state of the buttons.

```
public int getNumButtons()
```
◀ New in 1.2 ▶

This method returns the number of buttons associated with this SensorRead object.

11.3 Picking

Behavior nodes provide the means for building developer-specific picking semantics. An application developer can define custom picking semantics using Java 3D's behavior mechanism (see Chapter 10, "Behaviors and Interpolators"). The developer might wish to define pick semantics that use a mouse to shoot a ray into the virtual universe from the current viewpoint, find the first object along that ray, and highlight that object when the end user releases the mouse button. A typical scenario follows:

1. The application constructs a Behavior node that arms itself to awaken when AWT detects a left-mouse-button-down event.

2. Upon awakening from a left-mouse-button-down event, the behavior

   a. Updates a Switch node to draw a ray that emanates from the center of the screen.

    b.   Changes that ray's TransformGroup node so that the ray points in the direction of the current mouse position.

    c.   Declares its interest in mouse-move or left-mouse-button-up events.

3. Upon awakening from a mouse-move event, the behavior

    a.   Changes that ray's TransformGroup node so that the ray points in the direction of the current mouse position.

    b.   Declares its interest in mouse-move or left-mouse-button-up events.

4. Upon awakening from a left-mouse-button-up event, the behavior

    a.   Changes that ray's TransformGroup node so that the ray points in the direction of the current mouse position.

    b.   Intersects the ray with all the objects in the virtual universe to find the first object that the ray intersects.

    c.   Changes the appearance component of that object's shape node to highlight the selected object.

    d.   Declares its interest in left-mouse-button-down events.

Java 3D includes helping functions that aid in intersecting various geometric objects with objects in the virtual universe by

- Intersecting an oriented ray with all the objects in the virtual universe. That function can return the first object intersected along that ray, all the objects that intersect that ray, or a list of all the objects along that ray sorted by distance from the ray's origin.

- Intersecting a volume with all the objects in the virtual universe. That function returns a list of all the objects contained in that volume.

- Discovering which vertex within an object is closest to a specified ray.

Note: Picking and scene graph update are not synchronized. In Java 3D version 1.2, the elapsed time between a scene graph update and a pick (that uses the updated scene graph) is about three frames.

11.3.1   SceneGraphPath Object

A SceneGraphPath object represents the path from a Locale to a terminal node in the scene graph. This path consists of a Locale, a terminal node, and an array of internal nodes that are in the path from the Locale to the terminal node. The terminal node may be either a Leaf node or a Group node. A valid SceneGraphPath must uniquely identify a specific instance of the terminal node. For nodes that are not under a SharedGroup, the minimal SceneGraphPath consists of the Locale and the terminal node itself. For nodes that are under a SharedGroup, the minimal SceneGraphPath consists of the Locale, the terminal node, and a list of all Link nodes in the path from the Locale to the terminal node. A SceneGraphPath may optionally contain other interior nodes that are in the path. A SceneGraphPath is verified for correctness and uniqueness when it is sent as an argument to other methods of Java 3D.

In the array of internal nodes, the node at index 0 is the node closest to the Locale. The indices increase along the path to the terminal node, with the node at index length-1 being the node closest to the terminal node. The array of nodes does not contain either the Locale (which is not a node) or the terminal node.

During picking and intersection tests, the user specifies the subtree of the scene graph that should be tested. The whole tree for a Locale is searched by providing the Locale to the picking or intersection tests.

The SceneGraphPath object returned by the picking methods represents all the components in the subgraph that have the capability `ENABLE_PICK_REPORTING` set between the root of the subtree and the picked or intersected object. All Link nodes are implicitly enabled for pick reporting. Note that `ENABLE_PICK_REPORT-ING` and `ENABLE_COLLISION_REPORTING` are disabled by default. This means that the picking and collision methods will return the minimal SceneGraphPath by default.

When a SceneGraphPath is returned from the picking or collision methods of Java 3D, it will also contain the value of the LocalToVworld transform of the terminal node that was in effect at the time the pick or collision occurred.

Constructors

`public SceneGraphPath()`

Constructs and initializes a new SceneGraphPath object with default values:

Parameter	Default Value
root `Locale`	null
`object`	null
`nodeCount`	null
`transform`	identity

```
public SceneGraphPath(Locale root, Node object)
public SceneGraphPath(Locale root, Node nodes[], Node object)
```

These construct and initialize a new SceneGraphPath object. The first form specifies the path's Locale object and the object in question. The second form includes an array of nodes that fall in between the Locale and the object in question, and which nodes have their ENABLE_PICK_REPORTING capability bit set. The object parameter may be a Group, Shape3D, or Morph node. If any other type of leaf node is specified, an IllegalArgumentException is thrown.

Methods

```
public final void set(SceneGraphPath newPath)
public final void setLocale(Locale newLocale)
public final void setObject(Node object)
public final void setNode(int index, Node newNode)
public final void setNodes(Node nodes[])
```

These methods set the path's values. The first method sets the path's interior values. The second method sets the path's Locale to the specified Locale. The third method sets the path's object to the specified object (a Group node, or a Shape3D or Morph leaf node). The fourth method replaces the link node associated with the specified index with the specified newLink. The last method replaces all of the link nodes with the new list of link nodes.

```
public final Locale getLocale()
public final Node getObject()
```

The first method returns the path's Locale; the second method returns the path's object.

```
public final int nodeCount()
public final Node getNode(int index)
```

The first method returns the number of intermediate nodes in this path; the second method returns the node associated with the specified index.

```
public final void setTransform(Transform3D trans)
public final Transform3D getTransform()
```

The set method sets the transform component of this SceneGraphPath to the value of the passed transform. The get method returns a copy of the transform associated with this SceneGraphPath. The method returns null if there is no transform associated. If this SceneGraphPath was returned by a Java 3D picking and collision method, the local-coordinate-to-virtual-coordinate transform for this scene graph object at the time of the pick or collision is recorded.

`public final boolean isSamePath(SceneGraphPath testPath)`

This method determines whether two SceneGraphPath objects represent the same path in the scene graph. Either object might include a different subset of internal nodes; only the internal link nodes, the Locale, and the Node itself are compared. The paths are not validated for correctness or uniqueness.

`public boolean equals(SceneGraphPath testPath)`
`public boolean equals(Object o1)`

The first method returns `true` if all of the data members of path `testPath` are equal to the corresponding data members in this SceneGraphPath. The second method returns true if the Object `o1` is of type SceneGraphPath and all of the data members of `o1` are equal to the corresponding data members in this SceneGraphPath and if the values of the transforms are equal.

`public int hashCode()`

This method returns a hash number based on the data values in this object. Two different SceneGraphPath objects with identical data values (that is, `trans.-equals(SceneGraphPath)` returns `true`) will return the same hash number. Two paths with different data members may return the same hash value, although this is not likely.

`public String toString()`

This method returns a string representation of this object. The string contains the class names of all nodes in the SceneGraphPath.

11.3.2   BranchGroup Node and Locale Node Pick Methods

The following methods are in both the BranchGroup node class and the Locale node class:

`public SceneGraphPath[] pickAll(PickShape pickShape)`
`public SceneGraphPath[] pickAllSorted(PickShape pickShape)`
`public SceneGraphPath pickClosest(PickShape pickShape)`
`public SceneGraphPath pickAny(PickShape pickShape)`

These methods return either an array of SceneGraphPath objects or a single SceneGraphPath object. A SceneGraphPath object describes the entire path from a Locale to a node that intersects the specified PickShape (see Section 11.3.3,

"PickShape Object"). The methods that return an array return either all the picked objects or all the picked objects in sorted order starting with the objects "closest" to the eyepoint and ending with the objects farthest from the eyepoint. Methods that return a single SceneGraphPath return a single path object that specifies either the object closest to the eyepoint or any picked object (this latter method also implements the fastest pick operation possible). All ties in testing for closest objects intersected result in an indeterminate order.

11.3.3   PickShape Object

The PickShape object is an abstract class for describing a shape that can be used with the BranchGroup and Locale pick methods. The PickShape object is extended by PickBounds, PickCone, PickCylinder, PickPoint, PickRay, and PickSegment objects. The PickCylinder object is further extended by the PickCylinder and PickCylinderSegment objects. The PickCone object is further extended by the PickConeRay and PickConeSegment objects.

Constructors

```
public PickShape()
```

Constructs a PickShape object.

11.3.4   PickBounds Object

The PickBounds object provides a bounds to supply to the BranchGroup and Locale pick methods. See also Section 11.3.2, "BranchGroup Node and Locale Node Pick Methods."

Constructors

```
public PickBounds()
public PickBounds(Bounds boundsObject)
```

The first constructor creates a PickBounds initialized with the bounds set to null. The second constructor creates a PickBounds with the bounds set to boundsObject.

Methods

```
public void set(Bounds boundsObject)
public Bounds get()
```

These methods set and retrieve the boundsObject of this PickBounds.

11.3.5   PickPoint Object

The PickPoint object provides a point to supply to the BranchGroup and Locale pick methods. See also Section 11.3.2, "BranchGroup Node and Locale Node Pick Methods."

Constructors

```
public PickPoint()
public PickPoint(Point3d location)
```

The first constructor creates a PickPoint initialized to (0,0,0). The second constructor creates a PickPoint at the specified location.

Methods

```
public void set(Point3d location)
public void get(Point3d location)
```

These methods set and retrieve the position of this PickPoint.

11.3.6   PickRay Object

The PickRay object is an encapsulation of a ray that is passed to the pick methods in BranchGroup and Locale. See also Section 11.3.2, "BranchGroup Node and Locale Node Pick Methods."

Constructors

```
public PickRay()
public PickRay(Point3d origin, Vector3d direction)
```

The first constructor creates a PickRay initialized with an origin and direction of (0,0,0). The second constructor creates a PickRay from the specified origin and direction.

Methods

```
public void set(Point3d origin, Vector3d direction)
public void get(Point3d origin, Vector3d direction)
```

These methods set and retrieve the origin and direction of this PickRay object.

11.3.7   PickSegment Object

The PickSegment object is an encapsulation of a segment that is passed to the pick methods in BranchGroup and Locale. See also Section 11.3.2, "Branch-Group Node and Locale Node Pick Methods."

Constructors

```
public PickSegment()
public PickSegment(Point3d start, Point3d end)
```

The first constructor creates a PickSegment object with the start and end of the segment initialized to (0,0,0). The second constructor creates a PickSegment object from the specified start and end points.

Methods

```
public void set(Point3d start, Point3d end)
public void get(Point3d start, Point3d end)
```

These methods set and retrieve the start and end points of this PickSegment object.

11.3.8   PickCone Object

The PickCone object is the abstract base class for all cone pick shapes. PickCone is extended by the PickConeRay and PickConeSegment classes.

Constructors

◀ New in 1.2 ▶ `public PickCone()`

Constructs an empty PickCone. The origin and direction of the cone are initialized to (0,0,0). The spread angle is initialized to $\pi/64$.

Methods

◀ New in 1.2 ▶ `public void getOrigin(Point3d origin)`
◀ New in 1.2 ▶ `public void getDirection(Vector3d direction)`
◀ New in 1.2 ▶ `public double getSpreadAngle()`

These three methods return the origin, direction, and spread angle of this Pick-Cone, respectively.

11.3.9   PickConeRay Object   ◀ New in 1.2 ▶

The PickConeRay object is an infinite cone pick ray shape. It can be used as an argument to the picking methods in BranchGroup and Locale.

Constructors

```
public PickConeRay()                              ◀ New in 1.2 ▶
public PickConeRay(Point3d origin, Vector3d direction,    ◀ New in 1.2 ▶
    double spreadAngle)
```

The first constructor creates an empty PickConeRay. The origin and direction of the cone are initialized to (0,0,0). The spread angle is initialized to $\pi/64$ radian. The second constructor creates an infinite cone pick shape from the specified parameters.

Methods

```
public void set(Point3d origin, Vector3d direction,     ◀ New in 1.2 ▶
    double spreadAngle)
```

This method sets the parameters of this PickCone to the specified values.

11.3.10   PickConeSegment Object   ◀ New in 1.2 ▶

The PickConeSegment object is a finite cone segment pick shape. It can be used as an argument to the picking methods in BranchGroup and Locale.

Constructors

```
public PickConeSegment()                          ◀ New in 1.2 ▶
public PickConeSegment(Point3d origin, Point3d end,     ◀ New in 1.2 ▶
    double spreadAngle)
```

The first constructor creates an empty PickConeSegment. The origin and end point of the cone are initialized to (0,0,0). The spread angle is initialized to $\pi/64$ radians. The second constructor creates a finite cone pick shape from the specified parameters.

Methods

```
public void set(Point3d origin, Point3d end, double spreadAngle)  ◀ New in 1.2 ▶
```

This method sets the parameters of this PickCone to the specified values.

◀ New in 1.2 ▶ `public void getEnd(Point3d end)`

> This method gets the end point of this PickConeSegment.

◀ New in 1.2 ▶ ## 11.3.11 PickCylinder Object

The PickCylinder object is the abstract base class of all cylindrical pick shapes.

Constructors

◀ New in 1.2 ▶ `public PickCylinder()`

> This constructor creates an empty PickCylinder. The origin of the cylinder is initialized to (0,0,0). The radius is initialized to 0.

Methods

◀ New in 1.2 ▶ `public void getOrigin(Point3d origin)`
◀ New in 1.2 ▶ `public double getRadius()`
◀ New in 1.2 ▶ `public void getDirection(Vector3d direction)`

> These three methods return the origin, radius, and direction of this PickCylinder object.

11.3.12 PickCylinderRay Object

The PickCylinderRay object is an infinite cylindrical ray pick shape. It can be used as an argument to the picking methods in BranchGroup and Locale.

Constructors

◀ New in 1.2 ▶ `public PickCylinderRay()`
◀ New in 1.2 ▶ `public PickCylinderRay(Point3d origin, Vector3d direction,`
                        `double radius)`

> The first constructor creates an empty PickCylinderRay. The origin and direction of the cylindrical ray are initialized to (0,0,0). The radius is initialized to 0. The second constructor creates an infinite cylindrical ray pick shape from the specified parameters.

Methods

◀ New in 1.2 ▶ `public void set(Point3d origin, Vector3d direction, double radius)`

> This method sets the parameters of this PickCylinderRay to the specified values.

11.3.13 PickCylinderSegment Object

The PickCylinderSegment object is a finite cylindrical segment pick shape. It can be used as an argument to the picking methods in BranchGroup and Locale.

Constructors

```
public PickCylinderSegment()                        ◀ New in 1.2 ▶
public PickCylinderSegment(Point3d start, Point3d end,   ◀ New in 1.2 ▶
     double radius)
```

The first constructor creates an empty PickCylinderSegment. The start and end points of the cylindrical segment are initialized to (0,0,0). The radius is initialized to 0.

Methods

```
public void set(Point3d start, Point3d end, double radius)   ◀ New in 1.2 ▶
```

This method sets the parameters of this PickCylinderSegment to the specified values.

```
public void getEnd(Point3d end)                     ◀ New in 1.2 ▶
```

This method returns the end point of this PickCylinderSegment.

CHAPTER 12

Audio Devices

A Java 3D application running on a particular machine could have one of several options available to it for playing the audio image created by the sound renderer. Perhaps the machine on which Java 3D is executing has more than one sound card (for example, one that is a wave table synthesis card and the other with accelerated sound spatialization hardware). Furthermore, suppose there are Java 3D audio device drivers that execute Java 3D audio methods on each of these specific cards. The application would therefore have at least two audio device drivers through which the audio could be produced. For such a case the Java 3D application must choose the audio device driver with which sound rendering is to be performed. Once this audio device is chosen, the application can additionally select the type of audio playback on which device the rendered sound image is to be output. The playback device (headphones or speaker(s)) is physically connected to the port to which the selected device driver outputs.

12.1 AudioDevice Interface

The selection of this device driver is done through methods in the PhysicalEnvironment object (see Section C.9, "The PhysicalEnvironment Object"). The application queries how many audio devices are available. For each device, the user can get the AudioDevice object that describes it and query its characteristics. Once a decision is made about which of the available audio devices to use for a PhysicalEnvironment, the particular device is set into this PhysicalEnvironment's fields. Each PhysicalEnvironment object may use only a single audio device.

The AudioDevice object interface specifies an abstract audio device that creators of Java 3D class libraries would implement for a particular device. Java 3D uses several methods to interact with specific devices. Since all audio devices implement this consistent interface, the user could have a portable means of initializing, setting particular audio device elements, and querying generic characteristics for any audio device.

Constants

```
public static final int HEADPHONES
```

Specifies that audio playback will be through stereo headphones.

```
public static final int MONO_SPEAKER
```

Specifies that audio playback will be through a single speaker some distance away from the listener.

```
public static final int STEREO_SPEAKERS
```

Specifies that audio playback will be through stereo speakers some distance away from, and at some angle to, the listener.

12.1.1 Initialization

Each audio device driver must be initialized. The chosen device driver should be initialized before any Java 3D Sound methods are executed because the implementation of the Sound methods, in general, is potentially device-driver dependent.

Methods

```
public abstract boolean initialize()
```

Initializes the audio device. Exactly what occurs during initialization is implementation dependent. This method provides explicit control by the user over when this initialization occurs.

```
public abstract boolean close()
```

Closes the audio device, releasing resources associated with this device.

12.1.2 Audio Playback

Methods to set and retrieve the audio playback parameters are part of the AudioDevice object. The audio playback information specifies that playback will be through one of the following:

- Stereo headphones.

- A monaural speaker.

- A pair of speakers, equally distant from the listener, both at some angle from the head coordinate system *z*-axis. It's assumed that the speakers are at the same elevation and oriented symmetrically about the listener.

The type of playback chosen affects the sound image generated. Cross-talk cancellation is applied to the audio image if playback over stereo speakers is selected.

Methods

The following methods affect the playback of sound processed by the Java 3D sound renderer:

```
public abstract void setAudioPlaybackType(int type)
public abstract int getAudioPlaybackType()
```

These methods set and retrieve the type of audio playback device (HEADPHONES, MONO_SPEAKER, or STEREO_SPEAKERS) used to output the analog audio from rendering Java 3D Sound nodes.

```
public abstract void setCenterEarToSpeaker(float distance)
public abstract float getCenterEarToSpeaker()
```

These methods set and retrieve the distance in meters from the center ear (the midpoint between the left and right ears) and one of the speakers in the listener's environment. For monaural speaker playback, a typical distance from the listener to the speaker in a workstation cabinet is 0.76 meters. For stereo speakers placed at the sides of the display, this might be 0.82 meters.

```
public abstract void setAngleOffsetToSpeaker(float angle)
public abstract float getAngleOffsetToSpeaker()
```

These methods set and retrieve the angle, in radians, between the vectors from the center ear to each of the speaker transducers and the vectors from the center ear parallel to the head coordinate's *z*-axis. Speakers placed at the sides of the computer display typically range between 0.175 and 0.350 radians (between 10 and 20 degrees).

```
public abstract PhysicalEnvironment getPhysicalEnvironment()
```

This method returns a reference to the AudioDevice's PhysicalEnvironment object.

12.1.3 Device-Driver-Specific Data

While the sound image created for final output to the playback system is either only monaural or stereo (for this version of Java 3D), most device-driver implementations will mix the left and right image signals generated for each rendered sound source before outputting the final playback image. Each sound source will use N input channels of this internal mixer.

Each implemented Java 3D audio device driver will have its own limitations and driver-specific characteristics. These include channel availability and usage (during rendering). Methods for querying these device-driver-specific characteristics follow.

Methods

public abstract int getTotalChannels()

This method retrieves the maximum number of channels available for Java 3D sound rendering for all sound sources.

public abstract int getChannelsAvailable()

During rendering, when Sound nodes are playing, this method returns the number of channels still available to Java 3D for rendering additional Sound nodes.

public abstract int getChannelsUsedForSound(Sound node)

This method queries the number of channels that are used or would be used to render a particular sound node. This method returns the number of channels needed to render a particular Sound node. The return value is the same no matter if the Sound is currently active and enabled (being played) or is inactive.

12.2 AudioDevice3D Interface

The AudioDevice3D Class extends the AudioDevice interface. The intent is for this interface to be implemented by AudioDevice driver developers (whether a Java 3D licensee or not). Each implementation will use a sound engine of its choice.

The methods in this interface should *not* be called an application. The methods in this interface are referenced by the core Java 3D Sound classes to render live, scheduled sound on the AudioDevice chosen by the application or the use chosen by the application or user.

Methods in this interface provide the Java 3D core a generic way to set and query the audio device on which the application has chosen to perform audio rendering. Methods in this interface include

- Set up and clear the sound as a sample on the device.

- Start, stop, pause, unpause, mute, and unmute of sample on the device.

- Set parameters for each sample corresponding to the fields in the Sound node.

- Set the current active aural parameters that affect all positional samples.

Constants

```
public static final int BACKGROUND_SOUND
public static final int POINT_SOUND
public static final int CONE_SOUND
```

These constants specify the sound types. Sound types match the Sound node classes defined for Java 3D core for BackgroundSound, PointSound, and Cone-Sound. The type of sound a sample is loaded as determines which methods affect it.

```
public static final int STREAMING_AUDIO_DATA
public static final int BUFFERED_AUDIO_DATA
```

These constants specify the sound data types. Samples can be processed as streaming or buffered data. Fully spatializing sound sources may require data to be buffered.

Sound data specified as *streaming* is not copied by the AudioDevice diver implementation. It is up to the application to ensure that this data is continuously accessible during sound rendering. Futhermore, full sound spatialization may not be possible, for all AudioDevice3D implementations on unbuffered sound data. Sound data specified as *buffered* is copied by the AudioDevice driver implementation.

Methods

public abstract void setView(View reference)

This method accepts a reference to the current View and passes reference to the current View Object. The PhysicalEnvironment parameters (with playback type and speaker placement) and the PhysicalBody parameters (position and orientation of ears) can be obtained from this object and from the transformations to and from ViewPlatform coordinate (the space the listener's head is in) and Virtual World coordinates (the space the sounds are in).

```
public abstract int prepareSound(int soundType,
        MediaContainer soundData)
```

Prepares the sound. This method accepts a reference to the MediaContainer that contains a reference to sound data and information about the type of data it is. The soundType parameter defines the type of sound associated with this sample (Background, Point, or Cone).

Depending on the type of MediaContainer the sound data is and on the implementation of the AudioDevice used, sound data preparation could consist of opening, attaching, or loading sound data into the device. Unless the cached is true, this sound data should *not* be copied, if possible, into host or device memory.

Once this preparation is complete for the sound sample, an AudioDevice-specific index, used to reference the sample in future method calls, is returned. All the rest of the methods that follow require this index as a parameter.

```
public abstract void clearSound(int index)
```

Clears the sound. This method requests that the AudioDevice free all resources associated with the sample with index id.

```
public abstract long getSampleDuration(int index)
```

Queries sample duration. If it can be determined, this method returns the duration in milliseconds of the sound sample. For noncached streams, this method returns Sound.DURATION_UNKNOWN.

```
public abstract int getNumberOfChannelsUsed(int index)
public abstract int getNumberOfChannelsUsed(int index,
        boolean muted)
```

Query the number of channels used by Sound. These methods return the number of channels (on the executing audio device) that this sound is using if it is already playing or those it is expected to use if it were to begin playing. The first method takes the sound's current state (including whether it is muted or unmuted) into account. The second method uses the muted parameter to make the determination.

For some AudioDevice3D implementations,

- Muted sounds take up channels on the systems mixer (because they're rendered as samples playing with gain zero).
- A single sound could be rendered using multiple samples, each taking up mixer channels.

`public abstract int startSample(int index)`

Starts sample. This method begins a sound playing on the AudioDevice and returns a flag indicating whether the sample was started.

`public abstract int stopSample(int index)`

Stops sample. This method stops the sound on the AudioDevice and returns a flag indicating whether the sample was stopped.

`public abstract long getStartTime(int index)`

Queries the last start time for this sound on the device. This method returns the system time of when the sound was last "started." Note that this start time will be as accurate as the AudioDevice implementation can make it, but that it is not guaranteed to be exact.

`public abstract void setSampleGain(int index, float scaleFactor)`

Sets gain scale factor. This method sets the overall gain scale factor applied to data associated with this source to increase or decrease its overall amplitude. The gain `scaleFactor` value passed into this method is the combined value of the Sound node's initial gain and the current AuralAttribute gain scale factors.

`public abstract void setDistanceGain(int index,`
  `double[] frontDistance, float[] frontAttenuationScaleFactor,`
  `double[] backDistance, float[] backAttenuationScaleFactor)`

Sets distance gain. This method sets this sound's distance gain elliptical attenuation (not including the filter cutoff frequency) by defining corresponding arrays containing distances from the sound's origin and gain scale factors applied to all active positional sounds. The gain scale factor is applied to sound based on the distance the listener is from the sound source. These attenuation parameters are ignored for BackgroundSound nodes. The `backAttenuationScaleFactor` parameter is ignored for PointSound nodes.

For a full description of the attenuation parameters, see Section 6.9.3, "Cone-Sound Node."

`public abstract void setDistanceFilter(int filterType,`
  `double[] distance, float[] filterCutoff)`

Sets AuralAttributes distance filter. This method sets the distance filter corresponding arrays containing distances and frequency cutoff applied to all active positional sounds. The gain scale factor is applied to sound based on the distance the listener is from the sound source. For a full description of this parameter and how it is used, see Section 8.1.17, "AuralAttributes Object."

public abstract void setLoop(int index, int count)

Sets loop count. This method sets the number of times sound is looped during play. For a complete description of this method, see the description for the Sound.setLoop method in Section 6.9, "Sound Node."

public abstract void muteSample(int index)
public abstract void unmuteSample(int index)

These methods mute and unmute a playing sound sample. The first method makes a sample play silently. The second method makes a silently playing sample audible. Ideally, the muting of a sample is implemented by stopping a sample and freeing channel resources (rather than just setting the gain of the sample to zero). Ideally, the unmuting of a sample restarts the muted sample by offset from the beginning by the number of milliseconds since the time the sample began playing.

public abstract void pauseSample(int index)
public abstract void unpauseSample(int index)

These methods pause and unpause a playing sound sample. The first method temporarily stops a cached sample from playing without resetting the sample's current pointer back to the beginning of the sound data so that at a later time it can be un-paused from the same location in the sample when the pause was initiated. The second method restarts the paused sample from the location in the sample where it was paused.

public abstract void setPosition(int index, Point3d position)

Sets position. This method sets this sound's location (in Local coordinates) from the provided position.

public abstract void setDirection(int index, Vector3d direction)

Sets direction. This method sets this sound's direction from the local coordinate vector provided. For a full description of the direction parameter, see Section 6.9.3, "ConeSound Node."

public abstract void setVworldXfrm(int index, Transform3D trans)

Sets virtual world transform. This method passes a reference to the concatenated transformation to be applied to local sound position and direction parameters.

public abstract void setRolloff(float rolloff)

Sets AuralAttributes gain rolloff. This method sets the speed-of-sound factor. For a full description of this parameter and how it is used, see Section 8.1.17, "AuralAttributes Object."

public abstract void setAngularAttenuation(int index, int filterType, double[] angle, float[] attenuationScaleFactor, float[] filterCutoff)

Sets angular attenuation. This method sets this sound's angular gain attenuation (including filter) by defining corresponding arrays containing angular offsets from the sound's axis, gain scale factors, and frequency cutoff applied to all active directional sounds. Gain scale factor is applied to sound based on the angle between the sound's axis and the ray from the sound source origin to the listener. The form of the attenuation parameter is fully described in Section 6.9.3, "ConeSound Node."

public abstract void setReflectionCoefficient(float coefficient)

Sets AuralAttributes reverberation coefficient. This method sets the reflective or absorptive characteristics of the surfaces in the region defined by the current Soundscape region. For a full description of this parameter and how it is used, see Section 8.1.17, "AuralAttributes Object."

public abstract void setReverbDelay(float reverbDelay)

Sets AuralAttributes reverberation delay. This method sets the delay time between each order of reflection (while reverberation is being rendered) explicitly given in milliseconds. A value for delay time of 0.0 disables reverberation. For a full description of this parameter and how it is used, see Section 8.1.17, "AuralAttributes Object."

public abstract void setReverbOrder(int reverbOrder)

Sets AuralAttributes reverberation order. This method sets the number of times reflections are added to reverberation being calculated. A value of −1 specifies an unbounded number of reverberations. For a full description of this parameter and how it is used, see Section 8.1.17, "AuralAttributes Object."

public abstract void setFrequencyScaleFactor(float frequencyScaleFactor)

Sets AuralAttributes frequency scale factor. This method specifies a scale factor applied to the frequency (or wavelength). This parameter can also be used to expand or contract the usual frequency shift applied to the sound source due to

Doppler effect calculations. Valid values are ≥ 0.0. A value greater than 1.0 will increase the playback rate. For a full description of this parameter and how it is used, see Section 8.1.17, "AuralAttributes Object."

public abstract void setVelocityScaleFactor(float
     velocityScaleFactor)

Sets AuralAttributes velocity scale factor. This method specifies a velocity scale factor applied to the velocity of sound relative to the listener's position and movement in relation to the sound's position and movement. This scale factor is multiplied by the calculated velocity portion of Doppler effect equation used during sound rendering. For a full description of this parameter and how it is used, see Section 8.1.17, "AuralAttributes Object."

public abstract void updateSample(int index)

Explicitly updates a sample. This method is called when a Sound is to be explicitly updated. It is called only when all of a sound's parameters are known to have been passed to the audio device. In this way, an implementation can choose to perform lazy evaluation of a sample, rather than updating the rendering state of the sample after every individual parameter changed. This method can be left as a null method if the implementor so chooses.

12.3   Instantiating and Registering a New Device

A browser or applications developer must instantiate whatever system-specific audio devices that he or she needs and that exist on the system. This device information typically exists in a site configuration file. The browser or application will instantiate the physical environment as requested by the end user.

The API for instantiating devices is site-specific, but it consists of a device object with a constructor and at least all of the methods specified in the AudioDevice interface.

Once instantiated, the browser or application must register the device with the Java 3D sound scheduler by associating this device with a PhysicalEnvironment object. The `setAudioDevice` method introduces new devices to the Java 3D environment, and the `allAudioDevices` method produces an enumeration that allows examination of all available devices within a Java 3D environment. See Section C.9, "The PhysicalEnvironment Object," for more details.

CHAPTER 13

Execution and Rendering Model

J AVA 3D's execution and rendering model assumes the existence of a VirtualUniverse object and an attached scene graph. This scene graph can be minimal and not noticeable from an application's perspective when using immediate-mode rendering, but it must exist.

Java 3D's execution model intertwines with its rendering modes and with behaviors and their scheduling. This chapter first describes the three rendering modes, then describes how an application starts up a Java 3D environment, and finally it discusses how the various rendering modes work within this framework.

13.1 Three Major Rendering Modes

Java 3D supports three different modes for rendering scenes: immediate mode, retained mode, and compiled-retained mode. These three levels of API support represent a potentially large variation in graphics processing speed and in on-the-fly restructuring.

13.1.1 Immediate Mode

Immediate mode allows maximum flexibility at some cost in rendering speed. The application programmer can either use or ignore the scene graph structure inherent in Java 3D's design. The programmer can choose to draw geometry directly or to define a scene graph. Immediate mode can be either used independently or mixed with retained and/or compiled-retained mode rendering. The immediate-mode API is described in Chapter 14, "Immediate-Mode Rendering."

13.1.2 Retained Mode

Retained mode allows a great deal of the flexibility provided by immediate mode while also providing a substantial increase in rendering speed. All objects defined in the scene graph are accessible and manipulable. The scene graph itself is fully manipulable. The application programmer can rapidly construct the scene graph, create and delete nodes, and instantly "see" the effect of edits. Retained mode also allows maximal access to objects through a general pick capability.

Java 3D's retained mode allows a programmer to construct objects, insert objects into a database, compose objects, and add behaviors to objects.

In retained mode, Java 3D knows that the programmer has defined objects, knows how the programmer has combined those objects into compound objects or scene graphs, and knows what behaviors or actions the programmer has attached to objects in the database. This knowledge allows Java 3D to perform many optimizations. It can construct specialized data structures that hold an object's geometry in a manner that enhances the speed at which the Java 3D system can render it. It can compile object behaviors so that they run at maximum speed when invoked. It can flatten transformation manipulations and state changes where possible in the scene graph.

13.1.3 Compiled-Retained Mode

Compiled-retained mode allows the Java 3D API to perform an arbitrarily complex series of optimizations including, but not restricted to, geometry compression, scene graph flattening, geometry grouping, and state change clustering.

Compiled-retained mode provides hooks for end-user manipulation and picking. Pick operations return the closest object (in scene graph space) associated with the picked geometry.

Java 3D's compiled-retained mode ensures effective graphics rendering speed in yet one more way. A programmer can request that Java 3D compile an object or a scene graph. Once it is compiled, the programmer has minimal access to the internal structure of the object or scene graph. Capability flags provide access to specified components that the application program may need to modify on a continuing basis.

A compiled object or scene graph consists of whatever internal structures Java 3D wishes to create to ensure that objects or scene graphs render at maximal rates. Because Java 3D knows that the majority of the compiled object's or scene graph's components will not change, it can perform an extraordinary number of optimizations, including the fusing of multiple objects into one conceptual object, turning an object into compressed geometry or even breaking an object up into like-kind components and reassembling the like-kind components into new "conceptual objects."

13.2 Instantiating the Render Loop

From an application's perspective, Java 3D's render loop runs continuously. Whenever an application adds a scene branch to the virtual world, that scene branch is instantly visible. This high-level view of the render loop permits concurrent implementations of Java 3D as well as serial implementations. The remainder of this section describes the Java 3D render loop bootstrap process from a serialized perspective. Differences that would appear in concurrent implementations are noted as well.

13.2.1 An Application-Level Perspective

First the application must construct its scene graphs. It does this by constructing scene graph nodes and component objects and linking them into self-contained trees with a BranchGroup node as a root. The application next must obtain a reference to any constituent nodes or objects within that branch that it may wish to manipulate. It sets the capabilities of all the objects to match their anticipated use and only then compiles the branch using the BranchGroup's compile method. Whether it compiles the branch, the application can add it to the virtual universe by adding the BranchGroup to a Locale object. The application repeats this process for each branch it wishes to create. Note that for concurrent Java 3D implementations, whenever an application adds a branch to the active virtual universe, that branch becomes visible.

13.2.2 Retained and Compiled-Retained Rendering Modes

This initialization process is identical for retained and compiled-retained modes. In both modes, the application builds a scene graph. In compiled-retained mode, the application compiles the scene graph. Then the application inserts the (possibly compiled) scene graph into the virtual universe.

CHAPTER 14

Immediate-Mode Rendering

JAVA 3D is fundamentally a scene graph–based API. Most of the constructs in the API are biased toward retained mode and compiled-retained mode rendering. However, there are some applications that want both the control and the flexibility that immediate-mode rendering offers.

Immediate-mode applications can either use or ignore Java 3D's scene graph structure. By using immediate mode, end-user applications have more freedom, but this freedom comes at the expense of performance. In immediate mode, Java 3D has no high-level information concerning graphical objects or their composition. Because it has minimal global knowledge, Java 3D can perform only localized optimizations on behalf of the application programmer.

14.1 Two Styles of Immediate-Mode Rendering

Use of Java 3D's immediate mode falls into one of two categories: pure immediate-mode rendering and mixed-mode rendering in which immediate mode and retained or compiled-retained mode interoperate and render to the same canvas. The Java 3D renderer is idle in pure immediate mode, distinguishing it from mixed-mode rendering.

14.1.1 Pure Immediate-Mode Rendering

Pure immediate-mode rendering provides for those applications and applets that do not want Java 3D to do any automatic rendering of the scene graph. Such applications may not even wish to build a scene graph to represent their graphical data. However, they use Java 3D's attribute objects to set graphics state and Java 3D's geometric objects to render geometry.

A pure immediate mode application must create a minimal set of Java 3D objects before rendering. In addition to a Canvas3D object, the application must create a

View object, with its associated PhysicalBody and PhysicalEnvironment objects, and the following scene graph elements: a VirtualUniverse object, a high-resolution Locale object, a BranchGroup node object, a TransformGroup node object with associated transform, and, finally, a ViewPlatform leaf node object that defines the position and orientation within the virtual universe that generates the view (see Figure 14-1).

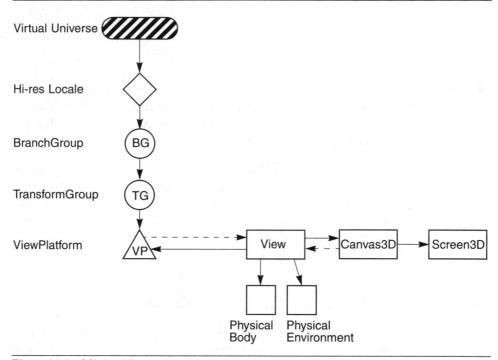

Figure 14-1   Minimal Immediate-Mode Structure

Java 3D provides utility functions that create much of this structure on behalf of a pure immediate-mode application, making it less noticeable from the application's perspective—but the structure must exist.

All rendering is done completely under user control. It is necessary for the user to clear the 3D canvas, render all geometry, and swap the buffers. Additionally, rendering the right and left eye for stereo viewing becomes the sole responsibility of the application.

In pure immediate mode, the user must stop the Java 3D renderer, via the Canvas3D object `stopRenderer()` method, prior to adding the Canvas3D object to an active View object (that is, one that is attached to a live ViewPlatform object).

14.1.2 Mixed-Mode Rendering

Mixing immediate mode and retained or compiled-retained mode requires more structure than pure immediate mode. In mixed mode, the Java 3D renderer is running continuously, rendering the scene graph into the canvas. The basic Java 3D *stereo* rendering loop, executed for each Canvas3D, is as follows:

```
clear canvas (both eyes)
call preRender()                         // user-supplied method
set left eye view
render opaque scene graph objects
call renderField(FIELD_LEFT)             // user-supplied method
render transparent scene graph objects
set right eye view
render opaque scene graph objects again
call renderField(FIELD_RIGHT)            // user-supplied method
render transparent scene graph objects again
call postRender()                        // user-supplied method
synchronize and swap buffers
call postSwap()                          // user-supplied method
```

The basic Java 3D *monoscopic* rendering loop is as follows:

```
clear canvas
call preRender()                         // user-supplied method
set view
render opaque scene graph objects
call renderField(FIELD_ALL)              // user-supplied method
render transparent scene graph objects
call postRender()                        // user-supplied method
synchronize and swap buffers
call postSwap()                          // user-supplied method
```

In both cases, the entire loop, beginning with clearing the canvas and ending with swapping the buffers, defines a frame. The application is given the opportunity to render immediate-mode geometry at any of the clearly identified spots in the rendering loop. A user specifies his or her own rendering methods by extending the Canvas3D class and overriding the preRender, postRender, postSwap, and/or renderField methods.

14.2 Canvas3D Methods

The Canvas3D methods that directly affect immediate-mode rendering are described here.

When a Canvas3D object is created, it is initially marked as being started. This means that as soon as the Canvas3D is added to an active View object, the rendering loop will render the scene graph to the canvas. In pure immediate mode, the renderer must be stopped (via a call to `stopRenderer`) prior to adding the canvas to an active View object.

Constants

```
public static final int FIELD_LEFT
public static final int FIELD_RIGHT
public static final int FIELD_ALL
```

These constants specify the field that the rendering loop for this Canvas3D is rendering. The `FIELD_LEFT` and `FIELD_RIGHT` values indicate the left and right fields of a field-sequential stereo rendering loop, respectively. The `FIELD_ALL` value indicates a monoscopic or single-pass stereo rendering loop.

Methods

`public GraphicsContext3D getGraphicsContext3D()`

This method retrieves the immediate-mode 3D graphics context associated with this Canvas3D. It creates a new graphics context if one does not already exist. It returns a GraphicsContext3D object that can be used for immediate mode rendering to this Canvas3D.

◀ New in 1.2 ▶ `public J3DGraphics2D getGraphics2D()`

This method returns the 2D graphics object associated with this Canvas3D. A new 2D graphics object is created if one does not already exist. See Section 14.3.2, "J3DGraphics2D."

`public void preRender()`

Applications that wish to perform operations in the rendering loop prior to any actual rendering must override this method. The Java 3D rendering loop invokes this method after clearing the canvas and before any rendering has been done for this frame. Applications should *not* call this method.

public void postRender()

Applications that wish to perform operations in the rendering loop following any actual rendering must override this method. The Java 3D rendering loop invokes this method after completing all rendering to the canvas for this frame and before the buffer swap. Applications should *not* call this method.

public void postSwap()

Applications that wish to perform operations at the very end of the rendering loop must override this method. The Java 3D rendering loop invokes this method after completing all rendering to this canvas, and all other canvases associated with the current view, for this frame following the buffer swap. Applications that wish to perform operations at the very end of the rendering loop may override this function. In off-screen mode, all rendering is copied to the off-screen buffer before this method is called. Applications should *not* call this method.

public void renderField(int fieldDesc)

Applications that wish to perform operations during the rendering loop must override this function. The Java 3D rendering loop invokes this method, possibly twice, during the loop. It is called once for each field (once per frame on a monoscopic system or once each for the right eye and left eye on a field-sequential stereo system). This method is called after all opaque objects are rendered and before any transparent objects are rendered (subject to restrictions imposed by OrderedGroup nodes). This is intended for use by applications that want to mix retained/compiled-retained mode rendering with some immediate-mode rendering. The fieldDesc parameter is the field description: FIELD_LEFT, FTFLD_RIGHT, or FIELD_ALL. Applications that wish to work correctly in stereo mode should render the same image for both FIELD_LEFT and FIELD_RIGHT calls. If Java 3D calls the renderer with FIELD_ALL, the immediate-mode rendering needs to be done only once. Applications should *not* call this method.

public final void startRenderer()
public final void stopRenderer()

These methods start or stop the Java 3D renderer for this Canvas3D object. If the Java 3D renderer is currently running when stopRenderer is called, the rendering will be synchronized before being stopped. No further rendering will be done to this canvas by Java 3D until the renderer is started again. If the Java 3D renderer is not currently running when startRenderer is called, any rendering to other Canvas3D objects sharing the same View will be synchronized before this Canvas3D's renderer is (re)started.

◀ New in 1.2 ▶ `public final boolean isRendererRunning()`

This method retrieves the state of the renderer for this Canvas3D object.

`public void swap()`

This method synchronizes and swaps buffers on a double-buffered canvas for this Canvas3D object. This method should be called only if the Java 3D renderer has been stopped. In the normal case, the renderer automatically swaps the buffer. This method calls the `flush(true)` methods of the associated 2D and 3D graphics contexts, if they have been allocated. If the application invokes this method and the canvas has a running Java 3D renderer, a `RestrictedAccessException` exception is thrown. An `IllegalStateException` is thrown if this Canvas3D is in off-screen mode.

14.3 API for Immediate Mode

The Java 3D immediate mode allows an application to set attributes directly and draw three-dimensional geometry using the same objects as in Java 3D scene graphs. An immediate-mode application renders by passing these objects to the set and draw methods of a GraphicsContext3D object.

14.3.1 GraphicsContext3D

The GraphicsContext3D object is used for immediate-mode rendering into a 3D canvas. It is created by, and associated with, a specific Canvas3D object. A GraphicsContext3D class defines methods that manipulate 3D graphics state attributes and draw 3D geometric primitives.

Note that the drawing methods in this class are not necessarily executed immediately. They may be buffered up for future execution. Applications must call the `flush(boolean)` method to ensure that the rendering actually happens. The flush method is implicitly called in the following cases:

- The `readRaster` method calls `flush(true)`.
- The `Canvas3D.swap` method calls `flush(true)`.
- The Java 3D renderer calls `flush(true)` prior to swapping the buffer for a double-buffered on-screen Canvas3D.
- The Java 3D renderer calls `flush(true)` prior to copying into the off-screen buffer of an off-screen Canvas3D.
- The Java 3D renderer calls `flush(false)` after calling the `preRender`, `renderField`, `postRender`, and `postSwap` Canvas3D callback methods.

A single-buffered, pure-immediate mode application must explicitly call `flush` to ensure that the graphics will be rendered to the Canvas3D.

Constants

```
public static final int STEREO_LEFT
public static final int STEREO_RIGHT
public static final int STEREO_BOTH
```
◀ New in 1.2 ▶
◀ New in 1.2 ▶
◀ New in 1.2 ▶

These constants specify whether rendering is done to the left eye, to the right eye, or to both eyes.

Constructors

There are no publicly accessible constructors of GraphicsContext3D. An application obtains a 3D graphics context object from the Canvas3D object into which the application wishes to render by using the `getGraphicsContext3D` method.

The Canvas3D object creates a new GraphicsContext3D the first time an application invokes `getGraphicsContext3D`. A new GraphicsContext3D initializes its state variables to the following defaults:

Parameters	Default Values
Background object	null
Fog object	null
ModelClip object	null
Appearance object	null
List of Light objects	empty
High-Res coordinates	(0, 0, 0,)
modelTransform	identity
AuralAttributes object	null
List of Sound objects	empty
buffer override	false
front buffer rendering	false
stereo mode	STEREO_BOTH

Methods

public Canvas3D getCanvas3D()

This method gets the Canvas3D that created this GraphicsContext3D.

```
public void setAppearance(Appearance appearance)
public Appearance getAppearance()
```

These methods access or modify the current Appearance component object used by this 3D graphics context. The graphics context stores a reference to the specified Appearance object. This means that the application may modify individual appearance attributes by using the appropriate methods on the Appearance object (see Section 8.1.2, "Appearance Object"). The Appearance component object must not be part of a live scene graph, nor may it subsequently be made part of a live scene graph—an IllegalSharingException is thrown in such cases. If the Appearance object is null, default values will be used for all appearance attributes—it is as if an Appearance node were created using the default constructor.

```
public void setBackground(Background background)
public Background getBackground()
```

These methods access or modify the current Background leaf node object used by this 3D graphics context. The graphics context stores a reference to the specified Background node. This means that the application may modify the background color or image by using the appropriate methods on the Background node object (see Section 6.4, "Background Node"). The Background node must not be part of a live scene graph, nor may it subsequently be made part of a live scene graph—an IllegalSharingException is thrown in such cases. If the Background object is null, the default background color of black (0,0,0) is used to clear the canvas prior to rendering a new frame. The Background node's application region is ignored for immediate-mode rendering.

```
public void setFog(Fog fog)
public Fog getFog()
```

These methods access or modify the current Fog leaf node object used by this 3D graphics context. The graphics context stores a reference to the specified Fog node. This means that the application may modify the fog attributes using the appropriate methods on the Fog node object (see Section 6.7, "Fog Node"). The Fog node must not be part of a live scene graph, nor may it subsequently be made part of a live scene graph—an IllegalSharingException is thrown in such cases. If the Fog object is null, fog is disabled. Both the region of influence and the hierarchical scope of the Fog node are ignored for immediate-mode rendering.

```
public void addLight(Light light)
public void insertLight(Light light, int index)
public void setLight(Light light, int index)
public Light getLight(int index)
public void removeLight(int index)
public int numLights()
public Enumeration getAllLights()
```

These methods access or modify the list of lights used by this 3D graphics context. The addLight method adds a new light to the end of the list of lights. The insertLight method inserts a new light before the light at the specified index. The setLight method replaces the light at the specified index with the light provided. The removeLight method removes the light at the specified index. The numLights method returns a count of the number of lights in the list. The getLight method returns the light at the specified index. The getAllLights method retrieves the Enumeration object of all lights.

The graphics context stores a reference to each light object in the list of lights. This means that the application may modify the light attributes for any of the lights using the appropriate methods on that Light node object (see Section 6.8, "Light Node"). None of the Light nodes in the list of lights may be part of a live scene graph, nor may they subsequently be made part of a live scene graph—an IllegalSharingException is thrown in such cases. Adding a null Light object to the list will result in a NullPointerException. Both the region of influence and the hierarchical scope of all lights in the list are ignored for immediate-mode rendering.

```
public void setHiRes(int x[], int y[], int z[])
public void setHiRes(HiResCoord hiRes)
public void getHiRes(HiResCoord hiRes)
```

These methods access or modify the high-resolution coordinates of this graphics context to the location specified by the parameters provided. In the first method, the parameters x, y, and z are arrays of eight 32-bit integers that specify the high-resolution coordinates point.

```
public void setModelTransform(Transform3D t)
public void multiplyModelTransform(Transform3D t)
public void getModelTransform(Transform3D t)
```

These methods access or modify the current model transform. The multiplyModelTransform method multiplies the current model transform by the specified transform and stores the result back into the current model transform. The specified transformation must be affine. A BadTransformException is thrown (see

357

Section D.1, "BadTransformException") if an attempt is made to specify an illegal Transform3D.

◀ New in 1.2 ▶ `public void setBufferOverride(boolean bufferOverride)`
◀ New in 1.2 ▶ `public boolean getBufferOverride()`

These methods set and retrieve a flag that specifies whether the double buffering and stereo mode from the Canvas3D are overridden. When set to true, this attribute enables the `frontBufferRendering` and `stereoMode` attributes.

◀ New in 1.2 ▶ `public void setFrontBufferRendering(boolean frontBufferRendering)`
◀ New in 1.2 ▶ `public boolean getFrontBufferRendering()`

These methods set and retrieve a flag that enables or disables immediate mode rendering into the front buffer of a double buffered Canvas3D. This attribute is used only when the `bufferOverride` flag is enabled. Note that this attribute has no effect if double buffering is disabled or is not available on the Canvas3D.

◀ New in 1.2 ▶ `public void setStereoMode(int stereoMode)`
◀ New in 1.2 ▶ `public int getStereoMode()`

These methods set and retrieve the current stereo mode for immediate mode rendering. The parameter specifies which stereo buffer or buffers are rendered into. This attribute is used only when the `bufferOverride` flag is enabled. The stereo mode is one of the following: STEREO_LEFT, STEREO_RIGHT, or STEREO_BOTH. Note that this attribute has no effect if stereo is disabled or is not available on the Canvas3D.

◀ New in 1.2 ▶ `public void setModelClip(ModelClip modelClip)`
◀ New in 1.2 ▶ `public ModelClip getModelClip()`

These methods set and retrieve the current ModelClip leaf node. The set method sets the ModelClip to the specified object. The graphics context stores a reference to the specified ModelClip node. This means that the application may modify the model clipping attributes using the appropriate methods on the ModelClip node object. The ModelClip node must not be part of a live scene graph, nor may it subsequently be made part of a live scene graph—an IllegalSharingException is thrown in such cases. If the ModelClip object is null, model clipping is disabled. Both the region of influence and the hierarchical scope of the ModelClip node are ignored for immediate-mode rendering.

```
public void setAuralAttributes(AuralAttributes attributes)
public AuralAttributes getAuralAttributes()
```

These methods access or modify the current AuralAttributes component object used by this 3D graphics context. The graphics context stores a reference to the specified AuralAttributes object. This means that the application may modify individual audio attributes by using the appropriate methods in the Aural-Attributes object (see Section 8.1.17, "AuralAttributes Object"). The Aural-Attributes component object must not be part of a live scene graph, nor may it subsequently be made part of a live scene graph—an `IllegalSharingExcep-tion` is thrown in such cases. If the AuralAttributes object is `null`, default values will be used for all audio attributes—it is as if an AuralAttributes object were created using the default constructor.

```
public void addSound(Sound sound)
public void insertSound(Sound sound, int index)
public void setSound(Sound sound, int index)
public Sound getSound(int index)
public void removeSound(int index)
public int numSounds()
public boolean isSoundPlaying(int index)
public Enumeration getAllSounds()
```

These methods access or modify the list of sounds used by this 3D graphics context. The addSound method appends the specified sound to this graphics context's list of sounds. The `insertSound` method inserts the specified sound at the specified index location. The `setSound` method replaces the specified sound with the sound provided. The `removeSound` method removes the sound at the specified index location. The `numSounds` method retrieves the current number of sounds in this graphics context. The `getSound` method retrieves the index-selected sound. The `isSoundPlaying` method retrieves the sound-playing flag. The `getAllSounds` method retrieves the Enumeration object of all the sounds.

The graphics context stores a reference to each sound object in the list of sounds. This means that the application may modify the sound attributes for any of the sounds by using the appropriate methods on that Sound node object (see Section 6.9, "Sound Node"). None of the Sound nodes in the list of sounds may be part of a live scene graph, nor may they subsequently be made part of a live scene graph—an `IllegalSharingException` is thrown in such cases. Adding a `null` Sound object to the list results in a `NullPointerException`. If the list of sounds is empty, sound rendering is disabled.

Adding or inserting a sound to the list of sounds implicitly starts the sound playing. Once a sound is finished playing, it can be restarted by setting the sound's enable flag to `true`. The scheduling region of all sounds in the list is ignored for immediate-mode rendering.

public void readRaster(Raster raster)

This method reads an image from the frame buffer and copies it into the Image-Component or DepthComponent objects referenced by the specified Raster object. All parameters of the Raster object and the component ImageComponent or DepthComponent objects must be set to the desired values prior to calling this method. These values determine the location, size, and format of the pixel data that is read. This method calls `flush(true)` prior to reading the frame buffer.

public void clear()

This method clears the canvas to the color or image specified by the current Background leaf node object.

public void draw(Geometry geometry)
public void draw(Shape3D shape)

The first `draw` method draws the specified Geometry component object using the current state in the graphics context. The second `draw` method draws the specified Shape3D leaf node object. This is a convenience method that is identical to calling the `setAppearance(Appearance)` and `draw(Geometry)` methods passing the Appearance and Geometry component objects of the specified Shape3D nodes as arguments.

◀ New in 1.2 ▶ **public void flush(boolean wait)**

This method flushes all previously executed rendering operations to the drawing buffer for this 3D graphics context. The `wait` parameter indicates whether to wait for the rendering to complete before returning from this call.

◀ New in 1.2 ▶ **14.3.2 J3DGraphics2D**

The J3DGraphics2D class extends Graphics2D to provide 2D rendering into a Canvas3D. It is an abstract base class that is further extended by a nonpublic Java 3D implementation class. This class allows Java 2D rendering to be mixed with Java 3D rendering in the same Canvas3D, subject to the same restrictions as imposed for 3D immediate-mode rendering: In mixed-mode rendering, all Java 2D requests must be done from one of the Canvas3D callback methods; in pure-immediate mode, the Java 3D renderer must be stopped for the Canvas3D being rendered into.

An application obtains a Java 3D 2D graphics context object from the Canvas3D object that the application wishes to render into by using the `getGraphics2D` method. A new J3DGraphics2D object is created if one does not already exist.

Note that the drawing methods in this class, including those inherited from Graphics2D, are not necessarily executed immediately. They may be buffered up for future execution. Applications must call the `flush(boolean)` method to ensure that the rendering actually happens. The flush method is implicitly called in the following cases:

- The `Canvas3D.swap` method calls `flush(true)`.
- The Java 3D renderer calls `flush(true)` prior to swapping the buffer for a double-buffered on-screen Canvas3D.
- The Java 3D renderer calls `flush(true)` prior to copying into the off-screen buffer of an off-screen Canvas3D.
- The Java 3D renderer calls `flush(false)` after calling the `preRender`, `renderField`, `postRender`, and `postSwap` Canvas3D callback methods.

A single-buffered, pure-immediate mode application must explicitly call `flush` to ensure that the graphics will be rendered to the Canvas3D.

Methods

public abstract void flush(boolean wait)   ◀ New in 1.2 ▶

This method flushes all previously executed rendering operations to the drawing buffer for this 2D graphics object.

public final Graphics create()   ◀ New in 1.2 ▶
public final Graphics create(int x, int y, int width, int height) ◀ New in 1.2 ▶

These methods are not supported. The only way to obtain a J3DGraphics2D is from the associated Canvas3D.

public final void setBackground(Color color)   ◀ New in 1.2 ▶
public final Color getBackground()   ◀ New in 1.2 ▶
public final void clearRect(int x, int y, int width, int height) ◀ New in 1.2 ▶

These methods are not supported. Clearing a Canvas3D is done implicitly via a Background node in the scene graph or explicitly via the `clear` method in a 3D graphics context.

Math Objects

MATHEMATICAL objects allow Java 3D users to represent and manipulate low-level mathematical constructs such as vectors and matrices. Math objects also define specific operations that allow users to manipulate them in appropriate ways.

Java 3D needs these vector and matrix math classes. It uses them internally and also makes them available to applications for their use. However, they are not part of Java 3D. Rather, they are defined here for convenience. These classes will become more widely distributed, which is why Java 3D defines them as a separate `javax.vecmath` package. Figure A-1 shows the math object hierarchy.

A.1 Tuple Objects

Java 3D uses tuple objects to represent and manipulate two-, three-, and four-element values.

A.1.1 Tuple2d Class

The Tuple2d class is used for points and vectors. This class is a two-element tuple that is represented by double-precision floating-point x,y coordinates.

Variables

The component values of a Tuple2d are directly accessible through the public variables x and y. To access the x component of a Tuple2d called upperLeft-Corner, a programmer would write upperLeftCorner.x. The programmer would access the y component similarly.

Tuple Objects
Tuple2d
    Point2d
    Vector2d
Tuple2f
    Point2f
    TexCoord2f
    Vector2f
Tuple3b
    Color3b
Tuple3d
    Point3d
    Vector3d
Tuple3f
    Color3f
    Point3f
    TexCoord3f
    Vector3f
Tuple3i
    Point3i
Tuple4b
    Color4b
Tuple4d
    Point4d
    Quat4d
    Vector4d
Tuple4f
    Color4f
    Point4f
    Quat4f
    Vector4f
Tuple4i
    Point4i
AxisAngle4d
AxisAngle4f
GVector

Matrix Objects
Matrix3f
Matrix3d
Matrix4f
Matrix4d
GMatrix

Figure A-1   Math Object Hierarchy

```
public double x
Public double y
```

The *x* and *y* coordinates, respectively.

Constructors

```
public Tuple2d(double x, double y)
public Tuple2d(double[] t)
public Tuple2d(Tuple2d t1)
public Tuple2d(Tuple2f t1)
public Tuple2d()
```

Each of these five constructors returns a new Tuple2d. The first constructor generates a Tuple2d from two double-precision floating-point numbers *x* and *y*. The second constructor generates a Tuple2d from the first two elements of array t. The third and fourth constructors generate a Tuple2d from the tuple t1. The final constructor generates a Tuple2d with the value of (0.0, 0.0).

Methods

```
public final void set(double x, double y)
public final void set(double[] t)
public final void set(Tuple2d t1)
public final void set(Tuple2f t1)
public final void get(double[] t)
```

The first set method sets the value of this tuple to the specified *xy* coordinates. The second set method sets the value of this tuple from the two values specified in the array t. The third and fourth set methods set the value of this tuple to the value of the tuple t1. The get method copies the value of the elements of this tuple into the array t.

```
public final void add(Tuple2d t1, Tuple2d t2)
public final void add(Tuple2d t1)
public final void sub(Tuple2d t1, Tuple2d t2)
public final void sub(Tuple2d t1)
```

The first add method sets the value of this tuple to the vector sum of tuples v1 and v2. The second add method sets the value of this tuple to the vector sum of itself and tuple t1. The first sub method sets the value of this tuple to the vector difference of tuple t1 and t2 (this = t1 − t2). The second sub method sets the value of this tuple to the vector difference of itself and tuple t1 (this = this − t1).

```
public final void negate(Tuple2d t1)
public final void negate()
```

The first `negate` method sets the value of this tuple to the negation of tuple `t1`. The second method negates the value of this vector in place.

```
public final void scale(double s, Tuple2d t1)
public final void scale(double s)
public final void scaleAdd(double s, Tuple2d t1)
public final void scaleAdd(double s, Tuple2d t1, Tuple2d t2)
```

The first `scale` method multiplies each element of the tuple `t1` by the scale factor `s` and places the resulting scaled tuple into `this`. The second method multiplies each element of this tuple by the scale factor `s` and places the resulting scaled tuple into `this`. The first `scaleAdd` method scales this tuple by the scale factor `s`, adds the result to tuple `t1`, and places the result into the tuple `this` (this = s*this + t1). The second `scaleAdd` method scales tuple `t1` by the scale factor `s`, adds the result to tuple `t1`, then places the result into the tuple `this` (this = s*t1 + t2).

```
public final void absolute(Tuple2d t)
```

This method sets each component of the tuple parameter to its absolute value and places the modified values into this tuple.

```
public final void clamp(double min, double max)
public final void clamp(double min, double max, Tuple2d t)
public final void clampMin(double min)
public final void clampMin(double min, Tuple2d t)
public final void clampMax(double max)
public final void clampMax(double max, Tuple2d t)
```

The first `clamp` method clamps this tuple to the range [`min`, `max`]. The second `clamp` method clamps the values from tuple `t` to the range [`min`, `max`] and assigns these clamped values to this tuple. The first `clampMin` method clamps each value of this tuple to the `min` parameter. The second `clampMin` method clamps each value of the tuple `t` and assigns these clamped values to this tuple. The first `clampMax` method clamps each value of this tuple to the `max` parameter. The second `clampMax` method clamps each value of tuple `t` to the `max` parameter and assigns these clamped values to this tuple. In each method the values of tuple `t` remain unchanged.

```
public final void interpolate(Tuple2d t1, Tuple2d t2, double alpha)
public final void interpolate(Tuple2d t1, double alpha)
```

The first method linearly interpolates between tuples t1 and t2 and places the result into this tuple (this = (1 − alpha) * t1 + alpha * t2). The second method linearly interpolates between this tuple and tuple t1 and places the result into this tuple (this = (1 − alpha) * this + alpha * t1).

```
public boolean equals(Tuple2d t1)
public boolean equals(Object t1)
```

The first method returns true if all of the data members of tuple t1 are equal to the corresponding data members in this tuple. The second method returns true if the Object t1 is of type Tuple2d and all of the data members of t1 are equal to the corresponding data members in this Tuple2d.

```
public boolean epsilonEquals(Tuple2d t1, double epsilon)
```

This method returns true if the L∞ distance between this tuple and tuple t1 is less than or equal to the epsilon parameter. Otherwise, this method returns false. The L∞ distance is equal to

$$\text{MAX}[\text{abs}(x1 - x2), \text{abs}(y1 - y2)]$$

```
public int hashCode()
```

The hashCode method returns a hash number based on the data values in this object. Two Tuple2d objects with identical data values (that is, equals(Tuple2d) returns true) will return the same hash number. Two objects with different data members may return the same hash number, although this is not likely.

```
public String toString()
```

This method returns a string that contains the values of this Tuple2d.

A.1.1.1   Point2d Class

The Point2d class extends Tuple2d. The Point2d is a two-element point represented by double-precision floating-point *x,y* coordinates.

Constructors

```
public Point2d(double x, double y)
public Point2d(double p[])
public Point2d(Point2d p1)
```

367

```
public Point2d(Point2f p1)
public Point2d(Tuple2d t1)
public Point2d(Tuple2f t1)
public Point2d()
```

Each of these seven constructors returns a new Point2d. The first constructor generates a Point2d from two double-precision floating-point numbers x and y. The second constructor generates a Point2d from the first two elements of array p. The third and fourth constructors generate a Point2d from the point p1. The fifth and sixth constructors generate a Point2d from the tuple t1. The final constructor generates a Point2d with the value of (0.0, 0.0).

Methods

```
public final double distanceSquared(Point2d p1)
public final double distance(Point2d p1)
```

The distanceSquared method computes the square of the Euclidean distance between this point and point p1 and returns the result. The distance method computes the Euclidean distance between this point and point p1 and returns the result.

```
public final double distanceL1(Point2d p1)
```

This method computes the L_1 (Manhattan) distance between this point and point p1. The L_1 distance is equal to

$$\text{abs}(x1 - x2) + \text{abs}(y1 - y2)$$

```
public final double distanceLinf(Point2d p1)
```

This method computes the $L\infty$ distance between this point and point p1. The $L\infty$ distance is equal to

$$\text{MAX}[\text{abs}(x1 - x2), \text{abs}(y1 - y2)]$$

A.1.1.2   Vector2d Class

The Vector2d class extends Tuple2d. The Vector2f is a two-element vector represented by double-precision floating-point x,y coordinates.

Constructors

```
public Vector2d(double x, double y)
public Vector2d(double v[])
```

```
public Vector2d(Vector2d v1)
public Vector2d(Vector2f v1)
public Vector2d(Tuple2d t1)
public Vector2d(Tuple2f t1)
public Vector2d()
```

Each of these seven constructors returns a new Vector2d. The first constructor generates a Vector2d from two floating-point numbers x and y. The second constructor generates a Vector2d from the first two elements of array v. The third and fourth constructors generate a Vector2d from the vector v1. The fifth and sixth constructors generate a Vector2d from the specified tuple t1. The final constructor generates a Vector2d with the value of (0.0, 0.0).

Methods

```
public final double dot(Vector2d v1)
```

The dot method computes the dot product between this vector and vector v1 and returns the resulting value.

```
public final double lengthSquared()
public final double length()
```

The lengthSquared method computes the square of the length of the vector this and returns its length as a double-precision floating-point number. The length method computes the length of the vector this and returns its length as a double-precision floating-point number.

```
public final void normalize(Vector2d v1)
public final void normalize()
```

The first normalize method normalizes the vector v1 to unit length and places the result in this. The second normalize method normalizes the vector this and places the resulting unit vector back into this.

```
public final double angle(Vector2d v1)
```

This method returns the angle, in radians, between this vector and vector v1. The return value is constrained to the range $[0, \pi]$.

A.1.2 Tuple2f Class

The Tuple2f class is a generic two-element tuple used mostly for specifying points and vectors made up of single-precision floating-point *x,y* coordinates.

Variables

The component values of a Tuple2f are directly accessible through the public variables x and y. To access the x component of a Tuple2f called upperLeftCorner, a programmer would write upperLeftCorner.x. The programmer would access the y component similarly.

```
public float x
public float y
```

The *x* and *y* coordinates, respectively.

Constructors

```
public Tuple2f(float x, float y)
public Tuple2f(float t[])
public Tuple2f(Tuple2f t1)
public Tuple2f(Tuple2d t1)
public Tuple2f()
```

Each of these five constructors returns a new Tuple2f. The first constructor generates a Tuple2f from two floating-point numbers *x* and *y*. The second constructor generates a Tuple2f from the first two elements of array t. The third and fourth constructors generate a Tuple2f from the tuple t1. The final constructor generates a Tuple2f with the value of (0.0, 0.0).

Methods

```
public final void set(float x, float y)
public final void set(float t[])
public final void set(Tuple2f t1)
punlic final void set(Tiple2d t1)
public final void get(float t[])
```

The set methods set the value of tuple this to the values provided. The get method copies the values of the elements of this tuple into the array t.

```
public final void add(Tuple2f t1, Tuple2f t2)
public final void add(Tuple2f t1)
public final void sub(Tuple2f t1, Tuple2f t2)
public final void sub(Tuple2f t1)
```

The first add method computes the element-by-element sum of tuples t1 and t2, placing the result in this. The second add method computes the element-by-element sum of this tuple and tuple t1, placing the result in this. The first sub method performs an element-by-element subtraction of tuple t2 from tuple t1 and places the result in this (this = t1 − t2). The second sub method performs an element-by-element subtraction of t1 from this and places the result in this (this = this − t1).

```
public final void negate(Tuple2f t1)
public final void negate()
```

The first negate method sets the values of this tuple to the negative of the values from tuple t1. The second negate method negates the tuple this and places the resulting tuple back into this.

```
public final void scale(float s, Tuple2f t1)
public final void scale(float s)
public final void scaleAdd(float s, Tuple2f t1)
public final void scaleAdd(float s, Tuple2f t1, Tuple2f t2)
```

The first scale method multiplies each element of the tuple t1 by the scale factor s and places the resulting scaled tuple into this. The second scale method multiplies each element of this tuple by the scale factor s and places the resulting scaled tuple into this. The first scaleAdd method scales this tuple by the scale factor s, adds the result to tuple t1, and places the result into the tuple this (this = s*this + t1). The second scaleAdd method scales tuple t1 by the scale factor s, adds the result to tuple t2, then places the result into the tuple this (this = s*t1 + t2).

```
public final void absolute()
public final void absolute(Tuple2f t)
```

The first absolute method sets each component of this tuple to its absolute value. The second absolute method sets each component of this tuple to the absolute value of the corresponding component in tuple t.

```
public final void clamp(float min, float max)
public final void clamp(float min, float max, Tuple2f t)
public final void clampMin(float min)
public final void clampMin(float min, Tuple2f t)
public final void clampMax(float max)
public final void clampMax(float max, Tuple2f t)
```

The first clamp method clamps this tuple to the range [min, max]. The second clamp method clamps the values from tuple t to the range [min, max] and assigns these clamped values to this tuple. The first clampMin method clamps each value of this tuple to the min parameter. The second clampMin method clamps each value of the tuple t and assigns these clamped values to this tuple. The first clampMax method clamps each value of this tuple to the max parameter. The second clampMax method

371

clamps each value of tuple t to the max parameter and assigns these clamped values to this tuple. In each method the values of tuple t remain unchanged.

```
public final void interpolate(Tuple2f t1, Tuple2f t2, float alpha)
public final void interpolate(Tuple2f t1, float alpha)
```

The first method linearly interpolates between tuples t1 and t2 and places the result into this tuple (this = (1 – alpha) * t1 + alpha * t2). The second method linearly interpolates between this tuple and tuple t1 and places the result into this tuple (this = (1 – alpha) * this + alpha * t1).

```
public boolean equals(Tuple2f t1)
public boolean equals(Object t1)
```

The first method returns true if all of the data members of tuple t1 are equal to the corresponding data members in this tuple. The second method returns true if the Object t1 is of type Tuple2f and all of the data members of t1 are equal to the corresponding data members in this Tuple2f.

```
public boolean epsilonEquals(Tuple2f t1, float epsilon)
```

This method returns true if the L∞ distance between this tuple and tuple t1 is less than or equal to the epsilon parameter. Otherwise, this method returns false. The L∞ distance is equal to

$$\text{MAX}[\text{abs}(x1 - x2), \text{abs}(y1 - y2)]$$

```
public int hashCode()
```

The hashCode method returns a hash number based on the data values in this object. Two Tuple2f objects with identical data values (that is, equals(Tuple2f) returns true) will return the same hash number. Two objects with different data members may return the same hash number, although this is not likely.

```
public String toString()
```

This method returns a string that contains the values of this Tuple2f.

A.1.2.1   Point2f Class

The Point2f class extends Tuple2f. The Point2f is a two-element point represented by single-precision floating-point *x,y* coordinates.

Constructors

```
public Point2f(float x, float y)
public Point2f(float p[])
public Point2f(Point2f p1)
public Point2f(Point2d p1)
public Point2f(Tuple2f t1)
public Point2f(Tuple2f t1)
public Point2f()
```

Each of these seven constructors returns a new Point2f. The first constructor generates a Point2f from two floating-point numbers x and y. The second constructor generates a Point2f from the first two elements of array p. The third and fourth constructors generate a Point2f from the point p1. The fifth and sixth constructors generate a Point2f from the tuple t1. The final constructor generates a Point2f with the value of (0.0, 0.0).

Methods

```
public final float distanceSquared(Point2f p1)
public final float distance(Point2f p1)
```

The distanceSquared method computes the square of the Euclidean distance between this point and point p1 and returns the result. The distance method computes the Euclidean distance between this point and point p1 and returns the result.

```
public final float distanceL1(Point2f p1)
```

This method computes the L_1 (Manhattan) distance between this point and point p1. The L_1 distance is equal to

$$abs(x1 - x2) + abs(y1 - y2)$$

```
public final float distanceLinf(Point2f p1)
```

This method computes the $L\infty$ distance between this point and point p1. The $L\infty$ distance is equal to

$$\mathrm{MAX}[abs(x1 - x2), abs(y1 - y2)]$$

A.1.2.2   Vector2f Class

The Vector2f class extends Tuple2f. The Vector2f is a two-element vector represented by single-precision floating-point x,y coordinates.

Constructors

```
public Vector2f(float x, float y)
public Vector2f(float v[])
public Vector2f(Vector2f v1)
public Vector2f(Vector2d v1)
public Vector2f(Tuple2f t1)
public Vector2f(Tuple2d t1)
public Vector2f()
```

Each of these seven constructors returns a new Vector2f. The first constructor generates a Vector2f from two floating-point numbers x and y. The second constructor generates a Vector2f from the first two elements of array v. The third and fourth constructors generate a Vector2f from the vector v1. The fifth and sixth constructors generate a Vector2f from the specified tuple t1. The final constructor generates a Vector2f with the value of (0.0, 0.0).

Methods

```
public final float dot(Vector2f v1)
```

The dot method computes the dot product between this vector and vector v1 and returns the resulting value.

```
public final float lengthSquared()
public final float length()
```

The lengthSquared method computes the square of the length of the vector this and returns its length as a single-precision floating-point number. The length method computes the length of the vector this and returns its length as a single-precision floating-point number.

```
public final void normalize(Vector2f v1)
public final void normalize()
```

The first normalize method normalizes the vector v1 to unit length and places the result in this. The second normalize method normalizes the vector this and places the resulting unit vector back into this.

```
public final float angle(Vector2f v1)
```

This method returns the angle, in radians, between this vector and vector v1. The return value is constrained to the range $[0, \pi]$.

A.1.2.3   TexCoord2f Class

The TexCoord2f class is a subset of Tuple2f. The TexCoord2f is a two-element vector represented by single-precision floating-point *x,y* coordinates.

Constructors

```
public TexCoord2f(float x, float y)
public TexCoord2f(float v[])
public TexCoord2f(TexCoord2f v1)
public TexCoord2f(Tuple2f t1)
public TexCoord2f()
```

Each of these five constructors returns a new TexCoord2f. The first constructor generates a TexCoord2f from two floating-point numbers x and y. The second constructor generates a TexCoord2f from the first two elements of array v. The third constructor generates a TexCoord2f from the TexCoord2f v1. The fourth constructor generates a TexCoord2f from the Tuple2f t1. The final constructor generates a TexCoord2f with the value of (0.0, 0.0).

A.1.3   Tuple3b Class

The Tuple3b class is used for colors. This class represents a three-byte tuple. Note that Java defines a byte as a signed integer in the range [−128, 127]. However, colors are more typically represented by values in the range [0, 255]. Java 3D recognizes this and, in those cases where Tuple3b is used to represent color, treats the bytes as if the range were [0, 255]—in other words, as if the bytes were unsigned. Values greater than 127 can be assigned to a byte variable using a type cast. For example,

```
byteVariable = (byte) intValue;// intValue can be > 127
```

If intValue is greater than 127, then byteVariable will be negative. The correct value will be extracted when it is used (by masking off the upper bits).

Variables

The component values of a Tuple3b are directly accessible through the public variables x, y, and z. To access the x (red) component of a Tuple3b called myColor, a programmer would write myColor.x. The programmer would access the y (green) and z (blue) components similarly.

```
public byte x
public byte y
public byte z
```

The red, green, and blue values, respectively.

Constructors

```
public Tuple3b(byte b1, byte b2, byte b3)
public Tuple3b(byte t[])
public Tuple3b(Tuple3b t1)
public Tuple3b()
```

Each of these four constructors returns a new Tuple3b. The first constructor generates a Tuple3b from three bytes b1, b2, and b3. The second constructor generates a Tuple3b from the first three elements of array t. The third constructor generates a Tuple3b from the byte-precision Tuple3b t1. The final constructor generates a Tuple3b with the value of (0.0, 0.0, 0.0).

Methods

```
public String toString()
```

This method returns a string that contains the values of this Tuple3b.

```
public final void set(byte t[])
public final void set(Tuple3b t1)
public final void get(byte t[])
public final void get(Tuple3b t1)
```

The first set method sets the values of the x, y, and z data members of this Tuple3b to the values in the array t of length three. The second set method sets the values of the x, y, and z data members of this Tuple3b to the values in the argument tuple t1. The first get method places the values of the x, y, and z components of this Tuple3b into the array t of length three. The second get method places the values of the x, y, and z components of this Tuple3b into the tuple t1.

```
public boolean equals(Tuple3b t1)
public boolean equals(Object t1)
```

The first method returns true if all of the data members of Tuple3b t1 are equal to the corresponding data members in this tuple. The second method returns true if the Object t1 is of type Tuple3b and all of the data members of t1 are equal to the corresponding data members in this Tuple3b.

```
public int hashCode()
```

This method returns a hash number based on the data values in this object. Two different Tuple3b objects with identical data values (that is, `equals(Tuple3b)` returns `true`) will return the same hash number. Two tuples with different data members may return the same hash value, although this is not likely.

A.1.3.1   Color3b Class

The Color3b class extends Tuple3b and represents three-byte color values.

Constructors

```
public Color3b(byte c1, byte c2, byte c3)
public Color3b(byte c[])
public Color3b(Color3b c1)
public Color3b(Tuple3b t1)
public Color3b(Color color)                              ◀ New in 1.2 ▶
public Color3b()
```

Each of these five constructors returns a new Color3b. The first constructor generates a Color3b from three bytes c1, c2, and c3. The second constructor generates a Color3b from the first three elements of array c. The third constructor generates a Color3b from the byte-precision Color3b c1. The fourth constructor generates a Color3b from the tuple t1. The fifth constructor generates a Color3b from the specified AWT Color object. The final constructor generates a Color3b with the value of (0.0, 0.0, 0.0).

Methods

```
public final void set(Color color)                      ◀ New in 1.2 ▶
public final Color get()                                 ◀ New in 1.2 ▶
```

The set method sets the R,G,B values of this Color3b object to those of the specified AWT Color object. The get method returns a new AWT Color object initialized with the R,G,B values of this Color3b object.

A.1.4   Tuple3d Class

The Tuple3d class is a generic three-element tuple represented by double-precision floating-point x, y, and z coordinates.

Variables

The component values of a Tuple3d are directly accessible through the public variables x, y, and z. To access the x component of a Tuple3d called upperLeft-Corner, a programmer would write upperLeftCorner.x. The programmer would access the y and z components similarly.

```
public double x
public double y
public double z
```

The *x*, *y*, and *z* coordinates, respectively.

Constructors

```
public Tuple3d(double x, double y, double z)
public Tuple3d(double t[])
public Tuple3d(Tuple3d t1)
public Tuple3d(Tuple3f t1)
public Tuple3d()
```

Each of these five constructors returns a new Tuple3d. The first constructor generates a Tuple3d from three floating-point numbers x, y, and z. The second constructor generates a Tuple3d from the first three elements of array t. The third constructor generates a Tuple3d from the double-precision Tuple3d t1. The fourth constructor generates a Tuple3d from the single-precision Tuple3f t1. The final constructor generates a Tuple3d with the value of (0.0, 0.0, 0.0).

Methods

```
public final void set(double x, double y, double z)
public final void set(double t[])
public final void set(Tuple3d t1)
public final void set(Tuple3f t1)
public final void get(double t[])
public final void get(Tuple3d t)
```

The four set methods set the value of tuple this to the values specified or to the values of the specified vectors. The two get methods copy the x, y, and z values into the array t of length three.

```
public final void add(Tuple3d t1, Tuple3d t2)
public final void add(Tuple3d t1)
public final void sub(Tuple3d t1, Tuple3d t2)
public final void sub(Tuple3d t1)
```

The first add method computes the element-by-element sum of tuples t1 and t2 and places the result in this. The second add method computes the element-by-element sum of this tuple and tuple t1 and places the result into this. The first sub method performs an element-by-element subtraction of tuple t2 from tuple t1 and places the result in this (this = t1 − t2). The second sub method performs an element-by-element subtraction of tuple t1 from this tuple and places the result in this (this = this − t1).

```
public final void negate(Tuple3d t1)
public final void negate()
```

The first negate method sets the values of this tuple to the negative of the values from tuple t1. The second negate method negates the tuple this and places the resulting tuple back into this.

```
public final void scaleAdd(double s, Tuple3f t1)
```

A deprecated method. See method below.

```
public final void scale(double s, Tuple3d t1)
public final void scale(double s)
public final void scaleAdd(double s, Tuple3d t1)
public final void scaleAdd(double s, Tuple3d t1, Tuple3d t2)
```

The first scale method multiplies each element of the tuple t1 by the scale factor s and places the resulting scaled tuple into this. The second scale method multiplies each element of this tuple by the scale factor s and places the resulting scaled tuple back into this. The first scaleAdd method scales this tuple by the scale factor s, adds the result to tuple t1, and places the result into tuple this (this = s*this + t1). The second scaleAdd method scales the tuple t1 by the scale factor s, adds the result to the tuple t2, and places the result into the tuple this (this = s*t1 + t2).

```
public String toString()
```

This method returns a string that contains the values of this Tuple3d. The form is (x, y, z).

```
public int hashCode()
```

This method returns a hash number based on the data values in this object. Two different Tuple3d objects with identical data values (that is, `equals(Tuple3d)` returns `true`) will return the same hash number. Two tuples with different data members may return the same hash value, although this is not likely.

```
public boolean equals(Tuple3d v1)
public boolean equals(Object t1)
```

The first method returns `true` if all of the data members of Tuple3d v1 are equal to the corresponding data members in this Tuple3d. The second method returns true if the Object t1 is of type Tuple3d and all of the data members of t1 are equal to the corresponding data members in this Tuple3d.

```
public boolean epsilonEquals(Tuple3d t1, double epsilon)
```

This method returns `true` if the L∞ distance between this tuple and tuple t1 is less than or equal to the `epsilon` parameter. Otherwise, this method returns `false`. The L∞ distance is equal to

$$MAX[abs(x1 - x2), abs(y1 - y2), abs(z1 - z2)]$$

```
public final void absolute()
public final void absolute(Tuple3d t)
```

The first `absolute` method sets each component of this tuple to its absolute value. The second `absolute` method sets each component of this tuple to the absolute value of the corresponding component in tuple t.

```
public final void clamp(float min, float max)
public final void clamp(float min, float max, Tuple3d t)
public final void clampMin(float min)
public final void clampMin(float min, Tuple3d t)
public final void clampMax(float max)
public final void clampMax(float max, Tuple3d t)
```

Deprecated methods. See the next six methods.

```
public final void clamp(double min, double max)
public final void clamp(double min, double max, Tuple3d t)
public final void clampMin(double min)
public final void clampMin(double min, Tuple3d t)
public final void clampMax(double max)
public final void clampMax(double max, Tuple3d t)
```

The first `clamp` method clamps this tuple to the range [`min`, `max`]. The second `clamp` method clamps the values from tuple `t` to the range [`min`, `max`] and assigns these clamped values to this tuple. The first `clampMin` method clamps each value of this tuple to the `min` parameter. The second `clampMin` method clamps each value of the tuple `t` and assigns these clamped values to this tuple. The first `clampMax` method clamps each value of this tuple to the `max` parameter. The second `clampMax` method clamps each value of tuple `t` to the `max` parameter and assigns these clamped values to this tuple. In each method, the values of tuple `t` remain unchanged.

```
public final void interpolate(Tuple3d t1, Tuple3d t2, float alpha)
public final void interpolate(Tuple3d t1, float alpha)
```

Deprecated methods. See the next two methods.

```
public final void interpolate(Tuple3d t1, Tuple3d t2, double alpha)
public final void interpolate(Tuple3d t1, double alpha)
```

The first `interpolate` method linearly interpolates between tuples `t1` and `t2` and places the result into this tuple (this = (1 − alpha) * t1 + alpha * t2). The second `interpolate` method linearly interpolates between this tuple and tuple `t1` and places the result into this tuple (this = (1 − alpha) * this + alpha * t1).

A.1.4.1   Point3d Class

The Point3d class extends Tuple3d. The Point3d is a three-element point represented by double-precision floating-point *x*, *y*, and *z* coordinates.

Constructors

```
public Point3d(double x, double y, double z)
public Point3d(double p[])
public Point3d(Point3d p1)
public Point3d(Point3f p1)
public Point3d(Tuple3d t1)
public Point3d(Tuple3f t1)
public Point3d()
```

Each of these seven constructors returns a new Point3d. The first constructor generates a Point3d from three floating-point numbers `x`, `y`, and `z`. The second constructor generates a Point3d from the first three elements of array `p`. The third constructor generates a Point3d from the double-precision Point3d `p1`. The fourth constructor generates a Point3d from the single-precision Point3f `p1`. The fifth and sixth constructors generate a Point3d from the tuple `t1`. The final constructor generates a Point3d with the value of (0.0, 0.0, 0.0).

Methods

```
public final double distanceSquared(Point3d p1)
public final double distance(Point3d p1)
```

The `distanceSquared` method computes the square of the Euclidean distance between this Point3d and the Point3d p1 and returns the result. The `distance` method computes the Euclidean distance between this Point3d and the Point3d p1 and returns the result.

```
public final double distanceL1(Point3d p1)
```

This method computes the L_1 (Manhattan) distance between this point and point p1. The L_1 distance is equal to

$$\text{abs}(x1 - x2) + \text{abs}(y1 - y2) + \text{abs}(z1 - z2)$$

```
public final double distanceLinf(Point3d p1)
```

This method computes the L∞ distance between this point and point p1. The L∞ distance is equal to

$$\text{MAX}[\text{abs}(x1 - x2), \text{abs}(y1 - y2), \text{abs}(z1 - z2)]$$

```
public final void project(Point4d p1)
```

This method multiplies each of the x, y, and z components of the Point4d parameter p1 by 1/w and places the projected values into this point.

A.1.4.2   Vector3d Class

The Vector3d class extends Tuple3d. The Vector3d is a three-element vector represented by double-precision floating-point *x*, *y*, and *z* coordinates. If this value represents a normal, it should be normalized.

Constructors

```
public Vector3d(double x, double y, double z)
public Vector3d(double v[])
public Vector3d(Vector3d v1)
public Vector3d(Vector3f v1)
public Vector3d(Tuple3d t1)
public Vector3d(Tuple3f t1)
public Vector3d()
```

Each of these seven constructors returns a new Vector3d. The first constructor generates a Vector3d from three floating-point numbers x, y, and z. The second constructor generates a Vector3d from the first three elements of array v. The third constructor generates a Vector3d from the double-precision vector v1. The fourth constructor generates a Vector3d from the single-precision vector v1. The fifth and sixth constructors generate a Vector3d from the tuple t1. The final constructor generates a Vector3d with the value of (0.0, 0.0, 0.0).

Methods

`public final void cross(Vector3d v1, Vector3d v2)`

The cross method computes the vector cross-product of vectors v1 and v2 and places the result in this.

`public final void normalize(Vector3d v1)`
`public final void normalize()`

The first normalize method normalizes the vector v1 to unit length and places the result in this. The second normalize method normalizes the vector this and places the resulting unit vector back into this.

`public final double dot(Vector3d v1)`

The dot method returns the dot product of this vector and vector v1

`public final double lengthSquared()`
`public final double length()`

The lengthSquared method returns the squared length of this vector. The length method returns the length of this vector.

`public final double angle(Vector3d v1)`

This method returns the angle, in radians, between this vector and the vector v1 parameter. The return value is constrained to the range $[0, \pi]$.

A.1.5 Tuple3f Class

The Tuple3f class is a generic three-element tuple represented by single-precision floating-point x, y, and z coordinates.

Variables

The component values of a Tuple3f are directly accessible through the public variables x, y, and z. To access the x component of a Tuple3f called upperLeftCorner, a programmer would write `upperLeftCorner.x`. The programmer would access the y and z components similarly.

```
public float x
public float y
public float z
```

The *x*, *y*, and *z* coordinates, respectively.

Constructors

```
public Tuple3f(float x, float y, float z)
public Tuple3f(float t[])
public Tuple3f(Tuple3d t1)
public Tuple3f(Tuple3f t1)
public Tuple3f()
```

Each of these five constructors returns a new Tuple3f. The first constructor generates a Tuple3f from three floating-point numbers x, y, and z. The second constructor generates a Tuple3f from the first three elements of array t. The third constructor generates a Tuple3f from the double-precision Tuple3d t1. The fourth constructor generates a Tuple3f from the single-precision Tuple3f t1. The final constructor generates a Tuple3f with the value of (0.0, 0.0, 0.0).

Methods

```
public String toString()
```

This method returns a string that contains the values of this Tuple3f.

```
public final void set(float x, float y, float z)
public final void set(float t[])
public final void set(Tuple3f t1)
public final void set(Tuple3d t1)
public final void get(float t[])
public final void get(Tuple3f t)
```

The four `set` methods set the value of vector `this` to the coordinates provided or to the values of the vectors provided. The first `get` method gets the value of this vector and copies the values into the array t. The second `get` method gets the value of this vector and copies the values into tuple t.

```
public final void add(Tuple3f t1, Tuple3f t2)
public final void add(Tuple3f t1)
public final void sub(Tuple3f t1, Tuple3f t2)
public final void sub(Tuple3f t1)
```

The first add method computes the element-by-element sum of tuples t1 and t2, placing the result in this. The second add method computes the element-by-element sum of this and tuple t1 and places the result in this. The first sub method performs an element-by-element subtraction of tuple t2 from tuple t1 and places the result in this (this = t1 – t2). The second sub method performs an element-by-element subtraction of tuple t1 from this tuple and places the result into this (this = this – t1).

```
public final void negate(Tuple3f t1)
public final void negate()
```

The first negate method sets the values of this tuple to the negative of the values from tuple t1. The second negate method negates the vector this and places the resulting tuple back into this.

```
public final void scale(float s, Tuple3f t1)
public final void scale(float s)
public final void scaleAdd(float s, Tuple3f t1)
public final void scaleAdd(float s, Tuple3f t1, Tuple3f t2)
```

The first scale method multiplies each element of the vector t1 by the scale factor s and places the resulting scaled vector into this. The second scale method multiples the vector this by the scale factor s and replaces this with the scaled value. The first scaleAdd method scales this tuple by the scale factor s, adds the result to tuple t1, and places the result into tuple this (this = s*this + t1). The second scaleAdd method scales the tuple t1 by the scale factor s, adds the result to the tuple t2, and places the result into the tuple this (this = s*t1 + t2).

```
public boolean equals(Tuple3f t1)
public boolean equals(Object t1)
```

The first method returns true if all of the data members of tuple t1 are equal to the corresponding data members in this Tuple3f. The second method returns true if the Object t1 is of type Tuple3f and all of the data members of t1 are equal to the corresponding data members in this Tuple3f.

```
public boolean epsilonEquals(Tuple3f t1, float epsilon)
```

This method returns true if the L∞ distance between this tuple and tuple t1 is less than or equal to the epsilon parameter. Otherwise, this method returns false. The L∞ distance is equal to

$$\text{MAX}[\text{abs}(x1 - x2), \text{abs}(y1 - y2), \text{abs}(z1 - z2)]$$

385

```
public final void absolute()
public final void absolute(Tuple3f t)
```

The first absolute method sets each component of this tuple to its absolute value. The second absolute method sets each component of this tuple to the absolute value of the corresponding component in tuple t.

```
public final void clamp(float min, float max)
public final void clamp(float min, float max, Tuple3f t)
public final void clampMin(float min)
public final void clampMin(float min, Tuple3f t)
public final void clampMax(float max)
public final void clampMax(float max, Tuple3f t)
```

The first clamp method clamps this tuple to the range [min, max]. The second clamp method clamps the values from tuple t to the range [min, max] and assigns these clamped values to this tuple. The first clampMin method clamps each value of this tuple to the min parameter. The second clampMin method clamps each value of the tuple t and assigns these clamped values to this tuple. The first clampMax method clamps each value of this tuple to the max parameter. The second clampMax method clamps each value of tuple t to the max parameter and assigns these clamped values to this tuple. In each method the values of tuple t remain unchanged.

```
public final void interpolate(Tuple3f t1, Tuple3f t2, float alpha)
public final void interpolate(Tuple3f t1, float alpha)
```

The first method linearly interpolates between tuples t1 and t2 and places the result into this tuple (this = (1 – alpha) * t1 + alpha * t2). The second method linearly interpolates between this tuple and tuple t1 and places the result into this tuple (this = (1–alpha) * this + alpha * t1).

```
public int hashCode()
```

This method returns a hash number based on the data values in this object. Two different Tuple3f objects with identical data values (that is, equals(Tuple3f) returns true) will return the same hash number. Two tuples with different data members may return the same hash value, although this is not likely.

A.1.5.1   Point3f Class

The Point3f class extends Tuple3f. The Point3f is a three-element point represented by single-precision floating-point x, y, and z coordinates.

Constructors

```
public Point3f(float x, float y, float z)
public Point3f(float p[])
public Point3f(Point3d p1)
public Point3f(Point3f p1)
public Point3f(Tuple3d t1)
public Point3f(Tuple3f t1)
public Point3f()
```

Each of these seven constructors returns a new Point3f. The first constructor generates a point from three floating-point numbers x, y, and z. The second constructor (Point3f(float p[]) generates a point from the first three elements of array p. The third constructor generates a point from the double-precision point p1. The fourth constructor generates a point from the single precision point p1. The fifth and sixth constructors generate a Point3f from the tuple t1. The final constructor generates a point with the value of (0.0, 0.0, 0.0).

Methods

```
public final float distance(Point3f p1)
public final float distanceSquared(Point3f p1)
```

The distance method computes the Euclidean distance between this point and the point p1 and returns the result. The distanceSquared method computes the square of the Euclidean distance between this point and the point p1 and returns the result.

```
public final float distanceL1(Point3f p1)
```

This method computes the L_1 (Manhattan) distance between this point and point p1. The L_1 distance is equal to

$$\mathrm{abs}(x1 - x2) + \mathrm{abs}(y1 - y2) + \mathrm{abs}(z1 - z2)$$

```
public final float distanceLinf(Point3f p1)
```

This method computes the $L\infty$ distance between this point and point p1. The $L\infty$ distance is equal to

$$\mathrm{MAX}[\mathrm{abs}(x1 - x2), \mathrm{abs}(y1 - y2), \mathrm{abs}(z1 - z2)]$$

```
public final void project(Point4f p1)
```

This method multiplies each of the x, y, and z components of the Point4f parameter p1 by 1/w and places the projected values into this point.

A.1.5.2 Vector3f Class

The Vector3f class extends Tuple3f. The Vector3f is a three-element vector represented by single-precision floating-point *x*, *y*, and *z* coordinates.

Constructors

```
public Vector3f(float x, float y, float z)
public Vector3f(float v[])
public Vector3f(Vector3d v1)
public Vector3f(Vector3f v1)
public Vector3f(Tuple3d t1)
Public Vector3f(Tuple3f t1)
public Vector3f()
```

Each of these seven constructors returns a new Vector3f. The first constructor generates a Vector3f from three floating-point numbers x, y, and z. The second constructor generates a Vector3f from the first three elements of array v. The third constructor generates a Vector3f from the double-precision Vector3d v1. The fourth constructor generates a Vector3f from the single-precision Vector3f v1. The fifth and sixth constructors generate a Vector3f from the tuple t1. The final constructor generates a Vector3f with the value of (0.0, 0.0, 0.0).

Methods

```
public final float length()
public final float lengthSquared()
```

The length method computes the length of the vector this and returns its length as a single-precision floating-point number. The lengthSquared method computes the square of the length of the vector this and returns its length as a single-precision floating-point number.

```
public final void cross(Vector3f v1, Vector3f v2)
```

The cross method computes the vector cross-product of v1 and v2 and places the result in this.

```
public final float dot(Vector3f v1)
```

The dot method computes the dot product between this vector and the vector v1 and returns the resulting value.

```
public final void normalize(Vector3f v1)
public final void normalize()
```

The first `normalize` method normalizes the vector `v1` to unit length and places the result in `this`. The second `normalize` method normalizes the vector `this` and places the resulting unit vector back into `this`.

```
public final float angle(Vector3f v1)
```

This method returns the angle, in radians, between this vector and the vector parameter. The return value is constrained to the range $[0, \pi]$.

A.1.5.3   TexCoord3f Class

The TexCoord3f class extends Tuple3f. The TexCoord3f is a three-element texture coordinate represented by single-precision floating-point x, y, and z coordinates.

Constructors

```
public TexCoord3f(float x, float y, float z)
public TexCoord3f(float v[])
public TexCoord3f(TexCoord3f v1)
public TexCoord3f(Tuple3d t1)
public TexCoord3f(Tuple3f t1)
public TexCoord3f()
```

Each of these six constructors returns a new TexCoord3f. The first constructor generates a texture coordinate from three floating-point numbers x, y, and z. The second constructor generates a texture coordinate from the first three elements of array v. The third constructor generates a texture coordinate from the single-precision TexCoord3f v1. The fourth and fifth constructors generate a texture coordinate from tuple t1. The final constructor generates a texture coordinate with the value of $(0.0, 0.0, 0.0)$.

A.1.5.4   Color3f Class

The Color3f class extends Tuple3f. The Color3f is a three-element color value represented by single-precision floating-point x, y, and z values. The x, y, and z values represent the red, blue, and green color values, respectively. Color components should be in the range $[0.0, 1.0]$.

Constructors

```
public Color3f(float x, float y, float z)
public Color3f(float v[])
public Color3f(Color3f v1)
public Color3f(Tuple3d t1)
public Color3f(Tuple3f t1)
```
◀ New in 1.2 ▶ `public Color3f(Color color)`
```
public Color3f()
```

Each of these six constructors returns a new Color3f. The first constructor generates a Color3f from three floating-point numbers x, y, and z. The second constructor (Color3f(float v[])) generates a Color3f from the first three elements of array v. The third constructor generates a Color3f from the single-precision color v1. The fourth and fifth constructors generate a Color3f from the tuple t1. The sixth constructor generates a Color3f from the specified AWT Color object. The final constructor generates a Color3f with the value of (0.0, 0.0, 0.0).

Methods

◀ New in 1.2 ▶ `public final void set(Color color)`
◀ New in 1.2 ▶ `public final Color get()`

The set method sets the R,G,B values of this Color3f object to those of the specified AWT Color object. The get method returns a new AWT Color object initialized with the R,G,B values of this Color3f object.

◀ New in 1.2 ▶ ## A.1.6   Tuple3i Class

The Tuple3i class is a generic three-element tuple represented by signed integer *x,y,z* coordinates.

Variables

The component values of a Tuple3i are directly accessible through the public variables x, y, and z. To access the x component of a Tuple3i called upperLeft-Corner, a programmer would write upperLeftCorner.x. The programmer would access the y and z components similarly.

◀ New in 1.2 ▶ `public int x`
◀ New in 1.2 ▶ `public int y`
◀ New in 1.2 ▶ `public int z`

The *x*, *y*, and *z* coordinates, respectively.

Constructors

```
public Tuple3i(int x, int y, int z)
public Tuple3i(int[] t)
public Tuple3i(Tuple3i t1)
public Tuple3i()
```

◀ New in 1.2 ▶
◀ New in 1.2 ▶
◀ New in 1.2 ▶
◀ New in 1.2 ▶

Each of these four constructors returns a new Tuple3i. The first constructor generates a Tuple3i from the specified *x*, *y*, and *z* coordinates. The second constructor generates a Tuple3i from the array of length 3. The third constructor generates a Tuple3i from the specified Tuple3i. The final constructor generates a Tuple3i with the value of (0,0,0).

Methods

```
public String toString()
```

◀ New in 1.2 ▶

This method returns a string that contains the values of this Tuple3i.

```
public final void set(int x, int y, int z)
public final void set(int[] t)
public final void set(Tuple3i t1)
public final void get(int[] t)
public final void get(Tuple3i t)
```

◀ New In 1.2 ▶
◀ New in 1.2 ▶
◀ New in 1.2 ▶
◀ New in 1.2 ▶
◀ New in 1.2 ▶

The first set method sets the value of this tuple to the specified *x*, *y*, and *z* coordinates. The second set method sets the value of this tuple to the specified coordinates in the array of length 3. The third set method sets the value of this tuple to the value of tuple t1. The first get method copies the values of this tuple into the array t. The second get method copies the values of this tuple into the tuple t.

```
public final void add(Tuple3i t1, Tuple3i t2)
public final void add(Tuple3i t1)
```

◀ New in 1.2 ▶
◀ New in 1.2 ▶

The first method sets the value of this tuple to the sum of tuples t1 and t2. The second method sets the value of this tuple to the sum of itself and t1.

```
public final void sub(Tuple3i t1, Tuple3i t2)
public final void sub(Tuple3i t1)
```

◀ New in 1.2 ▶
◀ New in 1.2 ▶

The first method sets the value of this tuple to the difference of tuples t1 and t2 (this = t1 − t2). The second method sets the value of this tuple to the difference of itself and t1 (this = this − t1).

◀ New in 1.2 ▶ `public final void negate(Tuple3i t1)`
◀ New in 1.2 ▶ `public final void negate()`

The first method sets the value of this tuple to the negation of tuple t1. The second method negates the value of this tuple in place.

◀ New in 1.2 ▶ `public final void scale(int s, Tuple3i t1)`
◀ New in 1.2 ▶ `public final void scale(int s)`

The first method sets the value of this tuple to the scalar multiplication of tuple t1. The second method sets the value of this tuple to the scalar multiplication of the scale factor with this.

◀ New in 1.2 ▶ `public final void scaleAdd(int s, Tuple3i t1, Tuple3i t2)`
◀ New in 1.2 ▶ `public final void scaleAdd(int s, Tuple3i t1)`

The first method sets the value of this tuple to the scalar multiplication of tuple t1 plus tuple t2 (this = s*t1 + t2). The second method sets the value of this tuple to the scalar multiplication of itself and then adds tuple t1 (this = s*this + t1).

◀ New in 1.2 ▶ `public boolean equals(Object t1)`

This method returns true if the Object t1 is of type Tuple3i and all of the data members of t1 are equal to the corresponding data members in this Tuple3i.

◀ New in 1.2 ▶ `public final void clamp(int min, int max, Tuple3i t)`
◀ New in 1.2 ▶ `public final void clamp(int min, int max)`

The first method clamps the tuple parameter to the range [low, high] and places the values into this tuple. The second method clamps this tuple to the range [low, high].

◀ New in 1.2 ▶ `public final void clampMin(int min, Tuple3i t)`
◀ New in 1.2 ▶ `public final void clampMin(int min)`
◀ New in 1.2 ▶ `public final void clampMax(int max, Tuple3i t)`
◀ New in 1.2 ▶ `public final void clampMax(int max)`

The first method clamps the minimum value of the tuple parameter to the min parameter and places the values into this tuple. The second method clamps the minimum value of this tuple to the min parameter. The third method clamps the maximum value of the tuple parameter to the max parameter and places the values into this tuple. The final method clamps the maximum value of this tuple to the max parameter.

```
public final void absolute(Tuple3i t)
public final void absolute()
```
◀ New in 1.2 ▶
◀ New in 1.2 ▶

The first method sets each component of the tuple parameter to its absolute value and places the modified values into this tuple. The second method sets each component of this tuple to its absolute value.

```
public int hashCode()
```
◀ New in 1.2 ▶

This method returns a hash code value based on the data values in this object. Two different Tuple3i objects with identical data values (that is, Tuple3i.equals returns true) will return the same hash code value. Two objects with different data members may return the same hash value, although this is not likely.

A.1.6.1   Point3i Class
◀ New in 1.2 ▶

The Point3i class extends Tuple3i. The Point3i is a three-element point represented by signed integer x, y, z coordinates.

Constructors

```
public Point3i(int x, int y, int z)
public Point3i(int[] t)
public Point3i(Tuple3i t1
public Point3i()
```
◀ New in 1.2 ▶
◀ New in 1.2 ▶
◀ New in 1.2 ▶
◀ New in 1.2 ▶

Each of these four constructors returns a new Point3i. The first constructor generates a Point3i from the specified x, y, and z coordinates. The second constructor generates a Point3i from the array of length 3. The third constructor generates a Point3i from the specified Tuple3i. The final constructor generates a Point3i with the value of (0,0,0).

A.1.7   Tuple4b Class

The Tuple4b class represents four-byte tuples. Note that Java defines a byte as a signed integer in the range [−128, 127]. However, colors are more typically represented by values in the range [0, 255]. Java 3D recognizes this and, in those cases where Tuple4b is used to represent color, treats the bytes as if the range were [0, 255]—in other words, as if the bytes were unsigned. Values greater than 127 can be assigned to a byte variable using a type cast. For example,

```
byteVariable = (byte) intValue;// intValue can be > 127
```

If intValue is greater than 127, then byteVariable will be negative. The correct value will be extracted when it is used (by masking off the upper bits).

Variables

The component values of a Tuple4b are directly accessible through the public variables x, y, z, and w. The x, y, z, and w values represent the red, green, blue, and alpha values, respectively. To access the x (red) component of a Tuple4b called backgroundColor, a programmer would write backgroundColor.x. The programmer would access the y (green), z (blue), and w (alpha) components similarly.

```
public byte x
public byte y
public byte z
public byte w
```

The red, green, blue, and alpha values, respectively.

Constructors

```
public Tuple4b(byte b1, byte b2, byte b3, byte b4)
public Tuple4b(byte t[])
public Tuple4b(Tuple4b t1)
public Tuple4b()
```

Each of these four constructors returns a new Tuple4b. The first constructor generates a Tuple4b from four bytes b1, b2, b3, and b4. The second constructor (Tuple4b(byte t[]) generates a Tuple4b from the first four elements of array t. The third constructor generates a Tuple4b from the byte-precision Tuple4b t1. The final constructor generates a Tuple4b with the value of (0.0, 0.0, 0.0, 0.0).

Methods

```
public String toString()
```

This method returns a string that contains the values of this Tuple4b.

```
public final void set(byte b[])
public final void set(Tuple4b t1)
public final void get(byte b[])
public final void get(Tuple4b t1)
```

The first set method sets the value of the data members of this Tuple4b to the value of the array b. The second set method sets the value of the data members of this Tuple4b to the value of the argument tuple t1. The first get method places the values of the x, y, z, and w components of this Tuple4b into the byte array b. The second get method places the values of the x, y, z, and w components of this Tuple4b into the Tuple4b t1.

```
public boolean equals(Tuple4b t1)
public boolean equals(Object t1)
```

The first method returns true if all of the data members of Tuple4b t1 are equal to the corresponding data members in this Tuple4b. The second method returns true if the Object t1 is of type Tuple4b and all of the data members of t1 are equal to the corresponding data members in this Tuple4b.

```
public int hashCode()
```

This method returns a hash number based on the data values in this object. Two different Tuple4b objects with identical data values (that is, equals(Tuple4b) returns true) will return the same hash number. Two Tuple4b objects with different data members may return the same hash value, although this is not likely.

A.1.7.1   Color4b Class

The Color4b class extends Tuple4b. The Color4b is a four-byte color value (red, green, blue, and alpha).

Constructors

```
public Color4b(byte b1, byte b2, byte b3, byte b4)
public Color4b(byte c[])
public Color4b(Color4b c1)
public Color4b(Tuple4b t1)
public Color4b(Color color)                          ◀ New in 1.2 ▶
public Color4b()
```

Each of these five constructors returns a new Color4b. The first constructor generates a Color4b from four bytes—b1, b2, b3, and b4. The second constructor generates a Color4b from the first four elements of byte array c. The third constructor generates a Color4b from the byte-precision Color4b c1. The fourth constructor generates a Color4b from the tuple t1. The fifth constructor generates a Color4b from the specified AWT Color object. The final constructor generates a Color4b with the value of (0.0, 0.0, 0.0, 0.0).

Methods

```
public final void set(Color color)                   ◀ New in 1.2 ▶
public final Color get()                              ◀ New in 1.2 ▶
```

The set method sets the R,G,B,A values of this Color4b object to those of the specified AWT Color object. The get method returns a new AWT Color object initialized with the R,G,B,A values of this Color4b object.

A.1.8 Tuple4d Class

The Tuple4d class represents a four-element tuple represented by double-precision floating-point *x, y, z,* and *w* coordinates.

Variables

The component values of a Tuple4d are directly accessible through the public variables x, y, z, and w. To access the x component of a Tuple4d called upper-LeftCorner, a programmer would write upperLeftCorner.x. The programmer would access the y, z, and w components similarly.

```
public double x
public double y
public double z
public double w
```

The *x, y, z,* and *w* coordinates, respectively.

Constructors

```
public Tuple4d(double x, double y, double z, double w)
public Tuple4d(double t[])
public Tuple4d(Tuple4d t1)
public Tuple4d(Tuple4f t1)
public Tuple4d()
```

Each of these five constructors returns a new Tuple4d. The first constructor generates a Tuple4d from four floating-point numbers x, y, z, and w. The second constructor (Tuple4d(double t[]) generates a Tuple4d from the first four elements of array t. The third constructor generates a Tuple4d from the double-precision tuple t1. The fourth constructor generates a Tuple4d from the single-precision tuple t1. The final constructor generates a Tuple4d with the value of (0.0, 0.0, 0.0, 0.0).

Methods

```
public final void set(double x, double y, double z, double w)
public final void set(double t[])
public final void set(Tuple4d t1)
```

```
public final void set(Tuple4f t1)
public final void get(double t[])
public final void get(Tuple4d t)
```

These methods set the value of the tuple this to the values specified or to the values of the specified tuples. The first get method retrieves the value of this tuple and places it into the array t of length four, in *x, y, z, w* order. The second get method retrieves the value of this tuple and places it into tuple t.

```
public final void add(Tuple4d t1, Tuple4d t2)
public final void add(Tuple4d t1)
public final void sub(Tuple4d t1, Tuple4d t2)
public final void sub(Tuple4d t1)
```

The first add method computes the element-by-element sum of the tuple t1 and the tuple t2, placing the result in this. The second add method computes the element-by-element sum of this tuple and the tuple t1 and places the result in this. The first sub method performs an element-by-element subtraction of tuple t2 from tuple t1 and places the result in this. The second sub method performs an element-by-element subtraction of tuple t1 from this tuple and places the result in this.

```
public final void negate(Tuple4d t1)
public final void negate()
```

The first negate method sets the values of this tuple to the negative of the values from tuple t1. The second negate method negates the tuple this and places the resulting tuple back into this.

```
public final void scaleAdd(float s, Tuple4d t1)
```

Deprecated method. See the following method.

```
public final void scale(double s, Tuple4d t1)
public final void scale(double s)
public final void scaleAdd(double s, Tuple4d t1)
public final void scaleAdd(double s, Tuple4d t1, Tuple4d t2)
```

The first scale method multiplies each element of the tuple t1 by the scale factor s and places the resulting scaled tuple into this. The second scale method multiples the tuple this by the scale factor s and replaces this with the scaled value. The first scaleAdd method scales this tuple by the scale factor s, adds the result to tuple t1, and places the result into tuple this (this = s*this + t1). The second scaleAdd method scales the tuple t1 by the scale factor s, adds the result to the tuple t2, and places the result into the tuple this (this = s*t1 + t2).

397

```
public void interpolate(Tuple4d t1, Tuple4d t2, float alpha)
public void interpolate(Tuple4d t1, float alpha)
```

Deprecated methods. See the following two methods.

```
public void interpolate(Tuple4d t1, Tuple4d t2, double alpha)
public void interpolate(Tuple4d t1, double alpha)
```

The first `interpolate` method linearly interpolates between tuples `t1` and `t2` and places the result into this tuple (this = (1 − alpha) * t1 + alpha * t2). The second `interpolate` method linearly interpolates between this tuple and tuple `t1` and places the result into this tuple (this = (1 − alpha) * this + alpha * t1).

```
public String toString()
```

This method returns a string that contains the values of this tuple. The form is `(x, y, z, w)`.

```
public boolean equals(Tuple4d v1)
public boolean equals(Object t1)
```

The first method returns `true` if all of the data members of tuple `v1` are equal to the corresponding data members in this tuple. The second method returns true if the Object `t1` is of type Tuple4d and all of the data members of `t1` are equal to the corresponding data members in this Tuple4d.

```
public boolean epsilonEquals(Tuple4d t1, double epsilon)
```

This method returns `true` if the L∞ distance between this Tuple4d and Tuple4d `t1` is less than or equal to the `epsilon` parameter. Otherwise, this method returns `false`. The L∞ distance is equal to

$$\mathrm{MAX}[\mathrm{abs}(x1 - x2), \mathrm{abs}(y1 - y2), \mathrm{abs}(z1 - z2), \mathrm{abs}(w1 - w2)]$$

```
public final void absolute()
public final void absolute(Tuple4d t)
```

The first `absolute` method sets each component of this tuple to its absolute value. The second `absolute` method sets each component of this tuple to the absolute value of the corresponding component in tuple `t`.

```
public final void clamp(float min, float max)
public final void clamp(float min, float max, Tuple4d t)
public final void clampMin(float min)
public final void clampMin(float min, Tuple4d t)
```

```
public final void clampMax(float max)
public final void clampMax(float max, Tuple4d t)
```

Deprecated methods. See the following six methods.

```
public final void clamp(double min, double max)
public final void clamp(double min, double max, Tuple4d t)
public final void clampMin(double min)
public final void clampMin(double min, Tuple4d t)
public final void clampMax(double max)
public final void clampMax(double max, Tuple4d t)
```

The first clamp method clamps this tuple to the range [min, max]. The second clamp method clamps this tuple to the range [min, max] and places the values into tuple t. The first clampMin method clamps the minimum value of this tuple to the min parameter. The second clampMin method clamps the minimum value of this tuple to the min parameter and places the values into the tuple t. The first clampMax method clamps the maximum value of this tuple to the max parameter. The second clampMax method clamps the maximum value of this tuple to the max parameter and places the values into the tuple t.

```
public int hashCode()
```

This method returns a hash number based on the data values in this object. Two different Tuple4d objects with identical data values (that is, equals(Tuple4d) returns true) will return the same hash number. Two Tuple4d objects with different data members may return the same hash value, although this is not likely.

A.1.8.1   Point4d Class

The Point4d class extends Tuple4d. The Point4d is a four-element point represented by double-precision floating-point *x*, *y*, *z*, and *w* coordinates.

Constructors

```
public Point4d(double x, double y, double z, double w)
public Point4d(double p[])
public Point4d(Point4d p1)
public Point4d(Point4f p1)
public Point4d(Tuple4d t1)
public Point4d(Tuple4f t1)
public Point4d(Tuple3d t1)
public Point4d()
```

◀ New in 1.2 ▶

Each of these eight constructors returns a new Point4d. The first constructor generates a Point4d from four floating-point numbers x, y, z, and w. The second

399

constructor (`Point4d(double p[]`) generates a Point4d from the first four elements of array p. The third constructor generates a Point4d from the double-precision point p1. The fourth constructor generates a Point4d from the single-precision point p1. The fifth and sixth constructors generate a Point4d from tuple t1. The seventh constructor generates a Point4d from the specified Tuple3d—the w component of this point is set to 1. The final constructor generates a Point4d with the value of (0.0, 0.0, 0.0, 0.0).

Methods

◀ New in 1.2 ▶ `public final void set(Tuple3d t1)`

This method sets the x, y, and z components of this point to the corresponding components of tuple t1. The w component of this point is set to 1.

`public final double distance(Point4d p1)`
`public final double distanceSquared(Point4d p1)`

The `distance` method computes the Euclidean distance between this point and the point p1 and returns the result. The `distanceSquared` method computes the square of the Euclidean distance between this point and the point p1 and returns the result.

`public final double distanceL1(Point4d p1)`

This method computes the L_1 (Manhattan) distance between this point and point p1. The L_1 distance is equal to

$$\text{abs}(x1 - x2) + \text{abs}(y1 - y2) + \text{abs}(z1 - z2) + \text{abs}(w1 - w2)$$

`public final double distanceLinf(Point4d p1)`

This method computes the $L\infty$ distance between this point and point p1. The $L\infty$ distance is equal to

$$\text{MAX}[\text{abs}(x1 - x2), \text{abs}(y1 - y2), \text{abs}(z1 - z2), \text{abs}(w1 - w2)]$$

`public final void project(Point4d p1)`

This method multiplies each of the x, y, and z components of the point p1 by $1/w$, places the projected values into this point, and places a 1 into the w parameter of this point.

A.1.8.2   Vector4d Class

The Vector4d class extends Tuple4d. The Vector4d is a four-element vector represented by double-precision floating-point *x*, *y*, *z*, and *w* coordinates.

Constructors

```
public Vector4d(double x, double y, double z, double w)
public Vector4d(double v[])
public Vector4d(Vector4d v1)
public Vector4d(Vector4f v1)
public Vector4d(Tuple4d t1)
public Vector4d(Tuple4f t1)
public Vector4d(Tuple3d t1)
public Vector4d()
```

◀ New in 1.2 ▶

Each of these eight constructors returns a new Vector4d. The first constructor generates a Vector4d from four floating-point numbers x, y, z, and w. The second constructor generates a Vector4d from the first four elements of array v. The third constructor generates a Vector4d from the double-precision Vector4d v1. The fourth constructor generates a Vector4d from the single-precision Vector4f v1. The fifth and sixth constructors generate a Vector4d from tuple t1. The seventh constructor generates a Vector4d from the specified Tuple3d—the w component of this vector is set to 0. The final constructor generates a Vector4d with the value of (0.0, 0.0, 0.0, 0.0).

Methods

```
public final void set(Tuple3d t1)
```

◀ New in 1.2 ▶

This method sets the x, y, and z components of this vector to the corresponding components of tuple t1. The w component of this vector is set to 0.

```
public final double length()
public final double lengthSquared()
```

The length method computes the length of the vector this and returns its length as a double-precision floating-point number. The lengthSquared method computes the square of the length of the vector this and returns its length as a double-precision floating-point number.

```
public final void dot(Vector4d v1)
```

This method returns the dot product of this vector and vector v1.

401

```
public final void normalize(Vector4d v1)
public final void normalize()
```

The first `normalize` method normalizes the vector v1 to unit length and places the result in this. The second `normalize` method normalizes the vector this and places the resulting unit vector back into this.

```
public final double angle(Vector4d v1)
```

This method returns the (four-space) angle, in radians, between this vector and the vector v1 parameter. The return value is constrained to the range $[0, \pi]$.

A.1.8.3   Quat4d Class

The Quat4d class extends Tuple4d. The Quat4d is a four-element quaternion represented by double-precision floating-point *x*, *y*, *z*, and *w* values.

Constructors

```
public Quat4d(double x, double y, double z, double w)
public Quat4d(double q[])
public Quat4d(Quat4d q1)
public Quat4d(Quat4f q1)
public Quat4d(Tuple4d t1)
public Quat4d(Tuple4f t1)
public Quat4d()
```

Each of these seven constructors returns a new Quat4d. The first constructor generates a quaternion from four floating-point numbers x, y, z, and w. The second constructor generates a quaternion from the first four elements of array q of length four. The third constructor generates a quaternion from the double-precision quaternion q1. The fourth constructor generates a quaternion from the single-precision quaternion q1. The fifth and sixth constructors generate a Quat4d from tuple t1. The final constructor generates a quaternion with the value of (0.0, 0.0, 0.0, 0.0).

Methods

```
public final void conjugate(Quat4d q1)
public final void conjugate()
```

The first `conjugate` method sets the values of this quaternion to the conjugate of quaternion q1. The second `conjugate` method negates the value of each of this quaternion's *x*, *y*, and *z* coordinates in place.

```
public final void mul(Quat4d q1, Quat4d q2)
public final void mul(Quat4d q1)
```

The first `mul` method sets the value of this quaternion to the quaternion product of quaternions q1 and q2 (this = q1 * q2). Note that this is safe for aliasing (that is, `this` can be q1 or q2). The second `mul` method sets the value of this quaternion to the quaternion products of itself and q1 (this = this * q1).

```
public final void mulInverse(Quat4d q1, Quat4d q2)
public final void mulInverse(Quat4d q1)
```

The first `mulInverse` method multiplies quaternion q1 by the inverse of quaternion q2 and places the value into this quaternion. The values of both quaternion arguments are preserved (this = q1 * q2^{-1}). The second `mulInverse` method multiplies this quaternion by the inverse of quaternion q1 and places the value into this quaternion. The value of the argument q1 is preserved (this = this * q1^{-1}).

```
public final void inverse(Quat4d q1)
public final void inverse()
```

The first `inverse` method sets the value of this quaternion to the quaternion inverse of quaternion q1. The second `inverse` method sets the value of this quaternion to the quaternion inverse of itself.

```
public final void normalize(Quat4d q1)
public final void normalize()
```

The first `normalize` method sets the value of this quaternion to the normalized value of quaternion q1. The second `normalize` method normalizes the value of this quaternion in place.

```
public final void set(Matrix4f m1)
public final void set(Matrix4d m1)
public final void set(Matrix3f m1)
public final void set(Matrix3d m1)
public final void set(AxisAngle4f a)
public final void set(AxisAngle4d a)
```

These `set` methods set the value of this quaternion to the rotational component of the passed matrix.

```
public final void interpolate(Quat4d q1, double alpha)
public final void interpolate(Quat4d q1, Quat4d q2, double alpha)
```

The first method performs a great circle interpolation between this quaternion and the quaternion parameter and places the result into this quaternion. The second method performs a great circle interpolation between quaternion q1 and quaternion q2 and places the result into this quaternion.

A.1.9   Tuple4f Class

The Tuple4f class represents a four-element tuple represented by single-precision floating-point *x, y, z,* and *w* values.

Variables

The component values of a Tuple4f are directly accessible through the public variables x, y, z, and w. To access the x component of a Tuple4f called upper-LeftCorner, a programmer would write upperLeftCorner.x. The programmer would access the y, z, and w components similarly.

```
public double x
public double y
public double z
public double w
```

The *x, y, z,* and *w* values, respectively.

Constructors

```
public Tuple4f(float x, float y, float z, float w)
public Tuple4f(float t[])
public Tuple4f(Tuple4d t1)
public Tuple4f(Tuple4f t1)
public Tuple4f()
```

Each of these five constructors returns a new Tuple4f. The first constructor generates a Tuple4f from four floating-point numbers x, y, z, and w. The second constructor (Tuple4f(float t[])) generates a Tuple4f from the first four elements of array t. The third constructor generates a Tuple4f from the double-precision tuple t1. The fourth constructor generates a Tuple4f from the single-precision tuple t1. The final constructor generates a Tuple4f with the value of (0.0, 0.0, 0.0, 0.0).

Methods

```
public final void set(float x, float y, float z, float w)
public final void set(float t[])
public final void set(Tuple4f t1)
```

404

```
public final void set(Tuple4d t1)
public final void get(float t[])
public final void get(Tuple4f t)
```

The first set method sets the value of this tuple to the specified x, y, z, and w values. The second set method sets the value of this tuple to the specified coordinates in the array. The next two methods set the value of tuple this to the value of tuple t1. The get methods copy the value of this tuple into the tuple t.

```
public final void add(Tuple4f t1, Tuple4f t2)
public final void add(Tuple4f t1)
public final void sub(Tuple4f t1, Tuple4f t2)
public final void sub(Tuple4f t1)
```

The first add method computes the element-by-element sum of tuples t1 and t2 and places the result in this. The second add method computes the element-by-element sum of this tuple and tuple t1 and places the result in this. The first sub method performs the element-by-element subtraction of tuple t2 from tuple t1 and places the result in this (this = t1 − t2). The second sub method performs the element-by-element subtraction of tuple t1 from this tuple and places the result in this (this = this − t1).

```
public final void negate(Tuple4f t1)
public final void negate()
```

The first negate method sets the values of this tuple to the negative of the values from tuple t1. The second negate method negates the tuple this and places the resulting tuple back into this.

```
public final void scale(float s, Tuple4f t1)
public final void scale(float s)
public final void scaleAdd(float s, Tuple4f t1)
public final void scaleAdd(float s, Tuple4f t1, Tuple4f t2)
```

The first scale method multiplies each element of the tuple t1 by the scale factor s and places the resulting scaled tuple into this. The second scale method multiples the tuple this by the scale factor s, replacing this with the scaled value. The first scaleAdd method scales this tuple by the scale factor s, adds the result to tuple t1, and places the result into tuple this (this = s*this + t1). The second scaleAdd method scales the tuple t1 by the scale factor s, adds the result to the tuple t2, and places the result into the tuple this (this = s*t1 + t2).

```
public String toString()
```

This method returns a string that contains the values of this Tuple4f. The form is (x, y, z, w).

```
public boolean equals(Tuple4f t1)
public boolean equals(Object t1)
```

The first method returns true if all of the data members of Tuple4f t1 are equal to the corresponding data members in this Tuple4f. The second method returns true if the Object t1 is of type Tuple4f and all of the data members of t1 are equal to the corresponding data members in this Tuple4f.

```
public boolean epsilonEquals(Tuple4f t1, float epsilon)
```

This method returns true if the L∞ distance between this Tuple4f and Tuple4f t1 is less than or equal to the epsilon parameter. Otherwise, this method returns false. The L∞ distance is equal to

$$\text{MAX}[\text{abs}(x1 - x2), \text{abs}(y1 - y2), \text{abs}(z1 - z2), \text{abs}(w1 - w2)]$$

```
public final void absolute()
public final void absolute(Tuple4f t)
```

The first absolute method sets each component of this tuple to its absolute value. The second absolute method sets each component of this tuple to the absolute value of the corresponding component in tuple t.

```
public final void clamp(float min, float max)
public final void clamp(float min, float max, Tuple4f t)
public final void clampMin(float min)
public final void clampMin(float min, Tuple4f t)
public final void clampMax(float max)
public final void clampMax(float max, Tuple4f t)
```

The first clamp method clamps this tuple to the range [min, max]. The second clamp method clamps this tuple to the range [min, max] and places the values into tuple t. The first clampMin method clamps the minimum value of this tuple to the min parameter. The second clampMin method clamps the minimum value of this tuple to the min parameter and places the values into the tuple t. The first clampMax method clamps the maximum value of this tuple to the max parameter. The second clampMax method clamps the maximum value of this tuple to the max parameter and places the values into the tuple t.

```
public void interpolate(Tuple4f t1, Tuple4f t2, float alpha)
public void interpolate(Tuple4f t1, float alpha)
```

The first `interpolate` method linearly interpolates between tuples `t1` and `t2` and places the result into this tuple (this = (1 – alpha) * t1 + alpha * t2). The second `interpolate` method linearly interpolates between this tuple and tuple `t1` and places the result into this tuple (this = (1 – alpha) * this + alpha * t1).

public int hashCode()

This method returns a hash number based on the data values in this object. Two different Tuple4f objects with identical data values (that is, `equals(Tuple4f)` returns `true`) will return the same hash number. Two Tuple4f objects with different data members may return the same hash value, although this is not likely.

A.1.9.1   Point4f Class

The Point4f class extends Tuple4f. The Point4f is a four-element point represented by single-precision floating-point x, y, z, and w coordinates.

Constructors

```
public Point4f(float x, float y, float z, float w)
public Point4f(float p[])
public Point4f(Point4d p1)
public Point4f(Point4f p1)
public Point4f(Tuple4d t1)
public Point4f(Tuple4f t1)
public Point4f(Tuple3f t1)                          ◀ New in 1.2 ▶
public Point4f()
```

Each of these eight constructors returns a new Point4f. The first constructor generates a Point4f from four floating-point numbers x, y, z, and w. The second constructor (`Point4f(float p[])`) generates a Point4f from the first four elements of array p. The third constructor generates a Point4f from the double-precision point p1. The fourth constructor generates a Point4f from the single-precision point p1. The fifth and sixth constructors generate a Point4f from tuple t1. The seventh constructor generates a Point4f from the specified Tuple3f—the w component of this point is set to 1. The final constructor generates a Point4f with the value of (0.0, 0.0, 0.0, 0.0).

Methods

public final void set(Tuple3f t1)   ◀ New in 1.2 ▶

This method sets the x, y, and z components of this point to the corresponding components of tuple t1. The w component of this point is set to 1.

```
public final float distanceSquared(Point4f p1)
public final float distance(Point4f p1)
```

The distanceSquared method computes the square of the Euclidean distance between this point and the point p1 and returns the result. The distance method computes the Euclidean distance between this point and the point p1 and returns the result.

```
public final float distanceL1(Point4f p1)
```

This method computes the L_1 (Manhattan) distance between this point and point p1. The L_1 distance is equal to

$$\text{abs}(x1 - x2) + \text{abs}(y1 - y2) + \text{abs}(z1 - z2) + \text{abs}(w1 - w2)$$

```
public final float distanceLinf(Point4f p1)
```

This method computes the $L\infty$ distance between this point and point p1. The $L\infty$ distance is equal to

$$\text{MAX}[\text{abs}(x1 - x2), \text{abs}(y1 - y2), \text{abs}(z1 - z2), \text{abs}(w1 - w2)]$$

```
public final void project(Point4f p1)
```

This method multiplies each of the x, y, and z components of the point p1 by $1/w$, places the projected values into this point, and places a 1 into the w parameter of this point.

A.1.9.2   Color4f Class

The Color4f class extends Tuple4f. The Color4f is a four-element color value represented by single-precision floating-point *x*, *y*, *z*, and *w* values. The *x*, *y*, *z*, and *w* values represent the red, blue, green, and alpha color values, respectively. Color and alpha components should be in the range [0.0, 1.0].

Constructors

```
public Color4f(float x, float y, float z, float w)
public Color4f(float c[])
public Color4f(Color4f c1)
public Color4f(Tuple4d t1)
public Color4f(Tuple4f t1)
public Color4f(Color color)
public Color4f()
```
◀ New in 1.2 ▶

Each of these seven constructors returns a new Color4f. The first constructor generates a Color4f from four floating-point numbers x, y, z, and w. The second constructor generates a Color4f from the first four elements of array c. The third constructor generates a Color4f from the single-precision color c1. The fourth and fifth constructors generate a Color4f from tuple t1. The sixth constructor generates a Color4f from the specified AWT Color object. The final constructor generates a Color4f with the value of (0.0, 0.0, 0.0, 0.0).

Methods

```
public final void set(Color color)                          ◀ New in 1.2 ▶
public final Color get()                                     ◀ New in 1.2 ▶
```

The set method sets the R,G,B,A values of this Color4f object to those of the specified AWT Color object. The get method returns a new AWT Color object initialized with the R,G,B,A values of this Color4f object.

A.1.9.3   Vector4f Class

The Vector4f class extends Tuple4f. The Vector4f is a four-element vector represented by single-precision floating-point *x*, *y*, *z*, and *w* coordinates.

Constructors

```
public Vector4f(float x, float y, float z, float w)
public Vector4f(float v[])
public Vector4f(Vector4d v1)
public Vector4f(Vector4f v1)
public Vector4f(Tuple4d t1)
public Vector4f(Tuple4f t1)
public Vector4f(Tuple3f t1)                                  ◀ New in 1.2 ▶
public Vector4f()
```

Each of these eight constructors returns a new Vector4f. The first constructor generates a Vector4f from four floating-point numbers x, y, z, and w. The second constructor generates a Vector4f from the first four elements of array v. The third constructor generates a Vector4f from the double-precision Vector4d v1. The fourth constructor generates a Vector4f from the single-precision Vector4f v1. The fifth and sixth constructors generate a Vector4f from tuple t1. The seventh constructor generates a Vector4f from the specified Tuple3f—the w component of this vector is set to 0. The final constructor generates a Vector4f with the value of (0.0, 0.0, 0.0, 0.0).

Methods

◀ New in 1.2 ▶ `public final void set(Tuple3f t1)`

This method sets the x, y, and z components of this vector to the corresponding components of tuple t1. The w component of this vector is set to 0.

`public final float length()`
`public final float lengthSquared()`

The length method computes the length of the vector this and returns its length as a single-precision floating-point number. The lengthSquared method computes the square of the length of the vector this and returns its length as a single-precision floating-point number.

`public final float dot(Vector4f v1)`

The dot method computes the dot product between this vector and the vector v1 and returns the resulting value.

`public final void normalize(Vector4f v1)`
`public final void normalize()`

The first normalize method sets the value of this vector to the normalization of vector v1. The second normalize method normalizes this vector in place.

`public final float angle(Vector4f v1)`

This method returns the (four-space) angle, in radians, between this vector and the vector v1 parameter. The return value is constrained to the range $[0, \pi]$.

A.1.9.4   Quat4f Class

The Quat4f class extends Tuple4f. The Quat4f is a four-element quaternion represented by single-precision floating-point *x, y, z,* and *w* coordinates.

Constructors

```
public Quat4f(float x, float y, float z, float w)
public Quat4f(float q[])
public Quat4f(Quat4d q1)
public Quat4f(Quat4f q1)
public Quat4f(Tuple4d t1)
public Quat4f(Tuple4f t1)
public Quat4f()
```

Each of these seven constructors returns a new Quat4f. The first constructor generates a quaternion from four floating-point numbers x, y, z, and w. The second constructor generates a quaternion from the four floating-point numbers of array q of length four. The third constructor generates a quaternion from the double-precision quaternion q1. The fourth constructor generates a quaternion from the single-precision quaternion q1. The fifth and sixth constructors generate a quaternion from tuple t1. The final constructor generates a quaternion with the value of (0.0, 0.0, 0.0, 0.0).

Methods

```
public final void conjugate(Quat4f q1)
public final void conjugate()
```

The first conjugate method sets the value of this quaternion to the conjugate of quaternion q1. The second conjugate method sets the value of this quaternion to the conjugate of itself.

```
public final void mul(Quat4f q1, Quat4f q2)
public final void mul(Quat4f q1)
```

The first mul method sets the value of this quaternion to the quaternion product of quaternions q1 and q2 (this = q1 * q2). Note that this is safe for aliasing (that is, this can be q1 or q2). The second mul method sets the value of this quaternion to the quaternion product of itself and q1 (this = this * q1).

```
public final void mulInverse(Quat4f q1, Quat4f q2)
public final void mulInverse(Quat4f q1)
```

The first mulInverse method multiplies quaternion q1 by the inverse of quaternion q2 and places the value into this quaternion. The value of both argument quaternions is preserved (this = q1 * q2^{-1}). The second mulInverse method multiplies this quaternion by the inverse of quaternion q1 and places the value into this quaternion. The value of the argument quaternion is preserved (this = this * q1^{-1}).

```
public final void inverse(Quat4f q1)
public final void inverse()
```

The first inverse method sets the value of this quaternion to the quaternion inverse of quaternion q1. The second inverse method sets the value of this quaternion to the quaternion inverse of itself.

411

```
public final void normalize(Quat4f q1)
public final void normalize()
```

The first `normalize` method sets the value of this quaternion to the normalized value of quaternion q1. The second `normalize` method normalizes the value of this quaternion in place.

```
public final void set(Matrix4f m1)
public final void set(Matrix4d m1)
public final void set(Matrix3f m1)
public final void set(Matrix3d m1)
public final void set(AxisAngle4f a)
public final void set(AxisAngle4d a)
```

These `set` methods set the value of this quaternion to the rotational component of the passed matrix.

```
public final void interpolate(Quat4f q1, float alpha)
public final void interpolate(Quat4f q1, Quat4f q2, float alpha)
```

The first method performs a great circle interpolation between this quaternion and quaternion q1 and places the result into this quaternion. The second method performs a great circle interpolation between quaternion q1 and quaternion q2 and places the result into this quaternion.

◀ New in 1.2 ▶ **A.1.10 Tuple4i Class**

The Tuple4i class represents a four-element tuple represented by signed integer *x*, *y*, *z*, and *w* coordinates.

Variables

The component values of a Tuple4i are directly accessible through the public variables x, y, z, and w. To access the x component of a Tuple4i called upper-LeftCorner, a programmer would write upperLeftCorner.x. The programmer would access the y, z, and w components similarly.

◀ New in 1.2 ▶ `public int x`
◀ New in 1.2 ▶ `public int y`
◀ New in 1.2 ▶ `public int z`
◀ New in 1.2 ▶ `public int w`

The *x*, *y*, *z*, and *w* values, respectively.

Constructors

```
public Tuple4i(int x, int y, int z, int w)          ◀ New in 1.2 ▶
public Tuple4i(int[] t)                             ◀ New in 1.2 ▶
public Tuple4i(Tuple4i t1)                          ◀ New in 1.2 ▶
public Tuple4i()                                    ◀ New in 1.2 ▶
```

Each of these four constructors returns a new Tuple4i. The first constructor generates a Tuple4i from the specified x, y, z, and w coordinates. The second constructor generates a Tuple4i from the array of length 4. The third constructor generates a Tuple4i from the specified Tuple4i. The final constructor generates a Tuple4i with the value of (0,0,0,0).

Methods

```
public final void set(int x, int y, int z, int w)   ◀ New in 1.2 ▶
public final void set(int[] t)                      ◀ New in 1.2 ▶
public final void set(Tuple4i t1)                   ◀ New in 1.2 ▶
public final void get(int[] t)                      ◀ New in 1.2 ▶
public final void get(Tuple4i t)                    ◀ New in 1.2 ▶
```

The first set method sets the value of this tuple to the specified x, y, z, and w coordinates. The second set method sets the value of this tuple to the specified coordinates in the array of length 4. The third set method sets the value of this tuple to the value of tuple t1. The first get method copies the values of this tuple into the array t. The second get method copies the values of this tuple into the tuple t.

```
public final void add(Tuple4i t1, Tuple4i t2)       ◀ New in 1.2 ▶
public final void add(Tuple4i t1)                   ◀ New in 1.2 ▶
```

The first method sets the value of this tuple to the sum of tuples t1 and t2. The second method sets the value of this tuple to the sum of itself and t1.

```
public final void sub(Tuple4i t1, Tuple4i t2)       ◀ New in 1.2 ▶
public final void sub(Tuple4i t1)                   ◀ New in 1.2 ▶
```

The first method sets the value of this tuple to the difference of tuples t1 and t2 (this = t1 − t2). The second method sets the value of this tuple to the difference of itself and t1 (this = this − t1).

```
public final void negate(Tuple4i t1                 ◀ New in 1.2 ▶
public final void negate()                          ◀ New in 1.2 ▶
```

The first method sets the value of this tuple to the negation of tuple t1. The second method negates the value of this tuple in place.

413

◀ New in 1.2 ▶ `public final void scale(int s, Tuple4i t1)`
◀ New in 1.2 ▶ `public final void scale(int s)`

> The first method sets the value of this tuple to the scalar multiplication of tuple t1. The second method sets the value of this tuple to the scalar multiplication of the scale factor with this.

◀ New in 1.2 ▶ `public final void scaleAdd(int s, Tuple4i t1, Tuple4i t2)`
◀ New in 1.2 ▶ `public final void scaleAdd(int s, Tuple4i t1)`

> The first method sets the value of this tuple to the scalar multiplication of tuple t1 plus tuple t2 (this = s*t1 + t2). The second method sets the value of this tuple to the scalar multiplication of itself and then adds tuple t1 (this = s*this + t1).

◀ New in 1.2 ▶ `public final void clamp(int min, int max, Tuple4i t)`
◀ New in 1.2 ▶ `public final void clamp(int min, int max)`

> The first method clamps the tuple parameter to the range [low, high] and places the values into this tuple. The second method clamps this tuple to the range [low, high].

◀ New in 1.2 ▶ `public final void clampMin(int min, Tuple4i t)`
◀ New in 1.2 ▶ `public final void clampMin(int min)`

> The first method clamps the minimum value of the tuple parameter to the min parameter and places the values into this tuple. The second method clamps the minimum value of this tuple to the min parameter.

◀ New in 1.2 ▶ `public final void clampMax(int max, Tuple4i t)`
◀ New in 1.2 ▶ `public final void clampMax(int max)`

> The first method clamps the maximum value of the tuple parameter to the max parameter and places the values into this tuple. The second method clamps the maximum value of this tuple to the max parameter.

◀ New in 1.2 ▶ `public final void absolute(Tuple4i t)`
◀ New in 1.2 ▶ `public final void absolute()`

> The first method sets each component of the tuple parameter to its absolute value and places the modified values into this tuple. The second method sets each component of this tuple to its absolute value.

◀ New in 1.2 ▶ `public String toString()`

> This method returns a string that contains the values of this Tuple4i.

414

public boolean equals(Object t1) ◀ New in 1.2 ▶

This method returns true if the Object t1 is of type Tuple4i and all of the data members of t1 are equal to the corresponding data members in this Tuple4i.

public int hashCode() ◀ New in 1.2 ▶

This method returns a hash code value based on the data values in this object. Two different Tuple4i objects with identical data values (that is, Tuple4i.equals returns true) will return the same hash code value. Two objects with different data members may return the same hash value, although this is not likely.

A.1.10.1 Point4i Class

◀ New in 1.2 ▶

The Point4i class extends Tuple4i. The Point4i is a four-element point represented by signed integer x, y, z, and w coordinates.

Constructors

```
public Point4i(int x, int y, int z, int w)
public Point4i(int[] t)
public Point4i(Tuple4i t1)
public Point4i()
```

◀ New in 1.2 ▶
◀ New in 1.2 ▶
◀ New in 1.2 ▶
◀ New in 1.2 ▶

Each of these four constructors returns a Point4i. The first constructor generates a Point4i from the specified x, y, z, and w coordinates. The second constructor generates a Point4i from the array of length 4. The third constructor generates a Point4i from the specified Tuple4i. The final constructor generates a Point4i with the value of (0,0,0,0).

A.1.11 AxisAngle4d Class

The AxisAngle4d class represents a four-element axis-angle represented by double-precision floating-point x, y, z coordinates and an angle of rotation in radians. An axis-angle is a rotation of angle radians about the vector x,y,z.

Variables

The component values of an AxisAngle4d are directly accessible through the public variables x, y, z, and angle. To access the x component of an AxisAngle4d called myRotation, a programmer would write myRotation.x. The programmer would access the y, z, and angle components similarly.

415

```
public double x
public double y
public double z
public double angle
```

The *x*, *y*, and *z* coordinates and the rotational angle, respectively. The rotation angle is expressed in radians.

Constructors

```
public AxisAngle4d(double x, double y, double z, double angle)
public AxisAngle4d(double a[])
public AxisAngle4d(AxisAngle4d a1)
public AxisAngle4d(AxisAngle4f a1)
```
◀ New in 1.2 ▶ `public AxisAngle4d(Vector3d axis, double angle)`
```
public AxisAngle4d()
```

Each of these six constructors returns a new AxisAngle4d. The first constructor generates an axis-angle from four floating-point numbers x, y, z, and angle. The second constructor generates an axis-angle from the first four elements of array a. The third constructor generates an axis-angle from the double-precision axis-angle a1. The fourth constructor generates an axis-angle from the single-precision axis-angle a1. The fifth constructor generates an axis-angle from the specified axis and angle. The final constructor generates an axis-angle with the value of (0.0, 0.0, 1.0, 0.0).

Methods

```
public final void set(double x, double y, double z, double angle)
public final void set(double a[])
public final void set(Matrix4f m1)
public final void set(Matrix4d m1)
public final void set(Matrix3f m1)
public final void set(Matrix3d m1)
public final void set(AxisAngle4f a1)
public final void set(AxisAngle4d a1)
public final void set(Quat4f q1)
public final void set(Quat4d q1)
```
◀ New in 1.2 ▶ `public final void set(Vector3d axis, double angle)`
```
public final void get(double a[])
```

The first set method sets the value of this axis-angle to the specified x, y, z, and angle coordinates. The second set method sets the value of this axis-angle to the specified *x,y,z* angle. The next four set methods set the value of this axis-angle to the rotational component of the passed matrix m1. The next two set

416

methods set the value of this axis-angle to the value of axis-angle a1. The next two set methods set the value of this axis-angle to the value of the passed quaternion q1. The last set method sets the value of this axis-angle to the specified axis and angle. The get method retrieves the value of this axis-angle and places it into the array a of length four in x,y,z,angle order.

public String toString()

This method returns a string that contains the values of this AxisAngle4d. The form is (x, y, z, angle).

public boolean equals(AxisAngle4d v1)
public boolean equals(Object o1)

The first method returns true if all of the data members of AxisAngle4d v1 are equal to the corresponding data members in this axis-angle. The second method returns true if the Object o1 is of type AxisAngle4d and all of the data members of o1 are equal to the corresponding data members in this AxisAngle4d.

public boolean epsilonEquals(AxisAngle4d a1, double epsilon)

This method returns true if the L∞ distance between this axis-angle and axis-angle a1 is less than or equal to the epsilon parameter. Otherwise, this method returns false. The L∞ distance is equal to

$$\text{MAX}[abs(x1 - x2), abs(y1 - y2), abs(z1 - z2), abs(angle1 - angle2)]$$

public int hashCode()

This method returns a hash number based on the data values in this object. Two different AxisAngle4d objects with identical data values (that is, equals(AxisAngle4d) returns true) will return the same hash number. Two AxisAngle4d objects with different data members may return the same hash value, although this is not likely.

A.1.12 AxisAngle4f Class

The AxisAngle4f class represents a four-element axis-angle represented by single-precision floating-point *x*, *y*, and *z* coordinates and an angle of rotation in radians. An axis-angle is a rotation of angle radians about the vector x,y,z.

Variables

The component values of an AxisAngle4f are directly accessible through the public variables x, y, z, and angle. To access the x component of an

AxisAngle4f called `myRotation`, a programmer would write `myRotation.x`. The programmer would access the y, z, and `angle` components similarly.

```
public float x
public float y
public float z
public float angle
```

The *x*, *y*, and *z* coordinates and the rotational angle, respectively. The rotation angle is expressed in radians.

Constructors

```
public AxisAngle4f(float x, float y, float z, float angle)
public AxisAngle4f(float a[])
public AxisAngle4f(AxisAngle4f a1)
public AxisAngle4f(AxisAngle4d a1)
```
◀ New in 1.2 ▶ `public AxisAngle4f(Vector3f axis, float angle)`
```
public AxisAngle4f()
```

Each of these six constructors returns a new AxisAngle4f. The first constructor generates an axis-angle from four floating-point numbers x, y, z, and `angle`. The second constructor generates an axis-angle from the first four elements of array a. The third constructor generates an axis-angle from the single-precision axis-angle a1. The fourth constructor generates an axis-angle from the double-precision axis-angle a1. The fifth constructor generates an axis-angle from the specified axis and angle. The final constructor generates an axis-angle with the value of (0.0, 0.0, 1.0, 0.0).

Methods

```
public final void set(float x, float y, float z, float angle)
public final void set(float a[])
public final void set(Matrix4f m1)
public final void set(Matrix4d m1)
public final void set(Matrix3f m1)
public final void set(Matrix3d m1)
public final void set(AxisAngle4f a1)
public final void set(AxisAngle4d a1)
public final void set(Quat4f q1)
public final void set(Quat4d q1)
```
◀ New in 1.2 ▶ `public final void set(Vector3f axis, float angle)`
```
public final void get(float a[])
```

The first set method sets the value of this axis-angle to the specified x, y, z, and angle coordinates. The second set method sets the value of this axis-angle to the specified coordinates in the array a. The next four set methods set the value of this axis-angle to the rotational component of the passed matrix m1. The next two set methods set the value of this axis-angle to the value of axis-angle a1. The next two set methods set the value of this axis-angle to the value of the passed quaternion q1. The last set method sets the value of this axis-angle to the specified axis and angle. The get method retrieves the value of this axis-angle and places it into the array a of length four in x,y,z,angle order.

public String toString()

This method returns a string that contains the values of this axis-angle. The form is (x, y, z, angle).

public boolean equals(AxisAngle4f a1)
public boolean equals(Object o1)

The first method returns true if all of the data members of axis-angle a1 are equal to the corresponding data members in this axis-angle. The second method returns true if the Object o1 is of type AxisAngle4f and all of the data members of o1 are equal to the corresponding data members in this AxisAngle4f.

public boolean epsilonEquals(AxisAngle4f a1, float epsilon)

This method returns true if the L∞ distance between this axis-angle and axis-angle a1 is less than or equal to the epsilon parameter. Otherwise, this method returns false. The L∞ distance is equal to

$$MAX[abs(x1 - x2), abs(y1 - y2), abs(z1 - z2), abs(angle1 - angle2)]$$

public int hashCode()

This method returns a hash number based on the data values in this object. Two different AxisAngle4f objects with identical data values (that is, equals(AxisAngle4f) returns true) will return the same hash number. Two AxisAngle4f objects with different data members may return the same hash value, although this is not likely.

A.1.13 GVector Class

The GVector class represents a double-precision, general, dynamically resizable, one-dimensional vector class. Index numbering begins with zero.

Constructors

```
public GVector(int length)
public GVector(double vector[])
public GVector(GVector vector)
public GVector(Tuple2f tuple)
public GVector(Tuple3f tuple)
public GVector(Tuple3d tuple)
public GVector(Tuple4f tuple)
public GVector(Tuple4d tuple)
public GVector(double vector[], int length)
```

Each of these nine constructors returns a new GVector. The first constructor generates a generalized mathematical vector with all elements set to 0.0: length represents the number of elements in the vector. The second and third constructors generate a generalized mathematical vector and copy the initial value from the parameter vector. The next four constructors generate a generalized mathematical vector and copy the initial value from the tuple parameter tuple. The final method generates a generalized mathematical vector by copying length elements from the array parameter. The array must contain at least length elements (that is, vector.length ≥ length). The length of this new GVector is set to the specified length.

Methods

```
public final void add(GVector v1)
public final void add(GVector v1, GVector v2)
public final void sub(GVector v1)
public final void sub(GVector v1, GVector v2)
```

The first add method computes the element-by-element sum of this GVector and GVector v1 and places the result in this. The second add method computes the element-by-element sum of GVectors v1 and v2 and places the result in this. The first sub method performs the element-by-element subtraction of GVector v1 from this GVector and places the result in this (this = this – v1). The second sub method performs the element-by-element subtraction of GVector v2 from GVector v1 and places the result in this (this = v1 – v2).

```
public final void mul(GMatrix m1, GVector v1)
public final void mul(GVector v1, GMatrix m1)
```

The first mul method multiplies matrix m1 times vector v1 and places the result into this vector (this = m1 * v1). The second mul method multiplies the transpose of vector v1 (that is, v1 becomes a row vector with respect to the multiplication) times matrix m1 and places the result into this vector (this = transpose(v1) * m1). The result is technically a row vector, but the GVector class knows only about column vectors, so the result is stored as a column vector.

```
public final void negate()
```

This method negates the vector this and places the resulting vector back into this.

```
public final void zero()
```

This method sets all the values in this vector to zero.

```
public final void setSize(int length)
public final void int getSize()
```

This method changes the size of this vector dynamically. If the size is increased, no data values are lost. If the size is decreased, only those data values whose vector positions were eliminated are lost.

```
public final void set(double v[])
public final void set(GVector v)
public final void set(Tuple2f t)
public final void set(Tuple3f t)
public final void set(Tuple3d t)
public final void set(Tuple4f t)
public final void set(Tuple4d t)
```

The first set method sets the values of this vector to the values found in the array v: The array should at least be equal in length to the number of elements in the vector. The second set method sets the values of this vector to the values in vector v. The last 5 set methods set the value of this vector to the values in tuple t.

```
public final double getElement(int index)
public final void setElement(int index, double value)
```

These methods set and retrieve the specified index value of this vector.

```
public final double norm()
public final double normSquared()
```

The norm method returns the square root of the sum of the squares of this vector (its length in n-dimensional space). The normSquared method returns the sum of the squares of this vector (its length in n-dimensional space).

```
public final void normalize(GVector v1)
public final void normalize()
```

The first `normalize` method sets the value of this vector to the normalization of vector v1. The second `normalize` method normalizes this vector in place.

```
public final void scale(double s, GVector v1)
public final void scale(double s)
public final void scaleAdd(double s, GVector v1, GVector v2)
```

The first `scale` method sets the value of this vector to the scalar multiplication of the scale factor s with the vector v1. The second `scale` method scales this vector by the scale factor s. The `scaleAdd` method scales the vector v1 by the scale factor s, adds the result to the vector v2, and places the result into this vector (this = s*v1 + v2).

public String toString()

This method returns a string that contains the values of this vector.

public int hashCode()

This method returns a hash number based on the data values in this object. Two different GVector objects with identical data values (that is, `equals(GVector)` returns `true`) will return the same hash number. Two objects with different data members may return the same hash value, although this is not likely.

```
public boolean equals(GVector vector1)
public boolean equals(Object o1)
```

The first method returns `true` if all of the data members of GVector vector1 are equal to the corresponding data members in this GVector. The second method returns true if the Object o1 is of type GMatrix and all of the data members of o1 are equal to the corresponding data members in this GMatrix.

public boolean epsilonEquals(GVector v1, double epsilon)

This method returns `true` if the L∞ distance between this vector and vector v1 is less than or equal to the `epsilon` parameter. Otherwise, this method returns `false`. The L∞ distance is equal to

$$\text{MAX}[\text{abs}(x1 - x2), \text{abs}(y1 - y2), \dots]$$

public final double dot(GVector v1)

This method returns the dot product of this vector and vector v1.

```
public final void SVDBackSolve(GMatrix U, GMatrix W, GMatrix V,
    GVector x)
public final void LUDBackSolve(GMatrix LU, GVector b,
    GVector permutation)
```

The first method solves for x in $\mathbf{A}x = b$, where x is this vector ($n \times 1$), b is an $m \times 1$ vector, and $\mathbf{A}$ is an $m \times n$ matrix, defined as $\mathbf{A} = \mathbf{U} * \mathbf{W} * \text{transpose}(\mathbf{V})$. U, W, and V must be precomputed and can be found by taking the singular value decomposition (SVD) of $\mathbf{A}$. The second method takes the LU matrix and the permutation vector produced by the GMatrix method LUD and solves the equation $\mathbf{LU} * x = b$ by placing the solution to the set of linear equations into this vector (x).

```
public final double angle(GVector v1)
```

This method returns the (n-space) angle, in radians, between this vector and the vector v1 parameter. The return value is constrained to the range $[0, \pi]$.

```
public final void interpolate(GVector v1, GVector v2, float alpha)
public final void interpolate(GVector v1, float alpha)
```

Deprecated methods. See the following two methods.

```
public final void interpolate(GVector v1, GVector v2, double alpha)
public final void interpolate(GVector v1, double alpha)
```

The first method linearly interpolates between vectors v1 and v2 and places the result into this vector (this = (1 – alpha) * v1 + alpha * v2). The second method linearly interpolates between this vector and vector v1 and places the result into this vector (this = (1 – alpha) * this + alpha * v1).

A.2   Matrix Objects

Java 3D uses matrix objects to represent rotations and full 3D transformations. The matrix classes (as well as the associated Tuple and AxisAngle classes) include code for accessing, manipulating, and updating the matrix, vector, and AxisAngle classes. Java 3D further subdivides the matrix classes into 3×3 matrices (mainly to store rotations) and 4×4 matrices (mainly to store more complex 3D transformations). These two classes in turn provide support for both single-precision floating-point representations and double-precision floating-point representations.

Matrix operations try to minimize gratuitous allocation of memory; thus all matrix operations update an existing object. To multiply two matrices together and store the result in a third, a Java 3D application or applet would write `matrix3.mul(matrix1, matrix2)`. Here `matrix3` receives the results of multiplying `matrix1` with `matrix2`.

The Java 3D model for 3×3 transformations is

$$\begin{bmatrix} m00 & m01 & m02 \\ m10 & m11 & m12 \\ m20 & m21 & m22 \end{bmatrix} \cdot \begin{bmatrix} x \\ y \\ z \end{bmatrix} = \begin{bmatrix} x' \\ y' \\ z' \end{bmatrix}$$

$$x' = m00 \cdot x + m01 \cdot y + m02 \cdot z$$
$$y' = m10 \cdot x + m11 \cdot y + m12 \cdot z$$
$$z' = m20 \cdot x + m21 \cdot y + m22 \cdot z$$

The Java 3D model for 4×4 transformations is

$$\begin{bmatrix} m00 & m01 & m02 & m03 \\ m10 & m11 & m12 & m13 \\ m20 & m21 & m22 & m23 \\ m30 & m31 & m32 & m33 \end{bmatrix} \cdot \begin{bmatrix} x \\ y \\ z \\ w \end{bmatrix} = \begin{bmatrix} x' \\ y' \\ z' \\ w' \end{bmatrix}$$

$$x' = m00 \cdot x + m01 \cdot y + m02 \cdot z + m03 \cdot w$$
$$y' = m10 \cdot x + m11 \cdot y + m12 \cdot z + m13 \cdot w$$
$$z' = m20 \cdot x + m21 \cdot y + m22 \cdot z + m23 \cdot w$$
$$w' = m30 \cdot x + m31 \cdot y + m32 \cdot z + m33 \cdot w$$

Note: When transforming a Point3f or a Point3d, the input w is set to 1. When transforming a Vector3f or Vector3d, the input w is set to 0.

A.2.1   Matrix3f Class

The Matrix3f class serves to contain 3×3 matrices mainly for storing and manipulating 3D rotation matrices. The class includes five different constructors for creating matrices and several operators for manipulating these matrices.

Variables

The component values of a Matrix3f are directly accessible through the public variables `m00`, `m01`, `m02`, `m10`, `m11`, `m12`, `m20`, `m21`, and `m22`. To access the element in row 2 and column 0 of matrix `rotate`, a programmer would write `rotate.m20`. A programmer would access the other values similarly.

```
public float m00
public float m01
public float m02
public float m10
public float m11
public float m12
public float m20
public float m21
public float m22
```

These public variables are the elements of the matrix.

Constructors

```
public Matrix3f(float m00, float m01, float m02, float m10,
        float m11, float m12, float m20, float m21, float m22)
public Matrix3f(float v[])
public Matrix3f(Matrix3d m1)
public Matrix3f(Matrix3f m1)
public Matrix3f()
```

Each of these constructors returns a new Matrix3f object. The first constructor generates a 3 × 3 matrix from the nine values provided. The second constructor generates a 3 × 3 matrix from the first nine values in the array v. The third and fourth constructors generate a new matrix with the same values as the passed matrix m1. The final constructor generates a 3 × 3 matrix with all nine values set to 0.0.

Methods

```
public final void set(Quat4d q1)
public final void set(Quat4f q1)
```

These two set methods set the value of the matrix this to the matrix conversion of the quaternion argument q1.

```
public final void set(Matrix3f m1)
public final void set(Matrix3d m1)
```

Sets the value of this matrix to the value of the argument.

```
public final void set(AxisAngle4d a1)
public final void set(AxisAngle4f a1)
```

These two set methods set the value of the matrix this to the matrix conversion of the axis and angle argument a1.

425

```
public final void set(float scale)
public final void set(float m[])
```

The first method sets the value of this matrix to a scale matrix with the passed `scale` amount. The second method sets the values of this matrix to the row-major array parameter (that is, the first three elements of the array are copied into the first row of this matrix, and so forth).

```
public final void setElement(int row, int column, float value)
public final float getElement(int row, int column)
```

The `setElement` and `getElement` methods provide a means for accessing a single element within a 3×3 matrix using indices. This is not a preferred method of access, but Java 3D provides these methods for functional completeness. The `setElement` method takes a row index `row` (where a value of 0 represents the first row and a value of 2 represents the third row), a column index `column` (where a value of 0 represents the first column and a value of 2 represents the third column), and a value. It sets the corresponding element in matrix `this` to the specified value. The `getElement` method also takes a row index `row` and a column index `column`. It returns the element at the corresponding locations as a floating-point value.

```
public final void setRow(int row, float x, float y, float z)
public final void setRow(int row, Vector3f v)
public final void setRow(int row, float v[])
public final void getRow(int row, Vector3f v)
public final void getRow(int row, float v[])
```

The three `setRow` methods provide a means for constructing a 3×3 matrix on a row basis. The row parameter `row` determines which row the method invocation affects. A row value of 0 represents the first row and a value of 2 represents the third row. The first `setRow` method specifies the three new values as independent floating-point values. The second `setRow` method uses the values in the Vector3f `v` to update the matrix. The third `setRow` method uses the first three values in the array `v` to update the matrix. In all three cases the matrix affected is the matrix `this`. The two `getRow` methods copy the matrix values in the specified row into the vector or array parameter, respectively.

```
public final void setColumn(int column, float x, float y, float z)
public final void setColumn(int column, Vector3f v)
public final void setColumn(int column, float v[])
public final void getColumn(int column, Vector3f v)
public final void getColumn(int column, float v[])
```

The three setColumn methods provide a means for constructing a 3×3 matrix on a column basis. The column parameter determines which column the method invocation affects. A column value of 0 represents the first column and a value of 2 represents the third column. The first setColumn method specifies the three new values as independent floating-point values. The second setColumn method uses the values in the Vector3f v to update the matrix. The third setColumn method uses the first three values in the array v to update the matrix. In all three cases the matrix affected is the matrix this. The two getColumn methods copy the matrix values in the specified column into the vector or array parameter, respectively.

```
public final void setZero()
```

This method sets this matrix to all zeros.

```
public final void setIdentity()
```

This method sets this Matrix3f to identity.

```
public final void add(Matrix3f m1, Matrix3f m2)
public final void add(Matrix3f m1)
public final void sub(Matrix3f m1, Matrix3f m2)
public final void sub(Matrix3f m1)
```

The first add method adds the matrix m1 to the matrix m2 and places the result into the matrix this. The second add method adds the matrix this to the matrix m1 and places the result into the matrix this. The first sub method performs an element-by-element subtraction of matrix m2 from matrix m1 and places the result into the matrix this. The second sub method performs an element-by-element subtraction of the matrix m1 from the matrix this and places the result into the matrix this.

```
public final void transform(Tuple3f t)
public final void transform(Tuple3f t, Tuple3f result)
```

The first method multiplies this matrix by the tuple t and places the result back into the tuple (t = this*t). The second method multiplies this matrix by the tuple t and places the result into the tuple result (result = this*t).

```
public final void transpose()
public final void transpose(Matrix3f m1)
```

The first method transposes this matrix in place. The second method sets the value of this matrix to the transpose of the matrix m1.

```
public final void invert()
public final void invert(Matrix3f m1)
```

The first method inverts this matrix in place. The second method sets the value of this matrix to the inverse of the matrix m1.

```
public final float determinant()
```

The determinant method computes the determinant of the matrix this and returns the computed value.

```
public final void rotX(float angle)
public final void rotY(float angle)
public final void rotZ(float angle)
```

The three rot methods construct rotation matrices that rotate in a counterclockwise (right-handed) direction around the axis specified as the last letter of the method name. The constructed matrix replaces the value of the matrix this. The rotation angle is expressed in radians.

```
public final void mul(Matrix3f m1, Matrix3f m2)
public final void mul(Matrix3f m1)
```

The first mul method multiplies matrix m1 with matrix m2 and places the result into the matrix this. The second mul method multiplies the matrix this with the matrix m1 and places the result into matrix this.

```
public final void mulNormalize(Matrix3f m1)
public final void mulNormalize(Matrix3f m1, Matrix3f m2)
```

The first mulNormalize method multiplies this matrix by matrix m1, performs an SVD normalization of the result, and places the result back into this matrix (this = SVDnorm(this · m1)). The second mulNormalize method multiplies matrix m1 by matrix m2, performs an SVD normalization of the result, and places the result into this matrix (this = SVDnorm(m1 · m2)).

```
public final void mulTransposeBoth(Matrix3f m1, Matrix3f m2)
public final void mulTransposeRight(Matrix3f m1, Matrix3f m2)
public final void mulTransposeLeft(Matrix3f m1, Matrix3f m2)
```

The mulTransposeBoth method multiplies the transpose of matrix m1 (left) times the transpose of matrix m2 (right) and places the result into this matrix. The mulTransposeRight method multiplies matrix m1 times the transpose of matrix m2 and places the result back into this matrix. The mulTransposeLeft method multiplies the transpose of matrix m1 times matrix m2 and places the result into this matrix.

```
public final void normalize()
public final void normalize(Matrix3f m1)
```

The first `normalize` method performs a singular value decomposition normalization of this matrix. The second `normalize` method performs a singular value decomposition normalization of matrix m1 and places the normalized values into `this`.

```
public final void normalizeCP()
public final void normalizeCP(Matrix3f m1)
```

The first `normalizeCP` method performs a cross-product normalization of this matrix. The second `normalizeCP` method performs a cross-product normalization of matrix m1 and places the normalized values into `this`.

```
public boolean equals(Matrix3f m1)
public boolean equals(Object o1)
```

The first method returns `true` if all of the data members of Matrix3f m1 are equal to the corresponding data members in this Matrix3f. The second method returns true if the Object o1 is of type Matrix3f and all of the data members of o1 are equal to the corresponding data members in this Matrix3f.

```
public boolean epsilonEquals(Matrix3f m1, float epsilon)
```

This method returns `true` if the L∞ distance between this Matrix3f and Matrix3f m1 is less than or equal to the `epsilon` parameter. Otherwise, this method returns `false`. The L∞ distance is equal to

$$MAX[i = 0,1,2, \ldots n; j = 0,1,2,\ldots n; abs(this.m(i,j) - m1.m(i,j)]$$

```
public final void negate()
public final void negate(Matrix3f m1)
```

The first method negates the value of this matrix in place (this = –this). The second method sets the value of this matrix equal to the negation of the matrix m1 (this = –m1).

```
public final float getScale()
```

This method performs an SVD normalization of this matrix to calculate and return the uniform scale factor. If the matrix has nonuniform scale factors, the largest of the x, y, and z scale factors will be returned.

```
public final void setScale(float scale)
```

This method sets the scale component of the current matrix by factoring out the current scale (by doing an SVD) and multiplying by the new scale.

```
public final void add(float scalar)
```

This method adds a scalar to each component of this matrix.

```
public final void add(float scalar, Matrix3f m1)
```

This method adds a scalar to each component of the matrix `m1` and places the result into `this`. Matrix `m1` is not modified.

```
public final void mul(float scalar, Matrix3f m1)
```

This method multiplies each component of the matrix `m1` by a scalar and places the result into `this`. Matrix `m1` is not modified.

```
public final void mul(float scalar)
```

This method multiplies each element of this matrix by a scalar.

```
public final void transform(Tuple3f t)
public final void transform(Tuple3f t, Tuple3f result)
```

The first method multiplies this matrix by the tuple `t` and places the result back into the tuple (`t = this*t`). The second method multiplies this matrix by the tuple `t` and places the result into the tuple `result` (`result = this*t`).

```
public int hashCode()
```

The `hashCode` method returns a hash number based on the data values in this object. Two different Matrix3f objects with identical data values (that is, `equals(Matrix3f)` returns `true`) will return the same hash number. Two Matrix3f objects with different data members may return the same hash value, although this is not likely.

```
public String toString()
```

The `toString` method returns a string that contains the values of this Matrix3f.

A.2.2 Matrix3d Class

The Matrix3d class serves to contain 3×3 matrices mainly for storing and manipulating 3D rotation matrices. The class includes five different constructors for creating matrices and several operators for manipulating these matrices.

Variables

The component values of a Matrix3d are directly accessible through the public variables m00, m01, m02, m10, m11, m12, m20, m21, and m22. To access the element in row 2 and column 0 of the matrix named `rotate`, a programmer would write `rotate.m20`. Other matrix values are accessed similarly.

```
public double m00
public double m01
public double m02
public double m10
public double m11
public double m12
public double m20
public double m21
public double m22
```

These public variables are the elements of the matrix.

Constructors

```
public Matrix3d(double m00, double m01, double m02, double m10,
        double m11, double m12, double m20, double m21, double m22)
public Matrix3d(double v[])
public Matrix3d()
public Matrix3d(Matrix3d m1)
public Matrix3d(Matrix3f m1)
```

Each of these constructors returns a new Matrix3d object. The first constructor generates a 3×3 matrix from the nine values provided. The second constructor generates a 3×3 matrix from the first nine values in the array v. The third constructor generates a 3×3 matrix with all nine values set to 0.0. The fourth and fifth constructors generate a 3×3 matrix with the same values as the matrix m1 parameter.

Methods

```
public final void set(Matrix3f m1)
public final void set(Matrix3d m1)
```

These methods set the value of this matrix to the value of the argument.

```
public final void set(double scale)
public final void set(double m[])
```

These methods set the value of the matrix this to a scale matrix with the passed scale amount.

```
public final void set(AxisAngle4d a1)
public final void set(AxisAngle4f a1)
```

These two set methods set the value of the matrix this to the matrix conversion of the axis and angle argument a1.

```
public final void set(Quat4d q1)
public final void set(Quat4f q1)
```

These two set methods set the value of the matrix this to the matrix conversion of the quaternion argument q1.

```
public final void setElement(int row, int column, double value)
public final double getElement(int row, int column)
```

The setElement and getElement methods provide a means for accessing a single element within a 3×3 matrix using indices. This is not a preferred method of access, but Java 3D provides these methods for functional completeness. The setElement method takes a row index row (where a value of 0 represents the first row and a value of 2 represents the third row), a column index column (where a value of 0 represents the first column and a value of 2 represents the third column), and a value. It sets the corresponding element in matrix this to the specified value. The getElement method also takes a row index row and a column index column and returns the element at the corresponding locations as a floating-point value.

```
public final void setRow(int row, double x, double y, double z)
public final void setRow(int row, Vector3d v)
public final void setRow(int row, double v[])
public final void getRow(int row, Vector3d v)
public final void getRow(int row, double v[])
```

The three setRow methods provide a means for constructing a 3×3 matrix on a row basis. The row parameter determines which row the method invocation affects. A row value of 0 represents the first row, and a value of 2 represents the third row. The first setRow method specifies the three new values as independent floating-point values. The second setRow method uses the values in the Vector3d v to update the matrix. The third setRow method uses the first three values in the array v to update the matrix. In all three cases the matrix affected is the matrix this. The two getRow methods copy the matrix values in the specified row into the array or vector parameter, respectively.

```
public final void setColumn(int column, double x, double y,
      double z)
public final void setColumn(int column, Vector3d v)
public final void setColumn(int column, double v[])
public final void getColumn(int column, Vector3d v)
public final void getColumn(int column, double v[])
```

The three setColumn methods provide a means for constructing a 3×3 matrix on a column basis. The column parameter determines which column the method invocation affects. A column value of 0 represents the first column, and a value of 2 represents the third column. The first setColumn method specifies the three new values as independent floating-point values. The second setColumn method uses the values in the Vector3d v to update the matrix. The third setColumn method uses the first three values in the array v to update the matrix. In all three cases the matrix affected is the matrix this. The two getColumn methods copy the matrix values in the specified column into the array or vector parameter, respectively.

```
public final void add(Matrix3d m1, Matrix3d m2)
public final void add(Matrix3d m1)
public final void sub(Matrix3d m1, Matrix3d m2)
public final void sub(Matrix3d m1)
```

The first add method adds the matrix m1 to the matrix m2 and places the result into the matrix this. The second add method adds the matrix this to the matrix m1 and places the result into the matrix this. The first sub method performs an element-by-element subtraction of matrix m2 from matrix m1 and places the result into the matrix this. The second sub method performs an element-by-element subtraction of the matrix m1 from the matrix this and places the result into the matrix this.

```
public final void add(double scalar)
```

This method adds a scalar to each component of this matrix.

```
public final void add(double scalar, Matrix3d m1)
```

This method adds a scalar to each component of the matrix m1 and places the result into this. Matrix m1 is not modified.

```
public final void transform(Tuple3d t)
public final void transform(Tuple3d t, Tuple3d result)
```

The first method multiplies this matrix by the tuple t and places the result back into the tuple (t = this*t). The second method multiplies this matrix by the tuple t and places the result into the tuple result (result = this*t).

433

```
public final void transpose()
public final void transpose(Matrix3d m1)
```

The first method transposes this matrix in place. The second method sets the value of this matrix to the transpose of the matrix m1.

```
public final void invert()
public final void invert(Matrix3d m1)
```

The first method inverts this matrix in place. The second method sets the value of this matrix to the inverse of the matrix m1.

```
public final double determinant()
```

The determinant method computes the determinant of the matrix this and returns the computed value.

```
public final void rotX(double angle)
public final void rotY(double angle)
public final void rotZ(double angle)
```

The three rot methods construct rotation matrices that rotate in a counterclockwise (right-handed) direction around the axis specified by the final letter of the method name. The constructed matrix replaces the value of the matrix this. The rotation angle is expressed in radians.

```
public final void mul(Matrix3d m1, Matrix3d m2)
public final void mul(Matrix3d m1)
```

The first mul method multiplies matrix m1 with matrix m2 and places the result into the matrix this. The second mul method multiplies matrix this with matrix m1 and places the result into the matrix this.

```
public final void mulNormalize(Matrix3d m1)
public final void mulNormalize(Matrix3d m1, Matrix3d m2)
```

The first mulNormalize method multiplies this matrix by matrix m1, performs an SVD normalization of the result, and places the result back into this matrix (this = SVDnorm(this · m1)). The second mulNormalize method multiplies matrix m1 by matrix m2, performs an SVD normalization of the result, and places the result into this matrix (this = SVDnorm(m1 · m2)).

```
public final void mulTransposeBoth(Matrix3d m1, Matrix3d m2)
public final void mulTransposeRight(Matrix3d m1, Matrix3d m2)
public final void mulTransposeLeft(Matrix3d m1, Matrix3d m2)
```

The `mulTransposeBoth` method multiplies the transpose of matrix m1 (left) times the transpose of matrix m2 (right) and places the result into this matrix. The `mulTransposeRight` method multiplies matrix m1 times the transpose of matrix m2 and places the result back into this matrix. The `mulTransposeLeft` method multiplies the transpose of matrix m1 times matrix m2 and places the result into this matrix.

```
public final void normalize()
public final void normalize(Matrix3d m1)
```

The first `normalize` method performs a singular value decomposition normalization of this matrix. The second `normalize` method performs a singular value decomposition normalization of matrix m1 and places the normalized values into `this`.

```
public final void normalizeCP()
public final void normalizeCP(Matrix3d m1)
```

The first `normalizeCP` method performs a cross-product normalization of this matrix. The second `normalizeCP` method performs a cross-product normalization of matrix m1 and places the normalized values into `this`.

```
public boolean equals(Matrix3d m1)
public boolean equals(Object t1)
```

The first method returns `true` if all of the data members of Matrix3d m1 are equal to the corresponding data members in this Matrix3d. The second method returns true if the Object t1 is of type Matrix3d and all of the data members of `t1` are equal to the corresponding data members in this Matrix3d.

```
public boolean epsilonEquals(Matrix3d m1, double epsilon)
```

This method returns `true` if the L∞ distance between this Matrix3d and Matrix3d m1 is less than or equal to the `epsilon` parameter. Otherwise, this method returns `false`. The L∞ distance is equal to

$$\text{MAX}[i = 0,1,2,; j = 0,1,2,; \text{abs}(\text{this.m}(i,j) - \text{m1.m}(i,j)]$$

```
public final void negate()
public final void negate(Matrix3d m1)
```

The first method negates the value of this matrix in place (this = –this). The second method sets the value of this matrix equal to the negation of the matrix m1 (this = –m1).

public final double getScale()

This method performs an SVD normalization of this matrix to calculate and return the uniform scale factor. If the matrix has nonuniform scale factors, the largest of the *x*, *y*, and *z* scale factors will be returned.

public final void setScale(double scale)

This method sets the scale component of the current matrix by factoring out the current scale (by doing an SVD) and multiplying by the new scale.

public final void mul(double scalar, Matrix3d m1)

This method multiplies each component of the matrix m1 by a scalar and places the result into this. Matrix m1 is not modified.

public final void mul(double scalar)

This method multiplies each element of this matrix by a scalar.

public final void transform(Tuple3d t)
public final void transform(Tuple3d t, Tuple3d result)

The first method multiplies this matrix by the tuple t and places the result back into the tuple (t = this*t). The second method multiplies this matrix by the tuple t and places the result into the tuple result (result = this*t).

public final void setZero()

This method sets this matrix to all zeros.

public final void setIdentity()

This method sets this Matrix3d to identity.

public int hashCode()

The hashCode method returns a hash number based on the data values in this object. Two different Matrix3d objects with identical data values (that is, equals(Matrix3d) returns true) will return the same hash number. Two Matrix3d objects with different data members may return the same hash value, although this is not likely.

public String toString()

The toString method returns a string that contains the values of this Matrix3d.

A.2.3 Matrix4f Class

The Matrix4f class serves to contain 4×4 matrices mainly for storing and manipulating 3D transformation matrices. The class includes seven different constructors for creating matrices and several operators for manipulating these matrices.

Variables

The component values of a Matrix4f are directly accessible through the public variables m00, m01, m02, m03, m10, m11, m12, m13, m20, m21, m22, m23, m30, m31, m32, and m33. To access the element in row 2 and column 0 of matrix rotate, a programmer would write rotate.m20. A programmer would access the other values similarly.

```
public float m00
public float m01
public float m02
public float m03
public float m10
public float m11
public float m12
public float m13
public float m20
public float m21
public float m22
public float m23
public float m30
public float m31
public float m32
public float m33
```

These public variables are the elements of the matrix.

Constructors

```
public Matrix4f(float m00, float m01, float m02, float m03,
       float m10, float m11, float m12, float m13,
       float m20, float m21, float m22, float m23, float m30,
       float m31, float m32, float m33)
public Matrix4f(float v[])
public Matrix4f(Quat4f q1, Vector3f t1, float s)
public Matrix4f(Matrix4d m1)
public Matrix4f(Matrix4f m1)
```

437

```
public Matrix4f(Matrix3f m1, Vector3f t1, float s)
public Matrix4f()
```

Each of these constructors returns a new Matrix4f object. The first constructor generates a 4×4 matrix from the 16 values provided. The second constructor generates a 4×4 matrix from the first 16 values in the array v. The third constructor generates a 4×4 matrix from the quaternion, translation, and scale values. The scale is applied only to the rotational components of the matrix (upper 3×3) and not to the translational components. The fourth and fifth constructors generate a 4×4 matrix with the same values as the passed matrix m1. The sixth constructor generates a 4×4 matrix from the rotation matrix, translation, and scale values. The scale is applied only to the rotational components of the matrix (upper 3×3) and not to the translational components of the matrix. The final constructor generates a 4×4 matrix with all 16 values set to 0.0.

Methods

```
public final void set(Quat4f q1)
public final void set(Quat4d q1)
public final void set(Quat4f q1, Vector3f t1, float s)
public final void set(Quat4d q1, Vector3d t1, double s)
public final void set(Matrix4d m1)
public final void set(Matrix4f m1)
public final void set(AxisAngle4f a1)
public final void set(AxisAngle4d a1)
```

The first two set methods set the value of this matrix to the matrix conversion of the quaternion argument q1. The next two set methods set the value of this matrix from the rotation expressed by the quaternion q1, the translation t1, and the scale s. The next two set methods set the value of this matrix to a copy of the passed matrix m1. The last two set methods set the value of this matrix to the matrix conversion of the axis and angle argument a1.

```
public final void set(Matrix3f m1)
public final void set(Matrix3d m1)
```

These methods set the rotational component (upper 3×3) of this matrix to the matrix values in the m1 argument. The other elements of this matrix are initialized as if this were an identity matrix (that is, an affine matrix with no translational component).

```
public final void set(float scale)
public final void set(float m[])
```

The first method sets the value of this matrix to a scale matrix with the passed scale amount. The second method sets the value of this matrix to the row-major array parameter (that is, the first four elements of the array are copied into the first row of this matrix, and so forth).

```
public final void set(Vector3f v1)
```

This method sets the value of this matrix to a translation matrix with the passed translation value.

```
public final void set(float scale, Vector3f t1)
public final void set(Vector3f t1, float scale)
```

These methods set the value of this matrix to a scale and translation matrix. In the first method, the scale is not applied to the translation, and all of the matrix values are modified. In the second method, the translation is scaled by the scale factor, and all of the matrix values are modified.

```
public final void set(Matrix3f m1, Vector3f t1, float scale)
public final void set(Matrix3d m1, Vector3d t1, double scale)
```

These two methods set the value of this matrix from the rotation expressed by the rotation matrix m1, the translation t1, and the scale scale. The translation is not modified by the scale.

```
public final void get(Matrix3d m1)
public final void get(Matrix3f m1)
public final float get(Matrix3f m1, Vector3f t1)
public final void get(Quat4f q1)
public final void get(Vector3f trans)
```

The first two methods perform an SVD normalization of this matrix in order to acquire the normalized rotational component. The values are placed into the matrix parameter m1. The third method performs an SVD normalization of this matrix to calculate the rotation as a 3×3 matrix, the translation, and the scale. None of the matrix values in this matrix is modified. The fourth method performs an SVD normalization of this matrix to acquire the normalized rotational component. The values are placed into the quaternion q1. The final method retrieves the translational components of this matrix and copies them into the vector trans.

```
public final void setElement(int row, int column, float value)
public final float getElement(int row, int column)
```

The setElement and getElement methods provide a means for accessing a single element within a 4 × 4 matrix using indices. This is not a preferred method of access, but Java 3D provides these methods for functional completeness. The setElement method takes a row index row (where a value of 0 represents the first row and a value of 3 represents the fourth row), a column index column (where a value of 0 represents the first column and a value of 3 represents the fourth column), and a value. It sets the corresponding element in matrix this to the specified value. The getElement method also takes a row index row and a column index column and returns the element at the corresponding locations as a floating-point value.

```
public final void getRotationScale(Matrix3f m1)
```

This method retrieves the upper 3 × 3 values of this matrix and places them into the matrix m1.

```
public final void setScale(float scale)
public final float getScale()
```

The first method sets the scale component of the current matrix by factoring out the current scale (by doing an SVD) and multiplying by the new scale. The second method performs an SVD normalization of this matrix to calculate and return the uniform scale factor. If the matrix has nonuniform scale factors, the largest of the x, y, and z scale factors will be returned.

```
public final void add(float scalar)
```

This method adds a scalar to each component of this matrix.

```
public final void add(float scalar, Matrix4f m1)
```

This method adds a scalar to each component of the matrix m1 and places the result into this. Matrix m1 is not modified.

```
public final void mul(float scalar, Matrix4f m1)
```

This method multiplies each component of the matrix m1 by a scalar and places the result into this. Matrix m1 is not modified.

```
public final void mul(float scalar)
```

This method multiplies each element of this matrix by a scalar.

```
public final void setRow(int row, float x, float y, float z,
      float w)
public final void setRow(int row, Vector4f v)
public final void setRow(int row, float v[])
public final void getRow(int row, Vector4f v)
public final void getRow(int row, float v[])
```

The three setRow methods provide a means for constructing a 4×4 matrix on a row basis. The row parameter row determines which row the method invocation affects. A row value of 0 represents the first row, and a value of 3 represents the fourth row. The first setRow method specifies the four new values as independent floating-point values. The second setRow method uses the values in the Vector4f v to update the matrix. The third setRow method uses the first four values in the array v to update the matrix. In all three cases the matrix affected is the matrix this. The two getRow methods copy the matrix values in the specified row into the array or vector parameter, respectively.

```
public final void setColumn(int column, float x, float y, float z,
      float w)
public final void setColumn(int column, Vector4f v)
public final void setColumn(int column, float v[])
public final void getColumn(int column, Vector4f v)
public final void getColumn(int column, float v[])
```

The three setColumn methods provide a means for constructing a 4×4 matrix on a column basis. The column parameter column determines which column the method invocation affects. A column value of 0 represents the first column, and a value of 3 represents the fourth column. The first setColumn method specifies the four new values as independent double-precision floating-point values. The second setColumn method uses the values in the Vector4f v to update the matrix. The third setColumn method uses the first four values in the array v to update the matrix. In all three cases the matrix affected is the matrix this. The two getColumn methods copy the matrix values in the specified column into the array or vector parameter, respectively.

```
public final void setRotation(Matrix3d m1)
public final void setRotation(Matrix3f m1)
public final void setRotation(Quat4f q1)
public final void setRotation(Quat4d q1)
public final void setRotation(AxisAngle4f a1)
```

These methods set the rotational component (upper 3×3) of this matrix to the matrix values in the passed argument. The other elements of this matrix are unchanged. In the first two methods, a singular value decomposition is performed on this object's upper 3×3 matrix to factor out the scale, then this object's upper 3×3 matrix components are replaced by the passed rotation components, and finally the scale is reapplied to the rotational components. In the next two methods, a singular value decomposition is performed on this object's upper 3×3 matrix to factor out the scale, then this object's upper 3×3 matrix components are replaced by the matrix equivalent of the quaternion, and finally the scale is reapplied to the rotational components. In the last method, a singular value decomposition is performed on this object's upper 3×3 matrix to factor out the scale, then this object's upper 3×3 matrix components are replaced by the matrix equivalent of the axis-angle, and finally the scale is reapplied to the rotational components.

```
public final void setRotationScale(Matrix3f m1)
```

This method replaces the upper 3×3 matrix values of this matrix with the values in the matrix m1.

```
public final void setTranslation(Vector3f trans)
```

This method modifies the translational components of this matrix to the values of the vector trans. The other values of this matrix are not modified.

```
public final void setIdentity()
```

This method sets this Matrix4f to identity.

```
public final void setZero()
```

This method sets this matrix to all zeros.

```
public final void add(Matrix4f m1, Matrix4f m2)
public final void add(Matrix4f m1)
public final void sub(Matrix4f m1, Matrix4f m2)
public final void sub(Matrix4f m1)
```

The first add method adds the matrix m1 to the matrix m2 and places the result into the matrix this. The second add method adds the matrix this to the matrix m1 and places the result into the matrix this. The first sub method performs an element-by-element subtraction of matrix m2 from matrix m1 and places the result into the matrix this. The second sub method performs an element-by-element subtraction of the matrix m1 from the matrix this and places the result into the matrix this.

```
public final void transpose(Matrix4f m1)
public final void transpose()
```

The first `transpose` method transposes the matrix m1 and places the result into the matrix `this`. The second `transpose` method transposes the matrix `this` and places the result back into the matrix `this`.

`public final void transform(Point3f point)`
`public final void transform(Point3f point, Point3f pointOut)`

The first `transform` method postmultiplies this matrix by the Point3f `point` and places the result back into `point`. The multiplication treats the three-element point as if its fourth element were 1. The second `transform` method postmultiplies this matrix by the Point3f `point` and places the result into `pointOut`.

`public final void transform(Vector3f normal)`
`public final void transform(Vector3f normal, Vector3f normalOut)`

The first `transform` method postmultiplies this matrix by the Vector3f `normal` and places the result back into `normal`. The multiplication treats the three-element vector as if its fourth element were 0. The second `transform` method postmultiplies this matrix by the Vector3f `normal` and places the result into `normalOut`.

`public final void transform(Tuple4f vec)`
`public final void transform(Tuple4f vec, Tuple4f vecOut)`

The first `transform` method postmultiplies this matrix by the tuple `vec` and places the result back into `vec`. The second `transform` method postmultiplies this matrix by the tuple `vec` and places the result into `vecOut`.

`public final void negate()`
`public final void negate(Matrix4f m1)`

The first method negates the value of this matrix in place (this = –this). The second method sets the value of this matrix equal to the negation of the matrix m1 (this = –m1).

`public final void invert()`
`public final void invert(Matrix4f m1)`

The first method inverts this matrix in place. The second method sets the value of this matrix to the inverse of the matrix m1.

`public final float determinant()`

The `determinant` method computes the determinant of the matrix `this` and returns the computed value.

```
public final void rotX(float angle)
public final void rotY(float angle)
public final void rotZ(float angle)
```

The three rot methods construct rotation matrices that rotate in a counterclock-wise (right-handed) direction around the axis specified as the last letter of the method name. The constructed matrix replaces the value of the matrix this. The rotation angle is expressed in radians.

```
public final void mul(Matrix4f m1, Matrix4f m2)
public final void mul(Matrix4f m1)
```

The first mul method multiplies matrix m1 with matrix m2 and places the result into the matrix this. The second mul method multiplies the matrix this with matrix m1 and places the result in matrix this.

```
public final void mulTransposeBoth(Matrix4f m1, Matrix4f m2)
public final void mulTransposeRight(Matrix4f m1, Matrix4f m2)
public final void mulTransposeLeft(Matrix4f m1, Matrix4f m2)
```

The mulTransposeBoth method multiplies the transpose of matrix m1 (left) times the transpose of matrix m2 (right) and places the result into this matrix. The mulTransposeRight method multiplies matrix m1 times the transpose of matrix m2 and places the result back into this matrix. The mulTransposeLeft method multiplies the transpose of matrix m1 times matrix m2 and places the result into this matrix.

```
public boolean equals(Matrix4f m1)
public boolean equals(Object t1)
```

The first method returns true if all of the data members of Matrix4f m1 are equal to the corresponding data members in this Matrix4f. The second method returns true if the Object t1 is of type Matrix4f and all of the data members of t1 are equal to the corresponding data members in this Matrix4f.

```
public boolean epsilonEquals(Matrix4f m1, float epsilon)
```

This method returns true if the $L\infty$ distance between this Matrix4f and Matrix4f m1 is less than or equal to the epsilon parameter. Otherwise, this method returns false. The $L\infty$ distance is equal to

$$MAX[i = 0,1,2,3; j = 0,1,2,3; abs(this.m(i,j) - m1.m(i,j))]$$

444

public int hashCode()

The hashCode method returns a hash number based on the data values in this object. Two different Matrix4f objects with identical data values (that is, equals(Matrix4f) returns true) will return the same hash number. Two Matrix4f objects with different data members may return the same hash value, although this is not likely.

public String toString()

The toString method returns a string that contains the values of this Matrix4f.

A.2.4 Matrix4d Class

The Matrix4d class serves to contain 4×4 matrices mainly for storing and manipulating 3D transformation matrices. The class includes nine different constructors for creating matrices and several operators for manipulating these matrices.

Variables

The component values of a Matrix4d are directly accessible through the public variables m00, m01, m02, m03, m10, m11, m12, m13, m20, m21, m22, m23, m30, m31, m32, and m33. To access the element in row 2 and column 0 of matrix rotate, a programmer would write rotate.m20. A programmer would access the other values similarly.

```
public double m00
public double m01
public double m02
public double m03
public double m10
public double m11
public double m12
public double m13
public double m20
public double m21
public double m22
public double m23
public double m30
public double m31
public double m32
public double m33
```

These public variables are the elements of the matrix.

Constructors

```
public Matrix4d(double m00, double m01, double m02, double m03,
        double m10, double m11, double m12, double m13, double m20,
        double m21, double m22, double m23, double m30, double m31,
        double m32, double m33)
public Matrix4d(double v[])
public Matrix4d(Quat4d q1, Vector3d t1, double s)
public Matrix4d(Quat4f q1, Vector3d t1, double s)
public Matrix4d(Matrix3d m1, Vector3d t1, double s)
public Matrix4d(Matrix3f m1, Vector3d t1, double s)
public Matrix4d(Matrix4d m1)
public Matrix4d(Matrix4f m1)
public Matrix4d()
```

Each of these constructors returns a new Matrix4d object. The first constructor generates a 4×4 matrix from the 16 values provided. The second constructor generates a 4×4 matrix from the first 16 values in the array v. The third through sixth constructors generate a 4×4 matrix from the quaternion, translation, and scale values. The scale is applied only to the rotational components of the matrix (upper 3×3) and not to the translational components. The seventh and eighth constructors generate a 4×4 matrix with the same values as the passed matrix. The final constructor generates a 4×4 matrix with all 16 values set to 0.0.

Methods

```
public final void get(Matrix3d m1)
public final void get(Matrix3f m1)
public final double get(Matrix3d m1, Vector3d t1)
public final double get(Matrix3f m1, Vector3d t1)
public final void get(Quat4f q1)
public final void get(Quat4d q1)
public final void get(Vector3d trans)
```

The first two methods perform an SVD normalization of this matrix in order to acquire the normalized rotational component. The values are placed into the passed parameter. The next two methods perform an SVD normalization of this matrix to calculate the rotation as a 3×3 matrix, the translation, and the scale. None of the matrix values is modified. The next two methods perform an SVD normalization of this matrix to acquire the normalized rotational component. The last two methods retrieve the translational components of this matrix.

```
public final void setElement(int row, int column, double value)
public final double getElement(int row, int column)
```

The setElement and getElement methods provide a means for accessing a single element within a 4×4 matrix using indices. This is not a preferred method of access, but Java 3D provides these methods for functional completeness. The setElement method takes a row index row (where a value of 0 represents the first row and a value of 3 represents the fourth row), a column index column (where a value of 0 represents the first column and a value of 3 represents the fourth column), and a value. It sets the corresponding element in matrix this to the specified value. The getElement method also takes a row index row and a column index column and returns the element at the corresponding locations as a floating-point value.

```
public final void setRow(int row, double x, double y, double z,
      double w)
public final void setRow(int row, Vector4d v)
public final void setRow(int row, double v[])
public final void getRow(int row, Vector4d v)
public final void getRow(int row, double v[])
```

The three setRow methods provide a means for constructing a 4×4 matrix on a row basis. The row parameter determines which row the method invocation affects. A row value of 0 represents the first row and a value of 3 represents the fourth row. The first setRow method specifies the four new values as independent floating-point values. The second setRow method uses the values in the Vector4d v to update the matrix. The third setRow method uses the first four values in the array v to update the matrix. In all three cases the matrix affected is the matrix this. The two getRow methods copy the matrix values in the specified row into the array or vector parameter, respectively.

```
public final void setColumn(int column, double x, double y,
      double z, double w)
public final void setColumn(int column, Vector4d v)
public final void setColumn(int column, double v[])
public final void getColumn(int column, Vector4d v)
public final void getColumn(int column, double v[])
```

The three setColumn methods provide a means for constructing a 4×4 matrix on a column basis. The column parameter determines which column the method invocation affects. A column value of 0 represents the first column and a value of 3 represents the fourth column. The first setColumn method specifies the four new values as independent double-precision floating-point values. The second setColumn method uses the values in the Vector4d v to update the matrix. The third setColumn method uses the first four values in the array v to update the matrix. In all three cases the matrix affected is the matrix this. The two getColumn methods copy the matrix values in the specified column into the array or vector parameter, respectively.

```
public final void setRotation(Matrix3f m1)
public final void setRotation(Matrix3d m1)
```

These methods set the rotational component (upper 3×3) of this matrix to the matrix values in the passed argument. The other elements of this matrix are unchanged. A singular value decomposition is performed on this object's upper 3×3 matrix to factor out the scale, then this object's upper 3×3 matrix components are replaced by the passed rotation components, and finally the scale is reapplied to the rotational components.

```
public final void setRotation(Quat4f q1)
public final void setRotation(Quat4d q1)
```

These methods set the rotational component (upper 3×3) of this matrix to the matrix values in the passed argument. The other elements of this matrix are unchanged. A singular value decomposition is performed on this object's upper 3×3 matrix to factor out the scale, then this object's upper 3×3 matrix components are replaced by the matrix equivalent of the quaternion, and finally the scale is reapplied to the rotational components.

```
public final void setRotation(AxisAngle4d a1)
```

This method sets the rotational component (upper 3×3) of this matrix to the equivalent values in the passed argument. The other elements of this matrix are unchanged. A singular value decomposition is performed on this object's upper 3×3 matrix to factor out the scale, then this object's upper 3×3 matrix components are replaced by the matrix equivalent of the axis-angle, and finally the scale is reapplied to the rotational components.

```
public final void getRotationScale(Matrix3f m1)
public final void getRotationScale(Matrix3d m1)
public final void setRotationScale(Matrix3d m1)
public final void setRotationScale(Matrix3f m1)
```

The two get methods retrieve the upper 3×3 values of this matrix and place them into the matrix m1. The two set methods replace the upper 3×3 matrix values of this matrix with the values in the matrix m1.

```
public final void setTranslation(Vector3d trans)
```

This method modifies the translational components of this matrix to the values of the Vector3d argument. The other values of this matrix are not modified.

```
public final void setScale(double scale)
public final double getScale()
```

The first method sets the scale component of the current matrix by factoring out the current scale (by doing an SVD) and multiplying by the new scale. The second method performs an SVD normalization of this matrix to calculate and return the uniform scale factor. If the matrix has nonuniform scale factors, the largest of the x, y, and z scale factors will be returned.

```
public final void add(double scalar)
```

This method adds a scalar to each component of this matrix.

```
public final void add(double scalar, Matrix4d m1)
```

This method adds a scalar to each component of the matrix m1 and places the result into this. Matrix m1 is not modified.

```
public final void mul(double scalar, Matrix4d m1)
```

This method multiplies each component of the matrix m1 by a scalar and places the result into this. Matrix m1 is not modified.

```
public final void mul(double scalar)
```

This method multiplies each element of this matrix by a scalar

```
public final void add(Matrix4d m1, Matrix4d m2)
public final void add(Matrix4d m1)
public final void sub(Matrix4d m1, Matrix4d m2)
public final void sub(Matrix4d m1)
```

The first add method adds the matrix m1 to the matrix m2 and places the result into the matrix this. The second add method adds the matrix this to the matrix m1 and places the result into the matrix this. The first sub method performs an element-by-element subtraction of matrix m2 from matrix m1 and places the result into the matrix this. The second sub method performs an element-by-element subtraction of the matrix m1 from the matrix this and places the result into the matrix this.

```
public final void set(double m[])
```

This method sets the value of this matrix to the row-major array parameter (that is, the first four elements of the array will be copied into the first row of this matrix, and so forth).

```
public final void set(Matrix3f m1)
public final void set(Matrix3d m1)
```

These methods set the rotational component (upper 3×3) of this matrix to the matrix values in the matrix argument. The other elements of this matrix are initialized as if this were an identity matrix (that is, an affine matrix with no translational component).

```
public final void set(Matrix4f m1)
public final void set(Matrix4d m1)
```

These methods set the value of this matrix to the value of the passed matrix m1.

```
public final void set(Quat4d q1)
public final void set(Quat4f q1)
```

These methods set the value of this matrix to the matrix conversion of the quaternion argument.

```
public final void set(AxisAngle4d a1)
public final void set(AxisAngle4f a1)
```

These methods set the value of this matrix to the matrix conversion of the axis and angle argument.

```
public final void set(Vector3d v1)
```

This method sets the value of this matrix to a translation matrix by the passed translation value.

```
public final void set(Quat4d q1, Vector3d t1, double s)
public final void set(Quat4f q1, Vector3d t1, double s)
public final void set(Quat4f q1, Vector3f t1, float s)
```

These methods set the value of this matrix to the rotation expressed by the quaternion q1, the translation t1, and the scale s.

```
public final void set(double scale)
```

This method sets the value of this matrix to a scale matrix with the passed scale amount.

```
public final void set(double scale, Vector3d v1)
```

This method sets the value of this matrix to a scale and translation matrix. The scale is not applied to the translation, and all of the matrix values are modified.

```
public final void set(Vector3d v1, double scale)
```

This method sets the value of this matrix to a scale and translation matrix. The translation is scaled by the scale factor, and all of the matrix values are modified.

```
public final void set(Matrix3f m1, Vector3f t1, float scale)
public final void set(Matrix3d m1, Vector3d t1, double scale)
```

These methods set the value of this matrix from the rotation expressed by the rotation matrix m1, the translation t1, and the scale s.

```
public final void negate(Matrix4d m1)
public final void negate()
```

The first method sets the value of this matrix to the negation of the m1 parameter. The second method negates the value of this matrix (this = –this).

```
public final void transpose(Matrix4d m)
public final void transpose()
```

The first transpose method transposes the matrix m and places the result into the matrix this. The second transpose method transposes the matrix this and places the result back into the matrix this.

```
public final void transform(Tuple4d vec)
public final void transform(Tuple4f vec)
public final void transform(Tuple4d vec, Tuple4d vecOut)
public final void transform(Tuple4f vec, Tuple4f vecOut)
```

The first two transform methods postmultiply this matrix by the tuple vec and place the result back into vec. The last two transform methods postmultiply this matrix by the tuple vec and place the result into vecOut.

```
public final void transform(Point3d point)
public final void transform(Point3f point)
public final void transform(Point3d point, Point3d pointOut)
public final void transform(Point3f point, Point3f pointOut)
```

The first two transform methods postmultiply this matrix by the point argument point and place the result back into point. The multiplication treats the three-element point as if its fourth element were 1. The last two transform methods postmultiply this matrix by the point argument point and place the result into pointOut.

```
public final void transform(Vector3d normal)
public final void transform(Vector3f normal)
```

```
public final void transform(Vector3d normal, Vector3d normalOut)
public final void transform(Vector3f normal, Vector3f normalOut)
```

The first two `transform` methods postmultiply this matrix by the vector argument `normal` and place the result back into `normal`. The multiplication treats the three-element vector as if its fourth element were 0. The last two `transform` methods postmultiply this matrix by the vector argument `normal` and place the result into `normalOut`.

```
public final void invert()
public final void invert(Matrix4d m1)
```

The first method inverts this matrix in place. The second method sets the value of this matrix to the inverse of the matrix `m1`.

```
public final double determinant()
```

The `determinant` method computes the determinant of the matrix `this` and returns the computed value.

```
public final void rotX(double angle)
public final void rotY(double angle)
public final void rotZ(double angle)
```

The `rot` methods construct rotation matrices that rotate in a counterclockwise (right-handed) direction around the axis specified as the last letter of the method name. The constructed matrix replaces the value of the matrix `this`. The rotation angle is expressed in radians.

```
public final void mul(Matrix4d m1, Matrix4d m2)
public final void mul(Matrix 4d m1)
```

The first `mul` method multiplies matrix `m1` with matrix `m2` and places the result into the matrix `this`. The second `mul` method multiplies matrix `this` with matrix `m1` and places the result into the matrix `this`.

```
public final void mulTransposeBoth(Matrix4d m1, Matrix4d m2)
public final void mulTransposeRight(Matrix4d m1, Matrix4d m2)
public final void mulTransposeLeft(Matrix4d m1, Matrix4d m2)
```

The `mulTransposeBoth` method multiplies the transpose of matrix `m1` (left) times the transpose of matrix `m2` (right) and places the result into this matrix. The `mulTransposeRight` method multiplies matrix `m1` times the transpose of matrix `m2` and places the result back into this matrix. The `mulTransposeLeft` method multiplies the transpose of matrix `m1` times matrix `m2` and places the result into this matrix.

```
public final void setZero()
```

This method sets this matrix to all zeros.

```
public final void setIdentity()
```

This method sets this Matrix4d to identity.

```
public boolean equals(Matrix4d m1)
public boolean equals(Object t1)
```

The first method returns true if all of the data members of Matrix4d m1 are equal to the corresponding data members in this Matrix4d. The second method returns true if the Object t1 is of type Matrix4d and all of the data members of t1 are equal to the corresponding data members in this Matrix4d.

```
public boolean epsilonEquals(Matrix4d m1, float epsilon)
```

Deprecated method. See the next method.

```
public boolean epsilonEquals(Matrix4d m1, double epsilon)
```

This method returns true if the L∞ distance between this Matrix4d and Matrix4d m1 is less than or equal to the epsilon parameter. Otherwise, this method returns false. The L∞ distance is equal to

$$\text{MAX}[i = 0,1,2,3, j = 0,1,2,3; \text{abs}(\text{this.m}(i,j) - \text{m1.m}(i,j)]$$

```
public int hashCode()
```

The hashCode method returns a hash number based on the data values in this object. Two different Matrix4d objects with identical data values (that is, equals(Matrix4d) returns true) will return the same hash number. Two Matrix4d objects with different data members may return the same hash value, although this is not likely.

```
public String toString()
```

The toString method returns a string that contains the values of this Matrix4d.

A.2.5 GMatrix Class

The GMatrix class serves to contain a double-precision, general, and dynamically resizeable $M \times N$ matrix. Row and column numbering begins with zero. The representation is row major.

The GMatrix data members are not public, thus allowing efficient implementations of sparse matrices. However, the data members can be modified through public accessors. The class includes three different constructors for creating matrices and several operators for manipulating these matrices.

Constructors

```
public GMatrix(int nRow, int nCol)
public GMatrix(int nRow, int nCol, double matrix[])
public GMatrix(GMatrix matrix)
```

Each of these constructors returns a new GMatrix. The first constructor generates an nRow by nCol identity matrix. Note that because row and column numbering begins with zero, nRow and nCol will be one larger than the maximum possible matrix index values. The second constructor generates an nRow by nCol matrix initialized to the values in the array matrix. The last constructor generates a new GMatrix and copies the initial values from the parameter matrix argument.

Methods

```
public final void mul(GMatrix m1, GMatrix m2)
public final void mul(GMatrix m1)
```

The first mul method multiplies matrix m1 with matrix m2 and places the result into this. The second mul method multiplies this matrix with matrix m1 and places the result into this.

```
public final void add(GMatrix m1)
public final void add(GMatrix m1, GMatrix m2)
public final void sub(GMatrix m1)
public final void sub(GMatrix m1, GMatrix m2)
```

The first add method adds this matrix to matrix m1 and places the result back into this. The second add method adds matrices m1 and m2 and places the result into this. The first sub method subtracts matrix m1 from the matrix this and places the result into this. The second sub method subtracts matrix m2 from matrix m1 and places the result into the matrix this.

```
public final void negate()
public final void negate(GMatrix m1)
```

The first method negates the value of this matrix in place (this = –this). The second method sets the value of this matrix to the negation of the matrix m1 (this = –m1).

```
public final void invert()
public final void invert(GMatrix m1)
```

The first method inverts this matrix in place. The second method sets the value of this matrix to the inverse of the matrix m1.

```
public final void setIdentity()
```

This method sets this GMatrix to the identity matrix.

```
public final void setZero()
```

This method sets all the values in this matrix to zero.

```
public final void identityMinus()
```

This method subtracts this matrix from the identity matrix and puts the values back into this (this = I – this).

```
public final void copySubMatrix(int rowSource, int colSource,
        int numRow, int numCol, int rowDest, int colDest,
        GMatrix target)
```

This method copies a submatrix derived from this matrix into the target matrix. The rowSource and colSource parameters define the upper left of the submatrix. The numRow and numCol parameters define the number of rows and columns in the submatrix. The submatrix is copied into the target matrix starting at (rowDest, colDest). The target parameter is the matrix into which the submatrix will be copied.

```
public final void setSize(int nRow, int nCol)
```

This method changes the size of this matrix dynamically. If the size is increased, no data values will be lost. If the size is decreased, only those data values whose matrix positions were eliminated will be lost.

```
public final void set(double matrix[])
public final void set(GMatrix m1)
public final void set(Matrix3f m1)
public final void set(Matrix3d m1)
public final void set(Matrix4f m1)
public final void set(Matrix4d m1)
```

The first set method sets the values of this matrix to the values found in the matrix array parameter. The values are copied in one row at a time, in row-major fashion. The array should be at least equal in length to the number of matrix rows times the number of matrix columns in this matrix. The second set method sets the values of this matrix to the values found in matrix m1. The last four set methods set the values of this matrix to the values found in matrix m1.

```
public final void get(Matrix3d m1)
public final void get(Matrix3f m1)
public final void get(Matrix4d m1)
public final void get(Matrix4f m1)
public final void get(GMatrix m1)
```

The first two methods place the values in the upper 3×3 of this matrix into the matrix m1. The next two methods place the values in the upper 4×4 of this matrix into the matrix m1. The final method places the values in this matrix into the matrix m1. Matrix m1 should be at least as large as this matrix.

```
public final int getNumRow()
public final int getNumCol()
```

The getNumRow method returns the number of rows in this matrix. The getNum-Col method returns the number of columns in this matrix.

```
public final void setElement(int row, int column, double value)
public final double getElement(int row, int column)
```

These methods set and retrieve the value at the specified row and column of this matrix.

```
public final void setRow(int row, double array[])
public final void setRow(int row, GVector vector)
public final void getRow(int row, double array[])
public final void getRow(int row, GVector vector)
public final void setColumn(int col, double array[])
public final void setColumn(int col, GVector vector)
public final void getColumn(int col, double array[])
public final void getColumn(int col, GVector vector)
```

The setRow methods copy the values from the array into the specified row of this matrix. The getRow methods place the values of the specified row into the array or vertex. The setColumn methods copy the values from the array into the specified column of this matrix or vector. The getColumn methods place the values of the specified column into the array or vector.

```
public final void setScale(double scale)
```

This method sets this matrix to a uniform scale matrix, and all of the values are reset.

```
public final void mulTransposeBoth(GMatrix m1, GMatrix m2)
public final void mulTransposeRight(GMatrix m1, GMatrix m2)
public final void mulTransposeLeft(GMatrix m1, GMatrix m2)
```

The mulTransposeBoth method multiplies the transpose of matrix m1 (left) times the transpose of matrix m2 (right) and places the result into this matrix. The mulTransposeRight method multiplies matrix m1 times the transpose of matrix m2 and places the result back into this matrix. The mulTransposeLeft method multiplies the transpose of matrix m1 times matrix m2 and places the result into this matrix.

```
public final void transpose()
public final void transpose(GMatrix m1)
```

The first transpose method transposes this matrix in place. The second transpose method places the matrix values of the transpose of matrix m1 into this matrix.

```
public String toString()
```

This method returns a string that contains the values of this GMatrix.

```
public int hashCode()
```

This method returns a hash number based on the data values in this object. Two different GMatrix objects with identical data values (that is, equals(GMatrix) returns true) will return the same hash number. Two objects with different data members may return the same hash value, although this is not likely.

```
public boolean equals(GMatrix m1)
public boolean equals(Object o1)
```

The first method returns true if all of the data members of GMatrix m1 are equal to the corresponding data members in this GMatrix. The second method returns true if the Object o1 is of type GMatrix and all of the data members of o1 are equal to the corresponding data members in this GMatrix.

```
public boolean epsilonEquals(GMatrix m1, float epsilon)
```

Deprecated method. See the next method.

```
public boolean epsilonEquals(GMatrix m1, double epsilon)
```

This method returns true if the $L\infty$ distance between this GMatrix and GMatrix m1 is less than or equal to the epsilon parameter. Otherwise, this method returns false. The $L\infty$ distance is equal to

457

$$\text{MAX}[i = 0,1,2, \dots n; j = 0,1,2,\dots n; \text{abs}(\text{this.m}(i,j) - \text{m1.m}(i,j))]$$

public final double trace()

This method returns the trace of this matrix.

public final int SVD(GMatrix U, GMatrix W, GMatrix V)

The SVD method finds the singular value decomposition (SVD) of this matrix such that $\text{this} = \mathbf{U} * \mathbf{W} * \mathbf{V}^T$, and returns the rank of this matrix. The values of U, W, and V are all overwritten. Note that the matrix V is output as $\mathbf{V}$ and not $\mathbf{V}^T$. If this matrix is $m \times n$, then $\mathbf{U}$ is $m \times m$, $\mathbf{W}$ is a diagonal matrix that is $m \times n$, and $\mathbf{V}$ is $n \times n$. The inverse of this matrix is $\text{this}^{-1} = \mathbf{V} * \mathbf{W}^{-1} * \mathbf{U}^T$, where $\mathbf{W}^{-1}$ is a diagonal matrix computed by taking the reciprocal of each of the diagonal elements of matrix $\mathbf{W}$.

public final int LUD(GMatrix LU, GVector permutation)

The LUD method performs an LU decomposition. This matrix must be a square matrix, and the LU parameter must be the same size as this matrix. The diagonal elements of $\mathbf{L}$ (unity) are not stored. The permutation parameter records the row permutation affected by the partial pivoting and is used as a parameter to the GVector LUDBackSolve method to solve sets of linear equations. This method returns $+1$ or -1, depending on whether the number of row interchanges was even or odd, respectively.

3D Geometry Compression

JAVA 3D allows programmers to specify geometry using a binary compressed geometry format. This compression format is used with APIs other than just Java 3D and can be used both as a runtime in-memory format for describing geometry, as well as a storage and network format. Eventually the full specification of the compressed geometry format described in this section will be part of its own stand-alone specification, but for completeness it is included as an appendix to the early specification of the Java 3D API.

Java 3D uses a compressed geometry format that allows 3D geometry to be represented in an order of magnitude less space than most traditional 3D representations, with very little loss in object quality. The compression is achieved through several layers of techniques.

For a binary format to be useful as an interchange format, it is essential that the format be thoroughly and unambiguously documented. This appendix attempts to completely specify all the details of the compressed geometry format. To ensure current and future compatibility, it is essential to use only the features explicitly specified in this document. For a binary format to be useful as an interchange format, it is essential that the format be thoroughly and unambiguously documented. This appendix attempts to completely specify all the details of the compressed geometry format. To insure current and future compatibility, it is essential to use only the features explicitly specified in this document. Any features, fields, usage, and so on. not specified in the document should be considered illegal, and their usage would result in *invalid* compressed geometry data. "Invalid" means that using such a construct will be incompatible with current implementations or will break future implementations. This document will point out many of the constructs that would cause the data to be invalid.

B.1   Compression

The process of geometry compression is as follows:

1. The geometry to be compressed is converted into a generalized mesh form, which allows a triangle to be, on average, specified by 0.80 vertices.

2. The data for each vertex component of the geometry is converted to the most efficient representation format for its type and then quantized to as few bits as possible.

3. These quantized bits are differenced between successive vertices, and the results are modified Huffman-encoded into self-describing variable-bit-length data elements.

4. These variable-length elements are strung together into a final compressed geometry block using compressed geometry's seven geometry instructions.

B.2   Decompression

For pure software implementations, upon receipt, compressed geometry blocks are decompressed into the local host's preferred geometry format by reversing the compression process. This decompression can be performed in a lazy manner, avoiding full expansion into memory until the geometry is needed for rendering.

B.3   Appendix Organization

Before the bit details of the compression can be specified, several of the concepts used in compressed geometry need elaboration. The first several sections are an expansion of our SIGGRAPH '95 paper on compressed geometry.[1]

- *Generalized Triangle Strip*. This section is a refresher on the concept and semantics of a generalized triangle strip.

- *Generalized Triangle Mesh*. This section introduces the concept and semantics of a generalized triangle mesh.

- *Position Representation and Quantization*. This section describes the fixed-point format used for 3D positional representation.

---

1. Deering, Michael. "Geometry Compression." *Computer Graphics Proceedings*, Annual Conference Series, 1995, ACM SIGGRAPH, pp 13–19.

- *Color Representation and Quantization.* This section describes the fixed-point format used for color representation.

- *Normal Representation and Quantization.* This section describes a novel folded table-based representation of surface normals, and the fixed-point format of the resultant normals.

- *Modified Huffman Encoding.* This section describes the variant of Huffman delta encoding used for compressed geometry.

- *Compressed Geometry Instructions.* This section gives an overview of the seven compressed geometry instructions.

- *Semantics of Compressed Geometry Instructions.* This section contains pseudocode to document the detailed semantics of compressed geometry instruction execution.

- *Compressed Geometry Assembly Syntax.* This section gives an overview of the assembly syntax for compressed geometry instructions.

B.4   Generalized Triangle Strip

A generalized triangle strip is a generalization of the concept of a "zig-zag" and triangle fan. It is a sequence of vertices in which each vertex contains a two-bit replacement code. This replacement code defines how the present vertex is to be combined with previous vertices to form the next triangle. The replacement bits can also be thought of as a generalization of the "move/draw" bit used for lines.

A stack of the last three vertices used to form a triangle is kept. The three vertices are labeled oldest, middle, and newest. An incoming vertex of type `replace_oldest` causes the oldest vertex to be replaced by the middle, the middle to be replaced by the newest, and the incoming vertex to become the newest. This corresponds to a PHIGS PLUS triangle strip (sometimes called a "zig-zag" strip). The replacement type `replace_middle` leaves the oldest vertex unchanged, replaces the middle vertex by the newest, and makes the incoming vertex become the newest. This corresponds to a triangle fan.

The replacement type `restart` marks the oldest and middle vertices as invalid, and the incoming vertex becomes the newest. Generalized triangle strips must always start with this code. A triangle will be output only when a replacement operation results in three valid vertices.

`Restart` corresponds to a "move" operation in polylines and allows multiple, unconnected, variable-length triangle strips to be described by a single data structure passed in by the user, greatly reducing the overhead. The generalized triangle

461

strip's ability to effectively change from "strip" to "fan" mode in the middle of a strip allows more complex geometry to be represented compactly and requires less input data bandwidth. The restart capability allows several pieces of disconnected geometry to be passed as one data block. Figure B-1 shows a single generalized triangle strip and the associated replacement codes.

Triangles are normalized such that the front face is always defined by a counter-clockwise vertex order after transformation (assuming a right-handed coordinate system). To support this, there are two flavors of restart: `restart` (counterclockwise and `restart_reverse` (clockwise). The vertex order is reversed after every `replace_oldest` but remains the same after every `replace_middle`.

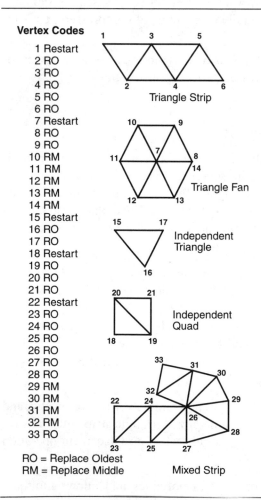

Vertex Codes

1 Restart
2 RO
3 RO
4 RO
5 RO
6 RO
7 Restart
8 RO
9 RO
10 RM
11 RM
12 RM
13 RM
14 RM
15 Restart
16 RO
17 RO
18 Restart
19 RO
20 RO
21 RO
22 Restart
23 RO
24 RO
25 RO
26 RO
27 RO
28 RO
29 RM
30 RM
31 RM
32 RM
33 RO

RO = Replace Oldest
RM = Replace Middle

Figure B-1   A Generalized Triangle Strip

B.5 Generalized Triangle Mesh

The first stage of compressed geometry is to convert triangle data into an efficient linear strip form: the *generalized triangle mesh*. This is a near-optimal representation of triangle data, given fixed storage.

The existing concept of a generalized triangle strip structure allows for compact representation of geometry while maintaining a linear data structure. That is, the geometry can be extracted by a single monotonic scan over the vertex array data structure. This is very important for pipelined hardware implementations. A data format that requires random access back to main memory during processing is problematic.

However, by confining itself to linear strips, the generalized triangle strip format leaves a potential factor of two (in space) on the table. Consider the geometry in Figure B-2.

While it can be represented by one triangle strip, many of the interior vertices appear twice in the strip. This is inherent in any approach wishing to avoid references to old data. Some systems have tried using a simple regular mesh buffer to support reuse of old vertices, but there is a problem with this approach in practice: In general, geometry does not come in a perfectly regular rectangular mesh structure.

The generalized technique employed by compressed geometry addresses this problem. Old vertices are *explicitly* pushed into a queue and then explicitly referenced in the future when the old vertex is desired again. This fine control supports irregular meshes of nearly any shape. Any viable technique must recognize that storage is finite; thus, the maximum queue length is fixed at 16, requiring a four-bit index. We refer to this queue as the *mesh buffer*. The combination of generalized triangle strips and mesh buffer references is referred to as a *generalized triangle mesh*.

The fixed mesh buffer size requires all tessellators or restripifiers for compressed geometry to break up any runs longer than 16 unique references. Since compressed geometry is not meant to be programmed directly at the user level, but rather by sophisticated tessellators or reformatters, this is not too onerous a restriction. Sixteen old vertices allow up to 94 percent of the redundant geometry to avoid being respecified. Figure B-2 also contains an example of a general mesh buffer representation of the surface geometry.

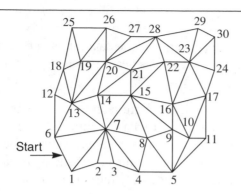

Generalized Triangle Strip
R6, O1, O7, O2, O3, M4, M8, O5, O9, O10, M11,
M17, M16, M9, O15, O8, O7, M14, O13, M6,
O12, M18, M19, M20, M14, O21, O15, O22, O16,
O23, O17, O24, M30, M29, M28, M22, O21, M20,
M27, O26, M19, O25, O18

Generalized Triangle Mesh
R6p, O1, O7p, O2, O3, M4, M8p, O5, O9p, O10, M11,
M17p, M16p, M-3, O15p, O-5, O6, M14p, O13p, M-9,
O12, M18p, M19p, M20p, M-5, O21p, O-7, O22p, O-9,
O23, O-10, O-7, M30, M29, M28, M-1, O-2, M-3,
M27, O26, M-4, O25, O-5

Legend
First letter: R = Restart, O = Replace Oldest, M = Replace Middle
Trailing "p" = push into mesh buffer
Number is vertex number, -number is mesh buffer reference
where -1 is most recent pushed vertex

Figure B-2   A Generalized Triangle Mesh

The language of compressed geometry supports the four vertex replacement codes of generalized triangle strips (replace oldest, replace middle, restart, and restart reverse) and adds another bit in each vertex header to indicate if this vertex should be pushed into the mesh buffer. The mesh buffer reference instruction has a four-bit field to indicate which old vertex should be rereferenced, along with the two-bit vertex replacement code. The semantics of a mesh buffer reference is that they do not have an option to repush their data into the mesh buffer; old vertices can be recycled only once.

Geometry rarely is composed purely of positional data; generally a normal and/or color are also specified per vertex. Therefore, mesh buffer entries are required to contain storage for all associated per-vertex information (specifically including normals, and colors.

For maximum space efficiency, when a vertex is specified in the data stream, (per-vertex) normal and/or color information should be directly bundled with the position information. This bundling is controlled by two state bits: *bundle normals with vertices* (bnv) and *bundle colors with vertices* (bcv). When a vertex is pushed into the mesh buffer, these bits control whether its bundled normal and/or color are pushed as well. During a mesh buffer reference instruction, this process is reversed. The two bits specify if a normal and/or color should be inherited from the mesh buffer storage or inherited from the *current normal* or *current color.*

There are explicit instructions for setting these two current values. An important exception to this rule occurs when an explicit "set current normal" instruction is followed by a mesh buffer reference, with the bnv state bit active. In this case, the former overrides the mesh buffer normal. This allows compact representation of hard edges in surface geometry. The analogous semantics are also defined for colors, allowing compact representation of hard edges in images embedded as geometry.

B.6   Position Representation and Quantization

The 8-bit exponent of 32-bit IEEE floating-point numbers allows positions literally to span the known universe: from a scale of 100 billion light years down to the radius of subatomic particles. However, for any given tessellated object the exponent is really specified just once by the current modeling matrix; within a given modeling space, the object geometry is effectively described with only the 24-bit fixed-point mantissa. Visually, in many cases far fewer bits are needed; thus the language of compressed geometry supports variable quantization of position data down to as little as one bit. The maximum number of bits supported is at most 16 bits of precision per component of position.

We still assume that the position and scale of the local modeling spaces are specified by full 32-bit or 64-bit floating-point coordinates. If sufficient numerical care is taken, several such modeling spaces can be stitched together without cracks, forming seamless geometry coordinate systems with much greater than 16-bit positional precision.

Most geometry is local, so within the 16-bit (or less) modeling space (of each object), the delta difference between one vertex and the next in the generalized mesh buffer stream is very likely to be less than 16 bits in significance. Indeed, one can histogram the bit length of neighboring position deltas in a batch of geometry and, based on this histogram, assign a variable-length code to represent the vertices compactly. The typical coding used in many other similar situations is customized Huffman code; this is the case for compressed geometry. The details of the coding of position deltas will be discussed later, in the context of color and normal delta coding.

B.7   Color Representation and Quantization

We treat colors similar to positions, but without using negative values. Thus RGBα color data is first quantized to 15-bit unsigned fraction components, and a zero sign bit is added to form a 16-bit signed number. These are absolute linear reflectivity values, with 1.0 representing 100 percent reflectivity. An additional parameter allows color data to be quantized effectively to any amount less than 16 bits; that is, the colors can all be within a 5-5-5 RGB color space. (The α field is optional, controlled by the *color alpha present* (cap) state bit.) Note that this decision does *not* necessarily cause mach banding on the final rendered image; individual pixel colors are still interpolated between these quantized vertex colors, and vertices also are subject to lighting.

The same delta coding used for color components is used for positions. Compression of color data is where compressed geometry and traditional image compression face the most similar problem. However, many of the more advanced techniques for image compression were rejected for geometry color compression because of the difference in focus.

Image compression makes several assumptions about the viewing of the decompressed data that *cannot* be made for compressed geometry. In image compression, it is known a priori that the pixels appear in a perfect rectangular array, and that when viewed, each pixel subtends a narrow range of visual angles. In compressed geometry, one has almost no idea what the relationship between the viewer and the rasterized geometry will be.

In image compression, it is known that the spatial frequency of the displayed pixels on the viewer's eyes is likely higher than the human visual system's color acuity. This is why colors are usually converted to yuv space, so that the uv color components can be represented at a lower spatial frequency than the y (intensity) component.

Usually the digital bits representing the subsampled uv components are split up among two or more pixels. Compressed geometry cannot take advantage of this because the display scale of the geometry relative to the viewer's eye is not fixed. Also, given that compressed triangle vertices are connected to four to eight or more other vertices in the generalized triangle mesh, there is no consistent way of sharing "half" the color information across vertices.

Similar arguments apply for the more sophisticated transforms used in traditional image compression, such as the discrete cosine transform. These transforms assume a regular (rectangular) sampling of pixel values and require a large amount of random access during decompression.

B.8 Normal Representation and Quantization

Probably the most innovative concept in compressed geometry is the method of compressing surface normals. Traditionally, 96-bit normals (three 32-bit IEEE floating-point numbers) are used in calculations to determine 8-bit color intensities. Theoretically, 96 bits of information could be used to represent 2^{96} different normals, spread evenly over the surface of a unit sphere. This is a normal every 2^{-46} radians in any direction. Such angles are so exact that by spreading angles out evenly in every direction from earth, you could point out any rock on Mars with subcentimeter accuracy.

But for normalized normals, the exponent bits are effectively unused. Given the constraint $|N| = 1$, at least one of N_x, N_y, or N_z must be in the range of 0.5 to 1.0. During rendering, this normal will be transformed by a composite modeling orientation matrix T: $N' = N \cdot T$.

Assuming the typical implementation in which lighting is performed in world coordinates, the view transform is not involved in the processing of normals. If the normals have been pre-normalized, then to avoid redundant renormalization of the normals, the composite modeling transformation matrix T is typically pre-normalized to divide out any scale changes, and thus

$$\mathbf{T}_{0,0}^2 + \mathbf{T}_{1,0}^2 + \mathbf{T}_{2,0}^2 = 1, \text{ etc.}$$

During the normal transformation, floating-point arithmetic hardware effectively truncates all additive arguments to the accuracy of the largest component. The result is that for a normalized normal being transformed by a scale-preserving modeling orientation matrix, the numerical accuracy of the transformed normal value is reduced to no more than 24-bit fixed-point accuracy in all but a few special cases.

Even 24-bit normal components are still much higher in angular accuracy than the (repaired) Hubble space telescope. After empirical tests, it was determined that an angular density of 0.01 radians between normals gave results that were not visually distinguishable from finer representations. This works out to approximately

100,000 normals distributed over the unit sphere. In rectilinear space, these normals still require high accuracy of representation; we chose to use 16-bit components that include one sign and one guard bit.

This still requires 48 bits to represent a normal. But since we are interested only in 100,000 specific normals, in theory a single 17-bit index could denote any of these normals. The next section shows how it is possible to take advantage of this observation.

B.8.1   Normals as Indices

The most obvious hardware implementation for converting an index of a normal on the unit sphere back into an $N_x N_y N_z$ value is by table look-up. The problem is the size of the table. Fortunately, several symmetry tricks can be applied to reduce the size of the table greatly (by a factor of 48).

First, the unit sphere is symmetrical in the eight quadrants by sign bits. In other words, if we let three of the normal representation bits be the three sign bits of the XYZ components of the normal, then we need only to find a way to represent one eighth of the unit sphere. The all positive sign bit octant of the unit sphere is shown in bold outline on the left half of Figure B-3. This 000 sign bit octant will be referred to as the *prime octant*.

Second, each octant of the unit sphere can be split into six identical pieces by folding about the planes $X = Y$, $X = Z$, and $Y = Z$. Such a division of the prime octant is shown in Figure B-3. The six possible sextants are encoded with another three bits. Now only 1/48 of the sphere remains to be represented.

This reduces the 100,000-entry look-up table by a factor of 48, requiring only about 2,000 entries, small enough to fit into an on-chip ROM look-up table. This table needs 11 address bits to index into it, so including our previous two 3-bit fields, the result is a grand total of 17 bits for all three normal components.

Representing a finite set of unit normals is equivalent to positioning points on the surface of the unit sphere. While no perfectly equal angular density distribution exists for large numbers of points, many near-optimal distributions exist. Thus in theory one of these with the same sort of 48-way symmetry described earlier could be used for the decompression look-up table. However, several additional constraints mandate a different choice of encoding:

- We desire a scalable density distribution in which zeroing more and more of the low-order address bits to the table still results in fairly even density of normals on the unit sphere. Otherwise a diffcrent look-up table for every encoding density would be required.

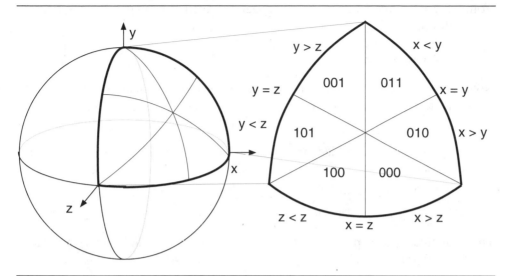

Figure B-3   **Encoding of the Six Sextants of Each Octant of a Sphere**

- We desire a delta-encodable distribution. Statistically, adjacent vertices in geometry will have normals that are nearby on the surface of the unit sphere. Nearby locations on the 2D space of the unit-sphere surface are most succinctly encoded by a 2D offset. We desire a distribution where such a metric exists.

- Finally, while the computational cost of the normal encoding process is not too important, in general, distributions with lower encoding costs are preferred.

For all these reasons, we decided to use a regular grid in the angular space within one sextant as our distribution. Thus, rather than a monolithic 11-bit index, all normals within a sextant are much more conveniently represented as two 6-bit orthogonal angular addresses, revising our grand total to 18 bits. Just as for positions and colors, if more quantization of normals is acceptable, then these 6-bit indices can be reduced to fewer bits; thus absolute normals can be represented using anywhere from 18 to as few as 6 bits. But as will be seen, we can delta-encode this space, further reducing the number of bits required for high-quality representation of normals.

B.8.2   Normal Encoding Parameterization

Points on a unit radius sphere are parameterized by two angles, θ and ϕ, using spherical coordinates. θ is the angle about the Y-axis; ϕ is the longitudinal angle from the $y = 0$ plane. The mapping between rectangular and spherical coordinates is as follows:

$$x = \cos\theta \cdot \cos\phi \qquad y = \sin\phi \qquad z = \sin\theta \cdot \cos\phi \qquad \text{(Eq. B.1)}$$

Note that many different incompatible definitions of spherical coordinates exist within mathematics and engineering. For the purposes of compressed geometry, spherical coordinates used are those defined by Eq. (B.1).

Points on the sphere are folded, first by octant and then by sort order of xyz into one of six sextants. All the table encoding takes place in the positive octant, in the region bounded by the half spaces:

$$x \geq z \qquad z \geq y \qquad y \geq 0$$

This triangular-shaped patch runs from 0 to $\pi/4$ radians in θ, and from 0 to as much as 0.615479709 radians in ϕ: ϕ_{max}.

Quantized angles are represented by two n-bit integers $\hat{\theta}_n$ and $\hat{\phi}_n$, where n is in the range of 0 to 6. The sextant coordinate system defined by these parameters is shown in Figure B-4, for the case of $n = 6$. For a given n, the relationship between these indices θ and ϕ is

$$\theta(\hat{\theta}_n) = \sin^{-1}(\tan(\phi_{max} \cdot (2^n - \hat{\theta}_n)/2^n))$$

$$\phi(\hat{\phi}_n) = \phi_{max} \cdot \hat{\phi}_n/2^n \qquad \text{(Eq. B.2)}$$

These two equations show how values of $\hat{\theta}_n$ and $\hat{\phi}_n$ can be converted to spherical coordinates θ and ϕ, which in turn can be converted to rectilinear normal coordinate components via Eq. (B.1).

To reverse the process, for example, to encode a given normal n into $\hat{\theta}_n$ and $\hat{\phi}_n$, one cannot just invert Eq. (B.2). Instead, the n must first be folded into the canonical octant and sextant, resulting in n'. Then n' must be dotted with all quantized normals in the sextant. For a fixed n, the values of $\hat{\theta}_n$ and $\hat{\phi}_n$ that result in the largest (nearest unity) dot product define the proper encoding of n.

Now the complete bit format of absolute normals can be given. The uppermost three bits specify the sextant, the next three bits specify the octant, and finally two n-bit fields specify $\hat{\theta}_n$ and $\hat{\phi}_n$. The three-bit sextant field takes on one of six values, the binary codes for which are shown in Figure B-3.

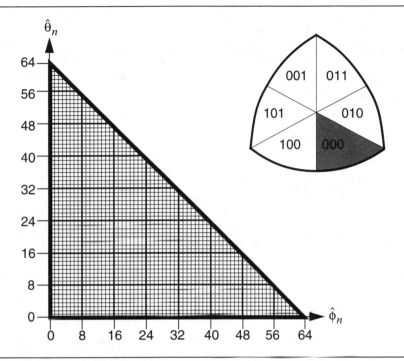

Figure B-4   Sextant Coordinates

This discussion has ignored some details. In particular, the three normals at the corners of the canonical patch are multiply represented (6, 8, and 12 times). By employing the two unused values of the sextant field, these normals can be uniquely encoded as special normals. The normal subinstruction describes the special encoding used for two of these corner cases (14 total special normals).

This representation of normals is amenable to delta encoding. Within a given sextant, the delta code between two normals is simply the difference in $\hat{\theta}_n$ and $\hat{\phi}_n$: $\Delta\hat{\theta}_n$ and $\Delta\hat{\theta}_n$.

B.8.3   Special Warping Rules for Delta Normals

With some additional work, this can be extended to sextants that share a common edge. First we must define how sextants border each other. Consider the three edges of the sextant coordinate system as defined in Figure B-4, and also examine Figure B-3 to see the sextant connectivity within an octant and between octants. The three possible neighbors of a sextant are shown schematically in Figure B-5.

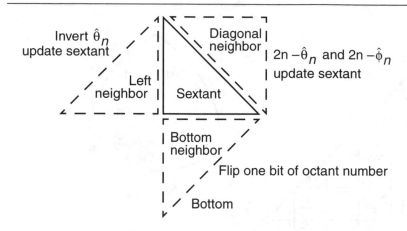

Figure B-5   Sextant Neighbors and Their Relationships

The left edge of a sextant will always be another sextant within the same octant, as will be the diagonal edge of a sextant. Note that the coordinate system of a sextant is defined only for coordinate values in the triangular region of the sextant.

For a given value of n (in the range of 1 to 6), where n is the number of bits of quantization of the sextant coordinates, the valid coordinates are bounded by $\hat{\theta}_n \geq 0$, $\hat{\phi}_n \geq 0$, and $\hat{\theta}_n + \hat{\phi}_n \leq 2^n$. For any given sextant number, the left and diagonal neighbors of that sextant are explicitly known. The bottom edge of a sextant will be the *same* sextant number, but in a different octant. The octant will differ from the current octant by the flip of exactly one of the sign bits. Which octant sign bit will be flipped is also explicitly known. The rules for finding each edge neighbor for any sextant are given in Table B-1.

Table B-1   Sextant Neighbors

Sextant	Left Neighbor	Diagonal Neighbor	Bottom Neighbor
sextant 000	sextant 100	sextant 010	flip octant y
sextant 001	sextant 101	sextant 011	flip octant x
sextant 010	sextant 011	sextant 000	flip octant z
sextant 011	sextant 010	sextant 001	flip octant z
sextant 100	sextant 000	sextant 101	flip octant y
sextant 101	sextant 001	sextant 100	flip octant x

In compressed geometry, all component delta fields and all component absolute fields (except component absolute normal fields) are represented by signed numbers. For each different coordinate component type, there are different wrap rules for what happens when a delta component overflows the absolute representation range. For positions, both positive and negative component values are legal, and overflowing past the largest positive component value is explicitly defined to wrap the coordinate to negative values while overflowing the most negative component value wraps to the positive values. For colors, negative component values are illegal, and wrapping out of the positive component values is illegal. For normals, special wrapping rules allow delta values to change the current sextant or octant in certain cases without explicitly specifying the new sextant or octant.

The special rules for wrapping during normal deltas follow:

- Normal Case:

  if $\hat{\theta}_n + \Delta\hat{\theta}_n \geq 0$, $\hat{\phi}_n + \Delta\hat{\phi}_n \geq 0$, $\hat{\theta}_n + \Delta\hat{\theta}_n + \hat{\phi}_n + \Delta\hat{\phi}_n \leq 2^n$:

  new $\hat{\theta}_n \leftarrow \hat{\theta}_n + \Delta\hat{\theta}_n$, new $\hat{\phi}_n \leftarrow \hat{\phi}_n + \Delta\hat{\phi}_n$,

  current sextant and octant are unchanged.

- Left Edge Wrap Case:

  if $\hat{\theta}_n + \Delta\hat{\theta}_n < 0$, $\hat{\phi}_n + \Delta\hat{\phi}_n \geq 0$, $-(\hat{\theta}_n + \Delta\hat{\theta}_n) + \hat{\phi}_n + \Delta\hat{\phi}_n \leq 2^n$:

  new $\hat{\theta}_n \leftarrow -(\hat{\theta}_n + \Delta\hat{\theta}_n)$, new $\hat{\phi}_n \leftarrow \hat{\phi}_n + \Delta\hat{\phi}_n$,

  current sextant is updated from left edge rules in Table B-1 and current octant is unchanged.

- Diagonal Edge Wrap Case:

  if $\hat{\theta}_n + \Delta\hat{\theta}_n \geq 0$, $\hat{\phi}_n + \Delta\hat{\phi}_n \geq 0$, $\hat{\theta}_n + \Delta\hat{\theta}_n + \hat{\phi}_n + \Delta\hat{\phi}_n > 2^n$:

  new $\hat{\theta}_n \leftarrow 2^n - (\hat{\theta}_n + \Delta\hat{\theta}_n)$, new $\hat{\phi}_n \leftarrow 2^n - (\hat{\phi}_n + \Delta\hat{\phi}_n)$,

  current sextant is updated from diagonal edge rules in Table B-1 and current octant is unchanged.

- Bottom Edge Wrap Case:

  if $\hat{\theta}_n + \Delta\hat{\theta}_n \geq 0$, $\hat{\phi}_n + \Delta\hat{\phi}_n < 0$, $\hat{\theta}_n + \Delta\hat{\theta}_n - (\hat{\phi}_n + \Delta\hat{\phi}_n) \leq 2^n$:

  new $\hat{\theta}_n \leftarrow \hat{\theta}_n + \Delta\hat{\theta}_n$, new $\hat{\phi}_n \leftarrow -(\hat{\phi}_n + \Delta\hat{\phi}_n)$,

  current sextant is unchanged, and current octant is updated from bottom edge rules in Table B-1.

Any wrap that does not fall into one of these categories is an illegal delta and is not allowed within a valid compressed geometry stream.

(Note that while the wrapping is defined here in terms of a given normal component quantization value n, in most implementations the wrapping would be applied after the current component values and delta values have been normalized into the greatest allowed values, e.g., $n = 6$.)

B.9 Modified Huffman Encoding

There are many techniques known for minimally representing variable-length bit fields. For compressed geometry, we have chosen a variation of the conventional Huffman technique.

The Huffman compression algorithm takes in a set of symbols to be represented, along with frequency of occurrence statistics (histograms) of those symbols. From this, variable-length, uniquely identifiable bit patterns that allow these symbols to be represented with a near-minimum total number of bits are generated, assuming that symbols do occur at the frequencies specified.

Many compression techniques, including JPEG, create unique symbols as tags to indicate the length of a variable-length data field that follows. This data field is typically a specific-length delta value. Thus the final binary stream consists of (self-describing length) variable-length tag symbols, each immediately followed by a data field whose length is associated with that unique tag symbol.

The binary format for compressed geometry uses this technique to represent position, normal, and color data fields. For compressed geometry, these <tag, data> fields are immediately preceded by (a more conventional computer instruction set) opcode field. These fields, plus potential additional operand bits, are referred to as *geometry instructions* (see Figure B-6).

Traditionally, each value to be compressed is assigned its own associated label; for example, an *xyz* delta position would be represented by three tag/value pairs. However, the delta *xyz* values are not uncorrelated, and we can get both a denser and simpler representation by taking advantage of this fact.

In general, the *xyz* deltas statistically point equally in all directions in space. This means that if the number of bits to represent the largest of these deltas is n, then statistically the other two delta values require an average of $n - 1.4$ bits for their representation. Thus we made the decision to use a single field-length tag to indicate the bit length of Δx, Δy, and Δz.

This also means that we cannot take advantage of another Huffman technique that saves somewhat less than one more bit per component, but our bit savings by not having to specify two additional tag fields (for Δy and Δz) outweigh this. A single tag field also means that a hardware decompression engine can decompress all three fields in parallel, if desired.

Similar arguments hold for deltas of $RGB\alpha$ values, and so here also a single field-length tag indicates the bit-length of the ΔR, ΔG, ΔB, and $\Delta\alpha$ (if present) fields.

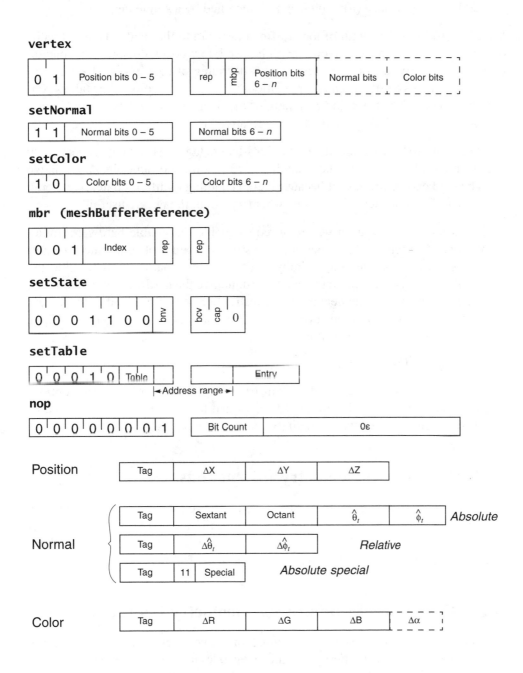

Figure B-6   Bit Layout of Compressed Geometry Instructions

The *u v* index fields of both absolute normals and delta normals are also parameterized by a single value (n), which can be specified by a single tag.

We chose to limit the length of the Huffman tag field to the relatively small value of six bits. This was done to facilitate high-speed, low-cost hardware implementations. (A 64-entry tag look-up table allows decoding of tags in one clock cycle.) Three such tables exist: one each for positions, normals, and colors. The tables contain the length of the tag field, the length of the data field(s), a data normalization coefficient (the up-shift), and an absolute/relative bit.

The tag field can be 0 to 6 bits in length. Zero-length tags are used when every entry in the table is identical: same data length, same up-shift, and same absolute/relative bit. The tag becomes irrelevant because there is nothing to differentiate. In general, there are only a few specialized cases where zero-length tags are useful.

One additional complication was required to enable reasonable hardware implementations. As seen in a later section, all instructions are broken up into an eight-bit header and a variable-length body. Sufficient information to determine the length of the body is present in the header. But to give the hardware time to process the header information, the header of one instruction must be placed in the stream before the body of the previous instruction. Thus the sequence ... B0 H1B1 H2B2 H3 ... has to be encoded as follows:

   ... H1 B0 H2 B1 H3 B2 ...

This *header forwarding* is applied to all instructions. The vertex instruction optionally had one or two subfields that need forwarded headers. In these special cases the headers are only six bits in length, because no opcode is present.

B.10 Compressed Geometry Instructions

Java 3D's compressed geometry protocol defines seven instructions to be used in specifying 3D geometry and certain affiliated attributes. Table B-2 gives a brief overview of these instructions and some of their semantics. More detail of these instructions, including their bit layout, is given in the following sections.

B.11 Bit Layout of Compressed Geometry Instructions

Figure B-6 shows the bit-level layout of the seven geometry decompression instructions. Each instruction has a unique opcode and then some (usually fixed number of) arguments. In the case of the setColor instruction, the number of arguments can be either three or four, depending on the current setting of the cap bit (set by the setState instruction). In the case of the vertex instruction, the number of arguments also varies by the current setting of the setState instruction.

Table B-2   Compressed Geometry Instructions

Instruction	Description
vertex	The primary instruction is vertex. A vertex instruction always specifies a 3D position, two generalized triangle strip replacement bits (rep), a mesh buffer push (mbp) bit, and it may optionally specify a normal and/or a color. The presence of normal or color data within a vertex instruction is controlled by two state bits known as the bundling bits: bnv and bcv, respectively.
setNormal, setColor	There are also two stand-alone instructions for specifying normals and colors: setNormal and setColor. These instructions may be freely interspersed with vertex instructions and semantically have (nearly) the same effect as normals or colors bundled directly with a normal. Once a color or normal value is specified, either directly or bundled with a vertex instruction, that color or normal will remain in effect as the current color or normal until a new value is specified. In this fashion, for example, a constant material color may be specified to apply to a forthcoming sequence of non-color-bundled vertices.
setState	The setState instruction updates the value of the three state bits. Two of these bits are the normal and color bundling bits; the third is color alpha bundling.
mbr	Mesh buffer reference. The mbr instruction allows any of the 16 vertices most recently pushed into the mesh buffer to be reused in place of a vertex instruction at this point. Two vertex replacement bits are also present.
setTable	The setTable instruction allows a range of entries in one of the three Huffman decompression tables, all to be set to the same new value.
nop	The variable length no-operation nop instruction allows the compression bit stream to be padded by a specified number of bits. This allows portions of the compression data to be 32-bit aligned when desired, as required at the end of a compressed geometry block.

The actual bit length of many of the components may vary, and, if so, a unique (dynamic) Huffman tag at the very start of any variable-length argument indirectly specifies the size of the argument.

B.12 Compressed Geometry Instruction Bit Details

The following subsections describe the bit details of the compressed geometry instructions as well as much of their associated semantics. Along with each instruction, its assembly (and disassembly) syntax is described.

B.12.1 nop Instruction

| 0 0 0 0 0 0 0 1 | Bit | 0 – 31 |

Assembly syntax: (nop <Bit count>)

The variable length no-operation (nop) instruction has an 8-bit opcode, a 5-bit count field, and a 0- to 31-bit field of zeros. The total length of the variable-length no-operation instruction is between 13 and 44 bits.

The variable-length nop instruction's primary use is to align compressed geometry instructions to word boundaries, when desired. This is useful if one wishes to "patch" a compressed geometry instruction in the middle of a stream without having to bit-align the patch.

B.12.2 setState Instruction

Assembly syntax: (setState {normalsBundled} {colorsBundled} {alphaBundled})

The setState instruction has a 7-bit opcode, 3 bits of state to be set, and a spare, for a total length of 11 bits. The first and second state bits indicate if normals and/or colors will be bundled with vertex instructions, respectively. The third state bit indicates if colors will contain an alpha value, in addition to the standard RGB. The final state bit is unused and reserved for future use.

In the assembly syntax, the specific unbundling of a value is indicated by three unbundling tags: {normalsUnbundled}, {colorsUnbundled}, {alphaUnbundled}. The six possible bundling tags can be combined in almost any order. If a tag is not present for either bundling or unbundling a value, then the value is implicitly unbundled. It is an error to have both a bundled and an unbundled tag present for the same value in the same setState instruction.

B.12.3   setTable Instruction

Assembly syntax: (setTable <Table> <start fill>-<end fill>
                   <Data Length> <Up-shift> <A/R>)

The setTable instruction has a 5-bit op code, a 2-bit table field, a 7-bit address/range field, a 4-bit data length field, an absolute/relative bit, and a 4-bit up-shift field. The total instruction length is fixed at 23 bits. The table and address/range fields specify which decompression table entries to update; the remaining fields comprise the values to which to update the table entries.

The 2-bit table specifies for which of the three decompression tables this update is targeted:

00   Position

01   Color

10   Normal

11   Unused—reserved for future use

The 7-bit address/range field specifies which entries in the specified table are to be set to the values in the following fields.

Address/Range	Semantics	Implicit Tag Length
$1a_5a_4a_3a_2a_1a_0$	set table entry $a_5a_4a_3a_2a_1a_0$	6
$01a_5a_4a_3a_2a_1$	set table entry $a_5a_4a_3a_2a_10$ through $a_5a_4a_3a_2a_11$	5
$001a_5a_4a_3a_2$	set table entry $a_5a_4a_3a_200$ through $a_5a_4a_3a_211$	4
$0001a_5a_4a_3$	set table entry $a_5a_4a_3000$ through $a_5a_4a_3111$	3
$00001a_5a_4$	set table entry a_5a_40000 through a_5a_41111	2
$000001a_5$	set table entry a_500000 through a_511111	1
0000001	set table entry 000000 through 111111	0

The idea is that table settings are made in aligned power-of-two ranges. The position of the first '1' bit in the address/range field indicates how many entries are to be consecutively set; the remaining bits after the first '1' are the upper address bits of the base of the table entries to be set. This also sets the length of the "tag" that this entry defines as equal to the number of address bits (if any) after the first '1' bit.

The data length specifies how large the delta values to be associated with this tag are; a data length of 12 implies that the upper 4 bits are to be sign extensions of the incoming delta value. Note that the data length describes not the length of the delta value coming in, but the final position of the delta value for reconstruction. In other words, the data length field is the sum of the actual delta bits to be read in plus the up-shift amount. For the position and color tables, the data length values of 1 to 15 correspond to lengths of 1 to 15, but the data length value of 0 encodes an actual length of 16, as a length of 0 makes no sense for positions and colors. For normals, a length of 0 is sometimes appropriate, and the maximum length needed is only 7. Thus for normals, the values 0 to 7 map through 0 to 7, and 8 to 15 are not used.

The up-shift value is the number of bits that the delta values described by these tags will be shifted up before being added to the current value. The up-shift is useful for quantizing the data to save space; it cannot be used to extend the range of the data represented. You are still limited to 16 bits (less for normals) for the resultant data even with a large up-shift value. The up-shift amount is essentially the number of low bits that you don't need to specify in the incoming data since they will always be zero. It is illegal for the up-shift to be greater than or equal to the data length.

So, there are three portions of the resultant data: the sign extension, the incoming data, and the up-shift. For example, if you have a position with a data length of 12 and an up-shift of 4, then the resultant data is made up of 4 sign extension bits in the high bits, 8 bits of incoming data, and 4 bits of zero in the low bits, for the up-shift.

The absolute/relative flag indicates whether this table entry describes values that are to be interpreted as an absolute reference or a relative delta—a 0 value indicates relative, a 1 value indicates absolute. Note that for normals, absolute references will have an additional six leading bits that describe the absolute octant and sextant.

B.12.4   mbr (meshBufferReference) Instruction

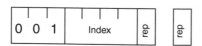

Assembly syntax: (mbr <rep> <index>)

Assembly syntax: <rep>:

RST	Restart
RSTR	Restart reverse
RMID	Replace middle
ROLD	Replace oldest

The mbr (meshBufferReference) instruction has a 3-bit opcode, a 4-bit mesh buffer index field, and a 2-bit vertex replacement field, for a total length of nine bits.

The index specifies which element of the mesh buffer should be used to define the current vertex. A value of 0 indicates to use the most recent vertex that has been pushed into the mesh buffer (before this instruction). Larger values indicate successively less recent pushes. Only the most recent 16 pushes are addressable.

The two-bit vertex replacement field has the same triangle semantics as it does within the vertex instruction:

0 0	Restart reverse
0 1	Restart
1 0	Replace middle
1 1	Replace oldest

There is no mesh buffer repush bit; mesh buffer contents may be referenced multiple times until 16 newer vertices have been pushed: if a vertex is still needed, it must be resent.

In general, the semantics of executing a mesh buffer reference instruction is nearly the same as executing a vertex instruction with data fields identical to those contained at the indicated mesh buffer location. There are, however, several subtle differences. First, as previously indicated, a mesh buffer reference never causes new values to appear in the mesh buffer, nor does it cause any mesh buffer values to go away.

Second, the effects of any intervening setState instructions changing the bundling bits need to be considered. If normals were bundled when the vertex was originally pushed into the mesh buffer, but normals are *not* bundled when the mbr instruction is executed, the old normal value *does not* replace the current normal value. Instead, the mbr instruction will use the current setting of the normal value. The same logic applies to colors and alpha. An mbr instruction accesses only the mesh buffer for those vertex components that are currently bundled.

The inverse case is considered an error: If normals were *not* bundled at the time the vertex instruction pushed a vertex into the mesh buffer, but normals *are* bundled at the time of execution of the mbr instruction, the normal value will be undefined. Such a sequence will result in an invalid Compressed Geometry object. Once again, the same logic applies for colors. A *push* in a vertex instruction causes only the currently bundled vertex components to be stored into the mesh buffer.

There is one more special case: when normals are bundled, if a `setNormal` instruction was executed before an `mbr` instruction and the instructions executed between these two do not include any `vertex` or `setState` (or `mbr`) instructions, the semantics of *normal override* apply. The semantics are that rather than inheriting all the data fields of the vertex from the stored mesh buffer values, the normal value is instead taken from the current normal value, as set by the `setNormal` instruction. This is to allow for hard edges in otherwise shared geometry. The idea is that otherwise there is no logical reason for a `setNormal` instruction that would have been invalidated by the inheritance within the `mbr` instruction. Once again, a similar logic applies to `setColor` instructions and the generation of a color override condition. This supports hard edges in colors. Note that any overrides are invalidated by `setState` or `vertex` instructions and also are no longer in effect after an `mbr` instruction is encountered.

Another effect of overrides is to override the invalidity of normals or colors having not been bundled with vertices at the time of vertices being pushed into the mesh buffer.

B.12.5   Position Subinstruction

0–6	1–16	1–16	1–16
Tag	ΔX	ΔY	ΔZ

Assembly syntax: (`Position` `<Tag>` `<ΔX>` `<ΔY>` `<ΔZ>`)

The `position` subinstruction can appear only within a compressed geometry `vertex` instruction and always as the first subinstruction. The tag field can be between 0 and 6 bits in length; all three delta (or absolute) fields will have the same length, between 1 and 16 bits, for a range of lengths between 3 and 54 bits.

As usual, the first six bits of the subinstruction are actually forwarded ahead of the rest of the instruction. Depending on the length of the tag and delta fields, the first 6 bits might contain only the tag or the tag and some of the X field bits or any subset up to the entire subinstruction, if short enough. However, it is possible for the entire subinstruction to be *too* short. It is not allowed for the tag together with the X, Y, and Z fields to be smaller than the six bits that get forwarded. There can be no "empty" bits in the forwarded header. If necessary, the tag and/or delta (or absolute) fields must be expanded so that the total number of bits used for the entire subinstruction is at least six. (Note that the expanded fields must be correctly described in the decompression table entry for the tag. One cannot simply add padding within a position subinstruction to a field that was previously specified with a shorter length in a `setTable` instruction.)

For clarity, because it is by far the most typical case, the three coordinate bit fields are labeled ΔX ΔY ΔZ, though more properly they are X, Y, and Z fields; their actual interpretation is absolute or relative depending on the setting of that bit in the decompression table entry corresponding to the tag field. In both cases the fields are signed two's-complement numbers.

You must always specify at least one absolute position before using any relative positions. It is illegal to have a relative position before the first absolute position.

It appears that, depending on the current position, half of the possible delta values are illegal. (For ease of understanding these examples, we will treat positions as integers.) For instance, going +10,000 from 30,000 will wrap past the positive limit of 32,767 for signed 16-bit two's-complement arithmetic. However, this turns out to be very useful. For example, if your current X position is –20,000 and the next X position is 30,000 then the difference that you'd like to use as a delta is +50,000, which is not directly representable. When you compute that difference using 16-bit arithmetic, the value wraps to –15,536, which *can* be represented as a delta. When –15,536 is added back to –20,000 on decompression, instead of getting –35,536, again the 16-bit arithmetic wraps and we get 30,000, which is the desired result.

B.12.6   Color Subinstruction

0–6	1–16	1–16	1–16	1–16
Tag	ΔR	ΔG	ΔB	$\Delta \alpha$

Assembly syntax: (Color <Tag> <ΔR> <ΔG> <ΔB> {<$\Delta \alpha$>})

The color subinstruction can appear within either a compressed geometry vertex instruction or a setColor instruction. The tag field can be between 0 and 6 bits in length; all three (or four) delta (or absolute) fields will have the same length, between 1 and 16 bits, for a range of lengths between 3 and 54 (or 70) bits. As usual, any subinstruction with a total length of less than 6 bits has trailing zeros added to pad the length to a minimum of 6 bits.

As usual, the first six bits of the subinstruction are actually forwarded ahead of the rest of the instruction. Depending on the length of the tag and delta fields, the first six bits might contain only the tag or the tag and some of the R field bits or any subset up to the entire subinstruction, if short enough. However, it is possible for the entire subinstruction to be *too* short. It is not allowed for the tag together with the R, G, and B (and α) fields to be smaller than the six bits that get forwarded. There can be no "empty" bits in the forwarded header. If necessary, the tag and/or delta (or absolute) fields must be expanded so that the total number of bits used for the entire subinstruction is at least six.

For clarity, because it is by far the most typical case, the color component bit-fields are labeled ΔR ΔG ΔB ($\Delta \alpha$), though more properly they are R, G, and B fields: their actual interpretation is absolute or relative depending on the setting of that bit in the decompression table entry corresponding to the tag field. In both cases the fields are signed two's-complement numbers. A sign bit is required for absolute color components. Negative color components make no sense and are ill-defined, so the sign bit on absolute components should always be zero. Similarly for delta color components, a negative result from adding a delta component to the current component makes no sense, and so negative results are also ill-defined.

If the most recent setting of the `cap` bit by a `setState` instruction is zero, then no fourth (alpha) field will be expected and must not be present. If the `cap` bit was set, then the alpha field will be processed and must be present.

You must always specify at least one absolute color before using any relative colors. It is illegal to have a relative color before the first absolute color.

The rest of the graphics pipeline and frame buffer following the geometry decompression stage may choose not to use all (up to) 16 bits of color component information; in this case, it is acceptable to truncate the trailing bits during decompression. What the geometry decompression format does require is that color setting of any size up to 16 bits be supported, even if all the bits are not used. Typically, implementations may use just 12 bits, 8 bits, or even 5 bits from each color component.

B.12.7 Normal Subinstruction

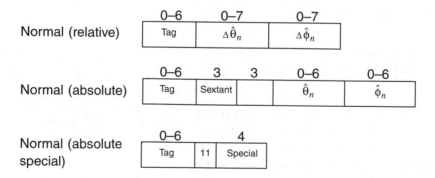

Assembly syntax: absolute: (`Normal` `<Tag><Sextant><Octant><`$\hat{\theta}_n$`><`$\hat{\phi}_n$`>`)

Assembly syntax: relative: (Normal <Tag> <$\Delta\hat{\theta}_n$> <$\Delta\hat{\phi}_n$>)

Assembly syntax: special: (Normal <Tag> <Special>)

Assembly syntax: <Sextant>: 0,1,2,3,4,5 (as specified in Figure B-3)

Assembly syntax: Table B-3 shows the assembly format for specifying octants in the <octant> field of Normal subinstructions (as well as setNormal instructions).

Table B-3   Syntax for Specifying Octants

Syntax	Octant
+++	+X +Y +Z
++-	+X +Y –Z
+-+	+X –Y +Z
+--	+X –Y –Z
-++	–X +Y +Z
-+-	–X +Y –Z
--+	–X –Y +Z
---	–X –Y –Z

Assembly syntax: Table B-4 shows the assembly syntax for specifying the special normals in the "Special" field of Normal subinstructions (as well as setNormal instructions).

The Normal subinstruction can appear within either a compressed geometry vertex instruction or a setNormal instruction. The tag field can be between 0 and 6 bits in length; the last two angle fields will have the same length, between 0 and 7 bits for deltas and between 0 and 6 bits for absolutes. Six more bits are always present for absolute normals. The range of sizes for a relative normal can be from 6 to 20 bits, and an absolute normal can be from 6 to 24 bits.

As usual, the first six bits of the subinstruction are actually forwarded ahead of the rest of the instruction. Depending on the length of the tag and delta fields, the first six bits might contain only the tag or the tag and some of the other field bits or any subset up to the entire subinstruction, if short enough. However, in the case of relative normals, it is possible for the entire subinstruction to be *too* short. It is not allowed for the tag together with the delta angle fields to be smaller than the six bits that get forwarded. There can be no "empty" bits in the forwarded header. If necessary, the tag and/or delta angle fields must be expanded so that the total number of bits used for the entire subinstruction is at least six.

Table B-4   Syntax for Specifying Special Normals

Syntax	Special	NX	NY	NZ	Comment
+00	0000	1.0	0.0	0.0	+X axis
–00	0010	–1.0	0.0	0.0	–X axis
0+0	0100	0.0	1.0	0.0	+Y axis
0–0	0110	0.0	–1.0	0.0	–Y axis
00+	1000	0.0	0.0	1.0	+Z axis
00–	1010	0.0	0.0	–1.0	–Z axis
+++	0001	$1/\sqrt{3}$	$1/\sqrt{3}$	$1/\sqrt{3}$	+X +Y +Z
++–	0011	$1/\sqrt{3}$	$1/\sqrt{3}$	$1/\sqrt{3}$	+X +Y –Z
+–+	0101	$1/\sqrt{3}$	$1/\sqrt{3}$	$1/\sqrt{3}$	+X –Y +Z
+––	0111	$1/\sqrt{3}$	$1/\sqrt{3}$	$1/\sqrt{3}$	+X –Y –Z
–++	1001	$1/\sqrt{3}$	$1/\sqrt{3}$	$1/\sqrt{3}$	–X +Y +Z
–+–	1011	$1/\sqrt{3}$	$1/\sqrt{3}$	$1/\sqrt{3}$	–X +Y –Z
––+	1101	$1/\sqrt{3}$	$1/\sqrt{3}$	$1/\sqrt{3}$	–X –Y +Z
–––	1111	$1/\sqrt{3}$	$1/\sqrt{3}$	$1/\sqrt{3}$	–X –Y –Z

A `Normal` subinstruction is interpreted as relative or absolute depending on the current setting of that bit in the decompression table entry corresponding to the tag field. Unlike the `Position` and `Color` subinstructions, the number of fields of a `Normal` instruction differs between the absolute and relative types.

When the subinstruction is relative, there are two delta angle fields after the tag field, both of the same length, up to seven bits. These two fields are signed two's-complement numbers. If, after delta addition, the resulting angle is outside the current sextant or octant, the sextant/octant wrapping rules (described elsewhere) apply. If zero-length angle fields are specified, this is equivalent to specifying a zero value for both fields, i.e., no change from the previous normal. It may be easier to use this method rather than turning off normal bundling for a small number of identical normals.

When the subinstruction is absolute, four bit fields follow the tag. The first is a three-bit (fixed-length) absolute sextant field, indicating in which of six sextants of an octant of the unit sphere this normal resides. The second field is also fixed at three bits, and indicates in which octant of the unit sphere the normal resides. The last two fields are absolute angles within the sextant and are unsigned positive numbers, up to six bits in length. If zero-length angle fields are specified, this is equivalent to specifying a zero for both fields.

At least one absolute normal must be specified before using any relative normals. It is an error to have any relative normals before the first absolute normal.

Note that sextants are triangular in shape; thus the range of valid angular coordinates within a sextant fills only half the square, plus the diagonal. Formally, after shift normalization, angular coordinates in ordinary absolute normals must obey the rule:

$$\hat{\theta}_6 + \hat{\phi}_6 \leq 64, \quad 0 \leq \hat{\theta}_6 < 64, \quad 0 \leq \hat{\phi}_6 < 64$$

A number of normals lie on the edges or corners where sextants meet (e.g., at $\hat{\theta}_n = 0$ and $\hat{\phi}_n = 0$). These normals do not have a unique encoding; the same normal can be specified using different sextants or octants. All of these encodings are legal; usually the choice of encoding is decided by using the one that makes it the easiest to compute deltas from the previous and/or to the following normal.

Fourteen special absolute normals are encoded by the unused two settings within the three sextant bits. This is indicated by specifying the angle fields to have a length of zero (not present) and the first two bits of the sextant field to both have a value of 1. Table B-5 lists the 14 special normals

Table B-5   The 14 Special Normals

Special	NX	NY	NZ	Comment
0000	1.0	0.0	0.0	+X axis
0010	−1.0	0.0	0.0	−X axis
0100	0.0	1.0	0.0	+Y axis
0110	0.0	−1.0	0.0	−Y axis
1000	0.0	0.0	1.0	+Z axis
1010	0.0	0.0	−1.0	−Z axis
0001	$1/\sqrt{3}$	$1/\sqrt{3}$	$1/\sqrt{3}$	+X +Y +Z
0011	$1/\sqrt{3}$	$1/\sqrt{3}$	$1/\sqrt{3}$	+X +Y −Z
0101	$1/\sqrt{3}$	$1/\sqrt{3}$	$1/\sqrt{3}$	+X −Y +Z
0111	$1/\sqrt{3}$	$1/\sqrt{3}$	$1/\sqrt{3}$	+X −Y −Z
1001	$1/\sqrt{3}$	$1/\sqrt{3}$	$1/\sqrt{3}$	−X +Y +Z
1011	$1/\sqrt{3}$	$1/\sqrt{3}$	$1/\sqrt{3}$	−X +Y −Z
1101	$1/\sqrt{3}$	$1/\sqrt{3}$	$1/\sqrt{3}$	−X −Y +Z
1111	$1/\sqrt{3}$	$1/\sqrt{3}$	$1/\sqrt{3}$	−X −Y −Z

Special normals are always absolute normals; they cannot be delta'd to from a previous normal. Unlike ordinary absolute normals, delta normals have the additional restriction that they cannot be delta'd *from*. Thus, the next normal after any special normal must always be an absolute normal (ordinary or special). In some cases, this overhead can be avoided by never landing on a special normal, when this perturbation of the data does not negatively impact the visual appearance of the object.

The rest of the graphics pipeline and frame buffer following the geometry decompression stage may choose not to use all (up to) 16 bits of normal component information; in this case it is acceptable to truncate the trailing bits during decompression. What the compressed geometry format does require is that normal settings of any size up to 18-bit absolute normals be supported, even if all the decompressed bits are not used.

B.12.8   vertex Instruction

Assembly syntax: `(vertex <rep> {push}`
`<position subinstruction>`
`            {<normal subinstruction>}`
`{<color subinstruction>})`

Assembly syntax: `<rep>`:

RST	Restart
RSTR	Restart reverse
RMID	Replace middle
ROLD	Replace oldest

The `vertex` instruction has a two-bit opcode, a `position` subinstruction (always), a two-bit vertex replacement field, a mesh buffer push bit, and, optionally, a `normal` subinstruction and/or a `color` instruction, depending on the current setting of the state bundling bits. The two-bit vertex replacement field has the same triangle semantics as it does within the `mbr` instruction:

0 0	Restart reverse
0 1	Restart
1 0	Replace middle
1 1	Replace oldest

The mesh buffer push bit indicates whether this vertex should be pushed into the mesh buffer so as to be eligible for later rereference.

The `Position`, `Normal`, and `Color` subinstructions have the semantics documented in their individual sections.

B.12.9   setNormal Instruction

| 1 ' 1 | Normal bits 0 – 5 | | Normal bits 6 – *n* |

Assembly syntax: absolute: (setNormal <Tag> <Sextant> <Octant> <$\hat{\theta}_n$> <$\hat{\phi}_n$>)

Assembly syntax: relative: (setNormal <Tag> <$\Delta\hat{\theta}_n$> <$\Delta\hat{\phi}_n$>)

Assembly syntax: absolute special: (setNormal <Tag> <Special>)

Assembly syntax: <Sextant>, <Octant>, <Special>: *same as for normal subinstruction.*

The `setNormal` instruction has a two-bit opcode and a `Normal` subinstruction.

The `Normal` subinstruction has the semantics documented in Section B.12.7, "Normal Subinstruction."

If a `SetNormal` instruction is present immediately before an `mbr` instruction, then the new normal value overrides the normal data present in the mesh buffer for that particular mesh buffer reference.

B.12.10 setColor Instruction

| 1 ' 0 | Color bits 0 – 5 | | Color bits 6 – *n* |

Assembly syntax: (setColor <Tag> <ΔR> <ΔG> <ΔB> {<$\Delta\alpha$>})

The `setColor` instruction has a two-bit opcode and a `color` subinstruction. The `color` subinstruction semantics are documented in Section B.12.6, "Color Subinstruction."

If a `setColor` instruction is present immediately before an `mbr` (`meshBufferReference`) instruction, then the new color value overrides the color data present in the mesh buffer for that particular mesh buffer reference.

B.13 Semantics of Compressed Geometry Instructions

The formal semantics of the compressed geometry format is best described by a state description of the decompression process. It must be emphasized that these state descriptions are given to show the formal semantics, not an efficient implementation.

The next few sections will present such a state description. While this description is intended to be a complete and unambiguous description of the compressed geometry format and decompression semantics, in practice studying both the compression process and the decompression process, and studying code examples for both, is a better approach for the human understanding process.

B.13.1 Header and Body to Variable-Length Instruction

Compressed geometry instructions have a minimum length of eight bits (six bits for subinstructions). This allows all geometry decompression instructions to be split into two physically separate bit sequences within the compressed stream. The first bit sequence is always of eight bits in length (six for subinstructions); the second bit sequence contains the remaining bits of the instruction (if any). Thus a logical stream of N compressed geometry instructions, where each instruction is split into two bit sequences H_i and B_i (i being from 0 to $N-1$), is physically represented as

$$H_0 \ B_{-1} \ H_1 \ B_0 \ H_2 \ B_1 \ \ldots \ H_{n-1} \ B_{n-2} \ H_n \ B_{n-1}$$

Okay, so what is this "B_{-1}"? All compressed geometry sequences have an implied (not physically present) H_{-1} of a nop opcode, thus B_{-1} is always present (starting at the eighth bit of the stream) as any valid variable-length nop body. (Just five zeros, the minimum-length nop, is a good default.) Thus the implied nop opcode "jump starts" the header-forwarded decompression process. This process is reversed at the end of the stream. H_n is a nop opcode, but no body is present, as B_{n-1} is the last bits of the stream. (As will be described, B_{n-1} must end on a 32-bit aligned boundary.)

This is viable because all compressed geometry streams are presented along with a total bit length of their contents, so no explicit end-of-stream marker is needed. Streams *must* be rounded up to the nearest full 64-bit word multiple by use of additional variable-length nop instructions of appropriate lengths (within the body of the stream, that is, their headers appear before H_n). This implies that H_{n-1} is usually a nop instruction used to force alignment.

This "header-forwarding" shuffled representation is necessary for hardware decompressors to operate efficiently. While this is not an issue for purely software-based decompressor implementations, in order to have one canonical format for both hard and soft decompressors, all decompressors must operate only on the header-forwarded representation; this is the only "official" compression bit-format specified. For a software decompressor, the extra unshuffling adds only slightly to the overall overhead of decompression; for hardware, it is essential.

Thus the first stage in the decompression process is to put the two separate bit sequences for each instruction back together. The next paragraph describes the flavor of this process, going around the loop approximately one and one-half times. The actual process is more accurately described in state machine semantics.

First, the fixed-length eight- (or six-) bit header for the next full instruction (or subinstruction) to be processed is detached from the current head of the compressed stream. Next, the variable-length body bits for the previous instruction (or subinstruction) are detached from the compressed stream and combined with the already extracted header for the previous instruction; the previous instruction is complete and can be processed. Now the fixed-length header for the instruction after the next is detached from the bit stream and then finally the variable-length body for the next full instruction can be detached; the next instruction is now complete and can be processed.

```
// pseudocode for converting bitstream into sequences of
// instructions
decompress(stream) {
    current_header <- nop
    while (not_empty(stream)) {
        next_header <- get_header_bits(stream)
        current_body <- get_n_bits(stream,
                                   body_length(previous_header))
        process_instruction(current_header, current_body)
        current_header <- next_header
    }
}
```

One slight complexity: The get_header_bits() extracts only six bits of header for color or normal subinstructions of a vertex instruction. It extracts a full eight bits of header in all other cases.

B.13.2   Variable-Length Instruction to Instruction

The three decompression tables contain entries for each different numeric tag describing whether the value in the stream is absolute or relative, and length and shift constants describing how to convert the variable-length bit field back into a fixed-length value. The fixed-length value for position and color components is 16 bits in length (sign, unit, 14 fraction); the fields for normal angles are 7 bits (signed) and 3 each for sextant and octant (if present).

B.13.3   Delta Position to Position

```
absolute_position(x, y, z):
   cur_x ← x, cur_y ← y, cur_z ← z

relative_position(Δx, Δy, Δz):
   cur_x ← cur_x + Δx, cur_y ← cur_y + Δy, cur_z ← cur_z + Δz
```

B.13.4   Delta Color to Color

```
absolute_color(r, g, b {, α}):
   cur_r ← r, cur_g ← g, cur_b ← b, {cur_α ← α }

relative_color(Δr, Δg, Δb {, Δα}):
   cur_r ← cur_r + Δr, cur_g ← cur_g + Δg, cur_b ← cur_b + Δb,
   {cur_α ← cur_α + Δα }
```

B.13.5   Encoded Delta Normal to Encoded Normal

State: cur_oct, cur_sex, cur_u, cur_v

```
absolute_normal(oct, sex, u, v):
   cur_oct ← oct, cur_sex ← sex, cur_u ← u, cur_v ← v

relative_normal(Δu, Δv):
```

```
   cur_u ← cur_u + Δu, cur_v ← cur_v + Δv,
   if (cur_u < 0)
      cur_u ← -cur_u, cur_sex ← flip_u[cur_sex]
   else if (cur_v < 0)
      cur_v ← -cur_v, cur_oct ← cur_oct <xor> flip_v[cur_sex]
   else if (cur_u + cur_v > 64)
      cur_u ← 64 - cur_u, cur_v ← 64 - cur_v,
      cur_sex ← flip_uv[cur_sex]

   flip_u[6]  = { 4, 5, 3, 2, 0, 1 }
   flip_v[6]  = { 2, 4, 1, 1, 2, 4 }
   flip_uv[6] = { 2, 3, 0, 1, 5, 4 }
```

B.13.6   Encoded Normal to Rectilinear Normal

```
nx ← norms[v,u].nx,   ny ← norms[v,u].ny,   nz ← norms[v,u].nz,
if (cur_sex & 4) t ← nx, nx ← nz, nz ← t
if (cur_sex & 2) t ← ny, ny ← nz, nz ← t
if (cur_sex & 1) t ← nx, nx ← ny, ny ← t
if (cur_oct & 1) nz ← -nz
if (cur_oct & 2) ny ← -ny
if (cur_oct & 4) nx ← -nx
```

The contents of the norms[] table is exactly specified, and the next revision of this specification will contain an exact listing of the values.

B.14 Semantics of Vertices

The formal semantics of the vertex processing is best described by a state description of the decompression process. Once again it must be emphasized that these state descriptions are given to show the formal semantics, not an efficient implementation.

B.14.1   Instruction to Vertex

This section describes the state change semantics caused by each instruction to generate the next output vertex, prior to assembly into triangles. The internal state consists of the three bundling bits, a current normal and current color, normal_override and color_override bits, the 16 mesh buffer vertices, and a current internal-cycling mesh buffer index.

```
normal(n):
    current_normal ← n, normal_override ← 1

color(c):
    current_color ← c, color_override ← 1

vertex(rep, mbp, p {, n} {, c}):
```

```
current_position ← p,
if (bnv) current_normal ← n,
if (bcv) current_color ← c,
output_vertex(rep, current_position, current_normal,
              current_color)
if (push) mesh_buffer[mesh_index].position      ← p
```

```
if (push && bnv) mesh_buffer[mesh_index].normal ← n
if (push && bcv) mesh_buffer[mesh_index].color  ← c
if (push) mesh_index ← (mesh_index+1) & 15
normal_override ← 0, color_override ← 0
```

mesh buffer reference(rep, i):

```
current_position ←
        mesh_buffer[(mesh_index - i - 1) & 15].position
if (bnv && !normal_override)
    current_color ← mesh_buffer[(mesh_index - i - 1) & 15].color
if (bcv && !color_override)
    current_color ← mesh_buffer[(mesh_index - i - 1) & 15].color
normal_override ← 0, color_override ← 0
output_vertex(rep, current_position, current_normal,
              current_color)
```

set state(new_bnv, new_bcv, new_cap):

```
bnv ← new_bnv,
bcv ← new_bcv,
cap ← new_cap,
normal_override ← 0, color_override ← 0
```

set table(address, range, entry):
        ...

nop(length):
        (null)

B.14.2   Vertex to Intermediate Triangle

This section describes the formal semantics of assembling vertices with replacement instructions into nearly finished triangles: the semantics of generalized triangle strips.

```
output_vertex(restart_reverse, newv):
    newest ← newv, number_of_vertices ← 1, rev = 1

output_vertex(restart, newv):
    newest ← newv, number_of_vertices ← 1, rev = 0
```

```
output_vertex(replace_middle, newv):
```

```
    if (number_of_vertices < 2)
        middle ← newest, newest ← newv, number_of_vertices++
    else if (number_of_vertices < 3)
        oldest ← middle, middle ← newest, newest ← newv,
        number_of_vertices++,
        intermediate_triangle(restart, oldest, middle, newest)
    else if (number_of_vertices == 3)
        middle ← newest, newest ← newv,
        intermediate_triangle(restart, oldest, middle, newest)
```

```
output_vertex(replace_oldest, newv):
```

```
    if (number_of_vertices < 2)
        middle ← newest, newest ← newv, number_of_vertices++
    else if (number_of_vertices < 3)
        oldest ← middle, middle ← newest, newest ← newv,
        number_of_vertices++,
        intermediate_triangle(restart, oldest, middle, newest)
    else if (number_of_vertices == 3)
        oldest ← middle, middle ← newest, newest ← newv,
        rev = 1 - rev,
        intermediate_triangle(restart, oldest, middle, newest)
```

B.14.3   Intermediate Triangle to Final Triangle

The final stage is to take into account the current reverse bit. This bit controls the order in which the vertices are output to ensure they all face the correct way.

```
intermediate_triangle(rev, v1, v2, v3):
```

```
    if (!rev)
        final_triangle(v1.position, v1.normal, v1.color,
                       v2.position, v2.normal, v2.color,
                       v3.position, v3.normal, v3.color)
    else if (rev)
        final_triangle(v2.position, v2.normal, v2.color,
                       v1.position, v1.normal, v1.color,
                       v3.position, v3.normal, v3.color)
```

B.15 Outline of Geometry Process

Java 3D formally defines only the compressed geometry format and the decompression semantics. Authoring tools are free to employ whatever compressed geometry algorithms they choose, as long as the results adhere to the specifications described in the previous sections.

However, to further document the semantics of the compressed geometry format, an overview of one particular compressed geometry algorithm is given here.

B.15.1   Compressing Geometry Data

Group the geometry to be compressed into separate rigid objects. Typically such objects will be individually culled during rendering, so you should not join objects too extensively prior to compression. In optimized systems, the granularity of object splitting will be computed by an algorithm that takes culling optimization into account (both frustum and occlusion culling).

B.15.2   Convert to Generalized Mesh Format

Once a group of geometry has been identified, it is next converted into generalized mesh format. This is a complex step, and a number of topological analysis-based algorithms have been applied to it. Note that to reduce compression time, when space is a less important issue than time, a compressor might only stripify, not meshify. Alternatively, the triangles have to have come from somewhere, and that in many cases is a tessellator of higher order surfaces. Such a tessellator will implicitly know the mesh connectivity and may be able to generate the triangle data directly in the generalized mesh format.

The next step is the quantization of the geometry positions, colors, and/or normals. All these quantizations can be varied within the geometry, but for simplicity a single fixed quantization of each is assumed here.

B.15.3   Position

Normalize the position data.

The containing bounding box for the object is computed. This is the minimal box such that all geometry vertices are contained within it. The vertices are then all normalized to be contained within this bounding box by first subtracting the XYZ location of the bounding box center from the vertex XYZ and then dividing all the XYZ vertex values by the half length of the longest side of the bounding box. Thus all normalized positions will be within the ±1 unit cube. A constant matrix transform corresponding to an offset to the center of the bounding box and an inverse scale by the half length of the longest side of the bounding box are created as a prologue for the geometry data. Note that in practice a little more care must be taken. The greatest positive value is actually $(2^{n-1}-1)/2^{n-1}$, when positions are quantized to n bits. By symmetry, the smallest negative value allowed is $-(2^{n-1}-1)/2^{n-1}$. The value -1 (only sign bit set, all other bits 0) is explicitly not allowed. Thus when computing the scale factor (and center) that will normalize the geometry, the actual representation range needs to be taken into account.

Quantize the position data.

Assuming that position data is to be quantized to n bits, each vertex position component should be multiplied by the value of 2^n and then rounded down to the nearest integer. If rounded to the nearest integer, or rounded up, the value may overflow the representation. Once again the goal is to take numbers from a given floating point range and represent all of them within an n-bit fixed point range.

B.15.4 Normals

Normalize the normals.

Each normal should be normalized to unit length.

Quantize the XYZ components of the normal to 14 bits accuracy.

Each normal component should be multiplied by 2^{14}, rounded to the nearest integer, and then converted back to floating-point representation and divided by 2^{14}.

Fold the XYZ components of the normal to the positive (prime) octant.

If an XYZ component of the normal is negative, invert it and save the original sign bits as a three-bit octant value. It is important when compressing always to strip the sign bits off first before applying sextant folding and to reverse the process when decompressing. Note that the octant bits read left to right: the upper bit is for the *x*-axis, the middle for the *y*-axis, and the lowermost for the *z*-axis.

```
oct = 0;
if(nx < 0.0) oct |= 4, nx = -nx
if(ny < 0.0) oct |= 2, ny = -ny
if(nz < 0.0) oct |= 1, nz = -nz
```

Fold the normal to the nX ≥ nZ ≥ nY sextant.

Check (in exactly the following order):

```
sex = 0;
if (nx < ny) t = nx, nx = ny, ny = t, sex |= 1
if (nz < ny) t = ny, ny = nz, nz = t, sex |= 2
if (nx < nz) t = nx, nx = nz, nz = t, sex |= 4
```

Match the nearest quantized normal representation.

Take the dot product of the normal with each of the quantized reference normals in the table for the specified number of quantized normal bits. That u,v normal index for the reference normal that gives the greatest (nearest unity) dot product result is the new quantized normal representation (along with the octant and sextant representation). (There are more efficient ways to compute the same results.) At this point there are no specific tie-breaking rules when two (or more) reference normals produce the same candidate dot product results. Technically this is purely a compressor internal issue.

Check for special normals.

The u,v normal index generated by the previous stage will generally be in the full 7-bit range of the normal grid space. In this space, the two classes of special normals occur when $u = 64$, $v = 0$, and when $u = 0$, $v = 64$. When this is detected, the sextant and octant bits must be examined to produce the proper special normal encoding:

```
if (u == 64 && v ==  0) {  /* Six coordinate axis case */
        if (sex == 0 || sex == 2) /* +/- x-axis */
            special = ((oct & 4)?0x2:0);
        else if (sex == 3 || sex == 1) /* +/- y-axis */
            special = 4 | ((oct & 2)?0x2:0);
        else if (sex == 5 || sex == 4) /* +/- z-axis */
            special = 0x8 | ((oct & 1)?0x2:0);
} else
    if (u ==  0 && v == 64) /* Eight mid point case */
        special = (oct<<1) | 1;
```

B.15.5   Colors

To begin with, the colors are assumed to be in a 0.0 to 0.9 representation.

Quantize the color values.

Assuming that color data is to be quantized to n bits, each vertex color component (R, G, B, and optionally α) should be multiplied by the value of 2^n and then rounded down to the nearest integer. Just as with positions, there is no true representation of positive unity.

B.15.6   Collect Delta Code Statistics

Make a pass in generalized mesh order through all vertices in the geometry. For each successive pair of vertices, compute the difference between their component values, compute the bit length of this (signed) difference, and histogram this bit length. Specifics for each component type are detailed in the following sections.

B.15.7   Position Delta Code Statistics

Compute ΔX, ΔY, and ΔZ. Determine which of these has the greatest magnitude. Compute the number of bits for this component, including one sign bit. This is the length to be histogrammed for positions.

B.15.8   Color Delta Code Statistics

Compute ΔR, ΔG, ΔB, and $\Delta\alpha$ (if present). Determine which of these has the greatest magnitude. Compute the number of bits for this component, including one sign bit. This is the length to be histogrammed for colors.

B.15.9   Normal Delta Code Statistics

For a given pair of normals, check to see if they have the same octant and sextant, and that neither is a special normal. If so, compute ΔU and ΔV. Determine which of these has the greatest magnitude. Compute the number of bits for this component, including one sign bit. This is the length to be histogrammed for this pair of normals.

If the normals have different sextants and/or octants, but neither is a special normal, check to see if their sextants share an edge. If so, the special normal wrapping rules from Section B.8.3, "Special Warping Rules for Delta Normals," can be applied. Depending on what type of edge they share, the delta including the change in edges is encoded in one of three ways: $U + \Delta U < 0$, $V + \Delta V < 0$, and $U + \Delta U + V + \Delta V > 64$. Each case is discussed in the following paragraphs. The sextant numbers are from the binary codes shown in Figure B-3.

499

Sextants 0 and 4, 1 and 5, and 2 and 3 share the U = 0 edge. When crossing this boundary, ΔU becomes ~U – `last_u`. This will generate a negative `cur_u` value during decompression, which causes the decompressor to invert `cur_u` and look up the new sextant in a table.

Sextants 0 and 2, 1 and 3, and 4 and 5 share the U + V = 64 edge. ΔU becomes 64 – U – `last_u`, and ΔV becomes 64 – V – `last_v`. When `cur_u` + `cur_v` > 64, the decompressor sets `cur_u` = 64 – `cur_u` and `cur_v` = 64 – `cur_v`, and a table lookup determines the new sextant.

Each sextant shares the V = 0 edge with its corresponding sextant in another octant. When in sextants 1 or 5, the normal moves across the X-axis, across the Y-axis for sextants 0 or 4, and across the Z-axis for sextants 2 or 3. ΔV becomes ~V – `last_v`. The decompressor inverts a negative `cur_v` and performs a table lookup for a mask to exclusive-OR with the current octant value.

Note: When using the normal wrapping rules, a subtle bug can be introduced due to the ambiguity of normals on a shared edge between two sextants. The normal encoding rules have unambiguous tie-breaking rules to determine which octant and sextant a given normal resides in. However, the wrapping rules assume by default that a delta'd normal is in the *same* sextant and octant as its predecessor if the delta landed only on an edge. This is subtly different than the sextant and octant that the encoding rules might have suggested. The proper procedure is to keep track of which octant and sextant a decompressor would believe that the normals being generated would lie in. When the normal to delta to lands on an edge of this region, change its sextant and octant from what the encoding rules suggest are the same as where it is now delta-ing from. This change in default encoding is permissible because the rectilinear normal encoded by values on a sextant edge is identical no, matter which sextant claims ownership.

Otherwise the normals cannot be delta encoded, and so the second (target) normal must be represented by an absolute reference to its three octant, three sextant, and 2 *n*-bit u, v addresses. This is the length to be histogrammed for this pair of normals.

Note: Slightly higher compression density can be achieved at a slight expense in representation accuracy by avoiding special normals when delta and wrapping differences are generating compact results. Instead of generating the special normal, a near-by nonspecial normal can be generated allowing for compact deltas. As with any compression technique that intentionally further modifies or distorts the input data, doing this normal perturbation must be a policy choice of the compressor itself and subject to quality constraints of the user.

B.15.10 Assign Huffman Tags

Encode data into variable-bit length compressed geometry instructions.

One can use an algorithm similar to the one used by the JPEG image compression standard. The main differences are how codes are reassigned when their lengths exceed the maximum code length, how the data bits are encoded in the compressed data stream, and also how they support additional attributes for codes (relative/absolute, how many bits of left shift).

The frequencies of the data lengths are used as leaf nodes in a binary tree. The algorithm used to generate the tree places the less-frequent codes deeper in the tree. After the tree is built, the traversal path to a leaf node becomes its Huffman code, and the depth in the tree becomes its code length.

Codes generated with a length greater than six, the maximum code length, must be shortened. These nodes are merged with more frequent nodes by increasing the number of sign bits included with the smaller data length.

B.15.11 Assemble the Pieces into a Bit Stream

Given the sequence of variable-bit-length compressed geometry instructions, shuffle the first eight (six) bits of each instruction ahead of its predecessor's body.

B.16 Compressed Geometry Assembly Syntax

This section describes the assembly syntax for both the input to an assembler for compressed geometry, and for the output of a disassembler of compressed geometry.

The concept of a verbose ASCII assembly syntax for a compressed binary format may seem like an oxymoron, but in fact a well-defined assembly format is an invaluable aid to debugging both compressors and decompressors. The ASCII assembly format is *not* meant to be a representation used for the transport of compressed geometry; rather, it is a debugging aid for those involved in programming compressors and decompressors and building hardware decompressors. The assembly format is also useful for generating and understanding test vectors. Both an assembler and a disassembler are available as stand-alone C programs as tools.

For generating compressed geometry programmatically, a number of C- and Java-based low-level compression tools are also available. With the possible exception of test vectors, software-based compressors should use these direct binary output routines; having a compressor generate an intermediate ASCII file representation only then to be assembled into binary is needlessly inefficient. If there is a need to examine the output of a compressor in a human readable form, a binary compressed geometry file can always be disassembled into ASCII by the disassembler when needed.

Because compressed geometry is a tightly encoded binary format, to make dissembled output more understandable, it is appropriate to perform some partial decompression optionally before generating the text output. Thus the compressed geometry disassembler supports multiple levels of decompression during disassembly. On the other hand, the compressed geometry assembler is not a compressor and thus supports as input the only lowest level syntax. There are five layers of successively more decompressed disassembly, with each level printed using either decimal or hex numbers. The five layers and two numeric formats are expressed as ten different levels of disassembly (with every other level just indicating that hex output for integer fields):

1. Nearly raw. After a symbolic opcode, decimal (or optionally, hex) numbers are printed for the modified Huffman tag field and for all data fields without any additional interpretation, scaling, or un-delta-ing, except that proper signed/unsigned semantics are followed. The only processing is to parse the incoming bit stream into bit fields and to undo the effects of header forwarding. The modified Huffman tag is used only to determine the length of the tag field and the following data fields. The opcode has no trailing letter modifiers (as documented below); this indicates level 1.

2. Same as level 1, but printed using hex numbers (preceded with a 0x suffix).

3. Modified Huffman tag expanded. The properties of the modified Huffman tag are shown in line: the length of the tag, the length of the data fields, and the left normalization shift for the field. The absolute/relative bit value is shown by appending the letter 'A' or 'R' to the opcode (or 'S' for absolute 'special' normals).

4. Same as level 3, but printed using hex numbers (preceded with the 0x suffix).

5. Normalized. The left normalization shift is applied to the data fields, and the specific properties of the modified Huffman tag are no longer shown. To differentiate from level 2, the letter 'N' is appended to the opcode name after the absolute/relative/special letter.

6. Same as level 5, but printed using hex numbers (preceded with the 0x suffix).

7. Un-delta'd. Like level 3, but relative values have had the running total added to them to show what the current full value is. Absolute values are unchanged from level 3. To differentiate from level 4, an 'A' suffix is added to the lengthening opcode name.

8. Same as level 7, but printed using hex numbers (preceded with the 0x suffix).

9. Floating point. While up to now all values have been subsets of 16-bit integers, before conversion to integer and quantization, most values were floating-point numbers in the 0 to 1.0 or −1.0 to 1.0 range. Level 5 shows the values as floating-point numbers, but it must be cautioned that these data fields, while similar to the input uncompressed unquantized values, will usually be slightly different in value than the original data. This floating-point output format is primarily included as a convenience when a user wants to understand the data closer to the original space.

10. Same as level 9, but non-floating-point numbers are printed using hex numbers (preceded with the 0x suffix).

Once again while the dissembler supports all 10 levels of output options, the assembler supports only levels 1 and 2.

The syntax is fairly simple. Because the setting Colors or Normals can be either standalone instructions or components of a vertex instruction, parenthetic instruction grouping (lisp style) is used to make the ownership of arguments clear.

As an example, following is the disassembly (print level 1) of a four-sided pyramid:

```
(nop  0)
(setTable Position 32-47  2  4 Rel)
(setTable Position 56-63  3  4 Rel)
(setTable Position  0-31 12  4 Rel)
(setTable Position 48-55 12  4 Abs)
(setTable Normal    0-31  5  0 Rel)
(setTable Normal   32-63  6  0 Abs)
(setTable Color    32-63  2  8 Rel)
(setTable Color     0-31  8  8 Abs)
(setState normalsBundled colorsUnbundled alphaUnbundled)
(setState normalsBundled colorsUnbundled alphaUnbundled)
(setColor  0    127     51     12)
(setState normalsBundled colorsUnbundled alphaUnbundled)
(setColor 32      0      0      0)
(vertex RST (Position 48  -2047   -2047    -205)
            (Normal 32 4 --+      44       0))
```

```
(vertex RMID (Position  0    2047        -2        0)
             (Normal 32 5 +++     44        0))
(vertex ROLD (Position  0       0   -2047      409)
             (Normal  0     14      0))
(vertex ROLD (Position  0    2047   -2047     -409)
             (Normal 32 4 +-+      44        0))
(vertex ROLD (Position 56       2        0        0)
             (Normal 32 4 --+      44        0))
(vertex RST (Position  0    2047        -2        0)
            (Normal 32 00-))
(vertex RMID (Position  0   -2047         2        0)
             (Normal 32 00-))
(vertex ROLD (Position 32      -2         0        0)
             (Normal 32 00-))
(nop 19)
(nop 29)
```

B.17 Compressed Geometry Instruction Verifier

This section describes the rules for determining if a given binary sequence is a valid compressed geometry block. These rules have been programmatically implemented in a compressed geometry verifier, a stand-alone C program that can validate a given file containing a Compressed Geometry object. The verifier is also available in a utility package in both C and Java for use within larger systems.

In theory, every producer of compressed geometry should run such a verifier on its output as a final check, and every consumer of compressed geometry should run such a verifier on any input as an initial check. In practice, for well-debugged programs and hardware implementations with error detection, a separate verification pass may not always be necessary, but it should always be available as an option. (It is also important to note that just passing the verifier is not sufficient to indicate that a compressed geometry compressor is functioning properly; the output must also be examined visually for other types of error.)

When the stand-alone verifier finds a violation, an appropriate error message is printed out. This is quite useful when debugging compressors. The implementation of the verifier is effectively an augmented decompressor, in which the uninitialized state is kept track of and additional error checking is applied.

For a Compressed Geometry object to be valid, it must adhere to at least the following rules, along with the restrictions described in the rest of this document:

Rule 1: Size, Alignment and Byte Order

Every compressed geometry is a sequence of binary data a multiple of four 8-bit bytes in size, starting on an aligned 32-bit boundary, represented in network byte order.

Rule 2: Beginnings

Every compressed geometry sequence starts with the body field of a nop instruction. Initial process proceeds as if a forwarded header of a nop instruction had just been seen. The length field of this nop instruction body can be of any legal length, though usually by convention the length field is 0; thus the first body consists of five zeros.

Rule 3: Endings

The last header in a compressed geometry sequence is a nop. This is followed by the body of the next-to-last instruction. This preceding instruction can be any instruction, and its body can be of any valid length for that instruction type, but the body must end on a four byte 32-bit word aligned boundary. To achieve this, usually the next-to-last and possibly the next-to-next-to-last instruction(s) are also nops, with lengths chosen to satisfy the ending requirement. Note that the body for the last instruction (the nop) is *not* present in the compressed geometry sequence. The end of the compressed geometry is determined from a separately specified size outside of the compressed geometry proper. Note that this ending convention is symmetrical with the starting convention; the sequential concatenation of two valid Compressed Geometry objects is also a valid Compressed Geometry object. For hardware, after a valid Compressed Geometry object has been executed, another valid compressed geometry can be executed without any pipeline flushes if desired.

Rule 4: Reserved Bits

Any bits or bit fields described as reserved in a compressed geometry instruction must be filled with zeros.

Rule 5: Valid Opcodes

Only the seven defined instruction opcodes may be present in a valid Compressed Geometry object.

Rule 6: No Defaults

All state used in the processing of compressed geometry must be defined before it is used; there are no implicit defaults for any of the state. The state includes the contents of the decompression tables as defined by the setTable instruction; the three bundling bits as defined by the setState instruction; the contents of the mesh buffer as defined by vertex instructions with push enabled; and the current position, normal, and color (and alpha), as defined by absolute settings in vertex instructions, setNormal instructions, and setColor instructions. Note that this does not mean that all possible state needs to be defined within a Compressed Geometry object. For example, only those portions of the decompression tables actually referenced by a vertex or setNormal or setColor instruction need be initialized first. The bits specified by setState always need to be referenced, unless there are no vertex instructions, which would occur only in a geometry-less Compressed Geometry object. Mesh buffer elements need only be defined if they are accessed by mesh buffer reference instructions. The current normal and the current color (and alpha) are special cases; if they are not used within a Compressed Geometry object, they may not need to be initialized, depending on the semantics of the outer incorporating graphics API.

Specifically in a valid compressed geometry sequence, no relative values for positions, normals, colors (or alpha) may appear in a vertex or setNormal or setColor instruction until after an absolute value has appeared for that particular item. There is no inheritance between different Compressed Geometry objects, each must be entirely standalone when it comes to state.

Rule 7: State Changes Immediately

State changed by setState and setTable instructions is in force and available as of next instruction. (This specifically disallows pipelined hardware implementations from changing the semantics to force user-visible delay slots.)

Rule 8: Valid XYZ Positions

Executing the position field of a vertex instruction will always result in a signed 16-bit fixed-point value for the current x, y, and z position state. All possible bit values are valid for these fields.

Rule 9: Valid Sextant Octant u v Normals

Executing a setNormal instruction, or executing (when present) the normal subinstruction of a vertex instruction, will result in updated sextant, octant, u and v fields. The wrapping semantics described earlier define the subset of valid values and delta operations allowed for these fields. If these fields are valid, then a valid conversion back to a rectilinear Nx, Ny, Nz value is defined.

Rule 10: Valid RGB{α} Color

Executing a setColor instruction, or executing (when present) the color subinstruction of a vertex instruction, will always result in a signed 16-bit fixed point value for the current R, G, B (and sometimes α) color state. Only positive values are valid for these fields.

Rule 11: What Is Outside the Scope of These Rules

The results of executing a sequence of compressed geometry instructions in a valid Compressed Geometry object is a sequence of specific vertex values and connectivity information for triangles (or lines or points). What further processing this output stream is subject to, and the semantics of this processing is outside the scope of the specification of compressed geometry. For example, the semantics of transformation, lighting, and shading are not specified by compressed geometry. Note that even the semantic interpretation of what type of color parameter the "color" values generated by compressed geometry is left undefined by the Compressed Geometry specification; this is up to the lighting equation (or for realistic rendering systems, more generally the programmable shader) of the outer incorporating graphics API. Specifically no implication is made as to whether the "color" value is an ambient color, a diffuse color, a specular color, an emissive color, some combination thereof, or a more generalized value used by a programmable shader. This, of course, also applies to any interpretation of the α value, which may or may not be an opacity value.

As described earlier, for a Compressed Geometry object to be valid, it must follow these rules *plus* adhere to the other constraints on individual compressed geometry instructions described in the rest of this document.

View Model Details

$\mathbf{A}$N application programmer writing a 3D graphics program that will deploy on a variety of platforms must anticipate the likely end-user environments and must carefully construct the view transformations to match those characteristics using a low-level API. This appendix addresses many of the issues an application must face and describes the sophisticated features that Java 3D's advanced view model provides.

C.1 An Overview of the Java 3D View Model

Both camera-based and Java 3D–based view models allow a programmer to specify the shape of a view frustum and, under program control, to place, move, and reorient that frustum within the virtual environment. However, how they do this varies enormously. Unlike the camera-based system, the Java 3D view model allows slaving the view frustum's position and orientation to that of a six-degrees-of-freedom tracking device. By slaving the frustum to the tracker, Java 3D can automatically modify the view frustum so that the generated images match the end-user's viewpoint exactly.

Java 3D must handle two rather different head-tracking situations. In one case, we rigidly attach a tracker's *base*, and thus its coordinate frame, to the display environment. This corresponds to placing a tracker base in a fixed position and orientation relative to a projection screen within a room, to a computer display on a desk, or to the walls of a multiple-wall projection display. In the second head-tracking situation, we rigidly attach a tracker's *sensor*, not its base, to the display device. This corresponds to rigidly attaching one of that tracker's sensors to a head-mounted display and placing the tracker base somewhere within the physical environment.

C.2 Physical Environments and Their Effects

Imagine an application where the end user sits on a magic carpet. The application flies the user through the virtual environment by controlling the carpet's location and orientation within the virtual world. At first glance, it might seem that the application also controls what the end user will see—and it does, but only superficially.

The following two examples show how end-user environments can significantly affect how an application must construct viewing transformations.

C.2.1 A Head-Mounted Example

Imagine that the end user sees the magic carpet and the virtual world with a head-mounted display and head tracker. As the application flies the carpet through the virtual world, the user may turn to look to the left, to the right, or even toward the rear of the carpet. Because the head tracker keeps the renderer informed of the user's gaze direction, it might not need to draw the scene directly in front of the magic carpet. The view that the renderer draws on the head-mount's display must match what the end user would see if the experience had occurred in the real world.

C.2.2 A Room-Mounted Example

Imagine a slightly different scenario where the end user sits in a darkened room in front of a large projection screen. The application still controls the carpet's flight path; however, the position and orientation of the user's head barely influences the image drawn on the projection screen. If a user looks left or right, then he or she sees only the darkened room. The screen does not move. It's as if the screen represents the magic carpet's "front window" and the darkened room represents the "dark interior" of the carpet.

By adding a left and right screen, we give the magic carpet rider a more complete view of the virtual world surrounding the carpet. Now our end user sees the view to the left or right of the magic carpet by turning left or right.

C.2.3 Impact of Head Position and Orientation on the Camera

In the head-mounted example, the user's head position and orientation significantly affects a camera model's camera position and orientation but hardly has any effect on the projection matrix. In the room-mounted example, the user's head position and orientation contributes little to a camera model's camera position and orientation; however, it does affect the projection matrix.

From a camera-based perspective, the application developer must construct the camera's position and orientation by combining the virtual-world component (the position and orientation of the magic carpet) and the physical-world component (the user's instantaneous head position and orientation).

Java 3D's view model incorporates the appropriate abstractions to compensate automatically for such variability in end-user hardware environments.

C.3   The Coordinate Systems

The basic view model consists of eight or nine coordinate systems, depending on whether the end-user environment consists of a room-mounted display or a head-mounted display. First, we define the coordinate systems used in a room-mounted display environment. Next, we define the added coordinate system introduced when using a head-mounted display system.

C.3.1   Room-Mounted Coordinate Systems

The room-mounted coordinate system is divided into the virtual coordinate system and the physical coordinate system. Figure C-1 shows these coordinate systems graphically. The coordinate systems within the grayed area exist in the virtual world; those outside exist in the physical world. Note that the coexistence coordinate system exists in both worlds.

C.3.1.1   The Virtual Coordinate Systems

The Virtual World Coordinate System

The virtual world coordinate system encapsulates the unified coordinate system for all scene graph objects in the virtual environment. For a given View, the virtual world coordinate system is defined by the Locale object that contains the ViewPlatform object attached to the View. It is a right-handed coordinate system with $+x$ to the right, $+y$ up, and $+z$ toward the viewer.

The ViewPlatform Coordinate System

The ViewPlatform coordinate system is the local coordinate system of the ViewPlatform leaf node to which the View is attached.

511

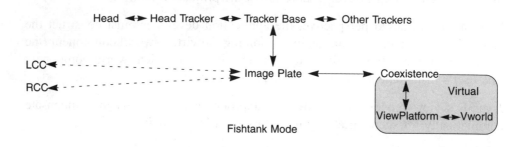

Figure C-1   Display Rigidly Attached to the Tracker Base

The Coexistence Coordinate System

A primary implicit goal of any view model is to map a specified local portion of the physical world onto a specified portion of the virtual world. Once established, one can legitimately ask where the user's head or hand is located within the virtual world or where a virtual object is located in the local physical world. In this way the physical user can interact with objects inhabiting the virtual world, and vice versa. To establish this mapping, Java 3D defines a special coordinate system, called *coexistence* coordinates, that is defined to exist in *both* the physical world and the virtual world.

The coexistence coordinate system exists half in the virtual world and half in the physical world. The two transforms that go from the coexistence coordinate system to the virtual world coordinate system and back again contain all the information needed to expand or shrink the virtual world relative to the physical world. It also contains the information needed to position and orient the virtual world relative to the physical world.

Modifying the transform that maps the coexistence coordinate system into the virtual world coordinate system changes what the end user can see. The Java 3D application programmer moves the end user within the virtual world by modifying this transform.

C.3.1.2   The Physical Coordinate Systems

The Head Coordinate System

The head coordinate system allows an application to import its user's head geometry. The coordinate system provides a simple consistent coordinate frame for specifying such factors as the location of the eyes and ears.

The Image Plate Coordinate System

The image plate coordinate system corresponds with the physical coordinate system of the image generator. The image plate is defined as having its origin at the lower left-hand corner of the display area and as lying in the display area's *XY* plane. Note that image plate is a different coordinate system than either left image plate or right image plate. These last two coordinate systems are defined in head-mounted environments only (see Section C.3.2, "Head-Mounted Coordinate Systems").

The Head Tracker Coordinate System

The head tracker coordinate system corresponds to the six-degrees-of-freedom tracker's sensor attached to the user's head. The head tracker's coordinate system describes the user's instantaneous head position.

The Tracker Base Coordinate System

The tracker base coordinate system corresponds to the emitter associated with absolute position/orientation trackers. For those trackers that generate relative position/orientation information, this coordinate system is that tracker's initial position and orientation. In general, this coordinate system is rigidly attached to the physical world.

C.3.2 Head-Mounted Coordinate Systems

Head-mounted coordinate systems divide the same virtual coordinate systems and the physical coordinate systems. Figure C-2 shows these coordinate systems graphically. As with the room-mounted coordinate systems, the coordinate systems within the grayed area exist in the virtual world; those outside exist in the physical world. Once again, the coexistence coordinate system exists in both worlds. The arrangement of the coordinate system differs from those for a room-mounted display environment. The head-mounted version of Java 3D's coordinate system differs in another way. It includes two image plate coordinate systems, one for each of an end-user's eyes.

The Left Image Plate and Right Image Plate Coordinate Systems

The left image plate and right image plate coordinate systems correspond with the physical coordinate system of the image generator associated with the left and right eye, respectively. The image plate is defined as having its origin at the lower left-hand corner of the display area and lying in the display area's *XY* plane. Note that the left image plate's *XY* plane does not necessarily lie parallel to the right image plate's *XY* plane. Note that the left image plate and the right image plate are different coordinate systems than the room-mounted display environment's image plate coordinate system.

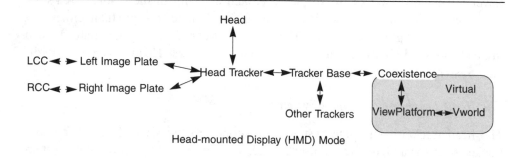

Head-mounted Display (HMD) Mode

Figure C-2   Display Rigidly Attached to the Head Tracker (Sensor)

C.4   The ViewPlatform Object

The ViewPlatform object is a leaf object within the Java 3D scene graph. The ViewPlatform object is the only portion of Java 3D's viewing model that resides as a node within the scene graph. Changes to TransformGroup nodes in the scene graph hierarchy above a particular ViewPlatform object move the view's location and orientation within the virtual world (see Section 9.4, "ViewPlatform: A Place in the Virtual World"). The ViewPlatform object also contains a ViewAttachPolicy and an ActivationRadius (see Section 6.11, "ViewPlatform Node," for a complete description of the ViewPlatform API).

C.5   The View Object

The View object is the central Java 3D object for coordinating all aspects of a viewing situation. All parameters that determine the viewing transformation to be used in rendering on a collected set of canvases in Java 3D are directly contained either within the View object or within objects pointed to by a View object (or pointed to by these, etc.). Java 3D supports multiple simultaneously active View objects, each of which controls its own set of canvases.

The Java 3D View object has several instance variables and methods, but most are calibration variables or user-helping functions.

Methods

```
public void setTrackingEnable(boolean flag)
public boolean getTrackingEnable()
```

These methods set and retrieve a flag specifying whether to enable the use of six-degrees-of-freedom tracking hardware.

```
public void getUserHeadToVworld(Transform3D t)
```

This method retrieves the user-head-to-vworld coordinate system transform. This Transform3D object takes points in the user's head coordinate system and transforms them into points in the virtual world coordinate system. This value is read-only. Java 3D continually generates it, but only if enabled by using the `setUser-HeadToVworldEnable` method.

```
public void setUserHeadToVworldEnable(boolean flag)
public boolean getUserHeadToVworldEnable()
```

These methods set and retrieve a flag that specifies whether to generate the user-head-to-vworld transform (initially `false`) repeatedly.

```
public String toString()
```

This method returns a string that contains the values of this View object.

C.5.1 View Policy

The view policy informs Java 3D whether it should generate the view using the head-tracked system of transformations or the head-mounted system of transformations. These policies are attached to the Java 3D View object.

Methods

```
public void setViewPolicy(int policy)
public int getViewPolicy()
```

These two methods set and retrieve the current policy for view computation. The `policy` variable specifies how Java 3D uses its transforms in computing new viewpoints, as follows:

- SCREEN_VIEW: Specifies that Java 3D should compute new viewpoints using the sequence of transforms appropriate to nonattached, screen-based head-tracked display environments, such as fishtank VR, multiple-projection walls, and VR desks. This is the default setting.

- HMD_VIEW: Specifies that Java 3D should compute new viewpoints using the sequence of transforms appropriate to head-mounted display environments. This policy is not available in compatibility mode (see Section C.11, "Compatibility Mode").

C.5.2   Screen Scale Policy

The screen scale policy specifies where the screen scale comes from. The policy can be one of the following:

- SCALE_EXPLICIT: Specifies that the screen scale is taken from the user-provided screenScale attribute.
- SCALE_SCREEN_SIZE: Specifies that the screen scale is derived from the physical screen according to the following formula. This is the default policy.

```
screenScale = physicalScreenWidth / 2.0
```

```
public void setScreenScalePolicy(int policy)
public int getScreenScalePolicy()
```

These methods set and retrieve the current screen scale policy.

```
public void setScreenScale(double scale)
public double getScreenScale()
```

These methods set and retrieve the screen scale value. This value is used when the screen scale policy is SCALE_EXPLICIT.

C.5.3   Window Eyepoint Policy

The window eyepoint policy comes into effect in a non-head-tracked environment. The policy tells Java 3D how to construct a new view frustum based on changes in the field of view and in the Canvas3D's location on the screen. The policy comes into effect only when the application changes a parameter that can change the placement of the eyepoint relative to the view frustum.

Constants

```
public static final int RELATIVE_TO_FIELD_OF_VIEW
```

This variable tells Java 3D that it should modify the eyepoint position so it is located at the appropriate place relative to the window to match the specified field of view. This implies that the view frustum will change whenever the application changes the field of view. In this mode, the eye position is read-only. This is the default setting.

`public static final int RELATIVE_TO_SCREEN`

This variable tells Java 3D to interpret the eye's position relative to the entire screen. No matter where an end user moves a window (a Canvas3D), Java 3D continues to interpret the eye's position relative to the screen. This implies that the view frustum changes shape whenever an end user moves the location of a window on the screen. In this mode, the field of view is read-only.

`public static final int RELATIVE_TO_WINDOW`

This variable specifies that Java 3D should interpret the eye's position information relative to the window (Canvas3D). No matter where an end user moves a window (a Canvas3D), Java 3D continues to interpret the eye's position relative to that window. This implies that the frustum remains the same no matter where the end user moves the window on the screen. In this mode, the field of view is read-only.

`public static final int RELATIVE_TO_COEXISTENCE`   ◀ New in 1.2 ▶

This variable specifies that Java 3D should interpret the fixed eyepoint position in the view as relative to the origin of coexistence coordinates. This eyepoint is transformed from coexistence coordinates to image plate coordinates for each Canvas3D. As in `RELATIVE_TO_SCREEN` mode, this implies that the view frustum shape will change whenever a user moves the location of a window on the screen.

Methods

```
public int getWindowEyepointPolicy()
public void setWindowEyepointPolicy(int policy)
```

This variable specifies how Java 3D handles the predefined eyepoint in a non-head-tracked application. The variable can contain one of four values: `RELATIVE_TO_FIELD_OF_VIEW`, `RELATIVE_TO_SCREEN`, `RELATIVE_TO_WINDOW`, or `RELATIVE_TO_COEXISTENCE`. The default value is `RELATIVE_TO_FIELD_OF_VIEW`.

C.5.4 Monoscopic View Policy

This policy specifies how Java 3D generates a monoscopic view.

Constants

```
public static final int LEFT_EYE_VIEW
public static final int RIGHT_EYE_VIEW
public static final int CYCLOPEAN_EYE_VIEW
```

These constants specify the monoscopic view policy. The first constant specifies that the monoscopic view should be the view as seen from the left eye. The second constant specifies that the monoscopic view should be the view as seen from the right eye. The third constant specifies that the monoscopic view should be the view as seen from the "center eye," the fictional eye half-way between the left and right eyes. This is the default setting.

Methods

◀ New in 1.2 ▶ `public void setMonoscopicViewPolicy(int policy)`
◀ New in 1.2 ▶ `public int getMonoscopicViewPolicy()`

These methods are deprecated. Use the `Canvas3D.setMonoscopicViewPolicy` and `Canvas3D.getMonoscopicViewPolicy` methods.

C.5.5   Visibility Policy

This policy specifies how visible and invisible objects are drawn.

Constants

◀ New in 1.2 ▶ `public static final int VISIBILITY_DRAW_VISIBLE`
◀ New in 1.2 ▶ `public static final int VISIBILITY_DRAW_INVISIBLE`
◀ New in 1.2 ▶ `public static final int VISIBILITY_DRAW_ALL`

These constants set the visibility policy for this view. The first constant specifies that only visible objects are drawn (this is the default). The second constant specifies that only invisible objects are drawn. The third constant specifies that both visible and invisible objects are drawn.

Methods

◀ New in 1.2 ▶ `public void setVisibilityPolicy(int policy)`
◀ New in 1.2 ▶ `public int getVisibilityPolicy()`

These methods set and retrieve the visibility policy for this view. The policy can be one of `VISIBILITY_DRAW_VISIBLE`, `VISIBILITY_DRAW_INVISIBLE`, or `VISIBILITY_DRAW_ALL`. The default visibility policy is `VISIBILITY_DRAW_VISIBLE`.

C.5.6   Coexistence Centering Enable

```
public void setCoexistenceCenteringEnable(boolean flag)          ◀ New in 1.2 ▶
public boolean getCoexistenceCenteringEnable()                   ◀ New in 1.2 ▶
```

These methods set and retrieve the coexistenceCentering enable flag. If the coexistenceCentering flag is true, the center of coexistence in image plate coordinates, as specified by the trackerBaseToImagePlate transform, is translated to the center of either the window or the screen in image plate coordinates, according to the value of windowMovementPolicy.

By default, coexistenceCentering is enabled. It should be disabled if the trackerBaseToImagePlate calibration transform is set to a value other than the identity (for example, when rendering to multiple screens or when head tracking is enabled). This flag is ignored for HMD mode or when the coexistenceCenterInPworldPolicy is *not* NOMINAL_SCREEN.

C.5.7   Eyepoint in Coexistence

```
public void setLeftManualEyeInCoexistence(Point3d position)      ◀ New in 1.2 ▶
public void setRightManualEyeInCoexistence(Point3d position)     ◀ New in 1.2 ▶
public void getLeftManualEyeInCoexistence(Point3d position)      ◀ New in 1.2 ▶
public void getRightManualEyeInCoexistence(Point3d position)     ◀ New in 1.2 ▶
```

These methods set and retrieve the position of the manual right and left eyes in coexistence coordinates. These values determine eye placement when a head tracker is not in use and the application is directly controlling the eye position in coexistence coordinates. These values are ignored when in head-tracked mode or when the windowEyepointPolicy is *not* RELATIVE_TO_COEXISTENCE.

C.5.8   Sensors and Their Location in the Virtual World

```
public void getSensorToVworld(Sensor sensor, Transform3D t)
public void getSensorHotSpotInVworld(Sensor sensor,
      Point3d position)
public void getSensorHotSpotInVworld(Sensor sensor,
      Point3f position)
```

The first method takes the sensor's last reading and generates a sensor-to-vworld coordinate system transform. This Transform3D object takes points in that sensor's local coordinate system and transforms them into virtual world coordinates. The next two methods retrieve the specified sensor's last hotspot location in virtual world coordinates.

C.6   The Screen3D Object

A Screen3D object represents one independent display device. The most common environment for a Java 3D application is a desktop computer with or without a head tracker. Figure C-3 shows a scene graph fragment for a display environment designed for such an end-user environment. Figure C-4 shows a display environment that matches the scene graph fragment in Figure C-3.

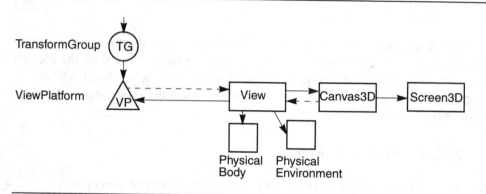

Figure C-3   A Portion of a Scene Graph Containing a Single Screen3D Object

Figure C-4   A Single-Screen Display Environment

A multiple-projection wall display presents a more exotic environment. Such environments have multiple screens, typically three or more. Figure C-5 shows a scene graph fragment representing such a system, and Figure C-6 shows the corresponding display environment.

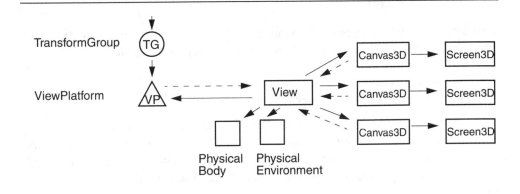

Figure C-5   A Portion of a Scene Graph Containing Three Screen3D Objects

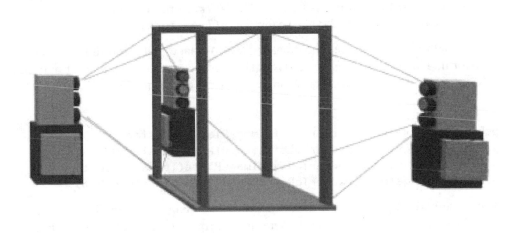

Figure C-6   A Three-Screen Display Environment

A multiple-screen environment requires more care during the initialization and calibration phase. Java 3D must know how the Screen3Ds are placed with respect to one another, the tracking device, and the physical portion of the coexistence coordinate system.

C.6.1   Screen3D Calibration Parameters

The Screen3D object is the 3D version of AWT's screen object (see Section 9.8, "The Screen3D Object"). To use a Java 3D system, someone or some program must calibrate the Screen3D object with the coexistence volume. These methods allow that person or program to inform Java 3D of those calibration parameters.

Measured Parameters

These calibration parameters are set once, typically by a browser, calibration program, system administrator, or system calibrator, not by an applet.

```
public void setPhysicalScreenWidth(double width)
public void setPhysicalScreenHeight(double height)
```

These methods store the screen's (image plate's) physical width and height in meters. The system administrator or system calibrator must provide these values by measuring the display's active image width and height. In the case of a head-mounted display, this should be the display's apparent width and height at the focal plane.

C.6.2 Accessing and Changing Head Tracker Coordinates

```
public void setTrackerBaseToImagePlate(Transform3D t)
public void getTrackerBaseToImagePlate(Transform3D t)
```

These methods set and get the tracker-base-to-image-plate coordinate system transform. This transform is typically a calibration constant. This is used only in SCREEN_VIEW mode. Users must recalibrate whenever the image plate moves relative to the tracker.

```
public void setHeadTrackerToLeftImagePlate(Transform3D t)
public void getHeadTrackerToLeftImagePlate(Transform3D t)
public void setHeadTrackerToRightImagePlate(Transform3D t)
public void getHeadTrackerToRightImagePlate(Transform3D t)
```

These methods set and get the head-tracker-to-left-image-plate and head-tracker-to-right-image-plate coordinate system transforms, respectively. These transforms are typically calibration constants. They are used only in HMD_VIEW mode.

C.7 The Canvas3D Object

Java 3D provides special support for those applications that wish to manipulate an eye position even in a non-head-tracked display environment. One situation where such a facility proves useful is an application that wishes to generate a very high-resolution image composed of lower-resolution tiled images. The application must generate each tiled component of the final image from a common eye position with respect to the composite image but a different eye position from the perspective of each individual tiled element.

C.7.1 Scene Antialiasing

```
public boolean getSceneAntialiasingAvailable()
```

This method returns a status flag indicating whether scene antialiasing is available.

C.7.2 Accessing and Modifying an Eye's Image Plate Position

A Canvas3D object provides sophisticated applications with access to the eye's position information in head-tracked, room-mounted runtime environments. It also allows applications to manipulate the position of an eye relative to an image plate in non-head-tracked runtime environments.

```
public void setLeftManualEyeInImagePlate(Point3d position)
public void setRightManualEyeInImagePlate(Point3d position)
public void getLeftManualEyeInImagePlate(Point3d position)
public void getRightManualEyeInImagePlate(Point3d position)
```

These methods set and retrieve the position of the manual left and right eyes in image plate coordinates. These values determine eye placement when a head tracker is not in use and the application is directly controlling the eye position in image plate coordinates. In head-tracked mode or when the windowEyepoint-Policy is RELATIVE_TO_FIELD_OF_VIEW or RELATIVE_TO_COEXISTENCE, this value is ignored. When the windowEyepointPolicy is RELATIVE_TO_WINDOW, only the Z value is used.

```
public void getLeftEyeInImagePlate(Point3d position)
public void getRightEyeInImagePlate(Point3d position)
public void getCenterEyeInImagePlate(Point3d position)
```

These methods retrieve the actual position of the left eye, right eye, and center eye in image plate coordinates and copy that value into the object provided. The center eye is the fictional eye half-way between the left and right eye. These three values are a function of the windowEyepointPolicy; the tracking enable flag, and the manual left, right, and center eye positions.

```
public void getPixelLocationInImagePlate(int x, int y, Point3d
     imagePlatePoint)
public void getPixelLocationInImagePlate(Point2d pixelLocation,   ◀ New in 1.2 ▶
     Point3d imagePlatePoint)
```

These methods compute the position of the specified AWT pixel value in image plate coordinates and copy that value into the object provided.

◀ New in 1.2 ▶ `public void getPixelLocationFromImagePlate(Point3d`
                    `imagePlatePoint, Point2d pixelLocation)`

This method projects the specified point from image plate coordinates into AWT pixel coordinates. The AWT pixel coordinates are copied into the object provided.

`public void getVworldToImagePlate(Transform3D t)`

This method retrieves the current virtual-world-to-image-plate coordinate system transform and places it into the specified object.

`public void getImagePlateToVworld(Transform3D t)`

This method retrieves the current image-plate-to-virtual-world coordinate system transform and places it into the specified object.

C.7.3   Canvas Width and Height

`public double getPhysicalWidth()`
`public double getPhysicalHeight()`

These methods retrieve the physical width and height of this canvas window, in meters.

C.7.4   Monoscopic View Policy

◀ New in 1.2 ▶ `public void setMonoscopicViewPolicy(int policy)`
◀ New in 1.2 ▶ `public int getMonoscopicViewPolicy()`

These methods set and retrieve the policy regarding how Java 3D generates monoscopic view. If the policy is set to `View.LEFT_EYE_VIEW`, the view generated corresponds to the view as seen from the left eye. If set to `View.RIGHT_EYE_VIEW`, the view generated corresponds to the view as seen from the right eye. If set to `View.CYCLOPEAN_EYE_VIEW`, the view generated corresponds to the view as seen from the "center eye," the fictional eye half-way between the left and right eye. The default monoscopic view policy is `View.CYCLOPEAN_EYE_VIEW`.

Note: For backward compatibility with Java 3D 1.1, if this attribute is set to its default value of `View.CYCLOPEAN_EYE_VIEW`, the monoscopic view policy in the `View` object will be used. An application should not use both the deprecated `View` method and this `Canvas3D` method at the same time.

C.8 The PhysicalBody Object

The PhysicalBody object contains information concerning the physical character-istics of the end-user's body. The head parameters allow end users to specify their own heads' characteristics and thus to customize any Java 3D application so that it conforms to their unique geometry. The PhysicalBody object defines head parameters in the head coordinate system. It provides a simple and consistent coordinate frame for specifying such factors as the location of the eyes and thus the interpupilary distance.

The Head Coordinate System

The head coordinate system has its origin on the head's bilateral plane of sym-metry, roughly half-way between the left and right eyes. The origin of the head coordinate system is known as the *center eye*. The positive X-axis extends to the right. The positive Y-axis extends up. The positive Z-axis extends into the skull. Values are in meters.

Constructors

public PhysicalBody()

Constructs a default user PhysicalBody object with the following default eye and ear positions:

Parameter	Default Value
leftEyePosition	(–0.033, 0.0, 0.0)
rightEyePosition	(0.033, 0.0, 0.0)
leftEarPosition	(–0.080, –0.030, 0.095)
rightEarPosition	(0.080, –0.030, 0.095)
nominalEyeHeightFromGround	1.68
nominalEyeOffsetFromNominalScreen	0.4572
headToHeadTracker	identity

```
public PhysicalBody(Point3d leftEyePosition,
        Point3d rightEyePosition)
public PhysicalBody(Point3d leftEyePosition,
        Point3d rightEyePosition, Point3d leftEarPosition,
        Point3d rightEarPosition)
```

These methods construct a PhysicalBody object with the specified eye and ear positions.

525

Methods

```
public void getLeftEyePosition(Point3d position)
public void setLeftEyePosition(Point3d position)
public void getRightEyePosition(Point3d position)
public void setRightEyePosition(Point3d position)
```

These methods set and retrieve the position of the center of rotation of a user's left and right eyes in head coordinates.

```
public void getLeftEarPosition(Point3d position)
public void setLeftEarPosition(Point3d position)
public void getRightEarPosition(Point3d position)
public void setRightEarPosition(Point3d position)
```

These methods set and retrieve the position of the user's left and right ear positions in head coordinates.

```
public double getNominalEyeHeightFromGround()
public void setNominalEyeHeightFromGround(double height)
```

These methods set and retrieve the user's nominal eye height as measured from the ground to the center eye in the default posture. In a standard computer monitor environment, the default posture would be seated. In a multiple-projection display room environment or a head-tracked environment, the default posture would be standing.

```
public double getNominalEyeOffsetFromNominalScreen()
public void setNominalEyeOffsetFromNominalScreen(double offset)
```

These methods set and retrieve the offset from the center eye to the center of the display screen. This offset distance allows an "over the shoulder" view of the scene as seen by the end user.

```
public void setHeadToHeadTracker(Transform3D t)
public void getHeadToHeadTracker(Transform t)
```

These methods set and retrieve the head-to-head-tracker coordinate system transform. If head tracking is enabled, this transform is a calibration constant. If head tracking is not enabled, this transform is not used. This transform is used in both SCREEN_VIEW and HMD_VIEW modes.

```
public String toString()
```

This method returns a string that contains the values of this PhysicalBody object.

C.9   The PhysicalEnvironment Object

The PhysicalEnvironment object contains information about the local physical world of the end-user's physical environment. This includes information about audio output devices and tracking sensor hardware, if present.

Constructors

public PhysicalEnvironment()

Constructs and initializes a new PhysicalEnvironment object with the following default parameters:

Parameter	Default Value
sensorCount	3
sensors	null (for all array elements)
headIndex	0
rightHandIndex	1
leftHandIndex	2
dominantHandIndex	1
nonDominantHandIndex	2
trackingAvailable	false
audioDevice	null
inputDevice list	empty
coexistenceToTrackerBase	identity
coexistenceCenterInPworldPolicy	View.NOMINAL_SCREEN

public PhysicalEnvironment(int sensorCount)

Constructs and initializes a new PhysicalEnvironment object.

The sensor information provides real-time access to continuous-input devices such as joysticks and trackers. It also contains two-degrees-of-freedom joystick and six-degrees-of-freedom tracker information. See Section 11.2, "Sensors," for more information. Java 3D uses Java AWT's event model for noncontinuous input devices such as keyboards (see Chapter 11, "Input Devices and Picking").

Audio device information associated with the PhysicalEnvironment object provides a mechanism that allows the application to choose a particular audio device (if more than one is available) and explicitly set the type of audio playback for sound rendered using this device. See Chapter 12, "Audio Devices," for more details on the fields and methods that set and initialize the device driver and output playback associated with the audio device.

Methods

The PhysicalEnvironment object specifies the following methods pertaining to audio output devices and input sensors.

public void setAudioDevice(AudioDevice device)

This method selects the specified AudioDevice object as the device through which audio rendering for this PhysicalEnvironment will be performed.

public AudioDevice getAudioDevice()

This method retrieves the specified AudioDevice object.

public void addInputDevice(InputDevice device)
public void removeInputDevice(InputDevice device)

These methods add and remove an input device to or from the list of input devices.

public Enumeration getAllInputDevices()

This method creates an enumerator that produces all input devices.

public void setSensorCount(int count)
public int getSensorCount()

These methods set and retrieve the count of the number of sensors stored within the PhysicalEnvironment object. It defaults to a small number of sensors. It should be set to the number of sensors available in the end-user's environment before initializing the Java 3D API.

public void setCoexistenceToTrackerBase(Transform3D t)
public void getCoexistenceToTrackerBase(Transform3D t)

These methods set the coexistence-to-tracker-base coordinate system transform. If head tracking is enabled, this transform is a calibration constant. If head tracking is not enabled, this transform is not used. This is used in both SCREEN_VIEW and HMD_VIEW modes.

public boolean getTrackingAvailable()

This method returns a status flag indicating whether tracking is available.

```
public void setSensor(int index, Sensor sensor)
public Sensor getSensor(int index)
```

The first method sets the sensor specified by the index to the sensor provided. The second method retrieves the specified sensor.

```
public void setDominantHandIndex(int index)
public int getDominantHandIndex()
```

These methods set and retrieve the index of the dominant hand.

```
public void setNonDominantHandIndex(int index)
public int getNonDominantHandIndex()
```

These methods set and retrieve the index of the nondominant hand.

```
public void setHeadIndex(int index)
public int getHeadIndex()
public void setRightHandIndex(int index)
public int getRightHandIndex()
public void setLeftHandIndex(int index)
public int getLeftHandIndex()
```

These methods set and retrieve the index of the head, right hand, and left hand. The index parameter refers to the sensor index.

Physical Coexistence Policy

```
public int getCoexistenceCenterInPworldPolicy()
public void setCoexistenceCenterInPworldPolicy(int policy)
```

These methods set and retrieve the physical coexistence policy used in this physical environment. This policy specifies how Java 3D will place the user's eyepoint as a function of current head position during the calibration process. Java 3D permits one of three values: NOMINAL_HEAD, NOMINAL_FEET, or NOMINAL_ SCREEN.

C.10 Viewing in Head-Tracked Environments

Section 9.5, "Generating a View," describes how Java 3D generates a view for a standard flat-screen display with no head tracking. In this section, we describe how Java 3D generates a view in a room-mounted, head-tracked display environment—either a computer monitor with shutter glasses and head tracking or a multiple-wall display with head-tracked shutter glasses. Finally, we describe how

Java 3D generates view matrices in a head-mounted and head-tracked display environment.

C.10.1 A Room-Mounted Display with Head Tracking

When head tracking combines with a room-mounted display environment (for example, a standard flat-screen display), the ViewPlatform's origin and orientation serve as a base for constructing the view matrices. Additionally, Java 3D uses the end-user's head position and orientation to compute where an end-user's eyes are located in physical space. Each eye's position serves to offset the corresponding virtual eye's position relative to the ViewPlatform's origin. Each eye's position also serves to specify that eye's frustum since the eye's position relative to a Screen3D uniquely specifies that eye's view frustum. Note that Java 3D will access the PhysicalBody object to obtain information describing the user's interpupilary distance and tracking hardware, values it needs to compute the end-user's eye positions from the head position information.

C.10.2 A Head-Mounted Display with Head Tracking

In a head-mounted environment, the ViewPlatform's origin and orientation also serves as a base for constructing view matrices. And, as in the head-tracked, room-mounted environment, Java 3D also uses the end-user's head position and orientation to modify the ViewPlatform's position and orientation further. In a head-tracked, head-mounted display environment, an end-user's eyes do not move relative to their respective display screens, rather, the display screens move relative to the virtual environment. A rotation of the head by an end user can radically affect the final view's orientation. In this situation, Java 3D combines the position and orientation from the ViewPlatform with the position and orientation from the head tracker to form the view matrix. The view frustum, however, does not change since the user's eyes do not move relative to their respective display screen, so Java 3D can compute the projection matrix once and cache the result.

If any of the parameters of a View object are updated, this will effect a change in the implicit viewing transform (and thus image) of any Canvas3D that references that View object.

C.11 Compatibility Mode

A camera-based view model allows application programmers to think about the images displayed on the computer screen as if a virtual camera took those images. Such a view model allows application programmers to position and orient a virtual camera within a virtual scene, to manipulate some parameters of the virtual camera's lens (specify its field of view), and to specify the locations of the near and far clipping planes.

Java 3D allows applications to enable compatibility mode for room-mounted, non-head-tracked display environments or to disable compatibility mode using the following methods. Camera-based viewing functions are available only in compatibility mode.

Methods

```
public void setCompatibilityModeEnable(boolean flag)
public boolean getCompatabilityModeEnable()
```

This flag turns compatibility mode on or off. Compatibility mode is disabled by default.

Note: Use of these view-compatibility functions will disable some of Java 3D's view model features and limit the portability of Java 3D programs. These methods are primarily intended to help jump-start porting of existing applications.

C.11.1 Overview of the Camera-Based View Model

The traditional camera-based view model, shown in Figure C-7, places a virtual camera inside a geometrically specified world. The camera "captures" the view from its current location, orientation, and perspective. The visualization system then draws that view on the user's display device. The application controls the view by moving the virtual camera to a new location, by changing its orientation, by changing its field of view, or by controlling some other camera parameter.

The various parameters that users control in a camera-based view model specify the shape of a viewing volume (known as a frustum because of its truncated pyramidal shape) and locate that frustum within the virtual environment. The rendering pipeline uses the frustum to decide which objects to draw on the display screen. The rendering pipeline does not draw objects outside the view frustum, and it clips (partially draws) objects that intersect the frustum's boundaries.

Though a view frustum's specification may have many items in common with those of a physical camera, such as placement, orientation, and lens settings, some frustum parameters have no physical analog. Most noticeably, a frustum has two parameters not found on a physical camera: the near and far clipping planes.

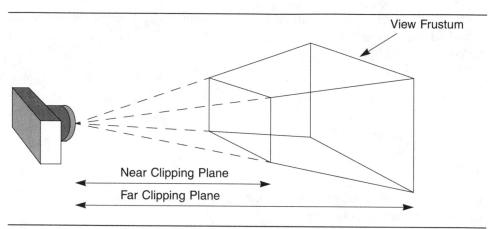

Figure C-7   The Camera-Based View Model

The location of the near and far clipping planes allows the application programmer to specify which objects Java 3D should not draw. Objects too far away from the current eyepoint usually do not result in interesting images. Those too close to the eyepoint might obscure the interesting objects. By carefully specifying near and far clipping planes, an application programmer can control which objects the renderer will not be drawing.

From the perspective of the display device, the virtual camera's image plane corresponds to the display screen. The camera's placement, orientation, and field of view determine the shape of the view frustum.

C.11.2 Using the Camera-Based View Model

The camera-based view model allows Java 3D to bridge the gap between existing 3D code and Java 3D's view model. By using the camera-based view model methods, a programmer retains the familiarity of the older view model but gains some of the flexibility afforded by Java 3D's new view model.

The traditional camera-based view model is supported in Java 3D by helping methods in the Transform3D object. These methods were explicitly designed to resemble as closely as possible the view functions of older packages and thus should be familiar to most 3D programmers. The resulting Transform3D objects can be used to set compatibility-mode transforms in the View object.

C.11.2.1 Creating a Viewing Matrix

The Transform3D object provides the following method to create a viewing matrix:

```
public void lookAt(Point3d eye, Point3d center, Vector3d up)
```

This is a utility method that specifies the position and orientation of a viewing transform. It works similarly to the equivalent function in OpenGL. The inverse of this transform can be used to control the ViewPlatform object within the scene graph. Alternatively, this transform can be passed directly to the View's VpcToEc transform via the compatibility-mode viewing functions (see Section C.11.2.3, "Setting the Viewing Transform").

C.11.2.2 Creating a Projection Matrix

The Transform3D object provides the following three methods for creating a projection matrix. All three map points from eye coordinates (EC) to clipping coordinates (CC). Eye coordinates are defined such that $(0, 0, 0)$ is at the eye and the projection plane is at $z = -1$.

```
public void frustum(double left, double right, double bottom,
        double top, double near, double far)
```

The frustum method establishes a perspective projection with the eye at the apex of a symmetric view frustum. The transform maps points from eye coordinates to clipping coordinates. The clipping coordinates generated by the resulting transform are in a right handed coordinate system (as are all other coordinate systems in Java 3D).

The arguments define the frustum and its associated perspective projection: (left, bottom, -near) and (right, top, -near) specify the point on the near clipping plane that maps onto the lower-left and upper-right corners of the window, respectively. The -far parameter specifies the far clipping plane. See Figure C-8.

```
public void perspective(double fovx, double aspect, double zNear,
        double zFar)
```

The perspective method establishes a perspective projection with the eye at the apex of a symmetric view frustum, centered about the Z-axis, with a fixed field of view. The resulting perspective projection transform mimics a standard camera-based view model. The transform maps points from eye coordinates to clipping coordinates. The clipping coordinates generated by the resulting transform are in a right-handed coordinate system.

The arguments define the frustum and its associated perspective projection: -near and -far specify the near and far clipping planes; fovx specifies the field of view in the X dimension, in radians; and aspect specifies the aspect ratio of the window. See Figure C-9.

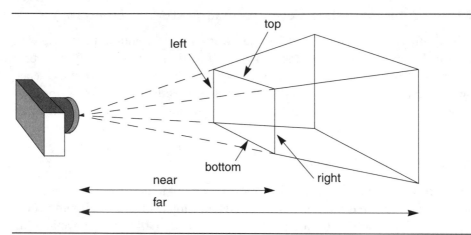

Figure C-8　A Perspective Viewing Frustum

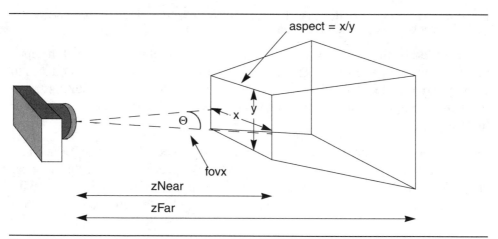

Figure C-9　Perspective View Model Arguments

```
public void ortho(double left, double right, double bottom,
        double top, double near, double far)
```

The `ortho` method establishes a parallel projection. The orthographic projection transform mimics a standard camera-based video model. The transform maps points from eye coordinates to clipping coordinates. The clipping coordinates generated by the resulting transform are in a right-handed coordinate system.

The arguments define a rectangular box used for projection: (`left`, `bottom`, `-near`) and (`right`, `top`, `-near`) specify the point on the near clipping plane that maps onto the lower-left and upper-right corners of the window, respectively. The `-far` parameter specifies the far clipping plane. See Figure C-10.

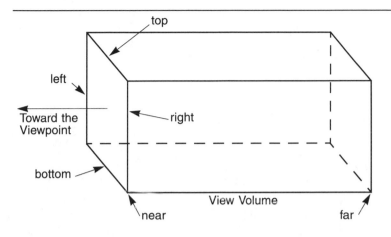

Figure C-10 Orthographic View Model

C.11.2.3 Setting the Viewing Transform

The View object provides the following compatibility-mode methods that operate on the viewing transform:

```
public void setVpcToEc(Transform3D vpcToEc)
public void getVpcToEc(Transform3D vpcToEc)
```

This compatibility-mode method specifies the ViewPlatform coordinates (VPC) to eye coordinates viewing transform. If compatibility mode is disabled, this transform is derived from other values and is read-only.

C.11.2.4 Setting the Projection Transform

The View object provides the following compatibility-mode methods that operate on the projection transform:

```
public void setLeftProjection(Transform3D projection)
public void getLeftProjection(Transform3D projection)
public void setRightProjection(Transform3D projection)
public void getRightProjection(Transform3D projection)
```

These compatibility-mode methods specify a viewing frustum for the left and right eye that transforms points in eye coordinates to clipping coordinates. If compatibility mode is disabled, a RestrictedAccessException is thrown. In monoscopic mode, only the left-eye projection matrix is used.

D

Exceptions

THE Java 3D API uses the standard Java exception model for handling errors or exceptional conditions. In addition to using existing exception classes, such as ArrayIndexOutOfBoundsException and IllegalArgumentException, Java 3D defines several new runtime exceptions. These exceptions are thrown by various Java 3D methods or by the Java 3D renderer to indicate an error condition of some kind.

The exceptions defined by Java 3D, as part of the javax.media.j3d package, are described in the following sections. They all extend RuntimeException and, as such, need not be declared in the throws clause of methods that might cause the exception to be thrown. This appendix is not an exhaustive list of all exceptions expected for Java 3D. Additional exceptions will be added as the need arises.

D.1 BadTransformException

Indicates an attempt to use a Tranform3D object that is inappropriate for the object in which it is being used. For example,

- Transforms that are used in the scene graph, within a TransformGroup node, must be affine. They may optionally contain a nonuniform scale or a shear, subject to other listed restrictions.

- All transforms in the TransformGroup nodes above a ViewPlatform object must be congruent. This ensures that the Vworld-coordinates-to-ViewPlatform-coordinates transform is angle- and length-preserving with no shear and with uniform scale. only

- Most viewing transforms other than those in the scene graph can contain translation and rotation only.

- The projection transform is allowed to be nonaffine, but it must be either a single-point perspective projection or a parallel projection.

Constructors

```
public BadTransformException()
public BadTransformException(String str)
```

These create the exception object that outputs the exception message. The first form uses the default message. The second form specifies the message string to be output.

D.2   CapabilityNotSetException

This exception indicates an access to a live or compiled Scene Graph object without the required capability set.

Constructors

```
public CapabilityNotSetException()
public CapabilityNotSetException(String str)
```

These create the exception object that outputs the exception message. The first form uses the default message. The second form specifies the message string to be output.

D.3   DanglingReferenceException

This exception indicates that during a `cloneTree` call, an updated reference was requested for a node that did not get cloned. This occurs when a subgraph is duplicated via `cloneTree` and has at least one leaf node that contains a reference to a node with no corresponding node in the cloned subgraph. This results in two leaf nodes wanting to share access to the same node.

If dangling references are to be allowed during the `cloneTree` call, `cloneTree` should be called with the `allowDanglingReferences` parameter set to `true`.

Constructors

```
public DanglingReferenceException()
public DanglingReferenceException(String str)
```

These create the exception object that outputs the exception message. The first form uses the default message. The second form specifies the message string to be output.

D.4   IllegalRenderingStateException

This exception indicates an illegal state for rendering. It is currently unused.

```
public illegalRenderingStateException()
public illegalRenderingStateException(String str)
```

These create the exception object that outputs the exception message. The first form uses the default message. The second form specifies the message string to be output.

D.5   IllegalSharingException

This exception indicates an illegal attempt to share a scene graph object. For example, the following are illegal:

- Referencing a shared subgraph in more than one virtual universe.
- Using the same component object both in the scene graph and in an immediate-mode graphics context.
- Including an unsupported type of leaf node within a shared subgraph.
- Referencing a BranchGroup node in more than one of the following ways:
  - Attaching it to a (single) Locale.
  - Adding it as a child of a Group node within the scene graph.
  - Referencing it from a (single) Background leaf node as background geometry.

Constructors

```
public IllegalSharingException()
public IllegalSharingException(String str)
```

These create the exception object that outputs the exception message. The first form uses the default message. The second form specifies the message string to be output.

D.6   MismatchedSizeException

This exception indicates that an operation cannot be completed properly because of a mismatch in the sizes of the object attributes.

```
public MismatchedSizeException()
public MismatchedSizeException(String str)
```

These create the exception object that outputs the exception message. The first form uses the default message. The second form specifies the message string to be output.

D.7   MultipleParentException

This exception extends `IllegalSharingException` and indicates an attempt to add a node that is already a child of one group node into another group node.

Constructors

```
public MultipleParentException()
public MultipleParentException(String str)
```

These create the exception object that outputs the exception message. The first form uses the default message. The second form specifies the message string to be output.

D.8   RestrictedAccessException

This exception indicates an attempt to access or modify a state variable without permission to do so. For example, invoking a `set` method for a state variable that is currently read-only.

Constructors

```
public RestrictedAccessException()
public RestrictedAccessException(String str)
```

These create the exception object that outputs the exception message. The first form uses the default message. The second form specifies the message string to be output.

D.9   SceneGraphCycleException

This exception indicates that one of the live scene graphs attached to a viewable Locale has a cycle in it. Java 3D scene graphs are directed acyclic graphs and, as such, do not permit cycles. This exception is thrown by the Java 3D renderer either at scene graph traversal time or when a scene graph containing a cycle is made live (added as a descendant of a Locale object).

Constructors

```
public SceneGraphCycleException()
public SceneGraphCycleException(String str)
```

These create the exception object that outputs the exception message. The first form uses the default message. The second form specifies the message string to be output.

D.10 SingularMatrixException

This exception, in the `javax.vecmath` package, indicates that the inverse of a matrix cannot be computed.

Constructors

```
public SingularMatrixException()
public SingularMatrixException(String str)
```

These create the exception object that outputs the exception message. The first form uses the default message. The second form specifies the message string to be output.

D.11 SoundException

This exception indicates a problem in loading or playing a sound sample.

Constructors

```
public SoundException()
public SoundException(String str)
```

These create the exception object that outputs the exception message. The first form uses the default message. The second form specifies the message string to be output.

Equations

THIS appendix contains the Java 3D equations for fog, lighting, sound, and texture mapping. Many of the equations use the following symbols:

- ·   Multiplication
- •   Function operator for sound equations;
Dot product for all other equations

E.1   Fog Equations

The ideal fog equation is

$$C' = C \cdot f + Cf \cdot (1 - f) \qquad\qquad \text{(Eq. E.1)}$$

The fog coefficient, f, is computed differently for linear and exponential fog. The equation for linear fog is

$$f = \frac{B - z}{B - F} \qquad\qquad \text{(Eq. E.2)}$$

The equation for exponential fog is

$$f = e^{-d \cdot z} \qquad\qquad \text{(Eq. E.3)}$$

The parameters used in the fog equations are

C =   Color of the pixel being fogged

Cf =   Fog color

d =   Fog density

F =   Front fog distance, measured in eye coordinates

B	=	Back fog distance, measured in eye coordinates
z	=	The z-coordinate distance from the eyepoint to the pixel being fogged, measured in eye coordinates
f	=	Fog coefficient

Fallbacks and Approximations

1. An implementation may approximate per-pixel fog by calculating the correct fogged color at each vertex and then linearly interpolating this color across the primitive.

2. An implementation may approximate exponential fog using linear fog by computing values of F and B that cause the resulting linear fog ramp to most closely match the effect of the specified exponential fog function.

3. An implementation will ideally perform the fog calculations in eye coordinates, which is an affine space. However, an implementation may approximate this by performing the fog calculations in a perspective space (such as device coordinates). As with other approximations, the implementation should match the specified function as closely as possible.

E.2   Lighting Equations

The ideal lighting equations are

$$Me + Ma \cdot \sum_i^{Numamb} (Lc_i) + \sum_i^{Numlt} (atten_i \cdot spot_i \cdot (diff_i + spec_i)) \qquad \text{(Eq. E.4)}$$

$$diff_i = (L_i \bullet N) \cdot Lc_i \cdot Md \qquad \text{(Eq. E.5)}$$

$$spec_i = (S_i \bullet N)^{shin} \cdot Lc_i \cdot Ms \qquad \text{(Eq. E.6)}$$

Note: If $(L_i \bullet N) \leq 0$, then $diff_i$ and $spec_i$ are set to 0.

$$atten_i = 1/(Kc_i + Kl_i \cdot d_i + Kq_i \cdot d_i^2) \qquad \text{(Eq. E.7)}$$

Note: For directional lights, $atten_i$ is set to 1.

$$spot_i = \max((-L_i \cdot D_i), 0)^{exp_i} \qquad \text{(Eq. E.8)}$$

Note: If the vertex is outside the spot light cone, as defined by the cutoff angle, $spot_i$ is set to 0. For directional and point lights, $spot_i$ is set to 1.

This is a subset of OpenGL in that the Java 3D ambient and directional lights are not attenuated and only ambient lights contribute to ambient lighting.

The parameters used in the lighting equation are

E	=	Eye vector
Ma	=	Material ambient color
Md	=	Material diffuse color
Me	=	Material emissive color
Ms	=	Material specular color
N	=	Vertex normal
$shin$	=	Material shininess

The per-light values are

d_i	=	Distance from vertex to light
D_i	=	Spot light direction
exp_i	=	Spot light exponent
Kc_i	=	Constant attenuation
Kl_i	=	Linear attenuation
Kq_i	=	Quadratic attenuation
L_i	=	Direction from vertex to light
Lc_i	=	Light color
S_i	=	Specular half-vector $= \| (L_i + E) \|$

Fallbacks and Approximations

1. An implementation may approximate the specular function using a different power function that produces a similar specular highlight. For example, the PHIGS+ lighting model specifies that the reflection vector (the light vector reflected about the vertex normal) is dotted with the eye vector and that this dot product is raised to the specular power. An implementation that uses such a model should map the shininess into an exponent that most closely matches the effect produced by the ideal equation.

2. Implementations that do not have a separate ambient and diffuse color may fall back to using an ambient intensity as a percentage of the diffuse color. This ambient intensity should be calculated using the following NTSC luminance equation:

$$I = 0.30 \cdot Red + 0.59 \cdot Green + 0.11 \cdot Blue \qquad \text{(Eq. E.9)}$$

E.3   Sound Equations

There are different sets of sound equations, depending on whether the application uses headphones or speakers.

E.3.1   Headphone Playback Equations

For each sound source, Java 3D calculates a separate left and right output signal. Each left and right sound image includes differences in the *interaural intensity* and an *interaural delay*. The calculation results are a set of direct and indirect (delayed) sound signals mixed together before being sent to the audio playback system's left and right transducers.

E.3.1.1   Interaural Time Difference (Delay)

For each PointSound and ConeSound source, the left and right output signals are delayed based on the location of the sound and the orientation of the listener's head. The time difference between these two signals is called the *interaural time difference* (ITD). The time delay of a particular sound reaching an ear is affected by the arc the sound must travel around the listener's head. Java 3D uses an approximation of the ITD using a spherical head model. The interaural path difference is calculated based on the following cases:

1. The signal from the sound source to only one of the ears is direct. The ear farther from the sound is shadowed by the listener's head ($\sin\alpha \geq De/2Dh$); see Figure E-1.

$$\begin{aligned} Ec &= |Vc| \\ Ef &= |Vt| + P \end{aligned} \qquad \text{(Eq. E.10)}$$

where

$$P = \frac{De}{2}\left(\frac{\pi}{2} - (\gamma - \alpha)\right)$$

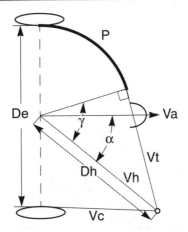

Figure E-1   Signal to Only One Ear Is Direct

2. The signals from the sound source reach both ears by indirect paths around the head ($\sin\alpha < De/2Dh$); see Figure E-2.

$$Ec = |Vt| + P'$$ (Eq. E.11)

$$Ef = |Vt| + P$$

where

$$P = \frac{De}{2}\left(\frac{\pi}{2} - (\gamma - \alpha)\right)$$

$$P' = \frac{De}{2}\left(\frac{\pi}{2} - (\gamma + \alpha)\right)$$

The time from the sound source to the closer ear is Ec/S, and the time from the sound source to the farther ear is Ef/S, where S is the current AuralAttribute region's speed of sound.

If the sound is closer to the left ear, then

$$ITD_l = Ec/S$$ *(Eq. E.12)*

$$ITD_r = Ef/S$$

If the sound is closer to the right ear, then

$$ITD_l = Ef/S$$ (Eq. E.13)

$$ITD_r = Ec/S$$

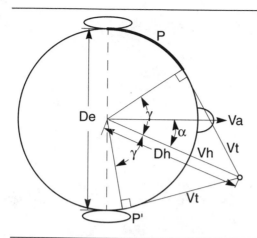

Figure E-2   Signals to Both Ears Are Indirect

The parameters used in the ITD equations are as follows:

α =   The smaller of the angles between *Vh* (or –*Vh*) and *Va* in radians

γ =   Angle between *Vh* and radius to tangent point on *Vt* in radians

De   =   Distance between ears (interaural distance)

Dh   =   Distance from interaural center to sound source

Ec   =   Distance from sound source to ear closer to sound

Ef   =   Distance from sound source to ear farther from sound

P, P'   =   Arc path around the head that an indirect signal must travel to reach an ear

S   =   Speed of sound for the current AuralAttribute region

Va   =   Vector from center ear forward parallel to *Z* axis of head coordinates

Vc   =   Vector from sound source to ear closer to sound

Vh   =   Vector from center ear to sound source

Vt   =   Vector from sound source to tangent point on the listener's head

E.3.1.2   Interaural Intensity (Gain) Difference

For each active and playing Point and ConeSound source, *i*, separate calculations for the left and right signal (based on which ear is closer to and which is farther from the source) are combined with nonspatialized BackgroundSound to create a stereo sound image. Each of the following equations is calculated separately for the left and right ear.

$$I(t) = \frac{\sum\limits_{i}^{numS} [G_i \cdot (F_i \bullet [ITD_i \bullet Sample(t)])]}{maxNumS} \qquad \text{(Eq. E.14)}$$

Note: For BackgroundSound sources, ITD_i is an identity function so there is no delay applied to the sample for these sources.

$$G_i = Gi_i \cdot Gd_i \cdot Ga_i \cdot Gr_i \qquad \text{(Eq. E.15)}$$

Note: For BackgroundSound sources $Gd_i = Ga_i = 1.0$. For PointSound sources $Ga_i = 1.0$.

$$F_i = Fd_i \bullet Fa_i \qquad \text{(Eq. E.16)}$$

Note: For BackgroundSound sources, Fd_i and Fa_i are identity functions. For PointSound sources, Fa_i is an identity function.

If the sound source is on the right side of the head, Ec is used for left G and F calculations, and Ef is used for right. Conversely, if the Sound source is on the left side of the head, Ef is used for left calculations, and Ec is used for right.

Attenuation

For sound sources with a single distanceGain array defined, the intersection points of V_h (the vector from the sound source position through the listener's position) and the spheres (defined by the distanceGain array) are used to find the index k where $d_k \leq L \leq d_{k+1}$. See Figure E-3.

For ConeSound sources with two distanceGain arrays defined, the intersection points of V_h and the ellipsi (defined by both the front and back distanceGain arrays) closest to the listener's position are used to determine the index k. See Figure E-4.

The equation for the distance gain is

$$Gd = Gd_k + \frac{(Gd_{k+1} - Gd_k) \cdot (d_2 - d_1)}{L - d_1} \qquad \text{(Eq. E.17)}$$

549

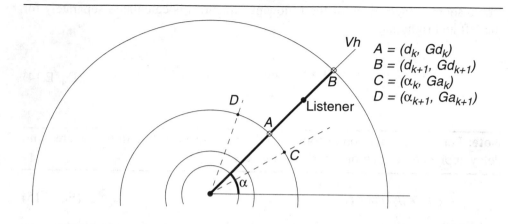

Figure E-3   ConeSound with a Single Distance Gain Attenuation Array

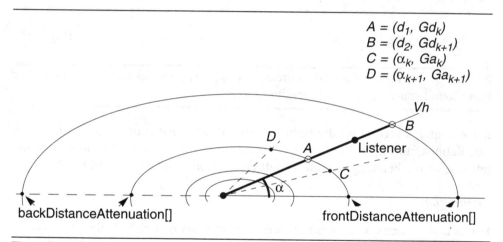

Figure E-4   ConeSound with Two Distance Attenuation Arrays

Angular attenuation for both the spherical and elliptical cone sounds is identical. The angular distances in the attenuation array closest to α are found and define the index k into the angular attenuation array elements. The equation for the angular gain is

$$Ga = Ga_k + \frac{(Ga_{k+1} - Ga_k) \cdot (\alpha_{k+1} - \alpha_k)}{\alpha - \alpha_k}$$
(Eq. E.18)

Filtering

Similarly, the equations for calculating the AuralAttributes distance filter and the ConeSound angular attenuation frequency cutoff filter are

$$Fd = Fd_k + \frac{(Fd_{k+1} - Fd_k) \cdot (d_2 - d_1)}{L - d_1} \qquad \text{(Eq. E.19)}$$

$$Fa = Fa_k + \frac{(Fa_{k+1} - Fa_k) \cdot (\alpha_{k+1} - \alpha_k)}{\alpha - \alpha_k} \qquad \text{(Eq. E.20)}$$

An N-pole lowpass filter may be used to perform the simple angular and distance filtering defined in this version of Java 3D. These simple lowpass filters are meant only as an approximation for full, FIR filters (to be added in some future version of Java 3D).

Fallbacks and Approximations

1. If more than one lowpass filter is to be applied to the sound source (for example, both an angular filter and a distance filter are applied to a Cone-Sound source), it is necessary only to use a single filter, specifically the one that has the lowest cutoff frequency.

2. There is no requirement to support anything higher than very simple two-pole filtering. Any type of multipole lowpass filter can be used. If higher N-pole or compound filtering is available on the device on which sound rendering is being performed, use of these is encouraged, but not required.

The parameters used in the interaural intensity difference (IID) equations are as follows:

A, B	= Triples containing DistanceGain linear distance, gain scale factor, and AuralAttribute cutoff frequency
C, D	= Triples containing AngularAttenuation angular distance, gain scale factor, and cutoff frequency
α	= Angle between Vh and Va in radians
Ec	= Distance from sound source to ear closer to sound from the ITD equation
Ef	= Distance from sound source to ear farther from sound source from the ITD equation
Fa	= Angular filter from ConeSound definition

Fd	= Distance filter from AuralAttributes
Ga	= Angular gain attenuation scale factor
Gd	= Distance gain attenuation scale factor
Gi	= Initial gain scale factor
Gr	= Current AuralAttribute region's gain scale factor
I	= Stereo sound image
L	= Listener distance from sound source
maxNumS	= Maximum number of sound sources for the audio device that the application is using for playback
numS	= Number of sound sources
sample	= Sound digital sample with a specific sample rate, bit precision, and an optional encoding and/or compression format
Vh	= Vector from center ear to sound source

E.3.1.3   Doppler Effect Equations

Between two snapshots of the head and the sound source positions some delta time apart, the distance between the head and source is compared. If there has been no change in the distance between the head and the sound source over this delta time, the Doppler effect equation is

$$f' = f \qquad\qquad\qquad\qquad \text{(Eq. E.21)}$$

If there has been a change in the distance between the head and the sound, the Doppler effect equation is

$$f' = f \cdot Af \cdot v \qquad\qquad\qquad\qquad \text{(Eq. E.22)}$$

When the head and sound are moving toward each other (the velocity ratio is greater than 1.0), the velocity ratio equation is

$$v = \frac{(S \cdot Ar) + (\Delta v(h, t) \cdot Av)}{(S \cdot Ar) - (\Delta v(s, t) \cdot Av)} \qquad\qquad \text{(Eq. E.23)}$$

When the head and sound are moving away from each other (the velocity ratio is less than 1.0), the velocity ratio equation is

$$v = \frac{(S \cdot Ar) - (\Delta v(h, t) \cdot Av)}{(S \cdot Ar) + (\Delta v(s, t) \cdot Av)} \qquad\qquad \text{(Eq. E.24)}$$

The parameters used in the Doppler effect equations are as follows:

Af = AuralAttribute frequency scale factor

Ar = AuralAttribute rolloff scale factor

Av = AuralAttribute velocity scale factor

Δv = Delta velocity

f = Frequency of sound

h = Listener's head position

v = Ratio of delta velocities

Vh = Vector from center ear to sound source

s = Sound source position

S = Speed of sound

t = Time

Note: If the adjusted velocity of the head or the adjusted velocity of the sound is greater than the adjusted speed of sound, f' is undefined.

E.3.1.4   Reverberation Equations

The overall reverberant sounds, used to give the impression of the aural space in which the active/enabled source sources are playing, is added to the stereo sound image output from equation E.14.

$$I'(t)_{[l, r]} = I(t)_{[l, r]} + \sum_{i}^{numS} R_i \qquad \text{(Eq. E.25)}$$

Reverberation for each sound is approximated in the following:

$$R_i = \sum_{j}^{fLoop} [(Gr^j \cdot Sample(t)_i) \bullet D(t + (Tr \cdot j))]^* \qquad \text{(Eq. E.26)}$$

Note that the reverberation calculation outputs the same image to both left and right output signals (thus there is a single monaural calculation for each sound reverberated). Correct first-order (early) reflections, based on the location of the sound source, the listener, and the active AuralAttribute's bounds, are not required for this version of Java 3D. Approximations based on the reverberation delay time, either suppled by the application or calculated as the average delay time within the selected AuralAttribute's application region, will be used.

The feedback loop is repeated until AuralAttribute's reverberation feedback loop count is reached or $Gr^j \leq 0.000976$ (effective zero amplitude, –60 dB, using the measure of –6 dB drop for every doubling of distance).

Fallbacks and Approximations

1. Reducing the number of feedback loops repeated while still maintaining the overall impression of the environment. For example, if –10 dB were used as the drop in gain for every doubling of distance, a scale factor of 0.015625 could be used as the effective zero amplitude, which can be reached in only 15 loop iterations (rather than the 25 needed to reach 0.000976).

2. Using preprogrammed "room" reverberation algorithms that allow selection of a fixed set of "reverberation types" (for example, large hall, small living room), which have implied reflection coefficients, delay times, and feedback loop durations.

The parameters used in the reverberation equations are as follows:

D	=	Delay function
$fLoop$	=	Reverberation feedback loop count
Gr	=	Reverberation coefficient acting as a gain scale-factor
I	=	Stereo image of unreflected sound sources
R	=	Reverberation for each sound sources
$Sample$	=	Sound digital sample with a specific sample rate, bit precision, and an optional encoding and/or compression format
t	=	Time
Tr	=	Reverberation delay time (approximating first-order delay in the AuralAttribute region)

E.3.2 Speaker Playback Equations

Different speaker playback equations are used depending on whether the system uses monaural or stereo speakers.

E.3.2.1 Monaural Speaker Output

The equations for headphone playback need only be modified to output a single signal, rather than two signals for left and right transducers. Although there is only one speaker, distance and filter attenuation, Doppler effect, elevation, and front and back cues can be distinguished by the listener and should be included in the sound image generated.

E.3.2.2 Stereo Speaker Output

In a two-speaker playback system, the signal from one speaker is actually heard by both ears, and this affects the spectral balance and interaural intensity and time differences heard by each of the listener's ears. Crosstalk cancellation must be performed on the right and left signal to compensate for the delayed attenuated signal heard by the ear opposite the speaker. Thus a delayed attenuated signal for each of the stereo signals must be added to the output from the equations for headphone playback.

The equations for stereo speaker playback assume that the two speakers are placed symmetrically about the listener (at the same off-axis angle from the viewing axis at an equal distance from the center of the listener's head).

$$I'(t)_l = I(t)_l + [D(t) \bullet [G(\bar{P}, \alpha) \cdot I(t)_r]] \qquad \text{(Eq. E.27)}$$

$$I'(t)_r = I(t)_r + [D(t) \bullet [G(P, \alpha) \cdot I(t)_l]] \qquad \text{(Eq. E.28)}$$

The parameters used in the crosstalk equations, expanding on the terms used for the equations for headphone playback, are as follows:

α = Angle between vectors from speaker to near and far ears

D = Delay function of signal variant over time

G = Gain attenuation scale factors function taking initial distance and angular gain scale factors into account

I = Sound image for left and right stereo signals calculated as for headphone output

P = Distance difference between near ear and far ear as defined for ITD, the speaker substituted for the sound source in equation

t = Time

E.4   Texture Mapping Equations

Texture mapping can be divided into two steps. The first step takes the transformed s and t (and possibly r) texture coordinates, the current texture image, and the texture filter parameters and computes a texture color based on looking up the texture coordinates in the texture map. The second step applies the computed texture color to the incoming pixel color using the specified texture mode function.

E.4.1   Texture Lookup

The texture lookup stage maps a texture image onto a geometric polygonal primitive. The most common method for doing this is to reverse map the s and t coordinates from the primitive back onto the texture image, then filter and resample the image. In the simplest case, a point in s, t space is transformed into a u, v address in the texture image space (Eq. E.29), then this address is used to look up the nearest texel value in the image. This method, used when the selected texture filter function is BASE_LEVEL_POINT, is called nearest-neighbor sampling or point sampling.

$$u = s \cdot width$$
$$v = t \cdot height$$
(Eq. E.29)

$$i = \mathrm{trunc}(u)$$
$$j = \mathrm{trunc}(v)$$
(Eq. E.30)

$$Ct = T_{i, j}$$
(Eq. E.31)

If the texture boundary mode is REPEAT, then only the fractional bits of s and t are used, ensuring that both s and t are less than 1.

If the texture boundary mode is CLAMP, then the s and t values are clamped to be in the range [0, 1] before being mapped into u and v values. Further, if $s \geq 1$, then i is set to $width - 1$; if $t \geq 1$, then j is set to $height - 1$.

The parameters in the point-sampled texture lookup equations are as follows:

width	=	Width, in pixels, of the texture image
height	=	Height, in pixels, of the texture image
s	=	Interpolated s coordinate at the pixel being textured
t	=	Interpolated t coordinate at the pixel being textured

u	=	u coordinate in texture image space
v	=	v coordinate in texture image space
i	=	Integer row address into texture image
j	=	Integer column address into texture image
T	=	Texture image

The above equations are used when the selected texture filter function—either the minification or the magnification filter function—is BASE_LEVEL_POINT. Java 3D selects the appropriate texture filter function based on whether the texture image is minified or magnified when it is applied to the polygon. If the texture is applied to the polygon such that more than one texel maps onto a single pixel, then the texture is said to be minified, and the minification filter function is selected. If the texture is applied to the polygon such that a single texel maps onto more than one pixel, then the texture is said to be magnified, and the magnification filter function is selected. The selected function is one of the following: BASE_LEVEL_POINT, BASE_LEVEL_LINEAR, MULTI_LEVEL_POINT, or MULTI_LEVEL_LINEAR. In the case of magnification, the filter will always be one of the two base level functions (BASE_LEVEL_POINT or BASE_LEVEL_LINEAR).

If the selected filter function is BASE_LEVEL_LINEAR, then a weighted average of the four texels that are closest to the sample point in the base level texture image is computed.

$$i_0 = \text{trunc}(u - 0.5)$$
$$j_0 = \text{trunc}(v - 0.5)$$
$$i_1 = i_0 + 1 \tag{Eq. E.32}$$
$$j_1 = j_0 + 1$$

$$\alpha = \text{frac}(u - 0.5)$$
$$\beta = \text{frac}(v - 0.5) \tag{Eq. E.33}$$

$$Ct = (1 - \alpha) \cdot (1 - \beta) \cdot T_{i_0, j_0} + \alpha \cdot (1 - \beta) \cdot T_{i_1, j_0}$$
$$+ (1 - \alpha) \cdot \beta \cdot T_{i_0, j_1} + \alpha \cdot \beta \cdot T_{i_1, j_1} \tag{Eq. E.34}$$

If the selected filter function is MULTI_LEVEL_POINT or MULTI_LEVEL_LINEAR, the texture image needs to be sampled at multiple levels of detail. If multiple levels of detail are needed and the texture object defines only the base level texture image, Java 3D will compute multiple levels of detail as needed.

557

Mipmapping is the most common filtering technique for handling multiple levels of detail. If the implementation uses mipmapping, the equations for computing a texture color based on texture coordinates are simply those used by the underlying rendering API (such as OpenGL or PEX). Other filtering techniques are possible as well.

Fallbacks and Approximations

1. If the texture boundary mode is CLAMP, an implementation may use either the closest boundary pixel or the constant boundary color attribute for those values of *s* or *t* that are outside the range [0, 1].

2. An implementation can choose a technique other than mipmapping to perform the filtering of the texture image when the texture minification filter is MULTI_LEVEL_POINT or MULTI_LEVEL_LINEAR.

3. If mipmapping is chosen by an implementation as the method for filtering, it may approximate trilinear filtering with another filtering technique. For example, an OpenGL implementation may choose to use LINEAR_MIPMAP_NEAREST or NEAREST_MIPMAP_LINEAR in place of LINEAR_MIPMAP_LINEAR.

E.4.2   Texture Application

Once a texture color has been computed, this color is applied to the incoming pixel color. If lighting is enabled, only the emissive, ambient, and diffuse components of the incoming pixel color are modified. The specular component is added into the modified pixel color after texture application.

The equations for applying that color to the original pixel color are based on the texture mode, as follows:

REPLACE Texture Mode

$$C' = Ct \qquad\qquad\qquad \text{(Eq. E.35)}$$

MODULATE Texture Mode

$$C' = C \cdot Ct \qquad\qquad\qquad \text{(Eq. E.36)}$$

DECAL Texture Mode

$$C'_{rgb} = C_{rgb} \cdot (1 - Ct_\alpha) + Ct_{rgb} \cdot Ct_\alpha$$

$$C'_\alpha = C_\alpha$$

(Eq. E.37)

Note that the texture format must be either RGB or RGBA.

BLEND Texture Mode

$$C'_{rgb} = C_{rgb} \cdot (1 - Ct_{rgb}) + Cb_{rgb} \cdot Ct_{rgb}$$

$$C'_\alpha = C_\alpha \cdot Ct_\alpha$$

(Eq. E.38)

Note that if the texture format is INTENSITY, alpha is computed identically to red, green, and blue:

$$C'_\alpha = C_\alpha \cdot (1 - Ct_\alpha) + Cb_\alpha \cdot Ct_\alpha$$

(Eq. E.39)

The parameters used in the texture mapping equations are as follows:

C = Color of the pixel being texture mapped (if lighting is enabled, then this does not include the specular component)

Ct = Texture color

Cb = Blend color

Note that C_{rgb} indicates the red, green, and blue channels of color C and that C_α indicates the alpha channel of color C. This convention applies to the other color variables as well.

If there is no alpha channel in the texture, a value of 1 is used for Ct_α in BLEND and DECAL modes.

When the texture mode is one of REPLACE, MODULATE, or BLEND, only certain of the red, green, blue, and alpha channels of the pixel color are modified, depending on the texture format, as described following:

- INTENSITY: All four channels of the pixel color are modified. The intensity value is used for each of Ct_r, Ct_g, Ct_b, and Ct_α in the texture application equations, and the alpha channel is treated as an ordinary color channel—the equation for C'_{rbg} is also used for C'_α.

- LUMINANCE: Only the red, green, and blue channels of the pixel color are modified. The luminance value is used for each of Ct_r, Ct_g, and Ct_b in the texture application equations. The alpha channel of the pixel color is unmodified.

- ALPHA: Only the alpha channel of the pixel color is modified. The red, green, and blue channels are unmodified.

- LUMINANCE_ALPHA: All four channels of the pixel color are modified. The luminance value is used for each of Ct_r, Ct_g, and Ct_b in the texture application equations, and the alpha value is used for Ct_α.

- RGB: Only the red, green, and blue channels of the pixel color are modified. The alpha channel of the pixel color is unmodified.

- RGBA: All four channels of the pixel color are modified.

Fallbacks and Approximations

An implementation may apply the texture to all components of the lit color, rather than separating out the specular component. Conversely, an implementation may separate out the emissive and ambient components in addition to the specular component, potentially applying the texture to the diffuse component only.

APPENDIX **F**

The Utility Packages

THIS appendix summarizes the Java 3D utilities packages.

F.1 The Utility Packages

The com.sun.j3d.* packages provide aids to assist the application programmer in setting up a user environment and getting a Java 3D application up and running as quickly as possible. The utilities packages contain classes that are not part of the formal Java 3D API specification. Since these packages are not part of the API specification, they are subject to change and will evolve over time.

The most useful of these packages are

- utils.universe – contains the SimpleUniverse class, which defines a minimal user environment that includes all of the necessary objects on the "view" side of the scene graph. See Section F.17, "utils.universe Package," for a description of this package.

- utils.geometry – contains geometry utilities, such as stripification, normal generation, tessellation, and primitive construction. See Section F.13, "utils.geometry Package," for a description of this package.

- utils.picking – contains the PickIntersection, PickTool, PickCanvas, and PickResult classes, which simplify the construction of picking routines. See Section F.15, "utils.picking Package," for a description of this package.

- loaders – contains the Loader and Scene interfaces, which can be used to implement a variety of Java 3D loaders in a standard manner. See Section F.5, "loaders Package," for a description of this package.

F.2   Package Overview

The Java 3D utilities packages are all in the `com.sun.j3d` hierarchy. Table F-1 lists the utilities packages.

Table F-1   Utilities Packages

Package Name	Description
`audioengines`	Useful only to people writing audio device drivers.
`audioengines.javasound`	Defines an audio output device that accesses JavaSound's sound mixer functionality.
`loaders`	Used in the construction of file loaders.
`loaders.lw3d`	Implements a loader for Lightwave 3D scene files.
`loaders.objectfile`	Implements a loader for Wavefront object files.
`utils.applet`	Enables creating Java applets that can also run as stand-alone applications.
`utils.behaviors.interpolators`	Enhances the Interpolator class with the TCB (Kochanek-Bartels) spline interpolation.
`utils.behaviors.keyboard`	Useful for controlling the scene graph behavior from the keyboard.
`utils.behaviors.mouse`	Useful for controlling scene graph behavior with the mouse, specifically, object rotation, translation, and zoom.
`utils.compression`	Useful for geometry compression.
`utils.geometry`	Includes geometry utilities, such as stripification, normal generation, tessellation, and primitive construction.
`utils.image`	Useful for loading Java 3D texture objects.
`utils.picking`	Useful for defining picking operations and retrieving information about the picked object.
`utils.picking.behaviors`	Combines picking with mouse-based rotation, translation, and zoom behaviors.
`utils.universe`	Useful for setting up a user environment to get a Java 3D program up and running quickly and easily.

F.3   audioengines Package

The `com.sun.j3d.audioengines` package is useful only to people writing audio device drivers. Java 3D application developers are not expected to use the classes in this package.

Table F-2 lists the classes in the `com.sun.j3d.audioengines` package.

Table F-2   audioengines Classes

Class	Description
AudioEngine	Extends: Object Implements: AudioDevice Encapsulates basic information about the AudioDevice, such as the playback type (headphones, monaural speakers, or stereo speakers) and the listener's distance from the speakers.
AudioEngine3D	Extends: AudioEngine Implements: AudioDevice3D Defines an audio output device that generates sound "image" from high-level sound parameters passed to it while the scene graph is active.
AuralParameters	Extends: Object Defines a set of fields that correspond to AuralAttribute fields.
Sample	Extends: Object Defines the data and methods associated with a sound sample played through the AudioDevice.

F.4   audioengines.javasound Package

The `com.sun.j3d.audioengines.javasound` package contains a single public class that implements a JavaSound-based audio device. Most programs should let the SimpleUniverse (or Viewer) class in the `universe` package construct the audio device.

Table F-3 lists the class in the `com.sun.j3d.audioengines.javasound` package.

Table F-3   audioengines.javasound Package

Class	Description
JavaSoundMixer	Extends: AudioEngine3D Defines an audio output device that accesses JavaSound's sound mixer functionality.

F.5   loaders Package

The `com.sun.j3d.loaders` package contains two interfaces, Loader and Scene, that can be used to implement a variety of Java 3D loaders in a standard manner. Base classes that implement these interfaces are also included as a convenience.

F.5.1   Interfaces

Table F-4 lists the interfaces in the `com.sun.j3d.loaders` package.

Table F-4   loaders Package Interfaces

Interface	Description
Loader	Used to specify the location and elements of a file format to load. The interface is used to give loaders of various file formats a common public interface.
Scene	A set of methods used to extract Java 3D scene graph information from a file loader utility. The interface is used to give loaders of various file formats a common public interface.

F.5.2   Classes

Table F-5 lists the classes in the `com.sun.j3d.loaders` package.

Table F-5   loaders Package Classes

Class	Description
LoaderBase	Extends: Object Implements: Loader Abstract base class that can be used as a starting point for a Loader. A specific file loader could extend this class and implement the load methods.
SceneBase	Extends: Object Implements: Scene Responsible for both the storage and retrieval of data from the Scene. Most loaders will not need to extend this class.

F.5.3 Exceptions

Table F-6 lists the exceptions in the `com.sun.j3d.loaders` package.

Table F-6   loaders Package Exceptions

Exception	Description
IncorrectFormatException	Extends: RuntimeException Indicates that a file of an incorrect type was passed to a loader.
ParsingErrorException	Extends: RuntimeException Indicates that the loader encountered a problem parsing the specified file.

F.6   loaders.lw3d Package

The `com.sun.j3d.loaders.lw3d` package provides a file loader that allows applications to load Lightwave 3D scene files.

Table F-7 lists the class in the `com.sun.j3d.loaders.lw3d` package.

Table F-7   loaders.lw3d Package

Class	Description
Lw3dLoader	Extends: loaders.lw3d.TextfileParser Implements: Loader Allows users to load Lightwave 3D scene files.

F.7   loaders.objectfile Package

The `com.sun.j3d.loaders.objectfile` package provides a file loader that allows applications to load Wavefront object files.

Table F-8 lists the class in the `com.sun.j3d.loaders.objectfile` package.

Table F-8   loaders.objectfile Package

Class	Description
ObjectFile	Extends: Object Implements: Loader Implements the Loader interface for the Wavefront .obj file format, a standard 3D object file format created for use with Wavefront's Advanced Visualizer™ and available for purchase from Viewpoint DataLabs, as well as other 3D model companies.

F.8   utils.applet Package

The `com.sun.j3d.utils.applet` package includes a single class, MainFrame, that enables the creation of Java applets that can also run as standalone applications. The MainFrame class was developed by Jef Poskanzer of Acme Labs <jef@acme.com>.

Table F-9 lists the class in the `com.sun.j3d.applet` package.

Table F-9   utils.applet Package

Class	Description
MainFrame	Extends: Frame Implements: java.lang.Runnable, java.applet.AppletStub, java.applet.AppletContext Allows a Java applet to run as an application.

F.9   utils.behaviors.interpolators Package

The `com.sun.j3d.utils.behaviors.interpolators` package provides spline-based interpolators using KCB (Kochanek-Bartels) splines (also known as the TCB or Tension-Continuity-Bias spline). Applications can use these interpolators to implement key-frame animation sequences.

Table F-10 lists the classes in the `com.sun.j3d.utils.behaviors.interpolators` package.

Table F-10   utils.behaviors.interpolators Package

Class	Description
KBCubicSplineCurve	Extends: Object A container class that holds a number of cubic spline segments.
KBCubicSplineSegment	Extends: Object Creates the representation of a KCB (Kochanek-Bartels) spline.
KBKeyFrame	Extends: Object Represents a Key Frame that can be used for Kochanek-Bartels spline interpolation.

Class	Description
KBRotPosScaleSplinePathInterpolator	Extends: KBSplinePathInterpolator Defines a behavior that varies the rotational, translational, and scale components of its target TransformGroup by using the Kochanek-Bartels cubic spline interpolation to interpolate among a series of key frames (using the value generated by the specified Alpha object). The interpolated position, orientation, and scale are used to generate a transform in the local coordinate system of this interpolator.
KBSplinePathInterpolator	Extends: Interpolator Defines the base class for all KCB (Kochanek-Bartels) Spline Path Interpolators.

F.10 utils.behaviors.keyboard Package

The `com.sun.j3d.utils.behaviors.keyboard` package contains classes that take keyboard events and turns them into transform changes that are suitable for use in modifying the ViewPlatform's transformation matrix for navigation.

Table F-11 lists the classes in the `com.sun.j3d.utils.behaviors.keyboard` package.

Table F-11   utils.behaviors.keyboard Package

Class	Description
KeyNavigator	Extends: Object Accumulates AWT key events (key press and key release) and computes a new transform based on the accumulated events and elapsed time.
KeyNavigatorBehavior	Extends: Behavior A simple behavior that invokes the KeyNavigator to modify the view platform transform.

F.11 utils.behaviors.mouse Package

The `com.sun.j3d.utils.behaviors.mouse` package contains classes that use mouse events to modify object or viewing transformations. Subclasses exist to perform rotation, translation, and zoom operations.

F.11.1 Interfaces

Table F-12 lists the interface in the `com.sun.j3d.utils.behaviors.mouse` package.

Table F-12 utils.behaviors.mouse Package Interface

Interface	Description
MouseBehaviorCallback	Allows a class to be notified when the transform is changed by one of the MouseBehaviors. The class that is interested in transform changes implements this interface, and the object created with that class is registered with the desired subclass of MouseBehavior using the `setupCallback` method. When the transform changes, the registered object's `transform-Changed` method is invoked.

F.11.2 Classes

Table F-13 lists the classes in the `com.sun.j3d.utils.behaviors.mouse` package.

Table F-13 utils.behaviors.mouse Package Classes

Class	Description
MouseBehavior	Extends: Behavior The base class for all mouse manipulators (MouseRotate, MouseZoom, and MouseTranslate).
MouseRotate	Extends: MouseBehavior A Java 3D behavior object that lets users control the rotation of an object via a mouse.
MouseTranslate	Extends: MouseBehavior A Java 3D behavior object that lets users control the translation (x, y) of an object via a mouse drag motion with the third mouse button (alt-click on PC).
MouseZoom	Extends: MouseBehavior A Java 3D behavior object that lets users control the z axis translation of an object via a mouse drag motion with the second mouse button.

F.12 utils.compression Package

The `com.sun.j3d.utils.compression` package includes classes for compressing geometry and for reading and writing compressed geometry resource files.

Table F-14 lists the classes in the `com.sun.j3d.utils.compression` package.

Table F-14 utils.compression Package

Class	Description
CompressedGeometryFile	Extends: Object Provides methods to read and write compressed geometry resource files. These files usually end with the .cg extension and support sequential as well as random access to multiple compressed geometry objects.
CompressionStream	Extends: Object Used as input to a geometry compressor. It collects elements such as vertices, normals, colors, mesh references, and quantization parameters in an ordered stream. This stream is then traversed during the compression process and used to build the compressed output buffer.
GeometryCompressor	Extends: Object Takes a stream of geometric elements and quantization parameters (the CompressionStream object) and compresses it into a stream of commands as defined in Appendix B, "3D Geometry Compression." The resulting data may be output in the form of a CompressedGeometry node component or appended to a CompressedGeometryFile.

F.13 utils.geometry Package

The `com.sun.j3d.utils.geometry` package contains geometry utilities, such as stripification, normal generation, tessellation (polygon triangulation), and primitive construction. The GeometryInfo class provides a common data storage format for the stripification, normal generation, and tessellation classes.

Table F-15 lists the classes in the `com.sun.utils.geometry` package.

Table F-15 utils.geometry Package

Class	Description
Box	Extends: Primitive A geometry primitive created with a given length, width, and height.
ColorCube	Extends: Shape3D A simple color-per-vertex cube with a different color for each face.

Table F-15   utils.geometry Package (Continued)

Class	Description
Cone	Extends: Primitive A geometry primitive defined with a radius and a height. It is a capped cone centered at the origin with its central axis aligned along the *y*-axis.
Cylinder	Extends: Primitive A geometry primitive defined with a radius and a height. It is a capped cylinder centered at the origin with its central axis aligned along the *y*-axis.
GeometryInfo	Extends: Object The object where you put your geometry if you want to use the Java 3D utility packages. Once you have your data in the GeometryInfo object, you can send it to any (or all) of several utilities to have operations performed on it, such as generating normals or turning it into long strips for more efficient rendering. Geometry is loaded just as it is in the Java 3D GeometryArray object, but there are fewer options for getting data into the object. GeometryInfo itself contains some simple utilities, such as calculating indices for nonindexed data ("indexifying") and getting rid of unused data in your indexed geometry information ("compacting").
NormalGenerator	Extends: Object Calculates and fills the normals of a GeometryInfo object. The normals are computed based on an analysis of the indexed coordinate information.
Primitive	Extends: Group The base class for all Java 3D primitives.
Sphere	Extends: Primitive A geometry primitive created with a given radius and resolution. It is centered at the origin.
Stripifier	Extends: Object Changes the primitive of the GeometryInfo object to triangle strips. The strips are made by analyzing the triangles in the original data and connecting them together.

Table F-15   utils.geometry Package (Continued)

Class	Description
Text2D	Extends: Shape3D Creates a texture-mapped rectangle that displays the text string supplied by the user, given the appearance parameters also supplied by the user.
Triangulator	Extends: Object Turns arbitrary polygons into triangles so they can be rendered by Java 3D. Polygons can be concave or nonplanar, and can contain holes (see GeometryInfo).

F.14 utils.image Package

The com.sun.j3d.utils.image package contains a single class, TextureLoader, that is used to load a Java 3D texture object from a file. It will automatically scale the image to a power of two and, optionally, compute mipmaps.

Table F-16 lists the class in the com.sun.j3d.utils.image package.

Table F-16   utils.image Package

Class	Description
TextureLoader	Extends: Object Used for loading a texture from an Image or BufferedImage. Methods are provided to retrieve the Texture object and the associated ImageComponent object or a scaled version of the ImageComponent object. The default format is RGBA. Other legal formats are: RGBA, RGBA4, RGB5_A1, RGB, RGB4, RGB5, R3_G3_B2, LUM8_ALPHA8, LUM4_ALPHA4, LUMINANCE, and ALPHA.

F.15 utils.picking Package

The com.sun.j3d.utils.picking package includes classes that construct a pick shape from a 2D mouse location, initiate a picking operation, and retrieve information about the picked object(s).

Table F-17 lists the classes in the com.sun.j3d.utils.picking package.

Table F-17   utils.picking Package

Class	Description
PickCanvas	Extends: PickTool Simplifies picking using mouse events from a canvas. This class allows picking using canvas *x,y* locations by generating the appropriate pick shape.
PickIntersection	Extends: Object Holds information about an intersection of a PickShape with a Node as part of a PickResult. Information about the intersected geometry, intersected primitive, intersection point, and closest vertex can be inquired.
PickResult	Extends: Object Stores information about a pick hit. Detailed information about the pick and each intersection of the PickShape with the picked Node can be inquired.
PickTool	Extends: Object The base class for picking operations. The picking methods will return a PickResult object for each object picked, which can then be queried to obtain more detailed information about the specific objects that were picked.

F.16 utils.picking.behaviors Package

The `com.sun.j3d.utils.picking.behaviors` package combines picking with mouse-based rotation, translation, and zoom behaviors. Once an object is picked, that object can be manipulated with the mouse.

F.16.1 Interfaces

Table F-18 lists the interface in the `com.sun.j3d.utils.picking.behaviors` package.

Table F-18   utils.picking.behaviors Package Interfaces

Interface	Description
PickingCallback	Allows a class to be notified when a picked object is moved. The class that is interested in object movement implements this interface, and the object created with that class is registered with the desired subclass of PickMouseBehavior using the `setupCallback` method. When the picked object moves, the registered object's `transformChanged` method is invoked.

F.16.2 Classes

Table F-19 lists the classes in the com.sun.j3d.utils.picking.behaviors package.

Table F-19 utils.picking.behaviors Package Classes

Class	Description
PickMouseBehavior	Extends: Behavior Base class that allows users to add picking and mouse manipulation to the scene graph.
PickRotateBehavior	Extends: PickMouseBehavior A mouse behavior that allows users to pick and drag scene graph objects.
PickTranslateBehavior	Extends: PickMouseBehavior A mouse behavior that allows users to pick and translate scene graph objects.
PickZoomBehavior	Extends: PickMouseBehavior A mouse behavior that allows users to pick and zoom scene graph objects.

F.17 utils.universe Package

The com.sun.j3d.universe package is useful for setting up a user environment to get a Java 3D program up and running quickly and easily. Specifically, this class creates a Locale, a single ViewingPlatform (with its associated ViewPlatform), and a Viewer object (with its associated View, PhysicalBody, PhysicalEnvironment, and AudioDevice). For many applications, the SimpleUniverse class will provide all of the necessary functionality.

Table F-20 lists the classes in the com.sun.j3d.utils.universe package.

Table F-20 utils.universe Package

Class	Description
MultiTransformGroup	Extends: Object A convenience class that effectively creates a series of TransformGroup nodes connected one to another hierarchically.
PlatformGeometry	Extends: BranchGroup Holds any geometry that should be associated with the ViewingPlatform object.

Table F-20   utils.universe Package (Continued)

Class	Description
SimpleUniverse	Extends: VirtualUniverse Sets up a minimal user environment to get a Java 3D program up and running quickly and easily. This utility class creates all the necessary objects on the "view" side of the scene graph. Specifically, this class creates a locale—a single ViewingPlatform, and a Viewer object (both with their default values). Many basic Java 3D applications will find that SimpleUniverse provides all necessary functionality needed by their applications.
Viewer	Extends: Object Holds all the information that describes the physical and virtual "presence" in the Java 3D universe.
ViewerAvatar	Extends: BranchGroup Holds geometry that should be associated with the View's *avatar*.
ViewingPlatform	Extends: BranchGroup Used to set up the "view" side of a Java 3D scene graph. The ViewingPlatform object contains a MultiTransformGroup node to allow for a series of transforms to be linked together. To this structure the ViewPlatform is added as well as any geometry to associate with this view platform.

CD-ROM Installation

T HIS appendix describes how to install the software on the CD-ROM that came with this book. For descriptions of the program examples on the CD-ROM, see Appendix H, "The Example Programs."

G.1 What's on the CD-ROM

The Java 3D CD-ROM contains the following:

- The Java 2 SDK, Standard Edition, v 1.2.2 for Solaris/SPARC systems (Solaris 2.6 or subsequent compatible version)

- The Java 2 SDK, Standard Edition, v 1.2.2 for Windows (Windows 98, Windows NT, and Windows 2000)

- The Java 3D API Version 1.2, including the com.sun.j3d.* packages, for Solaris/SPARC systems

- The Java 3D API Version 1.2, including the com.sun.j3d.* packages, for Windows systems (OpenGL version)

- Sun OpenGL 1.2.1 for Solaris

- Example programs

- The javadocs and *The Java 3D 1.2 API Specification* (this book) in a browsable format (both html and Adobe Acrobat)

The Java 3D CD-ROM does not contain OpenGL for Windows, which is required to run Java 3D applications. See Section G.2.1, "Requirements for Windows Systems."

The CD-ROM contains an index.html file with the latest information that may not have made it into this book. This file also has more detailed installation instructions, if you find the need.

The index.html file can be read with any browser. If any information in this appendix contradicts the index.html file, assume that the index.html file is correct.

The CD-ROM also contains the following directories:

doc/	Contains the javadocs and a browsable copy of this book
programs/	Contains example programs and demos
solaris/	Contains shell scripts for installing the Java 2 SDK, Java 3D, OpenGL, and any necessary patches on Solaris systems
win32/	Contains executable files for installing the Java 2 SDK and Java 3D on Windows systems

G.2   Installing the Software on Windows 98/NT Systems

G.2.1   Requirements for Windows Systems

The system on which the contents of the CD-ROM are installed should have

- At least 65 megabytes of free disk space for the Java 2 SDK
- At least 10 megabytes of free disk space for the Java 3D API

This version of Java 3D for Windows 98/NT requires OpenGL from Microsoft or a hardware accelerator that supports OpenGL 1.1 (or later). If you do not have OpenGL installed on your system, contact your hardware vendor or download OpenGL from

```
http://www.opengl.org/
```

G.2.2   Installing the Java 2 SDK on Windows Systems

The installation program creates a directory C:\jdk1.2.2 where it puts both the Java 2 SDK and the Java 3D SDK. It also creates a directory C:\Program Files\Javasoft\1.2 where it puts the Java 2 JRE and Java 3D runtime.

To install the Java 2 SDK and Java 3D on a Windows system, follow these steps:

1. If your system does not already have OpenGL installed, install it before installing the CD-ROM (see Section G.2.1, "Requirements for Windows Systems").
2. Insert the CD-ROM in your CD-ROM drive.

3. Install the Java 2 SDK and JRE.

   Open the `win32` folder on the CD-ROM and execute the `jdk1_2_2-001-win.exe` file. Follow the instructions the installer program provides.

4. Add the full path of the `jdk1.2.2\bin` directory to the PATH variable.

   Typically, the full path looks something like the following:

   ```
   C:\jdk1.2.2\bin
   ```

5. Check the CLASSPATH variable.

   Include "." in your CLASSPATH, or ensure that CLASSPATH is not set.

6. Verify that Java is installed by typing the following:

   ```
   > java -version
   java version "1.2.2"
   Classic VM (build JDK-1.2.2-001, native threads, symcjit)
   ```

   If you do not get the java version "1.2.2" message, verify that the jdk1.2.2/bin directory is in your path in Step 4 above. If you get the above message, proceed to Section G.2.3, "Installing the Java 3D API on Windows Systems."

G.2.3 Installing the Java 3D API on Windows Systems

To install the Java 3D API, follow these steps:

1. Install the Java 3D SDK.

   Execute the `java3d1_2-win-opengl-sdk.exe` file.

2. Install the Java 3D runtime.

   Execute the `java3d1_2-win-opengl-rt.exe` file.

3. Verify that Java 3D is installed by typing the following:

   ```
   > cd c:\jdk1.2.2\demo\java3d\HelloUniverse
   > java HelloUniverse
   ```

   You should see a window with a multicolored rotating cube.

4. See the `README.Java3D-jdk` file in the `jdk.1.2.2` directory for more information about this release.

G.2.4   Installing the Javadocs on Windows Systems

The javadocs for Java 3D may be installed on your system for ready access. Alternatively, you may choose to save the disk space by not installing the javadocs and reading them directly from the CD-ROM whenever needed (see Section G.4, "Accessing the Documentation from the CD-ROM").

You will need at least 10 megabytes of free disk space to install the Java 3D API javadocs.

The javadocs are stored on the CD-ROM in a compressed (zip) format. To install the javadocs on your system,

1. Create a directory on your system where you want to store the javadocs (for example, `C:\java3d\doc`).

2. Open the `win32` folder on the CD-ROM, and select the `java3d1_2-doc.zip` file.

3. Use a zip utility to unzip the `javadoc.zip` file into the directory you just created.

To read the javadocs, point your browser to the `index.html` file in the newly created `html` directory.

G.3   Installing the Software on Solaris Systems

G.3.1   Requirements for Solaris Systems

The system on which the contents of the CD-ROM are installed should have

- At least 38 megabytes of free disk space for the Java 2 SDK.
- At least 7 megabytes of free disk space for the Java 3D API.
- At least 32 megabytes of free disk space for Sun OpenGL 1.2.1 for Solaris.
- Sun OpenGL for Solaris/SPARC, version 1.2 (or later). Sun OpenGL 1.2.1 for Solaris is provided on the CD-ROM.
- A frame buffer with OpenGL support, such as Elite3D, Creator3D, or Expert3D.
- The Solaris 2.6 (or later) operating environment with the necessary patches installed (see Section G.3.3, "Installing Patches on Solaris Systems").

G.3.2 Installing Sun OpenGL 1.2.1 for Solaris

If you do not already have at least Sun OpenGL 1.2 for Solaris on your system, install Sun OpenGL 1.2.1 from the CD-ROM as follows:

1. Insert the CD-ROM in your CD-ROM drive.

2. su to root.

3. Run the installation program:

```
% /cdrom/solaris/opengl/ogl121.sh
```

4. Exit and restart your window system.

5. Run the ogl_install_check program to verify the installation:

```
% /usr/openwin/demo/GL/ogl_install_check
```

G.3.3 Installing Patches on Solaris Systems

Several patches are required to run Java and Java 3D on Solaris. These patches are included on the CD-ROM in the /cdrom/solaris/patches directory. A README file in this directory contains the complete list of patches for Solaris 2.6, Solaris 7, and Solaris 8.

To install the patches for your system, proceed as follows:

1. Insert the CD-ROM in your CD-ROM drive.

2. su to root.

3. Run the following script:

```
% /cdrom/solaris/patches/install_patches.csh
```

This script determines the version of Solaris that is running and installs all necessary patches for that version.

4. Reboot your system.

To show the installed patches, type the following:

```
% showrev -p
```

If you want to install an individual patch, rather than the entire set of patches, proceed as follows:

1. Insert the CD-ROM in your CD-ROM drive.

579

2. su to root.

3. Run `patchadd` with the path to the patch you want to install.

   For example,

   ```
   % patchadd /cdrom/solaris/patches/5.7/105181-17
   ```

4. Reboot your system.

G.3.4 Installing the Java 2 SDK on Solaris Systems

Note: You must have permission to write files in the directories where you want to install Java and Java 3D. If you do not have this permission, the installation program will run to completion, but Java and Java 3D will not be installed.

To install the Java 2 SDK on a Solaris system, follow these steps:

1. Change directories to where you wish to install the Java 2 SDK.

   For example, to install on /home/myhome,

   ```
   % cd /home/myhome
   ```

2. Run the installation program.

   ```
   % /cdrom/solaris/Solaris_JDK_1.2.2_05_sparc.bin
   ```

   This will create a `Solaris_JDK_1.2.2_05` directory containing the Java 2 SDK.

3. Update the PATH variable in your startup file.

   Put /home/myhome/Solaris_JDK_1.2.2_05/bin in your path ahead of any directory that may contain java, such as /usr/bin.

4. Check the CLASSPATH variable.

   Include "." in your CLASSPATH, or ensure that CLASSPATH is not set.

5. Verify that Java is installed by typing the following:

   ```
   % java -version
   java version "1.2.2"
   Solaris VM (build Solaris_JDK_1.2.2_05, native threads, sunwjit)
   ```

If you do not get the java version "1.2.2" message, verify that you have put the jdk1.2.2/bin directory in your path in Step 3 above. If you do get the above message, proceed to Section G.3.5, "Installing the Java 3D API on Solaris Systems."

G.3.5 Installing the Java 3D API on Solaris Systems

To install the Java 3D API, follow these steps:

1. Change to the jdk1.2.2 directory. For example,

```
% cd /home/myhome/jdk1_2_2
```

2. Install the Java 3D API. Type the following:

```
% /cdrom/solaris/java3d1_2-solsparc.bin
```

3. Verify that Java 3D is installed by typing the following:

```
% cd demo/java3d/HelloUniverse
% java HelloUniverse
```

You should see a window with a multicolored rotating cube.

4. See the README.Java3D-jdk file in the Solaris_JDK_1.2.2_05 directory for more information about this release.

G.3.6 Installing the Javadocs on Solaris Systems

The javadocs for Java 3D may be installed on your system for ready access. Alternatively, you may choose to save the disk space by not installing the javadocs and reading them directly from the CD-ROM whenever needed (see Section G.4, "Accessing the Documentation from the CD-ROM").

You will need at least 10 megabytes of free disk space to install the Java 3D API javadocs.

The javadocs are stored on the CD-ROM in a compressed tar format. To install the javadocs on your system, follow these steps.

1. Create a directory where you want to store the javadocs. For example,

```
% mkdir /home/myhome/java3d/doc
```

2. Change to the directory you just created. For example,

```
% cd /home/myhome/java3d/doc
```

3. Untar the file into the newly created directory:

```
% zcat /cdrom/solaris/java3d1_2-doc.tar.Z | tar xvf -
```

To read the javadocs, point your browser to the index.html file in the newly created html directory.

G.4 Accessing the Documentation from the CD-ROM

The javadoc-generated API documentation and the text of this book are included on the CD-ROM in a browsable (html) format. Additionally, the text of this book is included in a PDF format.

A browsable version of the javadocs is available in the /doc/java3d1_2-doc directory on the CD-ROM. Point your browser to the index.html file in this directory to view the Java 3D API documentation.

A browsable version of *The Java 3D API Specification* (this book) is available in the /doc/j3dbook directory on the CD-ROM. Point your browser to the index.html file in this directory to view the online version of this book. The text of this book is also available in Adobe Acrobat (PDF) format in the /doc directory as j3dbook.pdf. You can download a copy of the Adobe Acrobat Reader from

http://www.adobe.com/products/acrobat/readstep.html

The Example Programs

THIS appendix describes the example programs on the CD-ROM.

H.1 Introduction

Before you can compile Java 3D applications or run the example programs, you need to have installed or you need to install the following software on your system:

- Java 2 SDK version 1.2 or later (included on the CD-ROM)
- Java 3D API (included on the CD-ROM)
- OpenGL

The demo/java3d directory contains 37 subdirectories. All but two of these directories (geometry and images) contain at least one example program. Some directories contain several example programs.

Each example program consists of two files, a .java file and a .class file. For example, the ConicWorld directory contains the .java and .class files for six example programs: BoxExample, ConicWorld, FlipCylinder, SimpleCylinder, TexturedCone, and TexturedSphere.

H.2 Running the Example Programs

All of the example programs can be run as standalone applications from a UNIX shell or a DOS window. The syntax shown in this appendix is for UNIX. In DOS windows, you will need to replace "/" with "\" and specify the correct drive letter when referring to <jdkhome> (for example, "c:\jdk1.2.2").

For example, to run the HelloUniverse program, change your current directory ("cd") to the <jdkhome>/demo/java3d/HelloUniverse directory, where

<jdkhome> is the directory in which the Java 2 SDK is installed, and type the following:

```
% java HelloUniverse
```

Each of the other example programs can be run in a similar manner.

Some of the example programs require a larger heap size (memory pool) than the default provided by Java. To increase the maximum heap size to 64 megabytes, run java with the "–Xmx64m" option. For example,

```
% java –Xmx64m HelloUniverse
```

Several of the example programs can be run as applets, either within a browser (using Java Plug-in) or by running the applet from within the Java utility program called appletviewer.

H.2.1 Running within a Browser

Java 2 applets, including many Java 3D example programs, can be run within a browser using Java Plug-in. Special HTML tags are required to cause Netscape or Internet Explorer to use the correct version of the Java 2 platform via Java Plug-in. All of the Java 3D example programs that can be run as applets include HTML files that have been converted to use Java Plug-in. Refer to the following URL for information on using Java Plug-in 1.2.2 HTML Converter to convert your own applets to run in a browser:

http://java.sun.com/products/plugin/

On Windows, the Java Plug-in is automatically installed along with the Java 2 runtime environment. Applets can be run in either Netscape Communicator or Internet Explorer.

On Solaris, Java 3D applets can be run in Netscape Communicator 4.51 or later on Solaris 2.6 or later. After installing Netscape Communicator, you need to install Java Plug-in version 1.2 or later. Netscape Communicator and Java Plug-in may be downloaded for free from

http://www.sun.com/solaris/netscape/

Additional patches may be required (see the website for details).

In both cases (Windows and Solaris), Java 3D applets are run within the Java Plug-in by opening the Java Plug-in version of the associated HTML file. These files are of the form <demo-name>_plugin.html, where <demo-name> is the name of the particular Java 3D applet. For example, to run the HelloUniverse example program within a browser, open the `HelloUniverse/HelloUniverse_plugin.html` file in your browser.

The following page contains links to all of the Java 3D demos that can be run as applets:

```
<jdkhome>/demo/java3d/index.html
```

Just click on the link for a given demo to run that demo within your browser.

Some Java 3D applets require a larger heap size (memory pool) than the default provided by Java Plug-in. To increase the heap size to 64 megabytes, run the Java Plug-in Control Panel application (from the Start menu in the Programs section on Windows) and set the "Java Run Time Parameters" to "-Xmx64m".

H.2.2 Running within Appletviewer

To run Java 3D applets within `appletviewer`, open the original, unconverted version of the associated HTML file (not the "_plugin" version). For example,

```
% appletviewer HelloUniverse.html
```

Some Java 3D applets require a larger heap size (memory pool) than the default provided by Java. To increase the maximum heap size to 64 megabytes, run `appletviewer` with the "-J-Xmx64m" option. For example,

```
% appletviewer -J-Xmx64m HelloUniverse.html
```

H.3 Program Descriptions

Several example programs are included in the `demo/java3d` directory. All of the example programs are described here. Code fragments are listed for a few of the example programs.

The mouse can be used to manipulate the view in many of the example programs. In these examples, the left mouse button rotates the view, the middle mouse button zooms in and out, and the right mouse button pans the view.

H.3.1 AWT_Interaction

Directory: demo/java3d/AWT_Interaction

The AWT_Interaction program displays a cube in a window. A "Rotate" button at the top of the window rotates the cube in steps each time the button is selected. This program demonstrates modifying the scene graph directly from the AWT event thread using the ActionListener interface. This example is derived from the Hello-Universe example, but instead of being continuously modified by a RotationInterpolator behavior, the object's TransformGroup is set to a new value that is computed each time the "Rotate" button is pressed.

The relevant source code fragments from AWT_Interaction.java follow:

```
public class AWTInteraction extends Applet
                            implements ActionListener {
    TransformGroup objTrans;
    float angle = 0.0f;
    Transform3D trans = new Transform3D();

    Button rotateB = new Button("Rotate");
```

This code creates instance variables for the current angle, the TransformGroup that will be modified, and a button that will trigger the modification. The AWTInteraction class implements ActionListener so that it can receive button press events. The createSceneGraph method (not shown here) creates a root BranchGroup, an object TransformGroup, and a color cube, much as in HelloUniverse.

```
public AWTInteraction() {
    ...
    Panel p = new Panel();
    p.add(rotateB);
    add("North", p);

    rotateB.addActionListener(this);
    ...
}
```

The constructor puts the Rotate button in a panel and adds the AWTInteraction class as an action listener for the button.

```
public void actionPerformed(ActionEvent e) {
    if (e.getSource() == rotateB) {
        angle += Math.toRadians(10);
        trans.rotY(angle);
        objTrans.setTransform(trans);
    }
}
```

The `actionPerformed` method increments the `angle`, computes a new rotation matrix, and updates the object's TransformGroup. Since this is in an AWT event listener method rather than in a behavior, the transform update is not synchronized with the Java 3D renderer. In particular, if such an event listener method modifies two objects in the Java 3D scene graph, there is no guarantee that the effects of those two updates will be seen in the same frame. Also remember that it is never safe for two threads to modify the same Java 3D object simultaneously. This means that an object that is being updated by a behavior must not be modified by an AWT event listener.

H.3.2 AlternateAppearance

Directory: demo/java3d/AlternateAppearance

The AlternateAppearanceBoundsTest and the AlternateAppearanceScopeTest programs demonstrate the ability of the AlternateAppearance node to override the appearance of Shape3D nodes. The programs display a 5 × 5 matrix of spheres and a control panel. The control panel allows you to select different scopes and appearance colors. The AlternateAppearanceBoundsTest program allows you to choose one of three different sizes of BoundingSpheres for the region of influence of the AlternateAppearance node, select whether a bounds object or a bounding leaf is used, and enable or disable the appearance override enable flag in each of the objects. The AlternateAppearanceScopeTest program allows you to set the hierarchical scoping of the AlternateAppearance node and enable or disable the appearance override enable flag in each object in a group of objects.

H.3.3 Appearance

Directory: demo/java3d/Appearance

The AppearanceTest program displays an image background and nine rotating tetrahedron primitives. The tetrahedra are constructed with different material properties. The relevant source code fragments from `AppearanceTest.java` follow:

```
int row, col;
Appearance[][] app = new Appearance[3][3];

for (row = 0; row < 3; row++)
   for (col = 0; col < 3; col++)
      app[row][col] = createAppearance(row * 3 + col);

for (int i = 0; i < 3; i++) {
   double ypos = (double)(i - 1) * 0.6;
   for (int j = 0; j < 3; j++) {
      double xpos = (double)(j - 1) * 0.6;
      objRoot.addChild(createObject(app[i][j],
                       0.12,xpos, ypos));
   }
}
```

The above code, extracted from the createSceneGraph method, creates a 3 × 3 array of objects, each with its own Appearance, and adds them to the scene graph.

The createAppearance method takes in an object index from 0 to 8 and generates a unique Appearance for each object (using a switch statement). The objects are, in order from left to right and from bottom to top; an unlit solid, an unlit wire frame, unlit points, a lit solid, a texture-mapped lit solid, a transparent lit solid, a lit solid with no specularity, a lit solid with only a specular highlight (black ambient and diffuse), and a lit solid with a different material color. The code fragments for the texture mapped and transparent cases follow:

```
private Appearance createAppearance(int idx) {
   Appearance app = new Appearance();

   // Globally used colors
   Color3f black = new Color3f(0.0f, 0.0f, 0.0f);
   Color3f white = new Color3f(1.0f, 1.0f, 1.0f);

   switch (idx) {
   ...
   case 4:
      // Set up the texture map
      TextureLoader tex = new TextureLoader(texImage, this);
      app.setTexture(tex.getTexture());

      TextureAttributes texAttr = new TextureAttributes();
      texAttr.setTextureMode(TextureAttributes.MODULATE);
      app.setTextureAttributes(texAttr);
```

```
        app.setMaterial(new Material(white, black, white,
                            black, 1.0f));
        break;
```

For Appearance number 4, the TextureLoader utility is used to load a JPEG image from a file and create a Texture object. TextureAttributes are set up so that the lit color is blended with the texture map (MODULATE). Finally, a lighting Material object is created with a default color of white.

```
    case 5:
        // Set up the transparency properties
        TransparencyAttributes ta = new TransparencyAttributes();
        ta.setTransparencyMode(ta.BLENDED);
        ta.setTransparency(0.6f);
        app.setTransparencyAttributes(ta);

        // Set up the polygon attributes
        PolygonAttributes pa = new PolygonAttributes();
        pa.setCullFace(pa.CULL_NONE);
        app.setPolygonAttributes(pa);

        // Set up the material properties
        Color3f objColor = new Color3f(0.7f, 0.8f, 1.0f);
        app.setMaterial(new Material(objColor, black, objColor,
                            black, 1.0f));
        break;

    ...

    return app;
}
```

For Appearance number 5, TransparencyAttributes are set up to use blended transparency with the object being 60 percent transparent. Back face culling is disabled in the PolygonAttributes object so that the front and back faces of the transparent object are visible. Finally, a lighting Material object is created with the specified object color.

The createObject method (not shown) takes in an Appearance object, a scale value, and *x* and *y* position values. From these parameters, it creates a rotating tetrahedron that is positioned and scaled appropriately. The geometry for the tetrahedron is created by the Tetrahedron.java file.

H.3.4 AppearanceMixed

Directory: demo/java3d/AppearanceMixed

The AppearanceMixed program displays the same image background and nine rotating tetrahedra (with different material properties) as the AppearanceTest program described earlier. It adds a pair of triangles that are drawn in immediate mode; this immediate-mode rendering is mixed in with the retained-mode objects (the tetrahedra).

An application subclasses Canvas3D and overrides the renderField to render geometry in mixed-immediate mode. The relevant source code fragments from the MyCanvas3D class in AppearanceMixed.java follow:

```
static class MyCanvas3D extends Canvas3D {
    private GraphicsContext3D gc;
    ...

    private IndexedTriangleArray tri =
        new IndexedTriangleArray(4,
                IndexedTriangleArray.COORDINATES |
                IndexedTriangleArray.NORMALS, 6);

    private Point3f vert[];
    private Vector3f normals[];

    public void renderField(int fieldDesc) {
        computeVert();
        computeNormals();
        gc.draw(tri);
    }

    private void computeVert() {
        <modify vert[] array>
        ...
        tri.setCoordinates(0, vert);
    }

    private void computeNormals() {
        <compute new normals[] based on vert[] values>
        ...
        tri.setNormals(0, normals);
    }
```

The renderField method is called by Java 3D during the rendering loop for each frame. The AppearanceMixed example overrides this Canvas3D method to compute a new set of vertices and normals for the pair of triangles and to draw the triangles to the canvas. The computeVert and computeNormals update the vert and normals array and then call the methods to copy these changes to the IndexedTriangleArray object.

```java
public MyCanvas3D(GraphicsConfiguration gcfg) {
    super(gcfg);
    ...

    // Set up the graphics context
    gc = getGraphicsContext3D();

    // Create the appearance for the triangle fan
    Appearance app = new Appearance();
    ...
    gc.setAppearance(app);

    // Set up the global lights
    Color3f lColor1 = new Color3f(0.7f, 0.7f, 0.7f);
    Vector3f lDir1= new Vector3f(-1.0f, -1.0f, -1.0f);
    Color3f alColor = new Color3f(0.2f, 0.2f, 0.2f);
    gc.addLight(new AmbientLight(alColor));
    gc.addLight(new DirectionalLight(lColor1, lDir1));
}
```

The constructor for MyCanvas creates a Graphics3D object and initializes its appearance and lights. Note that even though the scene graph also contains light objects, they are not used for immediate mode rendering—lights must be created and added to the graphics context in order for immediate mode geometry to be lit.

H.3.5 Background

Directory: demo/java3d/Background

The BackgroundGeometry program demonstrates the use of background geometry. The inside of a Sphere is texture mapped and used as background geometry, which is rendered by Java 3D as if it were infinitely far away. The background is position- and scale-invariant—only rotations affect how the geometry is rendered. This demo demonstrates this with a group of boxes drawn in the virtual world. The viewing platform can be adjusted with the mouse buttons. Notice how translations do not affect the background, but rotations do.

591

H.3.6 Billboard

Directory: `demo/java3d/Billboard`

The Bboard and BboardPt programs demonstrate the use of Java 3D's Billboard behavior to rotate a billboard around the *y* axis and around a fixed point, respectively. Use the left mouse button to rotate the scene, the middle button to zoom, and the right button to translate.

Note: Billboard's functionality has largely been superseded by OrientedShape3D.

H.3.7 ConicWorld

Directory: `demo/java3d/ConicWorld`

This directory contains a README file and six demonstration programs:

- The ConicWorld program shows spheres, cylinders, and cones of different resolutions and colors.

- The SimpleCylinder program demonstrates a simple cylinder object. The left mouse button rotates the cylinder, and the middle button zooms.

- The BoxExample program demonstrates a rotating texture-mapped box. The left mouse button rotates the box, and the middle button zooms.

- The FlipCylinder program puts up a textured cylinder that can be rotated and zoomed with the mouse. The left mouse button rotates, the middle button zooms, and the right button translates.

- The TexturedCone and TexturedSphere programs demonstrate the use of texture mapping with the Cone and Sphere primitives, respectively.

These programs demonstrate the use of the geometry primitives in the `com.sun.j3d.utils.geometry` package.

H.3.8 FourByFour

Directory: `demo/java3d/FourByFour`

The FourByFour program is a three-dimensional game of tic-tac-toe on a $4 \times 4 \times 4$ cube. Once loaded, press the "Instructions" button for information on how to play the game.

H.3.9 GearTest

Directory: demo/java3d/GearTest

The GearTest program shows a single rotating gear. The GearBox program shows a rotating gear assembly with five gears and gear shafts. The entire gear assembly can be manipulated with the mouse. The geometry in this example program is mathematically computed and demonstrates the use of different Java 3D geometry types. The Gear, SpurGear, and Shaft classes contain most of the geometry creation methods.

H.3.10 GeometryByReference

Directory: demo/java3d/GeometryByReference

The GeometryByReferenceTest program draws a pair of triangles using the new geometry-by-reference API in the GeometryArray object. The geometry or color data is modified when the corresponding item is selected from the "Update Data" combo box.

The ImageComponentByReferenceTest program draws a small raster object in the upper left corner and a larger texture mapped square, using the same image as a texture, in the middle of the window. This program demonstrates the new by-reference API for passing image data to Java 3D. It also demonstrates the new y-up versus y-down attribute for images. Use the combo boxes at the bottom of the screen to select the desired mode for the raster image and the texture image.

The InterleavedTest program draws a pair of triangles using the new interleaved geometry-by-reference API in the GeometryArray object.

H.3.11 GeometryCompression

Directory: demo/java3d/GeometryCompression

The cgview program loads an object from a compressed geometry resource (.cg) file and displays it on the screen. The object can be manipulated with the mouse. Run the program with the following command:

```
java cgview <.cg file> [object-number]
```

You can use one of the .cg resource files in the demo/java3d/geometry directory. The following example will display a galleon (ship):

```
% java cgview ../geometry/galleon.cg
```

The obj2cg program reads one or more Wavefront .obj files, compresses them, and appends the corresponding compressed objects to the specified compressed geometry resource (.cg) file. Run the program with the following command:

```
java obj2cg <.obj file> [<.obj file> ...] <.cg file>
```

If the .cg file does not exist, it is created. If the file does exist and is a valid .cg resource file, the new object(s) are appended to the objects in the existing file. If it is not a valid .cg file, an exception is thrown.

The ObjectFileCompressor class provides the methods, used by obj2cg, to compress Wavefront .obj files into Java 3D CompressedGeometry nodes. The `Object-FileCompressor.html` file is the javadoc that describes the methods.

H.3.12 HelloUniverse

Directory: `demo/java3d/HelloUniverse`

The HelloUniverse program creates a cube and a RotationInterpolator behavior object that rotates the cube at a constant rate of $\pi/2$ radians per second. The code for this program is described in Section 1.6.3, "HelloUniverse: A Sample Java 3D Program."

H.3.13 LOD

Directory: `demo/java3d/LOD`

The LOD program demonstrates the use of the DistanceLOD behavior to select automatically from among four different resolutions of a shaded, lit sphere. The middle mouse button moves the object closer and farther away from the viewer. As the object gets farther away from the viewer, successively lower-resolution versions of the sphere are displayed.

H.3.14 Lightwave

Directory: `demo/java3d/Lightwave` directory

The Viewer program is a loader and viewer for Lightwave 3D scene files. This program implements only a subset of the features in Lightwave 3D. The `README.txt` file contains release notes for the loader. The Viewer program takes the name of a Lightwave 3D scene (.lws) file as its only argument. For example,

```
% java Viewer ballcone.lws
```

will display a red cone moving behind a stationary green ball.

H.3.15 ModelClip

Directory: demo/java3d/ModelClip

The ModelClipTest and ModelClipTest2 programs show model clipping. The ModelClipTest program draws an object that is clipped by a model clipping plane. The mouse can be used to manipulate the object. Note that the clipping plane moves with the object. The ModelClipTest2 program has a fixed object with a movable model clipping plane. The mouse can be used to manipulate the model clipping plane.

H.3.16 Morphing

Directory: demo/java3d/Morphing

The Morphing program displays at the bottom of the window a hand that morphs among the static views of the three hands at the top of the window. The Pyramid2Cube program is a simpler example that morphs among three cubes.

H.3.17 ObjLoad

Directory: demo/java3d/ObjLoad

The ObjLoad program loads Wavefront object files. Run the program with the following command.

java ObjLoad [-s] [-n] [-t] [-c degrees] <.obj file>

where the options are

-s   Spin (no user interaction)

-n   No triangulation

-t   No stripification

-c   Set crease angle for normal generation (default is 60 without smoothing group info, otherwise 180 within smoothing groups)

You can use one of the .obj files in the demo/java3d/geometry directory. The following example will display a galleon (ship):

```
% java ObjLoad ../geometry/galleon.obj
```

The relevant source code fragment from ObjLoad.java follows:

```
public BranchGroup createSceneGraph(String args[]) {
    ...
    int flags = ObjectFile.RESIZE;
    ...
    ObjectFile f = new ObjectFile(flags,
        (float)(creaseAngle * Math.PI / 180.0));
    Scene s = null;
    try {
        s = f.load(filename);
    }
    catch (FileNotFoundException e) {
        System.err.println(e);
        System.exit(1);
    }
    catch (ParsingErrorException e) {
        System.err.println(e);
        System.exit(1);
    }
    catch (IncorrectFormatException e) {
        System.err.println(e);
        System.exit(1);
    }

    objTrans.addChild(s.getSceneGroup());
```

The above code fragment creates an ObjectFile loader with the desired flags and crease angle, loads the specified filename (checking for file and parsing exceptions), and adds the loaded objects to the scene graph. This code fragment could easily be modified to accommodate a variety of loaders.

H.3.18 OffScreenCanvas3D

Directory: `demo/java3d/OffScreenCanvas3D`

The OffScreenTest program creates a scene graph containing a cube and renders that cube to an on-screen Canvas3D. In the `postSwap` routine of the on-screen Canvas3D, an off-screen rendering of the same scene is done to the off-screen buffer. The resulting image is then used as the source image for a Raster object in the scene graph.

The PrintFromButton program is similar to the OffScreenTest program, except that it doesn't automatically render to the off-screen buffer during the `postSwap` callback of its on-screen Canvas3D. The off-screen rendering is done when the "Print" button is pressed.

H.3.19 OrientedShape3D

Directory: `demo/java3d/OrientedShape3D`

The OrientedTest and OrientedPtTest programs demonstrate the use of Java 3D's OrientedShape3D nodes to create geometry that is oriented about the *y* axis and around a fixed point, respectively. These are essentially the same example programs used in the Billboard example, except that they use an OrientedShape3D node rather than a Billboard behavior. Use the left mouse button to rotate the scene, the middle button to zoom, and the right button to translate. Notice how the text does not jump around as it does when using a Billboard behavior.

H.3.20 PackageInfo

Directory: `demo/java3d/PackageInfo`

The PackageInfo program lists the package information for the Java 3D packages installed on the system. This can be used to determine which version of Java 3D you are running.

The QueryProperties program lists the values of the properties returned by the `queryProperties` method of the Canvas3D that is created from the preferred GraphicsConfiguration returned by SimpleUniverse.

H.3.21 PickTest

Directory: `demo/java3d/PickTest`

The PickTest program displays several 3D objects and a control panel. The control panel allows the user to change the pick mode, the pick tolerance, and the view mode. You can pick and rotate objects with the mouse. The PickTest program demonstrates the use of the PickMouseBehavior utility classes.

The IntersectTest program demonstrates the ability to get geometric intersection information from a picked object. Use the mouse to pick a point on one of the objects in the window. The program illuminates the picked location and the vertices of the primitive with tiny spheres. Information about the picked primitive and the point of intersection is printed. The IntersectTest program uses a mouse-based behavior, IntersectInfoBehavior, to control the picking. The relevant source code fragments from `IntersectInfoBehavior.java` follow:

```
PickCanvas pickCanvas;
PickResult[] pickResult;
public IntersectInfoBehavior(Canvas3D canvas3D,
        BranchGroup branchGroup,
        float size) {

    pickCanvas = new PickCanvas(canvas3D, branchGroup);
    pickCanvas.setTolerance(5.0f);
    pickCanvas.setMode(PickCanvas.GEOMETRY_INTERSECT_INFO);
    ...
```

The IntersectInfoBehavior class constructor creates a new PickCanvas object, initializes the PickCanvas with the desired tolerance, and sets the mode to allow geometry intersection information to be retrieved.

```
public void processStimulus(Enumeration criteria) {
    ...
    <check for mouse event>

    if (eventId == MouseEvent.MOUSE_PRESSED) {
        int x = ((MouseEvent)event[i]).getX();
        int y = ((MouseEvent)event[i]).getY();
        pickCanvas.setShapeLocation(x, y);
        Point3d eyePos = pickCanvas.getStartPosition();
        pickResult = pickCanvas.pickAllSorted();
        if (pickResult != null) {
            // Get node info
            Node curNode = pickResult[0].getObject();
            Geometry curGeom = ((Shape3D)curNode).getGeometry();
            GeometryArray curGeomArray = (GeometryArray) curGeom;
            // Get closest intersection results
            PickIntersection pi =
                pickResult[0].getClosestIntersection(eyePos);

            <get specific info from PickIntersection>
        }
    }
    ...
```

The processStimulus method checks for a mouse event and initiates a pick, via the PickCanvas object, at the selected location. It then looks for pick results and extracts the intersection information from the pick result (if any).

H.3.22 PickText3D

Directory: `demo/java3d/PickText3D`

The PickText3DBounds and PickText3DGeometry programs demonstrate bounds-based and geometry-based picking of Text3D objects, respectively. Both programs allow you to pick and rotate the text strings with the mouse. PickText3DBounds uses only bounds-based picking, so the string can be picked anywhere within the vicinity of its letters. PickText3DGeometry uses geometry-based picking, so the string can exactly be picked only on one of the letters in the string.

H.3.23 PlatformGeometry

Directory: `demo/java3d/PlatformGeometry`

The SimpleGeometry program displays two geometry objects: a sphere and a rotating cube. The sphere is created as PlatformGeometry using the universe utilities. This means that it is always in a fixed location relative to the viewer.

H.3.24 PureImmediate

Directory: `demo/java3d/PureImmediate`

The PureImmediate program demonstrates Java 3D's pure immediate mode. In this mode, objects are not placed into a scene graph but instead are drawn using the GraphicsContext3D drawing methods. The Java 3D renderer for the Canvas into which the immediate mode graphics are rendered must be stopped prior to immediate mode rendering. In this mode, the rendering is done from a user-controlled thread.

The relevant source code fragments from `PureImmediate.java` follow:

```
public class PureImmediate extends Applet implements Runnable {
    private Canvas3D canvas;
    private GraphicsContext3D gc = null;
    private Geometry cube = null;
    private Transform3D cmt = new Transform3D();

    // One rotation (2*PI radians) every 6 seconds
    private Alpha rotAlpha = new Alpha(-1, 6000);
```

The above code creates instance variables for a Canvas3D, the GraphicsContext associated with the canvas, a geometry object for drawing, a Transform3D object for rotation, and an alpha object to allow the rotation to be time-based. The Pure-Immediate class implements Runnable so that it can be run by a user-created drawing thread.

```
public void render() {
    if (gc == null) {
        // Set up Graphics context
        gc = canvas.getGraphicsContext3D();
        gc.setAppearance(new Appearance());

        // Set up geometry
        cube = new ColorCube(0.4).getGeometry();
    }

    // Compute angle of rotation based on alpha value
    double angle = rotAlpha.value() * 2.0*Math.PI;
    cmt.rotY(angle);

    // Render the geometry for this frame
    gc.clear();
    gc.setModelTransform(cmt);
    gc.draw(cube);
    canvas.swap();
}

public void run() {
    while (true) {
        render();
        Thread.yield();
    }
}
```

The render method renders a single frame. After ensuring that the graphics context is set up and the geometry is created, it computes the new rotation matrix, clears the canvas, draws the cube, and swaps the draw and display buffer. The run method is the entry point for our drawing thread. It calls the render method in a loop, yielding control to other threads once per frame.

```
    public PureImmediate() {
        <set layout of applet, get best graphics config>

        canvas = new Canvas3D(config);
        canvas.stopRenderer();
        add("Center", canvas);

        // Create the universe and viewing branch
        SimpleUniverse u = new SimpleUniverse(canvas);
        u.getViewingPlatform().setNominalViewingTransform();
        // Start a new thread that will continuously render
        new Thread(this).start();
    }
```

The constructor creates the 3D canvas, stops the Java 3D renderer, sets up the viewing branch (necessary even in pure immediate mode), and starts up the drawing thread.

H.3.25 ReadRaster

Directory: demo/java3d/ReadRaster

The ReadRaster program creates a scene graph containing a cube and renders that cube. In the postSwap routine of the Canvas3D, the contents of the canvas are read back using the Immediate mode readRaster method. The resulting image is then used as the source image for a Raster object in the scene graph.

H.3.26 Sound

Directory: demo/java3d/Sound

The SimpleSounds program shows a rotating cube and plays three different sounds, including a voice saying "Hello Universe."

The ReverberateSound program demonstrates different amounts of reverberation. It plays a voice saying "Hello Universe" in several different environments, including a closet, an acoustic lab, a garage, a dungeon (both medium and large), and a cavern.

The MoveAppBoundingLeaf program displays a large rotating cube and plays a single point sound source. Two Soundscape nodes are created and manipulated with a behavior. This results in one or the other being alternately selected.

H.3.27 SphereMotion

Directory: `demo/java3d/SphereMotion`

The SphereMotion program shows a lit sphere that is continuously moving closer to and farther from the viewer. The sphere is lit by two light sources, one fixed and one rotating around the sphere. Depending on a command line option, the two light sources are created as directional lights (the default), point lights, or spot lights. Run the program with the following command:

```
java SphereMotion [-dir | -point | -spot]
```

H.3.28 SplineAnim

Directory: `demo/java3d/SplineAnim`

The SplineAnim program demonstrates the use of KBRotPosScaleSplinePathInterpolator (see the description in Table F-10) to do spline animation paths using Kochanek-Bartels splines. A red cone is animated along a spline path specified by five knot points, which are shown as cyan spheres. Use the mouse to manipulate the scene.

A control panel allows you to toggle between spline and linear interpolation, a slider to adjust the speed of the animation, and an animation start/stop button.

H.3.29 Text2D

Directory: `demo/java3d/Text2D`

The Text2DTest program shows three different types of 2D text using the Text2D utility class.

H.3.30 Text3D

Directory: `demo/java3d/Text3D`

The Text3DLoad program permits you to enter your own text and see how it displays in 3D. The command for running Text3DLoad is as follows:

```
java Text3DLoad [-f fontname] [-t tesselation] <text>
```

The `fontname` variable allows you to specify one of the Java Font names, such as Helvetica, Times Roman, and Courier. The `tesselation` variable specifies how finely to tessellate the font glyphs. Once the text displays, the left mouse button rotates the text, the middle button zooms, and the right button translates.

H.3.31 TextureByReference

Directory: demo/java3d/TextureByReference

The TextureByReference program shows a set of animating textures using the image component by-reference feature. A control panel allows you to flip the image or to set the texture and geometry by-reference flag, the image orientation flag (*y*-up or *y*-down), and the image type. It also allows you to control the texture animation speed and to stop and restart the animation.

H.3.32 TextureTest

Directory: demo/java3d/TextureTest

The TextureImage program displays a rotating cube with a user-specified image file mapped onto the surface. The command for running TextureImage is

```
java TextureImage <image-filename> [-f ImageComponent format]
```

The ImageComponent format variable allows you to specify the format of the pixel data. If you do not specify an image file, the rotating cube will appear white. You can use one of the image files in the demo/java3d/images directory. For example,

```
% java TextureImage ../images/earth.jpg
```

will display the rotating cube with an image of earth mapped onto it.

The MultiTextureTest program displays a box with two textures applied to it. You can enable different combinations of one or two textures with the pop-up menu. Use the mouse buttons to manipulate the object.

H.3.33 TickTockCollision

Directory: demo/java3d/TickTockCollision

The TickTockCollision program shows an oscillating colored cube that collides with two rectangular objects. The rectangular objects change color when they collide with the cube.

H.3.34 TickTockPicking

Directory: demo/java3d/TickTockPicking

The TickTockPicking program displays a set of nine spinning tetrahedra and an oscillating colored cube. Picking the cube or one of the tetrahedra with the left mouse button causes it to change color.

H.3.35 VirtualInputDevice

Directory: demo/java3d/VirtualInputDevice

This directory contains another version of the HelloUniverse program with viewing position controls implemented via the InputDevice interface.

Glossary

avatar

The software representation of a person as the person appears to others in a shared virtual universe. The avatar may or may not resemble an actual person.

branch graph

A graph rooted to a BranchGroup node. See also scene graph and shared graph.

CC

Clipping coordinates.

center ear

Midpoint between the left and right ear of the listener.

center eye

Midpoint between the left and right eye of viewer. This is the head coordinate system origin.

compiled

A subgraph may be compiled by an application using the compile method of the root node—a BranchGroup or a SharedGroup—of the graph. A compiled object is any object that is part of a compiled graph. An application can compile some or all of the subgraphs that make up a complete scene graph. Java 3D compiles these graphs into an internal format. Additionally, Java 3D provides restricted access to methods of compiled objects or graphs. See also live.

compiled-retained mode

One of three modes in which Java 3D objects are rendered. In this mode, Java 3D renders the scene graph, or a portion of the scene graph, that has been previously compiled into an internal format. See also retained mode and immediate mode.

content branch

A branch graph that contains content-related leaf nodes, such as Shape3D nodes. No viewing-specific nodes are contained in a content branch.

DAG

Directed acyclic graph. A scene graph.

EC

Eye coordinates.

frustum

See view frustum.

group node

A node within a scene graph that composes, transforms, selects, and, in general, modifies its descendant nodes. See also leaf node and root node.

HMD

Head-mounted display.

image plate

The display area; the viewing screen or head-mounted display.

immediate mode

One of three modes in which Java 3D objects are rendered. In this mode objects are rendered directly, under user control, rather than as part of a scene graph traversal. See also retained mode and compiled-retained mode.

IID

Interaural intensity difference. The difference between the perceived amplitude (gain) of the signal from a source as it reaches the listener's left and right ears.

ITD

Interaural time difference. The difference in time in the arrival of the signal from a sound source as it reaches the listener's left and right ears.

leaf node

A node within a scene graph that contains the visual, auditory, and behavioral components of the scene. See also group node and root node.

live

A live graph is any graph that is attached to a Locale object, or a shared graph that is referenced by a live graph. A live object is any object that is part of a live graph. Live objects are subject to being traversed and rendered by the Java 3D renderer. Additionally, Java 3D provides restricted access to methods of live objects or graphs. See also compiled.

LOD

Level of detail. A predefined Behavior that operates on a Switch node to select from among multiple versions of an object or collection of objects.

polytope

A bounding volume defined by a closed intersection of half-spaces.

retained mode

One of three modes in which Java 3D objects are rendered. In this mode, Java 3D traverses the scene graph and renders the objects that are in the graph. See also compiled-retained mode and immediate mode.

root node

A node within a scene graph that establishes the default environment. See also group node and leaf node.

scene graph

A collection of branch graphs rooted to a Locale. A virtual universe has one or more scene graphs. See also branch graph and shared graph.

shared graph

A graph rooted to a SharedGroup node. See also branch graph and scene graph.

stride

The part of an interleaved array that defines the length of a vertex.

three space

Three-dimensional space.

view branch

A branch graph that contains a ViewPlatform leaf node and may contain other content-related leaf nodes for geometry associated with a viewer.

view frustum

A truncated, pyramid-shaped viewing area that defines how much of the world the viewer sees. Objects not within the view frustum are not visible. Objects that intersect the boundaries of the viewing frustum are clipped (partially drawn).

VPC

View platform coordinates.

Index

Page numbers in bold specify major references.

M

N

Q

R

641

T

Z

The Java™ Series

Ken Arnold · James Gosling · David Holmes

The Java™ Programming Language
Third Edition

ISBN 0-201-70433-1

The Real-Time Specification for Java™

ISBN 0-201-70323-8

Mary Campione · Kathy Walrath · Alison Huml

The Java™ Tutorial, Third Edition
A Short Course on the Basics

ISBN 0-201-70393-9

Campione · Walrath · Huml · Tutorial Team

The Java™ Tutorial Continued
The Rest of the JDK™

ISBN 0-201-48558-3

Patrick Chan

The Java™ Developers ALMANAC 2000

ISBN 0-201-43299-4

ISBN 0-201-43297-8

Patrick Chan · Rosanna Lee · Douglas Kramer

The Java™ Class Libraries Second Edition, Volume 1
java.io java.lang java.math java.net java.text java.util

ISBN 0-201-31002-3

Patrick Chan · Rosanna Lee

The Java™ Class Libraries Second Edition, Volume 2
java.applet java.awt java.beans

ISBN 0-201-31003-1

Patrick Chan · Rosanna Lee · Douglas Kramer

The Java™ Class Libraries Second Edition, Volume 1
Supplement for the Java™ 2 Platform Standard Edition v1.2

ISBN 0-201-48552-4

Zhiqun Chen

Java Card™ Technology for Smart Cards
Architecture and Programmer's Guide
Foreword by Patrice Peyret

ISBN 0-201-70329-7

Li Gong

Inside Java™ 2 Platform Security
Architecture, API Design, and Implementation

ISBN 0-201-31000-7

James Gosling · Bill Joy · Guy Steele · Gilad Bracha

The Java™ Language Specification, Second Edition

ISBN 0-201-31008-2

James Gosling · Frank Yellin · The Java Team

The Java™ Application Programming Interface, Volume 1
Core Packages

ISBN 0-201-63453-8

James Gosling · Frank Yellin · The Java Team

The Java™ Application Programming Interface, Volume 2
Window Toolkit and Applets

ISBN 0-201-63459-7

Jonni Kanerva

The Java™ FAQ

ISBN 0-201-63456-2

Nicholas Kassem · Enterprise Team

Designing Enterprise Applications with the Java™ 2 Platform, Enterprise Edition
Foreword by Jon Kannegaard

ISBN 0-201-70277-0

Doug Lea

Concurrent Programming in Java™ Second Edition
Design Principles and Patterns

ISBN 0-201-31009-0

Rosanna Lee · Scott Seligman

JNDI API Tutorial and Reference
Building Directory-Enabled Java™ Applications

ISBN 0-201-70502-8

Sheng Liang

The Java™ Native Interface
Programmer's Guide and Specification

ISBN 0-201-32577-2

Tim Lindholm · Frank Yellin

The Java™ Virtual Machine Specification Second Edition

ISBN 0-201-43294-3

Java™ 2 Platform, Enterprise Edition
Platform and Component Specifications

ISBN 0-201-70456-0

Henry Sowizral · Kevin Rushforth · Michael Deering

The Java 3D™ API Specification, Second Edition

ISBN 0-201-71041-2

Kathy Walrath · Mary Campione

The JFC Swing Tutorial
A Guide to Constructing GUIs

ISBN 0-201-43321-4

White · Fisher · Cattell · Hamilton · Hapner

JDBC™ API Tutorial and Reference, Second Edition
Universal Data Access for the Java™ 2 Platform

ISBN 0-201-43328-1

Steve Wilson · Jeff Kesselman

Java™ Platform Performance
Strategies and Tactics

ISBN 0-201-70969-4

Please see our web site (http://www.awl.com/cseng/javaseries)
for more information on these titles.